THE JEWS:

SOCIAL PATTERNS OF AN AMERICAN GROUP

THE JEWS

SOCIAL PATTERNS
OF AN AMERICAN GROUP

EDITED BY MARSHALL SKLARE

THE FREE PRESS, *New York*
COLLIER-MACMILLAN LIMITED, *London*

57-9318

PREFACE

THIS volume is intended to meet a need which has been described as follows by Dr. Louis Finkelstein of the Jewish Theological Seminary of America:

Some years ago, I undertook to prepare a comprehensive work describing the whole phenomenon of Judaism. It was to include a history of the Jews, a description of their present condition, a discussion of their contribution to civilization . . . and an outline of their beliefs and practices as Jews. . . . What surprised me . . . was the dearth of information about Jews today. There are probably a hundred people, and more, whose profession it is to discover all that can be known about the Jews in Jerusalem in the first century; there does not seem to be one who has the same duty for the Jews of New York in the twentieth century. So it comes about that we understand Judaism in the first century better than we understand Judaism in the twentieth.

As Dr. Finkelstein suggests, there are few if any scholars who devote their full efforts to the sociology of the American Jew. Nevertheless, many devoted and competent individuals have made worth-while contributions to the field. Their work is of interest to Jewish leaders and administrators charged with the formulation of communal policy; to the professional dealing with a Jewish clientele, be he a social worker, group worker, or therapist; to students and teachers in the field of ethnic and religious groups, and intergroup relations; and, finally, to the fraternity of research workers. In order that the needs of these various publics be served, the literature of the social sciences—and particularly that of sociology—has been the object of careful review.

Our materials are drawn from a variety of sources. First there are the M.A. and Ph.D. dissertations. Another source is the published works—the journal articles, the chapters in symposia, the contributions to yearbooks, the monographs. In most of the relevant dissertations, and in the general run of journal articles, Jews usually constitute the exclusive group under study. But this is not always the case, and thus we use a further source of material. These are the studies which are devoted to a *general* problem but in which Jews form a part of the community under investigation, a portion of the sample, or one of the groups tested. Because of the advantage of the comparative method, such studies offer particularly rich materials. Finally, there are the surveys and researches sponsored by Jewish organizations. Such material is frequently produced only in mimeographed form, and distribution is generally limited to a restricted public.

In summary, this volume consists only in part of material which is generally available, and thus it differs from the usual type of anthology. The editor approached numerous research workers, asking them to prepare material for the volume. In a number of cases we obtained materials for authors. In other instances the editor rewrote unpublished research reports. This volume necessitated close collaboration between some of the researchers and the editor. In several cases the authors of studies already published were asked to revise their material in the light of our needs. And when time permitted, certain materials prepared for this volume were first published elsewhere. Inasmuch as the book uses a good many articles either previously unpublished or specially revised, it is more than a reader in the conventional sense.

The stress in the volume is on empirical materials which report on research dealing with the contemporary scene, or on material which is essential for an understanding of contemporary life. In some cases we have included articles which would not ordinarily appear in a journal or monograph. However, we have attempted to utilize only those survey articles which are closely tied to empirical materials. Since this volume is not a source book, materials which are essentially documents are not included. The perceptive user will notice that not all subjects of interest are covered; in certain areas we could neither discover appropriate material nor locate a scholar who could devote himself to providing what was desired. This volume, then, is a reader *in* the sociology of American Jewry. By itself, it does not constitute a sociology *of* American Jewry.

Since there is no textbook in the field covered by this work, the organization of the book is not keyed to any particular volume. The present volume may be used as an aid in connection with a text on minority groups. The non-specialist will find that several such texts provide a worth-while overview of the group with which the volume is specifically concerned. The non-specialist may also obtain an overview in one or another of the recently published volumes which are specifically concerned with the Jewish group, and which offer survey articles covering various facets of American Jewish life and problems. Such volumes include *Jewish Life in America* edited by Theodore Friedman and Robert Gordis, Vol. IV of *The Jewish People—Past and Present,* and *American Jewry: The Tercentenary and After* edited by Eugene Kohn.

So much for the references which may interest those who wish to use this volume as a supplementary aid. Because of the fact that many books of this type are based on college courses for which texts are available, and are furthermore employed under the tutelage of instructors who can guide and interpret their contents to the student, editors have tended to avoid the presentation of very much in the way of interpretive comment. The inclination of the present editor has been in this direction, but the realization that many users of this book will employ it outside of the classroom situation has served to temper his desires. And it was also apparent that when used in college courses, the book may be recommended by teachers whose specialty lies in another area. In the light of these facts it was decided to present brief interpretive comments at the beginning of each section.

A deep debt of gratitude is owed to the authors and publishers who have co-operated with us in this venture. Our particular thanks go to those individuals who revised or wrote material especially for the volume. They were subjected to editorial conferences carried on by mail, telephone, or in person; their interest in this venture frequently involved taking time away from other pressing commitments. Some articles had to be rewritten by the editor for this volume, and the authors graciously gave me the freedom to do so.

A number of individuals have helped to provide materials, have suggested the inclusion of an article, or have given me the benefit of their opinion about a manuscript. They include Prof. Salo W. Baron, Prof. Abraham G. Duker, Prof. Erich Rosenthal, Prof. David Gold, Mr. Herbert Gans, and Mr. Nathan Glazer. It was indeed a pleasure to have the assistance of Dr. Aaron Antonovsky at various stages during the project. My colleagues at the American Jewish Committee, including Miss Iva Cohen, Mr. Harry Alderman, Mr. George Kellman, and Mr. Milton Himmelfarb, have been of substantial assistance. Staff members of other Jewish agencies who have co-operated in this venture include Dr. Zalmen Slesinger of the American Association for Jewish Education, Dr. Don Hager of the American Jewish Congress, Mr. Alvin Chenkin and Mr. Robert Morris of the Council of Jewish Federations and Welfare Funds; Mr. Alex Rosen, formerly with the National Jewish Welfare Board; Dr. Charles Winick, formerly with the Anti-Defamation League of B'nai B'rith; Mr. Joseph Willen of the Federation of Jewish Philanthropies of New York; Dr. Leon A. Feldman of the Jewish Education Committee of New York; and Dr. Walter A. Lurie, formerly with the National Community Relations Advisory Council. The interest and encouragement of Mr. Jeremiah Kaplan, Editor of The Free Press, was manifested throughout the period during which this volume was in preparation. I am fortunate indeed that my wife, Rose, possesses wide experience in the editorial field. Having her assistance has simplified my task considerably.

MARSHALL SKLARE

New York City
April, 1957

CONTENTS

you ARE an Beautiful pretty Angle.

4. *The Jewish Religion:*
Aspects of Continuity and Change

5. *Psychological Aspects: Group Belongingness and Jewish Identification*

6. *Some Cultural Aspects and Value Orientations*

1

The Historical Setting

INTRODUCTION

HOW much history must one know before he can fully comprehend the contents of this, or any similar volume? The answer to such a question would vary from sociologist to sociologist—there is no general agreement on the degree to which historical understanding is a prerequisite for studies of contemporary life. However, in the context of the present volume even those who are minimalists as regards history would agree that any student of the subject should acquire an overall view of Jewish immigration to the United States. We have thus included Bernard D. Weinryb's "Jewish Immigration and Accommodation to America," an article which provides the type of historical knowledge highly useful in placing any analysis of the contemporary scene in proper perspective. Perhaps the most notable aspect of Weinryb's treatment is his realistic appraisal of how Jewish immigrants actually felt about America once they arrived here, and how those who had preceded them reacted to the newcomers. Also, the footnotes to this article serve to suggest the wide range of source material available to the student.

Although the type of material presented by Weinryb is highly significant, it cannot stand alone; there is need for a broader analysis which seeks to portray American Jewry against the entire canvas of Western Jewry, and against the key historical developments of the modern era. This need is served by Ben Halpern's article, "America is Different." Halpern is one of the few authors represented in this volume who not only possesses a strong academic background in relevant disciplines, but who has the advantage of serving as a writer and editor of Jewish periodicals and as a participant in the ideological currents of American Jewry. Thus, his writing combines the "distance" unique to the academician with the warmth and the intimate acquaintanceship with the group characteristic of the ideologue and polemicist.

Halpern stresses the fact that American Jewry is a post-Emancipation Jewry, and that the continuity of European Jewish ideologies was broken in the United States. He emphasizes that the contrasting development of European and American Jewry is traceable to the different social and political conditions faced by these two Jewries. His treatment thus serves to supplement the article by Weinryb which stresses the experience of three hundred years of Jewish immigration to the United States. Essentially, the Halpern and Weinryb articles serve to explain the absence, the scarcity, and the pervasiveness of certain tendencies in American Jewish life. Such tendencies are stressed in many of the succeeding articles, particularly those in Section 3, devoted to aspects of the communal life of American Jewry.

BERNARD D. WEINRYB

JEWISH IMMIGRATION
AND ACCOMMODATION TO AMERICA

SINCE the first twenty-three Jews landed in New Amsterdam in September of 1654, some 3,000,000 Jews have entered the United States. During the century and a half after 1654, the entire number of Jewish immigrants amounted to about a thousand souls. Later, following the end of the Napoleonic wars, this trickle began to swell until it became a stream. In the third quarter of the nineteenth century the stream again began to widen, and probably an average of two or three thousand Jews came here annually.[1] Then, at the beginning of the 1880's, the stream became a torrent. Starting out with some 13,000 in 1882, immigration reached over 51,000 in 1891, and averaged over 100,000 in the years 1904-1914. During World War I the stream slowed down to a mere 12-15,000 annually, increased again to 119,000 in 1921, and totalled about 50,000 yearly in the following two years. Subsequently, the quota legislation of 1924 drastically reduced Jewish immigration; on an average, some 11,000 Jews arrived annually in the second half of the 1920's. This number was reduced to less than half in the 1930's—apparently as a result of the depression—but was to rise again at the end of the 1930's with the influx of Jews from Germany. This trend also continued during the war years. After the war, thousands of Jewish survivors of the Nazi holocaust found a home in America. Of the 3,000,000 Jews (the figure is admittedly a rough estimate) who immigrated to America during the years 1654-1954, some 90-95 per cent came here during the seventy-year period, 1880-1950. In terms of numbers, then, American Jewry today consists predominantly of first, second, and third generation individuals. However, the initial pattern set by the pre-1880 immigrants has had an important influence.

Formerly, Jewish historiography followed the concept of a tripartite division of the coming of the Jew to this country. It was maintained that there were three periods, each one marked by a difference in the origin of the Jews who arrived in the United States. Thus there was the Sephardic (i.e., descendants of Jews from Spain and Portugal) immigration during Colonial times and up to 1815, the German-Jewish immigration from 1815-1875 (or 1880), and East European since the 1880's. Lately this division has been challenged on the basis that in Colonial days many Jewish immigrants—perhaps even a majority—were Ashkenazim (i.e., Jews from West-

Reprinted from *Publication of the American Jewish Historical Society*, Vol. XLVI, No. 3-4 (May-June, 1957), by permission of the author and the publisher.

ern or Eastern Europe). It has furthermore been pointed out that in the nineteenth century Eastern European Jews arrived here before 1880 in considerable numbers.[2] However, granted that there was no period in which *all* the Jewish immigrants were of one and the same origin, the tripartite division is not only a convenient means of classification, but it is also sociologically sound. In each period a certain origin group formed the dominant strain in the Jewish immigration to America and impressed its pattern on the immigration wave. This was true even if the group may not always have comprised a numerical majority.[3]

Cultural and other differences between the immigration groups became more pronounced as a result of the social stratification which took place in connection with the time of arrival of each group. In America, as in other immigrant countries, social stratification and class structure[4] are connected with arrival date; the earlier arrivals form a sort of aristocracy. Original cultural differences between the groups are intensified by this "class division." The dominant group—the early arrivals—form the upper crust. They consider themselves superior to and distinct from the "minority" groups of later-comers,[5] and attempt to maintain social distance from them or to mold them into a certain pattern. When Philadelphia, for example, had a Jewish population of only two or three dozen families, conflicts between the old settlers and the newcomers were already taking place. In 1769, when Barnard Gratz—merchant and one of the founders of the Jewish community in Philadelphia—was in London, he received the following request in a letter from another "old-timer" in Philadelphia: "Pray prevent what is in your power to hinder any more of that sort to come!"[6] Even in our generation the German-Jewish arrivals of the last two decades are looked down upon and different accusations are advanced against them, accusations which are: ". . . not too much unlike the ideas about Jews generally harbored by anti-Semites."[7] They are allegedly ". . . conceited, they stick together and won't mix with the rest of us, they are arrogant, they are schemers, they are mercenary."[8]

On the other hand, individuals seek to assimilate into the "superior" group, thereby gaining standing and prestige. We find German Jews—and perhaps some Polish Jews—joining the Sephardic community organization or intermarrying with Sephardic Jews during the Colonial period; Russian and Polish Jews joining (German-Jewish) Reform temples and marrying upward into German-Jewish families during the nineteenth century. And in the last two decades, some German-Jewish immigrants of the Nazi period learned Yiddish—they "spoiled" their pure German language with the "jargon" of the "Ostjuden" in order to appear a step nearer to the now dominant group. And their younger generation frequently married into the Eastern European group—in one study it was found that 37.6 per cent of the German-Jewish immigrant males married outside the German-Jewish group.[9]

§ *Some General Considerations*

Immigration is a complicated process. People are separated from familiar surroundings and become strangers in a distant, cruel world:

> Emigration took the people out of traditional accustomed environments and
> replanted them in strange ground, among strangers, where strange manners
> prevailed. The customary modes of behavior were no longer adequate, for the
> problems of life were new and different. With old ties snapped, men faced the
> enormous compulsion of working out new relationships, new meanings to their
> lives, often under harsh and hostile circumstances.[10]

Immigrants do not usually arrive empty-handed in a new country; they
transport their ideas, culture patterns, and institutions. They try to implement their concepts so as to live in accordance with their own pattern
and to create for themselves the kind of organizations to which they have
been accustomed. But the new environment does not turn out quite
according to expectations; it calls for changes and modifications. From
this stem many conflicts affecting the group and the individual.

Even when mass psychology and hysteria exert pressure, migration is
the outcome of individual choice. The immigrant leaves his country with
some hope of being able to improve his lot in the new land. The physical
transformation from one society to another involves many frustrations
and gives rise to many social problems among the immigrants.[11] The
feeling of insecurity in a strange new environment, the separation from
the familiar surroundings, the necessity of adapting to the new, lack of
stability, failure to achieve status—all may lead to personal disturbances,
to aggression, to isolation, or to a desire to submerge oneself into the
dominant group.

Almost every contact in the new world bears the seeds of both adjustment and alienation. The first important contact arises from the necessity
of earning a living. In the pursuit of his daily bread, the immigrant is
forced almost immediately upon landing to find "a corner" in the economic
structure of the new land. He may bring with him ideas of his own, and
he may have accumulated experience and skills which he may try to use.
But he has to apply all of this to the realities of the new country. By virtue of taking his first job, or settling on a farm, or peddling his wares, or
opening a business enterprise, he must perforce integrate himself somewhat with the environment. On the other hand, this same economic function becomes—except in the case of those who are successful and move out
from the immigrant milieu—also a means of alienation. The immigrant is
deprived of choice. He usually has to accept the lower-paid jobs, and must
work long hours under the worst conditions. Peddlers and businessmen
often find it advisable to do their business among their own countrymen,
whose language and habits they understand and to whose needs they may
cater more successfully. Nevertheless, it is the economic function which
contributes the most toward "assimilation." Through his work the immi-

grant comes in contact with natives or assimilated immigrants. He observes their mores, their attire, their way of life, and he begins to imitate them. In many occupations he is forced to conform, at least externally, with the accepted code of behavior; he must know the language and acquire the forms of doing business.

Another primary necessity, a place to live, usually operates to alienate him from the larger environment. The immigrant is forced to seek the cheaper dwelling places. He is also likely to settle near his former fellow-countrymen, thus creating a ghetto. In need of mutual help, of security in case of sickness or death, and of comradeship, he may rely either on associations whose forms were brought over from abroad, or on ones copied from the new scene. In either case they serve, on the one hand, to help the immigrant associate himself more closely with the new country, while at the same time setting the group apart as such. The same holds true for the press, theatre, schools and religious institutions which the immigrant creates for himself. The general school, the general press, the street, and political life work in one direction—they all tend to alienate the immigrant from his own cultural background and they also serve to create a gulf between the immigrant and his children.

A further factor which has a definite influence upon the immigrant's emotions and behavior is the attitude of the native group or earlier immigrants toward him:

> Nothing annoys the foreigner or delays his assimilation more than a feeling of real difference . . . or of distinctions imposed on or sensed (social and professional inequality, xenophobia, racial discrimination, etc.). . . . One of the most unhappy fates is that of the man without nationality whose sense of being an outcast can amount to anguish. Every adaptation implies the acceptance of novel circumstances, but these must give the newcomer the feeling of being accepted, of enjoying material equality with all other members of the group.[12]

The disdain of the older settler forces the immigrant to adhere more closely to his own kind, to seek security in being proud of his origin, in the nationalistic tendencies of his group abroad. All of this leads to resistance to amalgamation. Actually, however, the immigrant's loneliness, shock, disorganization, alienation, resistance to the various pressures on the part of the "old-timers," his insecurity and lack of a sense of belonging, lead to a *variety* of reactions, many of them contradictory. Note, for example, the following: hopelessness, and an unscrupulous urge for achievement; resistance to change and willingness to give up the old ways and mores, and clinging to group identity and the urge for assimilation; nationalistic pride bordering on association with the ultranationalistic groups at home, and the drive to shed all group identity and submerge in the new country; severe criticism of the new country's order and mores, and readiness to accept everything as the best; religious piety and laxity; political conservatism and radicalism. All these and similar contradictions are an outcome of the specific situation into which the immigrant is thrown, with the individual immigrant reacting in one way or the other.

In the case of the Jewish immigrants to the United States, developments were influenced by two other forces: the fact that the Jews also comprised a minority—generally a persecuted or oppressed minority—in the countries from which they came, and the differentiation between the various waves of Jewish immigration. The first factor may have, on the one hand, preconditioned them somewhat to the role of a minority and to being uprooted and "replanted," but at the same time they were highly sensitive to anti-alien trends and group differences, seeing in them—rightly or wrongly— a repetition of European anti-Semitism. These sentiments and attitudes worked in two ways: they strengthened the feeling of alienation, frustration, and the desire for group life and, on the other hand, heightened the trends toward assimilation and the wish to shed as rapidly as possible all special group characteristics. All such tendencies became cumulative through the different waves of Jewish immigration, with each preceding wave both looking down upon those who followed and regarding them as of a lower species, while, at the same time, trying to force upon them the patterns which they believed would generate a minimum of anti-Jewish prejudice. Thus, the conflict between the older and the newer immigration was continually renewed.

Each of the Jewish immigrant groups had its own particular cultural pattern. Also, each wave came to a different America where, trying to continue with the former way of life in a strange environment, it was apparently subject to "social disorganization" and frustration:

> The greater the incompatibility between the cultural pattern of orientation of the immigrants and those of the absorbing country, and the stronger the immigrants' identification with their original patterns, the greater the tensions within the immigrants' own group, particularly between the generations.[13]

The Jewish immigration groups each felt the forcible uprooting to which every individual reacts with resentment and hope, with fear and longing. The difference between the first and the subsequent immigration waves was that the former left its initial imprint, and the subsequent groups had to accommodate not only to the outside world, but also to the generally strange pattern of the preceding Jewish group. The cleavage between their own pattern and the new environment was thus doubled. However, while the preceding Jewish group tried to impose its own patterns on the newcomers, shocking them by their manifestation of superiority, on the other hand it somehow helped to lessen the "cultural shock" by "explaining" the outside to the newcomers and serving as "interpreters" between the immigrants and the new social setting.

§ *The Sephardim and the German Jews*

The Sephardic Jews, who formed the dominant stream of Jewish immigrants during the century and a half after 1654, came with a distinctive

Jewish heritage. They were Marranos, or the descendants of Marranos. Some had experienced *de facto* political freedom in the Netherlands, England, or the West Indies before coming to these shores. Almost from the beginning they were indistinguishable with regard to their external appearance. The statements made by a German officer at the time of the Revolutionary War to the effect that Jews and Jewesses (in New York and Newport) were indistinguishable from others,[14] may have applied also to an earlier date. In other ways, too, they had always been steeped in general secular culture. After the first generation of the original Marranos, one authority states that "no knowledge of the traditional language of prayer" existed.[15] Furthermore, "the place of the voluminous [Jewish] ancient sacred literature was now taken by the Latin version of the Bible . . . the [prayers] of the Marranos were in the vernacular."[16] In Amsterdam, where the Marranos could return openly to their Jewishness, Spanish and Portuguese remained the official languages of the community and its literary means of expression, even though Menassah ben Israel established a Hebrew printing press in 1627.[17] Thus in America the group had only to transfer from Spanish culture to English culture. This was rapidly achieved—in fact, even before the adherents of the Dutch Reformed Church, or the German group, could make any such transition.[18]

In this connection it is significant to note that the minutes of Congregation Shearith Israel of New York City are written in Portuguese up to 1741, and later in a mixture of that language and English. However, by the end of the eighteenth century, English is employed exclusively. In 1757 the Congregation demands a cantor "who will be able to teach the children Hebrew with translation into English and Spanish," but five years later only Hebrew and English are required. Furthermore, the leadership was rapidly losing all contact with Hebrew. In 1728, of the seventeen people signing the regulation of Shearith Israel, only three (all having Ashkenazic names) employed Hebrew script. By 1746 it was only one out of forty-seven. In 1761 the first English translation of the holiday prayer book (*machzor*) was published in America. In the preface to the 1766 edition it is stated that many understand very little Hebrew, others none at all.[19] The *hazzan* (cantor), Gershom Seixas, no longer knew the Iberian tongue. In short, American Jews of the second half of the eighteenth century seem to have had much in common with the non-Jews with whom they frequently congregated and with whom they did business.

While the Judaism of the Sephardic immigrant was expressed not so much in terms of Jewish learning or even in strict observance, it *was* manifested through the following: (1) a strong organizational structure (the tradition of the Amsterdam Kehillah [community] with its *herem* [excommunication] powers), and (2) a strong hope of redemption. The Marrano had been unable, under the pressure of the Inquisition, to observe Jewish traditions, to learn Hebrew, or to study Torah. He used the same Bible as the Christian, but he concentrated on the Old Testament. The essence of his Jewishness was centered around a few doctrines, among which the denial of Jesus' claim to have been the Messiah was highlighted more than among other Jews. This stronger emphasis in turn placed in special focus the messianic hope of restoration of the "Land of Promise"—a hope which played such an important role in the Marranos' attitude toward Sabbatai Zevi: "They hoped eagerly for the final deliverance which they bound up with the recollection of the former national center in the Land of Promise."[20] From here a straight line leads to the strong tone of belief in *geulah* (redemption) which is to be found in the sermons of Seixas and in the writings, speeches, and plans for Ararat of Mordecai M. Noah. Organizationally, Shearith Israel in New York tried—by means of such sanctions as the *herem,* the denial of burial rights, and fines—to exercise power over individuals and to enforce a minimally religious way of life.[21] Only later, when a great many Jews became lax about observance, and when practice showed that they could exist without the Kehillah, did Shearith Israel relax its regulations (1790, 1805).

The original intention to build in America a Kehillah on the European model (i.e., one with compulsory powers) did not seem out of order, or in danger of making the American Jews of the eighteenth century "marginal men." Similarly, they, or their Americanized and Anglicized second generation, did not see any contradiction between their Americanism and Gershom Seixas' sermons filled with hope for return and for the "ingathering of exiles" to the Land of Israel.[22] Noah, who participated in American politics, journalism, and public life on a par with non-Jews, not only attempted to erect in America a Jewish state, but he regarded this as a preparation for the return of Jews to Palestine. He dreamt of a great "Jewish nation" by including the Samaritans, the Karaites, and the American Indians.[23] It may well be that Noah was an eccentric, or desired to use this affair for his own purposes, but the interesting point is that he belonged to the Jewish leadership group: he played a role in Congregation Shearith Israel and later in New York's Congregation B'nai Jeshurun (founded in 1825). Thus, his voice could mistakenly have been identified by non-Jews with that of the Jewish community. As far as it is known, the leaders did not find it necessary to disassociate themselves officially from his "nationalistic" proclamations and actions. One may possibly interpret the "exile" feeling, as expressed by Seixas and inferred by Noah, as having to do with Jewish religio-cultural matters, while in economic, social and political fields there was a feeling of belongingness. Thus, the pattern which evolved among the Sephardim was that of a group assimilated in terms of language and external way of life, being little versed in Jewish learning, becoming lax in ritual and religious observance, participating as individuals in the political life of the country and the social life of their neighbors, but nonetheless for the most part clinging to their religion, celebrating the Sabbath and holidays in their homes, and retaining their hope for redemption.

This picture did not hold for the Ashkenazim, the German and Polish Jews (mostly from Western Poland, which had become part of Prussia) who came to America during the eighteenth and the beginning of the nineteenth century. True, in the seventeenth and eighteenth centuries (and probably earlier) German Jews had little Hebrew learning and some had become lax in observance. Some committed sexual digressions; contrary to accepted concepts some were not far removed from secular pastimes and were on intimate terms with non-Jews. *Pinkesim* (minute books) of the communities, the moral literature of the time, and sermons attest to these trends.[24] Even so, the general outlook was traditional; Jews were legally separated from the non-Jewish environment and had their own dialect—the Judeo-German—in which the immigrants to America wrote their letters.

Following the Peace of Westphalia (1648), German Jewry was mobile, penetrating into new cities or into old ones in which their presence had formerly been prohibited. Some of these people on the move reached such port cities as Hamburg or Amsterdam. From there, some went on to England. And some dared to venture into the unknown, to undertake the long journey to the East Indies, or the North American English colonies. For the most part, these were single young men from poor homes. A number of them came here as indentured servants.

The make-up of the German Jewish immigrants during the first half of the nineteenth century, as well as afterward when the main stream of immigration came from Southern Germany, may be briefly described. The Jews there still lived, for the most part, in the traditional way, even though enlightenment and general schooling may have made inroads.[25] They also, in contrast with the general belief, still used to a great extent their Yiddish or Judeo-German,[26] although most of them may have also known German. The bulk of the immigrants comprised, at first, single young men—this fact is emphasized by the Jewish press of those years.[27] And even later, in the 1840's and 1850's, single young people seem to have predominated among the immigrants. Certainly this is true in the case of Württemberg, from which region we have official data.[28] These young people,[29] most of whom came from poor families of village and small-town horse and cattle dealers, storekeepers, artisans, farmers, and traders, were far from being learned in Torah. They were, just the same, attached to tradition even though they very often violated it in practice.

Still more was this the case with the Polish Jewish immigrants or those who came from Posen, a Polish province incorporated into Prussia at the end of the eighteenth century. The Polish Jewish immigrants, although mostly originating from the poorer, less educated groups and perhaps even from the less strictly Orthodox ones,[30] were more steeped in a Jewish way of life. They were also more learned in Hebrew than the Sephardic Jews, and had their own language, Yiddish.

These Ashkenazic immigrants of the nineteenth century (coming either

directly from their home countries or via London) were torn from their
environment and accustomed way of life, and transplanted to the strange-
ness of America. They encountered a most discouraging situation. Not
only was the outside world—the world of the Gentiles—unfamiliar, but so
were the rest of the Jews. Since the religious ritual in the synagogues was
Sephardic, it was different from the one to which they were accustomed.
Observance was much too lax even for the none-too-pious immigrants.
Instruction of the young was inadequate, knowledge of the Torah almost
nonexistent.[31] Socially, the Sephardim (and Sephardized Ashkenazim)
had added to their usual pride (a consideration of themselves as a sort
of Jewish aristocracy), the "right" of first-comers and of wealth. They
despised the poorer Ashkenazim and looked down upon the uncouth and
uneducated small-town German Jews. The shock of alienation and frustration, the protest against degradation, the reaction to being outcasts—all
this motivated criticism of the existing order. There were conflicts and
secessions from institutions, the foundation of new institutions, romantic
longings for the past and attempts to reconstruct its vestiges in institutions,
and warnings to countrymen at home not to come to America.

Thus, Haym Salomon in 1783, like Max Lilienthal in the 1840's and
Mose Weinberger in the 1880's, advised relatives and friends to remain
at home. Weinberger wrote: "For you, respected reader in Russia, Poland,
and Hungary I devoted this chapter. . . . You may have thought to come
here and seek your luck . . . [but my advice is to] . . . stay home."[32]
According to Lilienthal: "Jewish men who have families, a job, or a position may stay there. America needs men with industry, courage and
patience. . . . Lessons have to be conducted in English. *Shohatim* [ritual
slaughters] and *Chazanim* [cantors] must have some funds to be able to
wait for a position."[33] And Haym Salomon, like Eastern European immigrants a century later, complained about laxity in religious observance.
In a letter dated July 10, 1783 to a relative abroad, he wrote: "Your *Yikhes*
[family dignity] is worth very little here," and, "the nature of this country [is] *wenig yiddishkeit*" [little Jewishness].[34]

In Georgia, where the Ashkenazim came in some numbers, they had
founded a community of their own by the 1730's. During the Revolution
a number of newcomers came to Charlestown, most of them German and
Polish Jews, and they formed a "German-Jewish Congregation," though
it was in existence only a short time.[35] In Philadelphia, the Hebrew German Society Rodeph Shalom was founded about 1802 (perhaps a few
years earlier). In New York, after 1815 the newcomers began to challenge
the leadership of Shearith Israel. They claimed that the members of the
congregation were not sufficiently observant and did not care enough for
Jewish education. This was the group which broke away from Shearith
Israel and founded B'nai Jeshurun. They were reluctant to admit into
their congregation those who failed to observe the Sabbath.

This trend toward relaxing religious observance among the "old-timers," with a group of newcomers either dissenting or forming a newer, more Orthodox organization, was repeated many times during the nineteenth century. At the same time, individuals who succeeded in amassing fortunes tried to achieve status by "Sephardization."[36] Thus the Gratz family (of German-Polish extraction) and the Sheftall family were identified with the Sephardic group. Moses Levy and his brother Shmuel from Germany came to New York apparently at the end of the seventeenth century. They married into Sephardic families and became leaders in Shearith Israel (the inscription on the tomb of Moses is in Spanish as well as Hebrew). Isaac M. Wise relates in his memoirs that when he came to New York in 1846, he found that the oldest congregation was the Sephardic one (Shearith Israel), and that its oldest member was a Polish Jew.

By the 1840's changes had been taking place among the German-Jewish immigrants themselves. Both the general and the Jewish immigration waves from Germany began to bring in a number of intellectuals who had received a general German education. Among them were a few modern rabbis, and the so-called "forty-eighters" who had left Germany for political reasons. These people were steeped in German culture and thought.[37] They served as intermediaries here between the Germans and the German-Jewish group, "representing" the latter in German clubs and associations, voicing their sympathy with Germany and German culture, and celebrating the founding of the Reich at the beginning of the 1870's. As part of its Jewish heritage the German-Jewish group brought the fear of anti-Semitism and the sense of the long struggle for emancipation. In Germany this had involved, among other things, the desire for assimilation and the shedding of specific Jewish traits and national hopes, the leaning toward Reform, and probably also the prejudice against "Ostjuden."

Most of the immigrants were not intellectuals, but rather young people from tradition-bound homes in the villages and townlets of Germany, and at first they tried to continue to live according to tradition. But the difficult life in America plus the long trip from home to the port of embarkation and thence to America, led to laxity in Jewish observance.[38] More often than not, this laxity served to emphasize the immigrants' loneliness, alienation, and lack of a sense of belonging. The diary of Abraham Kohn, who came from Bavaria in 1842 and who later became a founder of Kehilath Anshe Maariv Congregation in Chicago and a friend of Abraham Lincoln, may be characteristic of this trend of feelings and attitudes. The fact that he is unable to observe the Jewish laws and commandments leads him to disappointment with America and acute longing for home, parents, and friends:

Leading such a life [as a peddler] none of us is able to observe the smallest commandment. Thousands of peddlers wander about America. . . . They no longer put on the phylacteries; they pray neither on working day nor on the Sabbath. . . . Is such a life not slavery rather than liberty?

From here he goes on to criticize the "celebrated freedom of American soil" where the right to peddle involves an expensive license and where one must "profane the holy Sabbath." The people in America appear to him to be funny, the land full of "hypocrisy, guile, and fraud," and he frequently thinks of his past:

> I long for the beautiful days in my beloved homeland. . . . Oh youth of Bavaria, if you long for freedom, if you dream of life here, beware, for you shall rue the hour you embarked for a country and a life far different from what you dream of . . . people who are credulous, filled with silly pride, cold toward foreigners and toward all who do not speak the language perfectly.[39]

These lonely, uprooted people, with their longing for home and the way of life they were accustomed to, and their alienation from the new environment, felt a craving both for some sort of belonging and for some Jewishness. The small group of Jewish intellectuals who were steeped in German culture gave direction to this craving. German culture,[40] which was at that time also highly valued in America, formed a shield; a minimum of Jewishness was encouraged in the synagogue which was mostly patterned after the non-Jewish church;[41] exclusive clubs and associations were organized; a new "aristocracy" was formed comprising the wealthy and privileged early arrivals. This group drew a social line between themselves and the Jews who came from Poland and other East European countries.[42] This tendency was strengthened by the general trend in America to differentiate between Northwest Europeans and East Europeans.

In line with the philosophy of similar circles in Germany, the elite group attempted to shed the traces of national identification. They declared themselves opposed to restoration in Palestine. They asserted that Jews are no longer a nation, they substituted another language for Hebrew in the prayers and they disclaimed the binding force of dietary laws and ceremonials (note the resolutions passed by the Reform rabbinical conferences held in Philadelphia in 1869 and in Pittsburgh in 1885). Being free of most of the attributes of Jewish group identification, this group of German Jews (we should not identify the elite with all German Jews in America) was easily able to change over from German to English (or, rather, to demand that other Jews do so) while privately, as it were, clinging to German culture.

The philosophy of Americanization propounded in the society at large became part and parcel of the philosophy of the German-Jewish leadership group. This was to serve two ends: (1) to assure recognition as a part of the larger community and thus avoid anti-Semitism, and (2) to facilitate acceptance among the higher American prestige groups by "civilizing" the "awkward and alien" religious Jews. The same motives

lay behind the German-Jewish opposition to the influx of East European
Jews, behind their attempts to remove and disperse them from the large
cities, and behind the Americanization-assimilationist trend given to the
whole system of assisting immigrants when the tide of immigration could
no longer be stemmed. Philanthropic activities were, however, also motivated by the Jewish heritage of welfare, by the feeling of kinship and
group ties, as were also the attempts to help in defense of Jewish rights
abroad.

§ *The Immigration from Eastern Europe*

The Eastern European immigrants, whose numbers began to increase
at the end of the 1860's, were different from the German Jews. They came
from a milieu where the feeling of homogeneity, of *Klal Yisrael* [unity of
Israel], was strongly entrenched, and where a set of Jewish values and
attitudes prevailed, including religious devotion and observance. In Eastern Europe, Jews lived in compact masses. Not only did they form a
majority of the population in many towns and hamlets, as well as a considerable percentage in the big cities, but the Jewish sections in these
settlements were generally "purely Jewish." In the smaller communities
the Jews usually occupied the central neighborhood surrounding the market place and business section, while the non-Jews lived in the suburbs.
In the big cities the Jewish population was mostly concentrated in a certain section with only a few living in the other neighborhoods.

In contrast with Western Europe, there was a definite sense of belonging to a "nation" or people. The mode of life was less a matter of individual
choice and more a matter of control by the group through the medium of
public opinion. If we take Thomas and Znaniecki's definition that social
opinion is the common factor which holds the community together, the
Jews of Eastern Europe lived in such a community. This was, however, a
community in the process of disintegration, though the exact degree of
disintegration varied from region to region, from community to community, and from group to group.[43] In the last quarter of the nineteenth
century, when the mass emigration began, the Jewish society of Eastern
Europe had already been torn by antagonisms for more than a century.
There were tensions between Chassidim and their opponents, the Mithnag-
dim, between Maskilim [enlighteners] and traditionalists, between poor
and rich—antagonisms which not infrequently found an outlet in overt
action. Conflicts between rich and poor, between those with prestige and
the depressed groups, were emphasized during the first half of the nineteenth century by the introduction of military service for Jews (Russia
1827, Poland 1844), for it was the poor and underprivileged who were
inducted, while the scions of the wealthier families found ways and means
of avoiding military service. Jewish society in Eastern Europe had also
been subject, for a century, to the forces of migration—forcible eviction

from villages as well as urbanization. Secularization was taking place and, in the era of mass migration, movements such as nationalism, Zionism, Socialism and the labor movement all became influential. From the viewpoint of the *shtetl* society, these were disruptive forces. This was especially true of Socialism, for its cosmopolitan ideology denied the existence of the Jewish people as a group.

The Jewish immigrants to the United States constituted in great part the "dissenters," the poor and underprivileged, the unlearned or less learned, and those who were influenced by secularism. The rich and well established, the learned and those with *yikhes*—with status—stayed at home. Moreover, the traditionalists feared to come because of the *weinig yiddishkeit* prevailing in America. Nevertheless, the majority of the immigrants *did* visualize themselves as wanting to live a Jewish group life with the traditional paraphernalia—somewhat relaxed perhaps, but not abandoned. Even the radicals were, in the final analysis and with minor exceptions, thrown back to the Jewish group, if only because they lacked a knowledge of English. Those who came over in the hope of working for the revolution in Russia—enlisting financial and other support—had to do this on East Broadway rather than among Russian immigrants who worked in the mines, in labor gangs, or on farms. The Jewish radicals fought tradition *within* the Jewish group—they arranged "Yom Kippur balls" (large parties on the Day of Atonement) in order to demonstrate their anti-religious attitude. Even though they refused to acknowledge it, they were living in a Jewish environment.

The East European Jewish immigrant found a doubly strange, unfamiliar, even hostile world. The cities in which they settled were dominated by a growing industrial economy which was interested in a fluid and cheap labor supply, but scarcely concerned with the laborer. The organized, or semi-organized, labor movement was opposed to immigration. And the dominant Protestant Anglo-Saxon group differentiated between the "old" and worthy immigrants, and the "new" unworthy ones.[44] The last quarter of the nineteenth century was also the period in which the beginnings of overt anti-Semitism and discrimination became observable, and when the American image of the Jew began to take the form of a stereotyped immigrant-peddler or old-clothes dealer, of a Shylock or parasite "producing nothing, fattened on the produce of land and labor and living on it" who was out somehow to subjugate the world financially.[45] These tendencies may or may not have been fully known to the new arrivals. The immigrants did, however, experience the prejudice of the Irish or German groups which found expression when boys or young people assaulted a Jewish peddler or passerby.

The Jewish environment in the United States was no less strange and unfriendly. The temples of the Reform Jews, with their Sunday services and uncovered heads, did not appear in the least Jewish to someone from

Eastern Europe. The leadership of the German Jews in America not only looked down on the new arrivals and emphasized the differences between themselves and the newcomers, but coupled their antagonism with the negative attitude of the non-Jews.

An anti-immigration tendency had been on the rise in the country since the 1870's. The debates in Congress in connection with President Grant's messages of December 4, 1871, and May 14, 1872, in which he demanded laws for the protection of immigrants, clearly showed a sentiment favoring control of immigration. Several states adopted laws to regulate immigration, but they were voided by the Supreme Court in 1876. In the following years the tide of immigration again rose after a drop in the mid-1870's. In April, 1880, a bill was introduced in Congress to limit entry of paupers and other undesirables, and it passed two years later. In 1884 New York State voted restrictive immigration laws. In 1891 there was a further extension of the federal exclusion of immigrants on grounds of health and morals; in 1896 a literacy test bill was passed but vetoed by the President. The general public saw in these and similar measures means of preventing (or limiting) the immigration of East and South Europeans—the "new immigrants" who were regarded as engulfing the country.

The German-Jewish leadership, their press and institutions, reflected these anti-immigration tendencies, and even applied the same terminology to the Eastern European Jews ("paupers").[46] Fearing anti-Semitism, or for other reasons, they opposed further arrivals. They tried to send back some of those who came, and were otherwise far from treating them as brothers. The following represent some of the reactions of Jewish organizations in America to the immigration in the wake of the Russian pogroms of 1881-1882: "Send no more immigrants." "America is not a poorhouse." "We would not be made an asylum for the paupers of Europe." "Emigration must cease. We'll not receive another refugee."[47] The Conference of Managers of the Associated Hebrew Charities in 1886 went on record with the following resolution: "We condemn the transportation of paupers into this country . . . all such as are unable to maintain themselves should be forthwith returned whence they came."[48]

The attitudes of the communities outside of New York were similar. To an inquiry from abroad in 1889, local charities replied: "They [the immigrants] are a bane to the country and a curse to the Jews;" [they] "are lazy and shiftless" . . . "very few . . . were able or had the inclination to do a day's hard work," and that until their Orthodox notions will be changed "there is little to be expected even from the children."[49] It is to be noted that the head of the United Hebrew Charities in Philadelphia tried, through denunciations, to stop Jewish immigration. He wrote first to the Secretary of the Interior, and later to the Secretary of the Treasury, complaining about the allegedly illegal influx of immigrants:

Philadelphia, July 26th, 1887.

Hon. Secretary of the Treasury.

Sir:— I respectfully beg leave to call your attention to a matter that, in my opinion, is in direct violation of the immigration laws. I have observed in my official capacity as Superintendent of the Young Men's Branch of the United Hebrew Charities of this city, the arrival of so many helpless men and women, and I am called upon nearly every day by immigrants who have been but a few days in this country, making demands upon our funds and applying for assistance otherwise. I learn from them that in very many cases their tickets are furnished them abroad through to Philadelphia, and inasmuch as the Association of Immigrants of this city has an agent who boards each and every incoming steamer to detect these paupers, I am led to believe that the difficulty occurs at the Port of New York; in fact, I have been told by many of them that such is the case. I have the honor to attach a letter from the Hon. Secretary of the Interior with whom I first communicated and who refers me to you.

Very respectfully your obedient servant,

E. Kleinsmith,[50]

Apparently only a relatively few men, such as Benjamin F. Peixotto (a leader of B'nai B'rith and at one time American Consul in Rumania) defended the Russian-Jewish immigrants.

That such negativism toward the immigrants had practical consequences is shown by the figures on returnees.[51] The Yiddish press of the time pointed out that the immigrants were being sent back on cattle steamers. The newspapers maintained that the Jewish agent of the United Hebrew Charities at the Port of New York was worse than the Irish Commissioner, for he was always advising "send him back."[52] The Eastern European Jew—as reflected in the Yiddish press—generally regarded the Charities as a lifeless machine which was out to degrade him and force him into Americanization or assimilation rather than to actually help him.

Another area of contact with American life—that of earning a living—was no less disappointing for the immigrant. If he had any hope of making money or a comfortable living in the "golden country," he saw his dreams evaporate immediately upon arrival. Although the percentage of skilled workers among the Jewish Eastern European immigrants was considerable, they could not all be absorbed in their previous occupations. The vast majority of the arrivals had two avenues open to them: (1) peddling, and (2) factory work in clothing or other light industries. Either one meant hard work, poor pay, an activity which the worker was frequently unaccustomed to, and even, to a certain extent, degradation. At least at first, peddling involved carrying heavy packs, knocking at many doors, often being abused, and earning but a pittance. The clothing shops, and to some extent also the cigar "factories," often comprised dirty, overcrowded, badly lit and ventilated rooms, in which tens or hundreds of workers toiled in a speed-up system for fifteen or even eighteen hours a day. Earnings were little, payment being uncertain and irregular:

Former *Yeshiva* students, store clerks, insurance agents, semi-intellectuals, Jewish teachers, bookkeepers . . . storekeepers, peddlers, became workers in tailoring shops. This was extremely individualistic human material, unaccustomed to discipline . . . all those people who in their home country had never done manual work, were here harnessed to the machine which ran, hurried, and speeded up until the last breath.[53]

The Eastern European Jew found himself at the opposite pole from the German Jew, or the "Germanized" Eastern European earlier immigrant. The latter group comprised the "bosses," the owners of the clothing and cigar factories, or of the stores which supplied the peddlers with their wares. Some of them were also on the boards of the charity institutions, and were obtaining cheap manpower through these organizations. The employer-employee relation only aggravated the tension between "East" and "West." And to add to this, there was the disappointment of the religious Jews who found it difficult, if not impossible, to observe the Sabbath, to obtain *really* Kosher meat, or to follow other religious observances. In summary, the documents of those days, the press, the fiction, the songs as well as the memoirs, are filled with descriptions of the sad plight, the poverty, and the dissatisfaction of the peddler and worker.

A common reaction to a new and unpleasant situation in a new country is to criticize, to negate it, and try to "escape" it:

There was no one who liked his work. All hated it and all sought a way of being free of it. All looked upon . . . the boss as upon their enemy, the exploiter who fattens up the marrow of his workers and gets rich on their account.[54]

This climate of opinion paved the way for the agitation of the socialists and anarchists. They found among these lower-middle-class (or declassed) people who had become workers, ready listeners to ideas condemning the existing conditions and promising a betterment of their lot. Depressed and underprivileged people do not, to be sure, make good material for a socialist organization or for a well-run trade union. But the negative approach, the criticism, found an open ear.

Disappointment, frustration, and loneliness motivated some to return to the countries of their origin. The majority, however, remained in America, and cursed Columbus for ever having discovered the land.[55] Through the European Hebrew newspapers they warned their countrymen to remain at home. They withdrew into themselves and into each other, tried to transfer their home environment to the new country which they refused to acknowledge. By these means they tried to create for themselves the feeling of belongingness. The immigrants had brought with them the image of their institutions, their way of life and ideas. The religious Jews made every effort to keep up their observances. They organized synagogues and chassidic *Shtiblech* (prayer and study houses). Frequently there was some form of mutual help organization or *landsmanschaft* connected with these institutions. The Orthodox element also attempted to form a Kehillah on the Russian-Polish model, and for this purpose they brought to New York at the end of the 1800's Rabbi Jacob Joseph from Vilna. They organized all sorts of religious schools: *Hadarim, Talmud*

Torahs, Yeshivoth. The small group of Hebraists organized Hebrew-speaking societies. The secularized, Russified intellectuals also sought to continue their tradition: "A very large number of the ghetto dwellers continued to live in Russian spirit, i.e., the intellectual and revolutionary Russia."[56] The nationalist-secularists wanted to develop a secular Jewish culture. This tendency characterized some of the Yiddish and Hebrew schools which were founded in the beginning of the twentieth century, and some of the Yiddish and Hebrew press and literature starting in the 1880's.

Institutions, organizations, and publications were, in fact, only physically located in America. In spirit they had little to do with America, having been transplanted from Poland and Lithuania to American soil. Praying was done according to the Polish ritual with the one difference that here there was less time to devote to study. The teachers in the *Talmud Torahs* and *Yeshivoth,* as well as in the modern Yiddish or Hebrew schools, came from Eastern Europe and used mostly textbooks brought over from there or arranged according to East European models. The method of instruction did not change except that, again, less time was devoted to these studies. This same tendency characterized the Yiddish (and Hebrew) periodicals. They were printed in America but the center of their interest lay in the old home. As the late Samuel Niger asserted:

> I read over the weekly *Forwerts* and *Zukunft* from 1897, *Nayer Geist, Naye Zeit* of 1898 and I was astounded to find that America occupied so little room in these important periodicals. Not only the articles, but also the news items, deal with America far less than with the old home. All these periodicals could, according to their content, have been printed in London and Paris, and not necessarily in New York.[57]

During World War I the Yiddish press reflected clearly a friendly attitude toward the Central Powers—a trend motivated by the old-world approaches and sympathies of the immigrants as well as the position taken by many Jews in Eastern Europe:

> We were persecuted in Russia, forced to leave . . . and we have a full moral right to hate our oppressors and to desire their defeat.[58]

By that time, however, a radical change was taking place among the East European immigrants. As a lower-middle-class group who had become workers out of sheer necessity, they were anxious to rise economically. Several avenues were open to them in the growing economy. The peddler could, in time, become a storekeeper. Also, the worker might open a candy store or a grocery, or become a jobber and eventually the owner of a factory. The carpenter or glazier sometimes became a building contractor or builder. Another possibility was to spend one's evenings studying so as to be able to take up a profession. Thus by 1914 a considerable number of East European immigrants were moving, or preparing to move, into the middle class. The Jews, coming from an urban

culture, had a head start over the other ethnic groups of the "new" immigration and they manifested a high occupational and class mobility. Thus,
during the last forty to fifty years, the Jews in America have changed from
a group comprising a majority of factory workers to one with a negligible
percentage of such workers. The old feeling of alienation and disappointment was destined to be moderated as the immigrant and his children
became part of the general urban middle class, and as they adopted its
code of behavior and mores.

The urbanized, industrialized middle-class society of America is, as
Erich Fromm, David Riesman, and others have pointed out, market-
oriented. One places on the competitive market "an externalized part of
the self" and not "the genuine self." The "personal non-marketable idiosyncrasy" has to be left at home if one would achieve success on the
market. In terms of the Eastern European Jew this might mean that he
could adjust his "artificial self" to the outside world by leaving his internal
"idiosyncrasy"—a part of his heritage, his sympathies and his group attachment—for his own "home consumption."

The Eastern European Jew and his American-born descendants have,
with some exceptions, preserved many emotional loyalties to their tradition
and heritage, vestiges of group identification, and a feeling of sympathy
and kinship with brethren abroad and with those in Israel. As the Americanized Eastern European Jew and his children have become the leaders
of Jewish organizations these trends make themselves felt in varying
degrees in contemporary Jewish community life. One may venture to say
that to a certain degree the immigrants have come to resemble the Sephardic or "Sephardized" Jew of a century and a half ago, for today we also
find a Jew who has accommodated in terms of socio-economic relations,
language, external way of life, who feels himself at home in the American
environment and participates in the life of the country. He is little versed
in Jewish learning and lax in religious observance, but clings to vestiges
of his heritage, activates Jewish values and survival, has an emotional
attachment to the group, and experiences the feeling of *Klal Yisrael*.

§ *Postscript: Recent Jewish Immigration*

The more recent waves of Jewish immigration include the immigrants
of the 1930's who came to America after the ascendance of the Nazis in
Germany, those who arrived during World War II, and the "remnants of
Israel" who immigrated after the war. These groups were relatively small;
it is estimated that an average of about 10,000 Jews came here annually
during the last quarter of a century (recent figures are not based on
official statistics—since 1944 the rubric "Hebrew" has been deleted from
the statistical classification scheme for immigration). The make-up of
these immigrants tended to be very different from those constituting the
preceeding waves. Many were middle-class and educated, and only those

with a certain status (such as community and party leaders, writers and rabbis), or those with "connections," were able to leave during the war or to gain admission to the country.

These new immigrants found ways and means of absorption through relatives or through organizations, and they avoided many problems of adaptation encountered by earlier immigrants. Clusters of immigrants were also not created to the extent that was true for earlier generations, although the German-Jewish immigrants of the 1930's and the extremely Orthodox groups which arrived since World War II, congregated in certain areas (the former in Washington Heights in New York City, and the latter in Williamsburg, Brooklyn). Both of these groups, however, did manifest some of the tendencies common to newcomers, namely, alienation, criticism of the existing society, withdrawal, and the creation of their own institutional framework. There was also the tendency to assimilate oneself into the existing Jewish community. Numerically, all the new groups are relatively small; they are (or will be) able gradually to fit themselves into the middle-class-oriented, Eastern-European-dominated, existing Jewish community structure. Any real impact coming from these newcomers has largely been confined to the Orthodox, who have succeeded in augmenting to a certain extent the strength of traditionalism in the area of religion.

BEN HALPERN

AMERICA IS DIFFERENT

THE tercentenary celebrations of the American Jewish community, held in 1955, chanced to come at a time when two conditions combined to heighten our sense of a peculiar destiny. We American Jews, after the destruction of the six million who were the main body of Jewry and the immediate source of our traditions, remain as the major part of all the Jews in the Diaspora. When we think of this, as we cannot help thinking, we are filled both with awe and with guilt at the blind whims of fortune through which we escaped, and we are both oppressed and uplifted by the leadership and new responsibilities we have inherited.

There is another source, too, of our sense of a special destiny. Since the Second World War, and especially since Eisenhower's election, all America has been overwhelmed with the feeling that now is our time of destiny, that this century is the American Century. For it is either that or it is the Russian Century, a thought that makes our distinction not only a proud boast but a grim obligation. To be sure, from the very beginnings of our history we Americans believed we were opening a new chapter, altering the whole character of everything that had gone before. With Wilson and F.D.R. we saw ourselves propelled into the center and forefront of world events; yet we sometimes felt that these great leaders were actually doing no more, though in the distinctively American pragmatic fashion, than forcing us to grow up to a point of social maturity the Old World had attained before us. The end of the Second World War saw the Old World in full collapse, while we (having elected Eisenhower) looked back at what we had built, up to and under the New Deal, and sealed it as concluded, fully formed, a new American way of life worthy to be emulated by other peoples. In the period following the Eisenhower election, a mass of books, pamphlets and periodical articles appeared, all sounding in varying accents the same refrain: America is different!

The American Jewish Tercentenary celebrations came in upon the crest of this wave. Jews in America at their three-hundred-year mark have their own very strong reasons to underscore the theme that "America is different," and when they orchestrate this music, it is to a counterpoint of peculiarly Jewish *motifs*. America is different—because no Hitler calamity is going to happen here. America is different—because it has no long-established majority ethnic culture, but is still evolving a composite culture to which Jews, too, are privileged to make their characteristic contributions. America is different—it is not Exile, and whatever may be the case with other Jewries, the open doors of the State of Israel do not beckon to us. With such a rich choice of harmonies, is it any wonder that the Tercentenary celebrations of the American Jews swelled to a powerful chorus, elaborately enunciating the single theme, "America is different!"

It seems, however, that the crucial respect in which American *Jewry* is different was missed altogether in the Tercentenary celebrations. That is not surprising, because if this difference were stressed it could have made the whole occasion seem artificial and contrived. American Jewry *is* different from other Jewries. It is younger than any other significant Jewry—with the exception of the State of Israel. In terms of *real,* effective history we are far from being three hundred years old. There is good sense in Croce's contention that only the history of free, rational, creative effort is real history, and that the chronicle of events in which man is passive is a different kind of thing altogether. At any rate, if American Jewry has a truly distinct and individual character, giving it a destiny different from that of other Jewries, there is only one way it can have acquired it: only by freely, rationally, and creatively grappling with the specific problems of its existence, and then handing down its distinctive working hypotheses for elaboration by succeeding generations. American Jewry has had nothing like three hundred years of this sort of history. If there are any native American Jewish institutions that were initiated before the Eastern European immigration of the 1880's, then most of these, too, are creations of the middle nineteenth century. The earliest idea evolved and perpetuated to this day in American Jewry can be nothing younger than the Reform movement, which goes back in this country to 1824. The characteristic American Jewish type today is a second or third generation American.

We are, then, one of the youngest of Jewries, one of the youngest even of the surviving Jewries. Our real history begins *after* the "solution" in America of the most critical problem that faced other Jewries in modern times, the problem of the Emancipation of the Jews. This was the problem that other Jewries had to grapple with when they entered the modern world, and the various solutions that they freely, rationally, and creatively evolved for it gave them each their individual character. French Jewry dealt with the issues and problems of Emancipation differently from German Jewry, German Jewry differently from Austro-Hungarian or from Russian Jewry; but all of them had to deal with the problem, and there was a continuity and connection between the solutions they found. What is characteristic of American Jewry, and what makes us different from all of these together, is that we began our real history as a post-Emancipation Jewry. Emancipation was never an issue among us: we never argued the problems it presented in America, nor did we ever develop rival ideologies about it and build our institutions with reference to them.

Because of this, the continuity of European Jewish ideologies is broken in America. We never had ardent groups of partisans who saw in Emancipation the whole solution of the Jewish problem. In Europe the Zionist movement arose in opposition to this thesis, and proposed "Auto-emancipation" instead of "Emancipation" as the solution of the Jewish problem. The theory of "Diaspora nationalism"—the advocacy of minority rights as a solution of the Jewish problem—likewise opposed to the Emancipation principle of individual enfranchisement the view that the Jews must be granted autonomy as a group, as an ethnic entity. All these theories existed in America only as pale copies of the European originals.

We have in America a small group who vociferously defend Emancipation, the American Council for Judaism. The pointlessness of their propaganda is obvious to anyone who asks himself who among the American Jews is opposed to Emancipation. There is no such group or person, for no one proposes to undo what has been the accepted basis of our life here since before we made any effort to shape our American Jewish history. Nor does the American Council defend Emancipation as a *solution* for the Jewish problem. Their view would be more accurately expressed by a classic statement of Abraham Cahan's, who declared in 1890:

> We have no Jewish question in America. The only question we recognize is the question of how to prevent the emergence of "Jewish questions" here.[1]

As for the opponents of this view, they, too, do not think in terms of a Jewish question which America has been vainly seeking to solve by the emancipation of the Jews, and for which we must seek alternative solutions other than Emancipation. We are only beginning to see what the Jewish question actually is in America.

§ *Anti-Semitism and Assimilation*

From a Jewish point of view, two elements are inseparable from any discussion of the Jewish problem: anti-Semitism and assimilation. For to a Jew the problem essentially is this: how can the Jewish people survive in the face of hostility which threatens to destroy us, and, on the other hand, in the face of a friendliness which threatens to dissolve our group ties and submerge us as a whole by absorbing us individually? Both phases of the Jewish problem are different in America than in Europe, and in both cases the reason is the same: in most countries of modern Europe the questions of anti-Semitism and the Emancipation and assimilation of the Jews were essentially connected with revolutionary crises in their national affairs, while no such connection existed in American history.

All we need do is consider what the Emancipation of the Negroes meant in American political and social history in order to measure the difference between a status that was never really contested, like that of the Jews, and one that it took a civil war to establish. Thus, when we think of anti-Semitism in such countries as France and Germany, Russia and Poland, we must remember that the great revolutions and revolutionary movements in those countries, at critical moments in their national history, placed the emancipation of the Jews upon their agenda for basic reform. Whatever has become part of the program of a national revolution not only divides the people at the first shock, but continues to divide them in the cycles of counter-revolution that always attend such upheavals in a nation's life. Hence, as Jewish Emancipation was an issue raised by the Revolution, so anti-Semitism had a natural place in the programs of European counter-revolutionary parties.

How different it was in America is quite clear. If the American Jews never had to divide ideologically over the issue of Emancipation, one of the reasons is that Emancipation of the Jews never became a revolutionary issue dividing the American people generally. For that matter, in the history of America the Revolution itself did not become a real (rather than academic) issue permanently dividing the people, since it was a revolution against outsiders—and the Loyalists remained in emigration. In England, on the other hand, the Cromwellian revolution was a crux in British history which still serves to determine opposed political attitudes. But at the time of that Glorious Rebellion there were practically no Jews in England. Consequently, at a later time, after the Jews had begun to arrive, the question of their Emancipation was debated in England (just as in America) in a relatively unimpassioned, desultory way. Whatever minor political struggles took place in spelling out the equal rights of the Jews had no inherent connection with, or essential place in, the major upheavals recorded in the national history. To be an anti-Semite in England, as in America, had no obvious, symbolic affinity with a counter-revolutionary ideology opposing the Glorious Rebellion or the American Revolution.

If one examines the American anti-Semitic movements, one cannot fail to appreciate how different they are from their European counterparts. Only in England do we find so anemic, so insignificant an anti-Semitic movement, a movement so unmistakably belonging to the "lunatic fringe."

The anti-Semitic movements of France and Germany, Poland and Russia may also have been fit subjects for psychopathological investigation; but no one will deny that they occupied a place in the forefront of the political affairs of their countries, and moved in (whether with or against) the mainstream of their national history. Far from being "fringe" phenomena, they had political power, or a reasonable chance to attain it. What we have in America in comparison is nothing but an aimless hate-mongering. The kind of anti-Semitism common in America is, and always has been, endemic throughout the Diaspora. It may be found in every social condition and in every political persuasion, from extreme right to extreme left. It is an anti-Semitism of impulse: the most characteristic thing about it is that it is not really organized on the basis of a clearly enunciated program providing what ought to be done about the Jews if the anti-Semites had their way.[2] This is something quite different from an anti-Semitism that was primarily political in vision. Modern European anti-Semitism was characterized from the beginning by large and active political aims, and it included, among other far-reaching social revisions proposed in its counter-revolutionary program, precise provisions for making the Jews second-class citizens, expelling them, or exterminating them. In comparison with these movements, American anti-Semitism (and, for the most part, British) has never reached the level of an historic, politically effective movement. It has remained, so to speak, a merely sociological or "cultural" phenomenon.

The question of assimilation also looks different in America, because the Jews never had an established status here other than that of our so-called Emancipation: there never were enough of us here before the nineteenth century to warrant giving us a special, institutionally established status. In Europe, on the other hand, Emancipation came as an effort to alter a hoary, time-honored status in which Jewish communities lived long before the Revolution.

The Emancipation seemed to promise the Jews that the difference between them and the Gentiles would be reduced to the private realm of religion. All public relations with the Gentiles would be carried on in the neutral area of citizenship, where Jews were guaranteed equality. Jews assumed that the public realm was identical with the whole social realm of intercourse between them and the Gentiles, and that in all other than purely Jewish religious affairs they would have full and free contact and equal status with Christians. This they soon found to be a delusion, for in all countries they discovered that Jewishness was a barrier and a disability in a wide range of social relations and that citizenship opened far fewer doors than they had imagined.

In most European countries the areas closed to Jews had been elaborated by centuries of custom and usage. When one had explored the precise extent of new freedoms opened to the Jews by the new status of citizenship, the barred contacts remained clearly and decisively, in fact, often quite formally, defined. The army, the higher government service, the magistracy, and the universities were all careers closed to Jews which, by quite explicit understanding, became open immediately upon baptism.

In all of Europe, Jews soon found that even after Emancipation actual relations in society continued to be governed by a series of restrictions taken from the religiously grounded stratifications of the *ancien régime*. To protests that all this was contrary to the new doctrine of citizenship, purporting to open all careers to talent and all doors of social intercourse to individual merit, an answer was soon provided: a still newer doctrine, the doctrine of romantic, organic nationalism, superseded the principle of citizenship. The national idea gave a new justification and pumped new life into practices which had theretofore survived as stubborn relics of feudalism and now all at once became grafted onto the modern idea of democracy. Fixed social positions, traditional folkways and culture, inheritance of privileges and obligations—all that had once been grounded in the divine will—now gained an organic sanction in the national history. The Jews found their assimilation even more rigidly opposed than under the purely religious criterion. If inheritance (that is, ethnic origin) became the key to admission into society and the license for participation in culture, then even the formal step of conversion was of no avail to the Jew.

In the beginning of the present century the actual social conditions that faced the Jew seeking to be part of his European nationality represented a shifting balance between divergent tendencies. One tendency was that of the Revolution, whose principle was to treat the Jew as an individual no different from all the rest. Actual social relations conformed to this principle only to the extent that the Revolution itself, or other forces, had succeeded in atomizing society. The Industrial Revolution and the development of trade allowed Jews to find new opportunities in business and thereby brought them into a new relation of equality with Gentiles. The Revolution succeeded in imposing its own principles in all political relationships except the bureaucracy. But the Jews could not simply move into these new positions unaltered. The grant of equality imposed its conditions and demanded its price. The "clannish" solidarity of the Jews had to be given up so that they could enter the body of citizens as individuals. They could keep their religion as a private cult, but not necessarily the kind of religion that was traditional among them. Jewish tradition was too organic in its own way, it incorporated too much historic distinctiveness and ethnic character, for the rigid individualism of radical revolutionary doctrine. Not that anyone expected to see the full consequences of egalitarian theory rigorously applied to Gentile society. But the revolutionary ardor to liberate the Jews had roots of its own in the anti-Semitism that is endemic in all Gentile society and expresses itself in all its divisions. The Jews might not get all they expected out of Emancipation, but the Emancipators were disposed to watch with a jealous eye how the Jews went about paying its price.[3]

The nobility, the army, the universities, all the corporate embodiments of privilege bearing upon them the stamp of consecration and tradition escaped the levelling influence of Revolution. As Jews rose in society through other channels they found their ultimate elevation blocked at these points. Some fought their way through to these positions as Jews, but most found that access to their goal, otherwise blocked, became magically open through a relatively simple and quite perfunctory (in most cases) operation. So they acquired new "convictions" and became baptized.[4] To the other Jews, this renegadism, as they regarded it, was their first great shocking disillusionment with the Emancipation, the first disclosure of the human degradation which is the price of assimilation.

The most serious strain upon Jewish-Gentile relations was the rise of counter-revolutionary anti-Semitism, which absorbed into an ethnic pattern the basic attitudes to the Jews implied in their old feudal, religiously determined status. Conservative anti-Semitism in an officially liberal society had contented itself with excluding Jews from those areas of corporate traditionalism which the Revolution had not succeeded in atomizing. But now nationalistic counter-revolution, seeking to turn the clock back, opposed the penetration Jews had already made into areas opened up by liberalism. Economic boycotts of the Jews were resorted to in order to bring industry and commerce "back" into the hands of the Germans or the Poles, or whatever the ethnic majority might be.

Particularly did the nationalists resent the great participation of Jews in all cultural activities. The organic doctrine of nationalism sought to overcome a cleavage between culture and tradition that had existed in Europe since the Renaissance. Modern culture had become a secular realm parallel to the traditional beliefs, art forms, ceremonials and etiquette still grounded in religion. The social framework of culture, the *Gelehrtenrepublik,* as the eighteenth-century Germans called it, was a liberal, international, individualistic, and secular intercourse between free spirits, which, even before the Revolution, existed side by side with the corporate social structures where the religious, feudal tradition was fostered. The Revolution was the signal that gave the Jews entrée into this world. It was a liberty that they eagerly embraced, shut out as they were on other sides from assimilation and its rewards. But it was a main object of counter-revolutionary nationalism to bring all culture back into an organic coherence based on the national tradition, even if both the religious and the secular were adulterated as a result. This meant imposing upon all forms of creative expression the same corporate principles and ethnic criteria that regulated participation in the religiously grounded forms. The participation of Jews in any cultural form was henceforth regarded as an illegitimate intrusion, or even a plot by the enemies of the people to corrupt its national spirit.

Thus there were forces in European society determinedly striving to undo even the amount of assimilation Jews had achieved. They were opposed not only to the integration of the Jew into such social relations as were governed by liberal principles but also to the admission of the Jewish convert into social relations still governed by corporate, religiously grounded criteria.

How different was the situation here in America! Here the bare conditions of geography and social statistics made liberalism the dominant principle of social organization. It was not so much revolution against an old regime that opened the door to assimilation for the Jews; it was the large extent of sheer formlessness in American society which allowed Jews and many other heterogeneous groups to live side by side, with the forms of their readjustment to each other to be determined.

Free entry into American society, of course, had its price and also its restrictions, just as did the assimilation of the European Jews after Emancipation. The price of the freedom to let the ultimate forms of mutual relationship between immigrant Jews (like all immigrants) and the whole American community remain for the future to determine was the willingness of the immigrant to give up old inherited forms. Just as settled America was willing, within limits, to be elastic, so it demanded of immigrants wishing to be naturalized that they first of all be elastic and accommodating. Not that there was any haste about the scrapping of outworn Old World customs. America was large enough to set aside "ghettoes" in its cities or even whole regions in its broad lands where immigrants could live undisturbed more or less as they had been accustomed to live in the Old Country. But this was a provisional form of living, in effect outside the real America, which everyone expected to be superseded as the forms of true American living were worked out by immigrant and native Americans in a continuing process of give and take.

The willingness to relinquish Old World habits was the *price* of assimilation in America. Its *limits* were defined by the established prerogatives of the older settlers. It is true that the ultimate forms of American life remained—as they still remain—in principle undetermined, and our assumption is that the cultural contributions of all America's components are equally welcome. Yet it is both implicitly and explicitly assumed that those who came here first are entitled to preserve and impose such forms of living as they have already made part of the American way. America is not only in essence free and democratic; it is also, in its established pattern, Anglo-Saxon, religiously multi-denominational, and dominated by the mentality of white, Protestant, middle-class, native Americans. However, this social dominance and cultural predominance are maintained not by delimiting any areas of social life under traditional, religiously grounded, and formally elaborated codes of exclusion which reserve them for particular families or religions, as in Europe. Our American history has not been long enough for that, perhaps, and in any case it has from the start consecrated the principles of complete social mobility, denying in theory all exclusions. But the claims and privileges of the older settlers are maintained by informal, almost tacit social covenants, which only rarely (as in our Immigration Act) need to be openly voiced.

Thus if liberal principles fail to be actually observed in America, just as in Europe, and if assimilation stops short at the barriers set up to protect inherited privilege, there is at least this difference: in Europe, the status with which we begin is the historical, quasi-feudal status, and liberalism rules only those areas which it specifically conquers; in America, the initial status is that of freedom, and only experience proves what areas privilege has successfully reserved for itself. Those in America who nurse a nostalgia for historically rooted social status have not been able to swim in the midcurrent of an American counter-revolutionary movement. The

American Revolution is the very beginning of our real history, and there is no one who more proudly flaunts it as his symbol than the American conservative. The self-conscious American opponent of the liberal revolution has no real alternative but to become an expatriate.

The result has been that while the history of American Jewish assimilation, too, has been full of disappointment and unanticipated checks, it has run a characteristically different course from the European experience. At the very outset of the European Emancipation, Jews were brusquely confronted with the price they must pay: for freedom of the individual, virtual dissolution of the group. The immigrant to these shores, too, found that the prize of Americanization was to be won at a price: by unreserved elasticity in discarding everything which America might find foreign. In both cases, only religion was reserved as a sanctuary of Jewish tradition. But there were these differences: in Europe, there was a fixed pattern that Jews were expected to adopt in discarding their own customs; in America, the ultimate American way of life was still in principle to be determined, taking into account what of their own immigrants might succeed in "selling" to the whole public. Besides, the demands of the European Emancipation upon the Jews were peremptory, they had to be conceded at once, and even through a formal declaration such as Napoleon extracted from the French Jews. In America, there was no urgency about the procedure. The Jews, like other immigrants, could make their way into the real American community as swiftly or as slowly as they themselves chose. They could, if they preferred, remain in their ghetto seclusion indefinitely.

In Europe, then, the stick; in America, the carrot. A parallel difference existed when the Jews came up against the unexpected barriers to assimilation, the reserved areas not governed by liberal principles. In Europe, the principle of exclusion was clear-cut, traditional—and quite simply overcome, if you wished, by conversion. There was no such clear choice in America. Established privileges were no less alien to this country than an established church. It was neither the accepted practice to demand conversion for specific social promotions, nor to grant them upon conversion. Thus, if American Jews went over to Christianity, it was no such concerted wave as arose in Germany, in the first eagerness to overleap the unexpected sectarian barrier to full assimilation. It was rather a final seal, in individual cases, upon assimilation otherwise complete.

§   *The Patterns of Modern Jewish Thought*

It is clear, then, that the typical situation faced by the American Jew was not the same as that characteristic of the European Continent. The differences apply to both major aspects of the Jewish problem, to anti-Semitism and to assimilation. But modern Zionism, and indeed all modern Jewish ideologies, arose when Jews began to confront, to take account of, and to understand—or try to "reach an understanding" with—the typical situation of Continental Europe. The characteristic American Jewish situation had hardly even begun to be faced—until the establishment of the Jewish State abruptly forced us to face it. It need not be surprising, then, if at precisely this time we witness a feverish effort to create a new American Zionism and new American Jewish ideologies generally; nor that these forced-draught efforts should in the beginning often bring more confusion than enlightenment.

What was the historical situation of Continental Jewry in the late nineteenth century, when the modern Jewish ideologies arose? As we have seen, it was characteristically a period of post-revolutionary or, if we may say so, neo-traditionalist nationalism, a period with a living memory of an *ancien régime,* a revolutionary movement, and a wave of post- or even counter-revolutionary reactions. Moreover, the Jewish problem was intimately involved with every phase of that living tradition.

The spirit of that time was critical of the Enlightenment and the Revolution, of rationalism, capitalism, and social relationships based on the undifferentiated equality of citizenship. For the modern European, the Jew became a symbolic embodiment of all these discredited traits. The out-and-out anti-Semites (but not only they) regarded the Jew as the head and fount of everything they despised in the liberal revolution—its rationalism, capitalism, and principle of civic equality. Similarly, of course, the eighteenth-century rebels against the *ancien régime* had seen in the ghetto a symbol of the medievalism they were determined to uproot. And just as the Revolution had proposed the assimilation of the Jews in all respects except as a reformed religious sect, so, by a reversal of history, the critics of the Revolution wanted to solve their Jewish problem by halting or annulling the assimilation that had already taken place and eliminating Jews and Jewish influence from the new order they hoped to set up.

What made one a modern Jew in the late eighteenth century was to understand and accept the attitude of Gentile contemporaries to social problems, and to the Jewish problem among them. The modern Jews of that time accepted the demands of the Enlightenment to change their habits and customs—those relics of medievalism—in order to enter a new enfranchised status; on the other hand, they could not understand or accept the exclusions still practiced against them after they had paid this entry fee. But the modern Jew of the late nineteenth century "understood" fundamentally, however much it may have pained him, why it was that he was not assimilated into full fellowship in his country. He shared with the modern Gentile the feeling that European society had not yet become what it should be, or that it had even gone quite astray from its true path. Thus, integration into society on the basis of the liberal principles of the Revolution no longer seemed to be the solution of his Jewish problem. In fact, the degree to which that integration had already taken place, in culture, in economic pursuits, and even in political participation, began to constitute for him, as for the Gentile, the very crux of the Jewish problem, the false position in which both danger and self-denial dwelt. He, like the Gentile, began to see or foresee other solutions of the Jewish problem as part of a new revolution of the whole structure of European society, in the course of which Jews would either disappear entirely as an entity or regroup in a new segregation from the Gentiles. "Modern" Jews hoped either for a radical revision of the liberal revolution, leading to Socialism and the disappearance of Judaism together with all other religions, or for a new nationalist era in which Jews would live as a distinct national entity, in the places where they then lived or in a new national territory. In other words, either total assimilation in a new, millennial secular society, without the eighteenth-century reservation of freedom to maintain a reformed Jewish religious community, or the total rejection of assimilation and an attempt to establish a new Jewish ethnic independence, in the several countries of Europe or in a new territory to be colonized by Jews.

The rejection of assimilation was a doctrine shared by Zionists with other ethnic autonomists. The failure of Emancipation, from this point of view, demonstrated that there had been a breach of faith by the Gentile Emancipators and a historical error on the part of the Jews; for after the latter had practically reformed themselves out of existence as a historic group, Gentile society had failed to keep its part of the bargain by assimilating the Jews individually. Zionism, however, viewed not only eighteenth-century Gentile liberalism with a disenchanted eye. It also had its reservations concerning those Gentile movements which, like itself, were critical of existing society and hoped to reconstruct it. In this respect, Zionism differed sharply from other modern Jewish movements. Jewish Marxism, regarding the Jewish problem as an expression of capitalism that would disappear in the classless society, implied faith that one's Gentile fellow-Socialists would not break their covenant as had the Gentile liberals. The advocates of national autonomy for minorities in Europe similarly trusted that Gentiles would abide by the covenants that were to embody this principle. Zionism had no faith in the willingness of the Gentiles to extend a welcome to Jews, under any definition, as free and equal brethren in the same land. It was a disillusionment built upon the experience that it was possible for revolutionists to regard Jewish blood spilt in pogroms as merely "grease on the wheels of the revolution."[5]

Zionism took anti-Semitism seriously and expected it to persist. This is the specific way in which it differed from other modern Jewish ideologies. The Socialists, who expected to submerge the Jews in a classless, cosmopolitan society, the Diaspora nationalists, who planned for minority rights —none could hope to succeed unless anti-Semitism vanished. The Zionist (and territorialist) solution of the Jewish problem, contemplating the removal of the Jews from Europe, remained intrinsically possible even if one were pessimistic or prudent enough to reckon with the persistence of anti-Semitism among the Gentiles.

Zionism, like other modern Jewish ideologies, felt it understood the critics of European liberalism (among them, the anti-Semites) and their disapproval of the liberal solution of the Jewish problem. Accepting, as they did, the organic, ethnic views of history and nationality, they felt it was a betrayal both of the Gentile and the Jewish national destiny for Jews to make themselves the protagonists of Gentile culture, for example, instead of fostering their own. Moreover, they appreciated that if it were the aim of a group to use all sources of power in a given territory for the preservation and propagation of its distinct national values, its traditional style of life and culture, its own ethnic variant of Christian culture, then it was bound to be resented when political and economic power came into the hands of Jews. Such an attitude left only one possibility for a compact between Jews and Gentiles that the two distinct groups could loyally uphold: those Jews who could not or would not assimilate must have a country of their own where they would be separate and independent.

Two things are characteristic of American Jewish ideologies. The first is that American Jews never faced directly the whole historic complex of problems, centering around Emancipation as a traumatic event, from which modern Jewish ideologies arose. The second is that only in our own time, actually in these very years since World War II, has American Jewry been compelled to face its own peculiar situation and to create its own history. One could conclude, then, that American Jewish ideological development may still not really have begun.

Whatever truth there may be in such a conclusion, it need not mean that we have had no differences of opinion, no debates until now. That is obviously untrue, for whatever ideology existed in Europe has had its adherents, few or many, here. Thus American Zionism, for example, arose by understanding and sharing in the typical attitudes, problems, and situation of Zionism in Europe—especially in the degree that American Zionists continued in America to live the life of the Old Country.

Now it was quite generally characteristic not only of American Zionism, or of American Jewry, or even of all immigrants, but of America itself to share and understand the life and thoughts, the trends of modern culture and politics in the Old World. Those newcomers who lived in the immigrant ghettos (at least, the cultural elite among them) shared the life of the Old World most directly and most specifically. Those older settlers (again, the cultural elite among them) who were establishing the permanent forms of American life also continued to live in the current of European political and cultural development, though with greater detachment and in a more general form. It was a more international European culture, and not so specifically a particular national culture, in which they shared. As for the culture arising in America itself, the specific "culture" native to the immigrant ghettos was based not only on an obviously transitory experience but also on an experience of suffering rather than of creation; "permanent" American culture remained intrinsically open and partially unformed, constituting, in a way, a set of defensible hypotheses rather than a body of axioms and absolute values.

It is important to note that only in our own time has the characteristic American Jewish type come to be the native-born American Jew. American Zionism, product of an earlier generation, was to a large extent a movement of the American immigrant ghetto.[6] Thus, intellectually, it shared in and understood the Zionism of the nineteenth-century "modern" European Jew, just as the other immigrant ghettos shared in and understood the social and intellectual movements of the Old Country they came from. The immigrant intellectuals who dominated American Zionism had a more direct and more specific understanding of the situation, problems and attitudes of the modern European Jew than is possible for the native American Jew. Yet even for them European Zionism was a *vicarious* experience.

It was natural, therefore, that even for the immigrants, new American experiences—the experience of the American immigrant ghetto, and the unfolding experience of the new American society in formation—began to color their Zionism. This tendency was heightened by the influence of native American leaders who were active in American Zionism from the very beginning. The nuances by which American Zionism was touched through its naturalization in America have now, in a time when American Jewry is largely native-born and remains as the major surviving Diaspora, become the dominant coloration of a new American Zionism.

The two major divisions of the Jewish problem, assimilation and anti-Semitism, look different against an American environment. The theory of assimilation as a solution of the Jewish problem was a revolt against an old-established historic status of the Jews in Europe, into which they had sunk vast creative energies. The "Ghetto" in Europe was not only an oppression the Jews suffered but a way of life they clung to. And when the reaction against assimilationism came in European Jewry, it paralleled, in a way, the post-revolutionary movements among the Gentiles: it saw itself as the synthetic conclusion of a Hegelian dialectical process. The Emancipation had been an antithesis of an original thesis, the Ghetto; and Zionism (like other modern Jewish movements), in transcending the Emancipation, intended to absorb what was valuable not only in the liberal revolution but in the primary status—the Ghetto—which assimilationism had rejected.

"Assimilationism" in America was a rejection of life in the immigrant ghetto. But life in the tenements had never been filled with any creative significance, no historic values had been placed upon it and institutionalized through it, it contained no unfulfilled promises, no high demands spontaneously arising from its own context to give historic dimensions to its past and historic perspectives to its future. The immigrant ghetto from the beginning was entered into only to be abandoned. For the Jewish immigrants it represented either the collapse and bereavement of the old values of the true, historic, European Ghetto—or, if they had already emancipated themselves from the historic Jewish values, it was a "melting pot," a grimy anteroom to the real America, a sordid extension of Ellis Island.

The generation that entered the immigrant ghetto was confronted by one overwhelming task: to get out, or enable the next generation to get out. This task they accomplished. But the generation that accomplished it had, in a way, stepped out of the frame of history, for history consists in whatever continues over a span of successive generations. The immigrant ghetto was not a continuation of the context of European Jewish life, whether Ghetto or emancipated; it was an interruption of that continuity, a break with that context. Nor did it, nor was it ever intended to, continue into the life of the next generation. It was a specific experience outside the frame of history and hence outside the frame of culture, at least in so far as culture is essentially historic.

There was nonetheless a very active cultural life and a vivid sense of history in the Jewish immigrant ghetto. That generation, in fact, reached an unsurpassed peak of historical awareness as Jews. And, concomitantly, they led a life of high cultural intensity. But the historical movements and cultural trends in which American Jews participated were European Jewish history and European Jewish culture, relevant to the situations and problems and expressing the values of European Jewry. The social reality of American Jewry was the one-generation experience of the immigrant ghetto, known from its very inception to be out of the frame of history and culture. Of course, American Jewry could never accept a merely vicarious participation in history and a merely nostalgic participation in culture, however intense these might be. The immigrant generation felt itself to be as much (if not more) a new beginning as a final chapter in the historic and cultural continuity of the Jews. They looked to the day when the threads of vicarious history and cultural nostalgia would weave into a new American pattern of continuity. But every American Jew, whatever his ideological sympathy—religious or secular, Zionist or non-Zionist, "survivalist" or "assimilationist"—knew beyond any question that the new hoped-for continuity that would transmit the American Jewish experience into history and culture must necessarily begin beyond the threshold of the immigrant ghetto.

If, then, "assimilationism" means radically to reject the "institutions" of the ghetto—in America, of the *immigrant* ghetto—then every American Jew, whatever his ideology, is an "assimilationist." And, in fact, the actual process of "assimilation" in the United States *is* the absorption of immigrants out of the immigrant ghettos. This is a movement in social relationships which it is common ground for every American Jew to accept. When "assimilation" served as an issue between American Jews it was not the actual process of assimilation out of the immigrant ghetto into the real

American society about which they were debating; their argument was about assimilation as it occurred in Europe.

The differences of opinion native to the American Jewish experience are only now beginning to be defined. They arise after assimilation out of the immigrant ghetto has not only been tacitly accepted in principle but carried out in practice. Assimilation can only become an issue, in terms of the actual experience dividing the American Jews, after the liquidation of the immigrant ghetto. At that point, when he is an "integrated" member of American society, the American Jew—now typically native-born—discovers that he still has a problem of assimilation. The problem is a totally new one, it presents the first challenge whose creative mastery might establish a continuous American Jewish historic tradition. If we may speak in terms of the Hegelian dialectic at all in America, then we are only at the point of establishing a thesis, not, as in Europe, capping an historic antithesis with its synthetic resolution.

In view of this fact it should not be surprising if American Jews are unwilling to begin their history with the disillusioned conclusion that they can come to no satisfactory terms with the Gentiles for the creative survival of the Jewish people in America. Nor should it be surprising that in looking backwards for its supports in history, no portion of American Jewry seeks to recapture any values institutionalized and expressed in the characteristic experience of the immigrant ghetto. Nor, finally, should it be surprising—however little gratifying we may find it—that the first attempts to set up American Jewish ideologies are based on a rather empty, almost defiant optimism about Jewish survival in the Diaspora and a somewhat boastful confidence in the values we will yet produce.

The question of anti-Semitism also looks different when viewed from an American perspective. In the past, to be sure, American Zionists and anti-Zionists have divided ideologically in their reactions to anti-Semitism almost entirely in relation to the nationalistic anti-Semitic movement of Europe. The anti-Zionist view was that, even if the Jewish status of Emancipation liberalism was inadequate, Jewish ideology must have as its premise the full confidence that anti-Semitism must and will disappear in a new Gentile society. The Zionist premise was that modern nationalistic anti-Semitism would not disappear, and that where it had once appeared Jewish life would increasingly become intolerable.

But the characteristic fact about America was that modern nationalistic anti-Semitism had not really appeared here. Moreover, the usual historic grounds for its appearance were lacking. The Jews in America did not come out of a medieval Ghetto through an act of emancipation, to find that, as a bourgeois people, they aroused nationalistic anti-Semitism. They filtered out of an immigrant ghetto not as a people but individually. They encountered anti-Semitism in America, but it was not based on a nationalistic reaction, rejecting the emancipation of the Jews. The native American anti-Semitism encountered here was the old perennial anti-Semitism in which Herzl discriminated the elements of "cruel sport, of common commercial rivalry, of inherited prejudice, or religious intolerance." This was a kind of anti-Semitism which neither Zionism nor any other modern Jewish movement could or would understand. It was the type of anti-Semitism with which only the medieval Ghetto had provided a certain established basis of understanding.

It is true, on the other hand—and very significant—that European anti-Semitism was able to extend its influence across the Atlantic and demonstrate, on numerous critical occasions, that the fate and destiny of American Jewry were intimately connected with the fate and destiny of European Jewry. But at other times, the global threat to the Jews having subsided, the American Jews who busied themselves with the matter were faced with the problem of their own, specifically American anti-Semitism.

This problem never really became an ideological issue between Zionists and non-Zionists in America any more than did the problem of American assimilation. At most there was a difference in the degree of concern about native anti-Semitism between Zionists and non-Zionists, a sort of temperamental difference rooted quite remotely in differences of ideas. The Zionist attitude, at bottom, assumes anti-Semitism to be ineradicable. With nationalistic secularist anti-Semitism, Zionism once hoped for an understanding through divorce. But where anti-Semitism remains theological, demanding perpetuation of the Jewish Exile until the Second Advent and the subjugation of Jews to Christians in the meantime, Zionism has no understanding to propose. Thus the characteristic attitude of American Zionism to this problem—that is to say, to native American anti-Semitism —is not to take it too seriously, to feel that it is essentially a Gentile, not a Jewish, problem. On the other hand, it is characteristic of non-Zionism to take precisely this problem seriously. Non-Zionists are inclined to turn a blind eye to the seriousness of nationalistic anti-Semitism such as we saw in Europe, rejecting the notion that Jews should attempt any "understanding" with Gentiles through emigration. The basis for this attitude is an underlying belief that anti-Semitism is not really a "modern" movement, with more vitality and contemporaneity than the Emancipation of the Jews, but only a medieval survival that should expire with the inevitable increase of rationality. Among the "missions" which non-Zionism has proposed for the Jewish Diaspora, one taken up with great earnestness in every country, and in America as well, is to cure the Gentiles of their vestigial anti-Semitism and so to consummate fully the Jewish Emancipation. But whether this is at all conceivable, assuming that Jews remain a distinct entity in the Diaspora, is a problem the new Zionist ideologists still have to face.

The crucial difference which has been brought about in the Jewish problem in the past generation is not only the rise of the State of Israel, but perhaps even more the destruction of European Jewry. This is a factor whose significance is likely to be overlooked because it is a negative factor —and one, of course, which it is anything but pleasant to remember. Without European Jewry, the face of the Jewish problem as it appears to American Jews is radically altered, and in a way simplified. Hitherto, views on the Jewish problem, in its two aspects of assimilation and anti-Semitism, were based on our European traditions and, no less, upon our involvement with the European Jewish situation. But now we live in a Jewish world where, essentially, we see only two main constitutents: ourselves—American Jewry—and the State of Israel. In Israel, the Jewish problem of assimilation and anti-Semitism does not exist, or only in the most indirect and transmuted forms. It continues to exist for us. But the problems of assimilation and anti-Semitism must now be approached in the forms native to America, without the overtones of significance previously lent them by their involvement with the developments in Europe. That simplifies the situation considerably.

We cannot say as confidently that it clarifies it as well. The nature of the Jewish problem characteristic of America has not yet been considered with the degree of rigor and incisiveness that were typical of our European ideologies. That was natural so long as the American situation was regarded as an atypical and not too significant variant of the Jewish problem. It now becomes the major exemplification of that problem in our times. That fact requires, as it is beginning to produce, a new focus in the direction of Jewish thought.

2

Demographic Aspects and
the Factor of Social Mobility

INTRODUCTION

SINCE the U. S. Decennial Census asks only for the individual's national origin, it is of diminishing utility to students of the sociology of the Jew. As is evident from other sections of this volume, the lack of such data is no insuperable barrier, for many types of productive investigations can be carried on in spite of wide gaps in demographic knowledge. These gaps, and especially the problem of selecting a sample at a reasonable cost, do of course offer continual harassment to the researcher. The articles presented in this section demonstrate, however, that substantial progress can be made even in the area of demography in spite of the lack of official statistics.

There have been two important sources in lieu of data from the Decennial Census. The first have been population surveys conducted by local Jewish communities. These "self-surveys" vary widely as to the methodology which they employ and the effectiveness with which their methodology is implemented. Frequently, the defects of such surveys are not immediately apparent, but perhaps the greatest limitation of "self-surveys" lies in the fact that they are seldom done in the largest Jewish communities. It is in this connection that the general study which is conducted for other than a Jewish purpose has particular value—such studies can be utilized to make real advances in knowledge about the demography of the Jewish community. These studies may be of limited utility in the smaller Jewish community, but in cities which have a fair proportion of Jews—the very cities where our knowledge is scantiest—they can yield valuable data.

Ben B. Seligman's "Some Aspects of Jewish Demography" uses a number of the more recent and more methodologically sophisticated "self-surveys" to suggest some overall demographic trends. His article is notable not only for the many cities which are presented, but also for the inclusion of relevant data from the Decennial Census. In communities where the ratio of Jews to non-Jews is not too sizeable, and where the Jewish survey is conducted at about the same time as the Decennial Census, a comparison of the data gathered by the two methods can be exceedingly helpful.

The widest gap in our demographic knowledge has been New York City. Even if reliable data were available for every other Jewish community in the country, the lack of material about New York City would mean that a valid demographic portrait of American Jewry would still be unavailable. There seems to be no immediate prospect of a "self-survey" in New York City. Fortunately, a research project on medical problems conducted by the Health Insurance Plan of Greater New York included both questions of a demographic nature as well as a query about religion. It is this material which forms the basis of the second article by Seligman, "The Jewish Population of New York City: 1952." The reader will note that the HIP Survey is confined to New York City alone—there are no data available about Jews who reside in the suburbs. In spite of this limitation, the article makes a highly important contribution to knowledge about a subject of basic importance.

The contribution of David Goldberg and Harry Sharp, "Some Characteristics of Detroit Area Jewish and Non-Jewish Adults," represents a further attempt to utilize data collected as part of a general research effort. One of the special merits of this material is the comparisons which are made between four different groups; frequently, studies compare merely Jews and non-Jews, or Jews and other whites. Another feature of the article is the data on income. Surveys sponsored by Jewish communal organizations have difficulty in obtaining valid information about income; the fact that fund-raising is an important activity of such bodies militates against frank disclosure. A note of caution is in order about the Goldberg and Sharp figures, however. Their top category is "$10,000 or more." We suspect that if this category were subdivided, a somewhat different picture would emerge; on the whole the largest incomes in the community are probably earned by non-Jews.

In focusing upon demographic aspects of American Jewish life, students have paid particular attention to comparisons between Jews and non-Jews in such areas as educational level, occupation, and income. The most apparent difference which emerged was that the rate of social mobility of the Jews was considerably higher than that of comparable non-Jewish groups. This fact was noticed by those who were primarily students of Jewish affairs as well as by those concerned more with stratification *per se*. Whatever the starting point, the discovery of an explanation for this phenomenon is of great importance. The first three articles in this section are primarily devoted to the presentation of data; only secondarily do they grapple with the problem of explanation. While the succeeding three articles—those by S. Joseph Fauman, Nathan Glazer, and Fred Strodtbeck—also present data on social mobility, they focus more explicitly on causal factors. Each of the three present a somewhat different approach, but all—in one way or another—look to Europe. That is, they seek for an explanation in the history and culture of the Jewish group. They do not believe that anti-Semitism alone, or the American situation alone, can explain matters fully. The orientations which they develop are helpful in understanding succeeding sections of this volume. In particular, they set the stage for the final section: "Some Cultural Aspects and Value Orientations."

BEN B. SELIGMAN
with the Assistance of
AARON ANTONOVSKY

SOME ASPECTS
OF JEWISH DEMOGRAPHY

§ *Introduction*

COMPRISING the largest Jewish community in the world, American Jews are as yet unable to ascertain with any degree of precision how many persons make up that grouping, where they live, how old they are, where they came from, and how they earn their livelihood. Full and detailed demographic information, comparable to the census data which are available about Canadian Jewry, is almost entirely lacking. While numerous attempts have been made to estimate the number of Jews in various localities in the United States, no nationwide census of American Jewry exists. The national estimates of Jewish population made by the Jewish Statistical Bureau in 1926 and 1936 in conjunction with the decennial Census of Religious Bodies of the United States Bureau (or the survey *Jews in the United States, 1945-46* made by the Office of Public Opinion Research at Princeton for the Federal Council of Churches), might have been thought by some lay people to be sufficient, but demographic experts have found them to be adequate only for purposes of rough calculation. Moreover, these studies do not provide detailed demographic data on the different religious groups, but only figures on church membership (roughly divided into two age groups), on congregations, on church property, and the like. In addition, no Census of Religious Bodies was held in 1946 for lack of Congressional appropriation, and it seems unlikely that such a census will be conducted in the near future.

Yet the importance of up-to-date, reasonably accurate data on Jewish communities is frequently recognized. Agencies serving Jewish communities, in addition to wanting a fairly reasonable estimate of the size of the Jewish population, would like to know its approximate age and sex distribution, the occupational distribution, whether the size of Jewish families

Published in this form for the first time. Much of the material has been adapted from: Ben B. Seligman and Harvey Swados, "Jewish Population Studies in the United States," *American Jewish Year Book*, Vol. 50, 1948-1949; Ben B. Seligman, "The American Jew: Some Demographic Features," *AJYB*, Vol. 51, 1950; *idem*, "Changes in Jewish Population in the United States, 1949-50," *AJYB*, Vol. 52, 1951; *idem*, "Recent Demographic Changes in Some Jewish Communities," *AJYB*, Vol. 54, 1953; and Benjamin B. Goldman and Alvin Chenkin, *The Jewish Population of New Orleans: 1953*, Council of Jewish Federations and Welfare Funds, 1954. Thanks are due to the publishers for permission to utilize this material.

is increasing or decreasing, whether there has been any change in longevity, whether population mobility is increasing in a way that shows a decided shift from one area to another, and the like. Obviously such questions are of prime importance to a community that intends to erect a community center, a hospital, a home for the aged, or a children's home, or that hopes to formulate long-range plans for community activity. In fact, the study of almost any problem in Jewish social research must either be based on population data, or needs population data as background.

It is not suggested here that knowledge of the demography of American Jewry is completely lacking. Local Jewish communities have from time to time conducted surveys to ascertain population size and characteristics. In 1948 an effort was made by the Council of Jewish Federations and Welfare Funds (CJFWF) to poll its member agencies in an attempt to discover the extent and intent of population studies that had been conducted in American Jewish communities in the previous decade. The present paper is based on data obtained in reply to this poll, subsequent data on other communities obtained in the years since 1949, comparable data on the total white population of those cities for which Jewish data were available, and, wherever feasible, comparisons with the demographic information as set forth in *Jewish Population Studies*, edited by Sophia M. Robison, a summary of surveys conducted in the 1930's.

At the time of the 1948 inventory there were 228 communities affiliated with the Council. A simple questionnaire was designed and mailed to them with the request that they return it together with a copy of any local study that might have been made. One hundred and fifty-two communities complied with the request, or about 67 per cent of those polled. This may not seem like a large enough percentage on which to base a series of conclusions, but it should be borne in mind that this 67 per cent represents approximately 90 per cent of a rough estimate of 4,500,000 American Jews.[1] The striking fact that 152 respondents can represent a concentration of 90 per cent of the population of the slightly more than 1,200 communities of which population estimates have been obtained, can be more easily grasped when it is understood that the thirteen largest Jewish communities in the United States—those reporting populations of 40,000 and over—comprise approximately 75 per cent of the total Jewish population: Baltimore, Boston, Chicago, Cleveland, Detroit, Los Angeles, Miami, Newark, New York City, Philadelphia, Pittsburgh, St. Louis, San Francisco.

The CJFWF study was not an attempt to obtain a precise count of the total Jewish population of the United States. Although the questionnaire did include several queries on total population estimates, it was recognized that the variety of ways in which these totals were arrived at would preclude the possibility of adding them up and attempting to present a scientifically accurate estimate of overall Jewish population. The object of the study was rather to survey local censuses, counts or studies that had been made in the previous decade, with the prospect of determining the approximate validity of current population estimates, of discovering the extent to which scientific methods were being utilized in local community studies, of learning whether there is a common basis for further demographic research on Jewish population, and of collecting suggestive data that might aid in marking out a program of national population and demographic research.

The recipients of the questionnaire, therefore, were asked not only for current local population estimates, but also for reasons why the current estimate varied (if at all) from earlier estimates, and the methods by which the current estimate was arrived at. In addition, they were given a list of possible sources of population information (synagogue lists, contributors' lists, etc.), and asked to check which of them they had used in compiling the current estimate. Finally, they were urged to indicate whether they intended to conduct a population survey in the near future.

The 152 communities replying to the questionnaires fell into three categories:

(1) Thirty-two communities of less than 1,000 Jewish population. They are scattered from coast to coast. Eight of them have conducted surveys in the past, consisting largely of counts based on master lists or other community listings. This primary dependence for population figures on listings or people in the community parallels that of the larger communities. But unlike the larger communities, those having 1,000 Jews or less specifically claimed that every Jewish individual in the reporting area was personally known to the respondent. Only three communities indicated that future population studies were contemplated.

(2) Fifty-four communities of 1,000 or more Jews in which population studies had not been made in the previous decade. In this category, the Jewish population ranges from 1,000 to 90,000. It does not include any of the five cities which have the largest concentration of Jewish population: New York, Chicago, Philadelphia, Los Angeles and Boston. In this group we find fifteen cities, almost a quarter of the total, reporting population estimates of 10,000 or more. (Half of this entire group reported that its estimates applied to metropolitan areas exclusive of environs.) This is a large fraction of the American Jewish group, and what strikes one most forcibly is that it is impossible to determine with any accuracy just how large a fraction it is, much less what kind of a fraction it is. As one respondent, answering for a community of about 20,000 Jewish persons, put it, "No one seems to know the origin of our estimate."

The devices employed to estimate Jewish population in these communities are varied: they include contributors' lists, alone and in combination with other lists, directories of various kinds, as well as individual guesses. In some instances, the number of Jewish families was estimated and arbitrarily multiplied by a figure which was believed to be representative of the average size of Jewish families in the community. This multiplier ranged from 3 to 3.7, depending on the predilection of the person making the estimate. In many of these cases, the average size of family for the general population was used, yet most students of Jewish population problems are agreed that in all probability the average Jewish family in this country is smaller than the average of the general population. Group pride would seem to be a strong factor in perpetuating overestimates both of family size and total population.

Of these 54 communities, 17, or 31 per cent, indicated that population studies were in progress or being contemplated. Each community, however, has its own interpretation of the term "population study," in the absence of a nationally directed series of surveys. It was clear that the value of the contemplated studies, insofar as population and demographic data were concerned, would vary enormously from city to city.

(3) There were 66 reporting communities which based their population estimates on surveys completed during the previous decade. Here again we find that there is far less homogeneity in survey techniques themselves, in findings, or in population estimates than we might at first expect. They do, however, exhibit features in common with the first two groups. For example, once again there is an almost even division between those communities restricting their estimate to the metropolitan area and those reporting for surrounding areas as well (obviously the variation in final population estimates can be significant, when large urban centers with sizeable Jewish populations in surrounding towns and residential areas are taken into account).

The population of these surveyed cities ranges from a reported 1,100 to a reported 2,000,000, and is distributed as follows: 55 of the cities report Jewish populations of 1,000 to 19,999, and 11 report populations of 20,000 and over. The table below breaks this down further.

Jewish Population Estimate	No. of Cities
1,000-4,999	31
5,000-9,999	20
10,000-19,999	4
20,000-39,999	1
40,000-99,999	5
over 100,000	5

These cities are, of course, scattered from coast to coast, and are representative of an excellent cross-section of large, medium and small Jewish communities.

All but one of the respondents in this surveyed cross-section report that the bulk of the surveys has been conducted between 1941 and 1948. Furthermore, 50 per cent of the surveys are credited—in whole or in part —to the National Jewish Welfare Board and its wartime subsidiary, the Bureau of War Records, which conducted a series of studies in American cities from coast to coast with the aim of establishing the percentage of Jewish men in military service, verifying their war service records and the like. Twenty-seven of the studies were conducted by local community councils, federations or similar organizations.

Seven principal survey techniques were utilized in these sixty-six studies. And even though seventeen respondents do not specify the techniques used, or indicate that the methods used are unknown to them, it can safely be assumed that this one-quarter of the responding communities in this group were surveyed in much the same manner as the three-quarters who list the following techniques:

Method	No. of Cities Employing Method
House-to-House Campaign*	24
Master List	23
Yom Kippur School Absence	7
Sampling	7
Death Records	3
Telephone Poll	3
Mail Poll	2

* Some refer to this as a door-to-door campaign, some as an "actual census," some as a "complete census," some as an "actual count," etc.

Before discussing the advantages and disadvantages of the above-listed methods, it would be well to point out that none of them are mutually exclusive. One can be certain that many more than twenty-three communities compiled master lists based on the rolls of communal organizations; surely many of those who conducted door-to-door surveys, or telephone polls, or mail polls or sample studies, began by making up an unduplicated list of all known Jewish families in their community.

Half a dozen of the respondents who report having conducted surveys compiled figures of the total number of Jewish families in their community, rather than of individuals. Once again, the multiplier used to determine total Jewish population varied with the community, from a low average family size of three to a high average family size of four.

A few words about techniques peculiar to Jewish population studies may be in order at this point. The problems of such studies are peculiarly complex and it is only natural that special efforts to solve them should have been made by demographers, statisticians and population experts. Each new technique that they have devised has its special merits, each new technique has its special difficulties and weaknesses. The Yom Kippur method involves a count of the number of pupils (generally between the age of 5 and 16) absent from the public school system on the Day of Atonement. From this number is subtracted the absences on an average school day. The difference, with corrections made for the somewhat smaller size of the average Jewish family, should give the number of Jewish school children; from this figure the total Jewish population can be estimated by comparison with the age composition of the general population. The complexity of this method renders it difficult for all but trained workers, and the possibilities of error in each step of the process, to say nothing of the assumptions that must be made at the outset, all conspire to make the final figures on Jewish population minimal, and subject to upward revision, as was recently demonstrated by Louis Rosenberg, a Canadian statistician (*American Jewish Year Book*, LVI, 1955, p. 298).

The death records method, as Dr. Robison puts it, "is based on the assumption that there is a similarity between the birth and death rates of the Jewish and non-Jewish population."[2] The problem is one first of identifying Jewish deaths in the community (by typically Jewish name, country of origin, undertaker or cemetery), and then of determining whether one is dealing with an aging population, which implies a changing death rate. The constantly changing death rate, the investigator's uncertainty as to whether he has actually selected an area containing a representative sample of the Jewish population and the questionable validity of "Jewish-sounding" death certificates, are all negative factors which must be weighed against the low cost and comparative simplicity of the operation. Here again only trained statisticians can be expected to conduct a death records survey with sufficient skill to make it a technically worthwhile operation. Demographically it is less worthwhile, for death certificates will not yield information on family size, occupation, employment status and the like.

Another method of population study utilized by a number of communities that may require explanation is the sample study (listed by seven respondents). Sampling can be a comparatively simple matter in a small community which is just a little too large for a complete door-to-door count of all Jews; in a great metropolis, it can be enormously complex, since care must be taken to insure the relative accuracy of the sample— both as to size and composition—for each section of the city that is enumerated. The great advantage of sampling is its flexibility; the sample can be drawn from lists of Jewish families, census lists, contribution lists and the like, and can be weighted so that it draws from heavy as well as light concentrations of Jewish population. The results, if the survey has been properly conducted, can have a gratifyingly high degree of accuracy, as witness the regular intercensal sample studies of the U. S. Census Bureau. But unfortunately, the sampling technique is most susceptible to distortion at the hands of inexperienced personnel. More than one community has begun a sample survey only to find complications mounting to such an extent that, even while enumerators were still in the field gathering data, the survey had to be abandoned.

In the completed sampling studies reported, the size of the sample has varied from 1.5 per cent to as high as one-third. In two instances (Newark, Pittsburgh) the size of the sample itself varied, depending on the intensity and estimated Jewish population of individual sampling areas. For example, the size of the sample in the Newark study varied in inverse ratio to the density of Jewish population in the individual area: in sectors known to be heavily Jewish, a 1/30th sample was used; in predominantly Gentile areas, practically the entire Jewish population was enumerated.

Obviously, not all of the numerous Jewish population studies made at different times and by different persons lend themselves to comparative analysis. In many, the gaps in the data were sufficiently serious as to require their elimination from the present survey. From among the 66 community studies of Jewish populations of over 1,000, reported in the 1948 CJFWF survey, and from subsequent studies, a number have been selected for detailed examination. These are listed in Table 1. The criteria employed for selecting these studies were based primarily on the fact that this group of studies is among the most recent, employed relatively comparable techniques, and presents data on Jewish communities which are more widely representative, geographically and numerically, than any summary published heretofore. While the bulk of the data utilized below has been drawn from the studies listed in Table 1, an effort has been made to relate this material to other researches undertaken by independent scholars on such special problems as Jewish birth rates and fertility. Where relevant, available data on other Jewish communities have also been cited. Finally, in an effort to make the Jewish data more meaningful, comparable data on the total white population of the respective cities have been presented.

Table 1—Jewish and Total White Populations of Selected Cities

City	Jewish Population	Year of Study[a]	Total White Population 1950[b]	Per Cent Jews of Total
Los Angeles	323,000	1950	1,758,773	18.4
Newark				
City	56,800	1948	363,149	15.6
Suburbs	29,500	1948	437,500	6.9
Miami	40,000	1949	402,530	10.0
Passaic	11,215	1949	54,691	20.2
Atlanta	10,217	1947	209,898	4.8
New Orleans	9,100	1950	464,587	1.9
Trenton	8,500	1949	113,477	7.5
Portland, Ore.	7,128	1947	360,388	1.9
Camden	6,517	1948	106,972	6.5
Indianapolis	6,268	1948	363,082	1.7
Utica	3,024	1948	99,861	3.0
Gary	2,500	1949	94,585	2.6
Port Chester, N. Y.	2,235	1950	22,528	10.0

a. These studies were most often conducted by The Jewish Welfare Board, Jewish Community Council or Jewish Federation.
b. From 17th U. S. Census. In all cases, figures are for cities or urban places.

§ II. Age Composition

One of the most striking sociological changes in recent years has been the unexpected shift in demographic trends. The population of the United States has altered markedly in its numbers, age structure, and marital status since 1940. While there is little evidence to demonstrate that the Jewish population has precisely followed the pattern set by general demographic changes, it may be surmised that shifts occurred in the Jewish population, although in all probability they were not so large. Past studies of Jewish populations in specific communities have provided fairly complete data on some demographic aspects, although on many significant matters the information has been fragmentary. In general, most of the Jewish communities for which studies have been made are aging ones and are clearly replenishing themselves at a rate slower than the general population. However, the general population has in recent years spurted so sharply that all the gloomy estimates and dour predictions of the 1930's and 1940's may now have to be revised. In fact, most demographic experts now hesitate to make the kind of predictions that were so common prior to World War II.

This remarkable growth in American population has been due to three factors: (1) a net in-migration greater than what was expected in the immediate postwar years; (2) fewer deaths than the experts anticipated; and (3) births that so far outstripped expectations that the impossibility of forecasting them for more than a year in advance is conceded. It is quite evident by now that population growth in the United States is not leveling off as was once thought, but that increases will continue, with a new flood of births to be expected in the 1970's.

Available data on the Jewish populations of the United States, albeit of a fragmentary nature, seems to indicate a condition of incipient decline. This was most evident during the 1930's, when Jewish population studies were made in a number of the larger Jewish communities (see Robison, *op. cit.*). These studies invariably showed the age group under five years as a relatively narrow one. When the data for more recent postwar studies are examined (see *American Jewish Year Book*, LI, 1950, p. 5 and LII, 1951, p. 5) one notes an expansion in the infant age groups for the Jewish population. At that time it was suggested that this spurt in the birth rate was a temporary phenomenon. However, with the persistent continued increase in the population of the United States, it seems likely that Jewish births have increased as well.

Most Jewish demographic studies begin, and justifiably so, with an analysis of the age structure of the population. While the United States for many years has enjoyed a relatively youthful population, specialists in recent years have become increasingly concerned with its progressive aging. Jewish community leaders too have had to address themselves to this question, for more and more communities have had to face up to the problem of pediatrics versus geriatrics. It is well known that with shifts in age composition and structure, there will occur changes in the likes, dislikes, and interests of the members of the community. With data on the nature of these population shifts, community leadership is more apt to anticipate such alterations in tastes.

Table 2 presents the percentage distribution of the Jewish and total white populations in the communities listed in Table 1 by age groups.[3]

A perusal of Table 2 should reveal to the reader some interesting aspects of the Jewish populations of these communities. Virtually all show significant gaps or "hollow classes" in the young and teen-age groups. That these "hollow classes" exist also in the general population is shown in the Census Bureau's data. Yet for the Jewish communities, the "hollowness" seems more marked and appears to extend beyond the 20-year group. While virtually all communities for which such data are presented here exhibit a strong pyramidal base, thereby indicating a larger number of births in recent years, the "hollow classes" often extend to the 35-year groups. This is in sharp contrast to the white general population where the largest class percentage occurs in the 25- to 29-year age group.

While some communities where more recent surveys were made (Trenton, Gary, New Orleans) exhibited a growth in the infant age groups, there has been a continual aging of the Jewish populations as evidenced by the median ages. In the earlier studies these were usually below thirty years, whereas at present the medians tend to be closer to thirty-five years.

Does this then indicate that American Jews began to have fewer children sooner than the general population? Or does it show that Jews marry at a later age than the rest of the population and consequently have smaller families? Or do Jews in this country curtail family size as a reponse to unfavorable economic conditions more quickly than is the case in the general population? While these possibly may be partial explanations for the demographic characteristics described above, they cannot be considered conclusively so without further detailed study. Furthermore, the extent to which wars, epidemics, or variations in births and deaths may affect specific Jewish age-sex patterns is difficult to assay.

Comparison with the age composition of Jewish communities a decade earlier presented by Robison shows clearly enough that the present "hollow classes" in the Jewish population were predominantly reactions to economic depression. Apparently the middle class, the largest part of the Jewish population included in these surveys, readily restricts family size during economic depressions. Thus invariably the age group under five years in the earlier studies was relatively a narrow one; this was true in Chicago, Detroit, Pittsburgh, Buffalo, Minneapolis, Passaic, Trenton, New London, Norwich, and San Francisco. The more recent studies show an expansion in the infant-age groups. This, of course, is also characteristic of the general population in the United States and is a result of the wartime spurt in the birth rate.

For Jewish communities, this relative increase in births may entail continuing responsibilities for such fields as Jewish education and youth programs. Any hasty de-emphasis of these aspects of community planning may prove to be premature, for in the next few years at least, and in the absence of any severe depressions, there may be increasing numbers to whom such programs are addressed. In the long run, however, the younger groups in the population, both general and Jewish, will in all probability continue to decline.

A decade or more ago the Jewish population, to judge by the early studies, was relatively a youthful one. In Chicago, for example, in 1930, considerably more than half (56.2 per cent) of the Jewish population was under the age of 30. The median age was under 30 in all cases except San Francisco. The more recent studies show median ages ranging from 28.4 for the Newark suburbs to 39.8 for New Orleans. This compares with an estimated median age in 1950 for the general white population in the United States of 30.8. Perusal of the figures given here emphasizes the continuous aging of the Jewish population, a process which appears to be more marked than in the general population in this country.

The age groups over 25 or 30 are relatively larger in the recent studies; this is true for Newark,[4] Atlanta, Portland, Camden, Indianapolis and Utica. Miami exhibits similar features, but in this instance the number of middle-aged persons has been increasing through in-migration. In Miami, male migrants apparently have been older than female migrants, while at the same time the latter have outnumbered the men, particularly in 20- to 50-year age groups.

It has also been shown that the almost exclusively urban concentration of American Jewry suggests a smaller average family size and a lower birth rate than in the general population. This, together with the fact that the few Jews in small communities may intermarry more readily or

Table 2—Age Composition of Jewish and Total White (1950)

Age Group	Los Angeles Jewish	Total	Newark (City) Jewish	Total	Newark (Suburbs) Jewish	Total	Miami Jewish	Total	Passaic Jewish	Total	Atlanta Jewish	Total	New Orleans[b] Jewish	Total
0- 4	8.2	8.5	7.5	8.5	12.5	8.2	8.6	8.5	7.2	8.3	7.7	9.2	8.8	10.7
5- 9	7.7	6.6	6.5	7.2	7.6	7.4	5.8	6.7	8.1	6.7	6.4	6.6	7.7	5.8
10-14	5.8	5.0	6.6	5.6	6.9	5.5	5.7	5.6	5.7	5.0	6.9	5.4	4.9	6.0
15-19	5.2	4.9	8.0	6.2	7.9	5.5	6.3	3.8	7.3	5.7	7.6	6.7	4.2	6.1
20-24	4.9	7.7	8.4	7.6	11.1	6.6	6.4	7.0	6.8	7.6	7.2	9.8	4.6	8.7
25-29	6.8	8.7	8.8	9.0	6.0	7.6	7.3	8.6	6.1	8.8	6.6	9.5	6.2	9.7
30-34	7.9	8.2	8.8	8.5	6.7	7.7	7.8	8.7	7.0	9.1	9.1	8.0	6.8	8.2
35-39	11.0	8.2	7.9	8.4	10.1	8.0	8.6	8.9	9.6	8.6	9.3	7.7	7.0	8.2
40-44	9.0	7.6	7.7	7.4	9.3	8.1	8.9	8.4	8.8	7.0	7.4	7.5	7.6	7.9
45-49	7.0	7.1	7.8	6.6	6.5	7.6	9.1	8.0	7.0	6.3	6.8	6.7	7.4	6.9
50-54	6.4	6.7	7.3	6.5	5.8	7.5	8.6	6.9	6.7	6.8	8.5	5.8	7.5	6.1
55-59	6.1	5.8	5.2	5.7	3.1	6.3	5.9	5.6	5.3	6.4	5.3	4.8	5.8	4.9
60-64	5.3	5.1	5.0	4.8	3.3	4.9	5.4	4.8	5.5	5.4	5.3	3.9	5.0	3.8
65 and over	6.9	10.1	4.5	8.0	3.2	9.1	5.6	8.5	6.6	8.3	5.9	8.4	12.7	7.0
	98.2[a]	100.0	100.0	100.0	100.0	100.0	100.0	100.0	97.7	100.0	100.0	100.0	99.2	100.0
Median Age	36.6		32.4		28.4		36.3		35.9		34.1		39.8	

a. Where totals do not add up to 100 per cent, this results from the exclusion of those whose ages were unknown as well as from rounding.
b. Age groups are 0-5, 6-10, 11-15, etc.

postpone marriage because of a lack of available partners, suggests further an inability of the smaller Jewish population centers to fill the gap created by the desire for smaller families. All this intensifies the aging process in the Jewish population.

This aging carries with it implications of considerable significance for local social planning. Aside from the broader problems such as types of housing, social security, and the effects on national productivity, there are such questions to be resolved as kinds of hospital services, institutional care for the aged, leisure-time programs for adults, and the like.

Comparison with several Canadian Jewish communities would seem to indicate that the American Jewish population is a somewhat "older" one.[5] Yet in Canada, too, the "aging" process was apparent; the teen-age groups invariably declined from 1931 to 1941 as a proportion of the total Jewish population.

In the case of Passaic, an opportunity presented itself for observing the actual growth of a Jewish population, for, as in the case of Trenton, Passaic made two Jewish population surveys at intervals of about a decade. In Passaic, a study made in 1937 reported a Jewish population of 10,066. The increase since then has been 11.4 per cent. The general white population of Passaic meanwhile suffered a 7.9 per cent decline, dropping from 59,365 in 1940 to 54,691 in 1950. Changes in the age structure of Passaic's Jewry are evident from a comparison of the 1937 data and the 1949 material. In 1937, the "under five" year age group was 6.1 per cent of the total, as compared to 7.2 per cent in 1949. Thus, the earlier study indicated

Population of Selected Cities: Percentages

Trenton Jewish	Total	Portland Jewish	Total	Camden Jewish	Total	Indianapolis Jewish	Total	Utica Jewish	Total	Gary[c] Jewish	Total	Port Chester Jewish	Total
9.0	8.7	9.2	9.0	9.7	9.8	9.6	10.1	9.5	9.1	11.0	10.4	7.9	9.5
8.2	6.9	5.7	6.8	7.8	7.9	6.6	7.3	5.7	7.0	6.9	8.1	9.5	7.5
5.4	5.7	5.0	5.3	6.2	6.2	5.0	5.8	6.4	5.9	6.9	6.5	7.2	5.9
5.8	6.1	6.5	5.1	5.6	6.1	6.0	5.9	6.6	5.9	7.1	6.0	5.1	6.2
7.0	7.9	7.6	6.6	6.2	7.8	7.0	8.0	6.7	6.8	7.6	7.8	4.7	7.3
8.7	8.8	6.8	7.8	8.1	9.1	8.5	9.0	7.2	8.0	7.7	9.1	6.0	8.3
8.7	8.8	8.3	7.4	9.2	8.7	9.5	7.9	9.4	7.8	7.8	9.0	7.8	8.4
9.5	8.2	9.1	7.8	10.8	7.9	9.1	7.4	9.7	7.7	7.8	8.4	8.9	8.6
8.9	7.2	8.3	7.2	9.9	6.7	8.5	7.1	9.3	6.8	7.8	7.0	7.7	7.8
7.3	6.4	7.9	6.6	7.2	5.8	7.0	6.6	8.7	6.1	7.7	6.2	7.0	6.8
6.8	6.4	7.4	6.5	6.5	6.0	7.2	5.0	8.0	6.4	8.0	5.9	6.0	6.6
4.9	5.7	6.1	6.2	5.1	5.6	5.8	5.3	5.1	6.2	7.8	5.6	4.4	5.2
4.7	4.9	4.8	5.7	4.0	4.6	4.3	4.4	2.7	5.3	5.9	4.5	3.7	4.2
5.1	8.3	7.3	12.0	3.7	7.8	5.7	9.2	5.0	11.0	—	5.5	5.5	7.7
100.0	100.0	100.0	100.0	100.0	100.0	99.8	100.0	100.0	100.0	100.0	100.0	91.4	100.0
32.4		35.4		33.5		33.7		34.0		30.8		36.0	

c. Figures given for age groups of 30 and over are estimates.

aging by virtue of the low concentrations in the "under five" age groups with high percentages in the twenty-five to forty-four year old groups. By the middle 1940's, however, this condition changed. The war and postwar period ushered in the usual high crop of war babies, and the Jewish birth rate increased together with the general birth rate. The data for Passaic, Post Chester, and Los Angeles would seem to indicate that while there has been a postwar slackening in the number of births, the drop has not reached the low levels shown for the 1930's, when in some communities the infant age group was 6 per cent or less of the total Jewish population. In Port Chester, the largest age group is the five- to nine-year olds. The relatively larger size of this group is also a result of the wartime growth in population. In this community too the postwar age groups declined somewhat, following the pattern set by other Jewish communities.

In contrast to the foregoing pattern, the Jewish population of Los Angeles shows a higher ratio for the group under five than for the succeeding age cohort, thus indicating a continued natural growth in the Jewish population. The major growth in the Jewish population of Los Angeles has, of course, come about through in-migration. But it is clear that this community's population is growing even aside from inward movements. The largest groups are in the age cohorts from thirty to forty.

In New Orleans,[6] the spurt in births since World War II was insufficient to offset the relatively narrow base in an age-sex distribution. The age groups from 10 to 25 there were the "hollow classes," evidence of the drop in births during the depression and prewar years. With the cessation of immigration it seemed most likely that the number of Jews over the age of 55 would increase in the next two to three decades while the number between the ages of 30 and 55 would decrease.

Thus it may be fairly stated that, despite lags, the Jewish population, at least in the larger cities (and this would include the bulk of American Jewry), conforms to the patterns exhibited by the general population. The age distribution of the general population now shows a larger proportion of children under the age of five; in many Jewish communities this class increased during and after the war and although there have been declines in this cohort, it is still sizeable. The percentage of older people has also been rising, and for Jewish communities perhaps even more rapidly than in the general population.

Additional data for comparative purposes are presented in Table 2, which gives percentage distributions for the general white population in certain cities for which there are Jewish data available. In comparing the age group 0-4 years for the Jewish and general data we note that the proportion of the total in that cohort is smaller in all but four of the Jewish communities, suggesting a lower degree of fertility. In the 20-24 age group, the so-called "depression class," only Portland and Newark (city) show higher percentages than that for the general white population in the 1950 census. Other comparisons seem to support virtually all of the observations and surmises indicated above.

§ III. Sex Ratios

The proportions of males and females in a population are important features of its composition, for these ratios markedly affect birth rates, death rates, marriages and migrations.[7] Where certain age groups are predominantly of one sex, it is conceivable that the character of community activities will be subject to change. In the case of Miami, for example, the proportion of females to males in the 20- to 50-year age groups is on the whole greater than in the other Jewish communities. In fact, for all age groups, except for those over 65, the Miami Jewish population appears to have a higher proportion of females to males. In terms of the total Jewish population, Atlanta, Passaic and New Orleans also exhibit sex ratios below 100, as shown in Table 3. Curiously enough, the high proportion of males in the over-70 groups, which is found in Miami and Worcester, does not at all conform to the general pattern, either for other Jewish communities or for the native-white general population of the United States. Such demographic peculiarities must influence community thinking on social planning questions.

Table 3—Sex Ratios: Jewish and Total White Populations*

City	Jewish Sex Ratio	Total White Sex Ratio, 1950	
Los Angeles	100.1	91.3	
Newark (City)	105.7	97.7	
Newark (Suburbs)	105.7	90.2	
Miami	97.9	95.7	
Passaic	96.9	94.6	
Atlanta	95.8	88.3	
New Orleans	95.0	90.0	
Trenton	100.8	96.7	
Portland, Ore.	103.6	92.8	
Camden	102.4	97.5	
Indianapolis	103.8	90.6	
Utica	103.1	92.1	
Gary	107.5	107.5	
Port Chester	103.5	97.8	
U. S. Total Population			99.2
U. S. Total White Population			99.4
U. S. Total Native White Population			99.0
U. S. Total Urban White Population			94.9

* Sources: Jewish population studies listed in Table 1, and data presented in 17th Census of the United States.

Comparison of the sex ratios for the general white population of certain communities as compared with the Jewish population of these communities, as shown in Table 3, suggests that the demographic influence of migration continues to exert a certain force. In all instances for which the comparisons were made the Jewish sex ratio figure is higher. While this might favor high marriage and fertility among the women in the more recent stock, it may lower the natural increase rate among them if many of the male immigrants were required to remain unmarried or even if they by force of circumstance had to marry late in life. In Gary, the preponderance of males in both the Jewish and general white population may be explained by the industrial environment which may tend to attract men more readily than women. Similarly, it is the economic, sociological and historical factors in the particular area that explain the divergent sex ratio patterns as between Jews and their neighbors in the other communities indicated here. In all, the influence of migration still persists.

More detailed data on sex ratios for certain Jewish communities are presented in: *American Jewish Year Book,* 1950 (Vol. LI) pp. 9-13; 1951 (Vol. LII) pp. 6-8; 1953 (Vol. LIV) pp. 6-8; and in *The Jewish Population of New Orleans: 1953,* published by the CJFWF (1954). These data show that in the main the communities conformed to the general sex ratio pattern, especially in the younger age groups. Toledo, however, exhibited a higher proportion of males in all age groups. The general population (native-white) in 1940 had a larger proportion of males to females in the under-20 age groups, a characteristic consistently true for six out of eight Jewish communities for which data after 1940 were available. In the Jewish communities which had population studies prior to 1940 and for which specific age group sex ratios could be obtained, four out of five conformed to this general pattern. As we move to the older age groups, we find the proportion shifting; the general (native-white, 1940) population shows more women than men in the age groups between 20 and 40. This appears to be currently true in four Jewish communities: Miami, Worcester, Portland, and Camden. The same condition apparently existed also in Detroit, Pittsburgh, San Francisco, and Norwich. In Indianapolis, Utica, Charleston, and Grand Rapids there appears a more equal male-female balance in this age group.

Beginning with about age 40, virtually all the studies indicate a marked shift in the sex balance toward the male side. This too approximates the pattern exhibited by the general (native-white) population in the United States. In the age groups over 60, however, the general population ratios again shift to the female side. This occurs also in the Jewish population, but for the two exceptions noted above. It is also interesting to note that all but three of the Jewish community studies reviewed (Norwich, New London, and Toledo) have lower sex ratios (and consequently a more even balance between the sexes) than the foreign-born white population residing in urban areas. The Jewish ratios, however, are higher than that for the native-white urban population.

The significance of these figures is emphasized when we realize that any disproportions or unbalance, particularly in the procreative age groups, reduces the possibilities of single people finding a suitable marriage part- ner. The large proportion of females in the 25-, 30-, and 35-year age groups in such Jewish communities as Camden, Worcester, and Utica can make it difficult for them to find husbands without crossing religious, cultural, and ethnic lines. Such disproportions consequently result in lower mar- riage rates and in all probability lead to lower birth rates for the Jewish population in the Unted States.

In Trenton, the data revealed a higher proportion of females in the 20-34 year age groups while the reverse is true for the age groups over 65. The reason for the latter was not determined. Nashville, on the other hand, showed a higher proportion of females for all groups of age 30 and over. There, too, no reason was adduced for the higher proportion of females. Gary, on the other hand, showed a slightly higher proportion of males, but there the proximity to heavy industry may have been an ex- planatory factor, although this was not necessarily a contributing element.

In Passaic, the sex ratio in the 1937 study was 100.1, indicating an al- most perfect balance between men and women. Twelve years later there was a decline in the proportion of men to women, the sex ratio being 96.9. This was true not only for the Jewish community as a whole, but also for all brackets up to age thirty-five. The shortage of men was particularly marked in the fifteen-nineteen age group as well as in ages below ten.

In Port Chester, the sex ratio data indicate an excess of men over women for the community as a whole (103.5) and particularly so for the age groups over fifty. This feature, while contrary to the experience of the general population, is in consonance with the experience of such Jewish communities as Miami, Worcester, Passaic, and Trenton. However, in the age groups between twenty-five and forty, the data indicate more women than men in Port Chester. In the infant-age group there are more girls than boys, while in the five-nine age group the reverse is true. The overall picture for Port Chester shows less imbalance in this population characteristic than is the case in a number of other Jewish communities.

In Los Angeles, on the other hand, the infant-age group shows a heavy predominance of males as compared to females, while the obverse holds for all groups through age nineteen. In fact, the age cohort fifteen to nine- teen shows the heaviest proportion of females of any Jewish community thus far included in these surveys, a feature that is probably accounted for by the great attraction that the entertainment industry has for young women. Again, the succeeding age groups up to age thirty-four show a greater proportion of males, shading off into a pattern in the higher age brackets that approximates that exhibited in the general population. For the entire community, the sex ratio in Los Angeles was reported at 100.1, indicating a fairly even overall balance between male and female.

It might be noted that the pattern of sex ratios in the age group over twenty in Port Chester and Los Angeles is somewhat erratic, thereby sug- gesting some response bias on questions concerning age. It would seem that the "21 plus" response favored by many women is employed even when the enumerator does not possess police powers. However, in the case of Port Chester (as well as Passaic) the "cluster" test for age response indicated a high reliability. In the case of Los Angeles, single-year age data were not available so that this test could not be made. Of course, biases in age response may affect the age composition pattern as well as the sex ratios.

In New Orleans, comparison of the Jewish sex ratios with those of the total white population (computed from 1950 census data) showed that there were fewer males than females for all age groups in the total white population (except those of 10-20) than there were in the Jewish population. It was adduced that the greater sex-ratio figure for the older Jewish population as compared with the total white population of New Orleans was rooted in the selective process of foreign immigration in which males were said to be more apt to migrate than females. It was especially noted that among the foreign-born there were more males than females.

§   IV. Marital Status

Information on marital status in Jewish populations is unfortunately neither as extensive nor as detailed as is the case with age composition. Community surveyors for one reason or another have evidently felt that this demographic measure was not nearly as important as age structure or occupational categories. While it is true that the ". . . married condition is the normal status for the majority of human beings who have reached the age of adulthood," and that this is equally true for the Jewish and for the general population, it must be recognized that variations might yield interesting and perhaps significant statistical facts.

Should there be, for example, an unusual proportion of single and widowed persons, such a fact ought to be taken into account by community leadership.[8] This might require certain emphasis on leisure-time programs or adult group activities. Or, if the data on married persons were shown with spouse present or absent, it would be possible to inquire further into certain group psychological problems. But to be most useful, the data would have to be tabulated according to age groups. While most modern censuses have recognized this, the studies examined here failed to analyze this aspect of their demographic problems. Only the studies of Passaic, Port Chester and New Orleans presented marital status by age. Useful analysis demands not only the kind of approach suggested above, but also tabulations of marital status by sex, by community areas, and perhaps by nativity.

Most of the studies suggest that for marital status Jewish communities conform to the pattern of the total population, as shown in Table 4, insofar as the majority of both is in the married class. One might suspect that, as would be expected from other data, e.g., the later marriage age of Jews, the Jewish populations would have a higher percentage of single persons than the general population, but such a generalization is not supported by the data. Comparison of the two groups suggests no striking differences. It should be noted, of course, that comparisons can be made at best in only rough ways, since not only are the relevant base years different, but the groups to which the data apply differ as well, since the census figures are for age 14 and over whereas this was not always the case in the Jewish studies.

Table 4—Marital Status of Jewish[a] and Total[b] Populations of Selected Cities (in Per Cent)

City		Single Male Female		Married[c] Male Female		Widowed or Divorced[d] Male Female		Not Reported Male Female		Total Number Male	Female
Los Angeles:	Jewish[e]	38.4	33.9	61.6	66.1	NS	NS	—	—	126,900	126,000
	Total	23.2	17.3	67.9	61.2	8.9	21.5	—	—	747,030	836,009
Passaic:	Jewish[e]	26.3	21.1	69.6	69.2	0.9	3.0	3.2	6.7	4,430	4,435
	Total	27.4	23.7	66.4	61.9	6.2	14.4	—	—	22,391	24,155
New Orleans:	Jewish[e]	23.9	19.9	68.4	57.4	5.2	21.3	2.5	1.4	3,425	3,814
	Total	26.0	20.5	67.8	61.6	9.6	23.1	2.4	1.8	200,040	233,240
Trenton:	Jewish[f]	40.0	35.2	57.0	56.5	2.9	8.2	0.1	0.1	4,128	4,105
	Total	30.4	24.1	63.2	61.1	6.4	14.8	—	—	50,574	52,464
Camden:	Jewish[g]	15.1		80.8		4.1		— — —		802	
	Total	26.3	20.8	67.0	64.5	6.7	14.7	—	—	46,597	48,839
Indianapolis	Jewish[e]	26.4	16.8	69.7	71.1	3.9	12.1	—	—	2,567	2,421
	Total	20.2	17.9	71.2	63.5	8.6	18.6	—	—	155,200	176,453
Gary:	Jewish[e]	25.2	16.0	70.6	74.5	2.3	7.8	1.9	1.7	693	654
	Total	23.7	16.6	68.9	70.3	7.4	13.1	—	—	51,302	49,206
Port Chester:	Jewish[e]	24.2	18.9	69.5	71.9	3.9	8.2	2.4	1.0	858	829
	Total	27.4	24.5	67.5	64.1	5.1	11.4	—	—	9,032	9,613

a. No data on Jewish marital status are given in the studies of Newark, Atlanta, Miami, Portland or Utica.

b. 14 years and over. *17th Census of the United States, 1950.* Percentages compiled from Table 34 in the separate parts of Volume II dealing with each state.

c. Differences between the number of married men and women are explained by interviewer or response errors which cannot be corrected statistically. For example, such errors or biases occur when widows or widowers will say in response to marital status questions that they are "married." Such a bias can be eliminated only by careful interviewing in the field. Errors of this nature are magnified when samples are used to estimate the characteristics of a universe.

d. For breakdown of divorced and widowed in the Jewish populations, see sources.

e. Age 15 and over.

f. Age group not given.

g. Age 20 and over.

NS—Not specified, included in "Single" category.

Table 4 indicates that the majority of persons are classified as married, thus bearing out the tentative conclusion offered earlier that Jewish populations conform to the general pattern, although there is the possibility that the percentage of divorces is smaller for Jews than for the general population.

In the Passaic and Port Chester studies marital status was cross-tabulated for the first time with age and sex, thus providing a more detailed analysis. These data revealed that for Passaic there were more single females than males in the fifteen-nineteen year old group; on the other hand, in Port Chester, there were more single young men than single young women. The data show, as might be expected, that the number of unmarried people declined as the population grew older. Comparison of marital status by age for men and women in both communities revealed the fact that men stay single longer than women.

The Passaic data showed the largest proportion of married persons to be in the thirty-five—forty-five year groups. The twenty-thirty year age groups in this community included only 10.2 per cent of the total number of married persons; when this was compared with the proportions of single persons in the same age group (40 per cent of the single persons) a basis was suggested for an incipient decline in population growth, to which postponed marriages are an important contributing factor. However, as in the general community, earlier marriage by females was indicated by an excess of married females over married males in all age groups up to age forty-five. Virtually the same observations, with but slight variations in the basic data, apply to Port Chester.

The New Orleans data revealed a relatively large proportion of women among those reported as widowed. This was ascribed to the greater female span of life and the supposed fact that widowers find it easier to remarry than widows. In this community, marital status data for Jews and the total white population were quite similar, although the Jewish population has more widowed and fewer divorced and separated. It is important to realize, however, that these data are affected by the different age distributions shown by the Jewish community and by the total white population. Since the latter is a younger population, and the incidence of widowhood is heaviest in the older years, the overall percentage of widowhood for the total white population is kept below the proportion reported for the Jewish population. An analysis, however, of the age groups 65 and on, revealed that 46 per cent of the total white population was widowed compared with 39 per cent of the Jewish population.

For the total age groups over 14 there were relatively fewer single individuals found among New Orleans Jews than among the total white population. However an analysis of the data for separate five-year age groups showed that there are proportionately *more*, not less, single Jews in the age groups under 35 than was the case for the total white population. In short, it was the greater proportion of older individuals in the Jewish population that gives the Jews relatively fewer single individuals over age 14 compared with the total white population, and not a greater tendency to marry.

These data bear out the thesis that Jews marry later in life than other elements in the population. This may reflect the problem of marrying within a small religious or ethnic group and may also be correlated with the high degree of educational attainment and professional aspirations of the Jewish population. In consonance with the above, there are proportionately fewer married Jews in each age group under 30 than there is in the total white population. After age 30, this reverses and there are more married individuals among Jews than among the total white population.

The New Orleans study is virtually the only one to concern itself with the question of intermarriage. Seven per cent of all married individuals among New Orleans Jewry were found to have non-Jewish spouses. There was a definite relationship between nativity, sex, and intermarriage. Over 90 per cent of those Jews who intermarried were native born, and of these males outnumbered the females more than three to one. A small number of foreign-born males and an almost nonexistent number of foreign-born females completed the count. These data appear to be on the conservative side. They do not include those considered Jews by other definitions than the one used in the study. Included were only those who retain identification with the Jewish community to the extent at least of answering the questionnaire. It may be asked whether the smaller proportion of female intermarriages reported was due in some measure to a greater tendency of women to adhere to their husbands' religious identification. Where a master list is employed from which a sample is drawn, identification is based for the most part on some interest, even if minimal, with Jewish activities. It is reasonable to assume that some portion of the intermarried families are consequently not included.

Considering households as apart from married individuals, it was found that 10 per cent of households in the New Orleans study included non-Jewish individuals. Data on this topic were not covered in exactly the same way by the recent Los Angeles study, but there, too, the evidence pointed to a greater number of mixed marriages in which the male partner was Jewish. In 1945 the Jacksonville Jewish community also inquired into this question and found that 10 per cent of their Jewish families involved intermarriages. In this study, also, most of the Jewish partners in intermarriages were native-born males.[9]

§ *V. Family Size*

The average size of the Jewish family has been a favorite item of discussion among population experts in Jewish social research. Prevailing opinion adopts the view that the Jewish family is smaller than that of the general native-white population. If this is so, then further evidence could be adduced concerning the relatively smaller growth of the Jewish as compared with the general population.

While size of family in the general population is important when decisions are to be made in types of housing to be provided or on the location of shopping areas, it is of particular interest for those local Jewish communities which are concerned with such questions as youth programs, leisure-time activities, location of Jewish center buildings, and related communal problems.

Median household size[10] in the United States declined between 1930 and 1940. In the latter year it was 3.28, and fell to 3.04 in 1950. Both as a proportion of the total number of families and in absolute numbers, six-

Table 5—Jewish Family Size: Percentage Distribution in Selected Cities[a]

Number of Individuals	Los Angeles[b]	Miami	Passaic	New Orleans[b]	Trenton[b]	Camden	Indianapolis	Utica	Gary	Port Chester
1	7.5	15.8	9.0	6.2	4.9	4.2	8.6	12.6	6.7	12.6
2	31.4	36.8	26.1	20.0	28.7	26.9	28.9	25.1	27.0	22.0
3	27.5	23.2	29.0	23.8	30.0	32.5	25.7	26.8	29.0	27.9
4	22.7	18.6	25.7	28.0	26.8	29.1	23.0	25.8	26.5	27.2
5	9.4	4.2	8.4	14.3	9.6	5.3	9.2	7.4	8.6	8.3
6	1.3	1.1	1.4	5.4	—	2.0	2.8	1.6	1.8	1.2
7	0.1	0.3	0.4	1.3	—	—	0.9	0.2	0.2	0.5
8 or more	0.1	—	—	1.0	—	—	0.9	0.5	0.2	0.3
Total	100.0	100.0	100.0	100.0	100.0	100.0	100.0	100.0	100.0	100.0
Number	107,600	13,302	3,680	9,566	2,658	357	2,060	1,028	566	736
Mean Jewish family size	3.00	2.63	3.04	2.84	3.10	3.10	3.13	2.98	3.10	3.00
Median Jewish family size	2.40	1.93	2.50	—	2.50	2.58	2.49	2.46	2.60	2.30
Mean per household, general white population, 1950	2.82	3.04	3.23	3.17	3.67	3.55	3.13	3.22	3.46	3.56

a. No data available for Newark, Atlanta or Portland.
b. Based on number of families. All other columns based on number of families.

persons-and-larger families in the general population have decreased. This trend is further emphasized by the fact that the number of persons in the total population per household declined from 4.9 in 1890 to 3.8 in 1940, and 3.5 in 1950.[11] Table 5 presents data on average family size in Jewish populations as revealed in the studies reviewed here.

A few exceptions to the uniformity of analysis which is being attempted here should be noted. In the Newark survey, the data were presented in terms of the "number of children ever born."[12] Thus, though a child had reached maturity, married, and established his own household, he was still to be counted into this particular enumeration, even though he might now be a parent himself. A similar approach was utilized in the Charleston study; several of the earlier studies also employed this approach. The United States Census Bureau also makes use of this classification; it is, however, broken down into age groups and is considered to be suggestive of fertility trends.[13]

As might be expected, such Jewish communities as Miami and Tucson tend to have smaller families than the others; in each of these the two-person family represents the largest group. While a community such as Indianapolis, which is less subject to inward migration than either Tucson or Miami, also has more two-person families than any other group, other Jewish communities, such as Worcester, Atlanta, Camden, Utica, Toledo, and Grand Rapids, have larger family groupings. It might be thought at first that the communities with more two-person family groupings are younger or have "incomplete" families, but the information on age structure belies this supposition. On the contrary, these communities are older and probably have a larger number of "completed" families. In these communities the median family size is considerably lower than in both the general population and in family size is considerably lower than in both the general population and the other Jewish communities, a fact which underscores a basically different sociological tendency; such a statistic indicates that it is the single-person and two-person families that migrate to these cities.

In Passaic, the three-person family was the most numerous type. Additional data on the "number of all children" emphasized the fact that Jewish families in Passaic tended to be small. The greatest concentrations of reported "all" children were in the one- or two-children group, forming 55 per cent of the total. However, the greatest distributions within these groups were in the ages below forty-five, indicating that there was a biological possibility for larger families. Only 40 per cent of the total number of Jewish mothers in Passaic were in the age group over forty-five. It is interesting to note also that the number of Jewish households in Passaic has increased 46 per cent since 1937.

In Port Chester, too, there was a skewness in the distribution of families toward the smaller sizes, with the three-person family being the most numerous type. Additional data on "number of all children" showed that the one- and two-children groups were 56 per cent of the total. Mothers below the age of forty-five, the biologically procreative ages, were 46 per cent of the total, indicating also a possibility for larger families.

In Los Angeles, the data indicated that the estimated 323,000 Jews were distributed among 107,600 households, with an average size of three (the median was smaller —2.4). Here the largest group was the two-person family, representing 31.4 per cent of the total number of households. Unfortunately, an analysis by age was not made available, so that it is not known whether this large two-person group consists of young people who have not started their families, older retired persons with completed families, or middle-aged people without children. In the absence of such an age analysis little can be surmised about the natural growth prospects of the Los Angeles Jewish community.

In New Orleans the average Jewish household comprised 2.84 individuals as compared with 3.17 for the total white population in 1950. The greatest number of Jewish households had two members, with three- and four-person families as the next largest group. As compared with other Jewish communities, the New Orleans average was low.

The median family size for the general urban population in the United States in 1950 was 3.42. Jewish communities generally exhibit a lower median family size than this average for the general population. This would seem to bear out the supposition that Jews tend to have smaller families.

For example, comparing the average household size of the general white population in certain communities with the mean family for the Jewish population in these localities, we find that in all but two cases the Jewish average is lower. For Indianapolis the figures are the same for both the general white and Jewish population, while in Los Angeles the Jewish figure is slightly larger, being 3.0 as compared with 2.82 for the general white population. It is possible that factors of population movement and local turnover account for this variation from the general pattern.

These facts, together with the statistics on age composition, underline the conclusion that American Jewry is replenishing itself at a very slow rate. In fact, if the number of newborn males is greater than the number of newborn females in the foregoing communities, then population growth may be said to be declining, since net reproduction rates are based on the extent to which one generation of child-bearing females reproduces itself. The high proportion of two-person and three-person families therefore may be indicative of a declining reproduction rate, although a cross tabulation by age and sex groups would be necessary for a definitive statement.

§ *VI. Vital Statistics: Fertility*

The central fact in all demographic studies is the rapidity with which a population reproduces itself. While statistics on age composition and changes in age structure lead to the surmise that the rate of Jewish population growth in this country is declining, conclusive evidence on this can be supplied only through specific measurements of births and deaths. Without such information it is virtually impossible to determine the dynamic changes taking place. Unfortunately, data on births are quite faulty; it is a known fact that birth registration statistics are often incomplete, especially in certain areas. This makes the ordinary birth rate of doubtful validity. Furthermore, for Jewish populations a birth rate would be even more dubious since the estimates of total Jewish population itself are so often open to question. In addition, registration of births by Jewish communities has seldom been attempted.

A more satisfactory approach at the present time is the fertility ratio, defined as the number of children under the age of 5 per 1,000 women of child-bearing age. An alternative concept is the number of young children per 1,000 *persons* of procreative age. These indices are easily derived from the data on age structure and are set forth in Table 6. In all but two cases (Los Angeles and Gary) the fertility ratios for Jewish populations computed on either basis are lower than the figure for the general white populations of the same communities. A second outstanding point is the fact that the earlier surveys revealed lower fertility ratios than those conducted in the 1940's. However, we should not conclude from this that Jewish births will continue to increase; the spurt in fertility may have been

Table 6—Fertility Ratios of Jewish and General White Populations (1950 Census) of Selected Cities

	Children under 5 per 1,000 females age 20-44		Children under 5 per 1,000 persons age 20-54	
	Jewish	General	Jewish	General
U.S. (white-general), 1940[a]	—	400.0	—	153.5
U.S. (white-general), 1950	—	622.0[b]	—	216.2
U.S. (white-urban), 1950	—	540.0[b]	—	195.5
Los Angeles	450.0[c]	408.0	160.0[c]	159.0
Newark (city)	—	406.0	134.1	159.0
Newark (suburbs)	—	428.4	189.1	164.2
Miami	380.0	391.0	147.4	152.0
Passiac	362.6	391.0	139.5	153.0
Atlanta	—	407.0	120.8	166.0
New Orleans	496.5	447.6	186.0	199.0
Trenton	412.8	419.0	158.2	163.0
Portland	387.7	461.0	139.3	179.0
Camden	354.6	468.0	138.0	196.0
Indianapolis	399.8	484.0	147.9	192.0
Utica	395.3	462.0	142.1	181.0
Gary	575.9	501.0	202.2	193.0
Port Chester	435.0	452.0	163.2	179.0

a. T. L. Smith, *Population Analysis*, p. 123; P. K. Whelpton and Associates, *Forecasts of the Population of the United States, 1945-75*, Washington, 1947.

b. Charles F. Westoff, "Differential Fertility in the United States: 1900 to 1952," *American Sociological Review*, Vol. XIX (Oct. 1954), p. 551. Data standardized for age of women and corrected for underenumeration and mortality of children.

c. Estimated.

a wartime phenomenon affecting Jewish as well as general populations. The probability is that the fertility trend in the Jewish population will at best but maintain the population size in the coming years.[14]

In Passaic, there was a considerable jump in the fertility ratio (per 1,000 persons) between 1937 and 1949, from 81.2 to 139.5. It seems evident that this trend was true for other Jewish communities as well. The Port Chester data appear higher than in other Jewish communities, but are lower than for the general community, a comparison that holds true for virtually all Jewish communities. The figure for Los Angeles (estimated from sample data) is high on the first basis, but not as high as in other Jewish communities for which data are available. The implication of this is the presence of relatively larger numbers of older persons.

Some further materials on Jewish population growth are available through the studies made by Nathan Goldberg.[15] Goldberg employs the data gathered by the U. S. Census Bureau on the "number of children ever born according to the country of origin of the female respondents." From this, Goldberg suggests that the birth rate for the Jewish population is declining. The younger generation of Jewish immigrants, he says, had a lower birth rate than the native-white population, and the downward trend in the birth rate for younger age groups was more pronounced for the Jewish than for the non-Jewish population. Goldberg states: "In the twenty years to 1940, the Jewish birth rate fell 37 per cent. This decline was more than double the 15 per cent fall in the birth rate of the native white population."

It is unfortunate that little more than the foregoing can be said about birth rates and fertility of the Jewish population in this country. Goldberg's analyses, while valuable, have become less useful with time because the number of persons reporting Yiddish as a mother tongue declines in each succeeding generation. Furthermore, these data cannot be employed to develop specifically Jewish mortality rates because the foreign-born population has now moved up the age ladder to a point where high death rates apply.

The kind of data on natural growth that should be developed is illustrated by the brief study of Jewish population increase in Montreal prepared by Louis Rosenberg of the Canadian Jewish Congress.[16] In this report vital statistics were available for Jewish and two other ethnic groups in Montreal; it was noted that the rate of natural increase decreased from 1911 to 1946 among all groups, but more so for the Jewish population. It has as yet been impossible to construct tables of life expectancy for Jewish populations such as was done for Canada by Mortimer Spiegelman, statistician of the Metropolitan Life Insurance Company.[17] To compute such tables it is essential to have age-specific mortality rates, data which again are lacking for Jewish communities in the United States.

Previous studies of Jewish mortality, aside from Canada, have all had inherent weaknesses which made their conclusions dubious. However, the one general pattern that seems to be characteristic is the relatively lower death rates for Jews as compared with other groups up to middle age, with mortality increasing in old age. This conclusion was arrived at in the Canadian study as well as by Goldberg.[18]

§ VII. Occupational and Industrial Classification: Economic Status

Although the analysis of occupational data is primarily useful in evaluating economic status, occupation exerts so strong and varied an influence on demography that it is difficult to exclude it from consideration in a population study. The nature of work affects the social and cultural environment of a people; the occupation and industry into which a person enters may be affected by a special system of values; personality traits and, in the long run, marital status, health, and reproduction rates are influenced by working conditions.

The community surveys offer at best but a partial picture of the occupational and industrial patterns of American Jewry, and as is true of many of the indices described here, their data must be employed cautiously. The communities which have conducted useful studies in recent years do not represent a majority of the Jewish population in the United States; as was indicated above, the survey methods utilized varied from study to study, again impelling caution.

The failure, for example, to classify Jewish mercantile and industrial establishments according to the number of workers employed and by volume of business, as is done in the Census Bureau investigations, makes it difficult to assay the relative position of Jewish entrepreneurs in the total business community. Most authorities suggest that Jewish businessmen are to be found largely in small enterprises, a conclusion that might be established without question by data on the number of workers and volume of business. Yet, lacking such information, it is patently unfair to compare the relative number of Jews and non-Jews engaged in industry and trade.

The labor force as usually defined includes persons 14 years old and over who are working or are seeking work at the time an enumeration is made. The 1950 census classified 53.2 per cent of the general white population as being in the labor force; this consisted of 79.0 per cent of males and 28.1 per cent of females. Jewish population statistics, even where community studies were made, do not yield such detail on the Jewish labor force. Whereas it is possible to say, for example, that 6.8 per cent of the white male labor force in the United States is in the age group 14-19,[19] no such statement can be made about the Jewish population. Were such information available it might show, for example, whether or not significant differences exist in the ages at which Jewish children enter employment.

Most of the data on labor force in the community studies reviewed here (see Table 7) are crude and lacking in sufficient detail to warrant comparative analysis. The only surveys in the older group (data for which are given in Robison and the *American Jewish Year Book,* Vol. LI, *op. cit.*) which presented fairly adequate labor force tables were those for Buffalo (gainfully employed), San Francisco and Detroit. Of the later studies, labor force data were available for Newark, Trenton, Gary, Passaic, Port Chester, Los Angeles and New Orleans.

Despite the paucity of data, a few generalizations seem to be warranted. Camden and Newark, heavily industrialized cities, have higher labor force ratios for the Jewish population than the other Jewish communities. This was also true in the earlier San Francisco study. Also, the data on Newark show a smaller proportion of the suburban Jewish population in the labor force. This raises the interesting question whether, for Jewish populations, inclusion in the labor force might not vary inversely with distance from industrial centers.

In a broad sense, it might be said that smaller proportions of total Jewish populations are part of the labor force than is the case in the general population. Whether this is due to a longer school period for Jewish children or to more Jewish women being engaged in housework, or other factors, is difficult to say in the absence of more information. Related to this finding is the fact that the later studies generally indicate smaller labor force percentages than the earlier ones. The former were conducted during a prosperous economic period. At such times there is less need to supplement a breadwinner's income; a housewife is not likely to seek work outside the home, thereby removing herself from the labor market.

Several of the studies reviewed here presented somewhat more detailed information than was made available in earlier community population studies. These were those for Passaic, Port Chester, Los Angeles and New Orleans. In Passaic 38.8 per cent of the total Jewish population was reported as part of the labor force. A similar percentage existed also in Port Chester. These were somewhat smaller ratios than were earlier reported for Newark, Trenton, Nashville, and Gary, where the proportion in the labor force was closer to the 50 per cent mark. Men in the Passaic and Port Chester labor forces outnumbered women in the ratio of about four to one. Salaried workers represented 20.8 per cent of the total Jewish population in Passaic, or 54 per cent of the labor force itself, while the self-employed were reported to be 44 per cent of the labor force. This relationship appeared to be about the same as in most large and intermediate Jewish communities, although in smaller towns the self-employed group is often the larger of the two. In Port Chester, for example, the self-employed were 19.9 per cent of the total population and 52 per cent of the labor force, while wage and salary workers were 41 per cent of the labor force. The fact that Port Chester is largely an upper-class residential community, while Passaic is an industrial community, is relevant here.

Housewives, who represented 26.8 per cent of the total Jewish popu-

Table 7—Jewish Labor Force, by Sex, of Selected Cities: Percentage Distribution[a]

MALE

	Los Angeles	Newark (City)[b]	Newark (Suburbs)[c]	Passaic	New Orleans	Trenton	Portland	Camden	Indianapolis	Gary[d]	Port Chester
Self-Employed	61.8	79.2	77.1	32.5	79.6	71.6	—	—	—	—	36.2
Wage and Salary Earners	1.5	2.6	1.4	30.3	2.7	2.4	—	—	—	—	22.2
Unemployed	—	—	—	1.3	—	—	—	—	—	—	1.6
Total in Labor Force	63.3	81.8	78.5	64.1	82.3	74.0	—	—	—	82.9	60.0
Housewife	—	—	—	—	—	—	—	—	—	—	—
Student	8.2	—	—	7.1	5.6	—	—	—	—	—	7.1
Retired	6.2	—	—	3.6	7.0	—	—	—	—	—	2.6
Others, No Answer	22.3	—	—	25.2	5.1	—	—	—	—	—	30.3
Not in Labor Force	36.7	18.2	21.5	35.9	17.7	26.0	—	—	—	17.1	40.0
Number	161,200	21,723	10,696	5,520	3,353	3,760	—	—	—	620	1,136

FEMALE

	Los Angeles	Newark (City)[b]	Newark (Suburbs)[c]	Passaic	New Orleans	Trenton	Gary[d]	Port Chester
Self-Employed	19.3	21.2	13.3	2.1	26.3	19.3	—	3.2
Wage and Salary Earners	1.2	0.9	1.0	11.7	2.9	1.9	—	10.7
Unemployed	—	—	—	0.2	—	—	—	1.9
Total in Labor Force	20.5	22.1	14.3	14.0	29.2	21.2	13.0	15.8
Housewife	49.9	—	—	52.7	59.5	—	—	47.0
Student	3.7	—	—	6.2	5.3	—	—	4.6
Retired	2.5	—	—	1.8	3.6	—	—	0.2
Others, No Answer	23.4	—	—	25.3	2.4	—	—	32.4
Not in Labor Force	79.5	77.9	85.7	86.0	70.8	78.8	87.0	84.2
Number	161,800	24,511	10,917	5,695	3,734	3,789	593	1,099

% Total Jewish Population in Labor Force: Los Angeles 41.7, Newark (City) 50.1, Newark (Suburbs) 46.1, Passaic 38.8, New Orleans 42.0, Trenton 47.5[e], Portland 40.0, Camden 57.9[f], Indianapolis 48.9[e], Gary 48.7[d], Port Chester 38.4

a. Unless otherwise indicated, based on population age 15 and over.
b. Age 14 and over.
c. Age 12 and over.
d. Age 19 and over.
e. Age 15 and over.
f. Over 21.

lation in Passaic, were also 52.7 per cent of the total number of females. In Port Chester, housewives were 23.1 per cent of the total population and 47 per cent of females. Students and retired persons were 9.2 per cent of the total Jewish population in Passaic and 7.3 per cent in Port Chester. (The "other" category included children not in the labor force.)

The Los Angeles study did not distinguish between salaried workers and self-employed in its labor force analysis, so that all that can be said is that 41.7 per cent of the population is included in the active labor force of the Los Angeles Jewish population. This is a smaller ratio than has been reported in the past for larger Jewish communities; it may be attributed in part to the fact that many people come to Los Angeles to retire. Men outnumber women in the Los Angeles Jewish labor force about three to one. Close to half the women are reported as housewives; this group represents 25 per cent of the Jewish population in Los Angeles.

What is required here is an analysis of the age and sex pattern of the Jewish labor force such as is done for the general labor force by the Census Bureau. Such data, too, could clarify the Jewish occupational pattern in relation to the general pattern. We do know that Jews as a group have a higher average age than their neighbors. We also know that the older age groups in this country tend to have higher proportions of professionals, semi-professionals, proprietors, managers, and officials. It seems reasonable, then, to suggest that the failure to take the age factor into account exaggerates, to some degree, the representation of Jews in such occupations.

Yet it is instructive to analyze occupational status; although not available for all the Jewish communities included here, it reveals some interesting disparities from general population characteristics. When the labor force was classified in 1950 into wage workers (including government workers), employers and self-employed, and unpaid family workers, the greatest proportion, 81 per cent of the general population, was to be found in the first category. The employing and self-employed group represented less than one-fifth of the total labor force. As would be expected, there were more female wage workers in proportion to the total female labor force than was the case among the male labor force. For urban areas the proportion of wage workers was even greater than for the general labor force in the United States. Male wage workers were 87.3 per cent of the male urban force; female wage workers were 94.0 per cent of the female urban labor force.[20]

In the Jewish populations for which data are available, only the female labor force approaches the proportions found in the 1950 general labor force. This appears to be the case in Newark (city), Atlanta, Worcester, Grand Rapids, San Francisco, and Buffalo. The Jewish male labor force in most of these communities appears to be much more in the employer and self-employed class; one interesting point to be noted is that the proportion of male wage workers increases as we come closer to industrial and commercial centers, with the highest percentage being found in Buffalo. If one were to attempt a broad generalization with respect to employment status, it might be suggested that in the middle-sized towns the tendency in the Jewish labor force is in the direction of the "employer and self-employed" category.

Classifications by industry, while not always of a uniform character, were made in most of the older studies and in a number of the more recent ones. They indicate a predilection on the part of the Jewish labor force for the wholesale and retail trades. Whether any definite geographic pattern underlies the rather wide range of participation in such industries (from 33 per cent in the city of Newark to 63 per cent in Jacksonville) is difficult to estimate at the present time. Yet it has been suggested that the emphasis on the trades tends to decline in the larger population and industrial centers. In the latter type of community (such as Worcester, Newark, Detroit, and Passaic), where some great manufacturing industry dominates the economic and social life of the town, a fairly large proportion of the Jewish labor force, together with general labor, will be found to be part of the community's industrial organization. Examination of the relevant data shows this to be true of Atlanta, Newark, and Norwich.

It has been often remarked that, in addition to the trades, Jews are to be found most heavily in the professions. Yet, in the community studies which provide such information (shown in Table 8, as well as in the Robison and *American Jewish Year Book* articles), the manufacturing group is greater than the professional group in most cases. This, taken together with the information in Table 9, indicates that the exclusive occupational emphasis of Jews on the professions as compared with other occupations is less than has been generally believed.

Examining the classification of the Jewish labor force by occupation we find the major clusters to be around "clerical, sales, and kindred workers," "proprietors, managers, and officials," and "professional and semi-professional workers." The other classifications are apparently less significant for the Jewish populations; on the other hand, population data for the United States show clerical work to be fourth in importance and professional positions seventh. Proprietorship ranks second generally, as was the case in four Jewish communities during the decade of the thirties. In more recent years proprietorship has been of first rank in virtually all of the Jewish population studies included here, with clerical occupations second and professional work in third position. Kingsley Davis once suggested that Jewish immigrants started in the trades and then educated their children for the professions; this, however, does not seem to be the complete explanation, for it overlooks the relatively high proportion of Jews in the clerical and sales field. Hence, this pattern requires some modification of the usual stereotype.

Aside from some percentage distributions for a few communities, the lack of complete and fully comparable data makes it virtually impossible

Table 8—Industrial Classification of Jewish[a] and Total White 1950 Labor Forces, Age 14 and Over, by Sex, of Selected Cities (in Per Cent)

ATLANTA

Category	Jewish	Male Total	Female Total
Extraction	0.2	0.4	0.2
Construction	1.5	10.6	0.7
Manufacturing	9.1	19.6	12.7
Transportation and Communication	0.9	11.8	4.9
Wholesale-Retail Trade	47.2	25.9	23.2
Finance, Insurance, and Real Estate	4.8	4.8	6.8
Business, Repair, and Personal Services	7.2	{ 16.2	{ 44.2
Professional, Related Services	13.8		
Government	1.5	6.9	5.2
Others, Not Reported	13.8	3.8	2.1
Total	100.0	100.0	100.0
Total Number	650		

NEWARK (City)

Category	Jewish	Male Total	Female Total
Extraction	—	0.2	0.1
Construction	2.5	7.2	0.4
Manufacturing	17.8	38.8	38.8
Transportation and Communication	5.2	7.2	3.4
Wholesale-Retail Trade	33.0	22.6	17.8
Finance, Insurance, and Real Estate	23.6	3.4	8.6
Business, Repair, and Personal Services	10.6	7.2	15.2
Professional, Related Services	—	5.1	10.8
Government	—	5.0	2.5
Others, Not Reported	7.3	3.3	2.4
Total	100.0	100.0	100.0
Total Number	22,383	121,953	61,908

PORTLAND

Category	Jewish	Male Total	Female Total
Extraction	0.1	1.4	0.5
Construction	0.7	9.3	1.0
Manufacturing	6.0	20.0	11.2
Transportation and Communication	1.5	15.6	5.6
Wholesale-Retail Trade	50.8	25.2	30.4
Finance, Insurance, and Real Estate	4.6	4.6	8.5
Business, Repair, and Personal Services	7.5	7.8	15.3
Professional, Related Services	13.7	7.3	21.2
Government	3.5	5.6	4.3
Others, Not Reported	11.6	3.2	2.0
Total	100.0	100.0	100.0
Total Number	2,518	105,091	53,279

LOS ANGELES

Category	Male Jewish	Male Total	Female Jewish	Female Total
Extraction	—	—	—	—
Construction	9.0	9.3	7.1	0.8
Manufacturing	21.7	24.5	19.8	19.8
Transportation and Communication	1.9	6.8	1.1	4.0
Wholesale-Retail Trade	37.8	24.1	29.8	24.0
Finance, Insurance, and Real Estate	6.2	4.7	9.9	7.9
Business, Repair, and Personal Services	{ 20.5	{ 20.3	{ 26.3	{ 36.9
Professional, Related Services				
Government	2.6	5.2	4.9	4.2
Others, Not Reported	0.3	5.1	1.1	2.4
Total	100.0	100.0	100.0	100.0
Total Number	99,500	526,656	31,000	272,940

PASSAIC

Category	Male Jewish	Male Total	Female Jewish	Female Total
Extraction	—	—	—	0.3
Construction	1.3	5.9	—	—
Manufacturing	14.2	50.8	6.8	56.5
Transportation and Communication	2.1	3.9	—	1.8
Wholesale-Retail Trade	43.6	20.8	23.6	15.0
Finance, Insurance, and Real Estate	2.5	2.4	0.6	2.8
Business, Repair, and Personal Services	{ 25.8	{ 10.6	{ 42.3	{ 21.3
Professional, Related Services				
Government	2.7	3.3	7.5	1.0
Others, Not Reported	7.8	2.3	19.2	1.3
Total	100.0	100.0	100.0	100.0
Total Number	3,515	17,289	805	9,780

PORT CHESTER

Category	Male Jewish	Male Total	Female Jewish	Female Total
Extraction	—	—	—	0.8
Construction	6.0	14.4	0.6	—
Manufacturing	14.4	31.0	15.8	41.2
Transportation and Communication	2.7	4.6	1.9	3.6
Wholesale-Retail Trade	48.2	22.9	39.3	17.6
Finance, Insurance, and Real Estate	3.9	2.6	1.3	2.8
Business, Repair, and Personal Services	{ 14.0	{ 16.6	{ 11.1	{ 30.1
Professional, Related Services				
Government	2.7	3.0	8.5	1.5
Others, Not Reported	8.1	4.9	21.5	2.4
Total	100.0	100.0	100.0	100.0
Total Number	663	7,049	153	3,459

NEW ORLEANS

Category	Male Jewish[b]	Male Total	Female Jewish[b]	Female Total
Extraction	0.3	2.9	—	0.5
Construction	2.8	9.0	0.7	1.0
Manufacturing	8.4	17.7	4.6	12.7
Transportation and Communication	2.2	17.4	3.6	8.0
Wholesale-Retail Trade	51.7	25.6	47.4	33.8
Finance, Insurance, and Real Estate	8.7	4.5	13.0	6.9
Business, Repair, and Personal Services	2.6	4.1	4.6	1.6
Professional, Related Services	18.3	5.8	14.5	20.5
Government	—	—	—	—
Others, Not Reported	5.0	13.0	11.6	15.0
Total	100.0	100.0	100.0	100.0
Total Number	2,670		981	

a. Data on the Jewish communities of Atlanta, Newark and Portland contained no breakdown by sex.
b. 17 and over.

to develop an adequate picture of trade or professional occupation breakdowns for all the studies included here. What seems to be characteristic,
despite the concentration on retail trade as opposed to wholesale trade
(as in the Newark suburbs, Worcester, Jacksonville, Portland, San Francisco,
Passaic, Trenton, and Norwich) is the smaller ratio for the former as compared with the United States as a whole. In most of the Jewish communities the proportion of those engaged in trade who were in retail enterprises
approximated 75 per cent; in the United States the number in retail trades
approximated 85 per cent. Where industry breakdowns were given, it
seemed clear that the most popular enterprises were food, clothing, furniture, and dry goods establishments. There are insufficient occupational
data, however, to set forth as a general or usual pattern.[21]

A few of the studies also classified that part of the Jewish labor force
engaged in manufacturing and mechanical industries in terms of specific
industries (Newark, Miami, Portland, Detroit, Passaic). Again, the food
processing, textile, and clothing industries appear predominant. In Detroit,
the automobile industry, the major industial activity, absorbed more than
one-third of the Jewish workers who were in manufacturing.

A detailed percentage classification of Jewish professional and semi-
professional workers is given in Table 10. This tabulation indicates that
the most popular professions are medicine, law, dentistry, and teaching.
This is not unexpected in view of the traditional system of values with
which Jewish persons have frequently measured these occupations. Aside
from teaching, which probably derives its high status value (despite the
notoriously low remuneration) from the characteristic respect for learning
to be found among Jewish parents, these professions possess certain common features: there is more latitude, more independent action, and more
freedom from petty discriminations in these professions than in others,
with the result that Jewish students tend to enter them.

Four of the later studies (Passaic, Port Chester, Los Angeles and New
Orleans) provided useful and interesting data on occupational classification. The occupational features of the small and intermediate communities
were emphasized in the material on Passaic and Port Chester. In the
former, the major groups were proprietors and managers (38.3 per cent),
clerical and sales (25.3 per cent), and professional and semi-professional
(12.0 per cent). The same pattern with slightly different proportions (proprietors, 49.5 per cent; clerical, 22.1 per cent; professional, 15.3 per cent)
existed for Port Chester. However, the data in Los Angeles show that the
clerical-sales and the proprietary groups are exactly the same in size, both
being 31 per cent of employed members of the Jewish labor force. If this
pattern holds true for other large Jewish communities, then the usual pre-
conceptions concerning Jewish occupational patterns will need revision.

In Passaic, the proportion of craftsmen, service workers, laborers, and
operatives was somewhat higher than in other Jewish communities, being
17.7 per cent. This may be due to Passaic's proximity to major industrial

areas. The original data revealed also that proprietorship in Passaic was heavily predominant among foreign-born males, while the clerical-sales group consisted largely of native-born females. A large male concentration in clerical-sales existed in Port Chester and in Los Angeles; in the latter city, men comprised more than 60 per cent of the clerical-sales category.

Information on specific professional occupations was made available in the Passaic and Port Chester surveys. The 1937 Passaic study indicated that the major professional group was "lawyers, judges, etc." with 20.5 per cent of all professionals, while "physicians, dentists, pharmacists" were second with 18.6 per cent. The 1949 study reversed this ranking; the latter group was in first place with 39 per cent while "lawyers, judges, etc." was second with 24 per cent. In Port Chester, too, physicians, dentists, and pharmacists were reported as the largest professional group, constituting 27.2 per cent of all professionals.

Table 9—Occupational Classification of Jewish and Total White (1950) Labor Forces, Age 15

	LOS ANGELES				PASSAIC			
	Male		Female		Male		Female	
Category	Jewish	Total White	Jewish	Total White	Jewish	Total White	Jewish	Total White
Professional and Semi-Professional	17.5	12.4	14.6	13.1	11.9	7.7	12.3	9.2
Proprietors, Managers Officials	36.9	15.6	13.0	6.3	43.6	13.7	13.5	3.9
Clerical, Sales, Kindred	24.9	18.0	50.3	41.3	18.8	12.9	55.4	26.8
Craftsmen, Foremen, Kindred (Skilled)	11.9	19.8	2.7	1.6	6.7	16.4	3.4	1.3
Operatives, Kindred (Semi-Skilled)	5.3	16.9	10.8	16.6	7.4	33.6	4.1	46.6
Service	2.0	9.1	8.1	19.4	2.3	7.1	0.7	10.3
Laborers	1.5	7.5	0.5	0.7	3.2	7.9	1.3	1.0
Others, Not Reported	—	0.8	—	1.0	6.1	0.7	9.3	0.9
	100.0	100.1	100.0	100.0	100.0	100.0	100.0	100.0
Total Number	99,500	526,656	31,000	272,940	3,415	17,289	740	9,780

	MIAMI			TRENTON			PORTLAND		
	Total Jewish	Total White Male	Female	Total Jewish	Total White Male	Female	Total Jewish	Total White Male	Female
Professional and Semi-Professional	13.4	8.3	10.4	19.2	7.4	9.8	15.1	10.0	14.0
Proprietors, Managers, Officials	26.1	15.9	5.7	43.2	11.2	3.6	37.2	16.9	6.6
Clerical and Sales	38.2	17.4	35.9	27.1	14.0	34.7	35.2	19.8	45.4
Craftsmen		20.6	1.2	5.7	18.3	1.5	3.3	19.9	1.4
	13.2								
Operatives		12.1	9.7	3.4	29.1	31.6	3.3	16.0	10.3
Service	8.6	14.5	34.5	1.1	8.6	15.6	2.2	8.1	20.6
Laborers	0.2	8.8		—	10.3	1.9	0.4	8.6	0.8
Others, Not Reported	0.3	2.4	2.6	0.3	1.1	1.3	3.3	0.7	0.9
	100.0	100.0	100.0	100.0	100.0	100.0	100.0	100.0	100.0
Total Number	4,336	76,022	40,177	3,426	36,780	19,615	2,392	102,091	53,279

Data on industrial classifications emphasize the concentration of the Jewish labor force in wholesale and retail trades in the three communities for which such information is available. In Passaic, the proportion is 40 per cent, while in Port Chester it is 46.5 per cent. This ratio is smaller in Los Angeles where the proportion of those in trades is 36 per cent, indicating a concomitantly more even distribution, especially in manufacturing enterprises and in business and professional services. It might be noted that in all three communities the manufacturing group was a sizeable proportion of the labor force. Specific data on the wholesale and retail trades for Passaic and Port Chester indicate that in this general field the major concentrations are in food establishments, apparel and shoes, and furniture and hardware. This pattern appears to be similar to that of other Jewish communities. (See Table 11.)

In the Passaic and Port Chester surveys certain cross-tabulations were

and Over, by Sex, of Selected Cities (in Per Cent)

| | NEW ORLEANS | | | | | | PORT CHESTER | | | | | NEWARK (CITY) | | |
| | Male | | Female | | | Male | | Female | | | Total | Total White | |
Jewish	Total	White	Jewish	Total	White	Jewish	Total	White	Jewish	Total	White	Jewish	Male	Female
23.5	10.6	14.5	15.4			14.9	7.7	17.1	11.0			14.0	6.4	7.3
46.0	17.6	25.1	6.0			56.3	14.8	20.3	3.7			32.0	10.8	3.1
22.0	21.9	53.4	54.3			16.1	13.0	47.8	32.8			26.3	15.0	33.7
2.7	20.1	1.0	1.5			5.9	23.4	1.9	2.1			9.6	19.5	2.4
1.3	15.5	1.7	11.0			3.3	23.0	9.1	34.0			5.8	27.8	34.3
2.3	7.0	3.3	10.1			0.8	8.1	—	15.0			1.4	9.5	16.9
0.5	6.4	—	0.6			1.5	9.1	1.3	0.3			2.2	9.8	0.9
1.6	0.9	1.0	1.1			1.2	0.9	2.5	1.1			8.7	1.2	1.4
100.0	100.0	100.0	100.0			100.0	100.0	100.0	100.0			100.0	100.0	100.0
2,670		981				663	7,049	153	3,459			22,383	121,953	61,908

| | CAMDEN | | | INDIANAPOLIS | | | UTICA | | | GARY | | |
| Total | Total White | | Total | Total White | | Total | Total White | | Total | Total White | |
Jewish	Male	Female	Jewish	Male	Female	Jewish	Male	Female	Jewish	Male	Female
18.8	5.5	6.8	12.4	9.4	10.8	9.4	6.5	13.4	18.4	5.7	12.6
47.0	8.9	3.0	50.8	11.8	4.0	46.5	14.2	3.6	44.0	7.1	5.0
24.8	13.8	32.4	28.7	18.5	41.4	29.9	17.0	33.3	20.6	10.0	40.7
4.6	25.2	2.0	2.9	21.3	2.1	4.8	19.7	1.6	10.7	27.8	2.0
3.2	26.3	35.4	4.1	21.2	19.5	1.3	25.5	32.7	—	25.0	14.6
1.6	8.6	18.0	1.0	8.5	19.5	1.5	8.8	13.8	—	5.3	21.7
—	11.0	1.5	0.1	7.9	1.0	3.6	7.6	0.8	6.3	17.9	2.0
—	0.7	0.9	—	1.4	1.7	3.0	0.7	0.8	—	1.2	1.4
100.0	100.0	100.0	100.0	100.0	100.0	100.0	100.0	100.0	100.0	100.0	100.0
432	33,656	15,625	2,429	123,180	63,288	1,239	26,638	13,880	591	41,729	12,709

Table 10—Classification of Professional Occupations: Percentage Distribution, Jewish Populations

	Newark City[a]	Suburbs[a]	Miami	Portland	Trenton	Passaic	Port Chester	New Orleans
Physicians	19.7	12.4	18.9	18.2	21.2	39.0	27.2	35.6[c]
Dentists	13.9	13.2	5.5	13.6	10.6			
Attorneys, Judges	16.6	26.1	19.2	21.4	20.4	24.0	14.4	18.0
Rabbis, Cantors,	4.4		2.7	2.6	b	19.0	16.0	14.4
Teachers	11.3	3.0	10.6	9.8	19.4			
Artists, Musicians,								
Writers	5.0	6.0	8.2	3.6	b	b	b	b
Accountants	b	b	16.5	b	b	10.0[d]	39.2[d]	8.6[d]
Social Workers	b	b	1.7	4.2	1.1	b	b	b
Nurses,								
Medical Assistants	b	b	8.9	3.9	b	b	b	b
Chemists, Pharmacists,								
Engineers, Architects	18.9	29.2	4.5	20.1	5.6	b	b	b
Semi-Professional,								
Others	10.2	10.1	3.3	2.6	21.7	8.0	3.2	23.4
	100.0	100.0	100.0	100.0	100.0	100.0	100.0	100.0

a. Figures given are for male population only.
b. Not classified separately.
c. Includes pharmacists.
d. Includes architects.

attempted for the first time which revealed significant relationships in the economic structure of these Jewish communities. When employment status was crossed with industry it was discovered that in Passaic 44.5 per cent of those in the "trades" category were wage earners. In Port Chester, the ratio was smaller, with 32.4 per cent of the "trades" group reported as wage earners. In the professional and business service groups, about half in Passaic were wage earners, while in Port Chester the proportion dropped to 30 per cent. The data on this, together with those for New Orleans, are given in Table 12.

Further light on economic structure was provided by a cross-tabulation of occupation and industry.[22] Here the Passaic data indicated that at least 30 per cent of the professionals were not independently engaged. The proprietorship group, as might be expected, was heavily concentrated in

Table 11—Wholesale and Retail Trades

	Passaic		Port Chester	
Trade	Number	Per Cent	Number	Per Cent
Food establishments	420	24.3	75	19.9
Eating and drinking places	110	6.4	9	2.3
Liquor	85	4.9	9	2.3
Apparel and shoes	375	21.8	75	19.9
Furniture, hardware, lumber	185	10.7	58	15.3
Auto and related	45	2.6	24	6.3
General merchandise	45	2.6	36	9.5
Other	320	18.6	63	16.6
No answer	140	8.1	30	7.9
Total	1,725	100.0	379	100.0

the trades. The clerical-sales group was to be found mainly in trades and services. A similar pattern was revealed for Port Chester.

In New Orleans, as in the other communities, there was a lack of "spread" among the various industrial classifications. One-half of the Jewish labor force is in the wholesale-retail trades, and this becomes almost 70 per cent when we add those in professional services. The emphasis on these two industrial groupings is further accentuated for those Jews who are self-employed, for almost 80 per cent of these are found here. The explanation for the preponderance of Jewish employment in these two industrial groupings is, of course, the fact that these offer greater opportunities for self-employment. Fully 62 per cent of the Jewish males in New Orleans engaged in wholesale-retail trades and in professional services were self-employed, compared with 38 per cent for the remainder of the Jewish labor force. Even for females, the proportion of self-employed in these two industrial classifications was 30 per cent, compared with 17 per cent for all other industries.

Shifting to occupational classifications, we find that four of every ten Jews in the New Orleans labor force list themselves as either proprietors or managers. The bulk of these were in the wholesale-retail trades, although there was a relatively large number in manufacturing. The next largest occupational grouping was clerical and sales with 30 per cent of the total labor force. While the largest proportion of these was once again found in wholesale-retail trades, there was a wider spread among the other industrial classifications. The last occupational grouping of any size was professional and semi-professional.

The professional and semi-professional occupations in New Orleans included four times as many males as females. The major fields for males are medicine, semi-professional occupations, and legal. Almost half of the females were teachers and 25 per cent each were in medicine and in miscellaneous professional activities.

The foreign-born segment of the labor force exhibited certain dissimilarities with the native born. Where almost a quarter of the native born

Table 12—Employment Status and Industry

	PASSAIC		PORT CHESTER		NEW ORLEANS	
	Self Employed	Wage Earner	Self Employed	Wage Earner	Self Employed	Wage Earner
Construction	25	15	27	14	31	56
Manufacturing	130	425	38	81	118	153
Transportation-communication	25	50	7	14	10	83
Wholesale-retail trade	970	775	256	123	933	912
Real estate, insurance	70	25	14	14	118	243
Professional and business services	635	630	77	33	465	280
Government	—	165	—	31	34	208
Other	15	25	4	8		
No answer	45	230	22	53	3	3
Total	1,915	2,340	445	371	1,712	1,938

are in professional and semi-professional occupations, we find only 13 per cent of the foreign born. On the other hand, a larger proportion of the foreign born are entrepreneurs and managers than are the native born, while the reverse is true for clerical and sales occupations. While the number of Jews engaged as craftsmen and foremen is small, we find a greater relative preponderance of foreign born. There seems to be a definite correlation between occupational pursuit and nativity especially for those occupations requiring higher education.

Comparison of the New Orleans data with the 1950 Census data shows a greater percentage of Jews listed as being in the professional and semi-professional and in the proprietor and manager occupations, and on the other hand, a much smaller percentage of Jews in all other occupations except clerical and sales. In these last two, the proportion of the labor force employed was approximately the same for both the total white and the Jewish labor forces. Especially noteworthy is the fact that the Jewish labor force in New Orleans had proportionately three times as many proprietors and managers as the total white labor force. For the skilled and semi-skilled occupations, the reverse was true, the total white labor force having proportionately more than seven times the number found in the Jewish labor force.

There are further interesting divergences within the professional occupations. The Jews were heavily represented in the medical and legal professions and also in the semi-professional occupations. The total white population has smaller proportions in these fields (particularly in the field of law) and a heavier representation in teaching and the other professions (the emphasis on the latter is particularly marked). It is thus evident that New Orleans Jewry, as is the case in other communities, tends to be limited to certain professional fields. In such professional occupations as engineers, architects, etc., are found but one per cent of the Jewish male labor force, compared with a figure of five per cent for the total white male labor force. This contrast is the more dramatic when we realize that the proportion of the Jewish male labor force engaged in all professional and semi-professional occupations was almost two and one-half times the proportion found in the total white male labor force.

The characteristics noted in Jewish occupational patterns when compared with the total white popuation of New Orleans are, as would be expected, still in evidence when industrial distributions are studied. Wholesale-retail trades employ 50 per cent of the Jewish labor force compared with 28 per cent of the total white labor force. In professional services also, a greater proportion of the Jewish labor force is employed compared with the total white labor force. In all other industrial groupings the Jewish labor force has proportionately fewer employed, with the minor exception of finance and real estate. Construction, manufacturing and transportation employed approximately 37 per cent of the total white labor force, compared with 12 per cent for the Jewish labor force. In general, industrial distribution of workers, when examined separately for male and female, did not vary significantly from the pattern discussed above.

Comparisons of data for labor force characteristics of the Jewish and general populations are difficult to draw, since such information as might have been gathered in the Jewish studies do not always employ the same classifications as utilized by the Census Bureau. Nevertheless some indications showing that the Jewish proportion in the labor force tends to be smaller are available. The 1950 census data indicated that in such cities as Newark, Portland, Camden, Indianapolis, Trenton, Gary, Passaic, Port Chester and Los Angeles, the general male white population generally had 80 per cent or more in the labor force. In the Jewish communities of Passaic, Port Chester and Los Angeles the proportion of males in the labor force was around 60 to 65 per cent. However, in three other communities (Newark, Trenton, Gary) it came close to the general population figure, even exceeding it by 2 percentage points in Newark.

Comparisons of employment status are difficult to make for lack of comparability in definitions and categories. In three cities (Passaic, Port Chester and Los Angeles) that part of the male labor force in the general white population that was classified as wage and salary earners ranged from 60 to 65 per cent, whereas for the Jewish populations in those cities the data showed about half of these figures. Generally speaking, it may be surmised that the Jewish communities exhibit a smaller proportion in the labor force and a smaller part of their labor force in the wage and salary earner categories than does the general community.

Tables 8 and 9 provide percentage distribution data from the 1950 census on industrial and occupational characteristics of the general white population in selected cities, compared to the Jewish populations of those cities. Perusal of these data suggests that there tends to be a greater emphasis on manufacturing pursuits than is the case in the Jewish communities, although there is a fair concentration in the wholesale-retail trades as is the case with the Jewish communities. Jewish communities also seem to be proportionately more heavily represented in real estate and insurance. However, the latter probably refers to agency representation rather than insurance company staff employment. Examination of the occupational data reveals a consistently greater representation in skilled and semi-skilled workers for the general population than for the Jewish, among whom representation in the professional and managerial group seems larger.

Occupation represents but one index of economic condition. To fully describe the position of Jews in the American economy, one would have to know the income levels of Jewish groups, their buying and consuming habits, and a variety of other indices of economic position. Such data, however, are extremely difficult to obtain in a survey; they are the kind of information that only the tax collector seems able to secure. Nevertheless, the Los Angeles study attempted to measure income levels among Jews in that community. On the basis of a subsample, a number of respondents were asked to indicate their income groups by means of a "secret ballot" device. While the interviewer explained the need for obtaining such data, the respondent was given a paper on which various income figures were listed and asked to check the correct figure. The paper was placed in an envelope by the respondent and sealed, thus making the source of the information entirely anonymous. The data in Table 13 indicate that the largest number of heads of households report moderate incomes.

Table 13—Percentage Distribution, Annual Income of Heads of Households, Los Angeles (Jewish Population)

	Less than $4,000	$4,000-$8,000	Over $8,000	Total
Professionals	27.4	27.5	45.1	100.0
Proprietors, managers	15.5	54.5	30.0	100.0
Clerical, sales	33.4	49.9	16.7	100.0
Other occupations	53.2	32.7	14.1	100.0
Retired persons	58.8	23.6	17.6	100.0

One further comparative measure of economic position, and that a rather crude one, is available for some of the population studies: home ownership. It is an incomplete measure, since considerably more information than the fact of home ownership would be required to evaluate economic position. One would need to know mortgage values, rentals, size of dwellings, and other such data. For the general population of the United States, owner-occupied dwelling units represent 51.0 per cent of all dwelling units as compared with 41.7 per cent for tenant-occupied units.[23] In the studies on Jewish population, tenant-occupied units range from 27.0 per cent in Camden to 60.7 per cent in the city of Newark. Owner-occupied homes, however, are more than 44 per cent in all but one of the cases (see Table 14). As said above, this information by itself does not lend itself to

Table 14—Home Ownership, Jewish Populations

City	TENANT-OCCUPIED		OWNER-OCCUPIED		NO REPORT	
	Number of Families	Per Cent	Number of Families	Per Cent	Number of Families	Per Cent
Newark (city)	9,829	60.7	3.969	24.5	2,402	14.8
Newark (suburbs)	4,166	55.5	3,344	44.5	—	—
New Orleans	1,467[a]	45.2	1,597[a]	48.7	196[a]	6.1
Atlanta	209	44.5	254	54.0	7	1.5
Utica	448	43.6	538	52.3	42	4.1
Indianapolis	816	40.5	1,201	59.5	—	—
Trenton	1,026	38.6	1,566	58.9	66	2.5
Camden	89	27.0	238	72.1	3	0.9

a. Estimated from data in original study which did not provide this figure.

further interpretation. The Los Angeles study also provided some data on home ownership which indicated that 58 per cent of Jewish persons in that city owned their own homes. The proportion of home ownership was higher for the professional and proprietary than for other occupational groups.

§ VIII. Secular Education

The various studies under review yield less and less information once the reader leaves behind such demographic measures as age, sex, and occupation. The reasons why investigators have not looked into such population characteristics as education, religious preference, and the like with the same thoroughness as with other measures of population, are varied: inadequately designed questionnaires, feelings that certain questions might be considered ill-advised in the enumeration, or simply a lack of funds and time. One investigator, after completing a detailed analysis of age composition and occupation, remarked: "This concludes the analysis of the statistics that were drawn from the schedules. Material of population mobility and length of residence . . . did not yield data of sufficient accuracy to justify statistical analysis." While this in itself might have indicated some weakness in the original questionnaire, the investigator apparently felt that age and occupational information were sufficient.

As for secular education, some data were available in some of the more recent studies; none of the older studies yielded usable information. To demographic experts, educational attainment represents a rough measure of population quality; it also indicates, in a large measure, the efforts a community makes on behalf of its growing generation.

Comparisons of educational attainment between the Jewish populations and the general white population in the United States are difficult: the data in the Jewish community studies are seldom set up by age groups, and there often exist inconsistencies in the lower age limits.[24] It would also have been useful if all the studies set up the information by sex.

For the general white population in the United States, the median number of years of school completed (for persons 25 years old and over) in 1950 was 9.7 years. To judge from the data in Table 15, the average for the Jewish population is a higher one. While a lack of sufficient data prevents the computation of exact medians, inspection indicates that the average in these studies would fall into the high school and/or high school graduate group. Furthermore, the proportions of the Jewish populations for high school and college are somewhat higher than in the general population. The few cases which show the data by sex reveal nothing that might be interpreted as a notable difference as between males and females. In Worcester, where data were available for native and foreign-born, the median year of general schooling completed for the latter group was from 2 to 3, with a large number reporting no formal general education. However, the data on Jewish education of adults in that community indicate a median age for Jewish schooling of 4.2 years, so that while the foreign groups in Worcester had little formal general education, Jewish education may have served as a substitute. In Port Chester 25 per cent of those age fifteen or over reported graduation from high school; in Los Angeles the per cent was 30.6. Those without formal education were in the main per-

Table 15—General Education, 1950, Total White and Jewish Populations of Selected Cities (in Per Cent)

	Los Angeles[a] Total	Jewish	Newark (City) Total	Jewish[b]	Atlanta Total	Jewish	New Orleans[d] Total	Jewish	Trenton Total	Jewish
No Formal Education	1.7	6.3	4.3	3.4	2.5	2.9	2.3	1.0	3.7	4.8
Some Elementary School	14.5	16.1	26.9	35.3	33.2	5.4	28.0	16.0	29.8	9.4
Elementary School Graduate	13.8	9.3	23.9		10.0	5.5[c]	15.2	6.1	15.9	7.9
Some High School	17.5	7.2	16.7	39.7	18.3	47.6	14.8	11.1	17.8	6.6
High School Graduate	28.4	30.6	17.2		17.4		21.4	25.4	16.3	32.3
Some College	12.3	12.5	3.6	19.6	8.7	25.1	7.4	16.7	5.3	8.6
College Graduate	8.6	11.7	4.0		7.1		7.5	11.0	4.9	18.1
Post-Graduate School		4.8				1.2		8.2		
Other, No Information	3.1	1.5	3.4	2.1	3.0	12.3	3.4	4.5	6.4	12.3
	99.9	100.0	100.0	100.1	100.2	100.0	100.0	100.0	100.1	100.0
Total Number	1,324,010		277,630		198,600		294,375		83,020	

Table 15—General Education, 1950, Total White and Jewish Populations of Selected Cities (in Per Cent) (Continued)

	Camden		Indianapolis		Gary		Port Chester		Miami	
	Total	Jewish	Total	Jewish[e]	Total	Jewish[f]	Total	Jewish[a]	Total	Jewish
No Formal Education	3.4	5.3	0.8	—	3.4	—	4.5	1.7	—	—
Some Elementary School	34.4	17.5	17.3	10.0	25.8	2.7	21.8	11.6	29.1	20.3
Elementary School Graduate	19.9		20.4	8.7	17.8	6.4	18.3	5.4		
Some High School	21.0	10.6	18.4	7.6	18.1	8.1	16.3	8.5	48.6	51.2
High School Graduate	14.4	35.6	24.2	36.1	22.0	27.4	23.6	24.9		
Some College	2.6	5.6	7.9	16.6	5.9	21.8	6.4	9.6	19.8	25.0
College Graduate	2.7	15.7	7.8	12.2	4.8	10.9	7.1	9.3		
Post-Graduate School			5.1		6.1			4.9	2.5	3.5
Other, No Information	1.4	9.8	3.1	3.7	2.2	16.6	2.1	24.1		
	99.8	100.1	99.9	100.0	100.0	100.0	100.1	100.0	100.0	100.0
Total Number	75,865		267,100		79,280		15,120		289,020	

a. Age 15 and over. Unless otherwise indicated, based on age 25 and over.
b. Age 5 and over.
c. Includes junior high school.
d. Age 6 and over.
e. Age 20 and over.
f. Does not give age limit.

sons over the age of 55. It is interesting to note that in Port Chester 18.5 per cent were still attending school, while in Los Angeles the proportion was a little over 20 per cent. From what is known of these characteristics in the general population, it would appear that with regard to general education Jewish communities seem to stand somewhat higher than the average for the entire population.

The New Orleans study provided more detailed data than did other surveys. The level of secular education attained by the Jewish population of New Orleans was high compared with both the total white population in New Orleans and with that of other Jewish communities where such information was available. The study compared the proportions of each five-year age group, from 6 through 30, of the Jewish and the total white populations enrolled in school. There is relatively little difference between the two up to the age of 15: 98.4 per cent of Jewish children aged 6 to 10, and 92.9 per cent (this latter figure excludes 6-year olds in kindergarten) of all white children were in school; the figures for the 11-15-year olds were 96.2 and 96.8 per cent, respectively. The next two older age groups, however, showed striking differences. Over three-quarters of Jewish youth aged 16-20 were enrolled in school, in contrast to only 47 per cent of all white youth. The contrast remains when sex is held constant. In the 21-25 group, there is a similar difference: while 32.1 per cent of Jewish young men were in school, only 20.5 per cent of all white young men were enrolled; for young women, the figures were 13.7 and 6.3 per cent, respectively.[25]

A further revealing comparison is the highest level of education obtained for the age groups 16-20 and 21-25. While the categories of educational level are very broad, they serve to underline the divergence between the level of attainment reached by the Jewish and the total white population. Almost no Jews failed to get further than elementary school, but one-fifth of all whites from 16-25 had had less than eight years of schooling. And whereas eight out of ten Jews in the age group 21 to 25 attended a minimum of a year at college, for the group 21 to 25 of the total white population the proportion was only one out of four. It might also be noted that the emphasis upon college attendance in the Jewish population has increased sharply with the passage of time. Of Jews 41 to 50, four out of every ten had had some college; of those 61 to 70, only two of ten had attended college.

§   IX. Nativity, Citizenship and Place of Birth

Although the Decennial Census makes no classification according to religious denomination, classification of the population by nativity is one of its major subdivisions. For the white population, a division is made into native white and foreign-born white, and in the 1930 census especially, the native white population was further subdivided into persons of native parentage and those of foreign or mixed parentage. Classifications by country origin and by mother tongue of the foreign-born population have also provided useful information.[26]

General data, other than local community studies, on the national origin of the American Jewish population are, of course, not available. At times, researchers have equated the Jewish population in an area with Russian immigrants.[27] This certainly is not a valid procedure, and in the absence of continued immigration from Eastern Europe becomes even less valid and less useful as time goes on. Also, the mother tongue classification in the decennial census is apparently becoming a less fruitful source of information.[28] The best source of information on this question, then, would be the various community population studies. Unfortunately, few of the surveys reviewed here sought information on nativity and citizenship. However, the data that were obtained are of considerable interest.

Table 16—Classification by Country of Birth, Jewish Population (in Per Cent)

	Los Angeles	Newark City	Suburbs	Passaic	New Orleans	Port Chester
Native-born	67.9	68.8	77.8	68.9[c]	83.1[e]	74.6
Foreign-born	32.1	31.2	22.2	31.1	16.9	25.4
	100.00	100.0	100.0	100.0	100.0	100.0
Foreign-born						
Russia	41.4	49.6	47.9	47.5	34.9	46.1
Poland	14.5	16.6	10.6	20.0	23.2	19.2
Austria	5.1	14.2[a]	11.4[b]	13.2[d]	2.7	4.2[f]
Rumania	4.7	4.3	3.3	1.6	9.0	3.2
Germany	3.8	3.7	5.5	2.0	14.4	3.3
Hungary	4.1	2.7	2.8	6.0	—	1.4
Great Britain	5.3	2.2	1.6	3.2	1.8	1.9
Other Eastern Europe	5.0	1.0	—	4.4	2.5	7.3
Other Western Europe	—	—	—	0.1	3.1	0.3
Other, Not Reported	16.1	5.7	16.8	1.8	8.6	12.9
	100.0	100.0	99.9	99.8	100.2	99 8
Total Native and Foreign	323,000	56,800	29,500	11,215	9,098	2,235

a. Includes 0.2 per cent from Czechoslovakia.
b. Includes 1.0 per cent from Czechoslovakia.
c. Includes 55 (0.5 per cent) of unknown nativity.
d. Includes 1.4 per cent from Czechoslovakia.
e. Includes 212 (2.3 per cent) of unknown nativity.
f. Includes 0.5 per cent from Czechoslovakia.

In the more recent surveys the proportion of the native born in the Jewish population ranged from 67.9 per cent to 83.1 per cent. As might be expected, the proportions of the native born in the three older surveys (Pittsburgh, San Francisco, and Buffalo) are smaller, yet in these communities, too, the native born represented over half the Jewish population. In five of the six studies, the largest proportion of foreign born, ranging from 34.9 per cent in New Orleans to 49.6 per cent in Newark (city), indicated that they came from Russia. Other major areas listed as birthplaces were Poland, Austria, Lithuania, Rumania, Germany, Czechoslo-

vakia, and Hungary. The three older studies which provided data on this
point indicated a similar pattern.

The increasing proportions of native born to foreign born show the
effects of lower migration; the influx under the Displaced Persons Act
of 1948, which amounts to a little over 1 per cent of the total estimated
Jewish population in this country, hardly altered this tendency. In Passaic, for example, the percentage of foreign-born persons in 1937 was 36.4;
this declined to 31.6 per cent in 1949. In this community, too, the
foreign-born group was relatively older than the native-born group. In
fact, an age pyramid for the foreign born alone would show all the characteristics of an old population, with a very narrow base and tending
toward a broad apex—a triangle pointing downward. The predominantly
foreign origin of the older group was evident also in other surveys. In
Port Chester the ratio of foreign born to native born was very low in the
younger age groups, rising markedly above the age of thirty-five, until
by age fifty-five there were more than twice as many foreign born as
native born.

In New Orleans the Jewish community is largely native born—less than
two out of ten Jews reporting a birthplace outside of the United States.
The foreign born are in the older age groups (their median age 55.0
years compared with 34.7 years for native born) so that in the next two
decades the proportion of native born will probably increase to over 90
per cent of the total Jewish population.

Port Chester and Los Angeles also inquired into the place of birth of
the native-born respondents in order to ascertain the degree of inward
migration. (See Table 17.) In the first of these cities about 95 per cent of
the native-born Jews reported the northeast regions of the United States
as their birthplace. These data together with the information on length of
residence suggest that in Port Chester perhaps 40 per cent of the Jews
are native to the community.

Table 17—Region of Birth, Per Cent of Native-Born Jews

Region of Birth	Port Chester	Los Angeles
New England	5.0	4.5
Central Atlantic	88.9	29.7
Middle West	0.4	26.6
Southwest	0.2	1.2
Southeast	0.2	3.0
Far West	a	35.0
No answer	5.2	—
Total	100.0	100.0

* Less than 0.1 per cent.

In contrast to such stability, the data on Los Angeles reveal a heavy
inward migration, which, of course, accounts for the spectacular growth
of that community in recent years. The Central Atlantic states were the

birthplaces of 29.7 per cent of present Los Angeles native-born Jewry, while 26.6 per cent reported coming from Middle Western states. Actually, 65 per cent of native-born Jews in Los Angeles reported coming from regions other than the Far West. As might be expected, the in-migrants from New York and Chicago are mainly adults, while most of the Los Angeles-born are children. The data on these aspects are given in Table 17.

New Orleans also inquired into these matters. There, the largest proportion of the native born (70 per cent) give New Orleans or other portions of Louisiana as their birthplace. Another 10 per cent were born in the Middle Atlantic states of New York, New Jersey, and Pennsylvania. Few Jews in New Orleans were born in the southern states along the eastern seaboard, although approximately 7 per cent come from the surrounding states of Kentucky, Tennessee, Alabama, and Mississippi. Excluding those Jews born in New Orleans, we find that more than a quarter of the native born last resided in Texas, Oklahoma, Arkansas, and other portions of Louisiana, before moving to New Orleans. Another quarter moved from the Middle Atlantic states (New York, New Jersey, Pennsylvania).

In a comparison of the countries of origin of the Jewish and total foreign-born population in these communities, the most striking point which emerges is the large percentage of the latter who come from countries which, in Table 16 on the Jewish foreign born, were grouped under "Other, not reported." In cities like Newark and Passaic, however, substantial numbers—though proportionately far less than among the Jewish foreign born—were born in Eastern Europe.

§ X. Internal Migration and Length of Residence

Movements of large masses of population have always been events of considerable meaning for society. The surge across the North American continent by the white man, the migrations of East Europeans in the 1880's, the exchanges of populations after the great wars, have affected social processes as well as individuals. In these gigantic waves in which people sought new homes and escaped old ones there arose problems of status, position, adjustment, and acclimatization. Today there are problems of carry-over from one generation to the next, with tension existing between parent and child, and movement from small cities to large cities, from large cities to suburbs.

However, the largest part of the movements of people consists of "milling around in local areas." This is probably true also for the Jewish populations. In the Jewish communities in which data on planning to move were obtained, those who indicated a move to some other city ranged from 2.3 per cent in Newark (suburbs) to 17.3 per cent in Camden (see Table 18). By far the greatest proportion having said that they would remain in their respective cities, although high "uncertain" percentages were recorded.

A number of the surveys also included data on length of residence.

Table 18—Families Planning to Move

	Newark (City)[a]		Newark (Suburbs)[a]		Camden[a]		Indianapolis[c]		Utica[a]	
	No.	Per Cent	No.	Per Cent	No.	Per Cent	No.	Per Cent	No.	Per Cent
Planning to Move										
Inside City	1,098	42.30	97[b]	43.71	45	60.00	303	88.60	100	44.64
Suburbs	293	11.29	445	9.53	—	—	—	—	—	—
Outside City	109	4.20	23	2.26	13	17.33	39	11.40	8	3.57
Other	187	7.20	34	3.34	—	—	—	—	—	—
No Information—Uncertain	909	35.01	419	41.16	17	22.67	—	—	116	51.79
Total Planning to Move	2,596	100.00	1,018	100.00	75	100.00	342	100.00	224	100.00
Not Planning to Move	13,604[d]	83.98	7,155[d]	87.54	252	70.59	1,408	68.35	599	58.21
Planning to Move	2,596	16.02	1,018	12.46	75	21.01	342	16.60	224	21.77
Don't Know	—	—	—	—	—	—	310	15.05	—	—
No Information	—	—	—	—	30	8.40	—	—	206	20.02
Total	16,200	100.00	8,173	100.00	357	100.00	2,060	100.00	1,029	100.00

a. Families.
b. Planning to move to Newark City.
c. Heads of families.
d. No definite number is given for families "not planning to move," so it is assumed that all families not listed as "planning to move" are "not planning to move."

Table 19 shows the median number of years of residence in the Jewish communities which presented such information. In the earlier studies, the median length of residence ranged from 13.2 in Norwich to 24.0 in New London; the more recent studies indicate a slightly higher average, with the exception of Miami, in which the median is but 5.1 years. About 70 per cent of the Miami Jewish population was estimated to have resided there less than ten years. This may be contrasted with Indianapolis where about one-fourth of the Jewish population has been in residence for ten years or less. Such figures, of course, emphasize the tremendously rapid growth of Miami's Jewish population in the last decade.

Table 19—Average Length of Residence

City	Median No. Years of Residence
Newark[a]	
City	25.08
Suburbs	18.75
Miami[b]	5.11
Atlanta[c]	23.10
Camden[c]	21.93
Utica[d]	17.17
Passaic[e]	16.26

a. Number of years of residence of family in Essex County.
b. Number of years of residence of family in Dade County.
c. Number of years of residence of family in city.
d. Foreign born by number of years in city.
e. Individuals by number of years in city.

Yet these data fail to tell us anything really significant about the internal migration of Jews in the United States. We cannot say that Jews are moving out of the large metropolitan areas to smaller communities, and if so, whether such persons are young or old, or middle-aged; nor can we say that young Jewish persons prefer the big city. In a general way, it is noted that Miami and Tucson's rapid growth in Jewish population is probably due to inward migration from other areas. But the character of that migration, an important local question, is unknown. Yet these are the questions which might have important implications for community planning. Internal migration, like the other demographic features of American Jews, remains to be explored.

Nevertheless, several community surveys did attempt more detailed analysis of residence and movement, as shown in Table 20. Thus in Port Chester about 38 per cent of the Jewish families indicated that they had moved within the last decade. Of those who reported residing in Port Chester twenty years or more, only 6 per cent reported that they resided at their present address that length of time. These data suggest a fairly high degree of movement within the community, a characteristic in the general population. In Passaic, where the analysis of residence was made according to nativity, the information revealed that 70 per cent of the foreign-born Jews

Demographic Aspects and Social Mobility

Table 20—Length of Residence, Per Cent of Jewish Population

Years	Passaic	Port Chester	Los Angeles[a]	Trenton[b,c]	Gary[c,d]
1- 5	15.4	17.7	21.6	21.9	18.4
6-10	14.7	17.5	22.9	16.6	11.2
11-15	10.8	10.7		13.1	11.4
16-20	10.0	8.1		9.5	8.6
21-25	10.5	9.2	55.5	8.6	13.7
26-30	11.2	6.8		9.2	36.7
Over 30	24.1	22.2		21.1	
No answer	3.3	7.8	—	—	—
Total	100.0	100.0	100.0	100.0	100.0

a. Heads of households.
b. Households.
c. The age breaks for Trenton and Gary were: "under 5, 5-9, 9-14. . . ."
d. Young adults and adults. Does not include children, youths and single young adults living with parents.

had been in the United States more than thirty years. The data further suggested an outward movement of native-born Passaic Jewry offset somewhat by an inward movement. For example, 20.7 per cent of native Jews residing in Passaic who were born elsewhere had been living in Passaic ten years or less. The tendency toward considerable moving about is further illustrated by the fact that about 18.5 per cent of Los Angeles Jewish households were planning to move at the time the survey was conducted. In New Orleans those planning to move were only 5 per cent of the total number of households.

§ *XI. Summary and Conclusions*

What, then, stands out in this large collection of seemingly conglomerate data? It is clear that the Jewish population is, on the average, an older one than the general white population, and one that is replenishing itself at a rate slower than the general population. Yet it is fairly certain that Jews benefited from the recent spurt in the birth rate, although the growth in population for Jews was in all probability not as large as for non-Jews. It is also fairly evident that Jews are a predominantly urban people: those who go to the smaller towns evidently do so for the sake of a greater measure of economic independence. It may very well be that the latter, too, motivates to some degree the urge to have smaller families. Most of the indications are that Jews do tend to have fewer children than non-Jews.

On marital status, virtually all the data suggest that Jewish communities conform to the national pattern. There is some evidence, however, that the Jewish population has more widowed and fewer divorced and separated persons, although such a generalization is obviously affected by the proportion of older persons in the population, as is the case amongst Jews. The only study that concerned itself with intermarriage, New Orleans, indicated that 7 per cent of married Jews had non-Jewish spouses: almost two-thirds of the Jewish members of the partnership were males. If this is the pattern in other communities (for which there are really no adequate data) it may be surmised that Jewish males tend to intermarry more readily than Jewish females.

Family size data reinforce the long-standing contention that Jewish families are smaller than non-Jewish families. This, together with corollary data on age composition, and completed vs. incompleted families (for the few cities where such data were compiled) suggests that American Jews are replenishing themselves at a somewhat slower rate than is the situation for the general population.

Data on labor force characteristics indicate that in cities outside New York and other large population centers, Jews tend to congregate in the proprietorship, managerial, professional and clerical occupations. The general reasons for this seem to be based on preferences for economic pursuits that allow for a greater measure of self-employment and independence and which may avoid situations of discrimination.

What ought to be especially noted is that virtually all of the foregoing observations are based on fragmentary information. Derived from a variety of community surveys which were initially designed for other than demographic studies, they are nevertheless the major source of factual data on the Jewish population in the United States and will remain the major source until such time as the U.S. Census Bureau may seek to include questions on ethnic or religious affiliation in its Decennial Census. The great advantage of the latter is that it would not only be a uniform, standard approach to Jewish demographic studies but would also allow for significant comparisons of the various subdivisions of the American population.

BEN B. SELIGMAN

THE JEWISH POPULATION
OF NEW YORK CITY: 1952

STATEMENTS on the demographic characteristics of Jews in America understandably must be qualified by whatever information is available on the Jewish population of New York City. Jews in that community comprise not only more than a fourth of the people who reside there, but represent approximately 40 per cent of all American Jews. Consequently, generalizations about the average age of Jews in this country, their sex ratio, the number of married or single persons, fertility tendencies, or occupational and labor force characteristics, can be made with some measure of completeness only if data are available on New York's Jewry.

Thus far virtually all information on American Jewish demography has been concerned with Jewish communities other than New York. Furthermore, very few of the larger communities of the size of Chicago or Los Angeles have been able to provide population data for their respective Jewish communities, and thus our picture of American Jewry has been based mainly on studies conducted in intermediate and small cities.[1] Now, for the first time, some demographic data on New York's Jewish population have been made available as a result of a survey of health and medical care of a representative sample of the New York City population. The survey was part of a special research project carried out in relation to the activities of the Health Insurance Plan of Greater New York (HIP). Included in the survey schedule were a number of questions of a specifically demographic character, such as age, sex, marital status, occupation, and industry. Thus, there was afforded an opportunity to obtain much of the necessary information that would provide a population profile of the New York Jewish community.

HIP's 1952 survey of residents of New York City reached 4,190 households and covered 13,558 individuals. Those respondents who identified themselves as Jewish came from 1,161 households, and included 3,581 individuals. Since the households were selected randomly from an area probability sample, it is possible to compute the range of error for the major characteristics. The sample did not include members of the families away from home who were serving in the Armed Forces or who were studying at institutions of higher learning, nor did it include permanently institutionalized persons. This article is based on material contained on the IBM cards of the Jewish respondents, and thus includes a sample of 3,581 Jews residing in the five boroughs of New York City in 1952.[2]

Published for the first time in this volume.

§ *Estimates of Size of Jewish Population*

In the past, estimates of the number of Jews residing in New York ranged from 1,500,000 to as many as 2,500,000. Sometimes these estimates were based on little more than informed guesses. At other times, special surveys—as, for example, the Youth Study conducted by the Welfare Council of New York—offered more reasonable bases for estimating the size of religious groups in New York.[3] Taking advantage of data on the number of Jewish students in both public and parochial schools made available through an unpublished study of the Jewish Education Committee of New York, the writer estimated in 1952 that New York's Jewry totalled 2,294,000, approximately 27 per cent of the entire population of the city. The HIP survey also provided data which would permit estimating the size of New York's Jewry. Since the HIP sample was in the ratio of one to a little less than 597 persons in the general population and since the latter was estimated to be a little over 8,000,000 in mid-1952, the estimate of the Jewish population of New York on this basis was set at 2,130,000.[4] Estimates made in 1955 by Henry Cohen for the Federation of Jewish Philanthropies of New York reduced this figure even further, to a total of 2,050,000.[5]

Utilizing estimates of migration movements and the rate of increase of the Jewish population,[6] Mr. Cohen predicted that the size of New York's Jewish population would continue to drop. This contention was based on the observation that migration to the suburbs consisted mainly of families still in the procreative age groups. With the reduction in the number of Jewish persons in these classes and with the virtual elimination of immigration, there does seem to be some basis for feeling that New York's Jewish population will continue to decline. This, however, may point to the need for expanding the range of population investigation from the strictly urban to that of the metropolitan area. In fact, there is growing recognition among those concerned with community services that the latter is the proper area concept today. However, should it be assumed that the movement to the suburbs may level off because of changes in present economic and social trends, it may very well be possible that the Jewish population of New York will have become stabilized.

§ *Age Composition*

Table 1 presents data on the distribution of the Jewish population by age groups and sex. As was the case in a number of recent studies (Port Chester, Passaic, New Orleans) the two youngest age groups in New York's Jewish population are proportionately larger than most of the older age groups, thus suggesting a larger number of births in more recent years. Nevertheless, there are some striking "hollow classes" in the New York data, notably the 20-24 age group for males and 15-19 age group for females. It is patent that this was a result of the reduced birth rate of the depression years. Perhaps, as Nathan Glazer suggests,[7] this illustrates the great volatility of social movements among Jews. As he notes, if there is a general movement away from manual work, among Jews it becomes a flight, and when the general birth rate drops, the Jewish birth rate plunges rapidly downward. While the lack of birth rate data for Jews through the years makes it difficult to document this contention, there seem to be various indications that the surmise is well founded.

Table 1—Age Composition by Sex (Per Cents)

Age Group	Male	Female
0- 4	4.6	4.4
5- 9	5.0	3.5
10-14	3.2	2.4
15-19	3.2	2.2
20-24	1.6	3.2
25-29	3.5	3.8
30-34	2.6	3.7
35-39	3.8	4.7
40-44	4.1	4.1
45-49	4.9	3.5
50-54	3.3	4.1
55-59	2.6	2.2
60-64	1.7	2.8
65-69	2.1	1.9
70-74	1.0	1.0
75-79	.5	.5
80 and over	1.8	2.5
Median Age	36.3	36.3
Total	49.5	50.5
	N = 1770	N = 1811

The median age for both males and females of New York Jewry was 36.3 years. This does not depart markedly from the range of median age indices shown in other Jewish communities, although it was less than the same index for New Orleans' Jewish population. Detailed comparisons with other religious groups in New York could not be made at the present time. However Dr. Deardorff's summary does indicate that while the Jewish group is somewhat older than the white Catholic group, it is not as old as the white Protestants.[8]

Table 2—Age Grouping: Jewish and Christian* (Per Cents)

	Catholic	Protestant	Jewish
Under 15	27.4	22.2	23.0
15-44	45.4	37.1	40.6
45-65	19.4	27.8	24.9
65 and over	5.9	9.3	7.6
No Report	1.9	3.6	3.9
	100.0	100.0	100.0

* From Deardorff, op. cit., p. 159.

Further data from the HIP study revealed that the Jewish group comprised almost a third of the 45-65 age groups and over 65 year age groups, while representing 27.2 per cent of those under age 15 in New York's population. Examination of age distribution data for other Jewish communities reveals modal clusters in the 35-45 age groups whereas for New York these are found in the 40-50 year age groups, thus suggesting that New York's Jewry is slightly older on the average than are Jews in other parts of the country.

§ *Sex Ratios*

Examination of sex ratio data for the various Jewish communities for which such information is available does not reveal any uniform pattern. While in Miami, for example, the proportion of males to females in middle age groups was low, this was not true for Los Angeles. It is evident that the particular underlying sociological characteristics of these cities affects this demographic index. The higher proportion of males in Gary, Indiana, for example, might be explained by the industrial character of that community.

For New York the data in Table 3 indicate that for in all age groups up to 15-19 there is a greater preponderance of males, while between the ages of 20-44 females exceed the number of males. Beyond the 40-44 year age group the pattern becomes erratic. What factors account for this are unclear. It may be that the postwar movement to the suburbs may have affected the sex ratio structure to some degree: it is known that such a movement affects the younger groups mainly. This, together with the data on marital status, may suggest that the suburban movement drains the male groups in the 20-44 year age group more heavily than it does the females.

Table 3—Sex Ratios by Age Group

Age Group	Ratios	Age Group	Ratios
0- 4	105.8	45-49	134.6
5- 9	139.6	50-54	80.1
10-14	129.8	55-59	116.4
15-19	147.3	60-64	61.0
20-24	41.0	65-69	111.9
25-29	91.2	70-74	94.8
30-34	72.1	75-79	100.
35-39	85.2	80 and over	72.2
40-44	99.3		
		Sex Ratio	97.7

The overall sex ratio for New York's Jewry in 1952 was 97.7 males per 100 females. This was less than for Los Angeles, Newark or Port Chester, but was higher than the same figure for the Catholic white population in New York (91.2) and the Protestant white group (86.5).[9] The disproportion in the latter was especially marked.

§ *Marital Status*

Few Jewish population studies have related marital status to age, but wherever this was done, as in the Passaic, Port Chester, and New Orleans studies, the pattern was revealed to be approximately similar: there was a tendency for women to marry earlier than men, a sharp drop in the number of single persons as age increases, a bulking of married men in the 35-45 age groups and of married women in the 25-44 age groups.

This pattern was also revealed in the New York data, as shown in Table 4. The modal groups in this table strikingly emphasize the point: for married females it is the 35-39 year age group, and for married males it is the 45-49 year age group, that show the underlying pattern. While suggestive of the possibility of an incipient population decline, we note

Table 4—Marital Status by Age and Sex (Per Cents)

	MALE					FEMALE				
Age Group	Single	Married	Widowed	Divorced or Separated	Unknown	Single	Married	Widowed	Divorced or Separated	Unknown
15-19	8.				.7	4.3	.5			.5
20-24	3.3	.9		.07	.07	2.7	4.9		.3	.2
25-29	2.1	6.9		.1	.4	1.4	7.7		.3	.1
30-34	1.1	5.8		.2	.1	1.2	7.6	.1	.1	.1
35-39	.6	9.9				.5	10.5		.2	
40-44	.7	10.1		.07		.4	9.2		.5	.07
45-49	.4	12.3	.1	.07		.4	7.5	.5	.4	.07
50-54	.3	8.4	.1			.5	7.6	1.4	.6	.07
55-59	.2	6.7		.07			4.6	.5	.4	
60-64	.07	4.2	.2	.07		.07	4.2	2.4	.1	.07
65-69		4.7	.7	.1		.2	2.5	1.9		.07
70-74	.1	2.	.6			.2	.9	1.6		
75-79		.8	.6			.07	.3	.8		.07
80 and over	.8	3.	.4	.07		1.6	2.3	1.8	.3	.2
Totals	18.	76.1	2.8	1.	2.1	13.7	70.6	11.1	3.	1.6
	N = 1316					N = 1443				

that the bulk of the single persons still is in the lower age groups. This contrasts with the picture in such a community as Passaic, where a large number of single persons was to be found in the 25-29 year age group rather than in the 15-19 year age group.

§ *Size of Household and Fertility Indices*

The general view is that the Jewish family tends to be smaller than that of the general native white population. In communities for which information is available the average size of family or household (arithmetic mean) has in no case been larger than 3.1. The 1952 data for New York City conformed to this general pattern. The average size of the Jewish household there is also 3.1. The modal group, however, was the two-person household (27.2 per cent of the total number of households) closely followed in size by four-person and three-person households. With over 80 per cent of the households classified as two, three or four persons in size, it is evident that there was no tendency for the size of the Jewish household in New York to increase as compared with other Jewish communities. Data compiled by Cohen indicate that among New York non-Jews there are a greater number of larger families than among Jews. He cites, for example, the fact that 18.7 per cent of white non-Jewish families had five or more persons, while for the Jewish population the ratio was 10 per cent.

Table 5—Household Size (Per Cents)

Size of Household	Number of Households	Number of Individuals
One person	7.8	2.5
Two persons	27.8	18.0
Three persons	26.7	26.0
Four persons	27.6	35.8
Five persons	7.1	11.5
Six persons	2.3	4.5
Seven persons	.4	1.0
Eight persons	.2	.4
Over eight persons	.1	.3
	100.0	100.0
	N = 1161	N = 3581

Arithmetic Mean	3.1
Median	2.5

Note may be taken of a recent attempt to estimate Jewish population in the suburban New York area by means of an average family size multiplier.[10] Respondents, consisting in the main of rabbis and center executives, were asked whether they thought a multiplier of 3.5 would be more accurate than 3.1. The majority replied in the affirmative. It may be noted that a multiplier of 3.5 would imply a preponderance of three- and four-person households with some fairly heavy representation in the five-person category. However, in the absence of any data that the Jewish population has increased in average household size to that extent, it would seem preferable to rely on available information and to continue to assert that the average Jewish household in the New York area still contains roughly 3.1 persons.

Little is really known of the dynamic changes in Jewish population growth. For this, information on birth rates and death rates is essential. The best one can do in this regard is to compute such an index as a fertility ratio defined as (1) the number of children per 1000 females age 20-44, or (2) the number of children per 1000 persons age 20-54. Comparison of New York's Jewish population fertility ratio (which were 460.2 and 176.1 respectively) with that obtaining in other Jewish communities shows the former to be somewhat higher than in such cities as Los Angeles, Miami, and Trenton. As compared with cities where studies were made in the early 1940's, New York's figure is, of course, higher, reflecting the increase in the general birth rate. The significance of the figure can be best appreciated by comparison with the other religious groups in New York. Such data, unfortunately, were not yet available to us, but the Cohen study compared the average size of Jewish households with the average size of white non-Jewish households. He found the former to be 3.1 persons as compared with 3.2 persons for the latter group. Cohen also found that there were more Jewish persons proportionately in the three- and four-person households than was the case among non-Jewish households. In the latter there were proportionately more persons in the larger households. For example, in the larger households of five or more persons there were included about 19 per cent of white non-Jewish households (comprising over a third of the white non-Jewish population) while only a little over 10 per cent of the Jewish households (comprising only 17.5 per cent of the Jewish population) were contained in this category.

Table 6—Fertility Ratios

Children/1000 females aged 20-44	460.2
Children/1000 persons aged 20-54	176.1

Table 7—Age of Mother by Number of People in Household (Per Cents)

NUMBER OF PEOPLE IN HOUSEHOLDS (N = 1089)

Age Group	1	2	3	4	5	6	7	8	Over 8	Total
15-19		.1								.1
20-24	.1	2.4	1.7	.9	.3					5.4
25-29	.1	2.7	3.1	3.1	.8	.1				9.9
30-34	.1	.8	3.	5.1	.6	.4		.1		10.2
35-39		.4	4.	5.9	2.	.8				13.2
40-44	.1	.6	3.8	5.4	1.8	.4	.4	.1	.1	12.6
45-49	.4	1.9	3.	4.1	.7	.1				10.4
50-54	.9	5.4	3.1	1.7	.4	.2				11.8
55-59	.3	3.7	1.7	.4	.3					6.4
60-64	.6	3.	1.6	.9	.4	.1				6.6
65-69	1.	2.9	.8	.2	.1	.1				5.2
70-74	.4	1.3	.3	.1		.2				2.2
75-79	.3	.4	.3	.1						1.
Over 80	.7	2.5	1.	.8						5.
Totals	5.	28.2	27.5	28.8	7.4	2.4	.4	.2	.1	100.

Another indication of fertility trends is the analysis of family data by age of mother: this is intended to compare the "completed vs. incompleted" families. Table 7, which presents such information for the New York Jewish population, indicates that the preponderance of mothers is in the four-person household category and shows also that most of them are past the age of 35. In the two-person category, which is the next largest group, the greater cluster of mothers is to be found in the over 45 year age groups. These observations suggest a higher ratio of "completed" families and do not encourage much prospect for a spurt in Jewish births.

§ *Labor Force Characteristics*

In New York the number of Jewish persons over the age of 15 who were reported to be part of the labor force comprised 51.3 per cent (or 40 per cent of the total Jewish population in that city). This was fairly close to the percentage for such cities as Passaic and Port Chester, although lower than for some of the other Jewish communities which have conducted studies, particularly in the late 1930's. There were reported to be almost three times as many men in the Jewish labor force of New York as women.

Henry Cohen reports that in general the proportion of New York's Jewish males who are working is the same as for non-Jews. While in the 14-24 age group there is a smaller proportion of Jewish males employed than is the case for non-Jews, this is counterbalanced by the fact that a higher proportion of Jewish males over age 25 are employed than among non-Jews.

Table 8—Occupational Distribution by Industry and Sex (Per Cents)

	MALE					
	Prof. and Semi-Prof.	Prop. and Mgrs.	Cler. and Sales	Craftsmen and Operatives	Service	Unknown
Construction	.4	.6	.1	2.		.1
Manufacturing	1.2	5.1	2.1	16.7	.1	
Transportation and Communication	.2	.6	.1	2.2		.1
Wholesale and Retail Trades	1.1	10.7	13.1	3.9	.6	.4
Insurance-Real Estate, etc.	9.3	3.7	2.4	2.5	.5	.6
Government	.3	.9	2.5	.1	.3	.3
Unknown	1.9	2.7	3.5	3.8	.2	3.1
Total	14.4	24.3	23.8	31.2	1.7	4.6

N = 1077

	FEMALE					
	Prof. and Semi-Prof.	Prop. and Mgrs.	Cler. and Sales	Craftsmen and Operatives	Service	Unknown
Construction			.6			
Manufacturing	.8	.8	8.1	14.5		
Transportation and Communication			2.2			
Wholesale and Retail Trades		5.9	17.3	1.7	.3	
Insurance-Real Estate, etc.	7.3	.8	13.4		4.4	
Government	.6		1.4			
Unknown		.6	11.7	1.1	.6	5.9
Total	8.7	8.1	54.7	17.3	5.3	5.9

N = 358

In sharp contrast to the situation in all other Jewish communities for which information has been made available, skilled and unskilled workers (craftsmen, foremen, operatives and laborers) in New York's Jewish labor force comprise the second largest group, being 28 per cent of the total. This was surpassed only by the clerical and sales group which was 31.5 per cent of the total Jewish labor force. Third and fourth, in order of importance, were proprietors and managers and the professional group. In all other studies, skilled and unskilled workmen were found in either fourth or fifth rank order of importance. When the data are classified by sex, we find that for males the workers category is the largest, exceeding by almost 7 percentage points that for proprietors and managers. The largest group of craftsmen and operatives was found in the manufacturing occupations. The pattern that this reveals for a demographic analysis of all American Jewry is quite significant since it indicates that insofar as the total picture is concerned, reliance solely on the data from cities outside New York may be somewhat misleading. Table 8 presents the data, by sex, on occupation and industry for the New York Jewish population.

What is even more striking than the foregoing is the fact that these data indicate that 62.4 per cent of the Jewish labor force in New York is engaged in private employment rather than in government or self-employment. This far exceeds the ratio of the privately employed wherever such data were available in other surveys. Those in New York Jewry who were self-employed or engaged in a family business without pay represented 26.5 per cent of the labor force. Only a little over 5 per cent were classified as government employees. In virtually all other Jewish communities for which data were available the self-employed category was well in excess of 30 per cent with the exception of Passaic, which, like New York, is an industrial center. The breakdown by sex (see Table 9) highlights the New York data: 58.1 per cent of the males and 75.7 per cent of the females are privately employed.

Interestingly enough, only about one-third of the professionals in the New York Jewish labor force were reported to be self-employed, while

Table 9—Employment Status by Occupation and Sex (Per Cents)

	MALE				FEMALE			
	Private Employment	Gov't. Employment	Own or Family Business	Unknown	Private Employment	Gov't. Employment	Own or Family Business	Unknown
Professional and Semi-Professional	7.4	.9	5.4	.6	4.4	3.4	.8	
Proprietors and Managers	7.3	.9	16.	.1	2.5		5.6	
Clerical and Sales	16.6	2.7	4.3	.3	48.1	2.2	2.5	1.9
Craftsmen, Operatives, etc.	24.7	.5	5.5	.6	15.1		1.1	1.1
Service	1.1	.4	.1	.1	4.8		.3	.3
Unknown	1.	.4	.6	2.5	.8			5.1
Totals	*58.1*	*5.8*	*31.9*	*4.2*	*75.7*	*5.6*	*10.3*	*8.4*

N = 1077   N = 358

63.4 per cent were privately employed or in government service. This exceeds the figure for either Passaic, where half of the professionals were privately employed, or Port Chester, where the percentage was 30 per cent. Over 65 per cent of the professionals were engaged in finance, real estate and insurance. On the other hand, the greatest concentration of the proprietor and managerial group was to be found in the wholesale and retail trades.

Table 10—Industry by Employment Status and Sex (Per Cents)

	Construc-tion	Manufac-turing	Transp. & Comm.	Wholesale & Retail	Insur. Real Est. Finance	Gov't.	Unknown
Male							
Private Employment	1.7	19.8	2.2	16.7	8.1		9.6
Government Employment		.4	.2		.6	4.4	.1
Own or Family	1.3	4.6	.7	12.7	9.6		.3
Unknown	.1	.4		.5	.6		2.7
Total	3.1	25.2	3.1	29.9	18.9	4.4	15.4
		N = 1077					
Female							
Private Employment	.6	23.5	2.2	17.6	19.3		12.6
Government Employment					3.1	1.9	.6
Own or Family		.8		6.4	2.5		.6
Unknown				1.1	1.1		6.1
Total	.6	24.3	2.2	25.1	26.	1.9	19.9
		N = 358					

In terms of industrial classification, the wholesale-retail trades were the largest category in New York with 29.9 per cent of the males and 25.1 per cent of the females so engaged. From the overall view, 28.7 per cent of the Jewish labor force was in the wholesale-retail trades. Those in manufacturing represented about 25 per cent, while 20 per cent were to be found in insurance, real estate and finance. Again, it should be stressed that the largest part of those so engaged were privately employed: in the wholesale-retail trades the privately employed were 59 per cent, while in manufacturing they were over 80 per cent. In real estate and insurance, the percentage dropped to 54 per cent. The percentage data, broken down by sex, are given in Table 10. One should note that when the data by sex are examined, those for the males engaged in real estate and insurance show a large ratio in the self-employed category. Labor force data are given in Table 11.

Table 11—Labor Force, Age 15 and over (Per Cents)

Working	49.4
Looking for work	1.9
Housekeeper	34.0
Attending School	8.0
Other	5.0
Unknown	1.7
Total	100.0

N = 2796

From the foregoing it is evident that the labor force characteristics of New York's Jewry deviates markedly from the pattern exhibited in other Jewish communities. Clerical and sales, skilled and unskilled workmen, proprietors and managers, and professionals represent in that sequence the occupational rank in New York. In virtually all other Jewish population surveys, it was found that proprietors and managers followed by clerical and sales were the major groupings. Most of the Jewish labor force in New York was found to be privately employed and not engaged in their own businesses, with the exception of males reported to be in real estate, insurance and finance. These, together with wholesale and retail trades and manufacturing, comprise the major industrial classifications for the New York Jewish population.

Cohen's review of the labor force data of the Jewish and non-Jewish population in New York City indicated that Jews are more heavily represented in the professions, proprietorships and sales categories than is the case for the white non-Jewish population. He states: "Though constituting only about one-fourth of the city's total population [Jews] constituted over 45 per cent in the proprietor and managerial category and 33 per cent of the professional and semi-professional categories. They constitute only 6.2 per cent of the services categories and 19.1 per cent of the craftsmen, operative and labor categories. Over two-thirds of employed Jews are in non-manual occupations compared to only one-half of employed white non-Jews."

§ *Nativity and Labor Force Characteristics*

The HIP survey elicited information on nativity for heads of households only. The responses were then grouped by United States, Other Western Hemisphere, Europe, and Other. For purposes of the present article these were cross tabulated with labor force characteristics. The results are given in Tables 12, 13 and 14. With but 49.2 per cent of the household heads identified as native born, it may seem as though here too New York's pattern diverges from other Jewish communities, where the native born have generally approximated three-fourths of the total Jewish population. However, it should be recalled that since the foreign-born group is doubtlessly older than the native born and since there has been no recent immigration of any substantial size, the likelihood is that for the native-foreign ratio New York's Jewish population approximates that of other Jewish communities.

It is interesting to observe that there is a greater preponderance of foreign-born household heads in the craftsmen-operatives category, while clerical and sales and proprietors and managers are the major groups for native-born heads of households. On the other hand, the wholesale-retail trades were first in industrial classification for both native- and foreign-born households heads although for the latter the manufacturing category was but one-tenth of one per cent less than the trades group. Both groups were predominately engaged in private employment. Of course, it would be interesting to know whether those who are not household heads are more heavily represented in self-employment than household heads, but the data did not lend themselves to such an inquiry.

§ *Other Data*

The HIP data on highest school grade attained (Table 15) revealed a pattern for New York's Jewish population that was fairly close to that

Table 12—Occupation of Head of Household by Place of Birth (Per Cents)

	United States	Other Western Hemisphere	Europe	Other	Unknown	Total
Professional & Semi-Prof.	8.7	.1	2.8	.3	.2	12.1
Proprietor & Mgrs.	12.3	.13	8.9	.25		21.58
Clerical & Sales	13.4		6.2	.25	.1	19.95
Craftsmen & Operatives	9.6		17.2	.1		26.9
Service	.5		1.			1.5
Unknown	1.8		.7		.2	2.7
Total	46.3	.23	36.8	.9	.5	84.73
Heads Not in Labor Force	2.9		11.9	.27	.2	15.27
Total	49.2	.23	48.7	1.17	.7	100.

N = 1161

Table 13—Industry of Household Head by Place of Birth (Per Cents)

	United States	Other Western Hemisphere	Europe	Other	Unknown	Total
Construction	1.2	.13	1.3			2.63
Manufacturing	9.		12.1	.3		21.4
Transportation & Communication	1.8		.9			2.7
Wholesale & Retail Trades	12.8	.05	12.2	.25	.2	25.5
Insurance, Real Estate, etc.	10.5	.05	6.3	.25	.1	17.2
Government	3.4		.2	.1		3.7
Unknown	7.6		3.8		.2	11.6
Total	46.3	.23	36.8	.9	.5	84.73
Heads not in Labor Force	2.9		11.9	.27	.2	15.27
Total	49.2	.23	48.7	1.17	.7	100.

N = 1161

Table 14—Place of Employment of Household Head by Birthplace (Per Cents)

	United States	Other Western Hemisphere	Europe	Other	Unknown	Total
Privately Employed	25.1		22.8	.8	.2	48.9
Government Employment	4.1		.7			4.8
Own or Family Business	15.4	.23	12.4	.1	.2	28.33
Unknown	1.7		.9		.1	2.7
Total	46.3	.23	36.8	.9	.5	84.73
Heads not in Labor Force	2.9		11.9	.27	.2	15.27
Total	49.2	.23	48.7	1.17	.7	100.

N = 1161

Table 15—Highest School Grade Attained, Age 5 and Over

No Formal Education	8.8%
First to seventh grade	15.4
Eighth grade	13.9
Ninth to eleventh grade	11.7
Graduated from high school	25.6
Attended college	9.1
Graduated from college	7.5
Post-graduate study	2.3
Unknown	5.7
Total	**100.0**

N = 3270

shown in other Jewish communities. Here too there was a greater proportion of those reporting attendance and graduation from high school and college than is the case in the general population. For example, in the latter about 4 per cent are reported to have attended and/or graduated from college, while reports from Jewish population surveys, including that for New York, set this figure at from 17 to 28 per cent.

The original schedule used in the HIP survey included a question on family income. However, for those households identified as Jewish, there were about 24 per cent "unknown" responses. It is understood that a similar bias applied to all of the 4,190 households included in the survey sample. Of the remainder in the Jewish group, 32 per cent reported household incomes between $3,000 and $5,000 a year, with about 9 per cent reporting family income over $8,000 per annum. In view of the large unknown bias, this was not cross tabulated with any of the labor force characteristics.

§ *Conclusion*

It is evident that the demographic picture of the American Jew is incomplete without data on the New York Jewish community. This observation must be especially emphasized in view of the fact that the latter's demographic features differ in many ways from those of other Jewish communities. This is underscored in the case of labor force and occupational characteristics, which in New York are less heavily weighted in the direction of professional and proprietorship endeavors than is the situation elsewhere. Since New York Jewry represents about 40 per cent of American Jewry, the resulting modifications of the usual image are significant. It cannot be said categorically, for example, that the Jewish businessman is always "self-employed," or that Jewish professionals are all doctors and lawyers. The New York data may very well imply that even the doctors and lawyers are salaried employees. Above all, what the data do suggest is the need for some caution before fully accepting the current characterizations being offered about the demographic features of American Jewry.

DAVID GOLDBERG
AND HARRY SHARP

SOME CHARACTERISTICS OF DETROIT AREA
JEWISH AND NON-JEWISH ADULTS

THE present paper consists of an analysis of the adult population of greater Detroit when classified by religious preference. Primary emphasis in the discussion which follows is placed upon the comparison between some characteristics of the Jewish and non-Jewish residents of the Detroit area. Catholics, white Protestants, and Negro Protestants are the three major non-Jewish groups used in this research.

As in most large metropolitan communities, the religious composition of greater Detroit is quite heterogeneous. Less than 4 per cent of the area's adults are classified as Jews in this study. With more than two and one-half million persons living in the city and its suburbs, the small proportion of Jews nevertheless represents a fairly large Jewish community.[1] Well over one out of every three persons in the Detroit area is a Catholic; a slightly higher proportion are white Protestants; and about 15 per cent of the residents are Negro Protestants.

§ *The Data*

The data upon which this research is based were collected through the facilities of the University of Michigan's Detroit Area Study. The Detroit Area Study is a continuing research organization which conducts an annual sample survey in metropolitan Detroit. Each year interviews are obtained with a probability sample of those residents of greater Detroit who are twenty-one years of age or older. Approximately two-thirds of the respondents live in the city and one-third live in suburban areas.[2]

Since the Jewish population of Detroit represents but a small fraction of the total population, statistics on Jews, or other subgroups of similar size, are subject to relatively wide sampling variation when derived from the Detroit Area Study's sample for any particular year. In anticipation of this problem, the sample was originally designed to permit the combination of data from several annual studies. The following report, therefore, is based on three separate studies conducted in 1951, 1954, and 1955. In each survey the interviewing period included the late winter and early spring months. In all three years a series of comparable questions was asked of the respondents. By cumulating the number of sample cases it

---

Published for the first time in this volume.

is possible to present information about Detroit area Jews with some confidence.

It must be emphasized that even with a combined sample the number of Jewish families (87) or Jewish adults (126) found in this research is quite small. Thus, the specific percentages reported for Jews should be interpreted with care. The differences between Jews and non-Jews which are discussed below, however, are usually so striking and so logically consistent throughout the analysis that it is unlikely that they are a result of chance variation.[3] The nature of the sample, moreover, affords a means for the comparisons of characteristics of Jews and non-Jews within a probability model which is usually not available in research of this type.

The classification of an urban population by religious preference could involve a considerable amount of research in itself. Although in many cases a functional classification based on behavioristic data would be most satisfactory, it is felt that the general descriptive purposes of the present report are quite adequately served through the self-identification of the population with a religious group. The classification utilized here is based on the answers of respondents to the question, "What is your religious preference?"

The Detroit Area Study material, within the limits of known sampling error, can be viewed as representative of the population of one large and highly urbanized community. It is not possible to determine to what degree the findings presented here may be generalized to the country as a whole. It is hoped, however, that this study will contribute to the growing body of research which will eventually permit general patterns to be isolated from those peculiar to a given community.

§ *Demographic Characteristics*

AGE. As a group, the adult Jews of Detroit are markedly older than are Catholics and Protestants (Table 1). The median age of Jewish adults (45.8) is four and one-half years greater than that of white Protestant adults, and seven to eight years greater than the median ages of comparable Catholics and Negro Protestants. Almost two-thirds of the adult Jews are forty years old or older; only one-half or less of the adult Catholics or Protestants are that old. Among the various factors contributing to the comparatively advanced age structure of Jews are the low birth and death rates of the Detroit Jewish population.[4]

MARITAL STATUS. There are very few differences in marital status among Detroit area Jews, Catholics or Protestants (Table 1). About three-quarters or more of the adult members of each group are married and live with their spouses; less than one out of every ten adult Jews or non-Jews has never married.

NUMBER OF CHILDREN EVER BORN. The small number of cases upon which this discussion is based allows only tentative conclusions to be drawn with respect to fertility patterns among the Jews of greater Detroit. Many of the findings of earlier research in fertility, together with at least one study currently being carried out, lend weight to the data presented here. The Indianapolis study of 1941, for example, found that the age-

Table 1—Selected Demographic Characteristics by Race and Religious Preference of the Adult Population of Metropolitan Detroit

Selected Demographic Characteristics	RACE AND RELIGIOUS PREFERENCE			Negro Protestant
	WHITE			
	Jewish	Catholic	Protestant	
Age (All Adults)				
21-29 years old	9%	24%	21%	29%
30-39 years old	26	30	26	29
40-49 years old	25	19	20	22
50-59 years old	19	14	17	12
60 or more years old	21	13	16	8
Total	100%	100%	100%	100%
Median age	45.8	38.8	41.4	37.5
Marital Status (All Adults)				
Married	74%	80%	81%	74%
Divorced, separated, widowed	17	11	13	17
Never married	9	9	6	9
Total	100%	100%	100%	100%
Mean Number of Children Ever Born to Married Women				
Women 40 years old or older	2.07	2.78	2.16	2.39
Number of sample cases	39	282	401	82
Women less than 40 years old	1.41	1.86	1.78	2.30
Number of sample sases	22	420	444	160
Detroit Area Migrant Status (All Adults)				
Native Detroiter	29%	42%	25%	8%
Not a native Detroiter	71	58	75	92
Total	100%	100%	100%	100%
Size of Place of Longest Previous Residence Before Coming to Detroit				
Rural farm: U.S.	3%	12%	23%	34%
Rural non-farm: U.S.	3	14	13	10
2,500-24,999: U.S.	3	15	18	14
25,000-99,999: U.S.	3	8	11	10
100,000 and over: U.S.	38	16	16	32
Non-U.S.	50	35	19	—
Total	100%	100%	100%	100%
Birthplace of Father of Head of Family				
United States	9%	34%	64%	100%
Place not in the U.S.	91	66	36	—
Total	100%	100%	100%	100%
Number of Adults in Sample	126	1283	1484	508
Number of Families in Sample	87	901	1076	330

standardized fertility rate of native Jewish couples was much lower than were those of natives in other religious groups in that city.[5]

In the Detroit area, when only women forty years old or older are considered (almost all of whom have completed their families), the mean number of children for both Jews (2.07) and white Protestants (2.16) lags considerably behind the number of children born to Catholic women (2.78). The mean number of children born to Negro Protestant women (2.39) occupies an intermediate position between those of Jews and Catholics.

There is some evidence that foreign-born Jews have a much larger family size than do native Jews.[6] Most of the Jewish women in Detroit over forty years old are foreign-born, whereas the majority of the Protestant women in these ages are natives. It would seem, therefore, that the similarity in the size of Detroit area Jewish and white Protestant completed families results in large part from the higher fertility of foreign-born women.

Without complex methods of analysis which necessitate a large number of cases, it is difficult to evaluate differences in fertility patterns among women less than forty years old, for these women have not yet completed their families. The Detroit data indicate, within these limitations, that young Jewish couples are currently having fewer children than are couples in any other religious group (Table 1). To this extent, Jewish families seem to be relatively unaffected by the post-World War II "baby boom."

The average size of the Jewish family in Detroit is not sufficient for population replacement. By taking into account the proportion of Jews who never marry and current mortality rates, the average Jewish married couple would have to have approximately 2.5 to 2.6 children in order to replace itself. As is shown, the mean number of children born to Jews of completed fertility is only a fraction above two. Moreover, the younger Jewish women's small mean number of children (1.41) would seem to indicate that they are not likely to surpass the older generation by an amount great enough to achieve replacement.

Although it is impossible to state definitely the kinds of fertility patterns that will develop as the younger women complete their families, there is other evidence that family size among Jews will remain relatively small. A recent survey, using a national sample of women in the child-bearing years, obtained an estimate of the total number of children each respondent expected to have. Unpublished data from this research indicate that Jewish women expect a much smaller mean number of children than do either Protestants or Catholics.

MIGRANT STATUS. Only about one-quarter of both the Jewish and white Protestant adults in the Detroit area were born in and have lived in Detroit all their lives (Table 1). It is the Negro Protestants, however, with but 8 per cent natives, who are the most migratory group. On the other hand, a relatively high proportion of Catholics (42 per cent) are native Detroiters.

SIZE OF PLACE OF LONGEST PREVIOUS RESIDENCE BEFORE COMING TO DETROIT. Among the Detroit area migrants, comparatively more Jews than non-Jews lived in foreign countries before moving to this city. Approximately one-half of those adult Jews who are not native Detroiters lived most of their lives in foreign places previous to their migration (Table 1). Catholic migrants and, to an even greater degree, white Protestant migrants are considerably less likely to have resided outside the United States than are Jews.

Very few Jewish or Catholic adults who are not native Detroiters lived on farms in the United States before coming to Detroit. Data not shown here indicate that about 93 per cent of all Jews and 87 per cent of all Catholics have never lived on a farm either in this country or in Europe. Detroit area Protestants, especially Negroes, have a much more extensive rural background than do Catholics or Jews.

Jewish migrants to Detroit come from large United States cities considerably more frequently than do Catholic or white Protestant migrants. Almost four out of every ten migrant Jews previously lived in U. S. cities of 100,000 or more population. Only 16 per cent of the Catholic or white Protestant migrants did so. A high proportion of Negro Protestants, like the Jews, also have migrated from the larger cities. The Negro movement, however, was almost completely from the South, while most United States Jewish migrants came from the eastern or midwestern states. Thus, as compared to other groups, many Jews have had the experience of living in a large northern United States metropolitan area before they entered the Detroit metropolis.

BIRTHPLACE OF FATHER OF HEAD OF FAMILY. The data on the birthplace of the family head's father clearly reveal the recency of Jewish migration to this country (Table 1). Only one-tenth of the Jewish family heads in Detroit are from families which have been in this country two or more generations. As compared with Jews, a much higher proportion of Catholics and, especially, white Protestants are "old Americans," in this sense.

Available data indicate that one out of every three Jewish adults in Detroit is an immigrant; this proportion is considerably higher than those of the other groups. The original nationality of one-half of Jewish families in greater Detroit is Russian. Poland and other central European areas acount for the remaining Jews. Both the country of origin and the low percentage of second or older generation Americans date the period of heavy Jewish migration between 1900 and 1920.

§ Socio-Economic Characteristics

It is reasonable to expect that many of the demographic differences found among the major religious groups of Detroit are associated with variations in socio-economic status. An analysis of Table 2 indicates that this is the case.

Table 2—Selected Socio-Economic Characteristics by Race and Religious Preference of the Adult Population of Metropolitan Detroit

Selected Socio-Economic Characteristics	RACE AND RELIGIOUS PREFERENCE			Negro Protestant
	Jewish	WHITE Catholic	Protestant	
Occupation of Family Head				
Operatives, service workers, laborers	13%	37%	29%	76%
Craftsmen and foremen	14	30	28	16
Clerical and sales workers	15	15	15	4
Proprietors, managers, officials	42	12	13	2
Professionals	16	6	15	2
Total	100%	100%	100%	100%
Self-Employment Status of Family Head				
Self-employed	48%	9%	10%	4%
Not self-employed	52	91	90	96
Total	100%	100%	100%	100%
Occupation of Father of Family Head				
Farmers	1%	19%	24%	46%
Operatives, service workers, laborers	3	36	20	30
Craftsmen and foremen	24	26	26	14
Clerical and sales workers	6	4	5	2
Proprietors, managers, officials	58	12	16	3
Professionals	8	3	9	5
Total	100%	100%	100%	100%
Annual Income of Family Head (1951-54)				
$2,999 or less	22%	17%	19%	40%
$3,000-4,999	16	40	34	50
$5,000-6,999	22	29	26	9
$7,000-9,999	6	10	13	1
$10,000 or more	34	4	8	—
Total	100%	100%	100%	100%
Median income	$6,200	$4,650	$4,800	$3,400
Educational Level (All Adults)				
Sixth grade or less	15%	17%	7%	21%
Seventh-eighth grade	16	18	19	24
Ninth-eleventh grade	10	23	22	26
Twelfth grade	41	34	34	22
Some college	18	8	18	7
Total	100%	100%	100%	100%

Table 2—Selected Socio-Economic Characteristics by Race and Religious Preference of the Adult Population of Metropolitan Detroit (Continued)

Educational Level (Adults Under 40 Years Old))				
Sixth grade or less	2%	5%	4%	16%
Seventh-eighth grade	5	8	9	15
Ninth-eleventh grade	7	29	24	34
Twelfth grade	59	47	43	27
Some college	27	11	20	8
Total	100%	100%	100%	100%
Home Ownership Status of Head of Family				
Home owner	52%	72%	71%	34%
Not a home owner	48	28	29	66
Total	100%	100%	100%	100%
Number of Adults in Sample	126	1283	1484	508
Number of Families in Sample	87	901	1076	330

OCCUPATION OF FAMILY HEAD. There are extremely large differences in the occupational structures of Jewish, Catholic, and Protestant families. A large majority of the heads of Jewish families hold white-collar jobs (73 per cent); the heads of non-Jewish families, especially Catholics and Negro Protestants, are heavily concentrated in the blue-collar occupations. Jewish family heads are particularly clustered in the "proprietor, manager, and official" classification. The proportion of Jews in these "tradesmen" jobs (42 per cent) is between three and four times greater than that for Catholics or white Protestants.

The occupational composition of the Jewish population of greater Detroit probably represents an intermediate position between the relatively proletarian Jews of New York City and the virtually complete white-collar concentration of Jews in some of the smaller communities of this country. The clustering of Jews in the high status occupations of many United States communities has been well documented.[7]

OCCUPATION OF THE FATHER OF THE FAMILY HEAD. For centuries the economic pursuits of the Jewish population in Europe were regulated by discriminatory laws which excluded Jews from farming and certain professions. These and other cultural factors produced a style of living among European Jews that was basically urban in character. This is reflected in the fact that almost none of the fathers of the heads of Detroit area Jewish families were farmers (Table 2); they were predominantly grouped in the trade and craft occupations—almost the only jobs left open to Jews.

The contrast in the occupational distribution of the fathers of Jewish and non-Jewish family heads is enormous. Approximately 75 per cent of the non-Jewish fathers were in farming or held blue-collar jobs, whereas almost the same proportion of Jewish fathers were in white-collar occupations. Many of the Jewish fathers who held white-collar jobs were probably hucksters, peddlers, or small traders and merchants; but the fact remains that their background was typically urban.

While modern American society has a comparatively high degree of social mobility, the occupation of the father, in most cases, will be closely related to that of his son. The influence of the father's occupation can be plainly seen in the current occupational distribution of the heads of Jewish and non-Jewish families in the Detroit community.

As compared to non-Jews, both Jewish fathers and sons are disproportionately found in the white-collar jobs. While the proportion of tradesmen and craftsmen among the Jews has declined during the last generation, this is not the case for non-Jews. There has been some increase in the comparative number of Jewish professionals and clerical workers between father and son, but the relative increase is no greater than that among Catholics and Protestants. Most of these generational changes in the occupations of Jews and non-Jews are concomitants of the continuing urbanization of American society.

SELF-EMPLOYMENT STATUS OF FAMILY HEAD. One of the most striking features of the economic status of Jewish families in Detroit is that almost one-half of the family heads are self-employed, although only 10 per cent or less of the heads of non-Jewish Detroit area families work for themselves (Table 2).

It is probable, as some writers have suggested, that the demands of religious life are among the various factors which have contributed to the high proportion of self-employed Jews. Many Jews in European communities, desiring to work under conditions where they could observe the Sabbath, daily prayers, and dietary laws, no doubt turned to self-employment as a means of meeting their religious obligations while earning a living.

Today, while self-employment is still characteristic of the Jewish working population, it seems unlikely that this is a direct result of current religious motivations. As is shown in the following section of this paper, Jewish people participate less frequently in religious services than do the members of any other major religious group. If synagogue attendance is a meaningful index of religious ties, orthodox religious codes are probably not too influential as determining factors in the economic life of most contemporary American Jews.

INCOME OF FAMILY HEAD. The median annual income of the heads of Jewish families during the 1951 to 1954 period was $6,200 (Table 2). This figure is considerably larger than are the median incomes of non-Jewish family heads. The high Jewish income, of course, is related to the upper occupational status of this group.

The large number of Jewish family heads who made $10,000 or more annually is striking. One-third of the heads of Jewish families earned this much money, as compared with less than one-tenth of the heads of the non-Jewish groups. At the other income extreme, about one out of every five Jewish, Catholic, and white Protestant family heads earned less than $3,000 a year from 1951 to 1954. Relative to Jews and Negro Protestants, Catholics and white Protestants are clustered in the middle income range ($3,000-$6,999). Negroes, for their part, are heavily over-represented in the very lowest income category.

EDUCATIONAL STATUS. Along with the occupational and income differences described above, the educational level of Detroit area residents is also related to religious preference. The relationship between education and religion, however, is not as clearly defined as was that found for occupation or income and religious preference.

Many students of Jewish history have commented about the emphasis placed upon intellectualism and scholarship in Jewish life—a value which probably had its origin in religious teachings. While the Jews of America are perhaps less religiously oriented now than in the past, this value seems to persist in the Jewish community.

As seen in Table 2, the Jewish educational level in the Detroit area is much greater than is that of Catholics or Negro Protestants. In general, however, white Protestants and Jews are quite similar in their educational achievements. Comparable trends in educational level have also been reported for a national sample of religious groups.[8]

The failure of Jews, as a whole, to evidence a significantly higher educational level than do white Protestants is undoubtedly related to the comparative concentration of Jews in the older ages. Older Jews have a low level of formal education, as judged by American standards. Often, this is due to the difficulty of equating a given number of years of non-secular foreign education with a given number of years in the American system. When only those adults less than forty years old are considered (as in Table 2), the educational level is higher for both Jews and non-Jews. But the gap between Jews and white Protestants is increased noticeably. Only 14 per cent of these younger Jews have failed to complete high school, as contrasted with 37 per cent of the white Protestants.[9]

HOME OWNERSHIP. Given the economic status of the Jewish population, it might be assumed that Jews are home owners to a greater extent than are non-Jews. As indicated in Table 2, however, this does not seem to be the case. While about one-half of the Jewish families own their homes, seven out of every ten Catholics and white Protestant families are home owners.[10]

The low degree of home ownership among the Jews was not expected, but data not shown here indicate that among the younger Jews the proportion of home owners is already as large as is that for the older Jewish population. It may be that as the younger Jews complete their life cycle they will surpass the older generation in home ownership. As of now, however, it is possible that in the Jewish pattern of consumption home ownership plays a less important role than is the case for non-Jews.

§ *Formal and Religious Participation*

In addition to economic relationships, an important aspect of the social structure of the human community is revealed in the participation of community members in formal groups and religious services. The final section of this paper is devoted to a brief analysis of these "non-economic" participational patterns as they are related to religious preference.

FORMAL GROUP PARTICIPATION. A large number of formal organizations[11] is characteristic of urban society. They are one of the means of carrying out the interests of the many groups which have developed through differentiation in the modern community. But not all urban residents are equally likely to join these organizations. For example, formal group membership is probably directly associated with economic status. It may be expected, therefore, that a generally high economic status and a long history of urban life will contribute to a higher formal group membership rate for Jewish adults than for non-Jewish adults.

The above expectation is generally substantiated by the data in Table 3. Seven out of every ten Jews are in formal groups other than unions, while about half of the non-Jews belong to such groups. Very few Detroit area Jews belong only to labor unions. On the other hand, a comparatively large number of Negro Protestants restrict their membership to a union. These trends are highly consistent with the occupational distributions of Jews and Negroes in greater Detroit.

The tendency for Jews to be joiners more than are non-Jews is also quite pronounced if the number of organizations in which memberships

Table 3—Formal Group Membership and Attendance at Religious Services by Race and Religious Preference of the Adult Population of Metropolitan Detroit

Formal Group Membership and Attendance at Religious Services	RACE AND RELIGIOUS PREFERENCE			Negro Protestant
	WHITE			
	Jewish	Catholic	Protestant	
Formal Group Membership				
No memberships	21%	34%	32%	35%
Labor union member only	8	17	14	25
Member of other groups	71	49	54	40
Total	100%	100%	100%	100%
Number of Sample Cases[a]	52	561	670	165
Attendance at Religious Services				
Attends every week	16%	69%	31%	38%
Attends a few times to once a month	10	12	21	35
Attends a few times a year	62	12	31	18
Never attends	12	7	17	9
Total	100%	100%	100%	100%
Number of Sample Cases	126	1283	1484	508

a. The data on formal group membership were obtained from one randomly selected respondent in each household for the years 1952 and 1954.

are held is the criterion of formal group participation. Data not presented here indicate that about 41 per cent of all Jewish adults hold multiple formal group memberships. Two or more memberships are held by less than one-third of the white Protestants, one-quarter of the Catholics, and only one-sixth of the Negro Protestants.

It would be valuable to see if Jews are in formal groups more than are non-Jews when socio-economic status is controlled. The size of the Jewish subsample, however, precludes this operation.

ATTENDANCE AT RELIGIOUS SERVICES. It is apparent from the data in Table 3 that Detroit area Jews presently do not attend religious services nearly as frequently as do non-Jews. Only 16 per cent of the Jewish adults go to their synagogues every week, and but one-fourth attend at least once a month. The most popular pattern of attendance among the Jewish population is to participate in services a few times a year, probably during the High Holidays (62 per cent do so).

Information not presented in the table shows that the one out of four Jews who attends services at least once a month represents the oldest segment of the Jewish population. The median age of those who attend this frequently is over sixty years.

One of the factors in the low level of synagogue attendance on the part of Jewish adults may be the relatively small number of second or older generation American Jews in the Detroit community. A large segment of the adult Jewish population consists of the children of immigrants, the element in which the rejection of old country practices is usually most pronounced.

The Catholic population of greater Detroit represents the opposite pole in religious attendance. Catholics are about as likely to go to church every week, as are Jews to attend synagogues a few times a year.

As compared to Jews or Catholics, white Protestants exhibit a great deal of variation in church attendance. About one-half of them go at least once a month, with the other half participating in services a few times a year or less. It may be noted that a considerably higher proportion of Negro Protestants attend church at least once monthly than is the case for white Protestants. It should also be pointed out that only a small proportion of Jews and non-Jews alike never attend religious services.

Recently there has been some comment on the return of many Jews to the synagogue. Evidence shown here would suggest that if this return movement has occurred, it has not resulted in frequent attendance at services. It is possible that any increase in the religious activity of Jews has resulted in more regular attendance at the High Holidays and greater participation in synagogue-affiliated functions other than services, but the Detroit data do not allow the investigation of these variables.

It should be stressed that the data on religious participation shown here are limited to the single dimension of church or synagogue attendance. A more complete picture would have to include participation in affiliated religious institutions as well as religious observances carried on in the home.

§ *Summary*

A descriptive study such as this cannot hope to present a full answer to the question of how socio-economic and other differences came into existence among the major religious groups in Detroit. At many places in the discussion a more intensive analysis would be highly desirable, but a limited number of sample cases of the Jewish population does not allow this to be done. It can be suggested, however, that some of the factors leading to the varying economic levels of the four major racial-religious groups in the Detroit area can be traced to a differential preparation for urban living.

The experience of many Detroit Negroes in the rural South, for example, is particularly difficult to use efficiently in the northern metropolis. This is not to deny, of course, that racial discrimination has also contributed to the Negro's generally low economic status. At the other extreme, Jews who migrated to this country did not represent a peasant class, but were overwhelmingly urban in origin. They were well prepared to fill the urban roles which they and their children so typically hold in Detroit's social structure.

The urban character of the Jewish population is seen not only in their economic pursuits, but also in associated characteristics such as a small family size and frequent participation in formal group structures. The unique history of Jews in European communities and the development of particular cultural values probably made their adjustment to metropolitan Detroit a simpler process than was the case among many other migrant groups of different ethnic origins.

S. JOSEPH FAUMAN

OCCUPATIONAL SELECTION
AMONG DETROIT JEWS

THIS study is an analysis of some aspects of occupational selection. The data presented demonstrate the extent to which, in one community, Jewish youth differ from non-Jewish youth in occupational distribution. The factors which produced these differences are analyzed. The data which show how and why Jewish and non-Jewish youth differ occupationally also suggest the extent to which Jews have been acculturated to the general American pattern of behavior. Since only the occupational adjustments of Jews are being studied, only those aspects of the socio-economic and socio-psychological life of Jews which are relevant to these problems are presented.

I

The population studies made of Jewish communities within the last fifteen years show, generally speaking, that about one-third of gainfully occupied Jews may be classed as professionals, proprietors, managers and officials; slightly more than a third as clerical workers; about one-tenth as skilled workers; and about one-fifth as semiskilled and unskilled workers.[1] Corresponding data for the population of the cities in which most Jews live show that proportionately, there are far more Jews than non-Jews in the professional, proprietary, managerial and official class; more Jews than non-Jews in clerical occupations; more non-Jews than Jews in skilled occupations; and far more non-Jews than Jews in semi-skilled and unskilled occupations. The occupational classification employed here and throughout this study is the Edwards scale as used in the U. S. Census.[2]

Within this framework of Jewish life as briefly noted, the occupational adjustments of Jews occur in conjunction with their adjustments in other areas of life. The integral part that occupational adjustments play in the total adjustment pattern of Jews has been assumed. There is good reason for assuming this relationship in all groups. In the case of Jews, the nature of their group life makes such an assumption desirable.[3] For the purposes of this study, the Jews are assumed to be a folk community. As defined here, a folk community differs from other groups only in degree. As compared to other groups a folk community has a greater conscious-

An earlier version of this article appeared in *Jewish Social Studies*, Vol. 14 (Jan. 1952), pp. 17-50, and is used here by permission of the author and the publisher.

[119]

ness of its identity and individuality, its members are more nearly similar in past historical experience, it is more integrated about a value system,[4] and it is more endogamous. (This definition is similar to that used by anthropologists.) Folk community characteristics of Jewish group life have been analyzed by many students; they point out that Jews differ from non-Jews in that Jews are more conscious of their mutual needs and more integrated about their group value system.

The utility of the concept of folk community becomes apparent when a theoretical analysis is made of the reasons for the occupational differences between Jews and non-Jews which are demonstrated in this study. Within this framework are analyzed the causal factors which have produced such occupational differences. The specific hypothesis of this study is that the occupational class distributions of Jewish and non-Jewish youth in Detroit differ because of differences between the Jewish and non-Jewish group in occupation of father, income of family, education of son and industry of son. The subsidiary hypothesis tested here is that the differences in the factors which are causally related to the occupational class distributions of Jewish and non-Jewish youth are the result of different environmental pressures facing Jews and non-Jews. Thus, it is concluded that if the effect of the assumed differences in environmental pressures can be controlled by controlling the factors through which it operates, then the occupational class distributions of Jewish and non-Jewish youth will be the same.

The pressures studied here are manifested in the four factors of (1) occupation of father, (2) income of family, (3) education of son and (4) industry of son. These four causal factors may be classified as to the amount of voluntary behavior that they contain for youths. They may be divided into two groups: the relatively fixed factors, which are the occupations of the father and the income of the family; and the relatively voluntaristic factors, which are the education of the son and industry of the son. The following analytical possibilities may occur. The fixed factors may have the greatest effect upon the occupational distributions of Jewish youth; or it may be that the voluntaristic factors have the greatest effect; or, finally, it may be that the occupations of youth are affected by a combination of fixed and voluntaristic factors.

If fixed factors (occupation and income of father) have the greatest effect upon the occupational adjustment of Jewish youth, it would be concluded that Jewish and non-Jewish youth actually behaved in the same way, but that the individual variations among parents had produced the difference. That is to say, for example, that Jewish and non-Jewish sons follow their fathers' occupations to the same extent, but that the facts of individual accident and circumstance, of preceding Jewish historical experience in Europe, of recency of migration, etc., have so affected the occupational patterns of fathers that the occupational patterns of sons are different. In such a situation it would be proper to conclude that the Jewish and the non-Jewish groups are not distinguished by a difference in value systems and hence that the folk-community aspect of Jewish group life may here be irrelevant.

To support such an explanation, Carpenter[5] points out that in 1920 foreign-born Jews in the United States were primarily a town people in origin, and that this is reflected in their occupational distribution. Warner and Srole[6] point out that those ethnic groups which have been urban for the longest period of time (in the community that they studied) seem to have an occupational distribution more heavily weighted in the professional and proprietary class and in the clerical class than those groups of more recent urban origin. If fixed factors are responsible for the occupational class differences between Jewish and non-Jewish youth, it might appear that the longer urban history of the Jewish group was mainly responsible. If the Jewish and the non-Jewish community respond similarly to the problem of occupational adjustment—a major aspect of group life—then it cannot be said that the Jewish community is possessed of a value system which is differently oriented than the general American value system.

If, on the other hand, the voluntaristic factors of education of son and industry of son appear to be the more significant factors in the process of occupational adjustment of Jewish and non-Jewish youth, then entirely different considerations are introduced. It is at this point that the concept of folk community has its greatest value. It is a valid conclusion that if Jewish and non-Jewish youth behave differently in areas of life where they have a choice, the reasons are to be found in some difference as to what is considered desirable behavior in the two groups. Such a difference is a difference in value systems, the main factor in which the folk community differs from the urban community within which it is contained.

One traditional characteristic of the Jewish community is that the highest status is accorded to the educated person. Many students of Jewish life have commented on the social status of the learned person and the reasons therefor.[7] It is apparent that the nature of Jewish life determined the very high status of the educated man. Psychologically, this valuation was transferred to the secular aspects of life when the legal ghetto was abolished. The group value oriented towards religious learning was transferred to the sphere of secular learning, without losing its hold upon the group.

Value elements are involved in industrial choices also. The Jews, as a group with different food, prayer, and religious habits than the peoples among whom they lived, have been affected by prejudice and discrimination. In such situations occupational choices were rigidly restricted. In addition to these restrictions the Jews needed occupations where they were able to behave as their religion required in terms of prayer and food habits. These restrictions operating together had a profound effect upon the occupational adjustments of Jews. Within the limits of choice allowed them they preferred those occupations in which they were able to behave religiously as they chose. Desirable occupations had to be ones that Jews could enter, where Jews had a freedom of choice of work-ing hours, and where, if Jews were expelled from the area, the activity could be carried on elsewhere.

II

The data for this study come from the Michigan Census of Population and Unemployment.[8] Detroit schedules for paired fathers and sons were separated into Jewish and non-Jewish groups. The sons used in the sam-ple were all sons who were living at home, had completed their educa-tion, were working or seeking work, and were from sixteen to twenty-five years of age.

Occupations were coded according to the Edwards scale and combined into the following groups; professional, proprietors, managers and officials; clerical, sales, and kindred workers; craftsmen, foremen and kindred workers; operatives and kindred workers, domestic and protective service workers, other service workers, laborers, no occupation. Industrial classi-fications were coded by the Edwards scale and then combined into three groups; manufacturing, trade, all others.

Education was coded in seventeen classes and recombined into five classes; 0-8 years of school; 9-11 years of school; 12 years of school; 13-15 years of school; 16 years or more of school.

In the original census income data were very clustered. Monthly rental of home was, however, reported by five-dollar intervals. Monthly rental was therefore used as an index of the economic status of the family. For homes owned, estimated rental was reported. The rental groups were combined as follows; homes renting from $0.00 to $19.00 per month; homes renting from $20.00 to $49.00 per month; and homes renting for over $50.00 per month.

Previous analysis of the methods used to draw the Detroit sample of the Michigan Census of Population and Unemployment indicated that the sample universe from which the study data were drawn was a truly random sample.[9] However, the sample for this study is not a random sample of all Detroit youth—it is a random sample of Detroit youth who were white, male, between the ages of sixteen and twenty-five, who had finished their education, who were working or seeking work, and who were living at home with a family head in residence. The effect of the differences between the sample as defined here, and the true Detroit sample of all youth, whether living at home or not, will be measured. It will be shown that the differences which do exist do not affect either the analysis or the conclusions drawn therefrom.

The sample, as described above, consisted finally of 750 Jewish sons and fathers and 7,321 non-Jewish sons and fathers. From Meyer's data[10] it is known what the numbers of Jewish youth should be in the sample drawn here. The sample Jewish youth form 90 per cent of the group of Jewish youth of the proper ages as specified by Meyer. Since the sample for this study contains only about 50 per cent of the youth in the labor force in Detroit, and since the Jewish youth in the sample are almost all of the Jewish labor force, the missing youth are non-Jewish.

It is assumed that the occupational class distribution of the youth in this sample should correspond to the true occupational class distribution of youth in Detroit. Table I presents the occupational class distribution of the sample youth, and of all Detroit youth in the same age group.

Table I—Occupational Class Distribution of Youth in Detroit by Religion, for Sample and Census Populations

Occupational Class of Son	SAMPLE SONS Jewish	Non-Jewish	Total	CENSUS SONS Total
Prof., Prop.	12.3	4.2	4.9	7.1
Clerical	45.6	21.4	23.6	34.1
Skilled	8.6	15.0	14.4	8.8
Semisk., Unsk.	33.5	59.4	57.1	50.0
Total	100.0	100.0	100.0	100.0

* Data for Census Sons are from *Michigan Census of Population and Unemployment 1935. First Series. Number 6, Table 5, p. 12.*

In addition to the differences in occupational class as presented above, those missing non-Jewish youth may differ in other characteristics from the sample of non-Jewish youth used here. It is not known what these differences may be. Two assumptions are made in the study which relate to this problem. It will first be assumed that the missing youth are the same in all characteristics studied as the non-Jewish youth in the sample. The result of making this assumption will be tested. Secondly, it will be assumed that the missing non-Jewish youth have the characteristics of the Jewish youth and their parents in the sample. The second assumption will also be tested. In using both of these assumptions, the missing youth will be added into the sample in such a way as to adjust marginal totals to the figures given in Table I.[11] This method is valid because it gives an estimate of error in the analysis which will be both the possible low point, and the high point of difference between Jewish and non-Jewish youth. These two adjusted samples are discussed in section IV. It may, in anticipation, be stated here that the effect of using the revised samples is such as to reinforce the conclusions drawn from the analysis of the original sample.

III

The analysis here is limited to the relationship of occupational class of son to the other variables of industry and education of son, and occupation and rental class of father.

It has generally been considered that the most important channel of social and occupational mobility in American society is education.[12]

Within the range of normal intelligence it appears that neither the level of education achieved nor occupation is dependent upon intelligence.[13] Since the sample as drawn was random, it has been assumed that the distribution of intelligence is a normal one.

Table II presents the data on education of sons and occupations of sons. The first striking difference noted is that Jewish sons are found three times as frequently in the professional and proprietary occupations as non-Jewish sons. Jewish sons in the clerical group outnumber non-Jewish sons by two to one; while in the skilled group they are only half as numerous as the non-Jewish sons. In the semiskilled and unskilled occupational class Jewish sons are slightly more than half as numerous as non-Jewish sons.

The number of Jewish sons with a completed college education is almost six times as large as the number of non-Jewish sons with the same education. Yet the number of Jewish sons with a completed college education who are found in the semiskilled class is only about half the number of non-Jewish sons with the same characteristics. The difference is explained by the fact that the percentage of Jewish sons with a completed college education who are in the professional and proprietary class is larger than the percentage of non-Jewish sons with the same characteristics. It appears then that college education produces less high occupational class for the non-Jewish son than it does for the Jewish son.

A similar situation is found among youth who have had some college but did not graduate. The fact is that Jewish sons have achieved more mobility through their education than non-Jewish sons, since three-fifths of the Jewish sons are in the clerical class, while only about two-fifths of the non-Jewish youth are in the same class.

Among the high-school graduates the situation is similar. Jewish high-school graduates are in professional and proprietary occupations almost twice as frequently as non-Jewish high-school graduates. In clerical occupations Jewish high-school graduates are found 50 per cent more often than non-Jewish high-school graduates. The differences that have been pointed out for college and high-school graduates are found in the lower educational classes as well. In general, it may be said that the lower the educational class, the greater the excess of Jewish sons over non-Jewish sons in the professional and the proprietary occupations. As the educational level increases, this disparity decreases, so that by the level of college graduates Jewish sons are only one-third more numerous than non-Jewish sons, whereas in the lowest educational class they were twice as numerous as non-Jewish sons. The same situation is found in the clerical class.

At the lowest occupational class level, differences between Jewish and non-Jewish youth show up in reversed form—the lower the educational class the less the difference between Jewish and non-Jewish youth. These differences are not as marked as in the professional and proprietary

Table II—Percentage Distribution of Occupation of Son by Education Class of Son, Detroit 1935

SON'S OCCUPATIONAL CLASS

Education of Son (years completed)	Prof., Prop. Mgr. & Off.		Clerical		Skilled		Semisk., Unsk. & No Occ.		Total		All Occ. Classes	
	Jewish Sons	Non-Jewish Sons	Jewish Sons	Non-Jewish Sons	Jewish Sons	Non-Jewish Sons	Jewish Sons	Non-Jewish Sons	Jewish Sons	Non-Jewish Sons	Jewish Sons	Non-Jewish Sons
0-8	5.3	2.1	30.7	10.5	17.3	14.0	46.7	73.4	100.0	100.0	7.5	20.7
9-11	9.0	2.5	37.2	16.3	11.2	15.9	42.6	65.3	100.0	100.0	22.3	40.4
12	8.8	4.7	50.0	31.6	7.7	15.2	33.5	48.5	100.0	100.0	50.7	33.3
13-15	11.6	13.0	60.6	37.4	4.3	13.6	23.5	36.0	100.0	100.0	9.5	3.9
16	42.6	33.4	39.6	37.1	5.0	6.8	12.8	22.7	100.0	100.0	10.0	1.7
Total	12.3	4.2	45.6	21.4	8.6	15.0	33.5	59.4	100.0	100.0	100.0	100.0

Table III—Percentage Distribution of Occupation of Son by Occupation of Father, Detroit, 1935

SON'S OCCUPATIONAL CLASS

Occupational Class of Father	Prof., Prop. Mgr. & Off.		Clerical		Skilled		Semisk., Unsk. & No Occ.		Total	
	Jewish Sons	Non-Jewish Sons	Jewish Sons	Non-Jewish Sons	Jewish Sons	Non-Jewish Sons	Jewish Sons	Non-Jewish Sons	Jewish Sons	Non-Jewish Sons
Prof., Prop., Mgr. & Off.	14.2	11.5	52.6	31.4	6.9	12.4	26.3	44.6	100.0	100.0
Clerical	10.2	5.5	55.5	36.4	5.5	12.8	28.6	45.3	100.0	100.0
Skilled	10.1	3.5	30.4	21.5	19.0	20.5	40.5	54.5	100.0	100.0
Semisk., Unsk. & No Occup.	11.4	2.4	36.0	16.6	7.3	13.5	45.3	67.4	100.0	100.0
Total	12.3	4.2	45.6	21.4	8.6	15.0	33.5	59.4	100.0	100.0

class. At the lowest educational level, in the semiskilled and unskilled class, Jewish youth are only five-eighths as numerous as non-Jewish youth, while at the college graduate level in the same class, Jewish youth are one-half as numerous as non-Jewish youth.

Occupations of sons are related, of course, to the economic status of their families which allows or prevents them from acquiring certain skills. (For economic status of the family, monthly rental is used as an index, as previously noted.) Such a relationship seems to be borne out by the data.

As the original study clearly shows (see Fauman, *op. cit.*), in the two higher occupational classes as father's rental decreases, Jewish sons enter these occupations at a greater rate than the non-Jewish sons. The exact reversal of this tendency is apparent in the lower occupational classes. In the two lower occupational classes the Jewish sons enter these occupations at a lesser rate than the non-Jewish sons as the rental level of the father decreases. These two summary statements hold true for each occupational class.

Meyer points out that the disparity in income distribution among Jews and non-Jews (rental in this study) is in reality *a concealed disparity of occupational distribution.*[14] *Incomes within occupational classes are similar for Jews and non-Jews, but since occupational distribution in the two groups differs, the income distribution in the two groups will also differ.* Thus, any effect of the fathers' rental in this study would seem to be a concealed effect of the occupational differences of Jewish and non-Jewish fathers. (The point is illustrated by Table IV, where the occupations of Jewish and non-Jewish fathers are compared.)

In the examination of Table III it is observed that for both Jewish youth and non-Jewish youth in each occupational class, the occupation of the father produces a greater number of sons in his class than any other occupation of father.[15] There are, nevertheless, many differences between Jewish and non-Jewish families revealed in this table. Among proprietary fathers, Jewish sons fall most frequently into the clerical class. But in this same group of fathers, twice as many non-Jewish sons are found in the skilled class as Jewish sons, more Jewish sons than non-Jewish sons are found in the professional and proprietary class, and far more Jewish sons than non-Jewish sons in the clerical class. On the other hand, among the unskilled sons, Jewish sons of professional and proprietary fathers are far less frequent than non-Jewish sons from the same category of fathers. Among the sons of clerical fathers, Jewish sons are found half as often in the skilled group as the non-Jewish sons. They are found far less often in the semiskilled and unskilled group than the non-Jewish sons. Similarly, in the analysis of the sons of skilled fathers, Jewish sons become proprietors and professionals almost three times as often as non-Jewish sons. Jewish sons of semiskilled and unskilled fathers have a far higher occupational class distribution than non-Jewish sons of semi-skilled and unskilled fathers.

In the lowest occupational class of fathers, Jewish sons reach the highest occupational class more than four times as frequently as non-Jewish sons whose fathers are in the same occupational class. In the skilled class, the Jewish sons reach the top occupational class almost three times as often as the non-Jewish sons whose fathers are in the skilled class. In the clerical class, the Jewish sons reach the top occupational class twice as often as the non-Jewish sons of fathers in the same class. On the other hand, in the professional and proprietary class, the Jewish sons are found in the lowest occupational class 60 per cent as often as non-Jewish sons whose fathers are in the professional and proprietary class. In all of the other classes of fathers Jewish sons are found in the lowest occupational class less often than non-Jewish sons. *Jewish sons, then, are more upwardly mobile than non-Jewish sons and less downwardly mobile than non-Jewish sons.*

In each of the four classes of occupation it is apparent that when mobility occurs among youth, Jewish youth not only move upward more frequently, but also farther than the non-Jewish youth. On the other hand, when there is downward mobility among youth, Jewish youth move downward less often than the non-Jewish youth, and less far than the non-Jewish youth.

These differences in mobility are again illustrated by the data in Table IV. It will be observed that the semiskilled and unskilled Jewish fathers produce almost the expected number of sons in the professional and proprietary class, but such is not the case among non-Jewish sons of fathers in the semiskilled and unskilled class. However, among the professional and proprietary sons, three times as many sons in the non-Jewish group come from fathers in the same group as would be expected. For Jewish sons, only slightly more sons in this class come from fathers in the class than would be expected. The greater preponderance of sons coming from fathers in the same class in the non-Jewish group relatively reduces the possibility of upward mobility for the sons of fathers in other classes. Thus, the professional and proprietary class is relatively more frozen among the non-Jewish group than among the Jewish group. This finding demonstrates vividly that the Rogoff approach (see note 15) is not equally valid for subgroups within a given population.

Table IV reveals also some interesting data for the skilled sons. The percentage of skilled Jewish sons and of skilled non-Jewish sons who have fathers who are skilled is almost the same. But the percentage of Jewish skilled fathers is only half the percentage of non-Jewish skilled fathers. What meaning may be attached to these differences?

Among Jewish skilled sons, 38.5 per cent come from fathers of the professional and proprietary class, while among non-Jewish skilled sons the corresponding percentage is 11 per cent. Most of the Jewish fathers in the professional and proprietary class are proprietors. Many are so by virtue of the fact that they possess a skill and have utilized it to enter a business career. Skills such as baking, butchering, sewing, are those which

Table IV—Percentage Distribution of Occupation of Father by Occupation of Son, Detroit, 1935

SON'S OCCUPATIONAL CLASS

Occupational Class of Father	Prof., Prop., Mgr. & Off.		Clerical		Skilled		Semisk., Unsk., & No Occ.		Total	
	Jewish Sons	Non-Jewish Sons	Jewish Sons	Non-Jewish Sons	Jewish Sons	Non-Jewish Sons	Jewish Sons	Non-Jewish Sons	Jewish Fathers	Non-Jewish Fathers
Prof., Prop., Mgr. & Off.	54.3	37.2	55.3	19.7	38.5	11.1	37.8	10.1	47.9	13.4
Clerical	10.9	10.5	15.5	13.6	7.7	6.8	11.2	6.1	12.8	8.0
Skilled	12.0	20.7	9.9	24.8	32.3	33.5	17.9	22.6	14.8	24.6
Semisk., Unsk. & No Occup.	22.8	31.6	19.3	42.0	21.5	48.6	33.1	61.2	24.5	54.0
Total	100.0	100.0	100.0	100.0	100.0	100.0	100.0	100.0	100.0	100.0

Table V—Percentage Distribution of Occupation of Son By Industry of Son

SON'S OCCUPATIONAL CLASS

Industrial Class of Son	Prof., Prop. Mgr. & Off.		Clerical		Skilled		Semisk., Unsk. & No Occ.		All Occ. Classes	
	Jewish Sons	Non-Jewish Sons	Jewish Sons	Non-Jewish Sons	Jewish Sons	Non-Jewish Sons	Jewish Sons	Non-Jewish Sons	Jewish Sons	Non-Jewish Sons
Manufacturing	3.6	1.7	24.7	12.4	22.1	21.1	49.6	64.8	25.9	55.6
Trade	13.6	8.0	66.1	52.4	4.0	9.0	16.3	30.6	50.8	19.9
All Others	18.9	6.1	24.0	15.9	3.4	6.1	53.7	71.9	23.3	24.5
Total	12.3	4.2	45.6	21.4	8.6	15.0	33.5	59.4	100.0	100.0

allow their possessors to become independent businessmen. The sons of these men are probably often going to follow in their footsteps, but in order to do so they must learn the skill. At the time that this study was made, the sons of this type had just acquired the skill, and hence are listed as skilled workers. When they are the ages of their fathers they perhaps will also be independent businessmen. This explanation, though speculative, seems to fit the facts of Tables III and IV. If it is sound, it explains why there is such a difference in percentage of Jewish fathers and sons in the professional and proprietary class.

From the occupational characteristics of youth presented so far it is noted that extreme differences exist between Jewish and non-Jewish youth. Such a situation could be due to the different characteristics of the industries that youth enter. For obviously trade has more opportunities for proprietors than does manufacturing and mechanical industry, since the units of business in the latter industry are larger.[16] It has also been noted that trade is traditionally the channel of mobility leading to independence. Table V presents the industrial classification of sons by their occupational classification. In both the Jewish and the non-Jewish group the percentage of proprietors is greater in trade than in manufacturing and mechanical industries. The same is true for the clerical class. On the other hand, the percentage of skilled workers is greater in mechanical and manufacturing industries than in trade for both Jewish and non-Jewish sons. The "all other industries" category has more semi-skilled and unskilled youth in it than any other category of industry.

Differences between Jewish and non-Jewish youth are found in each of the occupational classes. In manufacturing and mechanical industries, Jewish proprietors and professionals are twice as frequent as non-Jewish proprietors and professionals, and in trade Jewish sons are almost twice as frequent as the non-Jewish sons. In the "all other industry" category, Jewish professionals and proprietors are almost three times as frequently found as the non-Jewish youth in the same category. In the clerical class, Jewish youth are found in manufacturing and mechanical industries twice as frequently as non-Jewish youth. In trade, Jewish youth of the clerical class are somewhat more frequent than non-Jewish youth. Among skilled sons, Jewish and non-Jewish youth have about the same percentage in manufacturing and mechanical industries; while in trade, non-Jewish sons are twice as frequent in the skilled class as Jewish youth, and about the same distribution is found in the "all other industry" category. In all industrial categories Jewish youth are less frequent than non-Jewish youth in the semiskilled and unskilled class.

From the evidence previously discussed as to the relative ease of achieving independent occupations in the various industrial classes, it might be expected that Jewish sons would be far more highly concentrated in trade than non-Jewish sons. As a matter of fact the distribution of Jewish sons in trade is about the same as that of non-Jewish sons in manufacturing and mechanical industries. The reverse is true of Jewish and non-Jewish sons when manufacturing is considered. Here the Jewish sons have about the same percentage as the non-Jewish sons have in trade.

Other data in the original study[17] show that, relatively speaking, in the manufacturing and mechanical industries, there are far fewer Jewish professional and proprietary sons than would be expected. They are outnumbered by non-Jewish proprietor sons by over three to one, although non-Jewish sons are in the manufacturing and mechanical industries only twice as frequently. On the other hand, in trade the Jewish sons have more than their expected number of professionals and proprietors. But here again, the non-Jewish sons, while having fewer professionals and proprietors than the Jewish sons have twice as many as was to be expected of them. Jewish proprietors are mainly concentrated in trade and the "all other industries" class, while the non-Jewish proprietors are rather evenly spread over all three industrial classes. A similar situation exists in the clerical class.

In summary, in the analysis of the occupational adjustment of Jewish and non-Jewish youth certain factors stand out as the most important. It has been seen that the education of sons and industry of sons show the most difference as between Jewish and non-Jewish sons. It might, however, be thought that the greater difference between Jewish and non-Jewish sons in fixed factors as compared to voluntaristic factors influenced the education and industry of sons. Such a possibility will be explored. The problem that must now be attacked is the question of how the differences pointed out here affect the occupational distribution of Jewish and non-Jewish sons.

IV

In order to compare the effects of different variables upon the occupational class distribution of Jewish and non-Jewish sons, a technique should be used which makes no assumptions as to the nature of the variables. The method of standardization used here[18] requires only that the data can be tabulated in the form of a contingency table. No assumptions are made as to whether the variables are continuous or discrete. All of the standardizations have been calculated in the same manner as is used in the construction of mortality tables. The variables have been standardized singly, in pairs, and in triads, in order to eliminate multiple effects.

The effect of each variable upon the occupational class distribution of Jewish sons is shown by Table VI which presents the standardized occupational distribution of Jewish sons when each of the four variables has been held constant.

From these data, it appears that the most important single factor affecting the differences in occupational class distribution between Jewish and non-Jewish sons is the industrial class of the son. With the exception of the professional and proprietary class, this factor reduces the differential between Jewish and non-Jewish sons in the other classes more than any other factor that is held constant. The most important differential factor between Jewish and non-Jewish sons in the professional and proprietary class is the educations of the sons.[19] The least important of the four single factors that have been controlled is the rental class of father, for it reduces the differential between Jewish and non-Jewish sons the least of the four factors, except in the professional and proprietary class.

The range of reduction of the differentials between Jewish and non-Jewish sons' occupational class distribution is greatest in the skilled occupational class. Apparently this class is more affected by the variables being controlled than are any of the other occupational classes. Such a conclusion holds true when the variables are controlled in pairs.

It might perhaps be thought that the factor of education affects the clerical class more than any of the other occupational classes. Such is not the case. The greatest effect upon the differential between Jewish and non-Jewish sons in the clerical class appears when occupation of father or industry of son is held constant.[20] It is in the professional and proprietary class that the education factor has the most effect upon the differential between Jewish and non-Jewish sons.

Table VI—Percentage Distribution of Occupational Class of Son Specified Single Variables Held Constant for Jewish Sons

Occupational Class of Son	Jewish Sons	Non-Jewish Sons	CONSTANT VARIABLES JEWISH SONS			
			Educ. of Son	Occ. of Father	Rent of Father	Ind. of Son
Prof., & Prop.	12.3	4.2	8.8	11.4	10.8	9.2
Clerical	45.6	21.4	40.9	38.3	42.0	32.8
Skilled	8.6	15.0	10.9	9.9	9.2	13.3
Semisk., Unsk.	33.5	59.4	39.6	40.4	38.0	44.1
Total	100.0	100.0	100.0	100.0	100.0	100.0

Continuing the standardization, variables held constant in pairs reduce the difference in occupational class distribution between Jewish and non-Jewish sons much more than single variables held constant. When education of son and industry of son are held constant, 90 per cent of the difference in occupational class distribution between Jewish and non-Jewish youth disappears. Holding occupation of father and rental class of father constant reduces the difference by only 29 per cent. Data in the original study show these effects in detail.

When three variables are held constant, sample size is too small, in two of the combinations, to be significant. Significant results appear however in the other two combinations. The two cases that were analyzed held these factors constant: father's occupational class, father's rental class, son's education; and father's rental class, son's education and son's industrial class. The distribution of occupational class when these variables are held constant is shown in Table VII. The reduction of differences between Jewish and non-Jewish occupational class distribution is also shown.

Table VII demonstrates that the simultaneous standardization of three variables affects the differences in occupational distribution between Jewish and non-Jewish sons in a pronounced fashion. The differences between Jewish and non-Jewish youth are least reduced in the semiskilled and unskilled class. Even here the smallest reduction of difference is one-third. The greatest reduction of difference, as before, comes in the skilled class. With three-variable control, the differences between Jewish and non-Jewish sons in this occupational class become reversed.

Differences are reduced more when education of son and industry of son are controlled together than when they are controlled separately.

Since the differences have been reduced by 92 per cent on the average when one of the sets of three variable controls is applied, the conclusion is clear. If Jewish and non-Jewish youth did not differ in rental class of father, in education of son, and in industry of son, then Jewish youth and non-Jewish youth would have the same occupational distribution.

Table VII—Percentage Occupational Class Distribution, Jewish and Non-Jewish Sons, Three Variable Control for Jewish Sons; and Reduction of Differences between Jewish and Non-Jewish Sons

| | | | | JEWISH SONS, THREE VARIABLES CONSTANT | | | |
| | | | % Diff. Jewish & Non-Jewish Sons, | FATHER OCC. FATHER RENTAL SON EDUC. | | FATHER RENTAL SON EDUC. SON INDUSTRY | |
Occupational Class of Son	Jewish Sons	Non-Jewish Sons	Orig. Dist.	Stand. %	% Diff. Reduced	Stand. %	% Diff. Reduced
Prof., & Prop.	12.3	4.2	8.1	7.0	65.4	5.0	90.1
Clerical	45.6	21.4	24.2	34.4	46.3	25.1	84.7
Skilled	8.6	15.0	6.4	15.5	107.8	16.3	120.3
Semisk., & Unsk.	33.5	59.4	25.9	42.1	33.2	53.4	73.0
Total	100.0	100.0		100.0		100.0	
Average Reduction					63.2		92.0

It will be recalled that the sample used in this analysis was one which differed in occupational distribution from the true distribution of Detroit youth. Before it can be concluded that the differences between Jewish youth and non-Jewish youth have been explained, it is necessary to consider the effect of the sample error. In section II of this article two assumptions were made as to the possible revision of the sample. The first revision added the missing youth in the occupations in which they belonged. It also assumed that the distribution of their other characteristics was the same as that of the non-Jewish youth already in the sample. The second revision added the missing youth into the sample in their proper occupational class. It assumed that possibly these youth had non-occupational characteristics which differed from those of the non-Jewish youth already present in the sample. Since the distribution of education of son, rental of father, occupation of father and industry of son was so different for Jewish youth and non-Jewish youth in the sample, it was assumed that the missing youth would not differ from the present non-Jewish youth any more than the Jewish youth differed from the present non-Jewish youth. Hence the characteristics assigned to the missing non-Jewish youth were those which they would have had if they were Jewish. Thus, two different revised samples were made, the aim being to set the limits of error both downward and upward. Revised sample number one is the downward case, and the second revised sample is the upward case.

When the three variables are standardized in revised sample number one the occupational differences between Jewish and non-Jewish youth are reversed. Where in fact more Jewish youth than non-Jewish youth were found in the professional and proprietary class and the clerical class; with occupation of father, education of son, and industry of son held constant, fewer Jewish youth than non-Jewish youth are found in these classes.

Revised sample number two, which assumes that the missing non-Jewish sons had the characteristics of Jewish sons, after variables are standardized, demonstrates that occupational differences among Jewish and non-Jewish sons are not a function of sample error.[21]

The problem naturally arises as to the way in which the two most significant variables used in the standardization are related to the other two variables used. Do education of son and industrial class of son have the great effect upon son's occupation that they do because concealed within them is also the effect of father's occupational class and father's rental class? To find out the answer to this question the same standardization techniques are used.

The standardizations show that each of the variables considered has an effect upon the educational distribution of sons. But the effect of any of the variables is small. None of them materially affects the differences in education between Jewish and non-Jewish sons.[22] Thus, the educational differential between Jewish and non-Jewish sons cannot be explained by the other variables. Hence, also, educational differences which affect the occupational class differences between Jewish and non-Jewish sons are the effects of an independent variable, in terms of the variables that are being studied here.

Some factors remain which might explain the remaining discrepancy between the occupational class distributions of Jewish and non-Jewish sons. These suggestions cannot be established here. They are offered tentatively as possibilities. The effect of the income status of a family, as measured by rental class, might vary from family to family in an equal rental group, depending on the number of children. Similarly, the nativity of the families might vary between Jewish and non-Jewish families and have an effect upon our problem. Still another possible source of differences between Jewish and non-Jewish families might be the length of time the groups have lived in cities. These factors may have some effect upon the occupational differences studied here. But since the analysis thus far has shown that the major factors affecting the occupational differences between Jewish and non-Jewish sons are those which depend on the choice of the individual, the newly suggested factors, all deterministic for the individual, seem to be relatively unimportant.

Specific theoretical explanations of the different occupational adjustments of Jewish and non-Jewish youth were made earlier. The differences in fixed factors were the differences in the occupations and rental class positions of Jewish and non-Jewish fathers. It was pointed out that if these factors were responsible for the different occupational adjustment patterns of Jewish and non-Jewish sons, then the two groups of sons differed only because of previous group history. In such a case it was concluded that Jews and non-Jews are essentially alike in their value orientations, and will behave similarly when and if the effects of previous environments actually do disappear.

A quite different conclusion was derived when it was proposed that the voluntaristic factors studied were largely responsible for the differences in occupational adjustments of Jewish and non-Jewish youth. If the Jewish group assessed its sociological position differently than did the non-Jewish group, Jews would behave differently than non-Jews, even if the sociological position of both groups was, in fact, the same. The value orientation which the Jewish group possesses does lead them to react differently than non-Jews to their problems. The different behavior arising from such evaluation is shown by the differential educational and industrial pattern of Jewish sons as compared to non-Jewish sons. When such differences of value were controlled, the two groups did react similarly to their situation.

It has been shown that the occupational class differences between Jewish and non-Jewish sons vanish when the factors studied are held constant for the two groups of sons. It has also been shown that the sample errors are not responsible for the original occupational differences. These errors do not change the results of the standardization, nor do they affect the conclusions of the study.

In the discussion of the effect of the four variables upon the occupations of sons, education of son and industry of son appeared of great importance. The occupations of fathers and the rental class positions of fathers were less important factors. When variables were held constant these points were confirmed. It was found that the voluntaristic factors had a far greater effect upon the differential occupations of Jewish and non-Jewish sons than did the fixed factors. When single variables were controlled, voluntaristic factors were more effective in reducing difference than were the fixed factors. Similarly, when multiple factors were held constant the same effect appeared and in more extreme form. It must be remembered, however, that fixed factors did exert some pressure in reducing the differences in occupation between the two groups of youth. Such a finding is of sufficient importance that replications of this study should be made to see if the same results occur. Should this finding be confirmed, some of Rogoff's hypotheses would need reconsideration in the light of the differential group choices concealed in her data (see Rogoff, Natalie, *loc. cit.*, Ch. IV-VI).

Students have pondered for many years the problem of what produces the difference between the Jews and the peoples among whom they have lived. The more penetrating of the analytic studies which have been made point to several conditions of Jewish life which have operated to keep Jews alive as a distinct group. Historically, the Jews have had their life defined and circumscribed by the peoples among whom they live. This has produced among Jews a mode of life that can be characterized as urban, mobile, intellectual, and occupationally restricted. Dozens of volumes are filled with the details of laws which once regulated the economic pursuits of the Jew, banned his religious habits which affected non-Jewish life, regulated the clothes he wore, the areas he lived in, the kind of housing he was permitted, his citizenship, his legal status, the books he was allowed to print and to read, and the taxes he paid; they even specified how he was to be disposed of when he died. Unquestionably, all of these aspects of Jewish life—some of internal origin, others imposed by the host peoples among whom they lived—had an effect upon the Jew as well as the non-Jew.

There was, of course, the internal difference of life between Jew and non-Jew. The core of religious life which the Jew kept from the days of his earliest dispersion from his homeland soon grew to voluminous proportions. It is true that not all Jews believe the same things nor hold the same values. But the value of education is a concept which so permeates all aspects of Jewish life that it is doubtful if any Jew is unaware of it. The two factors of sociological position and value orientation produce the life characteristics of the Jewish community of our time as they produce the life characteristics of all other communities.

At the present time among Jews, as indicated by the results of this analysis, the voluntaristic factors are the most important factors in the complex of causes which produce Jewish occupational adjustment. The value items in Jewish life which produce this effect are the previously stated evaluation of education in and for itself, the desire for independence of position in economic life, and the differentiating effects of food habits, prayer habits, and Sabbath observances. Finally, the existence of discrimination or the expectation thereof also produces value orientations, as shown by the drive for economic independence.

As has been pointed out, the prestige of education is a function of the historical experiences of Jewish life. To maintain Jewish identity without a state, a portable state in the form of "Torah" was utilized. But "Torah" demands educated men, since there is not among Jews a hierarchy of priests who mediate between men and God. In Jewish life man must learn the laws of God as found in "Torah" and carry them out. The responsibility for education in the Jewish home was laid at the door of parents, not teachers. The life of parents was involved in the education of their children. The Jewish drive for education has been commented upon by most students of Jewish life.[23] Today, among many Jews it is mere perseveration. For it has continued to be a value long after it has ceased to have its original function in religious group survival. The drive for education once wholly contained in the ghetto life of the Jews was transferred to secular education when the ghetto was abolished in the nineteenth century in western Europe.

Similarly, the drive toward independence of economic position is easily traced. The Jews historically have been a mobile people. For centuries they were affected by the religious and economic discriminations that minorities often face in a strange home. As a defensive measure, self-employment was the answer. Another answer was to follow economic pursuits within the Jewish group. This latter alternative was a possible answer only for a few of the Jews in any one community. The independent operator of a business or a professional man could at any time move on with his capital and his skill. He was also not dependent upon being hired by someone who discriminated against Jews. More importantly, perhaps, in Orthodox Jewish life, an independent worker is able to arrange his working hours so that they correspond with the necessities of his religious life—with his thrice-daily prayers, with his Sabbath observance, and with his different food habits.[24]

The existence and expectation of discrimination are, of course, commonplace in Jewish life. They have an effect whether or not there is any actual discrimination against Jews, and long centuries of experience have led Jews to be sensitive to the possibility of new discrimination. Furthermore, this experience has led them to consider how they might best protect themselves against discrimination even before it arises. Independence of occupation or entrance into occupations protected by law are the customary defenses that have been built up in the Jewish communities.

It is possible to trace the complex interaction of all of these factors throughout Jewish history; the values that are discussed here are considered only in their relation to the occupational adjustment of Jewish and non-Jewish sons. The relation of these values to the problem of occupational differences is clear. Primarily, the occupational differences between Jewish and non-Jewish youth in Detroit are due to differences in evaluation of life among Jews and non-Jews and only secondarily due to their differences in sociological position.

In the light of the results of this study one problem raised implicitly can be considered. To what extent are the Jews in America the bearers of the culture of their past and to what extent are they bearers of the general American culture? It was assumed for this study that the Jews as a folk community represented a subculture enclaved within the general American culture. The concept of folk community was the framework within which the hypothesis of the study was set. The importance of the concept is shown by the fact that from it flows the theory of differing group values. The answer given here to the question of why Jewish and non-Jewish sons differ in occupational patterns provides a partial answer to the larger question. Upon the evidence adduced here it may be said that the concept of folk community appears to be a correct one. Similarly, since one major aspect of Jewish group life seems responsive to different forces than those operating in the same area of life in the non-Jewish urban community, the findings are consistent with the assumption that the Jews *are* a subculture in the general American culture, though the demonstration of that assumption was not a task of this study.

The extent to which the Jews represent a subculture can be only suggested here. The problem of how much of their traditional culture they possess and how much of the culture surrounding them can also be studied in the field of occupational adjustment. It has been concluded that the motivational pattern of Jewish behavior is a group pattern, a function of the group value system. Yet not all Jews possess the same set of values. It would be possible to study the Jewish group alone, differentiating it into fragments by the criterion of how many Jewish values each fragment possesses. If these fragments were compared, their occupational adjustments should vary. The variations should be similar to the variation found here between Jews and non-Jews. There are many ways to differentiate values within the Jewish group. For example, it might well be considered that values would be present in different quantity in various groups of Jews in relation to the length of time that they have lived in America, and also in relation to the hold of Jewish life upon various groups of Jews. Thus, a study which analyzed occupational class adjustment of Jews in terms of the factors considered above would be able to answer the dynamic problem that has been posed.

The present research can be the forerunner of such a new investigation. Theoretically, it should appear that differences between Jews in occupational class adjustment would be greatest where attachment to traditional Jewish life is greatest. It should also be greatest where length of stay in America was least. If such a study could be made, it would contribute greatly to an understanding of cultural assimilation and the place of values in group life. The work done here constitutes a beginning which is designed to open the problem to further analysis.

NATHAN GLAZER

THE AMERICAN JEW AND THE ATTAINMENT OF MIDDLE-CLASS RANK: SOME TRENDS AND EXPLANATIONS

IN the 1930's about half of those American Jews who were immigrants were still workers; only a slightly larger proportion of the second generation were clerks, office workers, salesmen, and the like. However, the fifteen years of prosperity from the end of the thirties to the mid-fifties have wrought great changes, and created the Jewish community we know today. The effect of these changes has been to raise the East European Jews—the immigrants of 1880-1924, their children and grandchildren—more or less to the level previously achieved by the German Jews. These changes have wiped out most of the economic and occupational distinctions between the two elements, and along with other developments, have in large measure merged the two formerly distinct elements into a single community.

In these fifteen years, the older generation of East European Jewish immigrants, with its large proportion of workers, has been further reduced by the natural effects of age, while the younger generation has risen in the social scale. Perhaps a majority of the younger generation is now composed of businessmen and professional men. This community of businessmen and professional men is better educated and wealthier than most of the population—probably as well educated and as wealthy as some of the oldest and longest established elements in the United States.

Outside of New York City, the homogeneous character of the Jewish communities is beyond dispute. Between 1948 and 1953 local Jewish communities conducted surveys in fourteen cities—Camden, N. J., Charleston, S. C., Gary, Ind., Indianapolis, Ind., Los Angeles, Cal., Miami, Fla., Nashville, Tenn., New Orleans, La., Newark, N. J., the suburbs of Newark (considered as a separate community), Passaic, N. J., Port Chester, N. Y., Trenton, N. J., and Utica, N. Y. This is a fair random sample of the existing types of Jewish communities. It was discovered that the proportion of Jews in the non-manual occupations (that is, of those working in the professions, as proprietors, managers, and officials, and as clerks and salesman) ranged from 75 to 96 per cent.[1] For the American population as a whole, the proportion engaged in this kind of work was about 38 per

Excerpted from "Social Characteristics of American Jews, 1654-1954," *American Jewish Year Book*, Vol. 56 (1955), pp. 3-41, by permission of the author and the publisher. (Copyright, 1955, by The American Jewish Committee and The Jewish Publication Society of America.)

cent of the gainfully employed in 1950. Even if we add to this group the
farm owners and tenants, who might be considered a rural social equivalent of the Jewish shopkeeper, we find that only 48 per cent of those
gainfully employed in the general population were in non-manual work
or owned and managed farms.[2]

Of course, it is only in the largest cities that one finds fairly substantial
proportions of Jewish workers. Yet it appears from a number of studies
that even in New York City two-thirds of the gainfully employed Jews,
both immigrants and native-born, are engaged in non-manual work. Certainly the proportion among the native-born elements alone is much
smaller. Among the non-Jews of New York, only one-half or fewer are
engaged in non-manual work.[3]

The distinction between manual and non-manual work is today considered a crucial one for determining the social status of individuals and
groups. (Of course, there is a considerable amount of movement across
the line.) Yet it is also important to know where in the non-manual group
American Jews fall. Here too the evidence is decisive: they are high in
the group, which is to say that a large proportion of them are professionals. Large as this proportion was in the 1930's, it is considerably larger
today. Thus, if we compare the fourteen communities that were surveyed
in 1948-53 with another group of ten communities surveyed during 1935-45
(Buffalo, N. Y., Detroit, Mich., Erie, Pa., Grand Rapids, Mich., Jacksonville, Fla., New Orleans, La., Passaic, N. J., Pittsburgh, Pa., San Francisco,
Cal., and Trenton, N. J.),[4] we find that the proportion of professionals has
risen, on the average, from about 11 per cent of the Jewish gainfully
employed in the earlier group to about 15 per cent in the later group. One
might argue that the two groups of cities are not strictly comparable.
However, three of the cities—New Orleans, Trenton, and Passaic—were
included in both groups. In New Orleans, the proportion of professionals
rose from 15 to 21 per cent of the Jews gainfully employed; in Trenton,
the proportion rose from 12 to 19 per cent; in Passaic, there was no change.
In 1950, about 8 per cent of the American population were professionals.[5]

This rise in the proportion of professionals has been accompanied by
a fall in the number of Jews engaged in the lower levels of white-collar
work—as clerks and salesmen. Comparing our two groups of Jewish communities, we find that in the 1935-45 group about 36.5 per cent of the
gainfully employed Jews were clerks or salesmen; in the 1948-53 group,
the proportion was only about 27 per cent. The rapid decline in the
numbers of Jewish secretaries and salesmen in recent years is a phenomenon apparent to the naked eye; the available figures support this
impression.

What has happened, in effect, is that the Jewish economic advantage,
already perfectly obvious in the thirties, in the form of superior education,
and a higher proportion of self-employed persons, has borne fruit in the
fifteen years of prosperity since 1940. The proportions of Jewish doctors

and lawyers has probably not risen greatly (it was very high in the thirties). For one thing, the number of Jewish doctors has continued to be artificially held down by discrimination. The greatest increase in the number of Jewish professionals has been in other categories—there are more Jewish journalists, authors, engineers, architects, college teachers. In short, one finds a rapid rise in the number of Jews engaged in all intellectual occupations in recent years.

One interesting example of this Jewish professionalization is afforded by Charleston. In the middle thirties, the Jews of Charleston—an element long established in the city, with a relatively low proportion of immigrants —included one doctor, one dentist, several lawyers, two pharmacists, three or four teachers, and one rabbi. In 1948, there were eight doctors, seven dentists, eighteen lawyers, five pharmacists, nine teachers, eighteen engineers, seven social workers, four accountants, three radio commentators, three writers and editors, three artists, an orchestra leader, and four rabbis. All this in a community of less than 2,000 persons.[6]

At the same time there has been little sign of change in another of the characteristics of Jewish occupational distribution. The Jews are largely still proprietors of their own business—whether they be pushcarts, junk yards, groceries, or factories—rather than managers and executives of enterprises they do not own. There are a number of reasons for this. The American Jew tries to avoid getting into a situation where discrimination may seriously affect him. In a great bureaucracy, he is dependent on the impression he makes on his superiors and, increasingly in recent years, dependent on the degree to which he approximates a certain "type" considered desirable in business. The Jew prefers a situation where his own merit receives objective confirmation, and he is not dependent on the good will or personal reaction of a person who may happen not to like Jews. This independent confirmation of merit is one of the chief charactreistics of business, as against corporate bureaucracy. In Abraham Cahan's *The Rise of David Levinsky,* we read how the young immigrant going into business could, despite his accent, produce clothing as good as that produced by longer established Americans, and more cheaply. Only a rare businessman would not buy Levinsky's goods because of his accent. But if David Levinsky had been trying to rise to the vice-presidency of a huge corporation, he would certainly have found the going harder.

Before we proceed, let us document two other aspects of the Jewish community which are closely related to this concentration in professions and business. We have spoken of the Jewish advantage in education. In New York City, two studies, in 1948 and 1953, showed that about one-sixth of the Jews over eighteen had completed college, compared with a little more than about one-twentieth of the non-Jews—and this even though considerably fewer of the Jews were native-born. In other cities, with smaller percentages of foreign-born Jews, the percentage of college graduates was even greater.[7]

As to the question of Jewish wealth: again, we may look at New York City, which has the largest proportion of Jewish workers and Jewish foreign-born. In 1951, according to one study, 12 per cent of the Jewish households of the city had incomes of more than $10,000 as compared with 5 per cent of the non-Jewish population. At the other end of the scale, 29 per cent of the Jewish households and 49 per cent of the non-Jewish households earned less than $4,000. It is true a larger number of the Jewish households than of the non-Jewish households refused to divulge their income—15 per cent as compared with 10 per cent. Yet this could hardly change the overall picture.[8] The evidence on this point would be multiplied *ad infinitum;* but it is most impressive that New York Jews, still the most varied and differentiated of all American Jews in their social range, nevertheless surpass their neighbors in wealth.

Finally, one other group of Jewish statistics is revealing evidence of the character of the Jewish experience in America. These statistics demonstrate that the rise in the social and economic position of the Jews has been extremely rapid, far surpassing that which can be shown for any other immigrant group, and indeed surpassing, for the same period, changes in the socio-economic position of long-settled groups. A study of American college graduates made in 1947 showed that more Jews than non-Jews became professionals (excluding teachers, who, though professionals, generally have a smaller income than other professionals); more Jews became proprietors, managers or officials; fewer Jews became any type of white-collar and manual workers.[9] Yet, if we were to look at their parents' occupations, we would find that *fewer* of their parents than of the parents of non-Jews had been professionals, and proprietors, managers, and officials.[10] This same point is demonstrated in a study of 1,500 gifted children in California during 1921-23. When studied twenty years later, the Jewish children showed the same more rapid rise than the non-Jewish. Of the Jewish children, 57.5 per cent became professionals; of the non-Jewish, 44 per cent. Yet only 15 per cent of the Jewish fathers, as compared with 35 per cent of the non-Jewish parents, had been professionals. In other words: in this group, in a single generation, the Jews had increased their proportion of professionals by close to 400 per cent, the non-Jews only by about 25 per cent.[11]

One further fact is interesting, and will prepare us to consider the causes of this prosperity of the Jews in America. In the study of Jewish and non-Jewish college students, it was found that, on the whole, the Jewish graduates tended to enjoy a higher income than the non-Jewish.[12] The careful researchers tried to determine the cause of this disparity. Knowing that Jews tend to settle in large communities, and that large incomes are more easily obtained in big cities, the researchers held the factor of size of city constant, and compared small-town Jews with small-town non-Jews, large-city Jews with large-city non-Jews. Again, the Jews had larger incomes in the small towns, as well as the large cities, and in every size of community. The researchers then tried to find out whether the higher Jewish income was a product of the fact that more Jews were concentrated in the high-paying professions. But even in the professions, Jews earned more than non-Jews. It appeared that the Jewish superiority in earning power could not be ascribed to any objective social character-istics—at least not to any that had come within the purview of this study.

In fact, the whole body of information on the socio-economic position of the Jews that we have attempted to summarize leaves us with one unanswered question: What is the explanation for the greater success—measured in the objective terms of income, and the commonly accepted status of different occupations—of the Jews in the United States?

The question is interesting not only in itself, but also because its answer will suggest whether we may expect this prosperity to continue. The modern student of social phenomena cannot stop at psychological expla-nations. We know that Jews get (or used to get) better marks in school. We know that Jews work (or used to work) harder at getting an educa-tion. It is also believed that they work harder at their trades, in their professions, in business. But again, what is the explanation for these traits?

Ultimately, social explanations must resort to history, and explain a present peculiarity by discovering an earlier one. We think that the expla-nation of the Jewish success in America is that the Jews, far more than any other immigrant group, were engaged for generations in the middle-class occupations, the professions and buying and selling. It has also been said that the urban experience helped them, but we think that experience is much less important. For in any case, very large proportions of Jews, German as well as East European, came from small towns and villages that were scarcely "urban." Now, the special occupations of the middle class—trade and the professions—are associated with a whole complex of habits. Primarily, these are the habits of care and foresight. The middle-class person, we know, is trained to save his money, because he has been taught that the world is open to him, and with the proper intelligence and ability, and with resources well used, he may advance himself. He is also careful—in the sense of being conscious—about his personality, his time, his education, his way of life. The dominating characteristic of his life is that he is able to see that the present postponement of pleasure (saving money is one such form of postponement) will lead to an increase in satisfaction later. Perhaps the most significant findings of Alfred Kinsey's study of male sexual behavior was on this point: the person who post-poned sexual pleasure, Kinsey discovered, was already essentially middle class; for even if such a person was now working class, he was going to rise into the middle class.

Now, since the end of the Middle Ages, and particularly since the

French Revolution, it has been those with training in the middle-class virtues who have reaped the greatest rewards in society. The world has indeed been open to persons with enterprise and capital, and the United States has been perhaps more open than most countries. The peasant and the worker, no matter what philosophers and moralists have to say about the virtue of manual work, never stand high in society. In primitive society, it is the chief and priest who dispose of the greatest wealth; in feudal society, it is the warrior and churchman; in modern society, it is the businessman and intellectual. Consequently, it is in modern society that the Jews, who had been stamped with the values that make for good businessmen and intellectuals, have flourished; and it is when society reverts to a more primitive state, where force and those who wield it receive the greatest rewards, that the Jews are again thrust back to a low social position.

But what is the origin of these values that are associated with success in middle-class pursuits? Max Weber argues that they originated in a certain kind of religious outlook on the world, the outlook of Calvinism. There is no question that Judaism emphasizes the traits that businessmen and intellectuals require, and has done so since at least 1,500 years before Calvinism. We can trace Jewish Puritanism at least as far back as the triumph of the Maccabees over the Hellenized Jews and of the Pharisees over the Sadducees. The strong emphasis on learning and study can be traced that far back, too. The Jewish habits of foresight, care, moderation probably arose early during the two thousand years that Jews have lived primarily as strangers among other peoples. Other features of Jewish religion and culture tended to strengthen the complex of habits leading to success in trade and the professions. One scholar has argued that the very strong interest of the Jews in medicine, both in ancient and medieval times and today, in the Arabic world as well as the Christian, comes from the orientation of Jewish religion to the good things of this world conceived not in hedonistic or epicurean, but in sober, moderate, Apollonian terms.[13]

These are the origins of what we have called the "middle-class" values held by Jews. But certainly Jewish economic experience since the beginning of the Christian era can only have strengthened the bent given to them by religion and culture. Until the nineteenth century the Jews were characteristically a group of traders and businessmen and scholars (the term professional is hardly applicable to the medieval doctor or teacher). They included too a large group of artisans, but, in contrast to the Christian artisans, the Jewish artisans were not members of guilds and corporations, but rather independent craftsmen and artists; consequently in large measure the Jewish artisans too were tradesmen. It is not easy to evaluate, in the creation of a Jewish character strongly influenced by middle-class habits, the relative influence of religion and that of occupations followed for centuries—both influences worked in the same direction.

The Jewish immigrants who came from Eastern Europe to the United States during 1881-1924 numbered as many workers, and as many impoverished workers, as any other ethnic group. But they carried with them the values conducive to middle-class success and could, under the proper circumstances, easily return to the pursuit of trade and study, and thus to the ways of their fathers and forefathers. What is really exceptional, in terms of the large perspective of Jewish history, is not the rapid rise of these Jews in America, but the degree to which, in the Czarist Empire and Eastern Europe in general, they had been forced out of their age-old pursuits and proletarianized. This process was to a certain extent a response to the industrial revolution: everywhere peasants and artisans and small traders were forced to become workers. But in the Czarist empire, where the bulk of East European Jews lived, artificial measures were taken to drive them out of their traditional occupations—Jewish taverns were closed, Jewish students were artificially limited in the schools, Jews were not permitted to live in the expanding capital cities.

As a consequence, then, of governmental anti-Semitism and the industrial revolution, the East European Jews arrived in this country either as workers or *luftmenshen*—businessmen and traders with neither stock nor capital. But they were not, like the other workers who immigrated with them, the sons of workers and peasants, with the traditionally limited horizons of those classes. The Jewish workers were the sons—or the grandsons—of merchants and scholars, even though the merchants had only their wits for capital, and the scholars' wits were devoted to feats of memory. This background meant that the Jewish workers could almost immediately turn their minds to ways and means of improving themselves that were quite beyond the imagination of their fellow-workers. Business and education were, for Jews, not a remote and almost foreign possibility, but a near and familiar one. They, or their friends or relatives, had the necessary experience and knowledge; with the prospect of success beckoning, it became worthwhile for the Jewish immigrants to work harder and save more than other immigrant groups.

In any case, the pattern of foresight and sobriety so essential for middle-class success was so well established in Jewish life that it was maintained even when there was no prospect of going into business. The Jews did not drink; the Jewish students were docile, accepting—as lower-class children rarely do today—today's restraints for tomorrow's rewards; the Jewish workers stayed out of jail. When we look at the working-class Jewish neighborhoods of the great American cities of the 1920's and 1930's, it is clear we are not dealing with ordinary workers. It was not dangerous to walk through the New York slums at night when they were inhabited by Jews. The Jewish workers violated most of the patterns of lower-class behavior, and were in many important ways indistinguishable from the non-Jewish as well as the Jewish middle class. Thus, a study of voluntary organizations in New York City in 1934-35 revealed—as other studies have—that the higher the class, the larger the number of persons active in organizations. But the Jewish workers break this pattern—more of them belong to organizations than do Jewish white-collar workers.[14] A study in Chicago six years later told the same story: "Whereas among Protestants and Catholics working-class persons belong to fewer associations, among Jews the relationship is reversed."[15] And a study of political activity in New York City in 1945 showed that low-income Jews wrote more often to their Congressmen than did even high-income Protestants and Catholics.[16]

In the early thirties, J. B. Maller compared the social characteristics of the solidly Jewish neighborhoods of New York City with those of the rest of the city. The Jewish neighborhoods were, economically speaking, representative of the city: the average rent in the Jewish neighborhoods was about that of the city as a whole. Yet no matter what statistics we look at, we find a more markedly middle-class pattern of behavior in the Jewish neighborhoods than elsewhere. Thus, the homicide and the accident death rates among Jews was half of that for the whole city (the lower class is much more subject to fatal accidents than the middle class). The infant mortality rate was lower, the IQ of school children higher, the school attendance rate higher, the juvenile delinquency rate less than half the general city figure.[17]

One more study is worth quoting on this point. In 1935, one out of every ten youths in the city of New York was interviewed. Here is a description of the leisure-time activities of the Jews among them:

> The principal recreational activities of Jewish and non-Jewish youth are the same, but more of the Jewish than the non-Jewish had participated in them. . . . more of them had participated in athletic games, had gone swimming, played tennis or golf, attended concerts and lectures. More (though the differences were not so great) had hiked, gone to dances, and visited museums. Fewer had spent any time on manual diversions such as sewing or knitting, or doing carpentering, or putting a radio in condition, or repairing a motor.[18]

What this means is that twenty years ago the Jewish youth of New York City, half of whom, according to this study, came from working-class homes, showed in their leisure-time activities the pattern of the middle class—just as their fathers, who would never be anything but workers, showed a middle-class pattern in their leisure-time activities. . . .

What is the significance of all of this for the relation of the Jews to the United States? We have pointed out those characteristics in which the American Jews have differed from the "general American population." It is useful to compare Jews with "average Americans" (3.5 per cent of whom are Jewish) because in this way we can define what is characteristic of Jews. But we should realize that the "average American" is even more of an abstraction than the "average Jew." If we were to leave out such underprivileged groups as the Negroes and Mexicans and Puerto Ricans, the Jewish advantages we have chronicled would become less striking. If we were to compare Jews with Episcopalians or Presbyterians, we might find that the proportion of Jewish professionals was lower than that of professionals in these high status denominations. Indeed, one study conducted in Madison, Wis., showed just that. Among the Episcopalians of that city, no less than 36 per cent of those gainfully employed were professionals, as compared with 16 per cent among the Jews.[19]

The groups that make up America differ very little from each other in their overt culture. But they do differ greatly from each other in many other respects. The fact of concentration in certain classes or occupations is not peculiar to the Jews; any group in the population which is relatively small, and whose arrival in this country has been concentrated in a relatively short span of time, is likely to have a special economic distribution, different from that of the abstraction we call "the general population." Two factors will determine what this distribution will be: the character of the group at the time of its arrival, and the structure of economic opportunity in the country at the time of its arrival. We have already shown how Jewish religion and culture and occupational experience fitted the Jewish immigrants for business and the professions; it should now also be pointed out that these non-manual occupations were expanding greatly during the period of the greatest Jewish immigration, and unskilled manual work and farming were employing a progressively smaller proportion of the labor force. Between 1910 and 1950, the proportion of the population engaged in non-manual work rose from 21 per cent to 38 per cent.[20] Certainly this offered great opportunity to the Jews. But one had to be of the proper social and psychological constitution to take advantage of it—which the Jewish immigrants were. Hence, while America in general became more markedly middle-class in its occupational structure, Jews became even more so.

There is a general tendency for the ethnic concentration in a single occupation or industry to suffer dilution in time, just as the ethnic neighborhood is gradually dissolved as the second generation and third generation moves away. This means that in the second generation of Norwegians we do not find so many farmers, in the second generation of Italians we do not find quite so many heavy manual workers, and so on. This dilution is actually a movement upward, occasioned by the better education and wider knowledge of opportunities available to a native-born generation. But in the case of the Jews, this dilution upward becomes a *concentration*, for the Jews begin to reach the upper limit of occupational mobility relatively early. In order to reflect the heterogeneity of "the general American population" more accurately, it would now be necessary for the Jews to actively oppose their natural inclinations, as well as the natural movement of American society itself, and artificially to attempt to increase the number of farmers and workers and maintain the proportion of office workers and salesmen among them. This is not going to happen: so we may expect the Jewish community to become more homogeneous in the future, as the number of first-generation workers, and the culture they established, declines.

FRED L. STRODTBECK

FAMILY INTERACTION, VALUES, AND ACHIEVEMENT

BY the early 1950's, progress on the problem of the identification, understanding, and development of talented persons was believed to have reached a plateau. The resources of the Social Science Research Council's Committee on Identification of Talent were thus to be used in a search for new perspectives. At Yale, the writer had been engaged in studies of family relationships and cultural values.[1] The implications of such research for the identification of talented persons or groups was believed to be a frontier area worthy of exploration.

It was not appropriate to think in terms of long-term designs. Terman had earlier, and inspiringly, demonstrated that to follow a set of young persons through a life career takes a life career. Like Terman, we faced the problem of relating whatever *analytic* variables we chose to work with to *outcome* variables, but the requirement of a "within-three-years" reporting date foreclosed to us the use of a longitudinal design. In retrospect, our ultimate decision on an outcome, or criterion, variable appears to have dictated the details of much of the remainder of the design.

The criterion problem consisted of a search for a way of evaluating performance in the larger community. We sought a community criterion which is as broadly understood and accepted as grades are in the academic community. The stubborn difficulty and appropriateness of the question, "What is talent?", was recognized and only uneasily resolved. The Committee came to use the term "talent" to refer to the *exercise* of an ability in a social setting, i.e., a talented performance. Mere possession of ability was not enough; activity of social consequence was required.

In small-group literature it has become commonplace to speak of social *rank* (in the group) as being a product of activities which have been carried out in conformity with group norms (4, p. 140). With regard to the larger society, although it is somewhat more difficult to demonstrate in particular cases, it is believed that rewards, prestige, and control of important resources also tend to be allocated in terms of the importance of the job and the length of training required to perform it. Through time, it appears that more responsible positions in society come to be coveted, in part, because of the consensus which exists concerning their worth to the group.

This paper is adapted from a larger research report. It is excerpted, by permission, from "Family Interaction Values and Achievement" by Fred L. Strodtbeck, in *Report of the Social Science Research Council's Committee on Identification of Talent*, by David C. McClelland and others.

Unusual attainment in community service, the professions, or business, generally results in high social status. More modest advances of the order of the shift from immigrant laborer to small business operator have similar, though not identical, status consequences. There is, of course, always some difficulty in distinguishing between status which is gained by personal effort and status which accrues from family membership. When the mobility of groups is under consideration, this difficulty is somewhat less serious. For example, if one of two groups who arrived in this country at about the same time has been markedly more upwardly mobile than the other, our inability to attribute the mobility exactly to the responsible generation does not foreclose a between-group comparison. The essential strategy in a "group" approach is that it enables us to utilize an indicant of performance which arises within society itself: status. The assumption is that the abilities of the more mobile groups have been used in activities of greater social consequence. Many difficulties, such as would arise when one attempts to compare the work of a chemist and a devoted nurse, are not squarely met. So long as the values of different men, or the same men at different times, are to be reconciled, it is doubtful that any fully satisfactory criterion can be found. "Relative rise in the status structure" appears to have the advantage of being a ubiquitous measure which both has application to many activities and implies the operation of a community-wide evaluation system. By this reasoning we have concluded that *status mobility* deserves serious consideration as a criterion of talented performance by groups.

This decision, made early in the research, at first seemed to create more problems than it solved. If social mobility were to be the criterion of differential talent development, how were we to get data helpful in understanding and identifying talented adolescents? Were we to be dependent in our research on the recall by adults of the attitudinal dispositions—and interpersonal relations—they believed themselves to have had as early adolescents? Since our time limitations no more permitted us to follow groups of adolescents in their status climb than in other forms of talent expression, was there an alternative to longitudinal research available? Could we not seek groups with differential mobility rates just as Durkheim had sought groups with differential suicide rates? Social group rates have the disadvantage that since they are based upon the average of acts by many persons, they ordinarily have low predictive value for particular individuals. It is nonetheless possible that theoretical understanding of factors involved in talent development may be advanced by the study of factors associated with difference in group rates. For even if group predictions fall far short of the desired predictive efficiency, the mechanisms believed to differentiate among groups may later be found to differentiate among families within particular groups and thus provide a more crucial test of our understanding.

To illustrate, there is a popular impression that Presbyterians, Quakers, and Mormons are outstandingly industrious and successful, and they are believed to have produced a disproportionately high number of public leaders and men of science. Presbyterians historically represented the prototype of ascetic Protestantism which Weber suggests is particularly consistent with the requirements for modern capitalism. Quakers and Mormons represent, in differing degrees, slight departures from ideal-type ascetic Protestantism, but there are still common emphases in the teaching of all three. From the standpoint of a research design, it would be desirable to have a classificatory typology of cultural groupings such that extreme cases could be selected with markedly different achievement rates. Hopefully, differences might be found between such groups which would clarify understanding of the requirements for achievement in particular situations. While such a design leaves much uncontrolled, it is to be considered first as a source of new hypotheses. Whatever findings result may be verified by other means.

In New Haven, where our research was to be conducted, there were only two large ethnic groups with similar periods of residence in this country: Southern Italians and Jews. Irish were also numerous, but they had been in New Haven a longer period. When it became apparent that for Italians and Jews it would be possible to locate second-generation families with early-adolescent (third-generation) sons in the public and parochial schools, an effort was made to review in detail the general demographic data relating to the time of arrival, respective economic situation upon arrival, and their subsequent socio-economic attainment. From the results of this inquiry we concluded that while Jews upon arrival had a slight advantage in terms of occupational status and urban skills, this original advantage has been appreciably widened during the period 1910-1940. Jews consistently have higher occupational status than the population at large, while, in contrast, Italians are consistently lower.

The next problem was to make decisions as to how to go about discovering what differences there might be between Italians and Jews in values, beliefs about nature, child-training practices, and family structure. To decide on research instruments, sample characteristics, and the like, it was necessary to be guided by working hypotheses suggested by the literature. Three sources were of particular importance: (a) studies of religion and social activity; (b) studies of child rearing and adult character; and (c) studies of small face-to-face group behavior. . . . [The section reprinted below follows a survey of the literature on these three topics—Editor.]

§ *Italian-Jewish Cultural Values*

It is to be assumed that the subsequent generations of Italians and Jews in this country have progressively become more acculturated and more like one another. For guidance in the formulation of hypotheses about the way in which value differences between these cultures may have influenced their differential achievement, one may turn first to the description of the original cultures from which they had emigrated. For the Southern Italian background there were some nine substantive sources (2, 3, 7, 8, 9, 10, 11, 12, 13). To the extent that they have been used in our quick overview, these sources were quite consistent. For the Jews, the relevant literature is much larger. In the present account, Zborowski and Herzog's *Life is With People* is the primary reference (16). Their treatment of *shtetl* culture is sympathetic—perhaps idealized—but sharply focused on attitude dimensions of great relevance to Italian-Jewish contrasts.

To begin with one of the most striking differences, Jews have traditionally placed a very high value upon *education and intellectual attainment*. The Jewish parent was expected to provide education, but not in a ritualistic manner. As much education was to be provided as the sons showed themselves capable of absorbing. Learning in the *shtetl* society gave the individual prestige, respect, authority—and the chance for a better marriage. The Jewish folk saying that "parents will bend the sky to educate their sons," and the heroic stories every first-generation Jewish parent can tell of the sacrifices made by fellow-parents to educate their children, illustrate the cultural legitimation of sacrifice for education.

The legitimation of education is further bound up with prestige associated with intellectual "brainwork," and the corresponding *lack* of prestige associated with physical accomplishments. This pattern of evaluation starts early in the child's career. Traditionally, a three- or four-year-old starting *kheyder* (elementary religious school) was regarded as a serious student. Brilliant students were treated with a deference ordinarily reserved for important adults. The weight of the opinion of the young scholar is reflected by the fact that a bearded man will not be ashamed to bring a difficult Talmudic question to a boy of thirteen.

Religious learning and the satisfactions of family life were not separated as they were in monastic Catholicism. It was the custom to arrange the young scholar's marriage while he was in his middle teens. In order that such scholars might give more attention to their studies, many of the economic responsibilities of the family were assumed by the wife.

In Southern Italian culture, the traditional attitude toward education was (and is) very different. School and book-learning environments were alien and remote from everyday experiences. Priests were taken from their families and villages to be educated. To the typical Southern Italian peasant, school was an upper-class institution and potentially a threat to his desire to retain his family about him. While education might well serve for some as a means of social advancement, the peasant was disposed to believe that this avenue was not open to his children—in their case education was not functional. For each age there is a proper behavior. Family life, local political power, and other objectives were stressed as alternative goals to learning.

Even in this country, the first-generation Southern Italian parents' attitude was, in part, negative to education. As an Italian educator reports: "Mother believed you would go mad if you read too many books and father was of the opinion that too much school makes children lazy and opens the mind for unhealthy dreams." Intellectualism, in itself, was not valued in Southern Italian communities. Learned men were of another class, or alternatively, they were men of the church. Status in the community changed slowly; property was in all cases more important. Property could be gotten faster by a trickster-trader than a scholar (1). Scholars were like monks: good men but not of the real world.

La famiglia in the Southern Italian culture was an inclusive social world. The basic mores of this society were primarily family mores—everyone outside the family was viewed with suspicion. The basic code was family solidarity, and there was strong feeling that the family should stay together—physically close together. The essence of the ethos has been most forcefully captured by Edward C. Benfield. He states the one premise from which the "family vs. all others" political orientation would seem to flow: "Choose so as to maximize the short-run advantage of the family and assume others will do likewise."[2]

The Jewish family was traditionally a close-knit one, but it was the entire Jewish *shtetl* community rather than the family which was considered the inclusive social unit and world. Although relatives were more important than friends, all Jews were considered to be bound to each other. The primary unit was the family of procreation. Physical proximity was not so heavily stressed. Mandelbaum (6, pp. 28, 31) and Joffe (5) have pointed out that the dynamics of benefice for the Jews was not of the reciprocal exchange nature. Parents' gifts to their children are to be parallel for the next generation. In the home, as in the community, giving must move in a descending spiral. Giving serves not only to enrich the donor and succor the recipient, but it also maintains the constituency of fundamentally equal persons—and in this way enriches the community. In American Jewish communities today, the sizeable and highly publicized charitable contributions owe much to this tradition.

For the Jewish parents there was in the *Alles für die Kinder* theme, an emphasis upon a bettered condition in the *future* which made them more willing to let children leave the community for opportunities elsewhere. Much less emphasis on the future existed in the Italian families' evaluation of alternatives.

The external world for the Jews was hostile to be sure, but it was by nature solvable. For all goods there is a proper price, for all labor there is a best way of doing it. For the Italian the equivalent phrasing is perhaps: "There is work which must be done." One might go further to say there are ways of doing the work which are more expeditious—but no matter how the work is done, there is always the chance that fate may intervene. The unpredictable intervention of fate may be for good or evil, but *Destino* is omnipresent. If a man works all his life for something which *Destino* may deny him, well then, why should men look so far ahead? There is always the present, and one might have a lucky break.

Zborowski, in his study in this country of the reactions of hospitalized Jewish and Italian veterans to pain, employs Florence Kluckhohn's well-known *time* orientation to differentiate the cultural responses (15). First, he finds that both Jews and Italians complain more about pain than "Old Americans." But, more importantly, sedation alone is enough to allay Italians. For the Jew sedation is not enough. He continues to be pessimistic and concerned about the implication of the sedation for his eventual recovery. For the Italian there is a *present-oriented* apprehension of the sensation of pain; for the Jew there is a *future-oriented* anxiety concerning the symptomatic meaning of the pain. Neither group wishes to suffer alone, neither group believes it is necessarily masculine to deny the existence of pain, and neither group believes that suffering is an end in itself.

In the use of folk medicines, belief in the "evil eye," and the like, Jewish and Italian culture shared many common irrational elements. Religious ritual was strong in both cultures. However, the complex of behavior involved in the individual's participation in his own salvation deserves separate attention.

In Italian folk theology, Catholic doctrine was popularly understood as requiring sheer obedience to arbitrary prescriptions for the sake of an arbitrary reward. Where the formula did not apply, the matter was of no real significance. Faith in the mystery of the Trinity and the timely interventions of the priest were all that was required. For the Jews, religious improvement was always possible and perfection always denied. The scholar proceeded at his own rate after becoming a rabbi. There was no one to grant the learned and respected man a more advanced degree; his job was ever undone. During the middle years he might have had to give more attention to business, but as he grew older he could spend his full time in discussion, study, and prayers.

In the East European *shtetl*, no man could occupy a position so humble that it could not in part be redeemed by his religious scholarship. Without the religious scholarship a man of means could be *prost*—simple, common, vulgar. A diploma of any type which signified learning in non-religious fields came to be accorded respect like that accorded religious scholarship. It is important to stress that if Talmudic scholarship taught precision, juridic care, and dedication, it taught attitudes toward learning which might, with a growth of heterodoxy, be transferred to other learning. So long as the ghetto confined the area of attainment, goals of religious scholarship were highly coveted. Upon release from the ghetto, the status and financial rewards available in the disciplines of law and medicine were also attainable by work of an intellectual character similar to Talmudic scholarship. Jewish mobility has in all probability been facilitated by the transformation of a complex of behavior which had not existed for the Italians.

A peasant's mistrust of books in contrast with the veneration of learning does not exist in isolation from other attitudes. Zborowski and Herzog tell us that in the *shtetl* the hair line of babies would in some instances be shaved back so that the child would have a high forehead—hence, appear intelligent. Short, thick hands were thought to be inappropriate and ugly—*prost*. The Jewish attitude toward the body was not ascetic, the body was neither ugly nor inherently evil. It was rather that the body was a vessel for containing the spirit. Rest, food, and procreation on the Sabbath were legitimated to keep the body at full efficiency, but a specialized interest in physical development *per se* was improper. For the Jews the mind was a great tool, but ever under discipline and purposeful direction. In the early morning prayers the mind is turned to sacred matters, on the Sabbath to non-business matters—it is never a question of whether the mind can win over impulse.[3]

It is perhaps equally true that the Italian emphasis on good food and proper relaxation is superficially similar to Jewish practice, and for that matter, to practices in many cultures. The essential difference as we perceive it is that the Italian manual worker was never ashamed of his strength; to keep his body fit was a desirable end in itself, for it was never perceived to be in competition with other necessarily more important activities.

To supplement the old-culture Italian-Jewish child training contrast there is just one comparative American study which has come to our attention. Field interviewers from the Harvard University Laboratory of Human Development contacted an area sample of families in greater Boston concerning methods of child rearing. With regard to second-generation Italians and Jews, the division of the families by social class was as follows:

	Italian	Jewish
Middle	7	64
Lower	36	15

This is consistent with the predicted differential status mobility: Jews are concentrated in the middle classes, Italians in the lower. Unfortunately, this distribution does not provide many middle-class Italian, and only relatively few lower-class Jewish families, though the frequencies for lower-class Italians and middle-class Jews are sizeable. Since this class distribution appears to be roughly "modal" for second-generation members of these ethnic groups, comparisons between these groups are of particular interest. To paraphrase slightly the language of the original manuscript, the main points made are as follows:[4]

(a) The amount of time spent in caretaking and in affectionate interaction with the child, the warmth of the mother-child relationship, and the amount of enjoyment in child-care is not different for the two groups. Both are relatively high in infant nurturance save only for the greater severity of the Italian mothers in toilet training. For sexual play with other children, masturbation, or nudity in the home, Italians are markedly less permissive than Jews.

(b) Italians are less permissive of aggression to parents and impose more requirements on the child's table manners, conversations with adults, acting as "boy" or "girl," caution around furniture, and freedom of movement from the home than do Jews. Italians were more prone to report they followed through and demanded obedience, although in terms of authority patterns such as mother-dominant, shared, father-dominant, or divided—no differences between Italian and Jewish families were reported. Family structure from the perspective of the child is reflected indirectly in the fact that Jewish children admit deviant behavior more frequently than Italian children, and, in addition, tend to require more attention from adults.

(c) In terms of current dependency, and this is focused at about the five-year level, both groups of children are about equally dependent, but the Jewish mother is significantly more accepting of dependent behavior. In general, the emotional atmosphere of parent-child relations is somewhat warmer in Jewish than in Italian families, while at the same time Jewish families place a higher evaluation on the benefits to be gained by spanking.

(d) In terms of expected school attendance, Jews expect much longer school attendance, but there is a corresponding lesser insistence on the child's "doing well in school." Perhaps this implies a disposition to permit the child to set his own level for quality of performance.

It should be noted that there were some marked differences between the 64 middle-class Jewish and the 15 lower-class Jewish families. While this latter number is small, the lower-class families were significantly more severe in weaning and toilet-training, took less pleasure in caring for babies, interacted less, and were less warm and nurturant when the child was an infant. At the current behavior level, they were also less demonstrative, much less permissive of sexual behavior, and in general more severe in their socialization practices. Italian-Jewish differences are greatly attenuated when class level is constant; hence, since class level is not controlled in the comparisons above, the exact contribution of "class" in contrast with "culture" cannot be ascertained.

Out of all this material, all too briefly summarized, we must now pick those values which appear most likely to have accounted for the differential occupational achievement of the two "old cultures" when they came to the United States. This task necessarily involves a comparison of Italian-Jewish value differences with the values we arrived at for a description of the Protestant-U.S. achievement ethic earlier [not included here—Editor]. It finally resolved itself into a comparison at five points, as follows:[5]

(1) *Man's sense of personal responsibility in relation to the external world.* The Protestant's world was the work of God, its mysteries were profound and not to be understood by the slacker. To work to understand

and transform this world was the true Christian's personal responsibility. Misfortunes have a definite place in the scheme; they are the tests which God sets before men. By such logic, hard work was understood to be behind all worldly accomplishment, but there was still no guarantee that even a lifetime of hard work would necessarily be rewarded.

For the "U. S. achiever"—the successful scientist, executive, or professional person—rational mastery of the situation has been equated with the "hard work" of the Protestants, and threat of almost continuous review of his record has been equated with anxiety over eventual salvation. There is no necessary personal deprivation which must be endured; one's accomplishment can be facilitated by "breaks," but importantly breaks are of the individual's own making. It is a matter of being available with what is needed at the right place and at the right time. Just as breaks are not given by a beneficent power, neither are failures. Whatever failure an individual has suffered could always have been foreseen and hedged against if the individual were sufficiently alert. One might commiserate with an unfortunate person, but for the "U. S. achiever" there is no legitimate excuse. His sense of personal responsibility for controlling his destiny is very great.

"Old-culture" Jewish beliefs appear to be congruent in many if not all respects with the "U. S. achiever" belief in rational mastery of the world presented above and at marked variance with that of the Southern Italian. For the "old-culture" Jew, there was the expectation that everything could be understood if perhaps not always controlled. Emphasis on learning as a means of control was strong. Religious or secular learning, once attained, unlike the Protestant's salvation and the "U. S. achiever's" status, was not in continual jeopardy. For men who were learned in trades but not specialized religious scholars, the expectations of charity to others of the community who were less fortunate was a continuing goad to keep working, but if misfortune befell a former benefactor, the community would understand. The "old-culture" sense of personal responsibility coexisted with a responsibility of the community for the individual which eases somewhat the precariousness associated with "all or none" expectations on the individual.

For the Italian, the best laid plans of man might twist awry. Misfortune originated "out there," not inside the individual. The term *Destino* suggests that it has been written that a particular event will or will not come to pass. A sort of passive alertness is inculcated; no one knows when he is going to get a lucky break, but at the same time there is no motivation for a heroic rational undertaking, for such an undertaking may be *destined* to fail.

(2) *Familism versus loyalty to a larger collectivity.* The essence of familism is an emphasis on filial obedience and parental authority. Calvinism was anti-familistic in its emphasis upon a first obedience to one's own soul and to God. Familistic social organization tends to involve a

particular locus of activity and a hierarchy of responsibility based upon age and kinship relations rather than upon impersonal technical requirements. For this reason the "U. S. achiever" tends to be anti-familistic like the Calvinist. That is, the desire to keep two or more generations together would compete with the job and educational opportunities which require residential moves. The "U. S. achiever" moves with his wife and children on the basis of his technical qualifications to wherever he believes he can maximize his opportunities. At the early stages of his career he may even avoid the line of work where his father might help him, so as to win for himself the privilege of being judged for his own competence.

The "old-culture" Jewish pattern involved separations for business and educational reasons and a heightened consciousness that a man's first responsibility was for his children. That is, obligations were primarily from those that have more to those that have less, which, practically speaking, meant that children need not always stay to nurture parents who might be better off than they were. The Jewish pattern of weaker ties to parents is not seen to be as extreme as the pattern for the "U. S. achiever," but in some ways it contrasts sharply with the Southern Italian pattern.

Under great economic duress the Southern Italian familial organization may shrink to the nuclear unit—but this is atypical. The successful Italian wishes to draw his extended family about him, and in the process some are lifted in status just as others are secured in the status of the large-family complex.

(3) *Perfectability of man.* An aspect of Calvinism, perhaps best captured for popular consumption in *Poor Richard's Almanac* by Benjamin Franklin, is the emphasis that at every moment of every day a person should work to improve himself. "Old-culture" Jewish emphases on religious scholarship and study represented a similar belief in the responsibility for self-improvement. For the "U. S. achiever" this perfectability requirement has, in one sense, been relaxed, but insofar as it remains, it has become even more stringent. Now, the improvement should take place in a relaxed manner with no apparent effort. The self-improvement should be "enjoyed," not "endured" as it might have been earlier. In all of these cases interest in education should be (and has been) high because it is one of the ways in which man obviously perfects himself.

For the Southern Italian there was considerable doubt as to whether man could perfect himself or, indeed, that he need try to. According to his interpretation of Catholicism, he must conscientiously fulfill his duties, but his "good works" did not form a rationalized system of life. Good works could be used to atone for particular sins, or, as Weber points out, stored up as a sort of insurance toward the end of his life, but there was no need to live in every detail the ideal life, for there was ever the sacrament of absolution. Furthermore, the Southern Italian really felt that man lived at an uneasy peace with his passions and that from time to time one had to expect them to break through. Man is really not perfectable—he is all too human, and he had better not drive himself or his mind too hard in trying to reach perfection.

(4) *Consciousness of the larger community.* The Protestants "each man his brother's keeper" has given way in the "U. S. achiever" to a less moralistic rationale for serial consciousness based upon a recognition of the interdependencies in modern society. Just as the "old-culture" Jewish community could vicariously participate in the charities of its wealthiest members, there is a sense in which the strengthening of various aspects of American society are recognized to contribute to the common good.

The "old-culture" Jew, enabled by his success to assume a responsibility for the community, had little choice in the matter. The social pressures were great, and they were ordinarily responded to with pride and rewarded by prominence in the community forum. The identification went beyond the extended family. The giver was not to be rewarded in kind; his reward came from community recognition. Such community identification—as contrasted with family identification—was not highly developed among Southern Italians. Reduced sensitivity to community goals is believed to inhibit the near-altruistic orientations which in adolescence and early maturity lead individuals to make prolonged personal sacrifices to enter such professions as medicine or the law.

(5) *Power relations.* Analysis of the requirements for success in America suggests that insofar as differences in status may be perceived to be legitimate because the high-status person is technically more competent, then the person in the subordinate position can still give his full commitment to organizational goals without feeling or acting as if he were being dominated by his superior. Early Protestantism laid the groundwork for such limited and specific relationships by insisting that each man had a post assigned him by God so that no one should feel inferior or superior. The modern bureaucracies create for "U. S. achievers" a greatly increased number of positions in our society where a person has a specific role in a larger impersonal system to perform.

On the other hand, the "old-culture" Jew did not see power in the context of some external system of pre-established impersonal relationships. He tended, like the Protestant, to reduce power questions to other terms, to the equity of a particular bargain, for example; but unlike the Protestant, these relationships were always specific both as to persons and content involved, and *not* part of a larger system. His primary concern was to make his relationships good with others with whom he was in close contact over a particular issue. The specificity of his relations with others, including his separation of business and family matters, is also like the functional specificity of modern bureaucratic society, but again unlike it in overlooking the *system* of such functional relationships.

The "old-culture" Italian tends to see power entirely in immediate interpersonal terms and as a direct expression of who can *control* the behavior of another rather than who knows more for a job in an impersonal system. He is constantly interested in "who's boss?" and with turning every relationship into a "for me-against me" or "over me-under me" polarity.

§ *The New Haven Sample*

In the process of developing the sampling frame in New Haven, certain further data were obtained which bear upon Italian-Jewish cultural differences. A questionnaire was administered to over 1,000 boys between 14 and 17 in the New Haven public and parochial schools (and a somewhat larger number of girls). Data obtained on this questionnaire were utilized primarily to identify a set of third-generation Italian and Jewish boys who were in turn stratified by their school performance and socioeconomic status. The questionnaire touched generally upon values and more particularly upon materials relating to occupational choice, parental expectations, parental control, educational aspirations, and balance of power in family interaction.

Boys from Catholic families who reported one or more paternal and one or more maternal grandparent born in Italy were considered Italian. Boys who reported the religion of both their parents as Jewish were considered Jewish. Determination of socio-economic status was made from information provided by the son relating to the parents' education and the father's occupation. Classification was made in terms of seven groupings [for an explanation of these groupings, see the larger report—Editor]. In terms of these two criteria the following frequencies were obtained:

Socio-economic Status	Italian	Jewish	Other
High (classes 1 and 2)	8	24	52
Medium (classes 3 and 4)	80	66	213
Low (classes 5, 6, and 7)	182	17	455
Unclassified	15	2	59
	285	109	779

It may be noted that there were very few *High* (major and minor professional, owners of very large business) Italians, and relatively few *Low* (laborers through skilled worker) Jews. For both groups there were a substantial number of families who owned or managed small businesses, or were engaged in white-collar or supervisory positions—here classified *Medium*.

To demonstrate more clearly the way in which this distribution confirms the differential status distribution of the two groups, one may construct an index number using the distribution of "others" as a base. For example, 52 of 720 (excluding unclassified "Others") are of high socio-economic status. On a pro-rata basis 19.5 Italians of high status would be expected. Actually significantly fewer than this, only 8, or 41 per cent of the expected, are observed. For the Jews of high status 310 per cent of the expected are observed. The full set of indices are as follows:

Socio-economic Status	Italian	Jewish
High	41%	310%
Middle	100	209
Low	107	25

It was desirable to use the boy's achievement in school as a criterion of his own performance just as the status of the family might be used as a criterion of the father's performance. Toward this end, each boy's performance on prior intelligence and school achievement tests was inspected and his grade performance in terms of the norms of the particular school predicted. When the boy's school grades exceeded the expected performance, he was considered an over-achiever and when his grades fell short of the predicted performance, he was classified as an under-achiever. . . . [A total of 48 Italian and Jewish boys, matched according to SES and divided equally as between over-achievers and under-achievers were selected for intensive analysis. In addition to the questionnaire administered in the schools, questionnaires were given to the father, mother, and son in each of these 48 households. An experimental procedure designed to measure family interaction was also utilized in each household. Details are contained in the original report. The section which follows presents some of the results of the original screening questionnaire—Editor].

§ *The V-Scale*

Fifteen items were included in the original screening questionnaire. These items, adapted from the Harvard Social Mobility seminar,[6] dealt very generally with the types of value differences which have been previously described as characterizing "old-culture" Italian-Jewish differences. Not all points in the value analysis were covered in the questionnaire because the analysis was completed only after the intensive study had been made and the questionnaire was used in selecting the subjects for intensive study. In the first stage of the analysis, search was made for items which would discriminate at the .05 level between over-achieving and under-achieving students (both Italians and Jews being excluded from this comparison). The original set of fifteen items was reduced to eight. In this process a set of items of uneven coverage resulted.

Since neither the Italians nor the Jews had been involved in the original computations, an inspection of Italian-Jewish differences on V-items provides an independent check on the distribution of one type of "achievement potential" in the two populations. As an operation to corroborate the inferences which had been made on the basis of status mobility, it was predicted that Jews would have higher achievement-related responses than Italians. It may be seen in Table 1 that this prediction was significantly confirmed for six of the eight items, and that no differences were observed in the other two cases.

Table 1—V-Scale Items, Factor Loadings and Italian-Jewish Response Levels

FACTOR LOADING			PER CENT DISAGREE BY ETHNICITY	
Factor I "Mastery"	Factor II "Independence of Family"	Items	Jews	Italians
.64	.00	Planning only makes a person unhappy since your plans hardly ever work out anyhow.	90	62
.49	.28	When a man is born, the success he's going to have is already in the cards, so he might as well accept it and not fight against it.	98	85
.58	.15	Nowadays, with world conditions the way they are, the wise person lives for today and lets tomorrow take care of itself.	(80)*	(79)
.04	.60	Even when teen-agers get married, their main loyalty still belongs to their fathers and mothers.	64	46
.21	.60	When the time comes for a boy to take a job, he should stay near his parents, even if it means giving up a good job opportunity.	91	82
.29	.68	Nothing in life is worth the sacrifice of moving away from your parents.	82	59
—.02	.28	The best kind of job to have is one where you are part of an organization all working together even if you don't get individual credit.	54	28
—.05	.00	It's silly for a teen-ager to put money into a car when the money could be used to get started in business or for an education.†	(65)	(63)

* The difference is not significant at the .05 level for pairs of values in parentheses; for the remaining values the differences are significant at the .05 level or greater.
† Per Cent "Agree" reported for this item.

A factor analysis reveals that items relating to the rejection of subjugation to fate—the first three—have a high loading on Factor I (Mastery), and the fourth through sixth items (relating to Independence of Family) have a high loading on Factor II. The item treating of organizational vs. individual credit discriminates between Italians and Jews and is not highly related to the other alternatives. The eighth item dealing with postponed gratification, which like the other seven had discriminated between over- and under-achieving students, did not discriminate between Italians and Jews nor did it correlate significantly with other items in the set. The third of the Mastery items also did not discriminate between Italians and Jews. The items dealing with control of one's destiny, separation from the family, and working for a group, differentiate between Italians and Jews as predicted in the introductory ethnographic contrasts. . . . [Subsequent sections detail father's V-scores, and relationships between type of family interaction as measured by a "power" score, school achievement levels, and V-scores—Editor].

§ *Summary*

Complicated though the task may be, we must now somehow integrate our empirical findings into the larger theoretical questions which lay behind our original research design. In its simplest terms, our plans started with the hypothesis that the American social system contained certain inherent requirements for the achievement of individuals in it, requirements inherited to a considerable extent from the Protestant Ethic as described by Weber, Parsons, and others, but also evolved into new forms. Then, since it was impractical to do longitudinal research, we decided to pick subcultures which had been conspicuously more and less successful in adapting *as groups* to the U. S. requirements for achievement of high status and to search their value systems and family life for clues as to why they differed in the production of achievant individuals in the United States.

Before summarizing the clues we discovered, it is necessary to stress that no one should impute an evaluative tone to our comparison of Italians and Jews—the two differentially achieving groups chosen for study. In the first place, the emphasis on status mobility as the criterion of "success" in this study should not be perceived as the only criterion by which one might recognize activities of social value. There are many alternative philosophies of life which would suggest quite different criteria of success to be investigated by the behavioral scientist. Our reason for choosing status mobility as the criterion rests primarily on the fact that it is a societal means of evaluating people which applies to a very broad range of social activities in the United States today.

Furthermore, we were not primarily motivated by a desire to study these subcultures *per se* with the notion of predicting which groups would show the most status mobility from now on. Rather our interest was in the extent to which each of these "old cultures" was *initially* adaptive to the U.S. social setting as we analyzed it. In fact, there is considerable evidence in our data to support the notion that whatever differences in values and family interaction initially existed, they are disappearing as both groups get more assimilated into American life. For example, we found no qualitative differences in family interaction between Italians and Jews using the Bales categories, and no V-score differences in our stratified sample (with effects of socio-economic status removed). Also, while Jews were more mobility-oriented in their favorable attitudes toward higher education and prestige occupations, there was no evidence that Italians differed from the rest of the population in this respect. Finally, we know that socio-economic status affects socialization practices and power balance in the family, both of which are factors which are related to subsequent achievement. But both ethnic groups are changing in socio-economic status. To take just one possible effect of this as an illustration: more Jews are moving into high status where the fathers are more power-ful and may therefore, according to our data, tend to produce sons who have values *less* conducive to upward mobility. On the other hand, more Italians may be moving into medium status where family power may be more conducive to mobility than in the lower status where many of them are now. Thus one might on this basis predict a reversal in the mobility rates of the past, with a trend toward greater mobility for the Italians in the future. So, lest the analysis be misunderstood, the interest in "old culture" differences is not at all to predict group mobility rates, but to identify clues which might have explained differences in their initial adjustment to American life.

The clues we found consist in part of the value differences based on ethnographic evidence summarized earlier, and whatever further support for them we uncovered in the empirical study. Each of these value differ-ences were selected because we thought it should promote status mobility in the United States, and not because it was necessarily the best way of comparing Italian and Jewish subcultures. In each case, our expectations were largely confirmed by the data. Three of the five expected value differences turned up in the V-scale which differentiated Italians from Jews and which also reflected differences in past status mobility (i.e., as represented by higher scores for fathers with higher social status) and probably *future* status mobility (i.e., as represented by higher scores for over-achieving sons). There is, then, evidence from three sources that the following three values contained in the V-scale are important for achieve-ment in the United States:

1. A belief that the world is orderly and amenable to rational mastery, and that, therefore, a person can and should make plans which will con-trol his destiny (three items in the V-scale). By way of contrast, the notion that man is subjugated to a destiny beyond his control probably impeded Southern Italians in their early adjustment to the United States, just as it impeded boys in school or less successful fathers in their occu-pations in this study. Unfortunately we cannot say with any assurance whether the poor performance of the Italians and of the less successful fathers or sons was the result of the belief in fate or whether the belief in fate was the result of the poor performance. However, since we know—in the case of the Italians—that the belief was part of the "old culture" and therefore antedated their performance, we may feel justified in pre-dicting that while beliefs and performance undoubtedly modify each other, it is the belief which came first so far as the adjustment of Southern Italians to the United States is concerned.

2. A willingness to leave home to make one's way in life. Again, by contrast, the South Italian stress on "familism" which we found evidence for in the V-scale should have interfered with upward mobility and con-

tributed to the lower occupational achievement of Italians as compared with Jews. Family balance of power also affects the willingness to leave home, a fact which demonstrates that one's position in life can produce a value disposition as well as the reverse. But whether the willingness to break up the family comes from an "old culture," from power balance in the family, from the father's or son's relative lack of success in job or school, it is certainly a value of importance in the "achievement complex."

3. A preference for individualistic rather than collective credit for work done. On the one item in the V-scale which dealt with this value, the Jews showed greater preference for individualistic, the Italians for collective rewards, as one would perhaps expect from the greater "familism" of the Italians. We have argued [in a section not reproduced here—Editor] that some loyalty to an abstract system of relations—to a collectivity—is essential in modern bureaucratic organizations. Hence, the greater collective emphasis of the Italians here would appear to have *favored* their quick adaptation to American life (although perhaps more now when bureaucracies are better developed than earlier). On the other hand these same bureaucracies stress individualistic rewards and impersonal relations between superiors and subordinates, both of which do not fit very well with the Italian emphases on *non-individualized* collateral loyalties and on very personal dominance-striving in face-to-face relationships. Although the questionnaire does not provide much information on this point, it is also clear that while the Jewish emphasis on individualized rewards *is* adaptive to the bureaucratic system, it also contains an element which does not fit the system so well—i.e., the stress on *personal* rather than impersonal individualistic relationships. But again, our main concern is not with Italian-Jewish differences, but with the elements in those differences which may explain their differential achievement. Here it seems to be the stress on individualistic reward among the Jews, although the case is not so clear-cut as with the other values in the V-scale, because there is only one item and because there are at this point elements in both "old cultures" working both for and against quick adaptation to the U.S. social system.

Aside from the V-scale results, which are most impressive because they reflect differential achievement of cultures (Jews over Italians), of fathers (high over low SES) and of sons (over- vs. under-achievement in school), there are two facts from the larger questionnaire study which relate to a fourth expected value difference between Italians and Jews— namely, the value placed on the *perfectability of man*. The Jews definitely had higher educational and occupational expectations for their sons. Practically speaking, this would appear to mean they believed that man could improve himself more by education and that one should not readily submit to fate and accept a lower station in life, the way the Italians were more prepared to do.

The fifth and final expected Italian-Jewish value difference had to do with power relationships. We had been led to believe by ethnographic reports and other studies that Italians would be more concerned than Jews with establishing dominance in face-to-face relationships, and such turned out to be the case. Both in the boys' reports of who was dominant at home and in the actual decision-winning in the 48 homes we studied intensively, the Italians showed greater variations from equality of power than the Jews. While this finding is probably of lesser importance than those presented above, it nonetheless sharpens our curiosity about what effects the power balance through time in particular families will have on the son's achievement. Is it possible that when relatively equalitarian relations persist in the home, the son can move to new loyalties in larger systems of relationships such as those provided by college or a job without an outright "rupture" of family controls? Or conversely, is such an adjustment to new institutions outside the home harder the more the home has tended to be dominated by one parent or the other? Furthermore, what would be the cost of such a rupture to the son in terms of performance and motivation to continue on his own? Would the conflict not be less, the frustration less, when the break came, and consequently the emotional and intellectual adjustment more efficient if he had come from a home where controls were already diffuse and equalitarian as they are in many situations in life? The present design involved only a single visit with the families; in subsequent research it is to be hoped more can be arranged as the child is growing up, so that one can follow the effects of power balance on the child's adjustment inside the family and subsequently to life outside it. . . .

Our purpose has been to break some new ground in the study of talent potential. We have tried to do so both theoretically and empirically by focusing on three fairly novel aspects of the problem: *the requirements of the U.S. social system for success, the role of values in achievement, and family power* as a determinant of some of the child's most fundamental adjustments to life. If our preceding pages have succeeded either through theoretical argument or empirical fact in convincing people that these are problems *relevant to talent identification and worthy of being pursued by further research along the same lines,* our major objective will have been reached.

References

1. Brown, N. O. *Hermes the thief*. Madison: Univer. Wisc. Press, 1947.
2. D'Alesandre, J. J. Occupational trends of Italians in New York City. *Italy American Monthly*, 1935, 2, 11-12.
3. Guilds' Committee for Federal Writers Publications. *The Italians of New York*. New York: Random House, 1938.
4. Homans, G. C. *The human group*. New York: Harcourt, Brace, 1950.
5. Joffe, N. F. The dynamics of benefice among East European Jews. *Social Forces*, 1948-49, 27, 239-247.
6. Mandelbaum, D. G. *Change and continuity in Jewish life*. Glencoe, Ill.: Oscar Hillel Plotkin Library, 1955.
7. Mangione, J. *Mount Allegro*. New York: Houghton Mifflin, 1942.
8. Mangione, J. *Reunion in Sicily*. New York: Houghton Mifflin, 1950.
9. Mariano, J. H. *The second generation of Italians in New York City*. New York: Christopher, 1921.
10. Pellegrini, A. *Immigrant's Return*. New York: Macmillan, 1951.
11. Radin, P. *The Italians of San Francisco: their adjustment and acculturation*, Monographs 1 and 2, S.E.R.A. Project, Cultural Anthropology, San Francisco, 1935.
12. Sangree, W. and Hybleum, M. A study of the people of Middletown of Sicilian extraction with special emphasis on the changes in their values resulting from assimilation into the Middletown community. Unpublished Master's thesis, Wesleyan Univer., 1952.
13. Sartorio, E. C. *Social and religious life of Italians in America*. New York: Christopher, 1918.
14. Snyder, C. R. Culture and sobriety. *Quart. J. Studies on Alcohol*, 1955, 16, 101-177, 263-289, 504-532; 1956, 17, 124-143.
15. Zborowski, M. Cultural components in responses to pain. *J. Social Issues*, 1952, 8, 16-30.
16. Zborowski, M. and Herzog, E. *Life is with people*. New York: International Univer. Press, 1952.

3

The Jewish Community: Institutions,
Social Patterns, Status Structure,
and Levels of Integration

INTRODUCTION

IT has become common in the United States to refer to the Jews as a *religious* group. Thus we employ such expressions as: "Protestant, Catholic, Jew." Yet students of the problem are aware of the fact that the Jews constitute much more than what is conventionally designated as a "religious" group. It is because of this fact that our section on community is placed before the series of articles on religion.

The papers in the present section make use of the concept of "Jewish community." The use of this term is fraught with a number of problems. The most important such problem is that—as regards the United States—by the most generous standards we can properly speak only of a Jewish *sub*community. And because affiliation with the subcommunity is not legally enjoined, because present-day American Jews do not have very high visibility as Jews, because people constantly leave (as well as enter) the group, it is not always simple to decide what are the criteria for affiliation. The most generally accepted yardstick is the individual's own definition of himself. In marginal cases importance must be attached to the definition of the larger community.

The fascinating problems which surround ambiguities in identification should not serve to detract attention from our central concern—that of analyzing what Jews do *as* a community, the various strata which compose the community, the changing patterns of affiliation and activity. The article by Herman D. Stein is an analysis of some of the main lines of activity which Jews have traditionally engaged in as an organized group. True, the author does not present material on the proportion of members of the Jewish community who participate in the services either as contributors to the "drives," or as recipients of the services, or as volunteer workers and board members. Studies on the extent of identification and participation are yet to be conducted. But the author succeeds very well in conveying the scope of Jewish social work, and in analyzing how the services have been changing in recent decades. The network of services, as presented in the Stein article, is one of the most elaborate maintained by any ethnic or religious group in the American community.

Two sections contained in Stein's contribution, "Overseas Aid" and "Refugees," merit special attention. American Jews are part of a larger group; insofar as a relationship with Jews in other countries is well-internalized, overseas developments exert an influence on what the American Jewish group does as a community. Realization of this fact serves as a corrective to the parochial approach which would neglect proper evaluation of the bonds between Jews in the United States and Jews in other lands.

As Stein stresses at the beginning of the article, his analysis is confined only to what is conventionally subsumed under the rubric "social work." Many organized groups in the Jewish community exist for other purposes. There are mutual benefit societies; organizations devoted to religious, educational and cultural pursuits; Zionist and pro-Zionist agencies; and community relations organizations. We should also bear in mind that the activities analyzed by Stein are those typically encountered in the well-established Jewish community of the central city. What is encountered in the suburb?

When a new movement toward the margins of the city started after World War II, Jews responded in vast numbers. Of course, their social mobility was the most important factor which powered this migration. The fact that they had been traditionally renters rather than home owners served on the one hand to slow the movement somewhat, but on the other hand to hasten it inasmuch as they were not tied to their old neighborhoods. Certain other cross-pressures would have to be examined in any full-scale analysis of the ecology of the present-day Jewish community. Our chief interest here is rather in the fact that in recent years large numbers of Jews have moved into new neighborhoods and suburbs. In each such place there was the problem: "Should a Jewish community be organized, and, if so, what institutional structures should have the greatest priority?" The first part of this question has been answered, on the whole, affirmatively. However, the type of community organized is generally characterized by a number of rather distinctive features, including the fact that at least in the initial stages of community organization the traditional social-work services and the older forms of Jewish endeavor are not strongly emphasized.

Herbert J. Gans' careful analysis of the origin and growth of a suburban Jewish community is a highly significant piece of work. The author combines a knowledge of suburbia generally with a keen comprehension of matters specifically Jewish. He properly stresses the desire of most Jews to continue their identification as Jews when they reach the suburb, and he points out that they desire to do so in a rather special way. He places emphasis on the fact that the socialization of the child as a member of the Jewish community becomes a predominant concern. The emergence of religion as a symbol of Jewishness, and the malleability of religious institutions, is also underlined. The extensive material on the various economic, social, and "brow" levels to be found in a homogeneous-appearing community serves to alert us to the many internal variations found within the Jewish group. Finally, Gans' presentation of minority-majority relations, and especially of the influence of the non-Jew on the formation and character of the emerging Jewish community, is exceedingly helpful. Chronically, the evaluation of the impact of this particular factor has varied greatly, being highly dependent upon the ideological orientation of the researcher.

One final word about the Gans article. Park Forest, Illinois, is hardly a typical Jewish suburban area. The predominant movement in Chicago, for example, appears to be not toward the southwest, the section where Park Forest is located, but rather to the north and northwest. If any one suburb in the area can be said to be typical, it is in all probability Skokie, Illinois. Here, the more traditional element is relatively stronger; the academicians, researchers, scientists, and writers of the type found in Park Forest exert less influence. The population of certain areas in this suburb is 80 per cent Jewish or more. Basically, however, the same forces are at work in both Park Forest and Skokie—the information included here is intended only to place the Gans article in proper perspective. As the author himself emphasizes in his concluding remarks, the research constitutes a clue to the coming major stage in Jewish adjustment to American society—that of a *second-third* generation community rather than a *first-second* generation community.

At several points Gans alludes to the importance, in the early stage of communal organization, of what he terms "Jewish professionals, men who work for American-Jewish agencies." In the article by Stein the professionalization of Jewish social work is a recurring theme. The paper by Solomon Sutker, on what he designates as the "organizational elite," is centrally concerned with this important area. While it is apparent that a definitive assessment of the overall role of the professional remains to be done, Sutker's analysis of the situation in one middle-sized Jewish community suggests some of the lines which require careful study in communities of various sizes, located in a number of different geographical areas.

The inference of the papers by Sutker and Stein is that philanthropy plays an exceedingly important role in the Jewish community. While this is a fact, it can easily serve to detract attention from one of the points made by Gans— that in a sense the formal structure of the Jewish community rests upon a base of *informal* and noninstitutionalized associational patterns. It is understandable that the importance of this factor became particularly noticeable when a community-in-the-making was under study. In more established places these sociability patterns tend to find some institutional expression, and because institutions and organizations have greater visibility than patterns of association, the emphasis tends to shift in the direction of describing the former. Sutker's article on social clubs—organizations which exist in community after community, though their purposes are not "complicated," as it were, by being connected with philanthropic, ideological, or religious agencies and motivations—serves as a needed corrective. The club pattern is seen in its most highly developed form in Atlanta —in this community, club membership is a rather common phenomenon in the middle and upper classes generally. Sutker portrays the activities of the Jewish clubs in detail. Such activities are a good indication of the high degree of acculturation of the members. Sutker's treatment is suggestive both in the presentation of some of the internal stratification existing in the Jewish community as well as in the estimation of the influence which the clubs (or rather the sociability patterns) exert upon the central institutional structure of the Jewish community. The emphasis of his presentation is upon the Jewish clubs as a resultant of discrimination and the consequent lack of opportunity to build social relationships with non-Jews, rather than as resultant of preference or of attitudes toward Jewish survivalism. Of course this view is essentially a hypothesis—though a highly credible hypothesis to be sure. It is one which is especially difficult to test under present conditions.

The influence of the Jewish upper class in the Jewish community, and the interaction of East- and West-European-derived Jews, has been noted in a number of articles. The contribution of E. Digby Baltzell is centrally concerned with these questions. Baltzell's thorough knowledge of the upper class and elite of Philadelphia help to place the Jewish developments in proper perspective, and his use of historical data (combined with an ecological approach) serves as an example of how the sociologist may properly utilize such materials. Baltzell appraises the importance and ramified consequences of philanthropy as an activity of the Jewish upper class. Some details about the role of the so-called "social discrimination" factor are presented. While Baltzell does not present the kinds of details about the Jewish clubs of Philadelphia which are included by Sutker for the Atlanta clubs, valuable material is suggested on the role which city and country clubs play in the stratification system. Baltzell briefly alludes to the significant example of an upper-class club which—though sponsored by Jews—aimed to appeal to Christians as well.

As we noted at the beginning of this introduction, Jews constitute a *sub-community*. John P. Dean's article serves the important purpose of stressing this fact, and of providing some details about the interaction between the Jewish community and the general community in middle-sized cities. His article blends survey material gathered from a large number of such cities with intensive data gathered in one community. The Dean article has the merit of subdividing the subject into manageable areas: participation in economic life, in political life, in social-service activities, in voluntary associations, in social cliques. His analysis also seeks to give due weight to the interacting factors of the exclusionary attitudes of the majority and the segregative and survivalistic attitudes of the minority. The concomitants of what the author calls "social insulation" are spelled out in some detail. His finding that communities which score *low* on social acceptability of Jews score *high* on Jewish participation in community affairs, has occasioned a good deal of comment. Some have drawn a hasty conclusion from this, namely, that participation is likely to have an adverse effect on the relationship of Jew to Gentile. Such conclusions, which are not in keeping with those of other investigators, should be regarded as highly tentative. As the author indicates, acceptability is also correlated with size of community; perhaps holding community size constant would modify the finding on the relationship of social acceptability and Jewish participation.

The article by Greenblum and Sklare bears some similarity to the Dean contribution in terms of the range of problems examined and the size of the communities used. It has been placed before the Dean material, however, because the focus is on the *"insider"* looking both "inside" and "outside" rather than the picture as seen from both the stance of the majority and the minority. Also, the article by Greenblum and Sklare has the rather special emphasis of seeking to discover sources of *disaffection* with the community.

HERMAN D. STEIN

JEWISH SOCIAL WORK IN THE UNITED STATES:
1920-1955

THE social work functions that have grown in the American Jewish community have been affected by general social work trends in the country as well as by internal developments in Jewish life. Such functions have become institutionalized along with the religious, the educational, and, most recently, the protective or "community relations" functions. While not all of Jewish social work has become highly institutionalized—there remain many small informal charities unrelated to larger social work developments—this paper will be confined largely to a consideration of those areas of Jewish social work which are so distinguished.

The years between 1920 and 1955 saw epic changes in American and Jewish life. Like all other Americans, Jews participated in and were strongly affected by the events of depression, wars, and postwar political and economic developments. The destruction of six million Jews by the Nazis produced a powerful effect on American Jewry, pervading all of their thinking and actions as a group. The memory of the recent European Jewish catastrophe impelled domestic Jewish agencies to work for objectives of Jewish group survival at home; it also evoked the widespread support of American Jews for the new State of Israel, which arose out of the ashes of World War II. The needs of refugees from Europe led to an expansion of overseas effort, and to the creation of special services for those refugees who entered the United States.

By the middle of the twentieth century, two-thirds of the five million Jews of the United States, constituting 3 per cent of the general population, were native-born. The need for special "Americanization" programs had greatly lessened; recent arrivals were being aided to adjust to American life by a whole complex of agencies serving the entire Jewish community—family counselling, vocational service, medical service organizations, community centers, as well as synagogues and temples and mutual benefit societies.

American Jews have moved up the economic ladder along with most Americans, and as a group have achieved a middle-income position. This has made it possible for American Jewry to support a variety of social

This paper is excerpted from Prof. Stein's article, "Jewish Social Work in the United States (1654-1954)," which appeared in the *American Jewish Year Book*, Vol. 57 (1956), pp. 3-98, by permission of the author and the publisher. (Copyright, 1956, by The American Jewish Committee and The Jewish Publication Society of America.) The excerpt is somewhat condensed; minor alterations have been made in a number of places.

services designed to serve Jewish communities, as well as to support non-Jewish health and welfare activities. Since World War II, as in many of the groups whose income position has changed, there has been a steady trend among Jews to move to the suburbs. This movement necessitates an examination of changing needs for service in new areas, the relocation of existing resources, and study of changing patterns of family living.

Another postwar phenomenon has been a tendency for the "return of the third generation" to its traditional cultural roots. This has been particularly noted among the younger members of the Italian and Jewish groups in the United States. In the Jewish community, this was reflected in the rising interest among American youth in Jewish education, in Israel, in Jewish cultural values, in books related to Jewish life. Whether or not we are now witnessing a true religious revival is open to question;[1] but membership in religious institutions has increased among American Jews, as it has among other religious groups in the United States. The trend toward the introduction of more vital Jewish content in Jewish institutions, particularly community centers, is in line with this new preoccupation with traditional values.

Conflicts and social distance among Sephardic, German, and East European Jews have become for the most part a thing of the past. Social services, in composition of their administration and clientele, reflect the disappearance of this source of divisiveness in Jewish life. Differences in ideologies and in commitments to religious observance remain, but support of the social services cuts across ideologies and religious identification. Jewish social work has become a centripetal, cohesive force in Jewish life.

§ Social Work Trends

The 1920's found Jewish social work in the United States basking in the glow of a decade of unparalleled growth and optimism. New "federations" for the purpose of centralized fund-raising and planning were emerging and existing ones were being strengthened. The community center movement was expanding and striking firm roots, making large capital outlays for building and equipment. Family welfare agencies, child care agencies, and hospitals all consolidated their financial position and invested in a greater refinement of services.

Professionalism had come to stay. In increasing numbers, social workers were entering the salaried class, many after having received a full two years of training in one of the graduate schools of social work. In 1919 there were fifteen such graduate schools, most of them attached to universities; by 1925 a full-fledged graduate school of Jewish social work was established in New York City. Trained social workers were given ever greater responsibility in administering and carrying out agency services. The prestige and authority of professional executives grew, the province of the lay administration shrinking commensurately.

The larger Jewish, as well as the nonsectarian, benevolent societies, no longer regarded themselves as, or called themselves, "charities." They became "family welfare societies," "social service associations," and "social service bureaus." The post-World War I development of psychiatry in social work, and the vision of social case work as a helping process, opened up new horizons for service. Family agencies (as they came to be known) still served the poorer elements in the community, but the way of helping was changing. More attention was paid to psychological and emotional problems "troubling" the "client," and to seeing how the family as a whole could be strengthened through help. Relief remained a major function, but administered more sensitively than before. Family agencies co-operated with employment and medical services, and tried to develop in the assisted individual greater self-awareness and capacity to handle his own problems.

The changing character of social need among Jews furthered this consolidation of services and gradual shift of function. In the garment industry, for example, where Jewish workers were concentrated, the growth of labor unions helped stabilize the industry. Garment workers no longer penniless between seasons, did not have to apply to philan-thropic agencies for relief in large numbers (unemployment insurance laws were not enacted in the United States until 1932).

Relief needs of new immigrants no longer were pressing, due to restrictive immigration legislation. Immigration from Eastern Europe, which had been dwindling since the beginning of World War I, became a mere trickle after the National Origins Quota Act of 1924, which brought Italian and East European Jewish immigration virtually to a halt.

The high-principled objectives of individuals who had headed social agencies during the previous period were incorporated more and more into the ongoing staff work of the agencies, giving these agencies new status. Executives such as Frances Taussig in New York City, Jacob Kepecs, Maurice J. Karpf and Harry Lurie in Chicago, Dorothy Kahn in Baltimore, John Slawson in Detroit and New York City, were able to infuse their organizations with professional methods and objectives. They worked with board members in developing policies which could take account of the fresh viewpoints and the newer knowledge and skills which social workers were bringing to their work.

In the decade between 1920 and 1930 social case work specialties proliferated from the new profession of social work, each specialty form-ing a national association. Psychiatric social work—in child guidance clinics, in school systems, in hospitals and clinics for the mentally ill—flourished, aided by foundations. Medical social work in hospitals, clinics, and work with the handicapped, spurted forward. Social group work began to emerge, along with community organization, as a basic process in social work. Jewish recreational workers formed their own national professional association; they were also active in general group work organizations. Jewish community organization was largely restricted to federation activity; but here, too, professionally trained social workers were increasingly in evidence.

With the new tools of psychological testing and interviewing, vocational guidance was rapidly becoming professionalized. Social workers who specialized in providing Jewish youth with individual educational and vocational guidance and job placement services established their own professional associations; communities organized new services to concentrate on this important work.

§ *Effects of the Depression*

The great depression that profoundly affected American life also revolutionized the character of social work in the United States.

Until the depression of the 1930's social work had given little attention to unemployment as such. Its leading agencies and spokesmen, however, were quick to realize the social implications of unemployment as the depression deepened and the number of the unemployed began to mount. Social workers encouraged the rapid development of public services, many of them helping to develop policy and administrative procedures in local, state, and Federal programs. At the 1931 meeting of the National Conference of Social Work Linton B. Swift took issue with President Herbert Hoover's statement that "the American method of assisting the unemployed is through private charity." It was clear to social workers who saw the faces and the numbers of relief applicants that the private agencies could not begin to cope with the vast needs of the unemployed.

Many prominent Jewish social workers forcefully spoke up to urge the Federal government to get into the "business of relief" and to develop a national social security program. . . . Before long public welfare departments in many states and local communities took over distribution of public assistance to the unemployed. In many cities where there were no public welfare departments, public funds were provided to the voluntary social agencies in order to assist relief applicants. Without the assistance of the public agencies, Jewish organizations could have barely succeeded in meeting the minimal needs for material relief.

Even with such assistance from public funds, the private family welfare agencies suffered severely from the depression. Standards of practice, developed in an atmosphere of "unprecedented freedom," had been sharply lowered by the fall of 1929. It was not easy to practice intensive and painstaking social case work when people were pounding at the door with stark emergency needs. Family agencies were hard put to cope with the problem of how far to individualize and how deeply to explore psychological problems at a time when case loads for social workers were rapidly growing. In addition, the demands for immediate relief were such that many untrained persons had to be engaged to act as social workers; as a consequence in many agencies staff morale was depressed.[2]

Child care agencies had to suspend new projects. Their income reduced, they were unable to raise salaries, and in some cases even had to cut salaries. But they still tried not to lower their standards of child care substantially. Community centers lost members by the hundreds, particularly among the unemployed, though most of the centers permitted the unemployed to register with no, or a mere token, payment. Community support declined severely, while pressure for service continued high. . . . The centers tried to provide whatever services they could day and evening, concentrating on less formal activities. Despite their lack of reserves and the burden of heavy mortgages, the community centers survived, having established themselves with sufficient roots and vitality in the communal structure. The National Jewish Welfare Board took leadership both in raising funds to meet the budgetary needs of local centers and in working out budgetary policies to allow for economies without sacrificing basic services.

One of the consequences of the depression was the loss of prestige suffered by some of the philanthropists who were leaders in Jewish welfare work. They had previously been respected, even by their critics, as motivated solely by humanitarian impulses; now they were attacked by some as autocratic "plutocrats" standing in the way of social work progress. A side effect of this depreciation of veteran leadership was the broadening of the base of philanthropic lay boards, through the inclusion of more representatives from the East European immigrant group.

The depression led many social workers to take greater interest in, and to identify themselves with, the expanding trade union movement, and with New Deal aspirations in general. This was also a period when thousands of college students and intellectuals flocked to various radical ideologies, and such ideologies were heavily represented in Jewish social work. In the larger cities, many social workers joined unions, and Jewish agencies were among the first social work agencies to be unionized. Better salaries, job security, and improved working conditions were motivating forces in unionization; another factor was undoubtedly sympathy among social workers for the nascent trade union movement in the United States as a whole.

To some Jewish social work executives one of the constructive developments arising from the depression experience was the necessity for close cooperation with nonsectarian as well as with public agencies. There was a generally heightened sense of the interdependence of social agencies, particularly in planning through such coordinating groups as community chests and community councils, and through major professional associations. Others viewed this trend with alarm, regarding it as decreasing the sense of Jewish identity among the case work agencies. Critics also felt that increased participation in community chests might lower the standards of Jewish agencies, because of the presumed need to strike a least common denominator with non-Jewish agencies. This fear has waned over the years.

One far-reaching change was undeniable. There was a traditional antipathy among Jews to accepting assistance from non-Jewish sources; the depression forced a change, if not in the attitude toward such assistance, certainly in the practice of acceptance. Early in the depression one Jewish social worker reported that "perhaps the most important lesson coming out of this emergency is the fact that an unwilling Jewish community has come to realize that relief work can, under proper safeguards, be financed by public funds without detriment to the Jewish families thus served."[3] Furthermore, Jewish leaders in social work, both lay and professional, worked diligently with their colleagues in the non-Jewish field to lead the government to assume responsibility for basic economic assistance.

§ *The Family Agency*

The family agency emerged from the depression with the awareness that relief was a public function. Except in very special cases, families or individuals requiring long-term financial assistance were now referred to public agencies. The emphasis was increasingly preventive; in order to forestall individual and family breakdown, case work or counselling service was provided in such problem areas as parent-child relations, marital difficulty, and nonpathological emotional distress. The family agencies gained confidence during the depression in their ability to be helpful to people other than the poor. World War II experience with families having war-related problems heightened this confidence, leading family agencies to widen their area of service to take in the whole Jewish community, including counselling for the "middle income family" that might not normally apply to a social agency for help. This expansion led, in turn, to the decision to set fees for case work or counselling service, so that middle-income groups need not feel that they were applying to a "charitable agency." Family agencies hoped to persuade these groups to look upon such service as professional help similar to that received from doctors and lawyers. The first experiment by a family agency in the systematic use of fees was made by the Jewish Family Service in New York (then the Jewish Social Service Association) in 1943, when it established its Consultation Center exclusively for paying clients. The success of this venture led to the gradual (and as yet incomplete) incorporation of fee scales into the family service field over the United States, particularly in the larger urban centers. Although the budgetary contribution of fees have occasionally been cited as a reason for their use by family agencies, at no point have fees even approximated the cost of service. The basic rationale for the use of fees has been its value as a way of introducing middle- and higher-income groups to case work service. . . .

The most important long-range question which fee-charging has raised, to which no definitive and universally acceptable answer has yet been found, has been the justification for philanthropic spending to aid middle- and upper-income families. The operating premise is that philanthropic giving by the Jewish community is still warranted because the service that is set up is available to all; that in this respect fee-charging resembles the contribution by a donor to a hospital fund, where the donor himself may be the recipient of the services the hospital affords. Nevertheless, case work for those who are economically self-sufficient, if not well-to-do, is a far cry from the traditional injunction to help the poor, and it has given pause to many lay and professional social work leaders. In effect, a changing concept of need is involved. The question of whether poor families or individuals may have to wait for service because of pressure to serve middle-income families coming for help has also been raised, but thus far there seems to be no clear-cut evidence that middle-class clients have been receiving preferential service. Jewish family agencies have been increasingly pressed for service by people from all walks of life, and waiting lists are common. There has been a recent development of group counselling, partly in response to this pressure.

Since World War II a number of the larger family agencies have become more and more active in programs of "family life education." Jewish agencies in Cleveland and New York have taken the lead. While in their early stages family life education programs took the form of lectures and parent education meetings, they have become more refined and have evolved into continuous discussion groups under the leadership of specially trained personnel. Such groups are designed to permit people to consider their current everyday problems cooperatively in order to prevent family breakdown and to minimize unrealistic anxieties through group reassurance. Subjects frequently discussed are marriage, in-laws, husband-wife relationships, and child behavior problems.

The basic purpose of the Jewish family agency has continued to be, on the one hand, to maintain the well-being and strength of the family, and, on the other hand, to prevent individual and family breakdown. Tensions arising out of marital conflict, or difficulties in parent-child relationships, or other aspects of individual adjustment, are among the problems with which the family agency can help. Jewish agencies have been in the forefront in developing case work and counselling techniques in this area. In addition, many family agencies provide a variety of more concrete services to the family. These include homemaker service, relief in certain cases, boarding care for the aged, psychological testing, and services to prisoners and paroleees.

Nevertheless, since the 1930's, the place of the Jewish family agency in "Jewish" social work has been sharply questioned. First of the agencies to professionalize by adopting the social case work process, the family agency has also been the first to become secularized. Hence, it has been subject to recurrent criticism as not being sufficiently Jewish to warrant a prominent place in Jewish social work; it has been maintained that support from Jewish funds could be justified only if the Jewish family agency concentrated on Jewish aspects of family life, and was related to Jewish religious and secular organizations. . . .[4]

However, exploratory efforts to make the family agencies more "Jewish" have been relatively ineffective. Exactly what the case work agencies should do other than what they have been doing has never been clarified to the agencies' satisfaction. To some extent, the attacks on the family agency's "non-Jewishness" represent an effort to engage all social services under Jewish auspices in furthering the aim of Jewish survival. However, it would be contrary to the major premises of professional practice for an agency to introduce any ideology into its actual rendering of service; critics have generally not gone so far as directly to propose it. The method of social case work, as distinct from its auspices or clientele, can no more be Jewish than the practice of medicine can. Besides, the very existence of the Jewish agency itself may be more relevant to Jewish group survival and group identity than "Jewishness" in the practice of social case work.[5]

The experience of the Jewish family agency in Springfield, Mass., is illuminating. In 1952 concern about "the place" of this agency in the Jewish community led to a study on attitudes towards it. As many Jews were applying to the nonsectarian family agency as to the Jewish family agency, and both agencies had high standards. The survey revealed no objective need for a family agency that could not be met by the nonsectarian agency; yet representative individuals in the Jewish community were reluctant to give up the Jewish agency. "In effect, the Survey Committee concluded that the intangible considerations of feeling and attitude which surround the existence of a Jewish social agency are still the decisive ones."[6]

It would appear that the Jewish social agency, however secular, remains a potent symbol of Jewish communal identity. The Jewish social agency's contributors, board members, social workers, and volunteers—whatever their own personal ideological leanings—are, by virtue of their activity, all engaged in furthering Jewish group identity and survival.

§ *The Aged*

In the United States, as in most Western countries, there has been a steady increase in the proportion of persons in the older age groups of the population. . . . Early attempts to deal with dependency in old age consisted of placing the aged poor in poor houses. These were barren institutions, generally pitifully inadequate in providing even the simple necessities. Religious, fraternal, and other organizations gradually provided more decent homes for the aged, but these could hardly meet the demand.

Industrialization during the nineteenth century was accompanied by a radical shift of population from farm areas to cities, contributing to a rapid increase in old age dependency. Older persons had fewer opportunities for work. In addition, a combination of factors encouraged married children to live apart from their parents, particularly among the urban middle classes.

Families were less able to care for the major needs of their members—in education, health, physical protection, recreation; parental control over choice of their children's spouses was weakened. Americans left their old homesteads in response to new economic opportunities; status was determined by economic and occupational position acquired through the individual's own efforts, rather than traditional family reputation. Concomitantly, the capacity to produce became a symbol of worth. As a consequence, the position of the urban aged became precarious, psychologically and emotionally as well as economically, with the withering of the prestige of old age. . . .

From the first, Jewish communities had no difficulty in accepting care for the aged as a traditional communal responsibility. Along with other sectarian groups, they established old age homes, maintained for the most part in a religious atmosphere. Like other groups, too, they found that the demand for such resources far exceeded available facilities. As an urban group Jews were particularly confronted with old age problems. While there was a strong tradition of family solidarity, and children felt a sense of obligation for the care of their parents, elderly Jews of East European background were culturally unprepared to be supported by their children. In addition, conflicts in values between first-generation parents and second-generation children created tensions which often led the aged to enter old age institutions as a place of last resort.

On the whole there were few social workers in these institutions until the 1940's. Partly this was due to the fact that old age homes did not tend to employ social workers, and, when they did, paid low salaries. It was also probably due to the feeling among social workers that they could make their best professional contribution (learn more, and advance farther) through working with youth and families; working with the aged seemed to offer no such prospects.

These conditions have sharply altered. Increasingly, homes for the aged have sought the help of professional social workers. And, as social workers learned more about the opportunities for helping in working with the aged, they sought employment in such programs.

Family agencies were reluctant to work with the aged until the 1940's, thinking primarily in terms of institutional placement, and tacitly assuming that "growth" ceases in the later years. During the last decade, however, Jewish agencies have helped lead the way to more creative and purposive interest in the aged.[7] Family agencies have begun to concentrate on providing special services for the aged, some services directly, others in cooperation with other agencies and institutions. By 1954, one client in every four in the Jewish family agencies was an aged person. Many agencies are offering direct counselling service by specially assigned experienced workers. The larger family agencies have also been concerned with living arrangements, and have assisted in the provision of boarding and nursing-home care and homemaker service, usually in conjunction with homes for the aged.

Jewish community centers have participated in many of these develop-ments, establishing "Golden Age" clubs and other types of community cen-ters. Jewish homes for the aged have expanded physically; they have also extended their services to aged people residing in their own homes. The emphasis has been on providing a variety of services to enable the aged to remain in their communities, where they can retain the satisfactions of nor-mal home and community life.[8] The concept of the old age home has changed from that of a permanent retreat to that of a resource to be used as needed, in time of incapacity, for longer or shorter periods. "The institu-tion for the aged is now viewed as a semi-hospital for the chronically ill and as a rehabilitation center, closely correlating case work, group work, psychiatric and other services."[9] The average age of persons admitted to facilities for the aged is therefore rising,[10] although many homes accept persons under age sixty-five if they are chronically sick and in need of cus-todial care. . . . Payments for service have more and more derived from public funds, current estimates being that 40 to 50 per cent of payments for services are derived from funds paid to residents of the homes.[11] Payments for service on the average account for 65 per cent of the operating receipts of homes for the aged. In addition, in some instances public funds are paid directly to institutions for special kinds of care. This situation has raised the question of how the voluntary, sectarian home for the aged is affected by such relationships to public sources of funds.

Another question is the effect of high-standard homes for the aged under philanthropic auspices on private nursing home facilities run for profit. This has not yet become a burning issue. But as both kinds of facilities grow, demand for old age resident care may lessen, and the question of competi-tion between private and public Jewish facilities may become more acute.

§ *Child Care*

Since the late 1930's there has been a trend for the populations of Jewish orphanages and other institutions for neglected children to decline, and for a diminution in foster home care. This has been due primarily to public assistance programs which permit widowed mothers to keep their children at home, and to the improvement in economic conditions. The emphasis throughout the child-care field has been on maintaining children in their own homes as long as possible. At the same time, there has been a tendency for child-care and family-agency services to merge. In 1955, of fifty-seven re-sources under Jewish auspices offering protective and foster care for children reporting to the Council of Jewish Federations and Welfare Funds, thirty-four were child-care departments within multiple-function family agencies and twenty-three were specialized child-care agencies.

There has also been a gradual decline in the average length of time dur-ing which children remain under agency care, attributable to greater recog-nition of individual needs of children, the development of specialized treatment programs, and the increased knowledge and skill of social workers. The result has been more effective service to children and their families and the placement of children in institutions or in foster homes only where such placement was needed. At the same time, Jewish agencies have been in the forefront of experimental programs for the treatment of children with special needs, particularly those emotionally disturbed. Residential treatment centers, specialized foster homes and group homes have all been established. . . .

A considerable proportion of the funds of child care agencies specializing in institutional and foster-home care come from public sources. Thus in 1954 an average of 25 per cent of the operating income of sixteen child-care agencies reporting to the Council of Jewish Federations and Welfare Funds came from public funds, with some agencies receiving over 50 per cent of their income from such sources. This was due essentially to the fact that municipalities were turning over to voluntary agencies certain types of care for children who normally would be eligible for public support. The government has been contributing an even higher proportion of the budgets of child care agencies of non-Jewish sectarian groups. The effects of this collaboration on the voluntary agencies, whether this might not constitute a problem in church-state relations, whether public auspices ought not directly to administer certain of these services, are becoming more and more important questions.

In 1930 the Jewish community of Cleveland transferred the responsibility of serving Jewish children eligible for foster home care to the newly formed public foster home agency. "The Cleveland Jewish community apparently accepted without question public services for Jewish children in foster home placements."[12] Few other communities have gone this far, and there is little doubt that none would be prepared to turn over institutional care to public agencies.

Jewish adoption agencies have been abreast, and sometimes in the forefront of, developments in the adoption field tending to improve practice and standards, particularly in making hitherto "unadoptable" children available for adoption. Even more than non-Jewish adoption agencies, Jewish agencies have had to meet a demand for adoptive children that far exceeds the supply. The result of this situation has been a "black market" in adoption that circumvents legal and social agency safeguards. In recent years, there has been both an increased public understanding of adoption service and more flexibility and self-study on the part of the agencies themselves.

§ *Vocational Services*

During the years of mass immigration, employment service became one of the functions of the large charities. . . . The 1920's brought specialization to this field, with psychological testing, vocational counselling, guidance for youth in the school systems, and professional training of workers. While Jewish family agencies continued to maintain vocational services for their clients, some as late as the 1930's and 1940's, distinct agencies in Jewish communities throughout the United States that were under federation auspices offered guidance, counselling, and placement.

Jewish vocational services were active in the 1920's and 1930's in guiding Jewish youth to those occupations where vocational opportunities existed for Jews, as well as those where the client's own aptitudes and interests could be employed. The services labored to break down barriers where discrimination existed. During the depression, they attempted to find jobs, worked closely with case-work and group-work agencies to meet the individual needs of persons referred for special psychological or medical reasons, and cooperated with public employment agencies. The agencies aided many thousands of refugees by finding jobs for them, or helping them support themselves through loans and business advice. To the immigrants arriving after World War II, the agencies have given intensive counselling.

When jobs became more plentiful, during and after World War II, the Jewish vocational services were able to try to meet the needs of men and women whose occupational opportunities were limited by medical or other problems. The vocational agencies entered the area of rehabilitation, where many have pioneered for years.

Workers in need of economic rehabilitation have been helped through sheltered workshops, protected work trials with sympathetic employers, and special services to individuals suffering from cardiac disorders, blindness, tuberculosis, or mental retardation. For more than a decade, agencies have offered special counselling, placement, and training programs for the aged. A number of agencies have established departments to handle hard-to-place individuals, such as prison parolees and "unemployable" individuals receiving public assistance. The vocational agencies have also begun to cooperate directly with institutions such as old-age homes and hospitals, as well as continuing their traditional cooperative activity with case work and group work centers. . . .

In an effort to serve the entire Jewish community, vocational services, like case work and group work agencies, have gradually been accepting clients able to afford fees.

The desirability of the Jewish agency's remaining in the field of placement, particularly at a time when public employment agencies can give appropriate placement service, has been questioned. There has, however, been no marked inclination as yet on the part of federations, or Jewish community groups generally, strongly to question the appropriateness of this kind of agency in the area of Jewish social work.

§   *Group Work and the Jewish Community Center*

During the 1930's four processes emerged in the American conception of social work as the basic methods by which social workers performed their functions, namely, social case work, social action, community organization, and social group work. Social group work was not defined easily; but by the 1930's it had become accepted as a legitimate process, referring to the development and adjustment of an individual through voluntary group association and the use of this association under professional guidance, as a means of furthering democratic values and other desirable social ends.

Interest in the methodology of social group work was widespread among Jewish social workers in such recreational and cultural settings as settlement houses, community centers, and summer camps—all of these coming under the general rubric of "group work agencies." Jewish community centers agreed on the values of the group work process as a method of leading its participants toward more democratic and socially adaptive behavior; they differed, however, on the extent of the emphasis on the clear-cut ideological objective of greater adherence to "Jewish values," and on the extent to which programs should center around this objective. Centers varied greatly in their incorporation of Jewish content in their programs. Many group workers felt that a strictly sectarian emphasis was antithetical to the underlying non-sectarian and humanistic values of social work which encouraged the individual to reach out from his own group to others, especially for purposes of social action. The radically uneven expressions of commitment to Judaism in the programs of community centers persisted for many years and was one of the influences that led to the survey of the Jewish Welfare Board and the community centers conducted by Dr. Oscar I. Janowsky in the early 1940's.[13]

The National Jewish Welfare Board (JWB) had been organized in 1917, later incorporating the federated YM and YWHA's; it promptly took the leadership in rallying the YMHA's and YWHA's to the war effort, coordinating all existing Jewish services in the Jewish recreational and adult educational field. As a representative of the Jewish community, the JWB was one of the six national American organizations participating in the morale program of the government during World War I, a precursor to its role in the United Service Organizations (USO) in World War II.

World War I led to the development of community branches of the JWB. These branches in turn became the beginnings of the community center movement, together with the existing YMHA's and YWHA's. From the beginning, the community centers were officially dedicated to the preservation of Jewish cultural values and group survival, and were influenced considerably by the philosophy of Mordecai Kaplan. The movement has been characterized by a close relationship to Jewish education (many centers housing daily or Sabbath instruction), as well as by a variety of recreational, educational, and cultural activities. The Jewish community center, however, differed from the synagogue center, or "institutional synagogue," which was frankly "religious" in its function.[14]

Through the 1920's and 1930's a body of trained center workers gradually came into being; a professional association was formed; and centers came to occupy a definite place in local communities.

During and after World War II and the Korean war, the JWB, through its national offices and affiliated centers, rendered outstanding service. It participated actively in every phase of the USO program, servicing the Jewish chaplain as well as the Jewish serviceman, and operating a large program in the United States and overseas. This program included religious service, social events, discussion and cultural groups, hospital visiting, and information service. The Jewish centers extended hospitality and introduced special programs for servicemen; they also worked with the young men of pre-draft age, whose problems were becoming widely recognized. By 1950, the JWB had 331 affiliated units among the community centers, YM & YWHA's, with approximately 502,000 members.

In 1947, many of the recommendations made as a result of the survey of the JWB were adopted. These focused on the center "as an agency of Jewish identification" and "as an agency of Jewish integration"—in short, one with a definite social ideology, rather than, for example, as an agency designed primarily to contribute group work services to the cause of individual and group betterment. Janowsky was in accord with the general philosophy of I. B. Berkson and Horace Kallen, who regarded the center as an expression of American democracy within which "cultural diversity" could flourish. The effect of the survey was to tighten organizational and program policies to underline clearly the *Jewish* character of the community center. With respect to "Jewish settlements," the Janowsky report had this to say:

> Jewish group work agencies, however denominated, must be Jewish or they have no reason for existence . . . a nonsectarian Jewish settlement or educational alliance is a contradiction in terms . . . nonsectarian agencies should be under nonsectarian direction, they should not be sponsored and financed exclusively or predominantly by the Jewish group.[15]

Whether or not influenced by this report, the national trend has been for Jewish "settlement houses" to be in fact reconstituted as Jewish community centers.

While the decisions taken as a result of the JWB survey settled many issues of policy, and made for more consistency in direction, they did not settle all problems. This was true particularly of professional commitments that might seem to conflict with stated community center values. Conferences, in-service training institutes, professional inter-association meetings as well as journals, are still working on a clarification of the issues. There is little question that the Jewish community center field has achieved greater clarity in its purpose, and that efforts to resolve inherent strains will continue.

In addition to working with many types of club and special interest groups, Jewish community centers have continued to offer a wide variety of activities: health and physical education, arts and crafts, dramatics, music, dance, forums, festival celebrations, and civic projects. Increasingly, centers have directed their activities to the entire Jewish community, seeking to include all social and economic levels and various ideological groups, as well as all age groups. Emphasis on service to the aged has led to closer relationships with old age homes and other community facilities in providing appropriate activity. Centers have reached out to offer advisory services to youth and adult groups through programs conducted in homes, schools, temples, and synagogues, and organized community-wide programs and councils. Also, community centers have co-operated closely with synagogue centers and Jewish education agencies. Jewish mobility has led to the extension of center programs to suburban areas, and to the purchase of large tracts on the outskirts of cities in preference to downtown city areas.[16]

§ *Camping*

Summer camping in the United States arose out of the conditions of city life, and the extension of the city school term. Urbanization was accompanied by a general breakdown in the traditional recreational and educational functions of the family. In rural areas the school term was originally limited to the three or four winter months, and supplemented the activity and education that children received from working with their parents and other adults on the home farm. In the city, the term was expanded to eight or nine months, leaving school children with virtually no experience in outdoor life, domestic science, or manual activities. Organizational camping in the Jewish field followed the general pattern in attempting to meet the health and recreational needs of impoverished and poorly nourished Jewish children through outdoor living. During the early period, many camps were attached to the general charities, as well as to Y's and settlement houses; today very few camps are attached to family agencies.

In the course of time the importance of camping in the general development of personality and in the enhancement of satisfaction and skills in group relationships became clearer. Its essentially educational character was perceived and many camps were organized or directed by educators. The influence of progressive education led to a stress on the potentialities in camping of "learning by doing." Group work centers, viewing camping as integral to the broad recreational and professional services they were offering, and consistent with group work skills and approach, characteristically began to operate summer camps themselves, many group workers developing specialized experience in camping.

The influence of psychiatry and the advances made in psychological knowledge during the 1920's added a new dimension to organizational camping; it came to be regarded as a potential contribution to the emotional well-being of children. New approaches to methods of helping the handicapped child gain maximum social adjustment led also to the forming of camps that specialized in programs for the handicapped.

By the 1930's, camps under philanthropic auspices had largely ceased to be primarily health-centered and had become institutions for enhancing general social adjustment. While Jewish, like non-Jewish, organizational camps served the poorer children throughout the depression, they became more and more available to middle-income groups with the rise of the Jewish economic position. Today, camps under the auspices of community centers and other social agencies characteristically charge fees —though the fees are modest in comparison with private camps. Poor Jewish children no longer have difficulty in securing at least a few weeks of summer camp. The problem has rather become one of justifying communally subsidized camps for children whose families might be able to afford to pay the higher fee of private camping. The general feeling is that such camps, like other Jewish social services, including the community centers themselves, should become increasingly available to the entire community, and that there is a value in not limiting such facilities to the lowest economic group. As in the case of the old age home *vs.* the private nursing home, however, there are possibilities that both institutional summer camps and the growing number of day camping facilities of community centers may come into competition with private facilities. . . .[17]

§ Health

During the period under review, the interest of Jewish communities in the development of health facilities steadily continued, while such facilities themselves became increasingly nonsectarian in service. In 1953 there were sixty-four hospitals under Jewish auspices in operation in the United States, and by that year all Jewish communities of over 30,000 population, except Washington, D.C., maintained hospitals. As of December 31, 1954, an average of 44 per cent of all patients admitted to such hospitals were Jewish, according to reports submitted to the Council of Jewish Federations and Welfare Funds.[18] The proportions varied widely from hospital to hospital, but general hospitals were almost uniformly nonsectarian in their admissions policy. In cities with the largest concentrations of Jewish population, Jewish hospitals naturally received the largest proportions of Jewish patients.

The financing of these hospitals is in marked contrast to other welfare services of Jewish communities. For all types of hospitals somewhat over 75 per cent of operating receipts are derived from payment for service (affected considerably by hospital insurance plans, which account for about half of the receipts). The proportion among general hospitals is 80 per cent; the lowest proportion, 2.4 per cent, is for specialized tuberculosis centers where contributions and membership dues constitute more than half of the receipts.

The number of Jews migrating to various parts of the United States for reasons of health has dwindled considerably since the turn of the century. Migration for health purposes to the National Jewish Hospital for Tuberculosis in Denver and in Los Angeles continue the pattern set many years before, but the number has sharply declined and applications have become more selective. There has continued to be some migration to mild, dry climates such as Arizona, Miami, Southern California, Texas, and New Mexico because of the alleged beneficial effects of climate on chronic arthritis, rheumatic fever, asthma, and various other diseases. The Council of Jewish Federations and Welfare Funds was asked to study the effect on the receiving communities of such migrants for health purposes, and it was found that the number seeking help from social agencies was beyond the local capacity to handle.[19]

Among the newer developments in which hospitals under Jewish auspices have been prominent is the hospital home care prorgam. Hospital services are extended to the home, thus enabling beds to be released for those patients who need hospital bed care, and resulting in improved opportunity for cure and rehabilitation. . . .

The Jewish community has continued to be concerned with special groups of handicapped, including the mentally retarded as well as the blind, the deaf, and otherwise physically disabled. While public programs have largely met minimal economic, and some of the training, medical, and custodial needs, a number of Jewish communities have maintained institutions and special programs for rehabilitation of handicapped groups, partly out of the conviction that public programs do not offer sufficient care. Vocational service agencies, as indicated previously, have played a special part in the occupational readjustments of the handicapped.

It is a far cry from the *hekdesh* of the European ghetto to the modern hospital of today. The traditional necessity to establish facilities for the Jewish sick because no one else would take care of them is no longer a prime motivation in the establishment of present-day facilities for health care, or in continuing the operation of those in existence. There appears to be a mingling of motivations: the desire of Jewish communities to make a direct contribution to the health of the entire community, to provide resources where Jewish doctors can be sure of acceptance for training, and in certain cases to provide a hospital atmosphere in which Jews, particularly those who are devout, may feel more at home. The fact that other sectarian denominations have also established hospitals may be still another motivation, or pattern, for Jewish behavior. One senses here a unique combination of a deep-seated traditional sense of communal responsibility for the sick and infirm within one's own group, with one of the most modern aspects of the American ethos—no racial or religious barriers to service. Curiously, despite the nonsectarian character of admissions to hospitals, the appropriateness of this kind of communal endeavor under Jewish auspices has been less subject to question than the Jewish family service agencies, whose clientele is almost uniformly Jewish (but whose *methods* are conceived of as nonsectarian).

§ *Overseas Aid*

The prodigious development of fund-raising for overseas aid has been termed "one of the greatest unifying forces in Jewish life." Such fund-raising has been essentially for the United Jewish Appeal, in which the American Jewish Joint Distribution Committee (commonly referred to in the United States as the JDC) and the United Israel Appeal (formerly United Palestine Appeal) have been the principal national partners. Federations and welfare funds bore the brunt of organizing and conducting the annual campaigns and of trying to develop rational relationships between overseas needs and domestic programs.

While a number of Jewish organizations representing labor, religious, and Zionist groups have been active in overseas aid, the JDC has been the organization charged with the overall task of the relief and rehabilitation of European Jewry. The JDC[20] carried staggering responsibilities at the close of World War II. JDC's previous history had given it structure and experience, but no prior experience could compare with that of coping with the ravages imposed on European Jewry by Nazi persecution and World War II.

This organization had been formed during World War I, and by 1925 JDC had begun to consider liquidating its operations. However, the economic crisis which swept Poland and nearby areas during that period militated against such liquidation. JDC continued its work with relief and reconstruction loans, establishing workshops and various other forms of rehabilitation in Eastern Europe and co-operating with organizations such as OSE, a group which operated medical institutions and child care programs in many parts of Eastern Europe. During the late 1920's a separate project called Agro-Joint was organized in the Soviet Union on behalf of Jews there. Agro-Joint's program included vocational training, loan funds for artisans, and workshops and cooperatives—all designed to help Jews settle on the land.

Again in the 1930's JDC considered liquidation, due to the success of its programs. But the advent of Hitler and the new European epoch he ushered in kept the JDC operating through the 1930's to bring relief to harried refugees, to help Jews emigrate from Germany, and to establish resettlement programs. Even after the Nazi invasion of Poland in 1939 JDC attempted as far as possible to bring relief directly to Jews in Germany and later in Eastern Europe. When the Nazis took Paris, JDC moved its European headquarters to Lisbon, where it continued on the alert to seize every possible opportunity for the rescue of the remnants of the massacred Jewish population of Europe.

When World War II came to a close, JDC representatives followed close behind the liberating armies, bringing food, clothing, and medical supplies directly to concentration camp victims, soon to be termed displaced persons, or "DP's."

When America's Jews came to realize what had happened to the Jewish communities of Europe—to near relatives, to brethren in cities and villages from which their parents and grandparents or they themselves had come; when the full story of concentration camps, crematory ovens, systematic slaughter and brutality became known, a wave of anguish swept through every Jewish community in the country. A huge outpouring of funds for rescue operations resulted. The JDC was faced with the task of moving in to help wherever it could. By supplying direct relief, in the form of food, clothing, and other articles; by bringing in doctors and nurses and medical supplies; by conducting an immigration service itself and in cooperation with the Hebrew Sheltering and Immigrant Aid Society (HIAS);[21] by working jointly with ORT (the Organization for Rehabilitation Through Training) in vocational training and rehabilitation; by bringing educational materials, religious books and teachers to DP's and local Jewish communities; by training social workers for local Jewish communities—by all these activities the JDC strove to meet its obligations.

As the years of crisis passed, and European Jews emigrated to Israel and to other lands, the JDC was able to turn its attention to needs in Moslem areas, particularly in the countries of North Africa. The lot of the Jewish populations in the unbelievably squalid ghettos—the *mellahs* of Morocco and Tunisia—was miserable beyond imagination. The situation became rapidly worse with the rise of nationalist sentiment in the North African countries and the friction between Israel and the neighboring Arab countries. Again JDC conducted rescue operations, cooperating with ORT and OSE in vocational training and rehabilitation and in health work, and with the Alliance Israélite Universelle and other groups in strengthening the personal and community resources of the Jewish populations of the Moslem countries.

When the State of Israel was established in May 1948, it had to depend very largely on philanthropic aid for its foreign exchange. In the course of time other resources have developed, and a "bond drive" has been launched; but philanthropic contributions through the United Israel Appeal have remained very important. The Jewish Agency for Palestine has been the major beneficiary of these funds. Sympathy for Israel's struggles, and concern for the welfare of the hundreds of thousands of victims of Nazi terror and war, have united Zionist and non-Zionist alike in contributing to the Israel causes, especially through the UJA.

§ Refugees

Shortly after Hitler came to power in 1933 Jews began to leave Germany. Many could not believe that the anti-Semitism of the Nazis could win a permanent footing, and fled later penniless and in panic. Those who were unable to leave before World War II eventually suffered the fate of

Central and East European Jewry. By 1934, German Jews were arriving in America in such numbers that a Greater New York Coordinating Committee was organized to coordinate the special refugee services of the two larger Jewish family agencies and the two local sections of the National Council of Jewish Women. The numbers grew larger year by year; thousands of the earlier refugees had resources or could quickly become self-maintaining, but financial assistance was necessary for others and many more required help in making their initial adjustments. By 1938 it had become clear that national support was necessary, and national planning. The National Coordinating Community Fund was organized to provide central financing for refugees and to assure a more general support.

By 1939, 40,000 Jewish refugees a year were entering the United States (some 200,000 all told came between 1933 and 1940); these later arrivals were older, poorer, more disturbed. In June 1939 the National Refugee Service (NRS) was set up to replace the predecessor organizations. The NRS offered migration service to the kin of German residents; resettlement help to new arrivals; subventions to physicians, scientists and other professionals to enable them to study for examinations and resume their professional careers; an employment and retraining program; loans to small business men; and assistance to refugees who were seeking permanent visas. As Eli Ginzberg has pointed out, the remarkable work of the NRS (and its successor organizations), through quiet and efficient assistance to refugees in becoming integrated into American life and the American economy, deterred the anti-immigration sentiment which was building up among powerful groups in the United States.[22]

At the peak of service, 900 community groups coordinated by the NRS were helping refugees throughout the nation. More than half of the refugees who arrived in the United States between 1939 and the entry of the United States into World War II in 1941 remained in New York City. The NRS assisted many thousands of others who wished, because of the presence of relatives and friends, or vocational opportunities, to "resettle" in smaller cities and towns throughout the country, to do so. While specialized refugee services were the pattern at first, gradually the tendency grew to "normalize" the newcomer's way of life by having him served through the same family, employment, and health services available to the general Jewish population in the communities where he came to settle.[23]

After World War II came the shattered, orphaned, widowed, maimed, and tortured remnants of the concentration camps and ghettos, the survivors of the incredibly ruthless extermination of 6,000,000 of their brethren. Abroad, they were assisted first by the liberating armies, then by the United Nations Relief and Rehabilitation Association (UNRRA), and then by the International Refugee Organization (IRO) and by the JDC. Emigration was slow, and the United States immigration laws restrictive, but in May 1946, the first of the "DP ships," the S.S. *Marine Flasher,* arrived in New York Harbor.

By then, the NRS had merged with the section on services to the foreign-born of the National Council of Jewish Women (which had been providing outstanding service at ports and docks, in naturalization and immigration advice, and in work for unattached women and girls) to form the United Service for New Americans (USNA). The new organization, receiving support (as did the NRS) from the United Jewish Appeal, was prepared to offer intensive help to the new arrivals through a variety of individual services including case work counselling, vocational help, and temporary relief. It was hoped that the DP Act of 1948 would open the gates of the United States to Jewish war victims, but implementation of the act was discouraging. In 1949, however, the movement increased, and the New York Association for New Americans (NYANA) was created to be responsible for local activity in New York City, while USNA remained the integrating agency on the national level, constantly widening the network of community resources available to help the arriving DP's.[24]

USNA became increasingly active in easing the possibilities of immigration, helping to break the slowdown in admissions under the amended DP Act of 1950. After the McCarran-Walter Immigration and Naturalization Act of 1952 was passed, USNA put all its resources into protecting the immigrant. The new act not only restricted immigration severely, leaving unchanged the national origins quota system of 1924, but increased the hazards of deportation.[25]

Between the end of World War II and 1954, about 150,000 Jewish refugees had resettled in the United States; more than 98 per cent were soon self-supporting, contributing to the economy, and to the social and cultural life of the nation.

The lessons of the previous experience of Jewish communities with the mass immigration in the years around the turn of the century had been well learned. For the tragic refugees and concentration camp victims of the new era, resources were mobilized quickly, unstintingly. Resettlement and "Americanization" proceeded amid hardships, but with full awareness of the implications for communities, and the needs of the newcomers. The consensus is that, despite crises and pressures from all sides, the effort to help the newcomers, keeping their best interests in mind, and without overburdening any particular community, was successful.

HIAS, with its more than forty years of experience in helping Jewish immigration, had been working alongside USNA in receiving new immigrants. Since HIAS's services resembled those of USNA, and those of the immigration department of the JDC, a merger among the three groups had repeatedly been broached. It was finally achieved in 1954, and a new organization, United HIAS Service, was formed, which was responsible for its own fund-raising. This represents "one of the last remaining examples of the bringing together of welfare institutions which had been founded in earlier years under the auspices of German and Eastern European Jewish groups."[26]

This paper cannot attempt to do justice to the story of American Jewry's contribution in social services to overseas communities. The full account needs telling; in such a document the work of the Zionist, as well as general organizations, would receive full treatment. The following is a listing of only some of the major Zionist and pro-Israel organizations which engage in social work for Israel and raise their own funds: Hadassah (the Women's Zionist Organization of America) and Junior Hadassah, which conduct independent health, medical, child rehabilitation, vocational, educational, and land reclamation activities in Israel; the Mizrachi Women's Organization of America, which maintains child care, vocational education, and other social service programs in Israel in the spirit of traditional Judaism; the Women's League for Israel, which provided shelter, vocational and social adjustment services for young women newcomers in Israel; the Federated Council of Israel Institutions, which acts on behalf of many educational and social welfare agencies of a traditional type in Israel; the American Red Mogen David for Israel, aiding the Israeli Red Mogen David.

§ *Financing*

Fund-raising for Jewish causes has been raised to elaborate heights, if not to a fine art. In addition to the armament of techniques common to fund-raising generally—such as "kickoff dinners," newspaper, radio and TV promotion; carefully gathered mailing lists; organization by occupational groups—in the Jewish field there is a fund-raising *tradition* to draw on. The professionals, who now constitute a new type of specialization within the Jewish community, may capitalize on self-generated pressures for giving—pressures stemming from Biblical and Talmudic precepts, from communal organization in the medieval city and in the East European *shtetl* to the American community of today. The readiness to give, the wherewithal to give, and the need, coupled with energetic fund-raising, have produced prodigious sums from American Jewry.

Amounts raised by campaigns of the federations and welfare funds (the latter being associations for nonlocal causes, both national and overseas), rose after World War II, primarily in response to overseas needs, to a peak of $200,721,000 in 1948. Since that time the sums have gradually declined; but in 1953 the total raised was about $44,000,000, still 60 per cent above the 1945 figure. Although uncertain economic conditions in 1950 and 1951 may have contributed to the decline in contributions, it is generally considered that other factors were even more important. One factor was the waning of the DP "problem"; a second, the success of Israel's War of Independence; a third, the desire of American Jews to engage in domestic projects, which had been delayed for several years.

The old conflicts between Zionists and non-Zionists were largely put aside during the 1940's and 1950's, when Jews of all ideologies united in their efforts for Hitler's victims. Israel not only became a state, but the new home of most of the new DP's. Hence, philanthropic support for Europe's Jews and Israel's Jews represented a single impulse.

A study of "multiple appeals" in fifteen cities established the fact that considerable funds were being raised outside of central community campaigns. In the cities investigated, the total was equal to 70 per cent of the aggregate amounts raised in the central campaign. These included local, national, and overseas projects in such fields as religion, education, and community relations, as well as health and welfare.[27]

Local agencies have been increasingly concerned with securing adequate financing through central Jewish campaigns, supplemented by community chest support, and fees for service. Increased payments for service have been sought for old age care and hospital care, in particular. This has been largely due to the extension of old age assistance and old age and survivors insurance, and to the prevalence of hospital insurance coverage. Public funds have come to constitute an appreciable share of the operating budgets of child care agencies.

It is impossible even to estimate the extent to which American Jews have contributed to general or non-Jewish causes in the health and welfare field. There is little question that these contributions have been and remain extensive.

§ *Research*

In speaking of "research," a distinction should be drawn between the fact-finding or survey variety, and the problem-solving type of research which begins with hypotheses to be explored or experimentally tested. The first has been widespread in social work for over fifty years, with increasing refinement of techniques; the second is a relatively recent development in social work, but the recognition of its importance has been growing.

Interest in objective fact-finding as a guide to policy and practice was expressed in Jewish social work as early as the 1880's and 1890's. This interest became more explicit around the turn of the century when Jewish social work leaders began to call for studies of the Jewish population of the United States, of needs, and of available resources. The pages of *Jewish Charity* are dotted with references to the need for research. This preoccupation led to the organization in 1917 of the Bureau of Jewish Social Research, which undertook studies for a variety of agencies. This bureau later became incorporated into the Council of Jewish Federations and Welfare Funds (CJFWF), established in 1924. The organization of such national agencies as the Jewish Welfare Board and the CJFWF made it possible for many local federations and welfare funds to secure expert assistance from national agencies; they also made regional and national surveys possible. Through the 1930's, 1940's and 1950's, the most frequent kind of research was the community survey. The CJFWF, the JWB, the Graduate School of Jewish Social Work, and the Conference on Jewish Relations (later called the Conference on Jewish Social Studies) were the principal organizations in the Jewish field to assume national responsibility in assisting local federations and welfare funds to carry out surveys.

Demographic studies of populations in cities such as Minneapolis and Trenton, economic and occupational research, administrative and financial studies, were also quite numerous. Evaluative studies that aimed principally at clarifying needs and resources, defining agency inter-relationships, and evaluating the work of given agencies, were less frequent though very important as a research emphasis.

Until the late 1940's, there was relatively little interest in Jewish, as in non-Jewish social work, in empirical research, particularly research that would draw fully on hypotheses as well as methods from the relevant social sciences. The continued pressure of lay leadership for a more definitive analysis of the contribution of service programs; the gradual availability of qualified research persons trained in or close to the social work field; and the greater security of social work agencies in the use of research, all have contributed to a gradual concentration on more sophisticated evaluative and experimental research in social work. Schools of social work have encouraged this development and have promoted research training through doctoral programs and other special programs for social workers qualified in social science research. Some agencies have, upon occasion, utilized the services of social scientists themselves in specific research programs.

At the same time, federations and welfare funds have been concentrating on research in planning ahead on the basis of the evaluation of the effectiveness of current programs. While scientific research has not yet received full recognition as a legitimate organizational investment in many individual agencies, the trend is clearly in that direction; the lack is in research manpower rather than in conviction or desire of executives and boards to engage in research activity. Jewish social work has been keeping abreast of social work research as a whole, and certain individual agencies have been leaders in this area.

BOARDS AND VOLUNTEER PARTICIPATION. With the rapid professionalization of the social work field starting with the 1920's, the authority of board members tended to recede, and that of the professional social work executive to be enhanced.[28] In a sense, the growing importance of the executive as a qualified technician, administering the services of other specialized personnel, was similar to the "managerial revolution" in industry, the tendency to turn over to the "manager" the technical reins of the industrial organization. For the social agency or federation, however, it sometimes meant the board's retreat from its appropriate authority and role, at the same time as it retained the official function of being responsible for policy. There was a real danger of the "strong" executive becoming too strong.

In one of the few attempts at a sociological analysis of the role of leadership in Jewish communal activity the thesis is developed that social prestige is the prime motivation for board membership, which . . . "is generally a reward for services already rendered; since the era of professionalization the board has been generally little more than a rubber stamp for the 'tradition' of the agency and the 'suggestion' of the executive. Nevertheless, board membership is *interpreted* as work."[29] This thesis has been accepted by some and disparaged by others as being perhaps locally true, or only superficially true, or not true at all. Two aspects of the thesis should be differentiated: motivation for board membership and the actual role of such membership. Analyzing motivation is always a hazardous occupation. It may, however, be possible to accept the desire for social prestige as one source of motivation for some board members, without imparting a negative connotation to this influence. There is nothing inherently unethical or psychologically unsound in a desire for higher social status, so characteristic of our culture. Moreover, such striving may not be an end in itself, and need not necessarily imply that the motivation is exclusively self-centered. The proper sociological question may rather be: "What makes board membership a channel for upward social mobility?" That board membership does imply high social status seems unquestioned.

There is little evidence that the motivations of lay leaders are in any wise different from those of others; only the channels through which motivation may be expressed may be different. Every community can point to individuals possessing the highest altruism and devotion to the best interests of the Jewish community, as well as to individuals who possess little of either quality. The record of Jewish communities in the development of welfare services in the United States attests to the fact that when all is said, their leadership has been effective and of a high order.

A negative attitude among social workers toward board members was much more characteristic of the 1930's than of the late 1940's and 1950's. Reacting sharply from earlier domination of social work activity by board members and volunteers during the 1920's and 1930's, professional social workers felt impelled to define and safeguard their newly assumed role and sphere of competence. Board members tended to be further isolated from professional staffs during the 1930's, if and when they associated themselves with economy-minded "business-like" principles which ran counter to the objectives and viewpoints of the social workers. As agencies became bureaucratized, with more clear-cut definitions of function, boards tended to accept the province staked out by the professional, while retaining their role as policymaking bodies. This is largely true today, with the exception of a few scattered smaller agencies that still adhere to a tradition of complete board control and operation.

The profusion of articles, books, and training seminars in the 1940's and 1950's dealing with the role of the board member would seem to attest to a re-evaluation and re-alignment of board members vis-à-vis professional staffs. The present tendency is for professionals to be much more ready to accept the legitimate responsibilities of boards, and for the executive to serve as a channel for more effective board-staff communication. The interest in accepting volunteers to perform direct service is another aspect of this trend.

Jewish agencies have seen every kind of motivation and every pattern of service among board members, from the most domineering to the most passive. There is also good evidence that the respective roles of boards and staffs are becoming more clearly defined in Jewish agencies, with a concomitant growth in mutual confidence and a decline in defensiveness over arrogated authority. As professional social workers have become secure both in their knowledge and skills and in the appreciation and confidence with which board members regard them, they have tended to relax their vigilance over their professional provinces. Conversely, as boards have been given more responsibility they have also tended to exercise it; the trend has been for executives to assume increasing authority, and the extent to which board members participate in formulating basic policy is often a reflection of the executive's leadership. The executive's influence, however, can spring not only from his professional leadership, but also from his ability to affect the status strivings of lay leaders. Like all power, that of the executive can be abused or well used—characteristically it is employed in the best interests of the organization and community he serves.

In addition to the lay leadership of the hundreds of local and national Jewish agencies in the United States, there is, of course, the participation of volunteers on every level of service. American society has been characterized both by an enormous profusion of voluntary groups and by the voluntary activities of Americans as individuals. There are an estimated 30,000,000 persons in the United States who offer unpaid help to various religious, social, political, civil, and service organizations. During World War II, 11,000,000 volunteers served in health and welfare programs alone to help the war effort.[30]

Like other Americans, American Jews have participated in both Jewish and general voluntary activities of all kinds. The National Council of Jewish Women is an outstanding example of a group of volunteers active in chapters throughout the country, to help the foreign-born, to give training scholarships to overseas students (and thus influence social services in Jewish communities abroad) and to develop cultural programs. The activities of Zionist organizations in the field of philanthropy to Israel have been cited. Synagogue and temple sisterhoods perform many volunteer functions. Fraternal orders such as B'nai B'rith offer many opportunities for volunteer service.

Volunteers have also been giving direct service to health and welfare agencies, to hospitals, child guidance clinics, and to institutions for children and aged. The volunteer no longer threatens the professional. On the contrary, the professional is more and more in a teaching and supervisory position with respect to the volunteer. But the volunteer can help in ways the professional cannot—not only by performing direct, concrete services for patients and clients under professional direction, but also by interpreting the work of the agencies and raising their prestige, by helping to raise funds, by making suggestions from a fresh point of view regarding policy and performance in their agencies. For these reasons, the volunteer is being sought today by the professional health and welfare agency, reversing a fifty-year trend.

§ *Jewish Social Work Training*

Following World War I there was a revival of interest in a Jewish school of social work; however, opinion was divided as to how generally social work-oriented, or specifically Jewish-centered, the school should be. The plan for the Graduate School of Jewish Social Work finally worked out in 1924 " . . . was a compromise between the view of those who could see no difference between Jewish and non-Jewish social work and regarded the separate system as being without justification, and those who pointed to the need for a positive Jewish ideology for social workers whose task included concern with Jewish cultural life."[31] The school, under the direction of Maurice J. Karpf, trained many of today's leaders in social work, and stimulated a great deal of research in Jewish life. Technical social work courses were given by the New York School of Social Work, while the Jewish part of the curriculum was taught directly at the Graduate School. The most successful attempt at separate training for Jewish social workers to date, the school finally succumbed in 1940 to divisions of points of view, to apathy, and to economic difficulties. . . . Attempts were made, particularly by the JWB, to introduce and pay for special courses in Jewish content in existing schools of social work, but these efforts were largely rejected by the schools on the basis that sectarian courses should not be offered in a general curriculum.

In 1941, Solomon Lowenstein called together a group of executives to consider the problem of training in Jewish social work. The result was a survey which found that the number of agencies definitely requiring their workers to have Jewish schooling was negligible, but that social workers in the expanding community organization and community center field were most aware of the Jewish content in their work.[32] This fact, in addition to the rapid development of central organizations in Jewish life (their number rose from 50 in 1930 to 300 in 1947, all with paid professional executives) led to the recommendation that Jewish social workers be trained to work in Jewish community organizations. This field includes community relations, planning services for the aged, and overseas work.

It was agreed that nonsectarian schools were preparing practitioners in the functional fields adequately. The final decision was to set up a Training Bureau for Jewish Communal Service to prepare experienced social workers for executive positions. Unfortunately, the number of staff released by agencies for training was too small to warrant the expense of the training, and this effort ended after a few years.

Recently, the Yeshiva University in New York City has set up a social work training program, and similar plans are afoot by other theological centers. This development is a reflection of the gradual mutual acceptance by the religious institutions of the place of organized social work and social work training in religious institutions, and by organized social work of the place of religion and traditional values in personality. Whether this mutual recognition will lead to social work training under permanently Jewish auspices, and whether this training will be sufficiently unique to clarify the nature of specifically Jewish social work, remains to be seen.

§ *Jewish Social Work in America: Retrospect and Prospect*

The handful of Jews living in the United States during the colonial period, while temporarily restricted from organizing synagogues in certain places, such as New Amsterdam, were able to do so by the end of the seventeenth century, and soon began to establish burial societies and other mutual aid activities. These organizations, under synagogue auspices originally, were a direct carryover from their previous traditions. As the number of Jews increased during the 1800's, with immigration, largely from Germany, they rapidly dispersed through the whole country. They prospered and entered fully into voluntary activities, within and without the Jewish fold. By 1880 Jews were represented in all walks of life, and in all forms of organized activity that were open to them—politics, trade associations, professional groups, fraternal orders. Within Jewish life they established such organizations as YMHA's, and charities and institutions for the orphaned, the sick, and the disabled. The East European immigrants also seized the opportunity to establish voluntary associations. They and their children formed not only replicas of synagogue-centered charities, but every kind of organization known to American life as well.

The Jewish community has in fact become essentially middle class in occupational terms; middle-class values—thrift, moderation, stress on education, postponement of immediate satisfactions—were implicit even among the most destitute of the arrivals on Ellis Island. The tradesmen and artisans of the colonial period, the itinerant peddlers of the 1880's, the tailors and shoemakers and dressmakers of the sweatshops and ghettos of the post-1880's, gave rise within one or two generations to groups of successful merchants, independent business men, professionals, white-collar workers. This is not to minimize the large numbers of poor Jews, or the sick and disabled; the misery of the hundreds of thousands of penniless new settlers in the crowded hovels of the lower East Sides in the major cities of the 1890's and early twentieth century, or the ravages of the depression of the 1930's on Jews and non-Jews alike. But the Jews of the United States have prospered as the country has prospered.

Jewish social work in the United States became strongly concerned with overseas aid both because it was traditional and because of overpowering facts of history. The immigration from Central Europe in the early 1800's and the mass immigration from Eastern Europe in the latter part of the century followed periods of intense persecution. From the 1880's the recurrent emergencies requiring aid to overseas communities built into Jewish welfare activity a structure of steady and organized effort for the aid of Jewish brethren in all lands. As the social position of the Jews in the United States became stronger with the growth of the American economy and the rise of the second- and third-generation to middle-class positions, American Jews became the major source of philanthropic effort for Jews in various parts of the world. Nazi persecution of Jews in Europe, the urgency of rescue, relief and rehabilitation of survivors after World War II, the need to help new emigrants from disaster areas in the 1930's and 1940's, and for philanthropic work in the new State of Israel, called forth prodigious outlays of funds, energy and expansion of overseas aid.

It is doubtful that there were specific relief needs peculiar to the Jewish population in the United States, aside from religious and cultural considerations, despite the recurrent concern that this might be the case. Thus, desertion in the early 1900's was considered to be a "Jewish problem" and a major cause of dependency in Jewish families. However, subsequent investigations proved that desertion was at least as common, if not more so, among non-Jewish famiiles. Tuberculosis, a scourge of the post-1880 immigration and the focus of much Jewish social work, was a blight wherever there was overcrowding, poor sanitation and poverty. Certain needs were probably more urgent for the Jewish population, but it would be difficult to demonstrate that these were specifically "Jewish needs." The concern, however, with preserving family life, with protecting the aged, and caring for children seems to have been relatively strong among the Jewish population, and to have derived in large measure from cultural influences.

The fact that there was general support in the United States for the growth of voluntary agencies created a climate in which private social agencies could flourish. Indeed, they sprang up in such profusion that attempts at self-regulation and coordination became the first order of the day in the 1870's with the charity organization movement. There was, however, no official discouragement to deter any segment of the population from starting "a charity" anywhere in the United States, and Jews were able to form whatever societies they wished without fear of state disapproval or special state regulation. Philanthropies mushroomed and fund raising became a huge problem. The "federation" movement was the response; it contributed not only to better financed but also to better co-ordinated, more stable and more permanent agencies for Jewish social work.

Sufficient numbers of Jews acquired financial security to make possible the Jewish philanthropies, the hospitals, the family agencies, the guidance clinics, the community centers, and the organizations for overseas aid. Other groups in the United States have, of course, conducted similar activities. But the extraordinary outpouring of voluntary funds for Jewish and general social work by the Jewish community cannot be accounted for by economics alone. This outpouring derives from more than financial ability to give, or even from effective fund-raising organization and techniques. It stems essentially from deeply ingrained humanitarian motivations, from traditions and patterns of giving centuries old, that depend not only on ability to contribute but also on the moral necessity to help one's brethren, regardless of personal sacrifice. The fact that the humanitarian impulse characterizes American life in general, that the individual citizen finds himself enjoined here to contribute to a variety of health, welfare and educational organizations—and is in fact encouraged to do so by the Federal government through tax deductions—has helped make Jewish social work in this respect, too, part and parcel of the American scene.

While cultural, historical, social, and economic factors contributed both to the development and the stability of Jewish social work, counter-influences tended to diminish the growth of "sectarian social work" (in the sense of auspices) both in the general community and specifically in the Jewish community.

One such influence has been the growth of governmental programs of assistance, and social security. These programs had the effect of virtually eliminating relief as a function of voluntary social service and of limiting private philanthropy to special fields. Another influence has been the ideology of many lay leaders and professional social workers, based on a secular humanism which regards "sectarianism" as inconsistent with or contradictory to social work values. These influences have restricted the growth of Jewish social work, created differences of opinion and approach that need continually to be reconciled.

What has happened to the traditional forms of charity as they existed among the Jews for hundreds of years? A few isolated groups have kept as close as possible to the traditional patterns of retaining social services as a synagogue function. But for the most part the traditional injunctions to clothe the needy, feed the hungry, shelter the homeless, are now being carried out by public services and are not confined to Jewish auspices. For the Jewish community in America is not self-enclosed and does not have to be self-sufficient. In fact, Jewish community leaders and professional social workers have helped in the development of public responsibility.

The orphanage has evolved into the cottage plan institution and foster care. Here, too, the government is taking on a larger share of the burden, and actual needs in the Jewish community have decreased. The *hekdesh* of the Jewish ghetto has become the modern hospital, under Jewish auspices, but increasingly open to all on a nonsectarian basis. The care of old people is more than ever a responsibility of the Jewish community. But all efforts are now being directed not to building institutions for the aged, but to developing special housing, extending medical service, boarding care, group activities, and individual counselling, in order to help elderly people to retain the satisfactions of normal community and home life, and to make the later years of life as rich as possible. The modern version of ransoming the captives is overseas aid—for the rescue, relief, and rehabilitation of oppressed brethren without resources of their own. To a greater degree than ever before, Jews in the United States have cooperated for this purpose.

Some needs are being met under new auspices, others have remained the same. But new needs have also arisen for which the Jewish community has assumed responsibility which it has delegated to Jewish social services: such needs as help in self-direction and self-fulfillment, the need of children for understanding and love, the need to locate one's group identity, the need for recreation and a social life.

These are not really new needs; indeed, they are very old. But they had not before been recognized by communal organizations as their responsibility to meet, but by family, friends, rabbi. Today, Jewish communities, along with those of other denominations, have established special resources to help meet them. Life has become complicated, and specialized functions are required; the social services have been developed to help family and rabbi and friends, when necessary, to meet these personal needs of individuals and families.

Among the long-range trends in Jewish social work one may discern the following:

1. The acceptance of direct material relief as a function of government rather than that of the voluntary agency.
2. The gradual extension of social service to wider segments of the entire community, rather than to the poor alone.
3. The increasing assumption of the responsibility to try new services, new ways of working, and to carry on research, with the premise that these are essential to the role of the voluntary agency. In turn, this assumes that governmental programs may eventually take over programs that are currently experimental.
4. The acceptance of persistent responsibility for the care of the aged as a traditional form of service of the Jewish community, while at the same time accepting help in financing, directly or indirectly, from public sources.
5. Emphasis on nonsectarian policies in service.
6. Increased use of volunteers for direct service under professional supervision.

7. Increased participation on boards of individuals from varying backgrounds. Such participation remains symbolic of high social status.
8. The decline of the isolated philanthropy unattached to existing federations or welfare funds.
9. Rapprochement between the organized religious elements in Jewish life and Jewish social welfare.
10. Concern with the issue of the Jewishness of Jewish social work. This concern is expressed differently in various agencies and professional groups.[33]

These trends add up to the continuation of deeply rooted cultural traditions, whose outward manifestations have changed but whose inner core remains the same. Jewish social work is no longer a matter of self-protection against a hostile environment; less than ever does it reflect lack of confidence in public or nonsectarian services; nor does Jewish social work represent the imposition of the will of a philanthropic oligarchy. Rather, this persistence of Jewish social work in the United States would seem to flow from the fact that after 300 years of living in this country, during which every diverse form of Jewish life has been able to appear, participation in social work under Jewish auspices has become the most universally accepted expression of Jewish communal feeling.

HERBERT J. GANS

THE ORIGIN AND GROWTH
OF A JEWISH COMMUNITY IN THE SUBURBS:
A STUDY OF THE JEWS OF PARK FOREST

URBAN residents have been moving to the suburbs almost as long as cities have existed in America. For many decades, this movement was limited to the upper-income groups, but since the 1920's and increasingly since the end of World War II, it has attracted middle-class families and even those of skilled workers.

The postwar housing boom was fed by returning G.I.'s. The new suburbs which sprang up to meet their housing needs followed traditional subdivision practices. However, the builders' search for the cheapest land located the new and low-priced settlements on the outskirts of the metropolitan areas, and placed the young veterans into one-age, one-class communities.

American Jews, stimulated by similar housing aspirations and needs, participated in this latest expansion of the city. In the new suburbs, they set up a distinctive type of Jewish subcommunity.[2] The new Jewish suburbanites are young members of the second generation (i.e., the first native-born one), and their children. Although they may be geographically and socially more mobile than their peers who remained in the city, they are typical in other respects, being mostly business and professional in occupation and overwhelmingly middle class in style of life.

The universal Jewish migration to the suburbs is very recent. However, unless American cities are redeveloped at a faster rate than is currently apparent, the middle class may become almost exclusively suburban. Among Jews as well the suburban community may thus become the norm. This report on one suburban Jewish subcommunity consequently is not only a case study of a new phenomenon, but perhaps a source of future trends. Furthermore, the main body of the study deals with a Jewish suburban community in its *first* year of existence; Park Forest thus presented a rare opportunity to study the processes which shape Jewish communal structure.

This article was written especially for this volume.

An abridged version of the study, under the title "Park Forest: Birth of a Jewish Community," appeared in *Commentary*, April, 1951, pp. 330-339; it was reprinted in *Commentary on the American Scene*, edited by Elliot E. Cohen, New York, 1953, pp. 205-223. Permission was given to *Commentary* to print parts of the final section of this article prior to its publication in this volume.

§ I. The Community and the Characteristics of the Jewish Residents

Park Forest, Illinois, the scene of the study described here, is not an ordinary suburb but rather a partially planned garden city.[3] Located thirty miles south of Chicago's Loop, it was envisioned both as a dormitory for Chicago white-collar workers (which it is), and a partially self-sufficient community with its own industries (which it still hopes to be). The plan called for 3,000 rental garden apartments, for 4,500 single-family homes available for sale, as well as for shopping centers, schools, churches, playgrounds and other community facilities.[4] The conversion of the golf course and farmland which were to be the site of the new town began in 1947, and the first tenants moved in on August 30, 1948. By April, 1949, the community had been incorporated as a village.

Like other postwar suburbs, Park Forest first attracted the people most sorely pressed for shelter—young couples with one or two children of pre-school age.[5] In 1949, the median age of the men was thirty-two, of the women somewhat less; anyone over forty was generally considered old. Many of the men were beginning their careers, and most of them were in professional, sales, or administrative and other business fields. Their educational level was high, and a majority of the men and many of the wives had some college education. Despite their recent graduation from the G.I. Bill of Rights, by 1949 the men were earning from $4000 to $10,000. Their median income was generally estimated at $5200. Consequently it seemed probable that the village was attracting the socially and geographically more mobile members of the generation of returning veterans.

In November, 1949, when the interviewing for this study was completed, about 1,800 families were living in the village. About 25 per cent of them were Catholic. The Jewish community then numbered just under 150 families. Of these, about twenty (fifteen of them mixed marriages) rejected all relationships with the formal Jewish community.[6] Another thirty families had not been in Park Forest long enough to have made contact with the established Jewish community. We interviewed a sample which consisted of forty-four of the remaining group of 100 families.[7] This sample was subdivided into families of people who had been *active* in the formation of Jewish organizations or were now in leadership positions, and those *inactive*, whether or not they were members of organizations.[8] Within the total sample, the median age of heads of households was thirty-five, and of their wives, thirty. As is indicated in Table 1, 43 per cent of the families had one or more school-age children, while 57 per cent had only younger children or were still childless. Although there were no age differences between the actives and the inactives, the former had a slightly higher proportion of older children.

Table 1—Family Status by Activity Status

Families With	Actives		Inactives		All	
	No.	%	No.	%	No.	%
School-Age Children	6	50	13	40	19	43
Preschool-Age Children Only	4	33	18	57	22	50
No Children	2	17	1	3	3	7
Total	12	100	32	100	44	100

The distribution of annual income for those who divulged such information is indicated in Table 2. The median family income was about $6400.[9] The actives' median income was only $6000, while that of the inactives totalled some $6400. However, since 40 per cent of the actives were in the highest income category, their mean income was about $7100 as compared with $6800 for the inactives.

Table 2—Family Income by Activity Status

Annual Income	Actives		Inactives		All	
	No.	%	No.	%	No.	%
Under 4500	1	10	0	0	1	3
4500-5400	3	30	7	27	10	28
5500-6400	2	20	6	23	8	22
6500-7400	0	0	4	15	4	11
7500-8400	0	0	7	27	7	19
8500-15000	4	40	2	8	6	17
Total	10	100	26	100	36	100

As is indicated in Table 3, about 90 per cent of the men in the sample had some college training. Some 57 per cent had graduated college, and 32 per cent held graduate or professional degrees. Again, the actives ranked somewhat higher: 75 per cent of the active men had four or more years of college as compared with 50 per cent of the inactive men.

Table 3—Educational Status by Activity Status and Sex

Education	MEN						WOMEN	
	Actives		Inactives		All		All	
	No.	%	No.	%	No.	%	No.	%
High School	0	0	4	13	4	9	11	25
College, 1-3 Years	3	25	10	31	13	29	8	18
College Graduate	3	25	8	25	11	25	15	34
Graduate Degree	3	25	5	16	8	18	6	14
Law Degree	2	17	2	6	4	9	0	0
M.D. Degree	1	8	1	3	2	5	0	0
N.A.	0	0	2	6	2	5	4	9
Total	12	100	32	100	44	100	44	100

As is indicated in Table 4, 36 per cent of the sample were professionals. A total of 48 per cent were in business and industry, though only 14 per cent were owners.

Eighty-eight per cent of the adults in the sample were native-born. Most of the parents of this group were foreign-born. Overwhelmingly, the families came from Eastern Europe. All but a few of our interviewees were brought up in large cities (60 per cent of them in Chicago); they come primarily from working-class or lower-middle-class areas of second

Table 4—Men's Occupational Status by Activity Status

Occupation	Actives		Inactives		All	
	No.	%	No.	%	No.	%
Business and Industry						
Owners, Family Partners	1 } 4	8 } 33	5 } 17	16 } 53	6 } 21	14 } 48
Managers, Supervisors	2	17	4	12	6	14
Other Employees	1	8	8	25	9	20
Government Employees	1	8	1	3	2	5
Professionals						
Academicians, Researchers	2 } 7	17 } 59	4 } 9	12 } 28	6 } 16	14 } 36
Physicians, Lawyers, Engineers, etc.	5	42	5	16	10	22
Semi-Professionals	0	0	4	13	4	9
Graduate Students	0	0	1	3	1	2
Total	12	100	32	100	44	100

settlement. While Park Foresters are mainly "second generation," *they are the children of later immigrants or of immigrants who themselves came to America as children, and must be distinguished from second generation descendants of Jews in the first waves of Eastern European immigration (before 1900) whose own children (third generation) are already adolescents or young adults.*[10] Table 5 shows the formal generational distribution using the classification system employed by Warner and Srole.[11] The comparison by activity status indicates that the percentage of F-2 (third generation) and mixed F-1, F-2 (second and third generation) among the actives was 25 per cent, as compared with 18 per cent among the inactives.

Table 5—Adult Generational Status by Activity Status

Generation	Actives		Inactives		All	
	No.	%	No.	%	No.	%
Mixed P-2, F-1	0	0	3	10	3	7
Both F-1	7	59	16	50	23	51
Man F-1, Wife F-2	2	17	2	6	4	9
Man F-2, Wife F-1	0	0	2	6	2	5
Both F-2, or F-3	1	8	2	6	3	7
Refugees	1	8	1	3	2	5
Man F-1, Wife Non-Jew	1	8	3	10	4	9
Man Non-Jew, Wife F-2	0	0	1	3	1	2
N.A.	0	0	2	6	2	5
Total	12	100	32	100	44	100

In summary, the Jewish sample can be described as a group of young, highly educated, second generation Jews of Eastern European parentage, most of whom have already achieved—or are likely to achieve—upper-middle-class income status, given continued prosperity.[12] The active members of the community rate somewhat higher on socio-economic characteristics than do the inactives.

Turning to the problem of cultural distinctiveness, it is apparent that many of the Jewish residents could not easily be distinguished from other Park Foresters. Although many of them could be said to "look Jewish," they wore the same fashions, ate the same dishes (except on special occasions), and participated with other Park Foresters in the ubiquitous American class and leisure culture of the "young moderns." They observed few of the old cultural and religious traditions. The village's isolation from synagogues and kosher butcher shops discouraged observant Jews from becoming tenants, and brought problems to those who did.

Not only did Park Forest Jews live like other Park Foresters; they lived *with* them. Whereas most American cities have neighborhoods which are predominantly Jewish (if not always in numbers, at least in atmosphere and institutions), such was not the case with Park Forest. The Jewish families were scattered at random, and only rarely were two Jewish families to be found in adjacent houses. The tenants, Jewish and non-Jewish, lived in so-called "courts"—*cul-de-sac* parking bays encircled by twenty to forty two-story garden apartments, built together in rows of five to seven, and renting in 1949 for $75-100 per month.[13]

The occupants of the courts described themselves as living in a goldfish bowl in which privacy was at a minimum. Depending on the make-up of the group, this court life ranged from that of "one big happy family" to a tense collection of unwilling neighbors, although with the passing of time people learned how to find privacy in a high-density world of picture windows. For many of the non-Jewish Park Foresters, the court was almost an independent social unit in which they found most, if not all, their friends, and from which they ventured only rarely, at least during the first year or two.[14]

§ II. The Formation of the Jewish Community

The Jews who came to Park Forest were impelled by the same need for housing, and a desire for a suburban environment in which to raise their children, as were their neighbors.[15] (Some of them also came to learn how to live in the suburbs before buying a house.) Soon after they arrived, they aligned themselves into a number of cliques. In a remarkably short period these formed an interrelated network by which news, gossip, and rumor could be communicated. Out of this informal community there developed a formal community of voluntary associations and religious organizations.

A. EVOLUTION OF THE INFORMAL COMMUNITY. The developmental processes of this informal community can be described in four stages: *contact, recognition, acquaintance,* and *friendship.*

Contact is the opportunity for face-to-face meeting. In order for interaction to develop beyond this point, there had to be the mutual recognition of each other's Jewishness and status position. *As an ethnic group, the Jews form a cohesive ingroup and tend to behave differently toward a member of the ingroup than towards a non-Jew, in many cases reserving the intimacy of friendship for the former.* Thus, before two persons can act in terms of the more personal ingroup norm, they must have a sign that identifies them to each other as fellow ingroup members. Without this recognition there can be no progress towards the formation of acquaintance and the regular interaction of an intimate nature (i.e., the exchange of personal facts, attitudes, and feelings which we call friendship).

Due to the fact that most of the officers of American Community Builders, Inc. (A.C.B.), the corporation that built Park Forest, are Jewish, and the further fact that several have long been active in Jewish affairs, a Jewish community in Park Forest was almost predestined.[16] Before the opening of the development, its officers had invited several friends to move out, and these were among the first tenants.

For those not personally known to the officers, the recognition process began in each court, as families stood beside their moving van and eyed the strangers who were to be their neighbors. Recognition was initiated even before contact was made, for with the first glance, Jewish people were attempting to figure out whether one or another person could be Jewish. This hypothesizing sometimes went on for days; or, if there was relative certainty, and one person was aggressive enough, it lasted a matter of minutes. Mrs. H. described it thusly:

> Mrs. F. came over and talked to me while we were outside with the moving van. It was not a question of religion, but of recognition, I knew she was Jewish by her name, and she looked Jewish, I don't know if the thing was ever discussed. I don't know if she knew I was Jewish that first day.

Mrs. F. said of that meeting:

> I didn't know Mrs. H. was Jewish, I kind of thought as much, by her looks.

In this case there were two signs of recognition, the Jewish "look" and a Jewish "name." Frequently people used a customary request for each other's names to test hypotheses of recognition based on the Jewish "look."

Anthropologists are agreed that there is no Jewish race. Nevertheless, many people, and especially Jews, tend to identify Mediterranean and Armenoid facial features as Jewish. This, plus the fact that certain names are almost monopolized by Jews, has created a stereotypical recognition formula which is realistic enough to be correct more often than it is not. This formula was used in a large number of cases for determining who were the other Jews in the court; its role in the formation of the Jewish community cannot be underestimated.

The look and the name were sometimes reinforced by what might be described as Jewish mannerisms, that is, a set of gestures or verbal expressions that are—again stereotypically—ascribed to Jews:

> It was obvious he was Jewish, by name and appearance. I thought he was from New York, by his speech and action. I've run into a lot of Brooklyn people and can tell them apart. Then I went into his house, and saw the candlesticks.

As the above respondent indicated, there were other signs of recognition, for some people displayed Jewish ritual objects which quickly resolved all doubts.

Sometimes, however, people turned to systematic techniques of exploration. For example, initial conversations were skillfully directed towards attempts to discover the other's religion, or to offer clues as to one's own. When that failed, or seemed imprudent, the conversation turned to food habits:

> . . . we have a taste for Jewish food . . . we told them what kind of food it was we liked: cornbeef, lox [smoked salmon]. . . .
> The day I moved in I advised that I was Jewish by asking for Jewish women who kept kosher. . . .

Sometimes there were no symbols or formulas which could be applied, and people found out by accident:

> My next-door neighbors, they didn't look Jewish, nothing Jewish about

them, but then I asked before Passover if they wanted to try some macaroons, and we found out.

I knew them as neighbors, knew them for a month, then the name was given me on a mailing list. I was amazed, I didn't know they were Jewish.

The recognition process was somewhat facilitated by the presence of a minister who conducted a religious survey soon after each court was occupied, and informed curious Jews who the other Jews in the court were. In addition, there were a number of Jewish men who made a point of getting to know the entire Jewish community, and thus they were able to introduce individuals to each other.[17]

There was no automatic progression from recognition to *acquaintance* without a desire for further association. In many cases, however, this desire for association with Jews was implied if not expressed already at the recognition stage, by the aggressiveness of one person or the other in creating conditions that allowed recognition when the Jewish-look-or-name formula alone was not conclusive.

Mutual recognition was followed by further exploration of each other's ethnic characteristics and affiliations. Neighbors asked each other where they were from, where they lived last, whom they knew there, what congregation or groups they belonged to, and later turned to discussing their attitudes towards Jewish traditions and observances. The question, "Did you know the So-and-So's in ————?" was perhaps most important. People who had mutual friends, or even mutual acquaintances in previous places of residence, very quickly passed to the acquaintance and friendship stages, thus accelerating the rate of community formation.

The abundance of these prior contacts is a function of the fact that the world of the middle-class Jew is comparatively small. Even in the larger cities, there are only a limited number of Jewish organizations, temples, and neighborhoods. Furthermore, Jewish families are still extensive, and maintain communication contacts even when kinship solidarity is much reduced. Consequently, people who are socially active tend to meet, or at least know about, a considerable proportion of their community's Jewish group. Many Park Forest Jews thus encountered neighbors with whom they could initiate relationships on the basis of some previous bond, even if it was nothing more than an introduction at some social function. In a new community of strangers, these prior contacts were invested with a greater significance than they would have elsewhere, and the relationships which grew from them achieved regularity and stability rather quickly. They became the foundations for the informal community, which was then completed by the slower development of social relationships among total strangers. The exchange of names also provided an opportunity for the parties involved to measure each other's social status and interests by those of the mutual acquaintance.

While it is difficult to determine at what point an acquaintance relationship became one of *friendship*, the overall time table of the process of informal community development was fairly uniform. Usually ten days to two weeks passed before any but the exceptionally gregarious and mobile people made any serious attempts at getting out of the house to make contacts. However, after this moving-in period, contact, recognition, and acquaintance relationships developed quickly. In general it was a matter of only four to eight weeks before people said they had friends whom they saw regularly. Some residents suggested that regularity did not yet mean intimacy: "We see the So-and-So's regularly but you really can't call them friends, we haven't been here that long." Nor was it certain that these relationships would persist. Nevertheless, in November of 1949 almost all of the families who were living in the village by July of that year had established some regular and stable sociability relationships with their fellow Jews.[18]

B. DEVELOPMENT OF FORMAL ORGANIZATIONS. The development of the formal community began with the organization of a B'nai B'rith lodge and a chapter of the National Council of Jewish Women.

Among the first arrivals in Park Forest were a handful of "Jewish professionals," men who work for American-Jewish agencies. They were interested in setting up Jewish organizations, and while their activity was voluntary, like that of any other resident, their interest was still more than purely social or civic. In March of 1949, when fifty Jewish families were living in the village, one of these professionals (employed as an organizer in Chicago) considered the time to be ripe and invited a small group of men to discuss the formation of a lodge. Several of the men had met each other previously in the course of a local political campaign. Many of those present at the meeting, although vaguely in favor of a group, were not interested in any specific organization. One of them said:

We were contemplating some kind of a social club, recreational, then we hit on . . . B'nai B'rith. The fact is that we were influenced, I guess, by fellows who are with B'nai B'rith.

Consequently, the group decided to form a lodge. Some thirty-five men were invited to the next meeting. There the lodge was organized, with the professionals and a handful of other actives taking over the decision-making positions.

The organization of the women's group took place about a month later. It was initiated by two women who had just entered the village. While they knew the Jewish residents of their court, they wanted to make contact with others. Through a mailing list already compiled by the men's group,[19] the women were contacted and invited to an organizational meeting. At this gathering the process which took place at the men's meeting was repeated. Most of those present expressed the desire and need for a women's group. The initiators proposed affiliation with Council. Their choice was approved, and they were named to leadership positions.

Attendance and active participation in the Council of Jewish Women was immediately greater than in B'nai B'rith, reflecting the women's greater desire for Jewish companionships. Furthermore, the Council meetings provided an efficient and easily available method for newcomers to make contacts with the older settlers. It facilitated the recognition process, and initially this was perhaps the group's major—though latent—function.

The early leadership structure of both groups in its relationships with the informal community was quite similar. The top leaders in both organizations were "lone wolves"—they belonged to no set clique in the village. The rest of the officers in both groups were drawn largely from a clique of the older, well-to-do people who had been active in formal organizational life elsewhere. This clique had become fairly well stabilized by the time the two formal groups were organized; consequently clique members worked actively together in the structuring of the formal community.

After the organizational period, both groups evolved in the direction of their urban counterparts. Thus B'nai B'rith had speakers, played poker, and offered refreshments; the Council ran a number of study groups, heard other speakers, conducted charity programs, and gave the Jewish women of the community a chance to dress up and meet. In November, 1949, each had enrolled about fifty members.

§ *III. The Child-Oriented Community:*
    The Organization of the Sunday School

From the point of view of gaining an understanding of the special nature of the Park Forest Jewish community, the most important process was the formation of the Sunday school. During the four months of organizing activity, the sociological and ideological splits already latent in the young community were brought to light. In the events that culminated in its organization, one may discern the growth of what will be described as the child-oriented Jewish community.

In June, 1949, eighty-six Jewish families were living in the rapidly growing community. Passover had come and gone—the handful of people who observed it traditionally having banded together to order "matzos [unleavened bread] and all the trimmings" from Chicago. The men who had organized the B'nai B'rith lodge, and who now constituted its decision-making group, had already begun to discuss among themselves the organization of a congregation. It was generally agreed that Park Forest's prime problem, however, was a Sunday school for the forty-odd eligible children then in the village. Both organizations had heard speakers on this subject.

A. THE ORGANIZATIONAL PROCESS: CHILD VS. ADULT ORIENTATION. The B'nai B'rith leadership met one evening and outlined the setting up of a Sunday school. This was to be part of a synagogue, either Reform or Conservative. But the project was short-lived. A meeting was arranged with a delegation from the Council. The women refused to help form a congregation, for they insisted that what Park Forest needed at present was a Sunday school; they believed that the organization of a congregation could be discussed later. The men's group had also considered and voted down this alternative. The leader of the group complained:

. . . they [the women] hadn't faced Jewish life, they didn't care for Jewish values, but they recognized that they were Jewish and they needed a Sunday school because the kids asked for it . . . they wanted a nonsectarian Sunday school.

Thus began four months of discussion, argument, and conflict, something previously unfamiliar to the community but easily understandable as institutional labor pains. In other groups such conflicts can often be explained in terms of power struggles between two socio-economic strata or ideological factions. In the Jewish community, however, they may signify conflicts between groups representing different stages in the ethnic adjustment to American life. In Yankee City's Jewish community, for example, the conflict over the synagogue was a struggle between generations. At issue were the rules to be followed in the institution and the amount of acculturation to be legitimated.[20] In Park Forest, where almost everyone is native-born and acculturated to a large and similar extent, the history of the conflict over the Sunday school may be explained as the ascendancy of a new type of formal Jewish community, the *child-oriented* one. This contrasts with the traditional Jewish community, which may be described as *adult-oriented.*

The adult-oriented community is one whose religious-cultural activities[21] are focused around its adult population, and in which the children's role is to learn to become adults, and to assume adult functions at the earliest opportunity. The child-oriented community is one in which the community's organizational energy is focused almost exclusively around the children's problems and needs as Jewish children (as perceived by the parents) *while at the same time most of the adults abstain from religious-cultural activities and involvement in the community.*

The Sunday school conflict in Park Forest was from the beginning a conflict between these two concepts of community organization. The men who wanted a congregation were thinking of an adult Jewish community training its children through a congregational Sunday school for eventual membership in the adult Jewish group. The women represented the child-oriented conception; they wanted a school for the children. As soon became clear, it was one that would not involve the adults in the Jewish community. Thus one man pointed out, very bitterly, that:

. . . the Jews are running away from each other, they don't want to stick out, and in a small community like this, they do stick out.

The women, equally bitter, accused the men of wanting a "Jewish Community Incorporated." Heated words revealed the underlying pattern. The women were accused of deserting the adult Jewish community; the men were said to be trying to overorganize it.[22]

The conflict between these opposing concepts became clearer in the weeks that followed. A steering committee consisting of four men and four women was formed to proceed with the actual organization of the school. While the men handled the administrative organization and the budget, the curriculum problem was left to a young Chicago rabbi who had first been invited as a speaker, and had then become interested in Park Forest. He supported the women in their rejection of the synagogue but suggested instead an adult-oriented Sunday school. He made this quite clear at a public meeting held early in October, 1949, when he said:

> As we train the children, you will have to train them yourself . . . you'll have to move towards a community center and a synagogue eventually . . . and give the children support.

The reaction to the rabbi's remarks came a week later at a meeting called to discuss the choice of texts, and to answer parents' questions. There quickly developed a spirited discussion of the curriculum. (The rabbi did not attend, having meanwhile accepted a post outside the Chicago area.) A large number of the parents voiced their dissatisfaction with the rabbi's ideas, and demanded what they described as a "secular" Sunday school which would teach the child *about* Jewish traditions. It would not tell him to put pressure on his parents to *observe* these in the home. Under the misnomer of "secular," the major concept of the child-oriented school was defined in public for the first time.[23]

The committee defended the rabbi's formulation. However, when feelings began to rise, some of the disagreement in the committee itself became public and finally the group resigned. In the heat of debate, one woman stated her belief that a locally staffed school could be set up, and she was asked to recruit a new committee. The group was voted into office after giving assurances that it would maintain a child-oriented approach.

The new committee felt it lacked sufficient Jewish background and experience to organize the school and sought help from a Jewish group worker (who had been away while the conflict raged) and his wife. He went to work and, after others had refused, he accepted the presidency of the group. His wife, an experienced Hebrew school teacher, agreed to become the superintendent of the school, which meanwhile had already announced an opening date.

While registration of children was taking place, the group worker met with the committee. Because of his previous experience, and the fact that he was a stranger to everyone concerned and had not been involved in the ideological and personal conflicts, he was able to get the various factions to work together. In talking with the parents of prospective students the couple found that:

> The chief objection seemed to be, they don't want the child taught that he must do this and that, light Sabbath candles, etc., so that when he comes home and his parents are not doing these things, there is no trouble.

They explained the curriculum to the parents, assuring them that:

The children will not be taught that parents have to light candles; the children will be informed of the background of candles. . . . We're teaching the child not that he must do these things; we just teach him the customs.

They also suggested to the parents that candles ought to be lit, if only to satisfy the needs of the child. In describing the major direction of the curriculum the couple unconsciously summarized the opposing points of view: "It was pointed out that the parents too play a role in the education, but we thought that *the historical approach*[24] was best." Parental pressure had thus resulted in a child-oriented school.

B. THE FUNCTION OF CHILD ORIENTATION IN THE ETHNIC PROCESS. The traditional Jewish community has always emphasized adult orientation, and adult-oriented activities. In the religious code, the period of childhood was terminated at thirteen and the young Jew was expected to take part in the intellectual and ritual activities of the adults. The traditional curriculum prepared youngsters for these activities, though the rigor of the training did not take into consideration that the student was a child. Reform and Conservative groups instituted many changes, but their organizational objectives and activities continued to be oriented toward adults. The American Jewish community remains officially adult-oriented. Major emphasis is placed on adult activities, although actual attendance and participation statistics would probably indicate a changing pattern. In Park Forest, however, adult Jews quite consciously rejected any involvement in the religious and cultural aspects of the Jewish community, while trying to teach the children to be Jews.

The source of this change seemed to lie in the American-Jewish middle-class family. The Sunday school is an institution which transmits norms of ethnic culture and symbols of identification, whereas the home and the family are run by secular, middle-class behavior patterns. The parents expected that the contradictions between the concept of the traditional Jewish home implicit in the Sunday school curriculum, and that of the actual one, would result in family tensions. Consequently, the parents were firm in not wanting the youngsters to bring the traditional patterns, plus the pressure of their youthful persuasiveness, into the house.

The group workers' advice to the parents to light Friday night candles for the satisfaction of the needs of the child appears as a significant redefinition of the traditional adult-oriented pattern. The statement accepted the fact that the parents were no longer emotionally involved in the ceremony. It redefined their role in a child-oriented manner—they became instruments which focused the ceremony exclusively toward the child. The traditional ceremony itself remained the same.

Why should the parents want to involve their children in the Jewish culture while withdrawing their own participation? Some explanations can be inferred from the reasons parents gave for sending their children to Sunday school.

Uppermost was the parental desire to develop and to reinforce Jewish identification through learning about Jewish history and traditions. That the child should internalize this identification was taken for granted. One parent explained:

> When a child grows up, you begin to let the child know what she is, and make her familiar with the Jewish people . . . to learn what Judaism is about. She might as well learn what she is, and what it means. . . .

The reinforcement pattern was stressed by parents of several six- and seven-year-olds, who hoped that the Sunday school would supply the children with answers about their identity. The interviewees indicated that such questions began to develop in the children's peer groups at this age. Sometimes the children were stimulated by a remark made in school, or by phrases picked up from the parental conversation. One child may have discovered that he is Protestant, and that there are also Catholics and Jews. He brought that information to the group, which then tried to apply these newly discovered categories to its members. Soon the Jewish children came home to ask their parents what they were, and "were they Jewish," or perhaps even to inquire, "Papa, why do I have to be Jewish?" Here the Sunday school was asked to came to the rescue, and to help the parents solve their children's problems. One father reported that his son, now in Sunday school, could:

> . . . probably tell me more [about Judaism] than I can. Sixty per cent of the Jews couldn't answer the questions their children ask.

Some parents were troubled by the children's questions because of their own ambivalence about the answers, but others were less concerned about their own ideas than with the fear that a wrong answer to the child might lead to undesirable emotional consequences.

Less sophisticated parents who wanted their children to learn about being Jewish complemented all of this by the qualification, "We want him to know what it's all about so that later he will have the background to make a choice." The notion that a Jewish child has a choice about being Jewish (at least in terms of public affiliation and overt social behavior), and that he could make his own decision in early adolescence or early adulthood, was voiced even by some parents who minutes later expressed their own continuing ambivalence about how to act and feel as regards to their identity.[25]

Another group of parents saw Sunday school preparation as a defense against later hardships arising out of the minority position of the American Jew. Two parents suggested that:

> . . . a Jewish child, he's something different, he's never one of the boys in a Gentile group; even if he's the best guy he's one of the outsiders, the first to get abused. And if he doesn't know why, it's going to be a great shock. It's part of his training, the Sunday school; he needs it.

> . . . I want him to have more security and acceptance in regard to his status and relationship with society—be better prepared than I was. . . .

Another reason for the parents' desire to have their children attend Sunday school stemmed from the latter's distinctive sociological position in the suburban Jewish community. While the parents selected their intimate friends from within the Jewish group, the children found their playmates in the court, without concern for ethnic origin.[26] In this respect they differed from big-city children who grow up in a peer group which is largely Jewish, partly for ecological reasons and partly because their parents try to bring them up among Jewish children. Furthermore, in Park Forest the Jewish children of grammar-school age soon saw their non-Jewish friends leave for school on Sunday mornings. They also heard about it from them later. Then, as one mother explained:

Our kids run around in the court, they want to get dressed up and go to church too. The Sunday school [the Jewish one] will give them something to do.

A number of children were actually sent to Protestant school a few times, but in general this pressure from the children was translated into an accelerated parental demand for a Jewish school.

For most of these parents, the Sunday school was not—like the traditional educational institution, the *cheder*—a religious or cultural school, and few considered the teaching of Jewish tradition to be an intrinsic end. Rather, the Jewish father in Park Forest who arises early on Sunday morning in order to deliver his youngster to Sunday school, conceived the institution to be a school in Jewish identity, in "*Jewishness*," not in *Judaism*.

C. THE CHILD-ORIENTED HOLIDAYS. The Sunday school was not alone in being child-oriented. During the fourteen months covered by this study, all of the adult activities of the formal organizations—aside from some sociability programs—were also oriented towards the children. The B'nai B'rith group nearly collapsed when its leadership was drawn into the attempt to organize a congregation, and later a Sunday school. After the school had been set up, the lodge immediately went to work on a Chanukah party which it planned to make an annual event of major proportions. The officers had realized that child orientation was dominant in Park Forest. One speculated hopefully that "perhaps the party will draw the parents closer together."

Even the future congregation, which then existed only as a discussion topic, was conceived of as child-oriented. In asking respondents whether or not they would like to see a congregation established in the village, we found that two-thirds responded favorably. Of those who gave a reason, 48 per cent explained that they wanted it exclusively for the children:

I just like to feel that I belong, as far as the childen are concerned. I'd like to keep it up, for them to think they should belong.

I want to give him the opportunity of witnessing something Jewish; he doesn't get too much at home.

Others were more emphatic in their child orientation:

You can't get me down . . . I don't believe in praying . . . in God . . . I want it for my son and daughter, I want them to know what it's like. I have had the background . . . I remember I enjoyed it at the time.

In Park Forest the Jewish holidays were major instruments for teaching and reinforcing Jewish identification, and in this process they too became child-oriented. Perhaps because of the age of most of the children, major emphasis was placed on what were called the "happy holidays": Sukkoth, Passover, Purim and Chanukah (traditionally commemorating the fall harvest, and victories over Egyptian, Persian and Syrian persecution, respectively).

Chanukah bulked largest of all. Even at Chanukah-time in 1948, when the Park Forest Jewish community numbered less than twenty families, the problem of Chanukah vs. Christmas had already concerned the parents. A year later the subject loomed large indeed. Thus the Council devoted its November meeting to ways of celebrating Chanukah; the apparent need to counteract the non-Jewish holiday encouraged the sale of $300 worth of religious materials.[27] The parental concern was understandable, for by late November the peer groups in which Jewish children participated were eagerly awaiting Christmas and Santa Claus. Naturally, the Jewish children attempted to share these expectations, and asked their parents for Christmas trees. The parents acted quickly:

My child wanted a Christmas tree, and we talked her out of it. . . . I make a fuss about Chanukah to combat Christmas, I build Chanukah up, and she appreciates Chanukah lights just as much. What we have done is to give her presents every night.

The F's had a big menorah in their window; that was very fine; maybe I'll do the same next year. . . . I could put my little menorah up there, I could wire it; is that O.K.? We could have different color lights—no, that's too much like Christmas.

Other parents explained that they decorated the menorah, and even the entire house, and used electric candles instead of wax ones. They tried hard to emphasize and advertise Chanukah to the child, and at the same time to exclude the Christmas tree and its related symbols from his environment. Parents were very bitter about the Jewish families who displayed Christmas trees. The names of these people were known throughout a large part of the Jewish community, and described in hostile terms. One mother explained:

The main trouble is with other Jews. In our house we do certain things, and in other Jewish houses they don't, and the children ask questions. . . . It's very confusing when Jewish people celebrate a definitely Christian holiday; I don't know what to tell my children when there are Jewish people with a Christmas tree on Chanukah.

During this conflict between the American and the ethnic culture, the ethnic festival undergoes marked changes. The traditionally simple menorah must compete with the visually more exciting Christmas tree; the gaiety and glitter of the Christmas season forces the parents to use a redecorated Chanukah to reinforce the child's Jewishness. Thus, Chanukah becomes increasingly a Jewish Christmas. In this process, the parents' already minimal participation in the holiday is forgotten. Chanukah, more so than any other festival, becomes completely child-oriented.

§ IV. The Adults: Secular Involvement in Sacred Patterns

Religion in Park Forest is thus primarily for the children; the adults have been pictured so far only as its somewhat unwilling handmaidens. However, their own religious activities, or lack of them, are equally important in shaping the suburban Jewish community, and will now be discussed.

Although Park Forest's isolation from religious facilities discouraged tradition-oriented residents, the village did attract two groups of people who wanted congregational affiliation. One group consisted of high-income families who had previously been active in congregations elsewhere. After the unsuccessful attempt to set up a synagogue in the village, about ten families equal in socio-economic position and status to the well-to-do store-owners and professionals in nearby Chicago Heights, joined the Reform congregation there. In addition, there were about ten families from Chicago's lower-middle-class Jewish areas[28] who maintained enough of the traditional religious complex of behavior patterns and attitudes to describe themselves as Orthodox or Conservative. They favored the establishment of a Conservative synagogue in the village.

The large majority made no effort at religious affiliation at this time, however. Judged by religious practices and synagogue attendance, most Park Foresters were not observant. As indicated in Table 6, 59 per cent of the families said that they had not attended religious services in recent years. The "break," if it can be described as such, generally came with the leaving of the parental home.

Table 6—Previous Adult Synagogue Attendance by Activity Status

Attendance	Actives		Inactives		All	
	No.	%	No.	%	No.	%
Regular	0	0	0	0	0	0
Occasional & High Holidays	1	8	4	12	5	11
High Holidays Only	5	42	8	25	13	30
No Recent Attendance	6	50	20	63	26	59
Total	12	100	32	100	44	100

While previous synagogue attendance was greater among actives than inactives, it was also higher among parents with children of Sunday school age. However, Table 7 suggests that the presence of older children was a more significant factor than activity itself.

Table 7—Proportion of Adults Previously Attending Synagogues by Activity and Family Status

	Occasional and Holiday Attendance	No Recent Attendance	Total	% Attending
Actives with School-Age Children	3	3	6	50
Actives without School-Age Children	3	3	6	50
Inactives with School-Age Children	5	6	11	45
Inactives without School-Age Children	7	14	21	33

After arriving in Park Forest, even the more loyal Sabbath worshippers ceased attending services. The nearest synagogues were in Chicago Heights, about fifteen minutes riding-distance away, but considerable social and cultural distance existed between that community's wealthy Reform temple, its Orthodox synagogue, and most of the residents of Park Forest. Geographical and social distance, lack of motivation, and the problem of baby-sitters all served to keep residents from attending services in Chicago Heights. Chicago's synagogues were one and one-half to two and one-half hours away, and only on the High Holidays did some ex-Chicagoans return to the city for services and family reunions.

For the observant few, the isolation from other Jewish institutions led to compromises, and eventual neglect of traditions that could be kept up only with extraordinary effort. Two examples suggest that forsaking of tradition appears to take place particularly at times of residential change. One of the housewives reported:

I used to buy kosher meat till about a year ago. . . . I just didn't like the kosher butcher in the neighborhood when we moved to Chicago; he gave me bad cuts. . . . I was just fed up, and everybody else was eating nonkosher meat, so I thought I'd try it. It took me two years to get used to it—many times I threw steaks away, I just couldn't eat them—but now I think nonkosher cuts are much better.

A Conservative resident explained his dilemma about one of the major holidays. Should he drive to the synagogue and violate one law, he wondered, or stay home and miss services, thus violating another commandment? In the absence of theological counsel, he finally decided it would be more fitting to drive to services than to stay away.[29]

For the majority of the residents, such problems were nonexistent. Their Friday nights were spent as others spend them in Park Forest—entertaining, going out, or staying home. Some people did light the Sabbath candles at dinner time, however. Saturdays were reserved for work around the house, shopping, visiting, and taking care of responsibilities and errands for which suburbanites have no time during the week.

Two types of Jewish religious patterns were still being observed. The first were the holidays and traditions that had become child-oriented. The others were those that related the Jew to his parents. Thus, several of the men remarked matter-of-factly that they were not interested in religious observances, but added, just as matter-of-factly, "except *Yahrzeit* [the annual remembrance of dead parents] of course." Others mentioned keeping certain holidays:

The only thing we did, at my son's birth we had a rabbi at the circumcision, mostly for my wife's parents; they would have felt bad.

Some people spent the holidays with parents, in-laws, or grandparents, celebrating them less as religious ceremonies than as family get-togethers. One respondent explained in jest:

I believe Rosh Hashanah [the Jewish New Year] should be two days, Passover too, for practical purposes. One day we go to his family, the other to mine.

Of the four housewives in the sample who were keeping kosher households, one explained:

I don't believe in keeping kosher . . . I do it for my parents now . . . I owe it to them to make my home welcome to them; I would prefer to go to the A & P . . . it's this weird sense of obligation to my parents.

Due to the fact that almost all Park Forest's Jewish residents came from more-or-less Orthodox homes, deference to the parents was expressed in these religious terms, even by those otherwise nonobservant. Many such individuals had broken away from all personal religious observance when they left the parental home. An Orthodox upbringing had left its mark, however, for the people who were no longer observant were conscious of this fact. The uneasiness and embarrassment which greeted the section of the interview on religious behavior suggested guilt feelings and indicated the extent to which the immigrant standards remained in force psychologically even though they were no longer implemented behaviorally.[30] In fact, some individuals viewed the desire to have children attend Sunday school as compensation for guilt feelings about personal religious deviations. One observer commented:

The parents aren't interested but they sort of give their kids Sunday school as a castor oil, a preventative for what ails the parents.

The parentally oriented religious observances created the first demand for a village religious institution. In January, 1949, when twenty-five Jewish families lived in Park Forest, the group already had a rabbi-substitute. A gregarious Jewish professional, although a layman, appointed himself on the basis of having had more religious training than any other resident. He ministered to occasional needs for technical religious advice, and reported that:

Someone needed Hebrew writing on a tombstone, they were told to call me; someone else wanted *Yiskor* [prayer for the dead] or *Yahrzeit* services, they called me.

When the Jewish population increased, other men served this function in other sections of the community.[31]

The religious needs were not strong enough to create sufficient demand for a synagogue. In September, 1949, after the first unsuccessful attempt to set up the congregation, two small groups of residents tried to organize High Holiday [New Year and Day of Atonement] services. However, because of poor communication between the newer courts, and the fact that the existing Jewish organizations in the older parts of the village were either engrossed in the Sunday school fight or had not yet resumed operations after the normal summer layoff, neither group was able to get a *minyan* [the quorum of ten needed to hold public services]. Some families went to Chicago to celebrate the High Holidays with relatives.

Reference has already been made to the desire for a congregation as: (1) an institution to maintain the adult-oriented Jewish community, (2) an instrument in a power struggle, (3) a child-oriented device for the inculcation of Jewishness, and (4) a religious institution (for a minority). A fifth function of the congregation in the suburban community became apparent after the High Holidays. At that time a small group of Jewish residents in what were then the newest courts had found each other, and decided after an evening's discussion that Park Forest should have a congregation. With the militancy of a newly established social movement, they planned to organize a mass meeting, run a fund-raising dance, and make a special financial appeal to the developer. While the project never materialized, a statement made by the group's leader is significant. He said as follows:

> We need a synagogue so they'll have more respect for us, to show that we have arrived, that we're not merely a bunch of individuals.

"They" referred to the non-Jewish neighbors. As it happened, the area in which the agitation arose was occupied by some small-town Midwesterners and Southerners who had already shown their distaste for their Jewish neighbors. The desire for physical evidence of Jewish group existence, and for a unifying symbol to negate inequality feelings in the face of aggression, was translated into the militant demand for a congregation.

This function of the congregation as a symbol of Jewish solidarity was also suggested during the interviewing by other residents in older parts of the village. Almost one-third of those who gave reasons for wanting a synagogue in Park Forest thought along the lines suggested by the following two respondents:

> I think it's sort of nice for the Jewish community to have a focal point; the religious congregation is a focal point.

> If the others are here, I don't see why a synagogue shouldn't be. . . . It's not competition as much as a matter of self-respect; I mean when the Catholic church is established, it'll have something to offer. . . . I would not like the Jewish community to have to rely on another church . . . it's a matter of self-respect. The Jews should carry their load.

The extent of the religious interests of the adult community was illustrated further by the responses to the previously mentioned interview question about a congregation. Some 66 per cent of the respondents were favorable toward the formation of a congregation. Since it was both psychologically and morally easier for a respondent to favor a synagogue than to oppose it, attitude intensity was also analyzed. Table 8 indicates that only 32 per cent of the sample could be described as personally involved in this problem (43 per cent if the unfavorable ones are included), and 57 per cent were indifferent, although most of them favorably so. Actives were considerably more favorable toward a congregation, and personally more involved than the inactives.

Table 8—Attitudes toward a Congregation by Intensity of Response and Activity Status

Attitude Intensity	Actives No.	%	Inactives No.	%	All No.	%
Favorable-Involved:						
("Yes, I want it for my child")	6	50	8	25	14	32
Favorable-Indifferent:						
("I'd like to see one, but for those in the community who want it")	4	33	11	35	15	34
Indifferent:						
("I never thought about it")	0	0	3	9	3	7
Unfavorable-Indifferent:						
("No, but I don't care")	0	0	7	22	7	16
Unfavorable-Involved:						
("I wouldn't belong to a synagogue")	2	17	3	9	5	11
Total	12	100	32	100	44	100

Attitudes toward a congregation were also more favorable among parents with school-age children (see Table 9). However, a separate analysis of the favorable-involved respondents showed that the presence of older children seemed to be more significant than activity.

Table 9—Proportion of Respondents Favorable-Involved towards a Congregation by Activity and Family Status

	Favorable-Involved	Other	Total	% Favorable-Involved
Actives with School-Age Children	3	3	6	50
Actives without School-Age Children	3	3	6	50
Inactives with School-Age Children	5	6	11	45
Inactives without School-Age Children	3	18	21	14

While the community climate in 1949 did not seem to be conducive to a congregation, the attitude analysis indicates that the favorable-involvement on the part of more than half the actives combined with the support of a quarter of the inactives, and the indifference of most of the others, might not present any major obstacles to the setting up of a congregation (although it might place a handicap on its ability to achieve widespread support).[32] The kind of congregation that might be set up could be guessed at by an analysis of the reasons given by the favorable-involved and the favorable-indifferent respondents. Of the respondents who gave any reasons, 48 per cent favored a child-oriented congregation; only 14 per cent, all of them favorable-involved, wanted a synagogue for the religious-cultural observances of the entire family (see Table 10).

Table 10—Reasons for Favorable Attitudes towards a Congregation
by Intensity and Activity Status

Reasons	FAVORABLE-INVOLVED			FAVORABLE-INDIFFERENT			Total	
	Actives	Inactives	All	Actives	Inactives	All	No.	%
Children's Needs	3	4	7	0	3	3	10	48
Family Needs	1	2	3	0	0	0	3	14
Community Cohesion	1	1	2	1	3	4	6	28
Other	1	0	1	1	0	1	2	10
Total	6	7	13	2	6	8	21	100

§ V. The Informal Community—
The Ethnic Cohesion of Sociability

While Jewish Park Foresters may have been child-oriented when concerned with Jewish religious life, and though they avoided involvement with adult Jewish activities, they were nevertheless willing and desirous of associating with other Jews. Groups were formed consisting usually of another couple or a clique[33] of couples. Together they composed the informal Jewish community.

A. SOCIABILITY PATTERNS. On the whole, the informal community existed only at night. In the daytime Park Forest was inhabited by housewives and the ever present children, and the Jewish women participated in the social life of the courts in which they lived. They interrupted their household duties to chat and "visit with" a neighbor over a morning cup of coffee, or while watching the children in the afternoon. They also belonged to the bridge and sewing clubs that were established in many courts. In these non-intimate, quasi-occupational relationships, which in many ways resembled their husbands' relationships at the office, ethnic distinctions were minimized.[34]

In the evening and weekend social relationships of couples, however, the Jewish husband and wife turned primarily to other Jews. One housewife summarized matters as follows:

My real close friends are Jewish, my after-dark friends in general are Jewish, but my daytime friends are Gentile.

Table 11 shows the sociability choices of thirty respondents who volunteered the names of their friends living in the village.

Although the figures are small, it is apparent that the actives chose their friends among other Jews to a greater extent than the inactives. *However, about half the people who named both Jews and non-Jews pointed out that their best friends were Jewish,* and two of the inactives who "saw" mainly non-Jews explained that they were merely visiting with

Table 11—Sociability Choices by Activity Status

"See Regularly Socially"	Actives		Inactives		All	
	No.	%	No.	%	No.	%
Jews Only	4	57	6	26	10	33
Mainly Jews, Some Non-Jews	1	14	9	39	10	33
Mainly Non-Jews, Some Jews	1	14	5	22	6	20
Non-Jews Only	1	14	3	13	4	14
Total	7	99	23	100	30	100

nearby neighbors and implied that the search for friends had not yet begun in earnest. Two of the respondents who named only non-Jews were attempting to avoid all relationships with Jews. Thus, for the purpose of "friendship" as distinguished from "neighboring," and especially for close relationships, the Jewish residents seemed to prefer other Jews. The informal Jewish community existed primarily for this function.

The cliques into which this community was subdivided varied in size from two to six couples. Sociometric factors as well as living room size set this as an upper limit. A superficial sociometric analysis indicated that these cliques were connected into a network (which existed primarily for communication) by people who belonged to more than one clique, and by a few others who maintained loose memberships with a large number. These latter people, who made few close friends, chose to get to know as many people as possible and derived pride and satisfaction from the acquisition of such relationships. During the time of the study, the informal community came together only once. This was at a village dance. As both Jews and non-Jews later reported, the Jews at this affair congregated in one section of the hall.

The formation of cliques was accelerated by the people with previous acquaintances. However, loose as these contacts may have been (a fleeting introduction at a meeting or party sufficed), such people established friendship relationships much more quickly than strangers who had first to explore each others' social attributes and interests. They generally became "charter members" of a clique which then attracted strangers into its circle. Of the approximately twenty-five cliques and combinations isolated in the sample, twenty had been formed, at least in part, on the basis of previous or mutual acquaintance. In this respect, the Jews differed sharply from other Park Foresters, most of whom knew no one when they arrived in the village.

Cliques were formed primarily on the basis of class, status, age, and ethnic background criteria. One of the largest and most powerful of the cliques was made up predominantly of relatively older, higher-income Park Foresters, many of them previously active in big-city Jewish congregations and groups. Most of the men held supervisory positions in business or industry, or were in the non-academic professions. A second clique consisted largely of academicians, researchers, scientists, writers, and their wives (many of whom were active on the community newspaper). A third was made up of families who had come to Park Forest from areas of second and third settlement. They were torn between their lower-middle-class and still partially tradition-oriented ways of life, and the upper-middle-class ways of the first clique.

Despite the class-status homogeneity of the cliques, members often harbored the most diverse attitudes toward Jewishness. Respondents reported frequent clique discussions on Jewish topics, and commented:

I don't start these discussions; it's a beautiful subject to steer away from; there are more fights about religion than anything else.

There's a couple with whom we're very friendly; we like each other very much. They don't believe the way we do, and if we discuss it, it would just lead to argument.

Whereas most non-Jewish Park Foresters chose their friends from within their courts, Jews tended to wander outside the court for their social relationships. Sometimes this was due to the absence of other Jews, but when this was not the case, clique membership and associated status and age criteria were more important than locational ones. One respondent described her relationship with the other Jewish women in the court:

We've never spent an evening together. Mrs. F. and I are good friends, we walk together, but she is a bit older. . . . She travels in a different circle of people . . . with an older, more settled crowd, better off; if they have children, they're beyond the preschool age. . . .

B. FRIENDSHIP AND INGROUP BEHAVIOR. Many factors must be considered in the explanation of this intraethnic friendship pattern. A fundamental one is the age-old segregation between Jew and non-Jew in Western society. Despite political emancipation, this segregation has been maintained by cultural differences. While many of these differences are being eliminated by acculturation, not enough time has elapsed for this change to affect adult social, and especially peer-group, relationships. As a consequence, current Jewish-non-Jewish relationships are still based largely on the historic segregation. Most Jews seem to assume its continued existence. Also, some feel they would be rejected in non-Jewish society, while others are not much interested in primary relationships with non-Jews.[35]

Perhaps most often, the long segregation has made association solely with other Jews almost habitual. The interview material indicated that most Park Forest Jews grew up in urban Jewish neighborhoods. Their parental circle, and their own childhood, adolescent, and adult peer groups, were predominantly Jewish. In the absence of any strong incentives or socio-economic and ideological pressures for greater social intimacy with non-Jews, these patterns of association were rarely questioned.

An important functional basis for the choice of Jewish friends was contained in the attitude shared by many Park Forest Jews that "it's easier being with Jews." *Since sociability is primarily a leisure activity, and in a suburban community one of the major forms of relaxation and self-expres-*

sion, the belief that there is likely to be less tension in social relationships with other Jews becomes all-important. A respondent who had both Jewish and non-Jewish friends pointed out:

> You can give vent to your feelings. If you talk to a Christian and say you don't believe in this, you are doing it as a Jew; with Jewish friends you can tell 'em point blank what you feel.

However ambivalent their feelings towards Judaism, in a group of friends the Jews form a strong ingroup, with well-verbalized attitudes toward the non-Jewish outgroup.[36]

The group cohesion, the ingroup attitude, and the anti-outgroup feeling that often accompanies it, are expressed frequently at the informal parties and gatherings where the friendly atmosphere and the absence of non-Jews creates a suitable environment. These feelings are verbalized through the Jewish joke, which expresses aspects of the Jew's attitude toward himself as well as toward the outgroup, or through direct remarks about the outgroup. At parties which are predominantly Jewish, it is necessary to find out if everyone is Jewish before such attitudes can be expressed overtly. When someone in the gathering who is assumed to be Jewish turns out to be otherwise, the atmosphere becomes very tense and the non-Jewish person may be avoided thereafter.

The manifestation of this ingroup attitude was described by one respondent who was converted to Judaism in his twenties. He told of becoming disturbed over a discussion at an informal party, the subject being how to inculcate Judaism into the children "and keep them away from the *goyim* (non-Jews)." This resident was very active in the Jewish community and feared the consequences of revealing his origin. Nevertheless, he felt the time had come to announce that he had been born and raised a Christian. The declaration broke up the party, and shocked many people. He said afterwards:

> From now on, they'll be on their guard with me in their presence. They've lost their liberty of expression, they don't express themselves without restriction now. At a party if anybody says something, everybody looks to see if I've been offended and people are taken into a corner and explained about me.

Despite the fact that this person had adopted the Jewish religion, was raising his children as Jews, and was active in Jewish life, he was no longer a member of the ingroup although he remained a member both of the community and of his clique.

In summary, ingroup feelings provided a solid base of emotional security for group members of the type which they felt they could not receive from strictly organizational and religious activities. It gave a cohesive function to the informal community.

C. Ethnic Cohesion Through Intellectual Positions and Leisure-Time Preferences. Some of the more highly educated members of the community rejected these ingroup feelings as "chauvinistic"; they pointedly responded that they did not distinguish between Jews and non-Jews in choosing friends. Nevertheless, they remained in the ingroup.[37] They made statements like the following:

The funny thing is, most of our friends are Jewish even though we say we don't care.

Or they said, on a note of guilt:

I think we should try to have friends that aren't Jewish. I don't like the fact that all my friends are Jewish.

Such Jews sensed that their failure to associate with non-Jews was not due to ethnic differences, but rather to their own special orientation toward American society and middle-class culture. Several reported such differences with honest misgivings and alarm:

I think most Jews feel they are a little better than others . . . they won't admit it, they think they're smarter than the rest. I almost guess Jews live by brain more than anyone else.

We're smarter, that's a prejudice . . . we have better intuition, but I know it's not true.

The Jews are more conscientious, they get more involved as in the League of Women Voters. . . .

These feelings were summarized in extreme form by one respondent:

I have a friend who is not Jewish who told me how fortunate I was in being born Jewish. Otherwise I might be one of the sixteen to eighteen out of twenty Gentiles without a social conscience and liberal tendencies. . . . Being Jewish, most of the Jews, nine out of ten, are sympathetic with other problems; they sympathize, have more culture and a better education; strictly from the social and cultural standpoint a man is lucky to be born a Jew.

These attitudes had some basis in reality, for there seemed to be proportionately more Jews than non-Jews in Park Forest who expressed strong feelings of social consciousness, a personal concern in the political, social and economic problems of the larger society, some interest in intellectual questions, and a tendency towards humanistic agnosticism.[38] Similarly, more Jews seemed to be interested in serious music and the fine arts, or at least the "highbrow" or "upper-middle brow" mass media fare,[39] in the so-called "higher quality" magazines, in the reading of books, and in membership in a Park Forest Cinema Club which showed foreign and art films.[40]

As a result, Jews who sought people sharing this subculture of intellectual interests and leisure preference tended to find them more easily among other Jews. In part this was due to the greater accessibility of other Jews. However, this was not a sufficient factor. Jews came together not only because they were Jews but because they shared the subculture, though it was actually devoid of Jewish themes. Furthermore, when Jewish problems were discussed by this group (and they *were* discussed), these were seen from a generalized world-view rather than from the ingroup perspectives described above.[41] Since the reasons for associating with other Jews were not primarily ethnic, ethnic distinctions were not made.[42] The Jewish scientists and academicians in the village formed a number of cliques organized on the basis of this shared culture. Membership, though predominantly Jewish, included non-Jews as well.[43]

The explanation for the fact that Jews seem to be more predominant in this culture than non-Jews is a complex one which can only be suggested here. In part, it stems from the fact that the second generation Jew is frequently a marginal person whose upbringing makes him sensitive to the world around him.[44] Furthermore, this culture is associated with upper- and upper-middle class circles,[45] and in Park Forest was shared by Jews who were either already upper-middle class, or moving in that direction. However, people did not choose this culture for its status implications, for they did not choose it consciously. Rather, they were drawn to it as much by their marginality as their mobility.

§ VI. Some Elements of a Young Suburban Jewish Community: A Summary

In 1949, Park Forest was a new, growing, and only partially completed community which could be expected to change significantly before stabilizing. Nevertheless, a number of elements in the make-up of the community, even after only a year of existence, seemed fundamental enough to remain unchanged.

First, the single theme which seems to characterize Park Forest Jews best is their child orientation. Second, in behavior and aspirations, they are solidly identified with one part or another of the ubiquitous middle-class consumption culture—even though they are likely to share this culture, especially in their intimate sociable activities, only with other Jews. *Their adjustment to American society and their present position in it can be described therefore as behavioral acculturation, but with continued social cohesion and isolation.*[46] Thus the Jews of Park Forest remain an ethnic group, albeit different from the parental one. As cultural differentiation has disappeared, ingroup cohesion depends increasingly on the feeling of Jewishness and identification with a group known as Jews. This cohesion in the face of cultural change cannot be better illustrated than by the angry comment of one Jewish resident about his Jewish neighbor:

He went to work on Yom Kippur [Day of Atonement]. That made me so mad. I think that's our day, I don't believe in Yom Kippur and I can't fast . . . but I do think it's an important day; that's not hypocrisy.

This feeling of Jewish identity provided the impetus for the parents' insistence on a Sunday school, for their transformation of the Chanukah holiday, and for the unending attempt to indoctrinate the child with a sense of Jewishness.

From a functional perspective, child orientation must be viewed as a

social mechanism by which Jewishness is transmitted to the next generation. In most societies, the group's *esprit de corps* is transmitted latently
through the children's imitation of, and partial participation in, adult
activities. In Park Forest, however, this transmission has become a manifest process, programmed for by the school. This has permitted parents
to select their own involvement pattern even while seeking ethnic allegiance from their children.

In the transmission of ethnic identification, the cultural tradition is also
passed on, though as an instrument and a by-product, and consequently
with alterations in content. Nevertheless, so long as Judaism is the curriculum for transmitting Jewishness, the traditional behavior patterns and
ideas will at least be discussed and taught, even though their incorporation
into the rules of daily life seems highly unlikely. *Child orientation is thus
a mechanism that guarantees the existence of the ethnic group and its
culture for another generation, despite the indifference, ambivalence, or
rejection of the culture by the adult carriers.*

Third, the community divides itself into "actives" and "inactives." In
1949, the actives made up about 27 per cent of the sample. However, this
proportion was probably temporarily high, for leaders of minority factions
would later withdraw from activity as the organizations crystallized
around majority points of view. As a group, the actives are distinguished
as having a somewhat higher average income, better education, and higher-
status occupation than the inactives. Actives are more likely to be upper-
middle class in consumption characteristics.

The inactives show a relative indifference to formal organizations,
especially if their children are not yet of Sunday school age. However, the
direction of this indifference tended to be favorable toward a proposed
congregation, especially if this was defined as a child-oriented institution.
The actives, on the other hand, are personally more involved in a congregation. They are likely to rank the existence and growth of the formal
organizations ahead of their personal religious-cultural attitudes, which
seem also to be primarily child-oriented.

Fourth, the developmental history of the Jewish community testifies
to the role of the Jewish professional as a spearhead, or "catalytic agent"
of the actives. Jewish professionals helped to bring Jewish residents together, they administered to their religious needs, started the lodge, tried
to organize a congregation, helped in forming the Sunday school, and have
since supervised Jewish education in the village. The Jewish professional
who replaced the citizen leader as the main cog in group formation seems
to be a new man on the Jewish scene, and his role may be another contribution to the trend of a functional rationalization of community life.
He is not a rabbi, but rather a youth worker, teacher, fund-raiser, social
worker, or public relations man whose occupational skills may be useful
in the extra-curricular task of starting a new community.[47] But even more
important, in Park Forest he is an expert at being Jewish, a skill many

other Park Foresters do not have. Sometimes this expert Jewishness is a part of his background, and his reason for becoming a professional. At times it results from a desire to work in the Jewish community rather than among non-Jews. Sometimes the expert's Jewishness may be expressed primarily in his career, so that after-hours activities in community organizations are a means of career advancement. Whatever his motivations, in Park Forest the Jewish professional directed the actives in a considerable part of formal Jewish community development. In the informal community, his influence was much smaller, for his professional techniques were not applicable.

Fifth, the sexual division of labor in the Jewish community has changed. In the suburb, and especially in the suburban dormitory, the men's daytime absence shifts a much greater role in its affairs to the women, except in functions requiring business skills, and aspirations such as power. In Park Forest, while the men still ran the financial and political aspects of community organization, the women participated in the ideological disputes and achieved their version of the Sunday school curriculum.

In the middle-class family, mothers generally play the major role in child-raising. As a result, their concern with Jewish education seems also to be stronger than that of the men. Furthermore, they are likely to be child-oriented, viewing the school mainly in terms of its consequences for the child. This is a major shift from the traditional Jewish family organization in which the father, as religious leader of the household, supervised the children's education for an adult community in which he himself was playing a role. Thus the traditional father was likely to be adult-oriented.

Furthermore, it seems clear that the women live a greater part of their life within the Jewish community, and are more concerned with matters relating to ethnic problems.[48] In Park Forest, they inaugurated social contacts with other Jews, set up the informal Jewish community, and put some pressure both on the men and on the children to keep their social contacts within the ethnic group. The men, on the other hand, seem to place less emphasis on ethnic association; B'nai B'rith was less successful than Council in developing an active program.

Finally, the Jewish community has been shaped also by the mobility aspirations of its members and the emerging class-status hierarchy. In Park Forest, this seemed to be developing into four major groups.[49] First, the upper-middle-class residents could be divided into two groups according to occupation of family heads. One consisted of men in business supervisory positions and non-academic professions, the other of those in the more academic professions. Between the two there was relatively little social contact. A third set included those residents in lower-middle-class white-collar occupations. The majority of the community was in the suburban middle-middle class (see footnote 13), although a number of families in this aggregate would eventually adopt the consumption and community activity patterns identified with the upper-middle class. A smaller group, who were living beyond their financial capacity and social skills, might have to relinquish their present status position in the event of setbacks.

The actual and potential upper-middle-class people originating from Chicago came to Park Forest from areas of third and fourth settlement. The lower-middle, and some of the middle-middle-class people, came primarily from those of second or third settlement, or had lived in such areas before the combination of marriage, desire to escape the ethnic neighborhood, and the postwar housing shortage, scattered them all over the city's transitional areas.[50]

Whether the Jewish residents of Park Forest were socially more mobile than other urban Jews of similar socio-economic levels, or their non-Jewish neighbors in the village, can be determined only through comparative studies. Various data indicate that the Jews in Park Forest were generally of a higher socio-economic level than the non-Jews. However, this can probably be explained by the fact that non-Jews with incomes at the higher levels might move to areas more prestigeful than Park Forest, and might be less interested in pioneering than in moving to areas whose status was already ascertained.

A similar explanation may be applicable to the Jews' proportionally high rate of activity in the village's political and civic affairs.[51] In November, 1949, only 9 per cent of the community's population, but 30 per cent of the candidates in the first two village elections, were Jewish. Furthermore, the Jews were more successful in getting elected, for five of the six members of the first Board of Education, and three of the six members of the first village government (including one who later became its president), were Jewish.[52] A proportionally large number of Jews were represented among the founders of the community newspaper, the American Veterans Committee (then the main voice of liberal political thought in the village), and the local affiliate of the Democratic party. However, these people did not participate as Jews, nor did their participation affect the Jewish community.

§ *VII. Postscript: Park Forest in 1955*

A. COMMUNITY GROWTH: 1950-1955. By 1955, Park Forest had grown almost to its originally planned size.[53] Some 6,300 families lived in the village, half of them as renters in the garden apartments built between 1947 and 1950 and the other half as owners of single-family homes built subsequently. The main shopping center had grown to include two department stores. Subsidiary centers, as well as schools and churches, interrupted the unending stream of streets and dwellings. A new village hall was being built to house the growing municipal functions. Next to it, a huge aqua-center was going up to reduce the discomforts of the Chicago summer.

The people that had come to Park Forest since 1950, while thought to be somewhat older and of a slightly lower socio-economic and educational level than the first residents,[54] were still primarily middle-class families with one or more young children. Turnover was high as compared with older suburban communities. But other indices, such as the decreasing turnout at local elections, the end of the boom in new organizations, and the nature of the dominant political issues, indicated that in many ways the village was settling down.

The Jewish community had kept pace with the growth of the village. It was estimated to consist of about 600 families, or 10 per cent of the total population. The Jewish arrivals of the previous five years were also said to be slightly older than the first settlers. Among them were a number of doctors and dentists (although there were fewer other professionals than before), and a large group of businessmen (many of them owning stores in the new shopping centers), salesmen and other white-collar workers. Family incomes were reported to be similar to those of old residents. Most of the newcomers were also second generation Jews from Eastern European backgrounds. The Jewish families were said to be less transient than the non-Jewish ones, and many of the old settlers had remained to become homeowners.[55] The organizational structure had been enlarged by the formation of a congregation in 1951. A temple Sunday school founded in 1955, and three more women's organizations (Hadassah, an auxiliary chapter of B'nai B'rith, and a temple sisterhood), completed the roster of new groups. After five years then, the Jewish community resembled the other suburban Jewish settlements which have mushroomed in the postwar era.[56] In this section the community's growth will first be described and analyzed in the light of the child-orientation hypothesis. Then it will be studied for evidences of a reversal of previous acculturation patterns in order to evaluate the frequently heard theory of a "postwar revival" of the American Jewish community.

B. THE FORMATION AND FUNCTION OF THE CONGREGATION. In 1950, High Holiday services were conducted in the village. Shortly thereafter, the small group which had attempted to set up a congregation in 1949 was instrumental in organizing Temple Beth Sholom. Late in 1951, a full-time rabbi was hired, and soon thereafter a building program was announced. In 1954, a $70,000 temple was erected through sizable contributions from the developer and his contractors, as well as smaller donations given by about one-fifth of the other residents. In 1955, the paid-up membership of the congregation numbered about 240 families, or 40 per cent of the total Jewish community.[57]

While the congregation's constitution proclaimed the membership's right to denominational diversity, officially the temple was affiliated with the Reform group. Its religious orientation could best be described as "Eastern European Reform." It combined permissiveness toward what many regard as deprivational practices in the home, with a quasi-Conservative array of ceremonies, Hebrew reading, and responsive singing at services. This cultural compromise was perhaps symbolized by the temple kitchen; it was not kept kosher, but no pork was served. The rabbi described this emphasis on ceremony as a "warm liberal Reform" agreeable to both Reform and Conservative members. The rabbi himself reflected the cultural career of his congregants, for he came from an Eastern European background, was trained as an Orthodox rabbi, and later changed his affiliation to Reform. While this similarity was not a manifest factor in his selection, it was perhaps no coincidence.

Friday night services generally attracted fifty to seventy-five people. A part of this attendance came from a core of forty more-or-less regular worshippers. The rest were celebrants of Yahrzeit services,[58] or came for other special reasons. Bar Mitzvahs [the rite of adulthood for boys], and social festivities often doubled or trebled attendance, with many of the extra worshippers coming from outside the village. High Holiday services attracted as many as 600 people.[59] A lecture series on secular Jewish topics was well attended, but adult education was limited to a Bible class which drew a comparative handful.

From the point of view of attendance, the religious-cultural functions of the synagogue ran a poor second to the social functions. Dinners, holiday dances, bazaars, and other "affairs" were very popular. Residents critical of the social functions of the temple noted that while Purim services had attracted fewer than fifty, the dance held that evening had brought 350 people to the temple.

Shortly after the organization of the congregation, nine women—several of them leaders of Council—set up a sisterhood. In 1955 it had enrolled about 300 members, or about half the adult women. Its main functions were fund-raising for the temple through parties and bazaars,[60] and provision of other assistance such as publication of the temple bulletin. Council had 180 members, and still functioned as a community-service agency. Organization of a temple brotherhood lagged. As one of the leaders explained it, this was because of the men's duties in the temple building program.[61] B'nai B'rith had a sizable though inactive membership. Because its chapter boundaries extended beyond the village, it did not play a major role in the community. This was true also of the B'nai B'rith auxiliary and the Hadassah chapter.

C. Child vs. Adult Orientation: The Organization of the Second Sunday School. For an understanding of the processes which shape the suburban Jewish community, we must focus again on the Sunday school, particularly on the organization of a second school in 1955. The first, or community school conducted by the Park Forest Board of Jewish Education, continued to operate under much the same leadership. In 1954-55, it had about 385 students, an estimated 85 to 90 per cent of the eligible Jewish children in the village.[62] When the congregation was organized, it had entered into an agreement by which members would send their children to the community school. The rabbi was appointed spiritual advisor, taught some courses, and presided at the Bar Mitzvah ceremonies. However, even at the time this arrangement was made, the group of temple leaders who had sought a congregation with a Sunday school in 1949 felt that the temple ought to have its own school. This position had been maintained over the years despite an adverse vote from a community meeting, and from a congregational committee on religious education in 1953. The influence of this group, which had been instrumental in organizing the congregation and in raising funds for the building, was such that in 1954 the congregational board voted to approve the organization of a school. The rabbi was selected partly because of his extensive training and experience in religious education, and was hired with the understanding that he would set up a congregational school. After the rabbi's attempts to incorporate the community school into the congregation had failed, the temple announced the formation of its own school.

Once again, the community leadership split openly into two camps, and through mass meetings and publications drew about half the community into the issue. By May, 1955, both schools had held pre-registration, and most of the parents had lost interest in the controversy. Some observers felt that such indifference indicated that many parents were satisfied as long as schooling was available, and cared little about curriculum or educational philosophy.

Underlying the public discussions was the question that had been debated in 1949: should the school teach children in a way that would encourage and even press parents to take part in religious-cultural activities, or should it teach them in a way that would leave parents uninvolved if they so choose. This question was basic to the larger problem of adult-versus child-orientation.

The community school explained its major principles in a pamphlet prepared for distribution for one of the public meetings:

[The school] emphasizes those elements of Judaism which are basically acceptable to all elements of Jewry. Differences of practice which exist are taught in a democratic climate encouraging acceptance of the diversity of opinion. . . . A community school permits the children to learn all facets of Jewish religion; the strength of Judaism lies in its breadth of outlook and range of inquiry . . . many . . . parents desire that their children be exposed to a broad cross-section of Jewish thought. . . .[63]

While the school encouraged the children's participation in the temple, the final decision was left up to the parents. As one of the school's lay leaders pointed out:

Its purpose is education, and the parents are not involved unless they want to be. Religion for the parents is not necessarily the main end of life; we want a school for our children, and the education they get here is excellent.

For the parents who took this position, the school fulfilled all the requirements of a child-oriented institution. Furthermore, its first objective was one which all parents ranked highly, that is, "to develop in the child pride and security in his Jewish identification."[64] Other parents probably accepted the community school's belief that:

A child who shares the experience with his parents in a temple and further enriches himself in an independent school will have a deeper insight that can be obtained from . . . a single viewpoint.[65]

The congregational leaders recognized the high quality of the school's educational program. However, they opposed the community school for its nondenominational orientation, and suggested that it was teaching the children *about* Judaism instead of emphasizing the *practice* of one kind of Judaism. The emphasis of the curriculum on the diversity within Judaism, they felt, was better suited for an adult education program; it did not sufficiently encourage loyalty to, and participation in, the congregation. The rabbi illustrated the differences he thought existed between the two schools:

. . . the community school teaches that Jews light candles on Friday night, and that the children *can* do this, but don't have to. Our curriculum will be more emphatic, we say you *ought* to do it.

As in 1950, the two groups differed over the role of "the home" in the transmission of Jewish identity and culture. The community school felt that the family had a central role in the children's education, Jewish or otherwise, and that parents should be free to determine their own position on religious matters. The school held workshops to help the parents integrate school program and home practice, but for those parents who rejected involvement, the teaching program could be limited to the child and the school.

The congregational school, on the other hand, felt that the parents' participation in Jewish education had become so minimal that the congregation had to take a more active role in training the child for religious participation.[66] For this purpose, the rabbi believed he had to assume a surrogate-father role. He explained:

I want to make personal contact with the children; otherwise I only get the volitional ones, and that's not many, and not good enough. I want to be able to identify with the children . . . I want them to accept the synagogue in their lives and to come to services. The school's program will be a "worship-curriculum." The children will have to come and help prepare services . . . the Saturday morning services will be part of their education.

The rabbi viewed the children not as students in a school, but as adults in miniature, playing their role in the temple. He justified this by pointing out:

My primary interest is in the adults, and I am opposed to a child-centered Judaism. However, here the people seem to be mainly interested in the education of the children. . . . We hope, though, the children will bring the parents . . . perhaps they will return the parents to Jewish life.

The rabbi's purpose was thus to maintain the adult-oriented congregation envisaged by the temple founders as early as 1949. *However, the community's child orientation necessitated a revised version, in which the children were to be asked to take over the position vacated by the adults.*[67]

D. THE SCHOOL ISSUE: LEADERSHIP FACTIONS. The formation of the second Sunday school forced the leaders and active members of the Jewish community to take sides on the issue. From an analysis of people supporting each school, there emerges a picture of the political-ideological structure of the Jewish community. Because of the similarity of the issues and the leadership to the 1949 controversy, this structure had probably changed very little.

It was explained previously that the congregation was from the beginning supported by a number of actives whose previous participation in a Jewish community had been centered around a congregation. They were families in the higher income categories. The men were employed in executive positions, businesses, and in law or medicine. They provided much of the community's share of the temple building costs and contributed to the extensive fund-raising apparatus developed by the sisterhood, which was led by their wives. The extent of the temple's financial needs, and the socio-economic level of those who organized the fund-raising affairs, tended to limit active participation in temple social activities to people with upper-middle-class incomes, or to those willing to make sacrifices to appear to have such earnings. One of the sisterhood leaders estimated that attendance at luncheons, parties, and other affairs had cost her family about $600 in addition to the $100 annual membership fee of the temple:

Many of the gals in the $6000-$7000 bracket can't afford to join it. They join the temple and the sisterhood, but they explain that they don't have time to participate, or some reason like that. Most of the gals have accepted the fact that they can't afford it; only a few got obnoxious about it. But to those who can't afford it, we don't have to sell the sisterhood. I myself have played this game for years, and since my husband works in the community, we have to do it for professional reasons anyway.

For some of these people, the temple-related social life was perhaps the preparatory and final step before affiliation with a higher income group and a style of suburban leisure often centered around a country club.[68]

The decision-makers of this group, however, were a small clique of Jewish professionals and other leaders, who were concerned with maintaining and increasing the strength and influence of the congregation. Their political and financial efforts were previously identified as being instrumental in the organization of the congregation, construction of the temple, and the opening of the second school. This group derived some of its influence from the support of American Community Builders and its officers, though the community grapevine differed in its estimates of the latters' role. The rest of the congregational leadership generally followed the line set by this group, which in turn tended to follow the national program of the Reform movement. On the whole, this group was concerned with the growth of the congregation and the fostering of participation by the rest of the community, rather than with theological or ideological problems. In so far as they were influentials, they fit Merton's conception of "locals."[69]

The community school, and the Park Forest Board of Jewish Education, was being supported by two groups. One consisted of a number of academic or academically oriented professionals, primarily teachers, lawyers, and scientists, some of whom were active in other aspects of village life. They, too, were already, or would some day, be described as upper-middle-class, though more so on the basis of occupation and amount of education than on income. Furthermore, their consumption style differed significantly from that of the congregation supporters, both in taste and "brow" levels. The differences between the two groups are perhaps best illustrated by the deprecatory labels they attached to each others' styles. The congregational supporters described the community school group as "pseudo-intellectuals," and the latter called the former "country-clubbers." While some community school supporters belonged to the congregation, they generally remained inactive. Most of their wives did not join the sisterhood.

Both groups grew up in Orthodox or ex-Orthodox backgrounds. However, the community school leaders felt that the Reform temple deviated too sharply from a religious-cultural tradition whose theological aspects some of them had rejected more completely than the congregational leaders. Their feelings of affinity to ethnic traditions were stronger than status considerations. Thus after the split with the temple, they proceeded to arrange for the holding of Bar Mitzvah services at an Orthodox congregation in Chicago Heights, whose membership was primarily lower-middle class.

Although some of these leaders did not participate in adult activities other than the Board of Jewish Education, they were highly interested in the content and quality of the children's Jewish education. Consequently, they provided the support for the intensive intellectual emphasis of the curriculum and the high teaching standards which the staff of the community school sought to achieve. Most of the people in this group would fit Merton's description of the "cosmopolitan."

Allied with them was the previously mentioned group of residents who were Conservative in religious outlook, lower-middle-class in occupation and style of life, and who had maintained some affinity with the immigrant culture. Despite their differences in background, they agreed with the cosmopolitans in their attitudes about the Reform temple, and on the religious and intellectual level of their school. The Jewish professionals and other leaders of the community school possessed characteristics and attitudes of both groups, which permitted them to bridge whatever differences in outlook appeared between the two.

E. The School Issue: Factors in Parental Choice. At the end of spring registration, the time when Park Forest was revisited, the congregational school had enrolled about 215 children, the community school about 125, and an estimated 150 children or more had not yet been registered.* Only an extensive study could discover to what extent these enrollment figures reflected a choice between the child-oriented and diffuse religious affiliation of the community school, and the adult-oriented and specific congregational-allegiance objectives of the temple group.

There could be at least three other considerations which parents might consider relevant to the decision to be made when the school year would actually begin. First, the system of fees was such that people with several eligible children would find it more economical to join the congregation and thus receive the benefit of a tuition-free institution. This appealed to those residents more concerned with the high cost of suburban living than with the ideological and organizational differences between schools. A second factor was the congregation's symbolic role as a community focus and, more importantly, as an instrument for teaching Jewishness to the children. The erection of a building had transformed this symbol into a physically real and imposing object, which allowed the residents to feel that they too had "arrived." According to one mother, it gave parents an opportunity to point out to their children that "they had a church now too, just like their non-Jewish friends."[70] Also, many parents had been brought up to expect a Sunday school within congregational confines, so that the organization of a temple school created little surprise on their part.[71] Furthermore, many of the parents who had grown up without any Jewish training were confronted with the necessity, and the wish, to teach their children to feel Jewish. To them, the rabbi loomed as a figure of authority and as an expert who could replace them in a role which they could not fill (and, judging by some of the parental comments made at pre-registration, a role which they did not especially cherish). On the other hand, some people felt that this transference of authority to the rabbi was undemocratic.[72]

A final factor was the difference in the status images of the congregation, with its upper-middle-class social activity, and the community school, where social functions were limited to educational events centered around the holidays and the children. Also, the latter's working agreement with a lower-middle-class Orthodox synagogue outside the community probably influenced a number of families, especially those with children of Bar Mitzvah age, toward the upper-middle-class temple.

Despite these considerations, if the congregational school follows its current aims and succeeds in training the children for participation in the temple in such a manner as to demand parental involvement, those parents who reject such participation may eventually be forced to choose between

* In October 1955, the congregational school had enrolled more than 500 students; the community school had only about 125 students from 80 families loyal to its program.

adult and child orientation. In families where the children's education, or the parents' desire to avoid participation, rank above all other considerations, the final decisions are predictable. In other homes, however, the family structure and the influence of the children's demands on parental authority may be significant factors in the final choice. For example, in families which William Whyte has described as "filiarchical,"[73] the events described by one mother might base the decision on the child's preference. This woman reported that:

> Here the children force you into things. If you send them to Sunday school and if a holiday comes up which you do not observe at home, the children tell you to participate and you have to. And if you don't send them to Sunday school, if your child is in that age group, he says, "Why can't I belong." . . . So I became interested; I had no choice.

On the other hand, the temple school, like the community school before it, may be able to carry on its teaching program in such a way that both its objectives and those of the child-oriented parents are satisfied at a level at which neither party feels a serious need to make changes. Furthermore, it is impossible to predict whether the children themselves will accept the program of participation to be offered them by the temple school.

For the student of the ethnic process, the most important question about both schools concerns the extent to which Sunday school education will induce students to participate in religious-cultural functions of the synagogue and the community when they reach adulthood. This problem cannot yet be studied in Park Forest, and it has not been investigated among third generation Jews in other communities. A reversal of acculturation processes seems unlikely, although some evidence of a "returning reaction" among the third generation members of other ethnic groups has been documented by Marcus Hansen. However, their return has been more on the ideological than the behavioral level; the resurrected cultural patterns do not seem to have affected basic aspects of their way of life.[74]

F. COMMUNITY GROWTH AS REVIVAL? Whatever the final outcome of the educational split, it is apparent that in the last five years the Jewish community in Park Forest has experienced considerable institutional growth. On the national scene, such things as the increase in synagogue affiliation, the organization of new congregations, the rise in Sunday and weekday school enrollments, and the increasing sales of Jewish consumer products, have all given rise to the suggestion that a Jewish revival was taking place, at least in the suburbs. If this revival were actually a reversal of the acculturation trends which had been reported in studies of urban Jewry, it would indicate that the reaction which Hansen described as a third generation phenomenon elsewhere was being anticipated among Jews by younger members of the second generation.

While the comprehensive study necessary to verify or reject this theory has not been made, the data collected in Park Forest do permit some tentative explanations of trends in the suburban Jewish community. These hypotheses, dealing with the influence of the suburban enviroment, the function of child orientation, the sociability patterns of the upper-middle class, the responsiveness to social pressure, and the adaptability of the suburban congregation, do not indicate a reversal of previous acculturation trends. *Instead, they suggest the transformation of a previously existing informal community pattern of urban origin into a new formal one.* It is this phenomenon which appears in the guise of a "revival."

1. INFLUENCE OF THE SUBURBAN ENVIRONMENT. To some extent, the growth of the suburban Jewish community is a response to suburban conditions. The move beyond the city limits, itself a function of the higher residential standards of today's urban middle class, has affected Jewish families with young children as much, if not more so, than others in their socio-economic category. In the suburbs, the environment is strange. The Jewish residents are no longer the majority or plurality which they were, or felt themselves to be, in the urban neighborhoods or blocks from which they came. Park Foresters describe themselves as now living in a "mixed community" and as "sticking out."[75] This may be as much a consequence of their own mobility as of their ecological situation (i.e., they are really "sticking out" in relation to a previous self-image). Nevertheless, these feelings make them responsive to formal "organizing" by more active Jewish residents.

The urban Jewish pattern of limiting sociability and friendship relationships primarily to other Jews has been carried over unchanged into the suburbs. This suggests that among adults at least, there has been no "return" to the Jewish community, since there had been no real "departure." Rather, the covert cohesiveness of the urban Jewish neighborhood has been transformed into an overt one in the suburbs by shifting sociability activities that previously took place in comparative anonymity to a set of formal and well-publicized organizations, primarily the congregation.

2. CHILD-ORIENTATION. The main functions of this formal organization are to make sure that the children grow up within a Jewish context and learn enough of it to identify themselves as Jews. Regardless of the objectives of the institutional leadership (which are generally still adult-oriented), from the perspective of the parents the Jewish organizations exist for the children.[76] One of the leaders of the sisterhood explained:

> People here don't have a need to join the congregation or the sisterhood until their children are old enough to join the Sunday school, and if there were no children, there'd be no temple or Jewish organizations.

Another leader indicated that while people without children are asked to join, they are not *expected* to do this. These observations are supported by a tabulation of the congregational membership. Of 180 member families with children, 85 per cent had at least one child of Sunday school age. Unfortunately, this tabulation could not be compared with the total number of Jewish families with one child of that age. However, data for a group of forty-three old and new residents who had recently purchased homes showed that 60 per cent of them had a Sunday-school-age child.[77] While 50 per cent of the families with eligible children had joined the temple, only 18 per cent of those without eligible children had done so.

The need to provide the children with manifest training in Jewish identification is partly a suburban substitute for the latent devices that existed in the immigrant family and the urban Jewish neighborhood. However, the suburban parents, trained by these latent means, feel themselves incapable of providing the proper learning environment for their children's identity. This function is shifted to various institutions.

3. THE ORGANIZATIONAL SOCIABILITY OF THE UPPER-MIDDLE CLASS. Although the children may provide the impetus for community organization, some parents use the groups which they have set up to reap the fruits of their socio-economic and educational mobility, and to live the "organization"- and "social affair"-centered life of the upper-middle class. This mobility must account at least in part for the higher organizational affiliation of the suburban as compared with the urban Jew, although the environmental and life-cycle conditions initiate formal organization, and channel it into institutions capable of serving the children's educational needs. These conditions do not, however, detract from the desirability of the organizational social life for the Jewish residents who can afford to participate. In Park Forest, this activity constituted the major, though latent, function of the temple sisterhood. Under its auspices, a part of the intense sociability of the Jewish community was transformed into temple activity. Informal get-togethers became committee meetings, parties became fund-raising affairs, and occasional night-club outings became community dances. Even so, the sisterhood president complained that there were not enough functions to keep the large proportion of active members occupied. The women who organized these activities are college-trained, with social and civic skills of various kinds. Unable to practice these skills in the professional world because of their family functions, they set up an active organization which permitted them self-expression in various nonfamilial roles. The affairs they scheduled seemed to be modeled on the extracurricular life of the college campus,[78] and were supported with high attendance by the rest of the Jewish community.[79]

4. SOCIAL PRESSURE AND INGROUP COHESION. Despite the plethora of organizations and activities, however, voluntary community participation in the formal organizations is not always widespread, or forthcoming when needed. Usually it is more likely to express itself in passive response than active support. The history of the congregation affords various examples of the sparsity of community interest. Its organization was due to the determined effort of a handful, although other residents joined once the institution was established. Fund-raising for the construction of the temple was partially planned by a professional public relations counsel, and in-

volved the sending of many letters and considerable personal coaxing on the part of the fund-raisers. Even so, informants suggested that the contributions of fifty people, and the ability of an additional person to secure a high mortgage, had built the temple. Continual fund-raising is required to support its current, though still expanding, operations. The setting up of the temple Sunday school also required extensive efforts aimed at overcoming community indifference and opposition.

As has already been indicated, the development of the organizational structure was due largely to the efforts of those residents whose power and community-service aspirations allowed them to apply the social pressure necessary to the development and functioning of organizations in a context of community indifference. In Park Forest, these persons were frequently Jewish professionals. However, it is easy to overlook a second component of the process, *the willingness of the community to accept social pressure*. Despite complaints, even from leaders, that the community was "over-organized," and that there was too much fund-raising, the cohesion of the Jewish group was such that appeals to group needs and pressures for aid and involvement were not, and indeed could not, often be denied. *On the one hand, the group's cohesion is so minimal that social pressure has to be applied to get things done, but on the other hand it is sufficient to tolerate the application of pressure.*

In Park Forest, the fact that the developer was also a high-ranking officer of the American Jewish community, that he was interested in the local Jewish group and provided free land and considerable financial support to the temple, and was said to wield considerable (though indirect) political influence in its affairs, no doubt affected the rate and direction of the development process. In this respect, then, Park Forest is not a representative community.

5. THE FUNCTIONAL ADAPTABILITY OF THE SYNAGOGUE. As in other suburban Jewish groups, much of the community's activity has centered around the Reform temple. This is due in part to the synagogue's traditional position and symbolic function in the Jewish community.[80] *However, the current effectiveness of the temple in this role is a result of its institutional diffuseness and flexibility and its ability, whatever its own objectives, to orient its program to the desires of its membership.* The rabbi commented on this in explaining the temple's policy towards newcomers:

We don't ask them for memberships until loyalties are built up, and until they've seen the services and benefits we can offer them.

This adaptability has been successfully achieved in four important areas.

First, the temple has been able to retain adult support by reducing or eliminating the traditional pressure for members' participation in religious activities, and by appealing to their sociability, status, and leisure interests in the religious program. Participation in Friday night services has been maintained in part through the *oneg shabbat,* or social hour, which follows it, the holding of Bar Mitzvahs, and ceremonies for new members.[81] As already indicated, the Reform ideology has also been flexible enough to permit the integration of ceremonial elements from Eastern European synagogue practices for the new Reform members.

Second, the temple has been able to exist despite minimal adult participation in its normal religious functions (except on the High Holidays) by redefining its adult-oriented program and aiming it also at the children. The organization of the temple Sunday school despite the lack of community support was thus perhaps a functional necessity for its survival as a religious institution.[82] By moving up the age of eligibility, and setting up a nursery Sunday school for the youngest children, the temple has been able to enlarge the clientele for these functions.

Third, the temple has not been unwilling to serve as the center for much of the community's social life. Thus it has been able to derive considerable financial support and membership loyalty to guarantee its survival. On the other hand, it is also the target for criticism from those residents loyal to a Jewish community that legitimizes only the manifest religious-cultural functions of the synagogue.

Finally, the temple has also adjusted itself to the sexual role shift that has taken place. A generation ago, synagogue activity was still primarily the role of the Jewish man, but today, and especially in the suburban Jewish community, the woman plays a major part. While men continue to monopolize political and financial leadership,[83] women carry out most of the other activities not handled by the rabbi.[84] The increase in the authority of the rabbi is related in part to the vacuum left by the departure of the men from religious-cultural affairs, and the lack of knowledge of the women in this field.

Only further studies can indicate whether this institutional adaptability is characteristic only of the Reform temple (and might thus help to explain why so many suburban congregations have affiliated themselves with the Reform movement), or whether it is also appearing among the other denominations.

G. THE UNAFFILIATED RESIDENTS. Because the analysis has been concerned with the factors behind the growth of a formal community structure, and the functional adaptation of the congregation at its center, major emphasis has been placed on the activities of the groups who provided the most consistent support. This has slighted the smaller number of residents described previously as the supporters of the Board of Jewish Education. While they sometimes attended congregational activities, more frequently they acted as critics of the temple, and participated in their own Jewish activities either on a familial basis, or in the administration and adult activities of the Board of Jewish Education.

Their role in the Park Forest Jewish community can perhaps be best understood historically. A set of leaders from these groups was instrumental in the formation of the community school and in its assumption of the central position in the community structure of the early years. With community growth, this position turned out to be disproportionate to their numerical, political-ideological, and financial strength among the later settlers. The competition for dominance that ensued between the school and the temple seems now to have been won by the latter. While in many communities minority elements later form their own congregations, only a part of this minority seeks such affiliation. Furthermore, much of the potential support for a second synagogue has been diminished by the temple's appeal to both Reform and Conservative worshipers and to the main sources of financial support.

Finally, however, it should be remembered that there are many Jewish families in Park Forest who, as the 1949 study showed, do not participate in any formal activities, although they maintain some relationship with the Jewish community through Jewish friends. Because there is no public evidence of their affiliation, they are often overlooked in the concern with formal organizations. The Jewish life of these people, who constitute close to half the Jewish population of Park Forest, was *not* studied in the 1955 revisit, and leaves a gap in the description of the total Jewish community.

H. The Suburban Revival: Some Conclusions. Events in Park Forest do not suggest any changes in acculturation or assimilation trends that might properly be described as a revival.[85] Synagogue attendance figures and community behavior generally offer no evidence for either a religious or a broader cultural "return."[86] Since the new suburban organizational structures are native to suburban middle-class America, and had no ancestors among Eastern European Jewry, they cannot be used to document an organizational revival. Finally, the fact that ingroup solidarity did not cease even during the most intense Americanization of the second generation rules out the possibility of a socio-psychological revival.

Instead, the growth of the new Jewish community can be explained as a transfer of traditionally intense ingroup sociability patterns from the informal cliques in which they were practiced in the cities, to a set of formal organizations in the suburbs. The fact that this sociability was hidden from public view in its unorganized urban state and suddenly burst forth into a plethora of organizations, budgets, and buildings in the new communities has suggested the possibility of a revival.

This transfer represents in part the increased organizational activity normally associated with achievement of upper-middle-class life styles, and the special conditions imposed by the suburban residential social structure in which it is happening. *Above all, however, it has taken place because of the need and desire of Jewish parents to provide clearly visible institutions and symbols with which to maintain and reinforce the ethnic identification of the next generation.*

The re-acceptance of some Judaic traditions at this time can be explained by the requirements of this objective. Even so, Park Forest Jews in their private lives have not adopted any religious or cultural traditions which would affect to any extent their upper-middle-class styles or aspirations. The changes that have taken place, therefore, seem to describe not a reversal of acculturation and assimilation tendencies but rather their continuation in new organizational contexts.

It is too early to tell whether the conditions which provide strength to the organizational structure of the Jewish community will continue as the postwar suburb matures, or whether the institutions can continue to be flexible enough to adapt to further changing conditions—for example, greater community interest in sociability functions as opposed to religious ones. Perhaps most important is the question whether the Judaic education and the social situations in which the children may find themselves will result in their congregational or other community affiliation in adolescence or adulthood, whatever the major function of specific institutions. The answers to these questions will be highly significant in determining the direction of the ethnic process in the next generation.

Although this article is based on the study of one suburban community, and one that is distinctive in several respects, the generalizations and hypotheses developed here are probably not unique to it. It is likely that they will be applicable not only to other suburban communities, but perhaps also to urban centers. In the latter, the existence of the phenomena described here may be masked by the fact that the Jewish population is not so distinctively limited to young middle-class couples with one or two children. However, there seems to be little reason why the phenomenon of child orientation, to mention just one, should be restricted to Park Forest. Indeed, it would seem reasonable to suppose that the developments described here must play an increasingly important role in the future Jewish community life in America. Consequently, the Park Forest Jewish community may be illustrative of a next major stage in the process of Jewish and ethnic adjustment to American society—the stage in which it is the relations between the second and third generations that are crucial, rather than those between an immigrant first and a native-born second generation. As a case study, then, this research on Park Forest is intended as a sequel to the many Jewish community studies which have been devoted largely to an analysis of relationships between the first and the second generation.

SOLOMON SUTKER

THE JEWISH ORGANIZATIONAL ELITE
OF ATLANTA, GEORGIA

THIS paper is concerned with the nature of the organizational elite (the professional community workers) of the Jewish community of Atlanta, Georgia,[1] and their interrelations with two other important segments of this community, the theological elite (the rabbinate) and the lay elite.[2] The lay elite consists of adult Jews who are not dependent for their livelihood as paid workers in Jewish community affairs and who have prestige and/or power in the social, political, economic or cultural life of the city of Atlanta or in Jewish affairs. Our concern is primarily with Jewish leadership on a local level. While many of the characteristics of local Jewish elite groups can be found among nationally and internationally organized Jewish groups, there are sufficient differences so that the material contained in this paper would be less applicable to them.

§ *The Functions of the Jewish Organizational Elite*

To an increasing degree, the more extended use of professional community workers and the bureaucratic mode of operation are becoming important aspects of Jewish communal life in the United States.[3] From the viewpoint that the religious base of Jewish community organization implied traditions and methods of operating its educational, social service and other important functions mingling personal, religious and communal rights, duties and obligations into a type of *Gemeinschaft* relationship, the rise of an organizational elite is spectacular in its implications. Yet the development of bureaucratic leadership in American Jewish community life is not surprising, since the Jews in this country are a city people who have been deeply affected by urban ways of living. Further, important parts of the social work, civic and social roles of the synagogue had been acquired earlier by the *landsmannschaften* or fraternal groups. In time, these latter groups yielded some of their major functions to professionalized secular agencies. Today most of the major organizations in the Atlanta

Reprinted. by permission, with some modifications from *Social Forces*, Vol. 31 (1952-1953), pp. 136-43. This paper is drawn from the writer's unpublished doctoral thesis, "The Jews of Atlanta: Their Social Structure and Leadership Patterns" (University of North Carolina, 1950).

The article is limited to those activities of the organizational elite that primarily concern the Atlanta Jewish community; certain peripheral associations which may have professional personnel, such as the National Conference of Christians and Jews, are excluded.

Jewish community, with the principal exception of the synagogues and some fraternal and women's groups, have local or regional professional guidance by members of the organizational elite.

Table 1 indicates the type of Jewish associations in Atlanta that have professional personnel and the general function or functions that the organizations handle. In terms of the territory served, the organizational elite of Atlanta can be divided into three major types: local, regional, and a mixture of local and regional. The local organizational elite are those whose work is confined to the Atlanta Jewish community. They may serve in other capacities in national organizations, but this situation would ordinarily stem from their position in the local community. This group includes the executives of almost all of the Jewish welfare service agencies, the local community council, the local bureau of Jewish education, the community center, as well as the social club managers.

Although the social clubs occupy a dominant role in local Jewish communal life, the managers of these organizations do not have an important function in general Jewish communal activities. The background and experience of the club manager are unlike these of other members of the organizational elite. He has only to provide technical direction of the social club, since the making and shaping of policy is handled by the boards and dominant cliques of each club. The club manager does not have to be a member of the Jewish group nor does he have to be imbued with a sense of Jewish culture. The other members of the organizational elite are concerned with ideological guidance as well as technical direction and co-ordination in thir spheres of activity. Unlike other formalized aspects of Jewish communal life, the social clubs are not concerned with ideologies, but primarily with activities that satisfy the recreational needs and desires of the club membership.

The regional organizational elite includes the professional representa-

Table 1—Functional Spheres of Operation of Jewish Organizations Employing Professional Personnel in Atlanta, Georgia, 1948*

Type of Organization Employing Professional Personnel	Case Work	Group Work	Community Organization and Relations	Social and Related Activities	Fraternal and Related Activities	Religious Activities	Other Types of Activities
Jewish Community Council			x				
Federation for Jewish Social Service	x						
Jewish community center		x		x			
Children's service agency	x						
Anti-Defamation League			x				
Zionist groups			x		x		x
Bureau of Jewish Education		x	x			x	
Jewish Welfare Board		x	x	x		x	
Council of Jewish Federations and Welfare Funds		x					
Social clubs				x			x

* Only the primary activities of each agency are included. There is an overlapping of agency listings at some of these organizations are principal divisions of some of the agencies included above.

tives of various national Jewish organizations who head the regional field offices of these agencies in Atlanta. The influence of this group on Jewish society in Atlanta is largely indirect, since they usually work with and through local agencies. Occasionally members of this small group may participate in local community activities, but such activity is usually on a personal rather than on an official basis. However, their positions are such that they can become local community participants with relative ease if they have the time and inclination to do so.

The mixed type of organizational elite includes those professional community workers whose agencies operate directly in both the region and in the local Jewish community. The regional office of the Anti-Defamation League is of this type, since its personnel is closely connected with the work of the public relations committee of the local Jewish community council and also handles duties that are region-wide in scope.

Even those members of the Atlanta Jewish organizational elite who operate local, independent agencies are now linked with workers from other cities who handle similar associations into a web of voluntary national organizations, such as a national Jewish social workers' association or the Council of Jewish Federations and Welfare Funds. Those members of the Atlanta Jewish organizational elite who are executives of such agencies as the Anti-Defamation League owe their primary allegiance to the national organizations which hire them. The important role of these national agencies is a relatively new trend in American Jewish community life, which in the past tended more toward local autonomy in its affairs. Now there is a drift in some important activities toward centralization of power on a national basis. But this situation also is obviously a near-universal trend in many important spheres of American life.

A CASE HISTORY. The rise of the professional community worker in Atlanta can be illustrated through a consideration of the development of bureaucratic leadership in the local Federation for Jewish Social Service, which is one of the oldest and most important Jewish community agencies in the city. The trends of Jewish social work are toward increasing secularization, experimentation, integration, professionalization and democratization of operation. The history of the Federation reflects a change in the control of operation of Jewish social service from the sometimes awkward efforts of the lay leader to the more experienced hands of the professional worker. It further indicates the transition of the paid worker from a subordinate position to a more equal status with the lay elite of the organization. Indeed, the technical superiority of the bureaucratic method in some ways gives the professional worker a focus of domination over the lay worker who has to be guided by the greater know-how of the organizational elite.

The nature of the administrative personnel in the Federation has changed considerably during the past forty years. The first employees often had been local residents who bore the title of *secretary to the board* or *superintendent* and who had a concern for welfare work but lacked training in this field. The various board members felt that it was within their province to operate as an administrative as well as a policy-determining body. They would determine if a sack of coal should be purchased rather than allow their employees to have any discretion in handling day-to-day items. The board also acted in the capacity of amateur social workers. They conducted their own investigations of welfare applicants and discussed each case among themselves. Any action that might be taken was based upon individual considerations and did not occur within the framework of a set of operational procedures as it does today.

The close supervision of the board over all activities in its early history is shown in the following excerpts which have been paraphrased from the minutes of the organization:

> The superintendent of the community center advised that he had been forced to buy a typewriter for his work even though the Federation has refused to grant funds for this purpose. The Federation then voted to pay for the machine and to reimburse the superintendent.

> At meetings of the relief association, each case was considered individually by the entire board that was present.

Clients frequently were called in to meetings of the board, and their problems were discussed with them. Indications of social control were evident when clients were advised to handle their personal problems in particular ways or when some Jewish person was arrested and members of the board of the relief association felt that it was their duty to take some action to assist the individual. The work of the association at this point consisted of a blending of the Old World stress on *mitzvas,* or blessings for good deeds, and increasing secularization.

By the mid-twenties, the Federation increasingly tended to acquire the services of trained personnel from northern cities. Fundamental changes in operating procedures on all levels of activity, including board meetings, became evident. The term *executive director* had superseded the old title of *scretary to the board* for the new administrative workers. In time, instead of reporting on individual cases, the executive director furnished statistics on activities and brought up questions involving general policy rather than requests for types of action needed to handle each investigation. A few cases were sometimes included as the last order of business to give a "human interest" angle to the statistical reports that were being offered. They merely illustrated the work of the agency, and unlike that which had transpired in the past, they were not being offered to secure the sanction of the board regarding the proper method of operation. The board continued to allocate additional functions to the executive director. The minutes now showed such items as:

> The question of vacations was left to the determination of the executive director.

The executive director was authorized to renew a loan with the Fourth National Bank.

The executive director was allowed to hire an office secretary. A regular bookkeeping system with inspections by an accounting firm was installed.

A new system of collecting accounts for the Free Loan Fund was devised with . . . the Committee determining the policies for operating the loan fund rather than the technical details of administration.

A decision was made to set up a budget system in the relief department and to inaugurate a standard family budget technique to insure better supervisory control of the activities of the department.

The executive director requested that individual members of the board assist the organization by not making any promises or arrangements with applicants for services that could not be carried out later or which might be deemed inadvisable by the social workers of the agency.

As late as 1931, there still were extended discussions on the proper functions of the board. The minutes of one meeting read:

> . . . One view was concerned with following the practice of deciding in each individual case the amount of relief to be granted; the other view stressed the importance of considering the problems presented by each situation, and that the Relief Board should act as a Case Advisory Committee and consider service cases where no material relief is a determining factor. A number of members felt that once a family budget is adopted as a basis of granting relief that the amount to be allowed is primarily an administrative function . . . it was understood that the Board was to be kept informed and regular statistical and financial reports would be submitted at meetings.

Particular case histories were cited to show the technicalities of case work which must consider psychological and cultural factors as well as the granting of material relief. The implications were that the trained social worker was the proper person to handle all aspects of case investigations and determinations.

Today this last view definitely prevails. The board determines overall policy and financing and secures its information about the workings of the organization largely from statistical reports. The executive director and his staff are no longer rigidly bound within a framework that tried to combine major policy determinations with administrative determinations. Likewise, the board is far more dependent upon its professional personnel to advise it regarding proper policy. The superiority of the bureaucratic technique has superseded the efforts of the voluntary worker.

§ *Characteristics of the Organizational Elite*

The number of persons who are members of the organizational elite are few and their staffs are relatively small, but their functional roles are of considerable importance to the Atlanta Jewish community. The members of the organizational elite, other than those who are managers of social clubs, exhibit similar characteristics. All of the organizational elite are college graduates who have had additional training in such fields as social work and law. Some were trained directly for their jobs, particularly those in the field of case work and group work. Thus the members of the organizational elite have what may be described as a social science background. It is to be expected that these persons would be well educated, for they are functioning as the bureaucratic leaders of a highly educated community.[4]

In political and economic philosophy, the organizational elite appear to be more articulately liberal in their ideas than the mass of the local Jewish community. Their social science training and general background would probably tend to accentuate a liberal attitude. This group more likely would be willing to support more "progressive" actions by the Jewish community than generally would be sponsored by the lay elite.

The various members of the organizational elite were born and/or reared either in the northern cities of the United States or Europe in practically every instance. Here are located the centers of training in Jewish social work and religion. Apparently there are very few persons in the South, even in proportion to its total Jewish population, that train either for the rabbinate or for any professional secular positions in Jewish communal life. Most of the organizational elite appear to have deeper roots in a more pervasive Jewish cultural background than ordinarily is to be found among the general Jewish population of Atlanta.[5]

The organizational elite tend to have a deeper awareness and interest in what is transpiring in present-day American Jewish community life than generally exists among the lay population whom they serve. Their concern with Jewish culture may be oriented toward a more secular approach than that of the lay membership. Their religious orientation often is less traditional than exists for the bulk of the lay leadership. Thus, while their synagogue affiliations vary somewhat, the highest percentage of the organizational elite are members of the Reform Temple despite the fact that their early training probably was in a more Orthodox tradition.

There is relatively little turnover among the organizational elite, except toward improvement of their status or transfers to other offices when they are connected with a national agency that operates regional offices throughout the country. Working hours and conditions and salary scales are on a comparable level with those of other Jewish workers in similar fields elsewhere. They receive salaries which are above the average usually paid to persons doing related work in community organization and other social services in non-Jewish community associations.

Although there are individual variations in the pattern, most of the organizational elite do not participate as active members in any of the Atlanta Jewish social clubs. The latter serve as an organized focal point that at least indirectly stresses some basic community differences. The organizational elite usually have to work with the entire community or with large segments of the community, so avoidance of club memberships helps to keep them from being labeled openly as adherents of particular groups and cliques. Also, the social clubs represent a conflicting set of patterns to the tasks that confront the organizational elite, since the clubs serve as indirect competitors of the community center movement and hinder the development of those movements and activities that the organizational elite would label "Jewish." Membership in the social clubs can be an expensive item that the organizational elite as salaried professional workers cannot afford. Their interests and inclinations are generally directed toward participation in more serious activities than the social club would offer. The organizational elite are members of B'nai B'rith, the Zionist Organization of America and related groups.

§ *Bureaucracy and the Organizational Elite*

The bureaucratic mode of operation that Weber described so well is essential if the organizational elite are to carry out their duties properly.[6] Thus the maintenance of systems of files and records is increasingly evident in the everyday functioning of the various offices operated by the organizational elite. It is particularly obvious in those agencies concerned with social casework, since elaborate case histories are required. This is in accordance with modern social work procedures and in distinct contrast to the traditional patterns of Jewish charity. Then there are the bulging files of the Anti-Defamation League office, crammed with correspondence and memoranda on the relationships of Jews and non-Jews within the southern region, as well as with a wide assortment of literature on intergroup relations. The Welfare Fund as an agency that is concerned with the collection and distribution of large sums of money to be expended for Jewish affairs requires an adequate bookkeeping and record system. The social clubs must operate in a "business-like manner" while the other community agencies, including synagogues, must maintain systems of records to operate effectively. Failure to do so now would be denounced as slipshod operation.

Weber spoke of the tendency of bureaucracy to follow general rules rather than to consider each case separately on a purely personal basis that would allow for the possible exercise of favoritism. Thus casework procedure follows somewhat general rules. Allowances are made on the basis of a previously devised budget system that estimates the price of different commodities and services involved in the "cost of living." The Atlanta Jewish Community Council and other organizations pass general resolutions that serve as guides to the organizational elite. However, there is occasional conflict between these two types of attitudes and methods of operation.

For example, the Community Council passed a resolution regarding ways of co-ordinating fund-raising campaigns among its members that gave precedence to the annual Welfare Fund drive. At a meeting of the Labor Zionists, a letter from a member of the organizational elite was read which deplored the efforts of this group to conduct a raffle to buy agricultural machinery for co-operative colonies in Palestine while the annual Welfare Fund campaign was in progress. The missive from the community executive brought a flood of protests from the members who spoke of other groups that "did as they pleased" and who also felt that they were doing something that was absolutely right. Some mildly slighting remarks were made about the organizational elite. "Go to their offices and ask to see them and maybe one of their secretaries will go and find out if they will see you."

Changes in procedure for handling transients further indicate the transition to a system which now stresses the use of general rules. Here the traditional society to aid strangers told of its religious duty to furnish food and lodging without question to any Jew who requested it, in contrast to the formalized procedures for handling transients that had been determined by the national and local Jewish social service agencies.

Again, in accordance with the characteristics of bureaucracy listed by Weber, the local organizational elite are dependent upon their jobs for their livelihood. Their positions are full-time tasks in which they have relatively secure tenure. However, in any real conflict between the organizational and lay elite, the latter would dominate since they control the financial resources of the local Jewish community and have a legitimate right to determine policy and personnel, despite the fact that they have sometimes largely relinquished such duties. But the lay elite still would be substituting one set of administrators for another, since they are so dependent on the latter to carry on the daily functioning of their organizations.

The organizational elite have a relatively high status in the community based primarily on their bureaucratic positions that give them important functional roles in community life. Their positions likewise provide entry into other important community roles. Some of these statuses have an ex-officio character, since the work of the organizational elite may require that they be placed automatically on various committees and boards. Other positions are acquired through the ability and desire of members of the organizational elite to engage in particular activities.

Weber wrote of the technical superiority of the bureaucratic structure and of the dependency of the elected office-holder on the specialized power of the expert even when he supposedly controls the latter. A familiar scene at meetings in the local Jewish community, or for that matter throughout our society, is the picture of the principal elected officers and the ranking members of the technical staff of the organization seated at the front of the table, with the latter providing the answers when issues become involved and complex. Thus one community leader commented:

> Our professional workers play an intellectual role in the community, for they provide guidance. When I need to know something, I call on the professional worker. I may not do as they suggest or indicate, but I do draw on them for information.

Another lay community leader spoke bitterly of his experiences at regional and national meetings of an organization in which he was deeply interested:

> Today we are so dependent on the professional community worker to tell

us what to do and how to do it. Particularly when I go to regional and national meetings, I encounter so many people, especially professional workers, who come up with clippings and documents to prove their points. They seem only to present the stuff that they want to prove and they have plenty of time to prepare their case beforehand. They know parliamentary procedure and how to confuse issues to get what they want. They play on words and we who are not so well prepared get lost.

It is likely that this lay leader, imbued with a traditionalist and personal approach in the solving of problems pertaining to his group, had not adjusted to the more rational and generalized approaches that had been developed in his organization.

When sites are to be selected for a community center or similar projects, when the Welfare Fund campaign is being organized, when an incident occurs that involves community relations or when any situation develops that requires technical assistance, then the organizational elite are consulted and utilized. In the past, the bureaucratic leader held a somewhat inferior position and was almost completely dominated by the lay elite. This was possible because of the more simplified tasks that were performed which could be handled by a layman, the lack of training and organization on the part of the paid community worker, and a general disdain of the paid worker as an equal participant. The organizational elite now are on a far more equal footing with the lay leadership in Jewish communities throughout the nation. Actually, the function of the latter group is frequently that of "followship" in which they furnish financial resources for community activities while the organizational elite furnish the creative leadership that sets policy, direction, and tone. Theoretically, part of the job of the organizational elite today lies in the encouragement of full participation in organizational affairs by the lay elite instead of complacent acquiescence to the suggestions of the paid community executive.

§ *Patterns of Co-operation and Competition*

The organizational elite exhibit patterns of co-operation and conflict among themselves as they jockey for power and prestige. On one policy the professional executives of various community agencies may be in conflict, while in connection with other programs they may be working together harmoniously. Often they serve on similar committees and thus present the general viewpoint of the professional community worker. Many of the members of the organizational elite and their associates meet irregularly as an informal association called the "Jewish Social Workers' Club." This loose organization serves as a medium for the exchange of ideas and for camaraderie. Also, there are occasional meetings of the executives of related agencies to co-ordinate policy. Actually, relations among the organizational elite as an entity are generally rather loose-knit. Except for those men whose organizations are directly connected, the organizational elite in a *collective* sense more often constitute a category than a group.

The patterns of conflict among the bureaucratic leaders usually are based upon ideological differences that are apparent in the purpose of the organizations which they administer, struggles for power that reflect changing community needs and corresponding efforts of organizations to meet these changing needs, and clashes of "personalities." The last factor may be a reflection of other factors. So-called "personality differences" can be of great importance in affecting community organization, particularly when an area of activity may be dominated by relatively few people. Sometimes members of the organizational elite will contend that the operations of a particular association represent a "negative" approach in solving a particular problem of Jewish community life, whereas their agency follows a more "positive" policy in this respect. This contention may be a rationalization, rather than an objective consideration of the ideologies involved, that will give their organization greater prestige. Yet these belief systems do provide some basis for conflict among the organizational elite. Competition can be engendered in situations involving scarcity and different value systems. The organizational elite must occasionally clash over the division of available funds. But they also may differ because of the particular approaches used by the organization that they head. Thus some of the organizational elite contend that the approach of the so-called civic-protective associations such as the Anti-Defamation League is essentially negative since its methods are basically defensive. They believe that the programs of these organizations involve an incomplete way of relieving frustrations and of accommodating to feelings of being different. Again, other ideological struggles are concerned with interpetations of what kind of agencies should handle particular kinds of social services and what should be proper social service policy. Also, some of the conflicts among the organizational elite revolve around the situation that certain members of this group have tended in the past to dominate many community functions which are now coming within the realm of new and expanding agencies that also utilize professional personnel.

There is no elaborate hierarchy of authority among the organizational elite of the Atlanta Jewish community although there are differences in the distribution and concentration of power and prestige among different bureaucratic leaders. Those members of the organizational elite who arrived earliest on the local scene and secured key positions in some instances have tended to build vested interests in the control of particular activities. In the meantime, the executives of other agencies are attempting to expand their functions or to secure a more autonomous and powerful status for their organizations. But so long as any community exhibits flux of either an expansive or retractive nature, such struggles for power and status are bound to continue. The needs of the community do not remain sufficiently stationary for clearly defined areas of operation to be made among the organizational elite.

§ *Interrelations with the Theological Elite*

Obviously there are occasions when the organizational and theological elites tend to be in either co-operation or competition. Thus social service had been an important aspect of the work of the rabbi in both Europe and the United States, but his control of this activity has diminished drastically as Jewish social work became increasingly secularized and professionalized. While a few associations that particularly evoke a religious character still remain within the orbit of the synagogue and its spiritual leader, major activities in this sphere have been taken over by the secular community agencies. Illustrative of the first type are societies for the burial of the dead, while an example of the secularized type would be a federation for Jewish social service that handles a full complement of case work and group work functions. One Atlanta rabbi told of the decline of his role in charitable work:

It used to be that *meshulochim* or collectors of charity for the many Jewish schools, orphanages and other agencies outside of the local community would come to see me to secure a letter of approval before they would start to make their rounds of the Orthodox Jewish group. Now I give no letters, for permission to solicit funds must come from the Welfare Fund and the Federation who exercise a tight control over the charitable work of the community. The Welfare Fund now is supposed to collect funds for these outside groups without the necessity of solicitation by the old-time *meshulochim*.

The position of rabbi brings with it an entire series of honorary and ex-officio statuses. The rabbinate almost automatically are placed on the boards of the various associations headed by members of the organizational elite. Few of these positions that are part of the office of the rabbi really are power positions in themselves. The rabbi who wishes to be participant and active in a particular function has entry because of his position as a member of the theological elite, but it is his own personality and interest that largely determines his importance in organizations apart from his congregation. The role of each rabbi then becomes an individually made proposition. He can be truly participant or nonparticipant in these groups as he pleases. Frequently the viewpoint of the rabbinate and the organizational elite coincide. Both tend to be more liberal in their approaches than the lay elite.

Sometimes the rabbis may stress activities that are not necessarily a requirement of their position. On occasion they may find themselves doing things that the organizational elite consider to be within their control. For example one rabbi has tended to stress goodwill work with non-Jews. He has become almost a symbol of the Atlanta Jewish community to the general populace, yet his methods tend to be antithetical to the approach advocated by the organizational elite concerned with combatting prejudice and discrimination.

With the increased emphasis on a more elaborate system of Jewish education as a method of developing a program of positive Judaism among the younger generation, the rabbinate find themselves in a new relationship with the organizational elite. In the past the formal religious education of the young was entirely under their supervision. Today the rabbis work with the various bureaus of Jewish education that exist in Atlanta and in other cities with large Jewish populations. The managers of these agencies exhibit more of the characteristics of the organizational elite than they do of the theological elite, and this means that even in the educational realm there is some competition between the two groups although the rabbis hold an important and even dominating voice in determining educational policy.

The rabbis recognize and deplore their declining role. They attempt to develop programs to counteract the decline in religious participation, but with indifferent success. The membership will furnish the financial and material resources for such programs, but their active participation is negligible. The social life of the community has been taken over by the social clubs, while the organizational elite operate the social service functions. The rabbis have to concern themselves largely with a residue of activity outside of their strictly religious and educational functions, for the Jewish population is characterized by a high ratio of synagogue membership and a low ratio of religious participation except on the High Holidays and on the ceremonial occasions which mark important phases of the life cycle. One rabbi sadly commented:

> The center of Jewish life was the home and the synagogue. Formerly the Jew was born in, married in, and buried from, the same house. Today he is born in a hospital, married in a social club, and his funeral takes place from a funeral parlor. This change in locale mirrors the decline of the synagogue, the rabbi, and the home in the life of the Jew.

§ *Conclusions*

The rise of the organizational elite is a reflection of a trend toward secularization and specialization that is occurring in Jewish community life. These managerial technicians provide technical direction and ideological guidance for Jewish association that are concerned with case work, group work, and community organization. Jewish communities such as the one in Atlanta are becoming increasingly dependent upon the organizational elite to operate basic community services other than purely religious functions.

The background characteristics of the organizational elite tend to be similar in such items as place of birth and type of education. In their political, economic, and social philosophy, the organizational elite are more articulately liberal in their ideas than the mass of the Jewish community. The existence of such attitudes in this group tends to have a liberalizing effect on the lay leadership of the community, since the latter so often turn to the organizational elite for guidance on Jewish community problems. The organizational elite utilize the methods of bureaucracy as an operating technique.

The patterns of conflict among the members of the organizational and theological elite in the Atlanta Jewish community are based chiefly on: (a) ideological differences, (b) struggles for status and power, (c) clashes of personalities, and (d) combinations of these categories, which frequently are reflections of the changing nature of Jewish community life. As the traditional functions of the synagogue and of folk groups are superseded by secular organizations, a decline in the influence of the former groups and a concurrent lessening of the influence of their leaders can be found. Also, despite their competitive struggles, the organizational elite often must cooperate with one another because of the nature of their work.

The strength of the organizational elite is to be found in their strategic positions, their training and their inclination to participate in community activities. Their general weakness can be found in their economic dependence on the lay elite (who have ultimate control over community activities) and in the maintenance of attitudes regarding methods of operation that may vary too greatly from those supported by the lay elite. Yet all the lay elite can do in case of a dispute is to find other managerial technicians to supervise the functioning of various key organizations in the modern Jewish community. The organizational elite have superseded many of the functions of both the theological and the lay elite and, in addition, have taken on new functions that put them in the forefront of personnel guiding the present-day American Jewish community.

THE ROLE OF SOCIAL CLUBS
IN THE ATLANTA JEWISH COMMUNITY

AN extremely high ratio of the families in the Atlanta Jewish community participate in the activities of the three local Jewish social clubs. In the 1940's, one of these organizations had over 1,200 members (mostly heads of households). The other two clubs were smaller since they secured their membership largely from the wealthier elements of the Jewish community. The number of families connected with social clubs represents an astonishingly high percentage of the (1946) estimated total Jewish population of over 10,000 persons, for approximately fifteen hundred *families* held membership in the three clubs. While over two thousand families belonged to the various synagogues in the community, many of these were nonparticipating. Synagogue attendance would hit its peak during the High Holidays, but club attendance was a week-to-week affair and often a daily one.

Economically the Jews of Atlanta are very middle class, for only one or two per cent of the Jewish working population are manual workers. The "clubbing" pattern pervades all levels of Atlanta Jewry, regardless of income level, country of origin, or synagogue affiliation. Social-club affiliation in our society generally begins with persons who are upper-middle class and continues into the upper levels of society (the Elks Club or the American Legion chapter-house might serve some of the social needs of the lower-middle class). However, in Atlanta, even those Jews who probably would be classified as lower-middle class belong to the P. Club. Also, the wealthier Jews of the city participate actively in their social clubs to a greater extent than the non-Jewish elite, who emphasize entertainment at home.

§ *The Functions of the Clubs*

A major reason for the existence of these Jewish social clubs lies in the fact that the Jewish population is excluded from the other major social clubs of the city. The by-laws of such organizations do not mention that "no Jews are allowed." Rather, unwritten rules dictate the pattern.[1] One rabbi, in discussing this situation, expressed the nature of social relationships in Atlanta between the prominent Jew and the prominent non-Jew

---

Published for the first time in this volume.

The article is based on the author's unpublished doctoral thesis, "The Jews of Atlanta: Their Social Structure and Leadership Patterns" (University of North Carolina, 1950). The data was gathered in 1948, and this article does not analyze trends since that time except where specifically indicated.

as follows: "A Jew is accepted anywhere in the city, with any group, up to six o'clock."

Actually there is some social intermingling between Jew and non-Jew, but it is not on a common club-membership basis. Social intercourse with non-Jews is most frequent with Jews who are wealthy and whose families have been resident in Atlanta for several generations. It also takes place between Jews and non-Jews who hold liberal points of view on social, economic and political issues. However, on the social level that constitutes "top society," the position of the Jew is very insecure—his status is that of an occasional guest but never that of the completely accepted member. One prominent Atlantan stated:

Although generally speaking Jews do not belong to some of the leading social clubs in the city they do have their own clubs that are very nice. I and some of my friends are sometimes guests at their clubs while they are guests of the non-Jewish clubs on occasion. In civic affairs the participation of Jews is more than welcome and is sought because of the high caliber of support that they give to such activities. Also they are invited into the "best" homes in the city.

One of the Jewish elite, who was described by both Jewish and non-Jewish groups as belonging to the Jewish coterie which sometimes operated on a social level with the leaders of Atlanta society, commented as follows:

The Jew isn't fully accepted in Atlanta social life. You have to have a particular talent such as being a good card player, golfer, or horseman in order to be invited into the homes of the "better" class in Atlanta. You get Gentile neighbors and they eventually learn that you don't have horns and that your food is good and then you get started along. But you are not generally accepted just as you are, but more because of your talents, wealth, and education.

The nature of these relationships probably builds up many feelings of insecurity for those members of the Jewish community who carry on some measure of social intercourse with the dominant elite of the city. Having the uncertain status of guest rather than the more stable position of member, it is not surprising that some Jews supported the formation of independent Jewish social clubs. Others who were not acquainted with non-Jews socially, or who did not wish to become a part of the non-Jewish group socially, also supported the formation of the Jewish social clubs. They desired a place where they could participate in social affairs with their Jewish friends who had similar interests.

In turn, the Jewish social clubs become an added inducement to remain within the Jewish group. The sense of uneasiness that may pervade some Jews in their social relationships with non-Jews—resting partly on the fear of being offended and partly on a lack of opportunity to build secure patterns of interaction with the outgroup—is lessened in an environment of familiar faces. The centripetal forces for remaining within the Jewish community on the social level are obviously strong.

The clubs have had a profound effect on the home life of many of the

Jewish families in the city. Many people confine their principal social participation to their clubs. The availability of card rooms, the frequent dances, the development of particular evenings as "club nights," the athletic facilities, the lack of a real community center[2] and the absence in the city of adequate recreational programs and leisure-time activities, commercial and public, have been factors promoting the clubhouses as important areas of social activity.

A typical day at the club will find it to be relatively quiet in the morning—except in the summer months, when the wives and children of members flock to the swimming pools. A few women's groups may be holding a morning meeting, but the staff is largely engaged in preparing for the luncheon hour and the evening activities. Often a luncheon group will meet at the clubs; certain cliques eat together frequently. The bars and slot machines do a steady business that reaches its peak in the evenings when the members and their guests are free to relax from their day's work. During these hours the card rooms, the eating rooms, and lounges become crowded. Except on club nights when the *pièce de résistance* is bingo, on dance nights, or on various other special occasions when the women can participate as vigorously as the men, more men than women frequent the clubs. A regular feature of the clubs are the special dances arranged for the younger generation.

No other Jewish association or group will attempt to put on a community-wide affair on "club" nights, for there would be inadequate attendance. Furthermore, various groups complain that the clubs are eliminating their ability to function properly. Most of the professional social workers, the rabbinate, the residents who are strictly orthodox in their religious views, and people who are interested in developing Jewish cultural activities feel that the social clubs have had the effect of lessening participation in certain areas of Jewish life. Thus one rabbi stated that:

> The Orthodox community in Atlanta is the P. Club, for everything in the community hinges around it. There will be about twenty-five men to a religious service in the evening or a handful of people to a business meeting or a cultural event, but there are always large groups of people at the clubs. Even our cultural activities have to be at the clubs since we lack a real community center. Further, none of the clubs maintain the Jewish dietary laws, which is having an additional effect on the local Jewish population. The food that is now served is not kosher [although much of it is "kosher-style"].

A leader in the labor Zionist movement characterizes the decline of his organization in the following way:

> We are an old organization, over thirty years old. We were stronger in the past but our membership has been dying out. We agree with the Arbeiter Ring [another labor group] in philosophy, but on the surface only. We are Zionists; they are not. We are interested in promoting literature, music, and culture, not athletics. But our membership, particularly the young ones, is declining in its interest. When we have a meeting, probably fifty per cent of the membership will be found at the P. Social Club instead. . . .

To most of the club members, the role of the social club is viewed from a different perspective. Many contend that the development of the social clubs—particularly the P. Club—has provided the Jewish resident of Atlanta with an opportunity for a dignified social life. They point out that some Jews were denied access to semi-public recreational facilities in Atlanta, and that the formation of the P. Club—with its excellent physical facilities —gave the Jew an area where he could act freely and enjoy himself without fear of insult. Note the following paraphrase of a statement volunteered by a prominent leader of the Jewish community:

In spite of those aspects of club life that some people consider 'bad,' they also offer many advantages to the Jewish community. For one thing, *the club can control the behavior of its members.* A man knows if he acts badly that he may not be able to get into a club or that he may be asked to resign. Since the club is such a prominent aspect of local social life, the possibility of nonmembership for failure to act properly tends to keep people in line. When you are in a club, you know that you have to act with a certain amount of decorum and you do so.

The members and officers of the club have a pretty good idea of the financial standing of its various members. So *the club is in a position to exert pressure on a member to give donations* to community needs in accordance with his economic position. Thus I recall one man who recently wanted to become a member of one of the clubs. He had given what we considered only a token contribution to charitable needs that was completely out of line with his financial position. He was not accepted for membership until he had increased his contribution to the [Jewish] Welfare Fund considerably.

The club provides a place for social life. There are relatively few places in Atlanta available for social life, for the regular population as well as the Jewish group. The clubs help to fill that void by providing entertainment and activities, food and drink, to meet the needs of those who wish to participate.

The club is a medium of advertising. When you have some important news that you wish to have circulated around, then the club is one of the best spots to do this. News gets around fast, because there are so many people at the clubs.

The social clubs are so important in the Atlanta Jewish community that they have representation on the local Jewish Community Council. The Jewish Community Council, the Welfare Fund, the Federation for Jewish Social Service, and many other important organizations in the Atlanta Jewish community use the clubs for their gatherings. However, it is only occasionally that a lecture on cultural activities will be held by one of the clubs. Furthermore, periodicals such as *Life* are found in the magazine racks in greater abundance than is true for Jewish journals. It is to be noted that the clubs close during the High Holidays and the Sabbath.

The clubs have filled the gap due to the lack of an adequate community center in many ways. The old center is too small, too far removed from the present concentration of Jewish population, and too poorly equipped to handle the current needs of Atlanta Jewry. The new center will bring with it a reassessment of the proper role of the clubs in the life of the community. The clubs may then become less communal in their orientation, and more involved in their own private affairs.

§ *Differences Among Clubs*

The oldest Jewish social club in the city is the S. Club. It is an outgrowth of a social organization that was started by a group of German Jews in 1867. Until recently its members almost invariably were of German or Central European descent, economically secure and even wealthy, and congregants of the local Reform temple. The homogeneity of descent and of synagogue membership is becoming less apparent since many of the newer members are persons of Eastern European descent who are on a similar economic cultural level. Possession of wealth is not an absolute criterion for membership, but it is important.

Although the S. Club is the oldest Jewish social club with the most prestige in the general community, some persons who today would meet its membership qualifications belong to another group, the M. Club. The M. Club is made up primarily of persons of Eastern European descent who generally have a high or above-average economic status in the Jewish community, but who belong to the moderate Orthodox synagogue rather than to the Reform congregation. They tend to support the Zionist movement and in many instances constitute some of the new leadership in the overall Jewish community. The antecedents of this organization are relatively new, for their charter dates from 1931. The present clubhouse was constructed in 1939. The S. Club has a somewhat larger membership than the M. Club. The M. Club represents the economically elite elements in the Eastern European Jewish population.

In 1948, the P. Club had the most elaborate physical plant of the various Jewish social clubs in Atlanta. Its membership was also larger than either of the two other organizations. The P. Club was started by approximately twenty men in 1914 as a means of organizing social and athletic activities for young males of Eastern European background who could neither afford to belong to the S. Club nor who would have been socially acceptable to the latter group. The early members were often clerical workers and proprietors of small business establishments. They erected a small clubhouse in the Jewish area of the city as it existed at that time. With improvement in the economic and educational status of the Eastern European Jew, membership grew. In 1939 a new building was erected. It cost over $250,000 and membership increased from over five hundred until it reached more than twelve hundred families by 1945. Elaborate additions to the building have been erected since that time. The membership probably includes more than 35 per cent of the families in the local Jewish community. *On the basis of numbers of active participants and the intensity of their participation in club activities,* the P. Club represents the most influential and potent Jewish organization in Atlanta. Almost 50 per cent of the members of the M. Club also belong to the P. Club; it is the M. and S. Clubs which appeal primarily to the wealthier persons in the Jewish community.

Large and attractive physical facilities characterize all three clubs. The installation of some improvement or device in one organization generally leads to changes and elaborations in the other clubs. Thus the S. Club recently constructed a new town and country club, complete with golf course; prior to this event the M. Club had a more modern plant than the S. Club.[3]

The operation of these organizations is expensive. Dues in both the M. Club and the S. Club are relatively high. In addition, members also are assessed according to their means to buy stock for capital improvements. The P. Club has a low membership fee, but this group has also resorted to selling stock to its members in order to finance a number of improvements to its facilities. Many services provided to members operate at a loss, although other services may be more profitable. Each club has a small group of men who tend to dominate the policies of the organization. One Atlantan observed: "If you want to see who controls a particular club, just watch the waiters. They know."

Just as there are those who are affiliated with more than one place of worship, families may belong to two or more social clubs. Business reasons, prestige factors, differences in facilities, and the desire to maintain social relationships with particular groups are some of the factors that may determine plural memberships. Some clubs are nearer to the business district and therefore are more convenient for dining during working hours. Another club may be the place which is frequented by friends and acquaintances, while the younger set in still another club may be more congenial to other family members. One man commented as follows on his plural memberships:

> I belong to the P. Club because it is convenient and my friends are there, I belong to the M. Club because my wife likes the social set there, and I am a member of the S. Club because my children want to go with the younger set who frequent that organization.

§ *Interrelations with Other Organized Jewish Activities*

The three social clubs reflect the social relationships that exist between different groups in the community. It is possible to tell with a considerable degree of accuracy the synagogue affiliations, fraternal memberships and other organized group relationships of club members. Table 1 attempts to indicate some of these interrelationships among the male members of the S. Social Club and the M. Social Club as well as their spouses. The two organizations were almost comparable in size when the study was made. About thirty individuals were members of both clubs. Most of this latter group had an Eastern European background, although a few German Jews also belonged to the M. Club.

The synagogue affiliations of the club members show distinct variations. The Reform Temple was started by the German Jewish population and it remains the principal place of worship for most of the membership of the S. Social Club; as is indicated in Table 1, 77 per cent of the male members of

Table 1—Jewish Organizational Affiliations of the Male Members of the S. Social Club
and the M. Social Club and Their Spouses, 1945-1946

Type of Organization	Percentage of Membership of the M. Social Club Holding Membership in the Following Organizations	Percentage of Membership of the S. Social Club Holding Membership in the Following Organizations
Reform Temple	37.0%	77.0%
Liberal Orthodox Synagogue	68.0	6.0
Strictly Orthodox Synagogues	4.0	.3
M. Social Club	100.0	9.0
S. Social Club	13.0	100.0
P. Social Club	45.0	21.0
B'nai B'rith	45.0	51.0
Zionist Organization of America	78.0	15.0
National Council of Jewish Women	32.0	49.0
Hadassah	80.0	21.0

Source: Membership lists of the above organizations for 1945-1946.

this organization belong to it. Only 6 per cent of the S. Social Club membership belonged to the liberal Orthodox synagogue, and these men were almost
entirely Eastern European Jews who in some instances also were members
of the Reform Temple. The distribution of synagogue membership at the
M. Social Club contrasts strikingly with the situation at the S. Social Club:
68 per cent of the members belonged to the liberal Orthodox synagogue and
37 per cent belonged to the Reform Temple. These particular people have
been climbing in social status. For some, this acceleration to a higher social
level involves membership in the Reform Temple. The members of both
social clubs were only slightly involved with the strictly Orthodox synagogues of the community, as such affiliations were practically nil for the
S. Social Club while less than 5 per cent of the members of the M. Social
Club held such memberships.

Differences in the ratio of membership in the P. Social Club by the constituents of the two elite social clubs also exist. The membership dues and
assessments of the P. Club are considerably lower than those of the other
social clubs, and it has a larger physical plant with excellent dining facilities.
It is located relatively near the business district of the city. These are some
of the factors that induce members of both the S. Social Club and the M.
Social Club also to retain memberships in the P. Social Club. In addition,
certain members of the M. Social Club belonged to the P. Social Club for
many years prior to the creation of the former organization. Since the bulk
of the membership of the P. Social Club is made up of persons of Eastern
European ancestry, it is understandable why the M. Social Club has a higher
percentage of its participants also belonging to it. Thus, 45 per cent of the
members of the M. Social Club also had joined the P. Social Club while
about one-fifth of the membership of the S. Social Club were in this category.

The B'nai B'rith represents an approach that is highly acceptable to both
German and Eastern European Jews. This acceptance is reflected in the more
uniform membership rate in this fraternal organization by the members of

the two social clubs: 45 per cent of the male members of the M. Social Club belong to B'nai B'rith while 51 per cent of the S. Social Club are in this organization. It should be remembered that B'nai B'rith was originally a fraternal order started by German Jews.

Affiliation with the local chapter of the Zionist Organization of America is in stark contrast with the mutual acceptance of B'nai B'rith. While over three-fourths of the male members of the M. Social Club belonged to the Zionist movement, only 15 per cent of the constituents of the S. Social Club held such memberships and many of these persons represented the overlapping affiliation between the two social clubs.[4]

A glance at the membership affiliations of the wives of the members of these two social clubs shows a similar patterning. The National Council of Jewish Women was originally created and operated by the German-Jewish group, but in time it broadened its membership base. This attempt at expansion was aimed largely at those women who represented the economically secure and socially prominent Eastern European families. Thus 49 per cent of the male members of the S. Social Club had spouses who belonged to the local chapter of the National Council of Jewish Women, while 32 per cent of the personnel of the M. Social Club were in this category. However, the contrast between the clubs becomes apparent when the factor of membership in Hadassah is considered: 80 per cent of the male members of the M. Club have wives who are members of Hadassah, compared with 21 per cent of the membership of the S. Club.

As a consequence of these patterings, it is possible to predict at which of the social clubs the various organizations will meet. The Zionists convene only at the M. Social Club or the P. Social Club, while the American Council for Judaism hold their gatherings at the S. Social Club. The National Council of Jewish Women most likely meet at the S. Social Club although they may use the facilities of the M. Social Club. B'nai B'rith functions are held at any of the clubs, as is also true for certain other organizations such as the Atlanta Jewish Community Council. In fact, the community-wide groups may deliberately spread their functions to take place at different clubs as a symbol of unity.

The patterns which we have described have multiple effects. An incident cited by a young college student whose parents were of German-Jewish ancestry and members of the S. Social Club illustrates one kind of problem:

I am attending the state university at Athens. Most of the boys from Atlanta who are in my crowd usually pledge a particular fraternity at the university, but we also get to know a lot of other Jewish boys and girls in the course of time, particularly at Hillel Foundation meetings. While I was at school I met a Jewish girl from Atlanta whom I had never known while home. She and I dated quite a bit at school and when vacation time came and we returned to Atlanta, we continued to date. However we finally broke up. An important factor was that I liked to take her to the S. Social Club where my friends went but she didn't like it too much because she didn't know many of the people. She wanted me to go with her to the M. Social Club which was the one that her parents belonged to, but I felt ill at ease there since I knew very few of the younger set who frequented that club.

Each of these individuals had been circulating within a particular orbit of the Jewish community while they were living in Atlanta; the patterns tended to close rather than open channels of circulation between the youth of the Eastern European and German Jewish groups.

Social clubs exist in many other Jewish communities, but the Jewish "clubbing" pattern existing in Atlanta appears to be unique in its elaborateness. Other communities may be as economically prosperous as the Atlanta Jewish community and therefore as capable financially of supporting a system of social clubs. However, they apparently did not have the type of lay leadership who for a time placed the development of social clubs (particularly of the type represented by the P. Club, designed for all levels of the community), as the principal community activity. Historically, the clubs may be viewed as in part filling the vacuum created by the lack of an adequate community center. The clubs have given the Jews of Atlanta an organized leisure-time program that places cultural and religious activity in a secondary position. As a consequence, these organizations profoundly affect all other major social institutions in the Atlanta Jewish community.

E. DIGBY BALTZELL

THE DEVELOPMENT OF A JEWISH UPPER CLASS IN PHILADELPHIA: 1782-1940

THE Jewish community in Philadelphia is one of the oldest and most influential in America. Isolated socially from the Gentile world in a variety of ways, this ethnic and religious community perpetuates an ancient and rich cultural tradition. Its well-developed institutional structure, which parallels that of the Gentiles, is supported by a highly articulate associational and class structure. Although primarily concerned with the historical development of the Jewish upper class in the city during the period 1782-1940, this paper forms only one part of a more inclusive analysis of the Philadelphia upper class and its relationship to the Philadelphia elite.[1] An outline of the conceptual framework used in this larger study will be found below; it is the one followed in the present paper and it will help us to integrate the present analysis of the Jewish upper-class structure in a larger framework:

> . . . the *elite* concept refers to those *individuals* who are the most successful and stand at the top of the functional objective class hierarchy. These individuals are leaders in their chosen occupations or professions; they are the final-decision-makers in the political, economic, or military spheres as well as leaders in such professions as law, engineering, medicine, education, religion, and the arts.
>
> . . . in any comparatively stable social structure, over the years, certain elite members and their families will tend to associate with one another in many and various primary group situations and gradually develop a consciousness of kind and a distinctive style of life. The *upper class* concept, then, refers to a group of *families*, descendants of successful individuals (elite members) of one, two, three, or more generations ago, who are at the top of the social (subjective) class hierarchy.[2]

Thus there are two analytically separable aspects of all class positions, the functional and the social; the elite and the upper-class concepts, in turn, refer to those individuals or families who are at the top in each of these aspects of the class hierarchy.

In more concrete terms, while Senator Joseph McCarthy was a member of America's governing elite, he was not a member of the upper class; Senators Lodge and Saltonstall, on the other hand, are members of both the elite and the upper class in America; and finally, the aristocratic graduate of Groton and Harvard, if employed as a minor functionary in a Boston bank, is a member of the upper class but not of the elite. In the never ending flux of history, new individuals rise to elite positions (Henry Ford I), their descen-

---

Published for the first time in this volume.

dants are ascribed an upper-class status, and sometimes but not always their sons or grandsons (Henry Ford II) also achieve elite status.

In order to test these theoretical concepts, *Who's Who*, a listing of successful individuals in America, and the *Social Register*, a convenient index of prominent families, were used to select the members of Philadelphia's elite and upper class.[3] In 1940, 770 residents of the city were listed in *Who's Who*, of whom 226 were also listed in the *Social Register* and 544 were not. A detailed analysis of the *Who's Who* biographies of the 770 members of the Philadelphia elite showed how the 226 members of the upper class differed from the rest of the elite. In brief, those listed in the *Social Register* were more likely to be descendants of well-known members of the Philadelphia elite from colonial times to the present; more likely to hold the highest positions in the most prominent banks and the leading law firms in the city; more likely to live in the fashionable Main Line and Chestnut Hill suburbs, where they belonged to the exclusive clubs; more likely to be educated at fashionable private schools and colleges; and as a final distinguishing characteristic, Proper Philadelphians—so-called—as over against the *Who's Who* group, were almost entirely Protestant, while the members of the inner circle of old Quaker families were part of the contemporary Quaker-turned-Episcopal gentry.

A small but important part of the Philadelphia elite in 1940 was drawn from the city's Jewish community (Table 1). Only one Jewish member of the elite, Dr. David Riesman, was also listed in the *Social Register*. Dr. Riesman, was born in Saxe-Weimar, Germany, where he attended the Ducal Gymnasium. He subsequently was brought to America where he obtained an

Table 1—Religious Affiliation of Philadelphians in Who's Who as Related to Social Class

	SOCIAL CLASS						
	Social Register		Non Social Register		Who's Who Total		Per Cent in Social
Religious Affiliation	No.	%	No.	%	No.	%	Register
Episcopalian	95	(42)	75	(14)	170	(22)	56
Presbyterian	30	(13)	107	(20)	137	(18)	22
Quaker	7	(3)	15	(3)	22	(3)	32
Baptist	2	(1)	22	(4)	24	(3)	8
Methodist	0	(—)	26	(5)	26	(3)	—
Other Protestant	10	(5)	70	(12)	80	(10)	13
Catholic	2	(1)	25	(5)	27	(4)	7
Jewish	1	(—)	26	(5)	27	(4)	3
No information	79	(35)	178	(32)	257	(33)	31
Total	226	(100)	544	(100)	770	(100)	29

M.D. degree at the University of Pennsylvania. Although he married the daughter of Penrose Fleisher, a member of one of the most prominent and aristocratic Jewish families in Philadelphia, Dr. Riesman's German background (members of the German Jewish elite were more likely to participate in the Gentile world) probably explains his participation in Philadelphia's fashionable society. The fact that he was a very popular physician whose patients were drawn primarily from the *Social Register* world was also important.

Although, with one exception, no members of the Jewish elite were a part of the upper-class Gentile world in 1940, a well-defined Jewish upper class existed in the city. Within the Jewish community, upper-class membership was based on German ethnic origins and family position, which, as in the Gentile community, meant "old wealth." Of the twenty-seven Jews listed in *Who's Who*, fourteen were also members of the Jewish upper class (these fourteen were isolated through personal observation as well as by means of checking with members of the Jewish elite). After a brief discussion of the members of the Jewish community who were listed in *Who's Who* in 1940, the historical development of the Philadelphia Jewish upper class will be analyzed in some detail.

The twenty-seven members of the Philadelphia Jewish community listed in *Who's Who* held important positions in a wide variety of occupations and professions: There were seven businessmen, five lawyers (two of whom were distinguished judges), two physicians, three journalists, three rabbis, plus a Congressman, college president, author, artist, historian, psychologist, and a world-famous bibliophile. While all fourteen of the Jewish upper class were born in the United States, seven of the thirteen remaining members of the elite were born in Russia or Poland. The members of the Jewish upper class were even less horizontally mobile than the upper class members of the Gentile elite: while 54 per cent of those listed in both *Who's Who* and the *Social Register* were born in Philadelphia, 57 per cent of the upper class members of the small Jewish elite were born in the city. Just about the same proportion of the Jewish elite were college graduates (74 per cent) as was the case for the entire Philadelphia elite (75 per cent). While eleven of the fourteen members of the Jewish upper class were college graduates, nine of the thirteen other members of the Jewish elite reported college degrees. Unlike the Quaker and Episcopalian upper classes, the Jewish community in Philadelphia did not have its own private schools. All save two upper-class members of the elite (both attended Quaker schools) were educated in the public school system.

The following members of the Jewish upper class were also prominent members of the Philadelphia elite in 1940: Abraham Simon Wolf Rosenbach, the famous bibliophile; Justice Horace Stern, of the State Supreme Court; Julius David Stern, publisher of the Philadelphia *Record,* the only Democratic newspaper in the city; Lessing J. Rosenwald, chairman of the board of Sears, Roebuck & Company; Dr. Solomon Solis-Cohen, poet and prominent physician; Morris S. Wolf, senior partner of the city's leading Jewish law firm; Howard A. Loeb, who followed his father as president of one of the city's principal banks; Samuel Fels and S. S. Fleisher, two of the city's leading philanthropists; Cyrus Adler, president of Dropsie College and a force in American Jewry as a whole; and Ellis Gimbel, distinguished department store executive, philanthropist, and civic leader.[4]

Howard Loeb, chairman of the board of the Tradesmen's National Bank, was the only member of this group to be connected with a Gentile institution. He and his father before him, in fact, were the only members of the Jewish community ever to attain the presidency of a large Proper Philadelphia banking institution; all the other members of this Jewish upper class were either heads of their own, or family, businesses, or they were independent professionals such as lawyers or physicians. In other words, with one exception even the most prominent Jewish members of the Philadelphia elite are connected occupationally only within their own group. This fact, of course, has important consequences. In the interlocking directorships within the Gentile business community, there are no members of the Jewish community to sponsor capable executives from Jewish firms. This system of parallel economic organizations, based on ethnic exclusiveness at the top levels, also ramifies down the managerial and employee hierarchy. Thus a Jewish department store hires Jewish clerks who have often been turned down by the rival Gentile department store.

§ *Historical Development of the Jewish Upper Class in Philadelphia*

The first Jewish colonists in America arrived at New Amsterdam in 1654. They were Sephardim who had originally gone to Brazil as crypto-Jews in the sixteenth century, or later, along with the early Dutch colonists. When the Portuguese conquered Brazil, the Jews spread north into the West Indies and into the British and Dutch colonies in North America. Eventually, in such colonial cities as Newport, Charleston, Savannah, and Philadelphia, there were a small number of Sephardic Jews.[5] In Philadelphia, the development of a Jewish elite and eventually an upper class can conveniently be divided into five historical periods: (1) before 1782 there were elite Jews in Philadelphia but too few of them to form a distinct Jewish community; (2) formation of an elite Jewish community with Jews still participating in both the social and business life of the Gentile upper class (1782-1840); (3) formation of the modern Jewish upper class composed of German (Ashkenazic) Jews (1840-1882); (4) mass Russian immigration resulting in a German-Russian caste-like division (1882-1920); (5) Russian Jews attaining elite status, followed by faint beginnings of acceptance into the Jewish upper class which was, in 1940, still almost entirely German in ethnic origins (1920-1940).

THE COLONIAL PERIOD UP TO 1782. For all practical purposes there was no coherent Jewish community in Philadelphia during most of the eighteenth century. During the early years of the century, however, there were probably a few leading Jews among the merchant elite. Early records are inadequate. In the 1740's, however, it is believed that a small group of Jews began holding religious services in a house in Sterling Alley.[6] On the other hand, with no synagogue or formal Jewish community, and little if any anti-Jewish prejudice, these early Philadelphia Jews participated as individuals in the social and economic life of the community. When the exclusive Dancing Assembly, the oldest organization of its kind in America was formed in 1748 by fifty-nine of the city's most prominent families, two Jews—David Franks and Samson Levy—were among the original subscribers.[7] To this day, an invitation to the annual Assembly balls is the ultimate criterion of acceptance within the inner circle of Proper Philadelphia society.

As the sex ratio was quite naturally unbalanced during this early period, many Jews were absorbed by the Gentile community. David Franks and Sampson Levy both married Christians and their children were baptized. Thus, although her father remained a Jew all his life, Rebecca Franks was baptized at aristocratic Christ Church. Once referred to by General Charles Lee as a lady with "every human and divine advantage," Rebecca Franks was one of the most popular belles of Revolutionary Society in Philadelphia. According to Dixon Wecter, she "visited and corresponded charmingly with Chews, Allens, and Penns, married Lieutenant-General Sir Henry Johnston, and finished her days as the *grande dame* of Bath, most aristocratic of English watering places."[8]

THE EARLY JEWISH COMMUNITY (1782-1840). The formal Jewish community in Philadelphia began with the construction of the first synagogue, Mikveh Israel. Mikveh Israel was Sephardic in ritual and language; there was a small nucleus of Sephardim in the original congregation, and the first rabbi, Gershom Mendes Israel Seixas, was a Sephardic Jew from New York. On the other hand, many of the founders, including such leading Philadelphians as Bernard Gratz, Manuel Josephson, Methias Bush, and Jonas Phillips, were of German origins. Haym Solomon, a Polish Jew who worked closely with Robert Morris during the Revolution, was also one of the original members of the Mikveh Israel synagogue.[9]

The fact that several of the founders of the Mikveh Israel synagogue had descendants who were leading members of Proper Philadelphia society in 1940 attests to the ease with which successful assimilation took place during the colonial period. Of course the Jewish community was small in size, and the sex ratio was presumably still unbalanced. These early Jewish families have kept their family names even though they have married Christians for four or five generations.

Although in colonial Philadelphia there was no anti-Semitism as we know it today, the construction of Mikveh Israel, and hence the formation of a visible Jewish community, resulted in the first overt expression of this phenomenon. The small Jewish congregation had purchased a lot in Sterling Alley where they planned to build a synagogue. The lot, however, was "contiguous" to a German Reformed congregation. Such vigorous protests were raised by this Protestant group that the Jewish leaders finally purchased a new lot in Cherry Alley between 3rd and 4th Streets. There the first Mikveh Israel synagogue was erected in 1782 (see Map 1).[10] Cherry Alley is north of Market Street. Although it is not clear why the Jewish congregation settled north of Market, it is interesting that Proper Philadelphians have always lived south of Market Street—near Washington Square in the early days and around Rittenhouse Square later on in the nineteenth century. This pattern of the Jewish neighborhood being north of Market prevailed until well into the twentieth century.

During the second half of the eighteenth century, Jewish immigrants continued to come to Philadelphia. They were almost overwhelmingly Ashkenazim. Those who were accepted were only too glad to join Mikveh Israel and thus "become" Sephardim. By 1810 the German Jews in the city formed the first Ashkenazic congregation, Rodeph Sholom.[11] Within a few years, interestingly enough, many of the founders of Rodeph Sholom rejoined Mikveh Israel. At this time Ashkenazi-Sephardic caste lines were not as sharply drawn as some would have liked to make out. In other words, the upper-class Jews in early Philadelphia were almost entirely Ashkenazim who were brought up in the Sephardic tradition. Bernard Gratz, parnas of Mikveh Israel, although an acculturated Sephardi, was from the upper-Silesian part of the Polish Kingdoms. Just as the Anglican ritual appealed to many of Philadelphia's Quaker-turned-Episcopal merchants, so the Sephardic ritual appealed to the more successful and socially acceptable Ashkenazim. The wealthy and fashionable, whether Gentile or Jew, have a way of joining the socially prominent churches and synagogues regardless of their own familial religious tradition.

The 1830's were a kind of watershed in upper-class Jewish history in Philadelphia. Although there was by then a definite Jewish community in the city, the families that had made their money and consolidated their position took their place in the social, cultural, and business life of the city and thus participated in the Gentile world. Five members of the Gratz family, for example, were taken into the Philadelphia Club before the Civil War. Founded by Biddles and Cadwaladers in 1832, the Philadelphia Club is the oldest upper-class city club in America.[12] Along with the Assembly, the Philadelphia Club was by far the most exclusive association in the city in 1940. Between 1845 and 1847, Hyman Gratz—wealthy merchant, respected civic leader, and member of Mikveh Israel—was president *pro tem* of the Philadelphia Club while its first president, Commodore James Biddle, was serving in the Mexican War.[13] Since the Civil War, no members of the Jewish community have been members of the Philadelphia Club. Moreover, it is interesting that even before this time, apparently none of the members of the Gratz family made any effort to propose their Jewish friends for membership in this exclusive organization.

The 1830's were also somewhat of a watershed in the relationship between the upper-class Jewish and Gentile communities in other American cities. Thus, according to Dixon Wecter, "the last Jew to enter the arcana

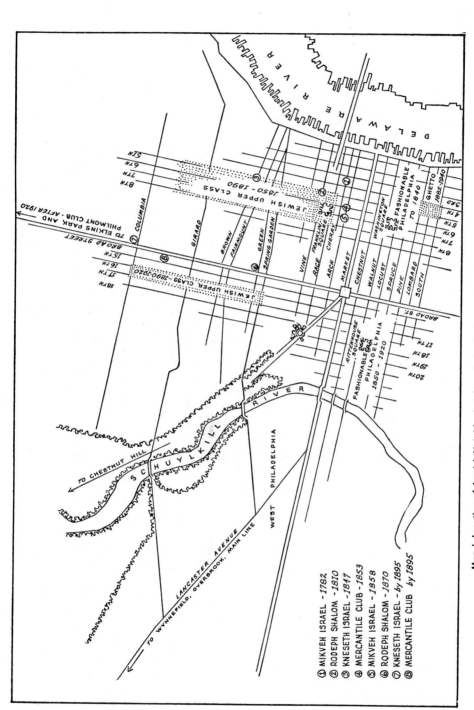

Map I. Location of Jewish Neighborhoods and Institutions in Philadelphia: 1782–1940

① MIKVEH ISRAEL – 1782
② RODEPH SHALOM – 1810
③ KNESETH ISRAEL – 1847
④ MERCANTILE CLUB – 1853
⑤ MIKVEH ISRAEL – 1858
⑥ RODEPH SHALOM – 1870
⑦ KNESETH ISRAEL – by 1895
⑧ MERCANTILE CLUB   by 1895

of smart New York Society before the bars went up was August Belmont."[14] Born in Germany, Belmont came to America as an agent of the Rothchilds and "after the panic of 1837—still with the approval of the greatest banking house in the world—he set up his own firm of August Belmont and Company."[15] He became a United States citizen, served as consul-general to Austria, minister to the Netherlands, and rendered valuable financial aid to the Union during the Civil War. The Belmonts have been leaders in New York Society for over three generations; August Belmont married a Miss Perry, of the family of naval heroes, and his grandson by the same name married a Boston Saltonstall.

FORMATION OF THE JEWISH UPPER CLASS (1840-1892). After the final defeat of Napoleon, settlers from Europe came to America in increasing numbers; the immigration of Jews along with other Germans was stepped up considerably during the three decades prior to the Civil War. For example, while 7,729 Germans entered America during the 1820's, this was increased to 152,454 during the 1830's.[16] Even more came in the forties and fifties. According to Carl Wittke, many of the Jewish forty-eighters of all classes were assimilated into the various German-American communities during this period.[17]

It is estimated that while there were some 4,000 Jews in America as of 1820, by 1860 there were close to 150,000.[18] Along with the increasing size of the Jewish community in Philadelphia, the modern upper class began to take shape in this pre-Civil War period. The three leading members of the original upper class were Isadore Binswanger, Abraham Simon Wolf, and Morris Rosenbach (ancestors of Abraham Simon Wolf Rosenbach and Morris Wolf—members of the 1940 elite). All three married sisters, the daughters of Hyman Polock; the sisters' brother was one of the city's leading booksellers and bibliophiles, Moses Polock. Hyman Polock, born in Amsterdam in 1786, had been married by the most fashionable German-Jewish rabbi in London in 1811, and came to America in 1813. He joined the Mikveh Israel congregation and was a moderately successful jeweler and a leader in the Jewish community for many years. He was an original member of the Hebrew Society for Visitation of Sick and Mutual Assistance, founded in 1813, and one of the founders and directors of the Hebrew Education Society in 1847.[19]

Before the Civil War, the Jewish upper class lived along 5th, 6th, 7th, and 8th streets, north of Franklin Square (see Table 2 and Map 1). In 1858, the Mikveh Israel congregation built a new synagogue at 7th and Arch streets (Abraham S. Wolf was on the building committee).[20] At the same time, upper-class social life centered around the Mercantile Club, founded in 1853 (Abraham S. Wolf, Morris Rosenbach, and Isadore Binswanger were among the eighteen charter members).[21] Located at 6th and Arch and thus just down the street from the synagogue, this exclusive club was limited to 400 upper-class Jewish families as late as the year 1894.[22] In the decade preceding the Civil War, partly due to exclusion from the Gentile community but primarily for convenience, this first Jewish upper class had developed a tightly organized community centering in the area north of Franklin Square.

Social position within the Jewish community is probably much more dependent upon the individual's charitable contributions than is the case with the Gentile community. Consequently, the members of the Jewish upper class in Philadelphia took the lead in founding various charitable organizations. The first Hebrew Charity Ball was organized in 1843 and soon became the most fashionable event of the year.[23] It was held annually until 1901, when the Federation of Jewish Charities was organized to re-

Table 2—Residene of Leading Jewish Upper-Class Families: 1859, 1890, 1914, 1940

Residential Areas[e]	1859 (N-14)[a]	1890 (N-41)[b]	1914 (N-37)[c]	1940 (N-58)[d]
	%	%	%	%
Franklin Square	100	80	8	—
North Broad	—	20	54	3
Old York Road	—	—	24	81[g]
Rittenhouse Square	—	—	6	13
Other Areas	—	—	8[f]	3[h]
All Areas	100	100	100	100

a. There were 18 founders of the Mercantile Club in 1853. These are the 14 family-heads who could be traced in McElroy's *Philadelphia City Directory*, 1859. The names of the founders of the Mercantile Club were taken from Henry Samuel Morias, *op. cit.*, p. 193.

b. These are the 41 traceable residences of the families of the men who founded the Philmont Country Club in 1906. For example, the residential address of Adam Gimbel, father of Ellis A. Gimbel, founder and president of the Philmont Club 1906-1946, is included here, as Ellis Gimbel was presumably living at home at that time. Similarly, N. Snellenburg, founder of N. Snellenburg and Company, the city's leading middle-class department store, is included here, although his descendants were Philmont founders. The addresses were obtained from *Boyd's Blue Book*, 1889-90.

c. This list includes 37 charter members of the Philmont Country Club. The charter members and their addresses were both taken from *Boyd's Philadelphia Blue Book, Elite Directory and Club List*, 1914.

d. There were 19 charter members of the Locust Club, founded in 1920. As many of these charter members were deceased in 1940, this list includes the residences of 58 members of their families. The addresses were obtained from the Philadelphia and Suburban telephone directories for the year 1940.

e. See Map 1.

f. All lived in West Philadelphia.

g. 31 of the 47 families living in this area lived in Elkins Park.

h. These families lived in the Whitemarsh Valley area.

place this informal method of raising money. The Jewish Hospital Association and the United Hebrew Charities were formed in 1865 and 1869 respectively, with Messrs. Binswanger, Wolf, and Rosenbach again among the founders of each institution.[24]

By 1882, then, there was a tightly structured German-Jewish upper class in Philadelphia. It centered around the Franklin Square neighborhood, north of Market Street, and its social life included the synagogue, the Mercantile Club, and charitable work. It has been shown how every upper-class institution was originally guided by members of the Wolf, Binswanger, and Rosenbach families. These first-family founders were, at the same time, the wealthiest members of the early Jewish community. In 1865, for example, the four richest Jews in Philadelphia were R. H. Gratz, Isadore Binswanger, Morris Rosenbach, and Abraham S. Wolf. In that year, Americans were blessed with an income tax, presumably to defray the costs of the war. The incomes of Philadelphians were published in a little pamphlet

entitled *Rich Men of Philadelphia;* R. H. Gratz's income was reported as
$102,042, Isadore Binswanger's as $65,143, Morris Rosenbach's as $25,452,
and Abraham S. Wolf's as $12,507.[25] All were sizeable incomes for that day.
The Gratz family were not only wealthier than the other three, but, as
descendants of the pre-1830's generation, they were less a part of the formal
Jewish upper class as it took shape at the time of the Civil War. According
to a Philadelphia City Directory of 1859, for example, while the Binswanger,
Wolf, and Rosenbach families all lived in the Franklin Square area, three
Gratz family-heads (an attorney, a merchant, and a gentleman) were living
west of Broad Street and north of Market Street (at that time the elite
new-rich, but not upper-class, Gentile neighborhood). A fourth Gratz listed
his address as 1309 Locust Street, and thus lived in a fashionable Gentile
neighborhood.[26]

In other words, the members of the Gratz family were no longer to be
considered part of the Jewish community. Many of them had married
Christians by this time and had themselves even been baptized. At the
upper-class level, the forces of assimilation were such that by the end of
the Civil War, most of the descendants of the eighteenth century Jewish
upper class who had been among the original founders of Mikveh Israel,
had become Christians and were completely accepted in fashionable
Gentile society. The prominent early nineteenth century familes, such as
Binswanger, Wolf, and Rosenbach, and not the Mikveh Israel founding-
families such as the Gratzes, constituted the leaders of the first coherent
Jewish upper class in the city.

RUSSIAN IMMIGRATION (1882-1920). In the year 1881, after Alexander
II was assassinated and his son Alexander III became Czar, anti-Jewish
pogroms became part of the policy of the Russian regime.[27] The central
problem confronting the Philadelphia Jewish community during the next
four decades was the assimilation of the mass of immigrants from Russia,
Poland, Hungary, and Rumania. Many were penniless when they arrived
in Philadelphia, and, of course, most of them were ignorant of American
language and customs. Fortunately, there was an established and prosperous Jewish community in the city with charitable habits based on an
ancient tradition of *noblesse oblige.* After 1882, most of the charitable
resources of the German-Jewish upper class went towards the aid of the
less fortunate Russian immigrants. The United Hebrew Charities in
Philadelphia, for example, obtained subscriptions from 682 individuals for
$14,773.32 in the year 1870; in 1894, on the other hand, 7,968 donors gave
$52,916.04.[28]

A great deal of financial aid also came from the more fortunate members
of the Russian-Jewish community in the city. For example, the Association
of Jewish Immigrants, all the officers of which were Russian-Jews, was
formed in 1884 at 931 South 4th Street.[29] During the year 1885, the association afforded shelter to 848 newly arrived immigrants, processed 900
applications for employment, and provided many other services including

protection from sharpers bent on taking advantage of ignorant immigrants.

Between 1882 and 1914, thousands of East European Jewish immigrants arrived in Philadelphia. They settled within a small area along 4th and 5th streets, south of Pine, which soon became known as Philadelphia's "East Side" (see Map 1). The Jews who poured into this South Philadelphia "ghetto" were a pious people with their own religious ritual, language, and traditions. They soon founded congregations and built their own synagogues. Of the eight synagogues in Philadelphia in 1882, for example, only one (417 Pine) was south of Market.[30] By 1900, the number of synagogues in the city had doubled; five of the eight new synagogues were located within an area of two city blocks in the Russian-Jewish Ghetto. (In addition to the existing synagogue at 417 Pine, five new ones were located at 4th and Lombard, 420 Lombard, 5th and Lombard, 518 South Street, and on 5th Street, between South and Lombard Streets.)[31]

At the same time that the "East Side" was developing in South Philadelphia, significant changes were taking place within the upper-class community, including several indications of increasing affluence. In the nineties the Jewish upper class began to move uptown to the elite area of the city, north of Market Street. At about the same time as the members of the Gentile North Broad Street elite were beginning to move out to the Old York Road, the Main Line, and Chestnut Hill, a new Jewish upper-class neighborhood was developing from North 17th to Broad Streets, between Spring Garden and Columbia Avenue (see Table 2 and Map 1). Members of the Wolf, Fleisher, and Binswanger families moved into this area in the nineties. In 1890, for example, Barnett Binswanger lived at 1414 North 16th Street, a few houses north of Meyer Guggenheim (1400 North 16th), founder of the Guggenheim dynasty and benefactor of the first Jewish hospital in Philadelphia.[32] Spring Garden Street, where the Gratz family lived in 1860 (see above), was one of the elite Gentile streets during and immediately after the Civil War. Charles T. Yerkes, the traction magnate who made the classic remark, "It's the straphanger who pays the dividends," lived on Spring Garden during this period (Theodore Dreiser, who fictionalized Yerkes's career in *The Financier,* had Copperwood living on Girard Avenue; both streets were elite addresses, and hence Dreiser's fiction rang true to the initiated).[33] In 1890, prominent Jews such as Penrose Fleisher and August and Edward Loeb had mansions on elite Spring Garden Street.[34]

By 1895, both the Rodeph Sholom and Keneseth Israel congregations had built large and impressive new synagogues on North Broad Street (see Map 1 and Table 3). The new Rodeph Sholom synagogue was situated at a point where Green Street, one of the most fashionable Jewish addresses at the turn of the century, ran into Broad Street. At the same time, the first summer resort synagogues along the New Jersey coast were built at Long Branch (1890), Atlantic City (1893), and Asbury Park (1896).[35]

The development of the Jewish summer resort was not solely due to the increasing affluence of the Jewish upper class. It was partly a reflection of the increasing anti-Semitism which characterized even the educated classes in America after the turn of the century. In the 1880's and early 1890's, for instance, many prominent Jewish Philadelphians spent their summers in such popular Proper Philadelphia resorts as Cape May.[36] The exclusion of members of the Jewish community from hotels, resorts, clubs, and neighborhoods, however, was more rigidly and overtly enforced after this period. (It was in the 1890's that the sign, "No Jews and Dogs Admitted Here," was supposed to have been displayed at fashionable Saratoga.)[37]

Table 3—Location of Upper Class Synagogues: 1860, 1895, 1940

	First Synagogue	1860	1895	1940
Sephardic				
Mikveh Israel	(1782)	7th & Arch	7th & Arch	Broad & York
Ashkenazic				
Rodeph Sholom[a]	(1810)	5th & Vine	Broad & Green	Broad & Green[c]
Keneseth Israel[b]	(1847)	5th & Brown	Broad & Columbia	Broad & Columbia

a. Rodeph Sholom, originally Orthodox, changed to the Reform service in 1870, when the new synagogue was built on North Broad Street.

b. Keneseth Israel was founded as a Reform congregation. This congregation led the "Radical Reform" movement in Philadelphia.

c. Since the 1920's, the members of Rodeph Sholom and Keneseth Israel have largely moved to the Old York Road suburbs. During the 1920's and 1930's the suburban members of the synagogues commuted to town for divine worship. Since World War II, these two congregations have organized a cooperative Sunday School for the children of their suburban members in Elkins Park. Keneseth Israel is planning to build in the Old York Road area as this is being written.

According to most observers, anti-Semitism was much more prevalent among the fashionable classes in America than was the case in France or England, where many ancient Gentile family lines had absorbed members of the Jewish community, and this has been explained in part by the timidity and conventionality so characteristic of the American open-class system. More important, however, was the fact that the masses of Jewish immigrants who came to these shores between 1882 and 1914 possessed quite alien cultural and religious traditions.[38] The tremendous growth of the lower-class Jewish community, moreover, coincided with the mass immigration of Southern Europeans who also differed in language, religion, and temperament from the dominant Anglo-Saxon majority. Thus, anti-Semitism was but one aspect of a growing antagonism towards all non-Anglo-Saxon Americans. According to H. L. Mencken, the prevalent use of such terms as *kike, bohunk,* and *wop,* originated in the last part of the nineteenth century.[39] In the twentieth century, old-stock Americans replaced the anti-Irish-Catholicism of their ancestors with a new, and sometimes more open, anti-Semitism.

Unfortunately, as with all forms of group prejudice, the dominant majority generally failed to differentiate between the various social, economic, or cultural levels which exist within all minority groups. Thus the cultivated Jewish aristocrat was often discriminated against because of a prejudicial stereotype derived from the behavior of lower-class immigrants. Quite naturally, this produced an all-too-human resentment and anti-Semitism within the Jewish community itself. The derogatory term, *kike*, for example, was first used in America by German Jews when referring to the less polished and often aggressive members of the East European Jewish community.[40]

There were, of course, no racial differences between the German and Eastern Jews. One need not go back too far in history to find similar ethnic origins. Many of the ancestors of the so-called German Jews in Philadelphia, as for example Hyman Polock or Hyman Gratz, were originally Polish. It was, then, primarily a different historical, and consequently cultural, experience which differentiated the Jews from Germany, Russia, or Poland. The Germans had the first and longest contacts with both Western European and American culture; the members of the German Jewish community, who came to America largely before 1870, were thus acculturated earlier than were the Jews from Eastern Europe. These historical and cultural differences were also reinforced by religious differences. In Philadelphia and elsewhere most of the upper-class German Jews belonged to Reform synagogues, while the Russian and Polish Jews were Orthodox. Within the Jewish community in the twentieth century, membership in a fashionable Reform congregation became a symbol of social and economic achievement and acculturation. It was much the same as the Quaker-turned-Episcopal or the Ashkenazi-turned-Sephardi process of an earlier Philadelphia. Today, several of the newest Reform synagogues in the city are made up primarily of East European Jews.

By 1900, most of Philadelphia's upper-class Jewish families had moved uptown to the new neighborhood west of Broad Street. In 1895, the Mercantile Club built an impressive new clubhouse on North Broad Street (1422 North Broad), located about halfway between the Rodeph Sholom and Keneseth Israel synagogues.[41] Several of the wealthier families, such as the Gimbels, had purchased mansions along Broad Street itself after the members of the Gentile elite had moved out to the suburbs. At the same time, a few Jewish families began to move out to the suburbs along the Old York Road. The first symptom of this Old York Road trend was the founding of the Philmont Country Club in 1906. Established by Gimbels, Snellenburgs, Loebs, and Wolfs, this was the original, and is still the most exclusive upper-class Jewish country club in the city.[42] As the figures in Table 2 suggest, by 1914 the movement to the suburbs was well under way.

EAST EUROPEAN JEWS ATTAIN ELITE STATUS (1920-1940). American ideals and aspirations are closely bound to the success saga. Most Americans strongly identify with the stories of Horatio Alger, with the lives of such men as Abraham Lincoln and Andrew Carnegie, and with the fabulous cinema Cinderellas of Hollywood. The rise of the East European Jewish community, within approximately half a century, from the American

Ghetto to middle-class comfort and even affluence is probably the most fabulous ethnic-group success story of all. At the turn of the century, most of the East European Jews were concentrated in the garment or handicraft industries or earning a precarious living as small shopkeepers, drummers, or peddlers. By the 1920's many had risen into the middle-class, white-collar world, and some had even attained elite status.[43]

In 1940, Albert Monroe Greenfield was the most powerful member of Philadelphia's Jewish community and one of the most influential men in the whole city. Born in the Ukraine in 1887, he was brought to America at the age of six. His father eventually became the proprietor of a small furniture store in North Philadelphia, where he probably never made more than $4,000 a year.[44] Young Albert graduated from Central High School, attended the University of Pennsylvania for two years, and entered the real estate business in 1903. In 1914 Greenfield married a Miss Kraus, who had studied at Bryn Mawr College and whose father was a successful building and loan magnate (Kraus was one of the original officers of the Association of Jewish Immigrants at its founding in 1884). By 1920, at the time of his father-in-law's death, Albert M. Greenfield had accumulated twenty-seven building and loan associations with total assets of approximately $35,000,000. He was also the owner (at the age of thirty-five) of the largest real estate business in the city—a firm that was one of the biggest in the nation (Albert M. Greenfield and Company was doing about $127,000,000 worth of business a year at that time).[45]

Perhaps partly as a reaction to outside pressures and partly due to developments within the Jewish community itself, the 1920's marked the beginning of a gradual breakdown of the caste-like barriers between the German and Russian Jewish communities in Philadelphia, at least at the elite level. The first signs of change came in 1919. Three days after the end of World War I, the Board of Directors of the Federation of Jewish Charities, following the leadership of their president, Louis Wolf, voted for "a hundred per cent federation." This meant that for the first time in Philadelphia leading German and Russian charitable institutions would be combined within one large organization.[46] Founded by upper-class German Jews such as Jacob Gimbel in 1901, the Federation—with eighteen affiliated agencies—had been raising about $200,000 per year in the decade before 1918. For the first "100 per cent campaign" in 1919, held under the chairmanship of Colonel Samuel D. Lit, a goal of $750,000 was set. A total of $800,000 was actually raised. By 1920, there were fifty-three German and Russian run charities included in the Federation.[47]

Charitable donations have always played an important role in the determination of social status within the Jewish community. As successful Russian Jews, symbolized by Mr. Greenfield, rose to influential positions within the city's business community, it was quite natural that they should assume their share of the charitable burden. It was also quite in accord with the mores and values of the Jewish community, and much more so here than in the Gentile community, to accept these new benefactors—or "big givers" as they were often called—within the higher associational levels of the social structure. In 1923, Albert M. Greenfield, who was now on the board of directors of the Federation, led the annual fund-raising drive.[48] Moreover, in 1925, while the most prominent upper-class members of the Jewish elite of 1940 (A. S. W. Rosenbach, Ellis Gimbel, Morris Wolf, Howard Loeb, Dr. Solis-Cohen, Judge Stern, Lessing J. Rosenwald, Samuel Fels, S. S. Fleisher, and Cyrus Adler) contributed a combined total of $52,775 to the drive in that year, Mr. and Mrs. Greenfield alone gave $31,000.[49] At about this time, the ethnic line was broken at the upper-class Mercantile Club when A. M. Greenfield became one of the first two members of the club who were not of German ethnic origin.[50] By 1940, Greenfield and other East European members of the Philadelphia elite listed membership in both the Philmont Country Club along the Old York Road, and the most exclusive Jewish urban men's club, the Locust, often known as the "Jewish Union League."

The Locust Club was founded in 1920 by leading members of the Jewish business community. In addition to Clarence Wolf, then president of the Mercantile Club, the charter members of the Locust Club included Gimbels, Fleishers, Lits, and Snellenburgs. This new urban men's club was somewhat different from the older Mercantile Club. In the first place, the older club, which was located in the heart of the Jewish community, was a center for family social life. With the suburbanization of the Jewish upper class, however, there was a need for a downtown club for businessmen. Of course, the leading members of the Jewish business community, unlike the Gratz family of an earlier day, were not accepted within the halls of such urban clubs as the Union League or the Philadelphia Club. Finally, while the Mercantile Club was voluntarily Jewish in membership, culture, and character, from the start the Locust Club was open to both Jews and Gentiles. As a gesture toward this ideal of avoiding exclusiveness, Francis Shunk Brown, one of the leading members of the Philadelphia bar and the grandson of two former governors of the state of Pennsylvania, was chosen to be the club's first president. Also, a promising young Irish-Catholic politician, a law partner of Morris Wolf, was one of the original directors. By 1940— although the original conception of the club still existed—only one non-Jewish member of the elite reported membership in the organization.

By 1929, most of the members of the Jewish upper class had moved out to the Old York Road suburbs, centering in Elkins Park. At the same time, but especially during the 1930's, many of the old Jewish families had moved into apartments in the Rittenhouse Square neighborhood (see Table 1). Also at this time, the more successful members of the East European community moved out of South Philadelphia and settled in West Philadelphia and Germantown. In 1940, the elite Russian-Jewish neighborhood in the city was Wynnefield-Overbrook, a West Philadelphia residential area just inside the city boundary from the upper-class Main Line. Albert

M. Greenfield moved into this area and in 1940 occupied a large mansion previously owned by Clarence Geist, one of Philadelphia's more colorful new-rich utility tycoons.

The residential distribution of the small Jewish elite in 1940 indicated that the caste-like divisions between the Russian and German communities were slowly dissolving (Table 4). It must be borne in mind, however, that these were older men with grown children, and therefore were less likely to reflect the neighborhood patterning of younger families.

Table 4—Residential Distribution of the Philadelphia Jewish Elite in 1940

Residence	Upper Class	Rest of The Elite
Rittenhouse Square	6	1
Old York Road	3	2
North Philadelphia	2[a]	2
Germantown	2	2
West Philadelphia	1[b]	3[c]
South Philadelphia	0	2
Swarthmore	0	1
	14	13

a. S. S. Fleisher lived in the same house, on once-fashionable Green Street, as his family did in 1890.

b. Samuel Fels lived at 39th and Walnut in a beautiful house which has since become the home of the Institute of Local and State Government of the University of Pennsylvania. The Institute was endowed and founded by Mr. Fels. The house was in the center of the "Drexel Colony" in the 1880's and 1890's, during which period the great A. J. Drexel lived there.

c. These three men lived in the Wynnefield-Overbrook section, the elite East European neighborhood in West Philadelphia.

POSTSCRIPT: THE SITUATION SINCE WORLD WAR II. Although our analysis of the Jewish upper class and elite ends as of 1940, a brief description of developments since the war will be helpful. Social change, of course, has been rather rapid. Any generalizations as to the direction of change must necessarily be highly tentative—more time is needed to gain historical perspective.

Perhaps the most important point that can be made about the postwar period is the following: although the caste-like line between the Gentile and Jewish community in Philadelphia at the elite level still remains as far as exclusive associations such as country clubs are concerned, residential exclusion appears to be definitely on the decline and possibly nonexistent. There are many examples of the new neighborhood pattern. In the first place, the Wynnefield-Overbrook area—during the 1920's and 1930's definitely an elite Jewish neighborhood in West Philadelphia just inside the city limits from the Main Line—is now heavily populated with affluent middle-class Jews of East European origin. At the same time, the wealthy elite Jewish families who formerly might have lived in this area now reside along the Main Line and in some of the other Gentile upper-class suburbs. For example, Mr. Greenfield, who is one of the leaders in the city's rejuvenated Democratic party (Philadelphia was the only large city to go overwhelmingly for Stevenson in 1952) and is retired from business and is the head of the Planning Commission, now lives in Chestnut Hill. This is the city's most exclusive suburban neighborhood. Furthermore, a member of the Wolf family is one of his neighbors. It is also significant to note that in the late 1940's the Radnor Valley Country Club, an elite club made up primarily of wealthy East European Jews, became the first Jewish club along the Main Line. Many affluent Jewish families, including the city's major motion picture theatre-owner, live nearby. It is significant that no members of the German-Jewish upper class have moved to the Main Line, although several prominent families have settled in Whitemarsh Valley, a fashionable rural area beyond Chestnut Hill.

On the whole, the old upper-class German-Jewish families have remained along the Old York Road. Since the War, a combined Sunday School for children from both the Rodeph Sholom and Keneseth Israel congregations has been established in the Old York Road area. At the time of writing, several religious buildings are being planned for the neighborhood. In February, 1955, for example, the Breyer Estate (a Philadelphia ice cream fortune) was purchased by the Beth Sholom congregation, which is now erecting a synagogue designed by Frank Lloyd Wright.

In this connection, it is interesting to note that a member of the old upper-class Binswanger family has once more gained an elite functional class position in Philadelphia. Frank G. Binswanger, one of the leading real estate agents in Philadelphia and a township commissioner in the Elkins Park area, handled the sale of the Breyer property.[52] It would appear that the upper-class Jewish community which was formed in the decades preceding the Civil War has been surprisingly vigorous; descendants of the old German families still live in Philadelphia and many of them have retained their position in the Jewish community.

JOSEPH GREENBLUM

AND MARSHALL SKLARE

THE ATTITUDE OF THE SMALL-TOWN JEW
TOWARD HIS COMMUNITY

ALTHOUGH Jewish population sta-
tistics are not very precise, it is generally agreed that 40-45% of American Jews live in or around New York City. It is further estimated that
70-80% reside in ten metropolitan areas. That the Jewish population is
concentrated in a handful of cities is a familiar fact, so familiar that the
implications of this concentration are seldom discussed. Certainly the rate
of intermarriage, the practice of the Jewish religion, the character of Jewish-Gentile relations, the nature of American Jewish culture, as well as
many other matters are influenced by the ecology of American Jewry. This
ecology involves the fact that in some of our largest cities the Jewish population—while in the minority—is still a significant group. Not only is the
population considerable, but it is concentrated in neighborhoods where
Jews constitute a majority. In such cities Jewish communal facilities are
both extensive and visible, and the general urban culture is modified by
the presence of a Jewish sub-culture.

This paper deals with that relatively small minority of Jews who live
in communities where the total population is less than 100,000, and the
number of Jews is under 1,000. These are cities where the Jewish group
does *not* constitute a numerically important segment of the population.
Furthermore, there are no "Jewish" neighborhoods and if Jewish communal
facilities are present, they are not very elaborate. There is little opportunity
for a minority-group culture to exist side-by-side with the general culture.
Our analysis is thus concerned with Jews who live in cities where the population, the institutions, and the culture is overwhelmingly non-Jewish.

The most obvious problem for study as regards the small-town Jew is
the question of intermarriage, and, by inference, the problem of assimilation.[1] Equally significant, however, is the more general problem of the
adjustment of the small-town Jew to his community. How does he view his
situation as a member of a minority group? How satisfied is he with the
community in which he lives?

The question of satisfaction with community, while of great importance,
constitutes a difficult research problem. To disentangle the Jewish com-

Published for the first time in this volume.

The authors are grateful to the B'nai B'rith Vocational Service Bureau, and to its
director, Mr. Robert Shosteck, for permission to utilize data from the Bureau's study of
Jews living in small and middle-size cities.

ponent, to estimate the extent to which Jewishness contributes to satisfaction-dissatisfaction with small-town life, is exceedingly complicated. Nevertheless, the nature of our data allows us to make a tentative approach to the problem.

§ A. *The Sample*

Our data originate from a nationwide survey of small-town Jews conducted in 1953 by the B'nai B'rith Vocational Service Bureau.[2] The Bureau wished to study the situation of the small-town Jew in order to gather information which would be of help to individuals interested in deciding whether or not to move from a large city to a smaller community.

The Bureau defined as its universe all communities in the United States and Canada—suburbs excluded—with fewer than 1,000 Jews and less than 100,000 total population.[3] The cost of obtaining a true sample of the estimated 175,000 Jews living in such communities in the United States was prohibitive, and thus a sample was selected from the membership roster of B'nai B'rith. Factors of size of Jewish and total community and of regional distribution were taken into account in developing the sample.

Inasmuch as the survey was limited to B'nai Brith members, all respondents are male Jews who are members of at least one Jewish organization. Some 6,300 questionnaires were mailed, and replies were received from 1,864 persons residing in 168 American towns. In order to check the representativeness of the sample, interviews were held with over 200 non-respondents—also B'nai B'rith members residing in small towns. In comparing the two groups, it was found that of those who responded by mail a greater proportion were younger, native-born, professional, and earning a lower income.

B'nai B'rith claims that about 70% of the adult male Jewish population residing in small towns hold membership in the organization. Observation suggests that this figure is approximately correct at least for several regions of the nation. Actually, in many smaller places affiliation with B'nai B'rith is *the* mark of Jewish identification.

In order to evaluate the differences between B'nai B'rith members and those outside the organization, interviews were held with 213 members and 213 non-members living in small towns. It was found that while 35% of the non-member group had been in the community 1-5 years, only 16% of the member group were in this category. In contrast to the non-members, the majority of individuals in the B'nai B'rith group had lived in the community over 10 years. As might be expected under these conditions, the income of the members was higher than that of the non-members. As a consequence, the sample is over-weighted in favor of the older and the more prosperous small-town Jew.

Is the non-member also more detached from the Jewish group? While there is no direct evidence on this point, it may be inferred that B'nai B'rith members are more closely identified with the Jewish group than are non-members. The findings of the study, then, can be generalized only to a limited extent. However, since the present analysis is largely devoted to comparisons between sub-groups, the problem of sample bias is not of crucial importance.

§ B. The Data

In keeping with our research problem, our primary interest in the B'nai B'rith study is in the data which bear upon attitude toward community. While most of the items in the questionnaire were designed to elicit demographic information, there are a number of attitudinal queries which yield information in the area of our concern. The first is a series of items in which respondents were asked to rate their community as either "good," "fair," or "poor" in respect to certain general as well as Jewish communal facilities and opportunities. The results are presented in Table 1.

Table 1—Small-Town Jews: Ratings of Their Facilities and Opportunities (N = 1,864)

	Good	Fair	Poor	Don't Know and No Answer
Opportunities To Satisfy Intellectual and Artistic Interests	23%	44%	27%	6%
Quality of Public Schools	57	31	6	6
Health Services and Facilities	63	30	4	3
Quality of Jewish Education	29	42	24	5
Opportunity To Marry within Faith	24	33	40	3
Chances of Feeling Comfortable as a Jew	68	28	2	2
Chances of Having Satisfactory Social Life	57	31	9	3
Chances of Jew To Obtain a Position of Prestige in Community	61	28	8	3
Chances of a Young Jewish Person To Achieve Economic Aspirations	45	34	6	15

We find that there are wide disparities between one area and another. Thus the item which receives the most favorable rating is: "Chances of feeling comfortable as a Jew." The response to this item would suggest that anti-Semitism is not a serious problem to the small-town Jew, or at least that whatever the extent of anti-Semitism it has not given him the feeling of being an alien in the community. In this connection we note that the great majority of respondents feel that Jews have either a "good" or "fair" chance of achieving a position of prestige in the community-at-large. Respondents also tended to rate their cities rather favorably in respect to economic opportunity: only 6% felt that a young Jewish person would not have much of a chance to achieve economic aspirations in the town where he resided. In respect to community facilities, the picture is mixed. While the majority rate school and health facilities as either "good" or "fair," almost 3 out of 10 rate cultural facilities as "poor." It is, however, the *Jewish* facilities which receive the lowest ratings. Thus, 57% rate the quality of their public schools as "good" but only 29% give a similar rating in the field of Jewish education. Similarly, only 24% rate their community as "good" in respect to opportunities to marry within the Jewish group.[4]

While these items are all suggestive in focussing upon the reactions of Jews to life in a small town, they leave much to be desired. Thus, it is difficult to know how respondents feel about the importance or salience of the various facilities and opportunities. It cannot be assumed that a respondent who rates the cultural facilities as "poor" necessarily has strong feelings of deprivation on this score. Furthermore, it is difficult to ascertain the effectiveness of the rated limitations of town facilities and opportunities. A favorable economic situation may make it possible for someone to take advantage of opportunities which are available in a not too distant metropolis. Again, a "poor" rating may not necessarily lead to feelings of deprivation.

The item which is most useful for our purposes—and the one which forms the basis for the major portion of our analysis—appeared in the questionnaire preceding the statements contained in Table 1. This item, which expressed more directly the respondent's feeling about his over-all adaptation to his community, read: "If you were a young Jewish person just starting your career, would you remain here or move elsewhere?"[5] A total of 53% elected to stay, 28% said that they would move, 16% were undecided, and 3% did not respond. Our interest is in the 28% who said that they would move. We conceived of this response as an indicator of general dissatisfaction, or what we have termed "community disaffection." We shall now proceed to analyze who the disaffected are and where they live, as well as to suggest situational factors which may account for their attitudes.

§ C. The Relationship between Community Disaffection and the Background Variables

We find that there is some relationship between disaffection with community and certain of the background variables, but most such relationships are not very striking (see Table 2). Older people tended to be slightly more dissatisfied with their communities than younger residents, but there is no consistent increase with age. There is a tendency for lower-income people to be more disaffected: almost one-third of those with incomes below 5,000 are disaffected compared to one-fourth of those in the highest income category (over $7,500).

Table 2 indicates that the natives (those born or reared in the community) and the in-migrants hold almost the same opinion: the in-migrants are only slightly more dissatisfied than the natives. The finding is particularly striking in view of the probability that most in-migrants originated from metropolitan areas.* In-migrants who settled because they were offered a job are slightly more dissatisfied than those who came to open, or take over, a business.

Increased length of residence reveals a cyclical tendency as regards disaffection with community. Newcomers (up to 5 years of residence) are almost as satisfied as old-timers (more than 20 years of residence). The proportion of disaffection rises among the 6-10 year group and declines among those who stay longer. The "length of residence" category, of course, includes only those who have remained in the community for a given number of years—presumably out-migrants leave behind those who have made some type of adaptation to small-town living. This line of reasoning does not explain the increase in disaffection between the first and the second half of the initial decade of residence in the community. Disaffection in this case might be the result of increased contact with the small community —contact which does not lead immediately to the drastic step of migrating from the community but which nevertheless helps to dramatize the limitations of the community.

Table 2—Community Disaffection According to Selected Variables

	%	N
Age		
21-35	24	(453)
36-50	30	(843)
Over 50	28	(547)
Socio-Economic Status		
Income:		
Over $7500	25	(702)
$5000-7500	30	(446)
Under $5000	32	(490)
Education:		
College	26	(959)
No College	30	(826)
Residential Status		
Reason for Coming to Community:		
Born or Reared in Town	24	(533)
In-migrated	30	(1326)
Business Opportunity	28	(703)
Offered Job	34	(338)
Relatives & Friends in Town	29	(243)
Other	29	(42)
Length of Residence:		
Up to 5 years	28	(340)
6-10	36	(184)
11-20	31	(397)
Over 20 years	25	(922)
Time-Generation in America:		
Immigrants	31	(475)
American-born: In-migrated	29	(844)
American-born: Born or Reared in Town	23	(487)

* A comparison with those from large cities could not be made because of lack of data on such origins.

The old-timer category (more than 20 years residence) requires further differentiation. It includes almost all who were born or reared in the community as well as in-migrants who have lived for more than twenty years in the town as adults. Our data indicate that there is virtually no difference in disaffection between these groups, showing that increased length of residence by in-migrants results in a level of satisfaction with community equal to, or approaching, that of natives.

These data also demonstrate that a cyclical tendency with increased length of residence is found among both immigrants and American-born in-migrants. When age is controlled, this tendency is accentuated in the 36-50 age group. Differences between length of residence categories tend to disappear among the younger residents.

What are the differences in community disaffection between immigrants to the United States and American-born Jews? Table 2 indicates that immigrants are more dissatisfied than those who were born or reared in the community, but they do not differ from American-born Jews who are in-migrants. The *children* of in-migrants who have been reared in the community are somewhat less dissatisfied than their parents. The significance of this finding is that the increasing rarity of the first-generation Jew as a migrant to the small community will not mean that in-migrants will no longer experience serious problems of adjustment. The problem of the Jew who is observant, who wears a beard and who has little facility in the English language may strike us as especially poignant. However, the third-generation Jew raised in New York, Boston, Philadelphia, or Chicago and convinced of the desirability of living in a metropolis, may have serious problems when the large corporation where he is employed in a professional or sales capacity decides to decentralize or expand by opening a branch plant or outlet in a small or medium-size community. While a transfer does not involve his learning a new language, or modifying his religious habits, it *may* mean a rather sharp break with his past.

§ D. Dynamics of Community Size

We find that dissatisfaction decreases as city size increases; 4 out of every 10 of those who reside in cities of under 10,000 would move if they were starting their careers (see Table 3). The residents of the largest communities (50,000-100,000) are relatively satisfied. Does this relationship have anything to do with the component of Jewishness, or is it simply a function of the fact that the smallest towns do not offer certain general advantages which are to be found in larger communities?

When our sample is categorized by size of *Jewish* population, the differences as regards community dissatisfaction are not as large or as consistent as in the case of city size. True, respondents in the largest Jewish communities (500-999) are least dissatisfied, but respondents in intermediate-size Jewish communities (100-499) are slightly more disaffected than those in

Table 3—Community Disaffection According to Community Structure Variables

	%	N
City Size		
Under 10,000	40	(173)
10,000-24,999	34	(763)
25,000-49,999	23	(529)
50,000-100,000	15	(358)
Jewish Population		
Under 100	29	(253)
100-499	33	(1002)
500-999	20	(571)
Proximity to Large Jewish Center		
Under 50 miles	31	(1041)
50-100 miles	26	(341)
Over 100 miles	24	(444)
Jewish Community Organization Index		
More	26	(1202)
Intermediate	31	(551)
Less	40	(65)

the smallest communities. However, more strikingly, we find the relationship between disaffection and size of Jewish community depends somewhat upon the size of the city in which the Jewish community is located (see Table 4). In the medium-size cities (city size was dichotomized into medium-size [25,000-100,000] and small-size [under 25,000]), dissatisfaction increases consistently with smallness of Jewish population. However, in the small-size cities, the effect of Jewish population size tends to be reversed; those in *larger* Jewish communities (over 100) are slightly more disposed to move. The expectation that the most dissatisfied individuals are to be found in the *smallest* Jewish communities in the small-size cities is not borne out in the data. Those in communities of more than 100 Jews in smaller cities are most disaffected, while—as expected—those in the largest Jewish communities in the larger cities are least dissatisfied.

Table 4 also indicates one additional fact of significance. It is that the effect of city size on disaffection varies with the size of the Jewish population—smallness of Jewish population diminishes and finally erases the difference in disposition to move which we found between the *smaller* and the *larger* city. Smaller city size produces greater disaffection *only* when the Jewish community numbers over 100 individuals; city size has no effect when the Jewish population is minimal.

Table 4—Community Disaffection According to Size of City and Jewish Community

	CITY SIZE			
	SMALL (Under 25,000)		MEDIUM (25,000-100,000)	
Jewish Population	%	N	%	N
Under 100	29	(194)	29	(58)
100-499	37	(626)	25	(375)
500-999	35	(116)	16	(454)

The above data suggest that greater size of minority community may become dysfunctional for personal satisfaction with community. Sheer size of Jewish population may have different consequences in small and medium-size cities. A minority community (assuming that other factors such as minority occupational structure are constant) may be more visible in small cities and towns than in larger cities. Furthermore, we may hypothesize that within smaller cities and towns increases in minority population may also heighten visibility. Under these circumstances, Jews might perceive such marked visibility as a threat to their social relations with Gentiles; in this sense, visibility may have dysfunctional consequences for the situation of the minority group. Thus the "comfortably small" Jewish community may be seen as a highly desirable community of residence. The point made by John P. Dean in his paper reprinted in this volume—that there is greater social acceptance of Jews in communities with a comparatively small proportion of Jewish to total population—may be seen as supporting this line of reasoning. However, in larger cities, it may be further hypothesized, increases in minority population may have minimal effect on its visibility. As there is less social acceptance by Gentiles—another finding by Dean in the paper cited above—larger minority communities may be welcomed because of greater possibilities for intra-group social contact. This contact can provide an alternative to the lack of social life with Gentiles, thus lessening social dissatisfaction and, in turn, disaffection with community.[6]

As noted previously, the questionnaire contained one item which served as a crude indicator of satisfaction with social life and relationships in the community (see Table 1 and footnote 4). If social satisfaction does indeed determine the differential variation of disaffection in the separate contexts of the small and the medium-size city (as found in Table 4), we would expect the level of social satisfaction to vary as did disaffection. However, we found that it did not: within each size city, the amount of social satisfaction is almost the same regardless of the size of the Jewish population. Therefore social satisfaction does not explain the pattern of differences in Table 4.

It does, however, *specify* the conditions for the emergence of these differences. Thus, Table 5 indicates that the tendencies observed in Table 4 occur only if the Jew is dissatisfied with social life in the community. Under this condition, increasing minority population is related to greater

Table 5—Community Disaffection According to City Size, Jewish Community Size, and Satisfaction with Social Life

| | SMALL CITY | | | | MEDIUM-SIZE CITY | | | |
| | Satisfied | | Dissatisfied | | Satisfied | | Dissatisfied | |
Jewish Population	%	N	%	N	%	N	%	N
Under 100	20	(99)	39	(92)	14	(35)	57	(21)
100-499	22	(337)	56	(271)	15	(213)	39	(150)
500-999	20	(64)	54	(50)	8	(300)	32	(141)

disaffection in smaller cities, and to less disaffection in medium-size cities. However, if Jews are satisfied with social life, the size of the Jewish population makes little or no difference in the level of disaffection, whether in the small or medium-size city. Thus social dissatisfaction is a necessary condition for the pattern of differences in Table 4.[7]

The finding in Table 5 can be read in another way. Irrespective of city or minority size, dissatisfaction with social life is consistently related to disaffection with community—there are always sizable differences in disaffection between the socially satisfied and dissatisfied. But in the small city this relationship (as measured by the increasing size of the differences) becomes stronger in the larger and more highly visible minority community. And in the medium-size city it seems to be weaker in the larger minority community, where the socially dysfunctional consequences of high visibility may be counterbalanced by greater possibilities for intragroup social contact.

§ E. Dynamics of Community Location and Structure

PROXIMITY TO LARGE JEWISH CENTER. Since we have found that size of Jewish community exercises some influence on attitudes, we must investigate the question of the distance from a large Jewish center (defined in the study as a community with over 1,000 Jews, i.e., with Jewish populations greater than any included in the sample). Presumably, greatest dissatisfaction should occur in communities which are more isolated from a large Jewish center. The figures in Table 3, however, suggest a trend in the opposite direction—those who reside near a large Jewish center are more disaffected than those who are isolated. When size of Jewish community is held constant, we find this relationship persists whatever the size of the minority community; it is especially marked among the smallest and largest Jewish communities (see Table 6). It cannot be claimed that the relationship between proximity to a larger Jewish center and community disaffection can be explained by the possibility that respondents in nearby communities tend to live in smaller Jewish communities than those in more isolated ones.[8] The unexpected finding that the most isolated are less dissatisfied than the most proximate will be further explored in a later section of this paper.

JEWISH COMMUNITY ORGANIZATION. We may next ask the question: "Is degree of minority community organization associated with attitude to

Table 6—Commmunity Disaffection According to Jewish Community Size and Proximity to Large Jewish Center

Proximity to Large Jewish Center	JEWISH POPULATION					
	Under 100		100-499		500-999	
	%	N	%	N	%	N
Near (under 50 mi.)	40	(90)	36	(532)	23	(419)
Isolated (50 & more mi.)	23	(163)	29	(470)	11	(152)

community of residence?" Our data contained three indicators of community organization: (a) extent of religious leadership (from a full-time rabbi to no rabbi), (b) frequency of religious services (from a weekly service to no services), and (c) extent of Jewish schooling facilities (from a weekday afternoon Hebrew School to no school). Since the three items were assumed to be highly correlated with the extent and amount of other Jewish community facilities, a single index of Jewish Community Organization was constructed from them.[9] The index was found to be associated with over-all attitude to community. Of those in communities with the greatest organization, a considerably smaller proportion is disaffected than in communities with the least organization (see Table 3).[10]

Perhaps the influence of minority community organization is conditioned by the factor of Jewish population size. The data indicate that smallness of Jewish population is associated with less minority community organization; we have already found some tendency for smallness of minority population to be associated with disaffection from community. Table 7,

Table 7—Community Disaffection According to Jewish Community Size and Organization

Index of Jewish	JEWISH POPULATION					
	Under 100		100-499		500-999	
Community Organization	%	N	%	N	%	N
More	25	(88)	31	(639)	20	(475)
Intermediate	29	(124)	35	(328)	17	(99)
Less	42	(36)	38	(29)	—	(0)

where size of Jewish population is controlled, specifies that the relation between minority organization and disaffection is true primarily in the smallest Jewish communities. As the minority population increases, variation in the extent of minority organization and facilities has less relation to disaffection: in communities of 100-499 the relationship is attenuated, while in the largest of our communities the difference disappears. Thus, extent of minority organization has little or no effect in the larger of our communities, though it makes for a wide difference in disaffection in the very small minority communities—in such communities the lack of formal minority organization predisposes the individual to disaffection. While in the very small Jewish community more elaborate minority facilities appear to minimize dissatisfaction, larger minority size, on the other hand, decreases disaffection independently of minority organization. With organization constant, increases in minority population (above 500) would appear to serve the same function as that of greater organization in the smaller minority community: greater group support to the individual minority member makes for less disaffection with his community.

DYNAMICS OF PROXIMITY AND MINORITY ORGANIZATION. We have shown that the relationship between proximity to a larger Jewish center and disaffection with community cannot be explained simply by size of Jewish community, and that the relationship is even more marked when minority

size is controlled. What accounts for this? Is it due to the possibility that
those who reside in communities nearer to a larger Jewish center have less
minority community organization and facilities than those more isolated?
Our data indicate the contrary: 74% of nearby respondents, compared to
55% of the more isolated, live in communities with the greater degree of
organization.

We suggest the following explanation: the residents of the nearby and
of the more isolated communities use *different* frames of reference in
evaluating their minority facilities and opportunities. These differential
frames of reference, we believe, help in determining satisfaction or disaffection with one's community as a place of residence. A person located
in a community *nearer* to a large Jewish center may compare his own
minority community facilities with the superior facilities of the nearby
population center. The more isolated resident lacks such a reference point.
Instead, he compares his community with neighboring cities much like his
own. The individual living near the large Jewish community finds his own
town wanting; the person living in an isolated community is less likely to
make an invidious comparison. Thus, community disaffection may stem
from feelings of "relative deprivation" which are engendered by comparisons with different "reference communities."[11]

Actually, we have no direct data on this point. Respondents were not
asked about their orientations and attitudes to neighboring Jewish communities; our explanation is an inference from the findings, and is suggested
as a hypothesis for further testing in the remainder of this paper, as well
as in future research. The proximity-isolation variable might be viewed
as a structural factor giving rise to differential reference group comparisons which in turn affect over-all attitude to community of residence. These
differential comparisons may mediate the relationship between the proximity-isolation variable and satisfaction with community.

At this point it may be of value to explore the consistency of the relationship between proximity and disaffection. Does it hold equally true
among communities with greater minority organization and facilities as
well as among communities with less or no organization? Table 8 compares
disaffection in near and isolated communities of different degrees of minority organization. We find that the relationship between proximity and
disaffection is true primarily among communities lacking minority organization. Here dissatisfaction in the near communities is relatively twice that
of the isolated (51% vs. 25%). The same tendency—somewhat modified—is
found among communities with intermediate organization. However, there
is virtually no difference between respondents in near and isolated communities with greater facilities and organization.

In the light of these relationships our statement about the effect of
"reference communities" requires some refinement. Invidious comparisons,
if any, with larger Jewish population centers by residents of neighboring
communities does not increase disaffection if one's community has a sub-

stantial complement of minority facilities. However, such comparisons maximize disaffection within minority communities which are located near a large Jewish center and which lack even minimal Jewish community organization. Apparently the discrepancy in minority facilities is most visible in these latter communities.

Table 8—Community Disaffection According to Jewish Community Organization and Proximity to Large Jewish Center

Proximity to Large Jewish Center	JEWISH COMMUNITY ORGANIZATION INDEX					
	Less		Intermediate		More	
	%	N	%	N	%	N
Near	51	(37)	36	(228)	28	(769)
Isolated	25	(28)	27	(323)	24	(433)

The process which we have suggested also helps explain a complementary finding in Table 8. It will be noted that extent of minority organization does not affect the rate of disaffection in *isolated* communities: there is hardly any difference between respondents in communities with less, and those with more, minority facilities. However, in the communities near a large Jewish center, a greater measure of minority facilities decreases dissatisfaction with the community.[12] Thus, lack of formal minority organization in communities near a large Jewish population center increases community disaffection since that center serves as a reference for the devaluation of one's own community. Attaining a degree of formal organization closer to, or identical with, that of the "reference community" tends to make for greater satisfaction with one's own community. The lack of even minimal facilities sharpens the discrepancy and makes for greater disaffection. However, in isolated towns such reference communities are lacking; standards of comparison are not geared to large Jewish community standards and degree of formal organization does not affect the individual's over-all attitude toward the community.

Do the relationships observed in Table 8 depend upon the size of the Jewish population? More specifically, we have already found that the relationship between the proximity-isolation variable and attitude to community was strengthened when size of minority community was controlled (see Table 6). Does this occur equally in communities with greater and lesser minority organization when minority size is held constant, thus suggesting further modification of our "reference community" hypothesis?

In Table 9 Jewish population size is controlled in order to test the consistency of the relationship found in Table 8. Because of the lack of cases with little community organization in cities of 500-999 Jewish population, our findings are restricted to the smaller and intermediate-size centers. The data contained in Table 9 indicate that the basic pattern of relationships in Table 8 tends to be confirmed whatever the minority population size—there are larger differences between near and isolated communities lacking minimal organization than between those with a greater degree of organization. As expected, among the more organized communities of under 100 Jews the more proximate have a higher percentage of disaffection than the isolated. However, the difference is considerably smaller than the corresponding difference among the less organized communities. Furthermore, for any given minority size, among communities near a large minority center those which lack minority organization yield higher frequencies of disaffection than those with more facilities, while in the isolated communities this difference, if any, is attenuated. Thus, the finding in Table 8 that greater minority facilities tend to reduce disaffection in the nearer communities but have little or no effect in the isolated communities, is found to hold true whatever the size of the minority population.

Table 9—Community Disaffection According to Jewish Community Organization and Proximity to Large Jewish Center: Jewish Community Size Held Constant

			JEWISH COMMUNITY ORGANIZATION INDEX			
		Less		Intermediate		More
Jewish Population Size & Proximity to Large Jewish Center	%	N	%	N	%	N
Under 100						
Near	58	(19)	34	(38)	35	(31)
Isolated	24	(17)	27	(86)	19	(57)
100-499						
Near	44	(18)	43	(141)	33	(369)
Isolated	27	(11)	30	(187)	29	(270)
500-999						
Near	—	(0)	20	(49)	22	(369)
Isolated	—	(0)	14	(50)	13	(106)

In spite of this, minority size appears to exert an effect on the relationship between proximity and disaffection. The differences in disaffection between respondents in near and isolated communities are considerably greater in the smallest rather than the larger (100-499) minority communities, and this is true for both "less" and "more" organized communities. (Those in the "intermediate" level of minority organization are not affected in this way.) Thus, although for a given size minority community lack of Jewish facilities among those near larger Jewish centers strengthens the feelings of deprivation engendered by reference community comparisons, there is also some evidence that differences in these feelings between those near and distant from a large Jewish center are accentuated in the smallest minority communities whatever the extent of minority facilities.

THE DEVALUATION OF JEWISH FACILITIES AS A PSYCHOLOGICAL VARIABLE. In order to explain our findings of the combined effects on community disaffection of proximity to larger minority center and extent of minority organization, we have inferred a psychological process of differential reference community comparisons and consequent feelings of relative deprivation in respect to the individual's evaluation of his minority community facilities. We have implied a devaluation of Jewish facilities as one expression of the minority member's feeling of such deprivation and have inferred that such devaluation contributes to disaffection with the community *qua* community. Thus, we have suggested that feelings of deprivation are greater among those located near rather than distant from large Jewish centers, although living in communities equally lacking minority organization. One would expect that devaluation of Jewish facilities would be greater among those similarly located and lacking in minority organization.

We may test this hypothesis by referring to the responses to the questions on the quality of Jewish education and the opportunity to marry within the group. An index, "Jewish Facilities Evaluation," was constructed from these items. Respondents were divided into three categories of high, intermediate, and low. This index was found to be highly associated with the "Jewish Community Organization" index. We found that three times as many in communities lacking minority organization devaluated minority facilities (i.e., were classified at the "low" extreme) as in communities with greatest organization (80% in the "less," 27% in the "more" organized). But there was also an over-all tendency for the *isolated* respondents to devaluate their Jewish facilities somewhat more frequently than those located near a large Jewish center (44% vs. 32%).

Table 10—*Devaluating Jewish Facilities According to Jewish Community Organization and Proximity to Large Jewish Center*

Proximity to Large Jewish Center	JEWISH COMMUNITY ORGANIZATION INDEX					
	Less		Intermediate		More	
	%	N	%	N	%	N
Near	84	(37)	56	(228)	23	(769)
Isolated	75	(28)	53	(323)	36	(433)

The test of our hypotheses is found in Table 10. When extent of Jewish community organization is held constant, the relationship between *isolation* and devaluation of Jewish facilities holds only in communities with the greatest degree of minority organization. With less organization this relationship tends to be gradually reversed. Among communities lacking organization there is a greater tendency to devaluation by those located near a large minority center. Although the number of cases is small and the differences not overly large, greater significance can be attached to the reversal of the differences.

Two different processes are suggested by this reversal. In the more highly organized communities there is a "realistic" appraisal of intra-group facilities and opportunities. And despite the same degree of minority organization, more isolated respondents visualize less intra-faith marriage opportunities and devaluate the quality of Jewish schooling in contrast to the near respondents with greater access to larger Jewish centers. However, when available minority facilities are scarce, the "realistic" attitude is counterbalanced by the process of reference community comparisons. Members of nearer communities experience the greatest strains in evaluating the adequacy of their minority facilities and opportunities.

Another finding related to the reference community process is contained in Table 10. Although differences in devaluation between "less" and "more" organized communities are great (whether they are near or isolated), the difference in the near communities is considerably wider. This can be expressed in the ratio of the "less" over the "more." In near communities it is almost four times, in isolated communities it is about two times. This suggests that the evaluation of one's minority facilities tends to be more extreme in communities with access to large Jewish centers. If minority facilities are scarce, nearby respondents are harsher in their devaluations than isolated respondents. Better facilities in near communities, on the other hand, result in a more moderate degree of devaluation than in isolated communities indicating perhaps the individual's pride in the intra-group facilities of his community.

Table 10 thus demonstrates that the psychological process of devaluation of one's minority facilities, like community disaffection, is heightened by a peculiar combination of the two community structure factors of proximity to large minority center and scarcity of minority organization. In addition, we have suggested above that this dissatisfaction with intra-group facilities and opportunities is channeled into the more generalized attitude of community disaffection. Some evidence in support of this relationship is given by the finding of a strong association between devaluation and disaffection: relatively three times as many of those who are "low" as are "high" on the index of Jewish Facilities Evaluation are disaffected with the community (41% of the "low," 30% of the "intermediate," 14% of the "high"). Available data also indicate that this association remains equally strong when proximity and minority organization are simultaneously controlled. Thus, concern with and evaluation of intra-group facilities and opportunities does affect adaptation to community.

Our discussion of the dynamics of location and organization of minority community may be stated in schematic form. The evidence points to the conclusion that the process of devaluation of minority facilities (and the reference community process implicit in it) may be a variable intervening between the minority structure factor (i.e., proximity and minority community organization) and general community disaffection. Thus:

PROXIMITY & MINIMAL MINORITY ORGANIZATION ⟶
DEVALUATION OF MINORITY FACILITIES ⟶
COMMUNITY DISAFFECTION

To arrive at this conclusion, we first demonstrated:

PROXIMITY & MINIMAL MINORITY ORGANIZATION ⟶
COMMUNITY DISAFFECTION

We then respecified this initial relationship in terms of intervening psychological processes, and demonstrated the following two relationships:

1. PROXIMITY & MINIMAL MINORITY ORGANIZATION ⟶
DEVALUATION

2. DEVALUATION ⟶ COMMUNITY DISAFFECTION

Further verification of the intervening role of the devaluation variable was not possible because of methodological limitations in the data.[13]

In this paper we have attempted:

1. to demonstrate the value of more intensive analysis of an already existing body of data, within the limitations presented by this data;
2. to extract knowledge about dynamic structural and psychological processes from variables ordinarily utilized as demographic indicators;
3. to delineate those factors emanating from *within* the Jewish community, whether these be "external" structural facts about Jewish communities or more internal processes about the behavior of Jews, and to evaluate their effects on some over-all measure of adaptation of the Jew to his minority existence—in the context of American small-town life.

JOHN P. DEAN

JEWISH PARTICIPATION IN THE LIFE
OF MIDDLE-SIZED AMERICAN COMMUNITIES

ALTHOUGH the history and background of American Jewry has been studied by noted scholars for some time, little research has been done on the status of Jews in the middle-sized communities across the land.[1] This paper will direct itself largely to two questions: (1) In American middle-sized communities, to what extent does the Jewish community participate in the life of the community at large? (2) What are the factors limiting that participation, both from the majority group and the minority group point of view?

These questions raise a problem in the definition of community, and the determination of the extent to which the Jewish minority in American cities can be considered a community. We may say that a community exists insofar as the following criteria are met: (a) it is localized in a geographic area; (b) there is continuity in the provision of life-sustaining activities; (c) there is a shared culture (folkways, mores, institutions); (d) it has an independent organizational and leadership structure. By definition, we have a minority group when the majority group (i.e., the dominant group controlling the major sources of wealth and power) reacts to an outgroup as having inferior status, and manifests this reaction by some kind of differential treatment. This minority group forms a minority community when it evolves a group life within, but independent of, the majority community, and thus to a greater or lesser degree itself meets the above criteria of community.

In most American cities, the Jewish minority is not localized in one section of the city. Originally, patterns of Jewish settlement resembled those of other foreign-extraction settlements in being localized in an area where relatives and familiar institutions could shelter the immigrants from the alien ways of a strange land. When the protective environment was no longer so necessary, Jews, like other ethnic groups, took up residence in such other sections of the community as their means could afford. Although at one time adherence to the religious requirement of walking to the synagogue helped to localize Jewish residences near the synagogue, this is no longer the case.

This paper appeared in *Jewish Social Studies*, Vol. VII, No. 3, under the title "Patterns of Socialization and Association between Jews and Non-Jews." It is used here by permission of the publisher. (Copyright, 1955, by the Conference on Jewish Social Studies.) By permission of the author and publisher, the article is printed here in a condensed and edited version.

Furthermore, the Jewish group is not distinct from the larger American community in the organization and provision of life-sustaining activities, such as the production and distribution of food, shelter, clothing, and the other necessities of life. It is true, however, that Jews participate in these activities in a pattern that is somewhat distinctive.

On the other hand, the Jewish group certainly meets the criterion of having a shared culture and common heritage. In Elmira, New York, for example, nine-tenths of the persons identified as Jews belong to either or both of the two religious congregations. Nearly nine-tenths of Elmira's Jews understand Yiddish, and two-thirds of them are able to speak it. Naturally there are wide variations in customs and beliefs, and it some-times seems that in a given community the only thing the Jews have in common is being considered Jewish. And at the peripheries of the com-munity, there may even be disagreement as to who is considered Jewish. But even if the shared culture may be blurred at the peripheries, we can surely agree that there is a core group that shares an awareness of minority group status, a feeling of interdependence with other group members within the community, and a sense of psychological unity.

Finally, we can clearly distinguish Jewish organizations and a Jewish leadership structure. About half of the organizations to which Jews in El-mira belong were classified as ethnic or religious organizations. In almost any Jewish community of reasonable size, informed citizens will largely agree on who the key ethnic leaders are. There is a strong tradition of "helping one's own" that tends to organize Jewish welfare activities some-what independently of the community at large. Thus, for middle-sized cities in America, it makes sense to speak of a Jewish community if we bear in mind that we are thinking primarily of a group that has a shared culture and a distinctive organizational and leadership structure.

It should be pointed out that particularly in the smaller cities, the Jews are a highly insignificant proportion of the population (see Table 1). In the majority of cities under 50,000, Jews form less than 1% of the popula-tion. But even in cities of 100,000-500,000, the Jewish population generally constitutes somewhere between 1-5 per cent of the population as a whole. It is within this context that we raise the following questions: (1) To what

Table 1—In the Smaller Cities under Study Jews Are Usually Just a Tiny Fraction of the Population

	POPULATION OF CITY					
	10,000-25,000	25,000-50,000	50,000-100,000	100,000-200,000	200,000-500,000	500,000 or more
Total Cities:	(42)	(51)	(48)	(48)	(32)	(18)
Percent of population that is Jewish:						
Less than 1%	65%	63%	42%	21%	6%	—
1%-2%	19	25	27	27	25	6%
2%-5%	9	6	23	29	50	25
over 5%	7	6	8	23	19	69
	100%	100%	100%	100%	100%	100%

extent do members of the Jewish minority participate largely within the Jewish community?, (2) To what extent do they participate in the life of the community at large? We will consider participation in *economic* life, in *political* life, in *community* services, and in the *social* life of the middle-sized American community. Since the main limitations to participation operate in the area of social relationships, only brief consideration will be given to the first three areas.

§ *Participation in Economic Life*

Comparative community studies of middle-sized American cities indicate that there are relatively few areas of economic life from which Jews are excluded. In those communities in which there is a convergence of local economic power in the hands of a Protestant Yankee old guard, there is limited participation not only by Jews but also by Catholics. In part this is because economic advancement by these groups has been recent, and established economic power tends to perpetuate itself. Thus, Jewish participation is most noticably absent in important locally owned industries, in local law firms that advocate for them, and in local centers of banking and finance. In the communities that the Cornell field staff visited, it was also rare for Jews to be found on the management level of major local industries, or on the boards of leading banks. Jews were seldom found on the executive levels of absentee-owned industry or in transportation, communication, or other utilities. Also, in these middle-sized American communities, there is a relative absence of Jews in wage-earning occupations, and therefore only a few in the inner circles of labor organization on the local level. Participation by Jews is most conspicuous in commercial enterprises—both wholesaling and retailing—and in the professions. These tend to be self-employed occupations, and therefore not subject to discrimination by employers. Discrimination in the professions occurs mainly at the training and licensing levels, and these are extra-community functions. There is no way to tell, of course, how much the concentration in merchandising is due to occupational inbreeding and how much is due to discrimination. Because of the concentration in merchandising, there is a conspicuous presence of Jewish-sounding names on the marquees of main street stores. This tends to give the Jewish group a spurious "visibility" that may feed the stereotype about Jews being "sharp operators in business." Although neither Jews nor Negroes constituted more than 3 per cent of Elmira's population, when asked to estimate the size of these two minority groups Elmira white Gentiles guessed a mean figure of 9 per cent for the Negroes and 27 per cent for the Jews.

Because of the relative prosperity of the professions and commercial enterprises in recent years, this occupational concentration of Jews has not handicapped the Jewish community economically. Jewish communities in small or middle-sized American cities tend to be middle class and upper class; in almost all instances Jewish families are better off economically than a cross-section of families in the community at large. Insofar as this economic prosperity is converted into business transactions evident to the community at large or into conspicuous manifestations of wealth such as fashionable homes, automobiles, clothing and accessories, it may also feed the stereotype of the Jews "knowing how to get their hands on the money."

§ *Participation in Political Life*

The participation of Jews in politics or in public office would appear to be relatively limited in comparison with individuals of Irish, Italian, or similar ethnic extraction. In the forty-eight communities of 50,000-100,000 population, only seven (15 per cent) had as many as two Jews in elected offices, and two-thirds of the communities had none. This picture varies tremendously with size of community, and with the proportion of the community that is Jewish. The larger the community and the higher the proportion of Jews, the more likely the Jews are to hold public office. Jewish participation is somewhat greater in *appointed* offices, there being more such participation at all levels of city size. Here, too, participation increases with city size and proportion of Jews. The most common type of participation is the appointment of lawyers to positions such as assistant district attorney, civil service commissioner, or housing commissioner.

We can hypothesize several reasons for this generally limited participation in public life: (1) Politics does not seem to be a part of the occupational tradition of Jewish families; (2) Jews may fear that identification with partisan causes conflicts with their professional standing or their business interests; (3) Political jobs may not appear especially rewarding to Jews; (4) Jews undoubtedly suffer in some instances from anti-Semitism. This last-named factor probably operates not so much at the level of the electorate as it does in the party councils that select the candidates or determine political appointments. Where Jews represent a substantial proportion of the community at large, representation in politics becomes essential and the limitation of participation by anti-Semitism is outweighed by practical political considerations.

§ *Participation in Community Service*

Although difficult to check systematically, it is our impression from interiews with Jewish leaders in a number of American communities that there has been a growing participation by Jewish leaders in general civic causes and community service activities. This must be attributed in part to the rising economic position of the Jew and the recognition of this fact by the policy-making bodies of civic organizations.

In a majority of communities at all city-size levels, Jews participate on the boards of Community Chests. This is true in 98 per cent of the com-

Table 2—*Jews Participate on the Boards of Non-Sectarian Family Casework Agencies at All Levels of City Size*

	POPULATION OF CITY				
	10,000-25,000	25,000-50,000	50,000-100,000	100,000-200,000	200,000 or more
Total Cities:	(22)	(42)	(43)	(47)	(48)
"Are there any Jewish members that belong to the board of the non-sectarian family casework agency?"					
YES	82%	64%	86%	89%	92%
NO	18	36	14	11	8
	100%	100%	100%	100%	100%

munities where the Jews represent between 1 per cent and 2 per cent of the population, and in 78 per cent of the communities where the Jews are less than 1 per cent of the total population. Similarly, there is marked Jewish participation on the boards of nonsectarian casework agencies. Even in communities where Jews constitute less than 1 per cent of the total population, over two-thirds of the nonsectarian family casework agencies have Jews on their boards (see Tables 2 and 3). This participation is important, since such agencies stem from the "Lady Bountiful" tradition in which socially elite women extend help to families in trouble. In most communities, these boards still have representatives from the social elite; board membership is frequently looked upon as a mark of high social status.

§ *Restrictions on Jewish Organizational Participation*

Jews are most seriously limited from assuming leadership roles in the community at large where these roles entail membership in groups governed by the norm of social exclusiveness. Sometimes economic power in a community is exercised by a group of old families among whom the traditions of social superiority still prevail. In such cities, Jews cannot hold strategic positions in the power structure. The canon of social exclusiveness prevails most noticeably, of course, in so-called "high society." It is here that restrictive practices against Jews are most prevalent even though Jews

Table 3—*Jews Participate on the Boards of Non-Sectarian Family Casework Agencies Even in Cities Where They Are a Small Proportion of the Population*

	PROPORTION OF JEWS IN POPULATION			
	Under 1%	1%-2%	2%-5%	5% or more
Total Cities:	(64)	(47)	(53)	(33)
"Are there any Jewish members that belong to the board of the non-sectarian family casework agency?"				
YES	70%	89%	93%	88%
NO	30	11	7	12
	100%	100%	100%	100%

may be leaders in the economic, political, and social-service life of the community.

In order to test the assumption that leadership participation *by* Jews and social acceptance *of* Jews are not synonymous, we contructed a score of social acceptability. This is based on whether Jews in a given community are accepted (1) in the Junior League, (2) in the most exclusive country club, and (3) in the most exclusive residential areas. We also constructed a score of Jewish leadership participation based on whether there were Jewish members (1) on the board of the Community Chest, (2) on the board of the nonsectarian casework agency, and (3) in elective and appointive public office. In Table 4 it is shown that communities which score *low* on social acceptability of Jews score *high* on Jewish participation in community affairs. Furthermore, both indices vary sharply with city size

Table 4—The Communities That Score Low on Social Acceptability of Jews, Score High on Jewish Participation in Community Affairs

| | SCORE ON ACCEPTABILITY OF JEWS | | | |
	Low	Medium Low	Medium High	High
Total Cities:	(83)	(93)	(52)	(20)
Score on Jewish participation in community affairs:				
High	33%	22%	19%	5%
Medium High	30	31	37	40
Medium Low	17	30	27	25
Low	20	17	17	30
	100%	100%	100%	100%

and with proportion of Jewish population. The larger the city and the larger the proportion of Jews in the community, the more Jews are excluded from socially elite organizations and residential areas.

Table 5—The Larger Communities Score Lower on the Acceptability of Jews

| | POPULATION OF CITY | | | | |
	10,000-25,000	25,000-50,000	50,000-100,000	100,000-200,000	200,000 or more
Total Cities:	(46)	(54)	(49)	(49)	(50)
Score on Acceptibility of Jews:					
Low	20%	20%	31%	45%	52%
Medium Low	48	24	47	37	34
Medium High	17	43	20	10	12
High	15	13	2	8	2
	100%	100%	100%	100%	100%

With respect to social exclusiveness, we note something resembling Myrdal's rank order of discrimination. Organizations can be ranked on the probability that in any given community they will exclude Jews. At the top would probably be the Junior League and any other special "society"

Table 6—The Higher the Proportion of Jews to the Total Population of the Community, the Lower the Community Scores on the Acceptability of Jews

| | PROPORTION OF JEWS IN POPULATION | | | |
	Under 1%	1%-2%	2%-5%	5% or more
Total Cities:	(91)	(56)	(54)	(38)
Score on Acceptibility of Jews:				
Low	22%	23%	45%	58%
Medium Low	33	41	46	29
Medium High	30	29	9	8
High	15	7	—	5
	100%	100%	100%	100%

organizations. Next would come the leading city club, then the country club. Perhaps next would be the service clubs, although the vast majority of chapters of Rotary and Kiwanis Clubs do not exclude Jews. Here discrimination most frequently takes the form of limiting participation to a few select members.

Even though specific instances that bring these restrictive practices to the attention of the Jewish community are rare in most communities, Jews appear to be fully aware of them. Furthermore, they appear to leave their mark on the self-esteem of Jewish leaders. Jewish leaders frequently refuse to accept social invitations to the city club or to the country club. One said:

> I sometimes feel like a prostitute. They'll call on me to lead their Community Chest campaign or help on the Red Cross. But when it comes to the country club, I'm not good enough for them.

When meetings of the local branch of the American Association of University Women, or of the County Medical Society, are scheduled at the country club, Jewish members are often in conflict and disagree among themselves about attending. Most Jewish leaders seem to take a sort of philosophical point of view: "I don't want to belong if they don't want me to belong, and I'm not going to go where I'm not wanted."

§ *Participation by Jews in Mixed Organizations*

How much does the average member of the Jewish community participate in mixed organizations, i.e., ones in which there are both Jewish and Gentile members? It is worth noticing first that Jews are more likely than members of the community at large to belong to organizations. Thus one-half of our sample of Elmira Jewry belonged to four or more organizations, in comparison with only 9 per cent of the members of the community at large. Furthermore, only one in fifteen Jews belonged to no organizations, compared with about half of the Gentile community. Slightly over half of the Jews belonged to mixed organizations, but nine-tenths belonged to a Jewish organization. Also, one-quarter of the Jewish community belonged to four or more Jewish organizations. This tendency was especially marked among the women, 44 per cent of whom belonged to four or more Jewish organizations. There appears to be little relationship between the number of ethnic organizations belonged to and whether or not a person belonged to a mixed organization. Whether one participates in a mixed organization *is* related, however, to several other factors. Males are twice as likely to belong to mixed organizations as females; persons in the 35-44 age group are more likely to belong than younger adult or older age groups; Jews born in the United States are twice as likely to belong to a mixed organization as Jews born abroad. And, as one might suspect, Orthodox Jews are less likely to participate in mixed organizations than Reform Jews.

Organizational contacts between Jews and Gentiles are likely to occur in fraternal and lodge organizations. They are equally likely to occur in patriotic organizations, and in organizations of a civic, charitable or business nature. For the most part these organizational contacts seem pleasant and comfortable, but they are occasionally disturbed by feelings of social distance or anti-Semitism. Among majority group members in Elmira who belonged to an organization that had Jewish members, only 9 per cent said they ever found themselves feeling different toward the Jews than toward other members. But among the Jews belonging to mixed organizations, 39 per cent said that they felt the Gentiles felt different toward them. Also about one in twelve said that they knew of instances in which Jewish members had been treated differently from other members in their organizations.

If Elmira can be considered at all typical, then we would conclude that members of the Jewish community participate fairly widely in the organizational life of the community at large, with the exception of the social elite organizations and the political, labor and church organizations. Their participation ranges through most of the other kinds of organizations the community provides.

§ *Social Cliques*

Participant observers in the Elmira community and in most other communities visited by the field staff reported virtually no social mixing between Jews and Gentiles. These observers were undoubtedly referring to the composition of social cliques. Out of the Elmira sample of 150 Jews, some eighty-nine individuals say they "go around with a certain bunch of close friends who visit back and forth in each other's homes." A total of fifty-eight of this group of "social participators" have all-Jewish social cliques. For another ten the Gentile participant in the social clique is the spouse of a Jew. An additional five have one-sex cliques and do not represent social mixing in the usual sense. Eight more have a Gentile couple in their social clique but it is predominantly Jewish, thus representing more the Gentile participation in the Jewish community than Jewish participation in the general community. This leaves a total of only eight persons —or less than 10 per cent of the group—who participate in predominantly Gentile cliques. These individuals are undoubtedly somewhat peripheral to the Jewish community. As Table 7 indicates, the number of Jewish organizations one belongs to is closely related to the composition of his social group. Those at the core of the Jewish community are people who are active in Jewish organizations and who have all-Jewish cliques.

Table 7—*The More Active One Is in the Jewish Community in Elmira, the More Likely He Is To Have an All-Jewish Social Circle*

| | NUMBER OF JEWISH ORGANIZATIONS RESPONDENT BELONGS TO | | | |
	None or one	Two	Three	Four or more
Total number of Jews who report they have a social circle:	(16)	(20)	(22)	(29)
Have an all-Jewish social circle	19%	55%	77%	90%
Have a social circle with a Gentile in it	81	45	23	10
	100%	100%	100%	100%

What are the reasons for this type of clique behavior? Is it non-acceptance by the Gentiles of Elmira? Unquestionably, it is this in part. About 15 per cent of the Gentiles who participate in an all-Gentile clique indicate they would have some negative feeling about Jews becoming a part of the group. But two-thirds of them say it would make no difference. In part the perpetuation of exclusively Jewish social cliquing is a function of the way the social machinery works. Women make most of the social arrangements. They are more likely to belong to all-Jewish organizations and less likely to belong to mixed organizations. Of the group of Elmira Jewish men who were interviewed on their community participation, only 12 per cent belonged only to Jewish organizations, whereas this was true of 48 per cent of their wives. For the most part the women do not work. They are much less likely than men to have contact opportunities with Gentiles. Consequently, the odds of their forming the kinds of extra-Jewish community relationships that might eventuate in social invitations are small. For some reason, perhaps because of close ingroup feelings, or feelings of social distance between Gentiles and Jews, those contacts that do occur seldom develop to the point where they break through this pattern of exclusive Jewish social life.

The tendency toward all-Jewish and all-Gentile social cliques is perhaps best viewed developmentally. Somehow, in the social process, people are sifted and sorted into cliques and social circles that are more or less well-knit, more or less homogeneous. We can hypothesize that particularly from the 'teen years on there is a strain toward homogeneity. The process, as we see it operating, is described in the paragraphs below.

Grade school and high school provide haphazard heterogeneous contacts under conditions favorable to friendship formation. Jews and Gentiles have opportunities to get to know each other—opportunities that their regular neighborhood, organization, and family contacts might fail to provide. Out of these recurring contact opportunities, friendships are formed that frequently carry over into social visiting and dating. But childhood and teen-age Jewish-Gentile relationships seldom weather the disruptive influences that sever them in the years following high school: going away to college, marrying someone from out of town and moving to another city, marrying a spouse whose own close friendships form the core of future social cliques, getting a job entailing new close friendships that replace former school ties.

After marriage, when new clique lines are formed, high school Jewish-Gentile relationships seldom are the basis for the married cliques. The joint social life of a married couple depends on who each of the spouses objects to and who each feels most "at home" with. If one spouse has acquaintanceship ties with an outgroup person that might develop into social visiting, the other spouse's prejudices, unfamiliarity with outgroup social habits, feelings of being ill-at-ease, or even outright objections will tend to throw invitation decisions toward ingroup couples with whom both spouses are comfortable. If at the time of marriage each spouse has an independent circle of friends, the couple will tend to become socially integrated into the circle least different in ethnic and prestige attributes from themselves. Furthermore, since Jewish boys probably have more leeway for heterogeneous social mixing and dating, their ties, more frequently than the girls' ties, would have to be the basis for postmarital Jewish-Gentile socializing. But women, for the most part, determine the social visiting since they more often handle the invitations and the arrangements.

Underlying many of these processes is, of course, the strong Jewish taboo on exogamy. Over half of Elmira's Jews said they would "find it distasteful to have a Gentile marry someone in (their) family." And the sentiment seems even stronger when it involves parents' reactions to their children's marital choices. As one Elmira father put it:

The basic worry of every parent is that their son will marry a *shikse* [non-Jewish girl]. Some mothers live in constant dread of it. When two mothers with marriageable sons get together you can be sure sooner or later they'll talk about it. They don't worry so much about their daughters. I guess they're more sure of them.

The continuous efforts of parents, not only during high school years but following high school, to avoid circumstances that might lead to intermarriage also promote homogeneous social visiting. Persons opposed to intermarriage are more likely to have an all-Jewish social clique (see Table 8). These factors are perhaps just as important as anti-Semitism in bringing about all-Jewish social circles.

Table 8—Jews in Elmira Opposed to Intermarriage Are More Likely To Have
an All-Jewish Social Clique

	FIND IT DISTASTEFUL TO HAVE SOMEONE IN THEIR FAMILY MARRY A GENTILE	
	Yes	No
Total cases:	(46)	(40)
Have an all-Jewish social clique	80%	50%
Have a mixed, Jewish-Gentile social clique	20	50
	100%	100%

§ *Other Jewish-Gentile Socializing*

From the homogeneous social cliques at the core of the Jewish community, one might get the mistaken impression that there is almost no socializing of any kind between Jews and Gentiles. When asked about their socializing with their closest Gentile contact, over half of our Elmira Jewish sample said that they had "visited back and forth in each others' homes fairly regularly." Another 22 per cent said they had "done something social together outside the home." Thus, about three-fourths of the Jewish community did some socializing with at least their closest Gentile contact.

Despite differences in contact opportunities, women had just as many of these more casual contacts with Gentiles as men. Socializing with one's closest Gentile contact occurred twice as much in the age group 35-44 as among persons over fifty-five. However, persons who were very active in the Jewish community (as judged by number of Jewish organizations belonged to) were just as likely to socialize with their closest Gentile contact as those who were less active or inactive. And there were no marked differences between the Orthodox and the Reform.

Which kinds of contacts between Jews and Gentiles are most likely to culminate in socializing? For Gentiles, organizational contacts were most likely to result in "doing something social together"; then came work contacts and then neighborhood contacts. For Jews, organizational and work contacts were both about twice as likely as neighborhood contacts to result in "doing something social together" (see Table 9).

However, in only about half of the situations where Jews have contacts with Gentiles at work or in organizations (even less in the neighborhood), do the relationships develop into active socializing. Therefore we must ask what the factors are that limit or promote warm social relationships between Jews and Gentiles.

For members of the majority group, the two major factors that determine whether Jewish-Gentile friendships develop are (1) anti-Semitism, and (2) opportunities for contact. The 274 persons in the Elmira cross section that did not mix socially with Jews were asked how they would *feel* about mixing socially with Jews. Fifty-four of them (or about 20 per cent) said they wouldn't like it. This does not, of course, tell us how many would actually let their feelings stand in the way of friendly interaction if the opportunity for interaction did occur.

We have rather impressive evidence from our high-school studies that shows the marked relationship between social visiting and the number of contact opportunities. This relationship holds both for students that express feelings of social distance toward Jews, and for those that do not. Among adults, too, persons prejudiced against Jews often have contact with them and frequently develop good friends that are Jewish—although not quite so frequently as the less prejudiced. Nevertheless, friendship formation does take place between prejudiced persons and persons from minorities they are prejudiced against. Our impression is that, given the opportunity, most persons will interact in a friendly way despite articu-lated attitudes of anti-Semitism. For example: A person who has stereo-typic misconceptions about Jews might join the Elks and find himself introduced through one of his brother Elks to a Jewish member. In order not to cause embarrassment or friction, his tendency will be to greet this Jewish person with the same gestures of friendliness as he would use to greet non-Jewish Elks. Most persons just do not have well-developed be-havior patterns for reacting anti-Semitically in common social situations. Thus they tend to react with the only social habits they have for handling social interaction (i.e., friendly gestures that promote pleasantness). It then frequently develops that the Jewish person they have met does not fit the stereotypic misconceptions they held about Jews. Do they yield their stereotypic misconceptions in the light of this new evidence? Not necessarily. More frequently, it would seem that they exempt from their prejudice the particular individual they have come to know. This "ex-emption mechanism" performs two functions for the anti-Semitic non-

Table 9—*Organizational and Work Contacts between Jews and Gentiles in Elmira Are More Likely To Eventuate in Socializing than Are Neighborhood Contacts*

	Place of Contact	% Having Done Something Social Together	(1949) Total Gentiles Having Contact with a Jew at Specified Places	(1951)
	Organizations	30%	(157)	30% (148)
Majority				
	Work	19%	(58)	16% (140)
Group				
	Neighborhood	8%	(153)	15% (126)
		% Having Done Something Social Together	Total Jews Having Contact with a Gentile at Specified Places	
	Organizations	48%	(79)	
Minority				
	Work	50%	(98)	
Group				
	Neighborhood	27%	(150)	

Jew: (a) It enables him to interact in a friendly way without friction when he meets a specific Jew, and (b) It enables him to maintain intact his prejudices against Jews in general. We are all familiar with the expression "Some of my best friends are Jews." This phrase obviously refers to the Jews which a prejudiced person has exempted. We just do not know how anti-Jewish prejudice affects the quality of a Jewish-Gentile relationship. We do know that the more prejudiced a person is and the closer the relationship is, the more psychological pressure there is for the person to exempt the Jewish contact from his prejudices. Respondents were asked whether they considered their closest Jewish contact typical of Jews or different in some respects. Those who were more prejudiced were somewhat more likely to give reasons that exempted their Jewish friend from the common stereotypic misconceptions about Jews.

It is our feeling, however, that the absence of contact opportunities is a much more serious limitation on friendship formation between Gentiles and Jews than is anti-Semitic prejudice. Contact opportunities are largely situational. In most neighborhoods, chance determines whether a non-Jew has a Jewish neighbor or not. It is true that restrictive practices cut down contact opportunities for the small segment of our population that lives in exclusive areas or belongs to exclusive organizations. But this is not true for the vast bulk of people. Contact opportunities vary tremendously with age, sex, socio-economic status and other such factors. But perhaps more important than any other single factor is the sheer numerical "scarcity" of Jews. With Jews representing such a small proportion of the total population of most communities (see Table 1), the mathematical probability of the average Gentile's having contact opportunities with Jews is exceedingly low. Most of our evidence indicates that where these opportunities are present, friendly interaction will generally take place.

Conversely, in most communities Jews have numerous opportunities for social contacts with Gentiles, and the social mixing of Jews with Gentiles appears to be clearly related to attitudes toward them. If we compare the Jews who have contact with Gentiles in their social cliques, in mixed organizations, or in other social settings, with those who do not, we find that the Jews that socialize more with Gentiles express more friendly feelings toward them (see Table 10). But in our Elmira cross section, one-quarter of the Jews did not develop their contacts with Gentiles to the point of socializing, either in the home or outside the home. For minority group members, then, what are the factors limiting contact?

Jews, due to their common background, locale, or origin, generally mix together and form, through *associational inbreeding*, common interests, similar cultural traits and mutual ties of acquaintance, friendship and affection. These common, like, and mutual bonds *perpetuate* the associational inbreeding and cut down contacts with Gentiles. Associational inbreeding is augmented by the avoidance techniques that form after rebuffs in contacts with the majority group, and lead to a *defensive insulation* that protects against further rebuff. Thus avoidance patterns tend to develop which promote evasion of situations in which the Jew might feel ill-at-ease.

THE CONCOMITANTS OF SOCIAL INSULATION. These protective reactions, working together with the close associational ties at the core of the Jewish community, bring about a social insulation that seems to produce certain characteristic reactions. One of these reactions is a tendency toward oversensitivity. For example, in one of the communities we studied, a Jewish woman was giving a birthday party for her son, many of whose playmates were Gentile. She did not invite those Gentile friends because she was afraid of being refused. So too, various members of the Jewish community will not accept invitations to social events at the country or city club because they are sensitive to their nonacceptability as *members* of these clubs. Of the group of seventy Jewish men interviewed in Elmira, nearly four-fifths agreed to the statement, "I find myself avoiding places like country clubs and other places where I feel Jews are not welcome." In this way sensitivity to rebuff leads to avoidance and the perpetuation of insulation. One woman in Elmira said:

> Oh, we see Gentiles all the time in organizations but not really socially. I'm sure we could if we wanted to. My daughter is different, though. Many of her friends are Gentile, and they are very fine girls, the highest type. I suppose we could be friends with their families—they are very nice people—because we live in the same neighborhood and our daughters are friends, but we've never really wanted to.

In league with certain personality characteristics, this sensitivity can lead to a perception of all Gentiles as *potentially* anti-Semitic. There is frequently the feeling that Gentiles will "treat you well enough until the chips are really down," at which point their true anti-Semitic feeling will crop out. Should such feelings on the part of Jews be reinforced by incidents (either experienced personally or communicated through family or friends), it is understandable that many Jews should seek to protect themselves from further rebuff.

Table 10—Jews in Elmira with More Social Contacts with Gentiles Are More Friendly to Them

	Has a Gentile in Social Clique	NO GENTILE IN SOCIAL CLIQUE			
		Belongs to Mixed Organization and Mixes Socially with a Gentile	Mixes Socially with a Gentile but Does Not Belong to a Mixed Organization	Belongs to Mixed Organization but Does Not Mix Socially with a Gentile	Belongs Neither to Mixed Organization nor Mixes Socially with a Gentile
Total cases:	(31)	(43)	(31)	(17)	(28)
"How friendly or unfriendly are your feelings toward Gentiles?"					
Per cent saying "Very friendly"	65%	63%	52%	41%	32%

In communities like Elmira, social insulation appears also to have the effect of intensifying social pressures *within* the Jewish community. This is true partly because the social pressures of a group of several hundred families concerned largely with the affairs of their own community operate much as they would in a small rural community. Although Elmira is a middle-sized community of over 50,000, social insulation makes the 400 Jewish families a primary community in which the detailed affairs of the community are prevailing topics of interest and conversation. News flies through the community with an almost magic speed. Public opinion is rapidly mobilized on community affairs. Membership in either the *Shul* or the Temple is almost mandatory. Strong pressures are brought to bear to belong to Jewish organizations. Strict sanctions operate to maximize financial contributions to Jewish causes. Because of these social pressures, the norms of achievement that are traditional in Jewish life are brought to bear on individual families in a way that appears to result in intensified status-striving. This intensified status-striving appears to be most characteristic of those social cliques that have most incorporated the upper-middle-class values of the community at large. Thus, the evidences of traditional Jewish life, especially those that are reminiscent of immigrant origins, are sloughed off in favor of attributes that are "typically American." These are the Jews that one participant observer aptly characterized as "frustrated Presbyterians."

Another result of the encompassing primary relationships within the Jewish community is the emotional impact of ideological conflicts. People one likes as friends and identifies with, may hold ideological positions about such things as Zionism or the assimilation of the Jews that are in direct conflict with one's own position. It is disturbing to be in conflict with close friends on deeply held values. Because of the strong need for interpersonal harmony in keeping the Jewish community functioning smoothly, these ideological differences tend to be repressed or internalized in favor of an apparent unanimity in the acceptance of common norms.

In a group the size of the Elmira Jewish community, there are relatively few people of similar age and status attributes. Thus, one's social circle tends to be dictated by similarities in age and status rather than by congenial personal qualities and common interests. In larger communities where there are many people of similar age and status, people can sift and sort themselves into congenial friendship groups that take account of personal qualities and interests as well as age and status.

Also, in a primary community of 400, affairs such as births, weddings, and burials, become community affairs, not merely family affairs. As community occasions, they must include people with such varying definitions of appropriate observance that there is no possibility of pleasing everybody. Uncertainty as to appropriate ritual and appropriate personal behavior tends to create anxiety.

Another effect of the insulation of Jewish community life is the occasional parallel development within the Jewish community of organizational forms or activities that emulate the majority group. If Jews are excluded from the country club, they will frequently form a Jewish country club. If Jews are not accepted in the Junior League, the Women's Council may adopt projects that are remarkably like Junior League projects. These organizations may fill some psychological need in providing a social exclusiveness that is unavailable to Jews in the community at large because of restrictive majority group practices.

The insulation of the Jewish community also results in situations in which there are virtual "ambassadors to the Goyim." For example, when the Jewish Community Center in one small town was about to apply for funds from the Community Chest, one Jewish board member on the Community Chest was cornered by other Jewish community leaders and impressed with the importance of his being a good spokesman for their group. The lone Jew who is on the board of a social agency or in an organization frequently sees his role as a representative of the Jewish group, and tailors his behavior so that it will not reflect badly on the Jewish community.

The presence of an insulated primary community that is the object of prejudice and discrimination leads to numerous incidents that illustrate Kurt Lewin's concept of the interdependence of fate. Partly because of ingroup ties that give Jews a feeling of psychological unity with other Jews and partly because many Jews perceive the majority group as having prejudiced misconceptions about the Jewish group, the attitude grows that unseemly behavior by one member of the Jewish community reflects badly on all members of the Jewish community. The social pressures of the primary community are particularly brought to bear on deviant behavior that is perceived as reinforcing stereotypic misconceptions. Incidents of overtipping, conspicuous consumption (particularly of the *nouveau riche* variety) and even certain business transactions are censured by members of the ingroup, who are afraid that the Jews will appear in a bad light in the eyes of the majority.

This brings us to the crux of the problem—the psychological position of the Jew in a community that is predominantly Gentile. For the self to be strong, one must see himself accepted in the eyes of the significant persons around him. The majority group person sees himself only through the eyes of the majority, while the Jewish person sees himself not only through the eyes of other Jewish persons but also through the eyes of the majority. Thus the psychological adjustment of Jewish persons is really a function of two self-images. To present this clearly, let us consider the problem in oversimplified, schematic form. What the Jewish community thinks of a given Jew is either important or unimportant to him. If it is unimportant to him, then his self-image is independent of what is thought of him by other Jews. If it is important to him then his self-image depends upon whether the Jewish community respects him or looks down on him. Likewise, his self-image depends on how important status in the Gentile group is to him and what he believes Gentiles think of him. As a result of his personal values, early life experiences, and the experiences he has in participating in Jewish community life and in the community at large, the Jewish person works out some kind of self-perception that represents a *more* comfortable or a *less* comfortable adjustment to his being a Jew in a Gentile community.

4

The Jewish Religion:
Aspects of Continuity and Change

INTRODUCTION

THE Jewish religion occupies a highly important place in the study of the sociology of the Jew. In addition to the significance of religion *per se,* many aspects of the subject of this volume touch upon religion at some point or other. Thus, religion is more than merely a facet of the area covered in this book—it is rather a central concern which merits detailed consideration.

It is helpful in any such consideration to stress the dynamics of Jewish religious experience in the United States. Thus, the assumption of new values and norms with a consequent departure from tradition needs thorough analysis. The question which first arises in this connection is: "Where do Jews stand in regard to Orthodoxy?" The article by Howard Polsky provides some information on this point. Polsky emphasizes the widespread disaffection from tradition and the fact that only a minority of the members of Orthodox synagogues carry out—in their personal lives—basic requirements of Jewish law. In order that his results be placed in proper perspective, it should be emphasized that Polsky studied a community located in the Midwest with a Jewish population of about 30,000. It is generally believed that the strength of Orthodoxy increases as one moves from the smaller-sized community to the larger-sized community, and that Orthodoxy is best-preserved in cities located in the Middle Atlantic and New England regions. Thus, no hasty conclusions should be drawn from this material. Rather, Polsky's article should be studied for its methodological contributions and the suggestive nature of the substantive findings.

The paper by Bernard C. Rosen represents an extension of the Polsky material, for it probes into the cross-pressures and conflicting values which work upon the individual to modify his pattern of religious belief and conduct. (Of course, the forces which serve to counter tendencies toward change, or to increase religious observance, are an equally important subject for research. Some of these forces are analyzed by Herbert Gans and other authors.) Rosen's paper has the advantage of inquiring into adolescent rather than adult attitudes; presumably at this stage of the life cycle cross-pressures and conflicting values have real impact. It is significant to note that both Rosen's and Polsky's respondents appear to emphasize adherence to ritualistic observance as *the* measure of religiosity.

The excerpt by W. Lloyd Warner and Leo Srole, reprinted from the well-known volume in the Yankee City series, serves to place the findings of the first two authors in the proper context. The Warner and Srole findings emphasize that whatever the deviations of Jews as individuals, such deviations are far from indicative of a desire to shed Jewish identification. Furthermore, whatever the individual's degree of secularization, the attitude prevails that the sacred order must be upheld. This feeling is greatly reinforced by the fact that the sacred order has very special symbolic value, for faith is identified with folk, and folk with faith. Thus, the end of Judaism is seen as the prelude to the end of the Jewish group.

This desire for Jewish survival—involving as it does the revival of flagging institutions—can only be met by a reorganization of such institutions. The subject of the Warner and Srole article is just such a reorganization. (Inasmuch as this particular reorganization took place in 1932, it cannot be ascribed to the psychological impact of the Hitler era. A number of students of Jewish problems have stressed such an impact as being largely responsible for the survivalistic temper which has been so characteristic of American Jewry in recent decades.)

Since the total population of the Jewish community of Yankee City numbers less than five hundred, changes were effected in a single congregation—all reforms had to be instituted without the founding of a new synagogue. We find several options in larger communities, such as the city studied by Polsky. Nontraditional congregations can be founded as Reform or Conservative synagogues, or they sometimes represent splinter groups which have left a traditional congregation, or they become nontraditional by stages which extend over a period of several decades. The special conditions present in Yankee City, serving as they do to telescope the changes, place in bold relief those innovations which have highest priority. An excerpt from Marshall Sklare's volume on Conservative Judaism serves to give a more detailed picture of these changes as they have occurred in many synagogues, to delineate the impelling forces behind the changes, and to point out some of the consequences which have ensued.

Up to this point the emphasis has been on attitudes and behavior patterns of adolescents and adults, and of practices in Orthodox and non-Orthodox synagogues. The study of continuities and changes in the Jewish religion may be seen from another vantage point—that of the most important religious functionary of the present era, the rabbi. The article by Jerome E. Carlin and Saul H. Mendlovitz, "The American Rabbi: A Religious Specialist Responds to Loss of Authority," not only adds much to the perspectives developed by the previous authors but it also contains valuable data in the special field of the sociology of professions. Perhaps the most striking aspect of the material is its scope. Since the authors interviewed many different types of rabbis, they actually describe the entire range of Jewish religious activity—Reform, Conservative, and Orthodox, as well as certain shadings within these categories. In this connection it is significant to note that Carlin and Mendlovitz include material on what they term the "Modern Orthodox Rabbi." Thus, they describe certain contemporary trends in Orthodoxy which are not suggested by Polsky and others. Such trends are in fact only apparent in the very large cities. Choosing to work in a metropolis, as Carlin and Mendlovitz did, has great advantages. With such a high proportion of American Jewry being concentrated in a half-dozen communities, researchers who work in smaller cities inevitably impose upon themselves certain limitations in the area of typicality. Problems of manageability and limited resources may, of course, dictate such a choice. There is no denying, however, that projects conducted in the largest centers have certain advantages—advantages which are clearly illustrated by the Carlin and Mendlovitz article.

Ira O. Glick's "The Hebrew Christians: A Marginal Religious Group" lies quite outside of the stream of other contributions in this volume. The Hebrew Christians are clearly Christians. However, Glick's material, though it deals at first glance with what appears to be a subject of peripheral interest, serves to stimulate thinking about a number of very crucial questions. The first is that of assimilation—especially the barriers and the facilitating factors to assimilation. The second, and perhaps the more significant question, is that of the articulation between religion and ethnicity, a matter which has been alluded to before in this Introduction. The Hebrew Christians represent a highly interesting type—a case of conversion without complete assimilation, and thus an instance where Jewish religion and Jewish ethnicity are not perfectly articulated. Furthermore, Glick's fascinating case study suggests some of the forces which play upon the the marginal Jew.

It should be recognized that a Jew who is on the way to leaving the Jewish group does not typically convert to Christianity. And it is perhaps true that even when a Jew takes on another faith, he typically does not do so via the Hebrew Christian movement. Thus, the material by Glick is highly useful in the discussion of what we might call theoretical problems in the sociology of American Jewry. In its strictly case-study aspects it describes a very special, even exotic, movement.

HOWARD W. POLSKY

A STUDY OF ORTHODOXY IN MILWAUKEE: SOCIAL CHARACTERISTICS, BELIEFS, AND OBSERVANCES

THIS article is part of a larger study of Jewish Orthodoxy in Milwaukee, Wisconsin.[1] The objective of the study was to analyze the interaction between the religious system of Orthodoxy and the pattern of the American social system. In the overall approach, the cultural ease method was utilized. The basic tenets of Jewish Orthodoxy were analyzed in terms of their significance for ordering the social system of the East-European *shtetl*. The transitional period in America (1880-1920) was depicted, during which the sacred norms and organizations were challenged as the Orthodox immigrants took over American values in the daily endeavor of American living. The focus of the analysis of the contemporary period centered upon changing religious values and a detailed description of the disintegration of the binding quality of traditional norms.

The Guttman scalogram, described in detail in the original version and briefly summarized in the following pages, was the chief research tool employed. Interviews were held with 905 male members of the eight Orthodox synagogues in Milwaukee. The total unduplicated membership of the synagogues numbered 1,197. As regards a number of demographic characteristics, the 24 per cent who did not respond closely resemble those who answered the questionnaire.

Although it is true that there are more people in the Jewish community who have an allegiance of some sort to Orthodoxy than there are members of Orthodox synagogues, it would have been very difficult to attempt to tap the group of non-members. The Orthodox population is defined in the present study as those individuals who have a commitment to Orthodoxy to the extent of formally belonging to one of the eight Orthodox synagogues. All of these synagogues solicit members, and those who attend regularly are likely to be enrolled on the membership roster. There are no doctrinal or behavioral tests for membership, and thus the most practical procedure was to count an individual as "Orthodox" who belonged to an Orthodox synagogue. Male members were questioned because, traditionally, Orthodoxy considers the male the head of the family. Formally, the male is the person who is responsible for the family leading an Orthodox way of life.

The technique employed to secure interview data has been little used in social science research, but is one that was found to be very effective. Each Orthodox family received a letter asking the respondent for his co-operation

Published for the first time in this volume.

in a research project, the object of which was to learn more about what was happening to Jewish people in America. The credentials of the research person in charge were mentioned. The communication also stated that several days after receiving the letter the male head of the family would be telephoned and that the interviewer who would conduct the interview over the telephone would not know the name of the party. The issue of anonymity was stressed in the letter, which was printed both in English and Yiddish. Every means of mass communication in the Jewish community was used to publicize the project. Those members whom rabbis and other officials thought could not be reached effectively on the telephone (primarily because of their advanced age) or people who had no phone, were interviewed at home. Interviewing took place between December, 1955 and February, 1956.

§ *Demographic Characteristics of the Orthodox Population*

Place of residence is often a good indicator of socio-economic status. We find that members of the Orthodox synagogues are concentrated in three areas in Milwaukee: 60 per cent are found in the Northwest area, 14 per cent in the Northeast, and 11 per cent in an immigrant area which we shall call the "Old Settlement." The Jewish population residing in the first two of these sections live in areas of high economic status, while the Old Settlement is located in a deteriorating section of town. The median rental averages for those sections of the areas in which the Jewish population is concentrated are as follows: Northwest: $85.00; Northeast: $104.00; Old Settlement: $49.00.[2] The disparity between the Old Settlement area and the other two areas of Jewish concentration is apparent, and we must conclude that Orthodox Jews have prospered along with the rest of Milwaukee Jewry and are located in middle and upper-middle class residential areas.

Of the eight Orthodox synagogues in Milwaukee, five are located on the Northwest side where 60 per cent of the membership is located; three are in the Old Settlement area where 11 per cent live; none is located on the Northeast side where 14 per cent of the Orthodox membership reside. There is, therefore, a decided imbalance in the location of Orthodox synagogues vis-à-vis their membership.

The occupational distribution of Orthodox Jewry supports our inference of the middle-class character of the Orthodox population (see Table 1). Some 60 per cent of the population are included in the catagories "proprietor," "salesman," and "professional." The other striking figure is the 20 per cent who are in the "retired" category. It is apparent that being a salesman, professional, or proprietor can interfere with the observance of traditional norms such as the prohibition against working on the Sabbath. A retired individual, on the other hand, is not forced by economic circumstance to violate Orthodox norms.

Table 1—Occupation of Orthodox Members*

Occupation	Per Cent
Proprietor	34.4
Salesman	13.2
Professional	12.6
Retired	20.9
Clerical	1.9
Manager, Official	4.2
Craftsman, Foreman	5.5
Laborer	4.1
Peddler	3.1
Other	.1
No information	.1
Total	100.0

* In all tables N = 905 unless otherwise indicated.

Less than 20 per cent of our Orthodox families have an income of less than $5,000 per year (see Table 2). Since we received enough "no information" replies to possibly distort the overall picture, the "no information" group was compared—background-wise—with the other income groups. It was found that the group most nearly resembles the middle-income grouping—those with incomes of $5,000-10,000.

Taking all these data together, there would appear to be little doubt of the middle-class character of the Orthodox membership. What has not been apparent thus far is that within this apparently homogeneous middle-class grouping there exists important cultural differences. For example, only 32 per cent of the total population were born in the United States. Furthermore, 37 per cent of the group have had no secular education, and 77 per cent have not attended college. On the other hand, 53 per cent have had eight or more years of Jewish education while only 4 per cent have had no Jewish education whatsoever.

There is little doubt too that Jewish Orthodoxy is an aging group which is not reproducing itself. Over 60 per cent of the membership is over 50 years of age; only 10% is under 40 (see Table 3).

Many of the differences noted above are split along age levels. Whereas over 90 per cent of those over 60 years of age were born in Europe, 82 per cent of those under 40 were born in the United States. Some 80 per cent of Orthodox Jews over 60 received 0-2 years of secular schooling and 97 per cent of the same group had no college whatsover. In contrast, 90 per cent of those under 40 years of age received 8 or more years of public school instruction, and 43 per cent received four or more years of college.

Table 2—Orthodox Members' Yearly Family Incomes

Income	Per Cent
Under $5,000	16.6
Between $5-10,000	38.6
Over $10,000	27.3
No information	17.5
Total	100.0

Table 3—Age of Orthodox Family Heads

Age	Per Cent
0-29	1.8
30-39	9.4
40-49	25.3
50-59	23.3
60-69	22.3
70-79	14.6
80 & over	2.7
No information	.6
Total	100.0

What is striking is the extent of Jewish education which all age groups have received. Thus, of those under 40 years of age, over 80 per cent received four or more years of Jewish education: this climbs to 83 per cent for those between 40-59 years of age and to 94 per cent for Orthodox Jews over 60. Although the younger elements within the present Orthodox movement have had considerably more secular schooling than the older people, they have had a fair amount of Jewish education as well. Perhaps this grounding in Jewish culture and religion has had something to do with this younger group maintaining membership in an Orthodox synagogue. However, our data do not permit us to make a statement of causality. In summary, the Orthodox group in Milwaukee is made up of largely middle-class elements with varying backgrounds who tend to be over 40 years of age and who make their living as self-employed businessmen, salesmen, or professionals. One-fifth are retired. One-third were born in the United States, and this in turn is reflected in varying degrees of public school and college education. All age groups, however, have had a considerable Jewish education.

§ *Affiliation and Attendance*

Some 91 per cent of the Orthodox membership belong to one Orthodox synagogue, while 8 per cent belong to two Orthodox synagogues and less than 1 per cent to three or four synagogues. More significant, however, is the fact that almost 15 per cent of the 905 Orthodox members retain dual membership in an Orthodox as well as a Conservative or Reform temple.[3]

Table 4—Attendance at Worship in Orthodox Synagogues

Attend	Per Cent
Daily (kaddish)	3.2
Daily (with or without kaddish)	7.0
Once a week	11.5
Once a month	4.1
Several times a year in addition to holidays	30.2
Mostly on important holidays	39.9
Other	3.9
No information	1.2
Total	100.0

What is the level of attendance at Orthodox synagogues? For the strictly Orthodox Jew, prayer is required thrice daily. Although one can pray at home, it is more meritorious to pray in the synagogue. The *kaddish* is a prayer said by one who has lost a member of his family; it is recited daily for 11 months from the day of death. Despite the existence of such obligations, attendance at prayer in the Orthodox synagogue is at a low level (see Table 4). We find that there is a three-way split within the Orthodox population. Some 70 per cent attend the synagogue only several times a year and on the important holidays; approximately 20 per cent attend at least once a week; only 10 per cent or 92 individuals, scattered in eight Orthodox synagogues, attend daily.

§ *The Orthodoxy Scalogram*

Our schedule contained fourteen items relating to attitudes and behavior vis-à-vis traditional Orthodox norms. A total of ten of the fourteen items were employed to test the degree of cluster. Each of the items was dichotomized into favorable or unfavorable responses, depending on whether they conformed to the Orthodox norm. The basic hypothesis of the scalogram is of course that if on any item the individual has responded favorably, he will respond favorably also to all the preceding items; if on any item the individual has responded unfavorably, he will respond unfavorably also to all items that follow. The ten items were ordered according to degree of favorable response (see Table 5). The *mitzvah*, or religious commandment, which was observed most widely was that of fasting on Yom Kippur, while the wearing of *tsitses* received the fewest positive responses.

It is significant to note that two items were not considered for the scalo-

Table 5—Number of Favorable Responses to Ten Items Measuring
Adherence to Norms of Orthodoxy*

Items	Per Cent Favorable
Do you fast on Yom Kippur?	81.6
Do you believe that God gave the Torah (Bible) to Moses on Mt. Sinai?	79.5
Do you buy your meat from kosher meat shops?	71.0
Are Sabbath candles lit Friday night in your home?	66.5
Do you keep separate meat and milk dishes in your home?	62.1
Do you eat meat in non-kosher restaurants? ("no" is "favorable")	33.7
Do you think it is all right for men and women to sit together in the synagogue or temple? ("no" is "favorable")	22.1
Do you always wear a hat when you eat?	16.8
Do you handle money on the Sabbath (Saturday)? ("no" is "favorable")	12.0
Do you wear *tsitses* (prayer fringes) every day?	7.5

* "No information" responses averaged less than one-half per cent. They were classified with the unfavorable responses.

gram because of the overwhelming majority who responded favorably. These items, dealing with circumcision and intermarriage, help to locate the value systems of practically the entire Orthodox membership (see Table 5A). The results of these two questions place the Orthodox popu-

Table 5A—Favorable Responses to Two Items Measuring Adherence to Norms of Orthodoxy

Items	Per Cent Favorable
Do you (would you) definitely prefer your child to marry a Jewish person?	96.8
Did you (would you) have your child circumcised according to Jewish law?	99.5

lation squarely behind the idea of Jewish survival. Thus, whatever the extent to which this group has abandoned the sacred norms, its behavior should not be interpreted as abandonment of Jewish identity. While the results of our questionnaire reveal that the nature and content of Jewishness (*Yiddishkeit*) has undergone far-reaching changes in the short span of one and two generations, the changes going on within Jewish life should not be uncritically regarded as assimilation.

Returning to the scalogram, five of the ten items were selected as exceptionally relevant to forming a scale with the least amount of error (the third, fifth, sixth, eighth, and ninth items in Table 5). The average probability beyond chance for all the items taken together to be "clustered" in scalable form is .90. Thus the six scale types run true to form in about nine out of every ten individuals in the Orthodox population sampled (see Table 6). We find that one out of every four Orthodox Jews has abandoned Orthodoxy to the extent of not buying from kosher butcher shops. Only 65 per cent maintain the most elementary procedure in a kosher home—keeping separate meat and milk dishes. Only 35 per cent refrain from eating meat in non-kosher resturants; only 18 per cent always wear

Table 6—The Number, Percentage and Explanation of Six Orthodox Scale Types

Scale Types	Number	Per Cent	Explanation
0	231	25.5	Responds favorably to no item
			Responds unfavorably: 3, 5, 6, 8, 9
1	93	10.3	Responds favorably: 3
			Responds unfavorably: 5, 6, 8, 9
2	268	29.6	Responds favorably: 3, 5
			Responds unfavorably: 6, 8, 9
3	147	16.2	Responds favorably: 3, 5, 6
			Responds unfavorably: 8, 9
4	57	6.3	Responds favorably: 3, 5, 6, 8
			Responds unfavorably: 9
5	109	12.0	Responds favorably: 3, 5, 6, 8, 9
			Responds unfavorably to no item
Total	905	100.0	

Items

3. Do you buy your meat from kosher meat shops?
5. Do you keep separate meat and milk dishes in your home?
6. Do you eat meat in non-kosher restaurants?
8. Do you always wear a hat when you eat?
9. Do you handle money on the Sabbath?

a hat when they eat; only 12 per cent follow a fundamental aspect of Sabbath observance.

§ *Relationships between the Orthodoxy Scalogram and Selected Orthodox Attitude and Behavior Items*

The Orthodoxy scalogram reveals some significant relationships with items that were not included in the scale (see Table 7). All of the items in Table 7 run in the expected direction. It is interesting to note that fully two-thirds of the respondents in scale types 0, 1, and 2 believe that most Orthodox synagogues in the United States will become Conservative and one-half to one-third of the respondents in the other three scale types also believe this to be true. One-third of even the most extreme conforming group, scale-type 5, have no objection to men and women sitting together in the synagogue. However, almost two-thirds of the people in the extreme deviant scale type 0 believe in the Sinaitic revelation. Fasting on Yom Kippur appears to remain a widely prevalent practice in all of the scale types, ranging from 57 per cent in the most deviant type to 98 per cent in the most conforming type.

Table 7—Relationship of Orthodox Scale Types to Selected Questionnaire Items

Item	PER CENT AFFIRMATIVE IN EACH SCALE TYPE					
	0	1	2	3	4	5
Are Sabbath candles lit Friday night in your home?	28.6	48.4	76.5	86.4	94.7	96.3
Do you believe that in time most Orthodox synagogues in the U. S. will become Conservative?	66.2	65.6	65.3	55.1	42.1	37.6
Do you think it is all right for men and women to sit together in the synagogue or temple?	97.8	89.2	96.5	75.5	61.4	33.9
Do you believe that God gave the Torah (Bible) to Moses on Mt. Sinai?	61.9	77.4	81.3	85.0	96.5	97.2
Do you fast on Yom Kippur?	57.1	64.5	93.3	91.2	96.5	98.2

As expected, many more in the deviant scale types have joined Conservative and Reform temples than in the conformist group. Also, attendance at Orthodox synagogues follows very closely the scale types in the expected direction: over 90 per cent of those in scale type 0 attend less than once a month while over two-thirds of those in scale type 5 attend the synagogue daily or once a week. The other types run proportionately between these two extremes in the expected direction and proportions.

Examining the relationship between demographic characteristics and scale types, we find the following:

1. With increased deviation from Orthodox norms (scale types 5-0), there is an increase in the number born in the United States; however, the scale types are evenly distributed among those born in Europe.

2. Conformity increases proportionately with age.

3. Deviancy is inversely proportional to the number of years of Jewish education; conformity is directly proportional with the number of years

of Jewish education. The opposite is true with public school and college —deviancy is associated with more public school and college education.

4. Increase of income is associated with deviancy.

5. Occupationally, the categories "proprietor," "salesman," and "professional" are associated with deviancy; being retired is associated with conformity.

Thus, deviancy is associated with being born in the United States, receiving a public school education, attending college, entering the ranks of business or a profession and gaining an income of over $5,000. Conversely, those who have retained traditional norms are mainly foreign-born, over sixty years of age, retired businessmen and workers who have had a considerable Jewish education but relatively little secular schooling. What is most revealing in the correlation of scale type and demographic factors is that the above generalizations apply with unusual regularity as one moves across the scale types from the extreme deviant to the extreme conformist. In summary, we note that although Jewish Orthodoxy is a monolithic sacred culture, those who have been imbued with its cultural norms gradually give them up in the daily business of making a living and imbibing the cultural values of the American society. The first to go are Sabbath observances; eating out sooner or later includes eating non-kosher food; then procedures within the home no longer follow the traditional commandments. The rituals retained by Orthodox members are those which require least interference with daily living but do serve as important identifying links with the Jewish people and the Jewish religion. These rituals include the annual fast day of repentance, Yom Kippur, and the circumcision rite. Abstract ethical beliefs are retained much longer than specific ritual commandments. Essentially, then, an increasingly secularized membership faces the crystallized dogma of rabbinical authority.

§   *Orthodoxy and Generation Differences*

The dramatic shift in observance of Orthodox norms by generation is summarized in Table 8.

Table 8—Normative Observance of Three Generations as Reported by Orthodox Members

Norms	Respondent's Father	Respondent	Respondent's Married Son
Sabbath observance	67%	12%	2%
Kashruth outside home	86	34	2
Kashruth inside home	94	62	19
Number of cases	905	905	559

Not only is there abandonment of rituals, but many of the married sons of Orthodox parents are leaving the Orthodox synagogue for Conservative and Reform temples. Although 80 per cent of all the married sons retain membership in the Orthodox synagogue, another one-third (37 per cent) are lost to the Conservative and Reform movements. Another one-third apparently do not affiliate with any religious institution (see Table 9).

Table 9—Married Sons' Synagogue Affiliations as Reported by Orthodox Members

Synagogue	Number Belonging	% Belonging
Orthodox	169	30.2
Conservative	110	19.7
Reform	95	17.0
Non-Affiliated*	185	33.1
Total	559	100.0

* Includes ''no information'' replies

§ *Retrospect and Prospect*

Our questionnaire has demonstrated the abandonment of specific rituals and the retention of certain religious beliefs. Thus the wearing of *tsitses*, an indispensable part of the Orthodox Jew's wardrobe, is rapidly becoming extinct. Only 68 of our respondents, or 7.5 per cent of the total, wear the garment. This is in sharp contrast to the 80 per cent who respond favorably to the query: "Do you believe that God gave the Torah (Bible) to Moses on Mt. Sinai?" (see Table 10).

Table 10—''Do You Believe that God Gave the Torah (Bible) to Moses on Mt. Sinai?''

Response	Per Cent
No	4.3
Yes	79.5
Don't know	14.8
Other	.2
No information	1.2
Total	100.0

We have noted that over 70 per cent of the Orthodox membership now attend the Orthodox synagogue only a few times a year, mostly on the few important holidays during the year. Furthermore, our respondents indicated a wavering position regarding one of the most critical issues in Orthodoxy at the present time—the problem of the seating arrangement in the synagogue during the worship services. The separation of the sexes has become the focus of Orthodox resistance to the Conservative movement. How long can this resistance endure when 77 per cent of all of our respondents do not object to men and women sitting together in the synagogue? But perhaps the most important point in this connection is the attitude toward the future. We find that a majority of the respondents believe that in time most Orthodox synagogues will become Conservative (see Table 11).

In the manifold individual adjustments of the Orthodox cultural heritage to the exigencies of contemporary American society there is revealed a remarkable regularity of religious behavior among Orthodox members.

Thus, individuals can be ordered into cumulative scale types ranging from extreme conformists to extreme deviants in terms of their observance of Orthodox rituals. Our respondents, the great majority of whom have had four or more years of Jewish education, have absorbed in various degrees the values in the American culture to the detriment of the retention of traditional norms. Because of the impact of American social, economic and cultural conditions, normative Orthodox consensus is insufficient to deter considerable numbers of Orthodox members from violating traditional norms. A very small band of the faithful (less than 8 per cent of the total) sustains traditional Orthodoxy in theory and in practice.

Table 11—"Do You Believe that in Time Most Orthodox Synagogues in the United States Will Become Conservative?"

Response	Per Cent
No	21.1
Yes	59.1
Don't know	19.3
No information	.4
Total	100.0

The future of Jewish Orthodoxy becomes even more problematic when the scale types are correlated with social, economic and cultural differences among the Orthodox members. Conformists, generally, are over sixty years of age, foreign-born, retired, with considerable Jewish training and very little general education, and reside near the Orthodox synagogues. Deviants, as defined by the Orthodoxy scalogram, are relatively younger, native-born, professional men and self-employed businessmen with some Jewish education, but considerably more general education. Many live on the Northeast Side where there are three Reform temples and not one Orthodox synagogue. As would be expected, the deviants are more liberal than the conformists in their attitudes toward changing traditional procedures in the synagogue. However, significant numbers among the conformists are also receptive toward such changes in hallowed institutional practices as men and women sitting together during worship. Thus the conformists appear to be influenced by the deviants regarding liberalization of synagogue procedures. Within the individual synagogues there is a rather even distribution of conformists and deviants, which indicates that the abandonment of Orthodox norms is a problem generic to all of the synagogues in Milwaukee.

Traditional forms in the Orthodox synagogue can be retained for many years after members have abandoned traditional norms in their personal lives. This is because the extreme conformists supported by the rabbis feel more strongly about maintaining the traditional norms than the deviants feel about changing procedures in the synagogue. However, when the abandonment of traditional norms has become so uniform and widespread among members of all kinds of socio-cultural backgrounds, the question can seriously be posed as to whether these religious changes in members' individual lives do affect the Orthodox synagogue itself. As already has been noted, one-third of the married sons of Orthodox members are not affiliated with any synagogue or temple; another one-third have joined Conservative and Reform temples; only one-third became members of Orthodox synagogues.

The objective assessment of the changing religious trends among the Orthodox Jews of Milwaukee, the "traditionalists" in the Jewish community, is an indication of the widespread secularization of religious observances that is taking place among Jews in America. Acceptance, rather than resistance to cultural change, is becoming the norm. Jewish Orthodoxy, having at its source an age-old tradition, has balanced to some extent the secularizing tendencies of the American social system. However, if Milwaukee is any kind of indication of what is happening to Orthodox Jews in similar-sized communities, it appears that American Jewish life will continue its unique development without a significant Orthodox movement in its midst. This will result in an acceleration of the process of secularization of Jewish religious traditions and raise new problems and challenges for the survival of Judaism in America.

BERNARD C. ROSEN

MINORITY GROUP IN TRANSITION:
A STUDY OF ADOLESCENT
RELIGIOUS CONVICTION AND CONDUCT

RELIGION is a relatively neglected area in American social research. While there have been several comprehensive studies of small deviant sects, as yet social scientists have made few empirical inquiries of the membership of large religious groups, especially in terms of their levels of religious conviction and conduct.[1] This paper is an attempt to fill in a small part of the lacunae that exist in our knowledge of one of these groups—the Jews. More specifically, it examines certain salient characteristics of the religious attitudes and behavior of one age stratum of American Jewry, a stratum whose present religious position is only roughly understood—the high-school-age adolescent. For the most part, our knowledge of Jewish adolescent religiosity has been based upon data that are highly impressionistic or are almost two decades old. The more recent studies in this area are concerned largely with college students, an older and more select population than the generality of Jewish adolescents.[2]

Adolescents are appropriate objects for a study of religious attitudes and behavior, for it is often in adolescence that the individual first questions the traditional religious tenets taught him as a child. When the adolescents are Jews, they are of additional interest, in part because of the particular role of religion in Jewish life, and in part because of the adjustments in religious orientation Jews have made in adapting themselves to the majority culture of American society. We propose in this paper to examine certain tendencies in Jewish adolescents' religious conviction and conduct which reflect their conceptualization of and reaction to certain traditional religious beliefs and practices, and which illustrate their adaptation of religious traditionalism to American majority group culture. More specifically, the aspects of the adolescent's religious conviction and conduct with which we will concern ourselves are as follows:

1. the tendency to stress ritual components in their definition of religiosity and its relationship to the religious self-image;
2. the tendency toward scientific rationalism and its impact upon traditional practices;

Published for the first time in this volume.

The writer is grateful to the Anti-Defamation League of B'nai B'rith whose Sigmund Livingston Fellowship helped make this research possible, and to Robin Williams and Edward Suchman of Cornell University for their guidance and encouragement.

[336]

3. the tendency to avoid particularistic beliefs and its relationship to American equalitarianism;

4. the tendency toward discrepancy between attitude and behavior.

These data do not, of course, cover the full range of the adolescent's religious life. Nor do the beliefs and practices examined here encompass the entire traditional system. Also, we recognize that there is no common position among all Jews on these particular religious elements. Indeed, the fact that these beliefs and practices are controversial makes it especially pertinent to determine where adolescents stand.

§ *Research Procedure*

Three samples were used in this study—two in Philadelphia, and one in Elmira, New York. The first and largest sample, 513 respondents, was secured in Philadelphia by visiting youth groups, predominantly high-school fraternities and sororities, B'nai B'rith clubs, and one Zionist group. As a check upon the first sample, a second group of forty-nine Philadelphia adolescents who did not belong to youth groups were interviewed. The third sample consisted of the entire population of Jewish children of high-school age in Elmira during the school year 1950-51. With the aid of information obtained from a census of the Jewish community conducted a year before by the Jewish Center, it was possible to locate and interview every recognizable Jewish adolescent—a total of fifty individuals. The fact that the Elmira sample contains the universe of Jewish adolescents in that community makes it especially valuable as a check upon the other samples.

As can be seen in Table 1, the typical respondent in these samples is between fifteen and seventeen years of age, the child of middle-class parents

Table 1—Composition of Samples*

	1st Philadelphia	2nd Philadelphia	Elmira
Total	513	49	50
Sex			
Female	242	23	28
Male	271	26	22
Age			
14-15	147	17	17
16-17	267	25	25
18-19	72	7	8
Economic Status			
Professional-Managerial	121	6	11
Merchant-White Collar	268	27	30
Workers	102	16	9
Religious Affiliation			
Orthodox	76	19	35
Conservative	295	11	—
Reformed	51	5	15
None	77	14	—

* Rows do not always add up to full number because of questions left unanswered.

belonging to a Conservative or Orthodox synagogue. The proportion of boys to girls is about even. We believe that these adolescents reflect the sentiments of a sizeable proportion of American Jewry, although without adequate census data it is not possible to say how representative they are of all American Jewish adolescents.[3]

A common core of questions was asked of all three samples, although with each group a somewhat different survey instrument was used. In the case of the first sample a self-administered questionnaire was employed; two roughly similar personal interview schedules were used with the other samples. Each interview lasted an hour and a half. Only a portion of the data collected will be examined here. Inasmuch as the data on the religious conviction and conduct considered in this paper were very similar for all three samples, in order to simplify presentation in most cases we shall give only the responses of our large Philadelphia sample.

§ Research Findings

RITUAL OBSERVANCE AND THE RELIGIOUS SELF-IMAGE. We were interested in learning how the adolescent viewed himself as a religious person, and what were the components that determined his religious self-image. Adolescents were asked first to estimate their religiosity and then to explain how they arrived at this self-estimation. Since Judaism is a system of beliefs, practices, and ethical concepts, it might be anticipated that the adolescent's self-estimation would be formed within the framework of these three components. We find, however, that for the overwhelming majority of adolescents, ritual observance is the primary element in the frame of reference within which they perceive their own religiosity and the religiosity of others. In most instances self-estimations were justified *only* in terms of ritual observance; a relatively small number went on to discuss the ethical dimensions of religiosity, while in not one case were beliefs spontaneously mentioned.

This is not to say that adolescents are unaware that Judaism contains beliefs and ethics. We were often told, on further questioning, that a religious person must believe in God, and that a religious person *should* be a good person. However, being a religious Jew is not perceived as necessarily meaning that one is a good person. Adolescents frequently cite instances of persons known to them whose ethics are dubious but whose religiosity they rate high because of the individual's close adherence to traditional ritual. Typical of this emphasis upon ritual observance is the explanation of a self-estimation given by a sixteen-year-old girl who described herself as only "slightly" religious:

If I was really religious, if I was a *good* Jew I would keep all the rules. I wouldn't eat *tref* [non-kosher food]. When I was younger I wouldn't ride on Saturday, but now . . . I don't abide by all the rules. I don't go to the synagogue on Saturday, but I do keep the High Holy Days.

This close relationship between ritual observance and ritual self-image can be clearly seen in Table 2. Adolescents who describe themselves as "strongly" or "moderately" religious are proportionately much more likely to approximate the traditional ritual norm in the observance of the dietary laws and synagogue attendance than are adolescents who describe themselves as being "slightly," or "not at all" religious. Thus of the adolescents who think of themselves as being "slightly" or "not at all" religious, only 15 per cent attend religious services weekly or monthly, and 25 per cent say they eat non-kosher food "never" or "sometimes." However, of those who describe themselves as "moderately" or strongly" religious, 46 per cent say they attend services weekly or monthly and 47 per cent report they eat non-kosher food "never" or "sometimes." The difference between these two groups is statistically significant at the .001 level.

Table 2—Relationship between Adolescent's Religious Self-Estimation and His Religious Service Attendance and Observance of the Dietary Laws

| | ADOLESCENT DESCRIBES HIMSELF AS: | |
Frequency of Religious Service Attendance:	Strongly, or Moderately Religious	Slightly, or Not At All Religious
	%	%
Once a week, or monthly	46	15
High Holy Days only or less	51	83
Never	3	2
TOTAL PER CENT	100	100
TOTAL CASES*	260	249
	$\chi^2 = 52.9732$	$P < .001$
Frequency of Use of Non-Kosher Food:		
Never	6	2
Sometimes	41	23
Often	53	75
TOTAL PER CENT	100	100
TOTAL CASES*	260	249
	$\chi^2 = 25.1506$	$P < .001$

* Not including respondents who left questions unanswered.

The emphasis upon ritual observance in definitions of religiosity cuts across all three movements in contemporary Judaism. Even adolescents affiliated with a Reform congregation estimate their religiosity within the traditionalist frame of reference, despite the fact that most of the Orthodox rituals have been discarded by Reform Judaism. For the Reform, the Conservative, and the Orthodox affiliated adolescent in our samples, a *religious* Jew is, in the words of a fourteen-year-old Reform affiliated boy,

. . . the kind who goes to *Shul* [synagogue] every day, never eats *tref.* You know the kind with the white beard and prayer shawl who holds up every law of the Jewish religion.

Given this emphasis upon traditional ritual as the primary component of their religion, it is not surprising that few adolescents give a high estimate of their religiosity. Only 2 per cent feel that they are "strongly" religious, while 49 per cent describe themselves as "moderately" religious, 41 per cent as "slightly" religious, and 8 per cent as "not at all" religious. Seventy-four per cent of these self-defined strongly religious persons are children of Orthodox parents. None of them is Reform. Seemingly, the use of the traditionalist frame of reference makes it difficult for Reform-affiliated respondents to consider themselves strongly religious.

One consequence of this stress upon ritual observance is that it is probably difficult for all but a few adolescents to find much ego-satisfaction in their religious self-images. The majority will possess the self-disparaging picture of themselves as deviating to a considerable extent from the standard which they use in defining religiosity. Our observations in Philadelphia and Elmira over a period of a year revealed that few adolescents seek to change this situation by striving to conform more closely to the traditional norms. The majority would prefer to change the religion to suit their own particular needs. Thus, when the question: "It has been suggested that some of the things in the Jewish religion be changed—how do you feel about this?" was put to the respondents, 68 per cent voted for change. (Paradoxically, these adolescents regard the traditional norms as too demanding while at the same time they are used in determining the self-estimation.) Others, perhaps in an effort to maintain a more satisfying picture of themselves, delete or relegate religion to a minor position in their conception of the good life. Thus, 32 per cent of the adolescents disagreed with the statement: "Religion is necessary in order to lead a good life."

This concern with ceremonial practice is, of course, not without precedence in Jewish history. However, in American society the stress upon ritual has quite different consequences for the adolescent than it had in other societies. In the East European *shtetl* communities for example, rituals were integrated into everyday religious and secular life. From the moment he arose in the morning the *shtetl* Jew entered into a regimen of ritual practices which did not cease until he closed his eyes in sleep at the end of the day. These practices stood in intimate and recognizable relationship to his religious beliefs and to the major institutions of his society.[4] In this country ceremonial observance is peripheral to the main stream of life, and, as we have noted, segmentalized from religious beliefs. In a situation such as this ritual observances may become, as they have for many of our respondents, an end in themselves, sometimes to the point of excluding other elements of religion. We believe that an unanticipated consequence of this situation for the future religious orientation of many adolescents is that it may increase the strong effect of scientific rationalism upon their total religious outlook.

SCIENTIFIC RATIONALISM. In the ghetto or *shtetl*, the Jew had been relatively isolated from the influence of scientific rationalism.[5] The Jewish school, which was for most East European Jews the only kind of school they attended, was primarily an institution for the transmittal of traditional religious learning and values; science played no role in the curriculum. Not until the Jew was permitted to move freely in the general society —in Western Europe as early as the eighteenth century, but not until the twentieth century for Eastern Europe—did he feel the full impact of scientific rationalism. This influence has been especially strong in American society, where the virtues of modern science are daily extolled in the schools and in the mass media of communication.[6]

It was perhaps inevitable that scientific rationalism should affect the religious outlook of Jewish adolescents, as it has young people of other faiths.[7] Many Jewish adolescents in our samples find it difficult to reconcile what their biology or physics teachers tell them with what they read in the Bible. Skepticism is readily apparent in the reaction of adolescents to the statement, "Modern science has shown many things in the Bible are not true." Over half the sample (57 per cent) agreed with this statement. In the second Philadelphia survey this problem was examined more directly with the question put this way, "Have your studies in science ever caused you to wonder whether some of the things in the Bible are true?" Almost half of the respondents (47 per cent) answered "yes," 41 per cent said "no," and 12 per cent "don't know." To a second question, "Do you think science has shown that some of the things in the Bible could not be true?" 52 per cent said "yes," 41 per cent said "no," and 7 per cent "don't know." Somewhat similar results were achieved when the same question was asked of Elmira adolescents: 68 per cent said "yes," 20 per cent said "no," and 12 per cent "don't know."

Skepticism which results from exposure to scientific rationalism is, of course, not limited to a questioning of the Bible's accuracy; it tends to be diffused through other areas of religious beliefs and practices as well. In Table 3 responses are cross-tabulated with attitudes toward religious beliefs and practices as indexed by two latent structure scales. The first scale concerns the adolescent's attitude toward six traditional beliefs (i.e., a belief in a personal God, in heaven and in hell, in a literal interpretation of the Bible, in a literal Moses, and in the Jews as a Chosen People). The second scale deals with attitude toward four traditional practices (i.e., the use of ritualistically acceptable foods, frequency of attendance at religious services, study of sacred books, and observance of the Sabbath).[8] For purposes of analysis adolescents who gave traditional responses to three or more beliefs and two or more practices, will be considered as relatively "traditionalist." We find a relationship between skepticism as indexed by a feeling that science has thrown in doubt the accuracy of the Bible, and the adolescents' attitudes towards traditional beliefs and practices. Thus, of those respondents who agreed with the statement, "Science has shown that many things in the Bible are not true," 36 per cent were relatively traditional in their attitudes toward beliefs and 50 per cent in their attitudes toward the practice; whereas of those who disagreed with the statement, 55 per cent were traditionalist on beliefs, and 66 per cent on practices.

The difference between the two groups is statistically significant at the .001 level.

Despite these data, it may be argued that scientific rationalism can have a benign influence on the religiosity of Jewish adolescents in that it provides adolescents with scientific legitimation for conduct that had been previously legitimated only in theological terms. This type of legitimation is seen in the tendency of many adolescents to ascribe modern hygienic purposes to the dietary laws. Thus, ritual washing of the hands before eating is explained as a recognition by ancient Jewish seers of the danger of infection from bacteria; ritual slaughtering of cattle is regarded as a hygienic measure safeguarding the health of the Jew from sick livestock. The ban against pork stems, they say, from a recognition of the possibility of infection by trichina. We find, then, that 36 per cent of the adolescents agreed with the statement, "The main reason Jews are not allowed to eat pork is because it is frequently diseased." One sixteen-year-old boy noted that, "Kosher means clean and cleanliness is for health. The food laws keep you healthy." A sixteen-year-old girl, explaining why she would observe the dietary laws when she became married, said, "I know that kosher meat is clean. We were told that pork is not healthy because of a disease— I forget its name."

However, religious conduct based upon scientific rationalization alone is subject to certain hazards from which religious behavior based on faith is exempt. When faith is directed toward supra-empirical reality, practices based on this faith are beyond refutation by sensory data. Religious practice based upon scientific rationalization, on the other hand, can be challenged by new scientific data. This is precisely what seems to have happened to the dietary laws. A number of adolescents (implicitly accepting the rationalistic approach) argue that modern methods of sanitation and

Table 3—Response to Statement: "Modern Science Has Shown Many Things in the Bible Are Not True," by Attitudes toward Traditional Beliefs and Practices

	Agree With Statement	Disagree With Statement
Attitude toward Beliefs	%	%
Traditionalist	36	55
Nontraditionalist	64	45
TOTAL PER CENT	100	100
TOTAL CASES*	293	191
	$\chi^2 = 17.3329$	$P < .001$
Attitude toward Practices		
Traditionalist	50	66
Nontraditionalist	50	34
TOTAL PER CENT	100	100
TOTAL CASES*	293	191
	$\chi^2 = 10.9243$	$P < .001$

* Not including respondents who left questions unanswered.

food inspection have made the dietary laws unnecessary. A sixteen-year-old Philadelphia boy explained, "I am against the kosher foods and dietary laws, as these laws were based upon facts millions of years ago, no refrigerators, etc. Dietary and food laws are completely without logical reason." A fifteen-year-old girl expatiated in a similar vein, "Many years ago the pig was a dirty animal and Jews do not eat anything that is not clean. However, it is all right now as all meat is government-inspected."

Viewed in this context, several consequences of the interrelationship of scientific rationalism and the stress upon rituals for the future religiosity of Jewish adolescents can be seen. What will be the reactions of those adolescents who stress rituals, and who also employ science as a rationale for ritual observance, when they come to believe that science has demonstrated that the rituals are no longer functionally appropriate? One type of reaction is that some adolescents abandon the rituals. For example, only 3 per cent of the respondents say they never eat non-kosher food; 64 per cent say they eat it often; whereas 14 per cent attend weekly religious service, 48 per cent report that their religious service attendance never exceeds two or three times a year (i.e., during the High Holy days).

Some adolescents react more extremely by abandoning both rituals *and* religion, viewing the two as being basically synonymous. This reaction is less common than the previous one—only 7 per cent of the sample say they are "not at all" religious. However, it is a reaction which may increase as time provides more opportunity for science to affect those adolescents who stress ritual observances and who also tend to legitimate observance in rationalistic terms. Thus, the data indicate that the drift away from religion is greatest among the older respondents: all of the adolescents who described themselves as "not at all" religious were over sixteen years of age. In effect, for some adolescents the emphasis upon rituals, while ostensibly an affirmation of traditional norms, may have the unexpected consequence of placing in greater jeopardy their adherence to tradition. For other adolescents this focus of attention upon ceremonial observance to the exclusion of beliefs and ethics represents a simplification of religious thinking to a point where scientific rationalism may affect adversely the adolescent's total attitude toward religion.

EQUALITARIANISM AND THE CHOSEN PEOPLE CONCEPT. There is a marked tendency among our respondents to reject religious beliefs which they regard as suggesting in-group superiority. To illustrate this point let us examine their attitude toward a basic belief of traditional Judaism (one of which has currency in modified form in Conservative and Reform Judaism as well[9]), the Chosen People concept.

When adolescents are questioned about their attitude toward the Chosen People concept, we find that only 29 per cent believe the Jews are a Chosen People, 38 per cent reject the idea, 28 per cent do not know what to think and 5 per cent give no answer. The relatively large percentage of "don't know's" possibly results from the fact that a considerable number of respondents claim to be unfamiliar with the idea. However, many of the answers appeared to be made by teen-agers with an eye to the world about them. They appear cognizant of the fact that for many non-Jews there is implicit in the Chosen People concept the assumption that to be Chosen is to be better or more deserving than others. This reaction was common even in countries and in centuries in which group particularism was regarded as God-ordained. It is even more likely to occur in a society, such as our own, which extols equalitarianism as one of its major value themes. As Myrdal has noted, equalitarianism is part of the American Creed.[10] In American society the equality theme stresses the similar intrinsic value of every man and is combined with a resentment of any claim to social distinction or special status not earned or based upon particular merit—a factor which Gorer argues militates especially against the Jews.[11]

Since equalitarianism is often equated with democracy, the belief that one's group is Chosen (and by implication better than other groups) is open to the charge of being undemocratic. That many adolescents in our samples have internalized this type of thinking is evidenced by the fact that 54 per cent of the adolescents agreed with the statement, "It is undemocratic for Jews to consider themselves a Chosen People." Moreover, when the answers to this statement are cross-tabulated with the respondent's attitude toward the Chosen People concept, as in Table 4, we find that respondents who consider the Chosen People concept undemocratic are considerably less likely to believe the Jews are a Chosen People than are adolescents who do not consider the concept undemocratic. Of those adolescents who regard the Chosen People idea as undemocratic only 15 per cent say they believe the Jews are a Chosen People, whereas 47 per cent of the adolescents who do not feel the concept is undemocratic accept the idea. The difference between these two groups is statistically significant at the .001 level.

These data lend support to the contention that some Jewish adolescents are reluctant to accept the Chosen People belief because of a fear of being accused of harboring illusions of "racial superiority." This may explain why only 29 per cent of the sample accept the belief. Like the non-Jew,

Table 4—Belief that the Jews Are a Chosen People, by Feeling
Chosen People Concept Is Undemocratic

"Are Jews a Chosen People?"	IS CHOSEN PEOPLE CONCEPT UNDEMOCRATIC?	
	Yes %	No %
Yes	15	47
No	53	19
Don't Know and No Answer	32	34
TOTAL PER CENT	100	100
TOTAL CASES*	275	214

$$\chi^2 = 61.7574 \qquad P < .001$$

* Not including respondents who left questions unanswered.

many Jewish adolescents think the concept possesses latent assertions of Jewish pre-eminence. Reasoning of this sort is quite explicit in a comment by a fourteen-year-old Philadelphia boy who rejected the concept because he felt that:

> All men are created equal. If the Jews feel they are a Chosen People it will bring about prejudices.

Said another boy, seventeen years of age:

> There is no superiority of races. The Jews are no more God's Chosen People than any other religious sect. We are all God's children.

DISCREPANCY BETWEEN ATTITUDES AND BEHAVIOR. Jewish adolescents in fairly large numbers find it more difficult to practice than to espouse verbally many of the traditional elements of their religion—an observation, of course, that can be made of adolescents in other religious groups as well. On the whole, adolescents in our samples tend to be more traditionalist in their attitudes than in their behavior, especially with respect to the practices pertaining to food habits and Sabbath observance. For example, although none of the adolescents attend daily services, we find that 3 per cent of them favor such attendance by others. Also, of the 48 per cent whose attendance never exceeds three or four times a year 27 per cent feel that weekly attendance at religious services is important. The same pattern exists for food practices: almost none of the adolescents is thoroughly traditionalist in his observance of the food practices, yet 8 per cent believe that Jews should never eat non-kosher food at any time, and 36 per cent feel that non-kosher food may be eaten outside of, but never in, the home. Furthermore, in what appears to be somewhat incongruous projection of their own urge toward traditionalism, 30 per cent of the adolescents who do not themselves accept any of the food laws state that Jewish boys in the armed services should not be excused from observing the food practices.

It might be expected, if Murphy's assertion that there is an urge toward consistency between behavior and attitude is correct,[12] that these inconsistencies would create feelings of guilt, strain, and eventually a call for change. To some extent this appears to be the case. As we have noted, a majority of adolescents (68 per cent) favor changes in religion. When asked to specify the changes, they invariably mention the rituals, particularly the food practices. It is also true that the more nonobservant the individual is, the more likely he is to favor this change. However, a significant proportion (28 per cent) of the nonobservant (e.g., those adolescents who state they eat non-kosher food often) are opposed to change.

While the reasons for this apparent inconsistency between attitude and behavior are not entirely clear, two factors which may afford a partial explanation were uncovered through intensive interviewing. First, many adolescents have a strong respect for tradition. They feel a sentimental attachment to ritual as the embodiment of tradition and they object to change as a violation of tradition. Thus one fifteen-year-old girl who does not observe the dietary laws opposed any change because, as she told us, "That's the way it's always been; I don't know, it just seems wrong to change them. After all, those laws were made long ago; what right have I to change them." Second, some nonobservant adolescents believe that rituals are a positive factor for group survival and should be preserved for that reason. Their attitude is that though rituals are meaningless for them, they are a "good thing for other people" and for the group. This attitude is summed up in a remark by a seventeen-year-old Elmira boy, a member of a Reform congregation, who said "Keeping kosher is a lot of ritual, like doing a lot of monkey dances; but I think they ought to keep it. It helps the Jews keep closer together."

On the whole, inconsistency in behavior and attitude appears to produce little psychological stress. Adolescents in our samples evince very little, if any, guilt when their behavior does not conform to the standards implicit in their attitudes. At any rate, direct questioning uncovered no overt verbalization of guilt feelings. Of course, many adolescents say that it would be a good thing if they were more religious, but—interestingly enough—such professions were more numerous among the observant than the nonobservant. In general, adolescents seem either to have segmentalized their attitudes from their behavior so that they are not aware of any discrepancy between the two, or they have rationalized this discrepancy by noting similar behavior among their peers. Typical of the latter is the remark of a girl who does not observe the food laws herself but feels that other people should do so. She describes her first reaction to eating non-kosher food in this way: "You know when I first ate *tref*, I almost got sick. Really I almost vomited, I felt so bad; but now I've got so used to it I don't even notice it. You see, all the girls in my crowd do it." These data suggest that when the norms are being generally violated among one's peers, any guilt feelings which may arise from the violation of the norms are quickly dissipated and there is little sustained discomfort.

§   *Summary*

Certain aspects of the religious conviction and conduct of three samples of Jewish adolescents in two communities have been examined. The data indicate that for adolescents in our samples the stress upon ritual components in defining religiosity may adversely affect the adolescent's religious self-image and increase the already noticeable impact of scientific rationalism upon his total religiosity. We noted that the tendency for adolescents to reject a belief which seemed to them anti-equalitarian and antidemocratic. Finally, we noted the discrepancy between the attitude and the behavior of many adolescents, manifesting itself in greater traditionalism in attitude than practice.

W. LLOYD WARNER
AND LEO SROLE

ASSIMILATION OR SURVIVAL: A CRISIS IN THE JEWISH COMMUNITY OF YANKEE CITY

THIS was the state of affairs [an ever increasing rate of defection from religious norms] in the Jewish community when in the summer months of 1932 three of the elder P[1] generation[1] men died, reducing the daily congregation close to the minimum of ten. During and immediately after the high holidays in September, the community suddenly galvanized itself into a burst of organized action. In a period of a few weeks, through a series of mass meetings, close to $10,000 was raised within the community itself, and a church edifice, vacated by the merger of two Protestant churches, was purchased outright.

Let us consider the wider context of this phenomenon. The year was 1932, the second of the "Great Depression"; the Jews had lost heavily on their property and were all gloomy about business. The Hebrew school committee had just met and decided that it could no longer continue paying the teacher his salary unless he was willing to take a sizable reduction in pay. In these circumstances, and with one synagogue building more than adequate to accommodate the entire adult group, not to speak of the bare handful of old men who were daily worshipers, the community could arouse itself to the point of pouring out more than $100 per family, on the average, in order to purchase a new synagogue edifice.

The incident appears to be incongruous and completely non-logical. Several pertinent facts must be presented in order to prove how sociological were these extreme measures.

The synagogue edifice then being occupied had been bought in 1907, when the Jews were concentrated in residential Section I-A. . . .[2] It was a plain frame building, fronting on a narrow, unpaved alley-like street. Families of new ethnic groups lived all around it. The attitudes of all but the elder P[1] men toward this synagogue building were derisive. One P[2] woman said: "I attend the synagogue only on the high holidays. It's an ugly place to go." An F[1] boy, asked why he didn't attend synagogue services, replied: "The synagogue is dirty and the services are dull."

A P[2] man remarked at greater length: "The community will not stay in the present synagogue because it is below their dignity. They are ashamed of themselves to bring their own children to it. The present building was

Reprinted from *The Social Systems of American Ethnic Groups*, pp. 205-217, by permission of the authors and the publisher. (Copyright, 1945, by the Yale University Press.)

acquired twenty years ago, when the Jews were all 'greenhorns' and once belonged to the Salvation Army [lower class]. The reason that the synagogue is below the dignity of the Jewish community is the fact that it is situated in an old, plain house, on the second floor, with very bad furnishings, and is in the very poorest section of town."

The newspaper article announcing the purchase of the vacant church, however, offered the explanation that "the present building has been outgrown and a structure that is larger was wanted."

The new edifice is in Section II-B of the city's residential structure, close to Zone III, on a paved, tree-shaded street whose residents are predominantly middle-class natives. One of the speakers at the dedication of the building as a synagogue spoke of it as being "in a desirable section of the city . . . one that will make every Jew proud."

In the *Herald* article announcing the dedication, the remodeling of the church interior was described, with this addendum: "In making the changes, the Jewish people took care to follow the old architecture of the building. They believe they have one of the most beautiful places of worship in the city."

In the period immediately before the 1932 high holidays, the community was in a state of dysphoria, or collective melancholia, over the status of the synagogue structure. Interviews that touched on religion inevitably struck the note indicated below. One younger P[1] Jew said: "You ask about the ritual observances. Actually very few of the Jews observe the ritual, and, in all, no more than ten hold observance at all strictly. But I think that the Jews will maintain themselves in America because my faith takes precedence over logic. I feel that there will always be Jews."

An elder P[1] Jew said, "Sometimes we haven't even got enough men for a *minyan,* and we have to run out into the street to pull in somebody to make ten. Who knows what will happen to the Jews in America? But it says in the Bible that 990 Jews out of a thousand may be lost, but if only ten out of the thousand remain, God is satisfied. But always when the Jew was about to be assimilated, for example, in Babylonia, always when things were too good something happened. They were driven out and this made the Jews come together again. The Jew must always be reminded by suffering and, let me tell you, it will happen in America. You will see."

Both of these Jews despair of the future, since, as another informant expressed it: "If you take away religion from the Jew, there is nothing left for him by which he can be a Jew." That is, the disintegration of the synagogue structure implies ultimate disintegration of the community system. In view of these facts, one Jew had recourse to faith over logic, and the other cited Jewish history to prove that the Jews have persisted, notwithstanding that they were often "about to be assimilated." The implication that "things were too good" seems to point to class mobility as also a factor in the present situation. The elder P[1] Jew's historical statement, "always . . . something happened," proved prophetic only a month later.

From this general condition of dysphoria, the "drive" to secure the new building put the entire community into a condition of euphoria. In the interest of the "United Jewish Community," a mass meeting was held to plan for a new synagogue. The Jewish community turned out en masse, the investigator reporting that "every family was represented, with only one exception, namely, the one considered intellectual." Close to $6,000 was either paid or pledged on this occasion alone, the contributions ranging from $250 from the fathers to $5 and $10 from adolescents and single dollar bills from children as young as five.

Typical comments made by adults to the investigator at the close of the meeting were: "This is the happiest day of my life. It's grand." "This is a new chapter in the history of the Yankee City Jews. The spirit was simply wonderful." "Everybody pledged more than they could pay. Especially in times like this, how people can scrape together the money for the new shul I don't know." A Jewish ex-resident of the city who was at the meeting said: "The community is certainly not normal now. Everybody is enthusiastic, inspired."

During the meeting a younger P[1] male arose to suggest "that Gentiles [of Yankee City] be approached for subscriptions." The suggestion was almost unanimously voted down, and the consensus of opinion after the meeting was expressed by the president of the Jewish Ladies' Aid Society when she said derisively: "It should not have been even mentioned." This attitude reflects an extreme tightening of the internal relations of the community around the internal crisis so that reference to the group's external relations was incongruous and not even to be "mentioned."

How these internal relations of the community system were all focused around the synagogue may be gathered from the fact that almost every adult above the age of twenty-five was represented on the various subcommittees working under the building committee.

Similarly, in the process of remodeling the building in order to convert it into a synagogue, many of the men volunteered their labor in order to avoid spending money for hired help. These were thanked publicly at a meeting by the president of the congregation.

Most striking of all, however, was the mobilization of the community associations. The Jewish Ladies' Aid Society started "the ball rolling" in the fund-raising campaign by giving the first donation—$1,000. Speaking for all the associations, an officer of the Junior Hadassah declared: "Now all organizations will be one—the shul. The Junior Hadassah will not have a chance to raise any money for itself. All contributions and all affairs will be for the shul. We won't make our quota [annual contribution to the national office] of $236. We will just hold affairs and turn over our profits to the shul fund."

Finally, we may quote from an interview with a member of the building committee: "We have never at any time in the last twenty-five years gotten all the Jews in the town to agree about anything. The new synagogue is something that all agree about. Every Jew in Yankee City has pledged money to it. And a number of Gentiles offered money. We tried to sidetrack it, since the Jewish community felt that they themselves should pay for it. If they make a sacrifice themselves, they would enjoy it better. They thought it was wrong to take Christian money.

"We took down young fellows who hang around the corners and showed them the new building, told them of our plans for the community center. They were all willing to work and were enthusiastic. They had worked for the Y.M.C.A., why shouldn't they do it for themselves? It woke up the entire Jewish community; it gave them something to look forward to. You know, the day of the meeting there were thirty-five people there to help clean up, even the older people." And he concluded: "Yes, everything is revolving around the synagogue. Everybody is working for it."

To understand this phenomenon, we must again turn to our generation classification. In the first place, it should be stated that the campaign, from first to last, was engineered not by the older P^1 men who had been the effective congregation, but by the P^2 and younger P^1 men who had not been members of the congregation and whose only articulation to the synagogue had been manifested on the high holidays.

The beginnings of the affair were described by the chairman of the building committee, who is of the P^2 generation and in the upper-middle class: "Recently this place on Jefferson Street came on the market. The first day of Rosh Hashana five of us [three P^2 and two younger P^1 men] went down to look at it, and from then on the thing grew. A committee was appointed with full authority and began negotiations. We wanted to know if the community was behind us, so we turned in a report not to buy the building because of the obstacles, and the moment we did this they all wanted it; in fact, the same group which was opposed to it before were now all for it. We said that we have no money and the people all said that the Jews are ready to give the money.

"We got the old men to turn their power over to the younger men so that we could reorganize things, elected officers, and we took in fifty-five new members [into the congregation] in one night. At our meetings there have been Jews who were never in a synagogue before."

The new officers of the congregation included five P^2, five younger P^1, and two elder P^1 men. At the time of this election, the members of the congregation had reached a new high of eighty, only twelve of whom were of the elder P^1 generation. But what were these younger men doing leading a campaign for a new synagogue building when some of them "were never in a synagogue before"? This question, in the course of intensive interviewing, was put in a less direct form to these very men. Their answers are illuminating.

One younger P^1 man replied: "We hope that the new shul will enthuse the younger people so they will come [to the synagogue] willingly." Another of this generation said: "A lot of us are not orthodox, but we all want the new shul. It will be a community center, plenty big, in a good neighborhood, and respectable. The middle-aged Jews are afraid of the younger generation, and are therefore taking [the synagogue] into their own hands."

These individuals seemed to say that the purpose of the community effort was to articulate the F^1 generation to the synagogue structure, but since the largest part (65 per cent) of this generation is still subadult and ineligible for membership in the congregation, there must be more to the situation than these answers reveal.

A few informants came closer to the truth in their replies. One P^2 Jew asserted: "The older people began to pass away and the younger people began to feel the responsibility, especially in the last few weeks."

In essence, therefore, a basic aspect of the phenomenon is the community crisis of age-grade movement. The elder P^1 generation, alone represented in the congregation, served to maintain the synagogue structure and to articulate the community with the extended religious system which is identified with the whole Jewish society. The dying out of these men carried the threat of extinction of the synagogue structure. This implied that the community would be severed first from the larger Jewish society; second, from its extended religious system; and third, from its traditional past. It would mean the collapse of the community as a Jewish community.

Under this threat, as several informants actually expressed it, of being left adrift and lost, the pressure of the community system compelled the age grades below the elder P^1 generation, i.e., the younger P^1 and P^2, to move up into the synagogue structure in order to keep it active in the community system. Every man in the younger P^1 and P^2 generations joined the congregation, fifty-five of them in one night.

The frequent emphasis upon bringing the F^1 generation into the synagogue fits into this interpretation. In any movement of an age-grade system, the lower age grades must be carried along. In this instance, unless the F^1 generations, who had dropped the traditional religious behaviors almost altogether, were somehow related to the synagogue structure, they would fail to move into the structure when the present younger P^1 and P^2 generations passed away. Therefore, it was necessary not only for the adults below the elder P^1 generation to establish relations, somewhat less formal, to the synagogue structure. When the men interviewed said, "We must bring our children into the synagogue," they meant in effect, "We must bring our children into the synagogue *along with us.*"

There is a sentence in the souvenir program issued at a benefit affair for the Synagogue Fund which reads: "They [the Yankee City Jews] realized that they were building not only for the present, but for posterity."

It was symbolic that, at the dedicatory ceremonies of the new building, the four-year-old grandson of one of the leading P^1 elders was chosen to

kindle the perpetual light which hangs over the Holy Ark in every synagogue.

Another highly important element of this age-grade movement, the
attitude of the P^1 elders to their displacement from control positions in the
synagogue structure, will be considered later in this chapter.

What is the relevance of the history of the new synagogue building to
the movement of the age-grade generation system? The answer lies in the
functions of both the old and new buildings as status symbols. The older
building, in a lower-class area, was associated with the phase of the
Jewish community when it was concentrated in this area and was largely
lower class in status. By 1932, however, the Jewish group was residentially
scattered, largely in Zone II, and the younger P^1 and P^2 generations were,
with few exceptions, in the middle class. If these young adults were to move
into the community synagogue structure, it was necessary that it be housed
in an edifice that had adequate status value. The original building definitely lacked that value. It was therefore necessary to secure a new building, and this was found in the Protestant church building in the upper part
of Section II-B. In the souvenir program already mentioned the need is
expressed in somewhat rhetorical terms: "Even as a child outgrows its
clothes, and the sleeves of its garments become too short, and the buttons
will no longer fasten and keep the body warm and healthy—even so did
the Jewish people of Yankee City outgrow their spiritual garment. There
soon arose a demand for a larger, finer, and more noble edifice. Something
greater was needed to keep the body of the community functioning properly."

Purchase and remodeling involved an outlay of close to $10,000, which
for the size of the group and the condition of the times was a prodigious
amount. Yet given the absolute necessity for movement of the younger
adults into the synagogue structure and also the need for a structure that
represented an adequate status symbol, the community worked itself up to
the highest pitch of euphoria in order to acquire the new building and
facilitate the age-grade movement into the synagogue structure.

The status value of the new building was important in relating the F^1
generation to the synagogue structure, as the chairman of the mass meeting
stated in his speech: "The old people depended on the old building, but
the young people were not interested. They came only on the high holidays and they would say, 'you are in the worst section of town,' and so they
stayed away."

This seems to ascribe the religious desuetude of the F^1 generation entirely to the status value of the old synagogue building, a condition which,
if corrected, would restore the religious orientation of this youngest generation. The behaviors of the Jews, however, indicate that their reason is
less simple than this. Throughout the entire affair, their plans were directed to converting the new building not only into a house of worship
but also—and explicitly—into a "community center," principally for the F^1

generation. One Jewish informant said: "We are only working for the shul because of the young people, in order to bring them in somehow, by giving them a nice place where they can dance and play." Providing recreational facilities has often been described in Jewish circles as "bringing the Jewish young people into the synagogue through the back door."

An expression of the recreational function of the synagogue is found in the following enthusiastic remarks of an officer of one of the F[1] associations: "You know, we, the Junior Hadassah, had our dance there [in the new synagogue], and it was a grand feeling. This auditorium and building was our own; we felt at home in it. It wasn't as if it were at the Masonic Temple, where we rent the hall and know that it is ours only for the evening. In the shul it is as if we are in our own home."

An entirely new development for the community, whose weddings had heretofore been held in Boston, is reported in the following: "Did you hear about the wedding that we had? It was the first wedding we had here in the shul and believe me, everybody was excited and thrilled. I think absolutely everybody in the community came."

Regarding the age-grade aspect of the situation as it affected the elder P men, it was immediately evident that the attitudes of some were ambivalent and that others were guardedly hostile, explicitly to the purchase of the new building, and implicitly to their displacement from the control offices in the congregation. One of them, a merchant who still lives in Section I-A, as do most of the elder P[1] families, said: "Ach, I don't know what to think of the new shul. What good is it? It's too far away. Here it is near, but there it is far. It takes a half hour to get there. You stay an hour, so that means two hours, and I can't take two hours. I have to open the store in the morning. We have to live, you know, so I won't be able to go. And the same thing with the others [P[1] elders]. So if they don't come every day, what good is the new shul?"

His statement, "I won't be able to go," in the face of his past behaviors in attending the synagogue daily seems to be an empty threat of withdrawal from the synagogue. Since the opening of the new synagogue, in fact, his attendance has been as regular as before.

"The new shul will bring in the young people—yes, to dance, to play cards. Put in a swimming pool and maybe they'll come. What good is it if they don't believe? In Europe when I was a boy the shul, *davening* [prayer], and the Sabbath was a holy thing. Here the boys laugh at it. It doesn't mean anything to them. If they don't believe, they won't come to the shul."

Another of the elder P[1] generation made this remonstrance: "We haven't many going to shul now. Why do we need a new shul? This one is big enough and good enough."

At one point after the new building was purchased, a few of these elders threatened secession on an issue of seating arrangements. An informant reports: "Mr. Leiber got sore and tried to get a group together to form a separate congregation in the old building. When the young men heard this—they are very smart—they went to the old building and took out the Torah [the Holy Scroll of the Law without which a synagogue is profane], which could have stayed a while, and everything else. That is, they stripped the building of all its holiness and therefore it was no longer a shul."

This antagonistic attitude on the part of the elder P[1] men must be considered in connection with their behaviors in contributing to the synagogue fund to the limit of their means and their verbal recognition of the community crisis. Their hostility is a corollary of the age-grade movement, which pushed them out of control of the synagogue structure.

However, this movement pushed them not only out but up, as seen in the attitudes of the younger men who treated the elders, for all the latter's antagonisms, solicitously, in a manner analogous to that used toward the "dying fathers" of Chinese society. For example, at the first mass meeting, contributions from two P[1] elders evoked this remark from the P[2] chairman: "I am happy to say that the older people are with us. Mr. Berg gives $50. Here is another contribution from the older generation that we are afraid about satisfying. One hundred dollars from Mr. Marcus." In the course of his address that evening the chairman said: "To the older men, I want to assure that we do not intend to disturb the ways of your worship. We want you to continue as you have in the past in your religious life."

More especially is this solicitous attitude seen in the compromises of the new synagogue officers on issues of "liberalizing" the synagogue. Not only were the younger men predicating their entrance into the synagogue structure on the acquisition of an edifice with adequate status value, but, in the beginning at least, they were determined to change the synagogue services from the strictly orthodox modes of the past. . . . A P[2] Jew's remarks indicated the direction these younger men were taking: "The orthodox synagogue has had no influence at all on the young people. You see, religion must be modernized to be accepted. I don't believe personally in going to the other extreme of Reform; but I believe that liberal Judaism can be a great influence. If you take away religion from the Jew, there is nothing left for him by which he can be a Jew. The Nationalists feel that the Jewish nation in Palestine alone will keep the Jew. But even with the Jewish state, the Jew in the Diaspora must have religion. Without it he loses all of his Jewishness. Judaism has applicability in modern times. But I mean liberal Judaism. It happens that because I am in an orthodox community I have to belong to the orthodox synagogue. But it's all very halfhearted. It's only lately that orthodoxy has come to a standstill. We have stopped fitting ourselves to the environment and to modern times, which orthodoxy in the past has always done before. The Catholic Church in America has adapted itself—has fitted itself to conditions—and it is one of the strongest religious bodies in the country. Jewish orthodoxy will not yield one iota, although in the past it has always adapted itself, else it could not have lived as long as it has. The Judaism of Babylonia was altogether different from that of Russia. I cannot explain why orthodoxy no longer adapts itself. Orthodoxy at present is a European orthodoxy, whereas American liberal Judaism is really an adapted form of orthodoxy.

"Martin Luther, just as Moses Mendelssohn, attempted to modernize and to bring religion into the common language of the people. The young people of today need the Bible in the language that they can understand. Of course Reformed Judaism has gone too far, has become an ethical culture society, rather than a religion. I have the most respect and veneration in the world for the Reformed rabbis; they are great scholars. But I cannot accept Reformed Judaism. It is too Christianized."

Here is seen a clear instance of the change of content in a church structure. For the changes proposed, while not altering the fundamental representations of Jewish orthodoxy, reflect the changing elements in the personalities of these younger Jews, especially those of the P^2 generation. By adaptation of Judaism "to the environment and to modern times," the informant means adaptation to his type of personality, which, containing American elements to an important degree, has radically moved away from Orthodox Judaism. For this type of personality to return to the synagogue it has left, the synagogue must be altered to "fit" that personality. It must be "liberalized": it must relax its unbending, rigorous prescription of behavior after an ancient pattern in a social system that can make no place for such a pattern. Evidence from the informants is that the movement of the P^2 social personality toward the American type has not proceeded so far as to eliminate its fundamental orientation to the Judaistic religious system.

It is noteworthy that the movement of the P^2 Jews, who had been so markedly dissociated from it, into the synagogue structure was justified by their relations to the American social system. For example, a P^2 upper-middle-class Jew, a leader in the campaign, after discussing how the younger Jews had thrown over their Jewishness, said: "The young men have found out that even to have the Christians like us, we should go to the synagogue. A Jew who is an honest Jew and takes an interest in his synagogue, that is, in his community, is really liked better by the Gentiles. A Christian who is a customer of mine told me that he would have more faith in one who was an observing Jew than in one who denied his religion." This is a man who, previous to the community's "drive" for a new synagogue building, had been described as being "removed from the shul and the community."

These remarks refer to personality development in ethnic communities generally and specifically to its second and third phases. . . . After having dissociated themselves from their community system and oriented themselves instead to the American social system, a process designated as the second phase, the P^2 personalities have returned to their community and synagogue.

In spite of the determination of the younger men to change the new synagogue structure to conform with their own personality pattern, they did so only in certain significant details. The evidence indicates that they were constrained by consideration for the P[1] elders. Throughout the speeches and press notices during the campaign, no mention was made of reforms in the direction of what is called Conservative Judaism. However, cautious reference was made to "semi-orthodoxy," "liberal orthodoxy," and "modern orthodoxy." The larger view of the younger men, however, is revealed in the remark of one P[2] Jew: "The older people, of course, are strict, but the younger ones are liberal. However, the new congregation is not going to be liberal because the younger people still have their parents and they [the parents] cannot break away from their practices. But when the old people die they will change the synagogue to the liberal ritual."

Nevertheless, certain members of the P[2] generation were frankly impatient with the congregation officers at delaying "liberalization" out of regard for the older men. One P[2] woman said petulantly: "I don't see why they insist on keeping the synagogue orthodox when almost everybody except the old are liberal."

On the issue of the seating arrangements of the sexes the P[2] men, under the prodding of their wives, pushed through a compromise reform. . . .[3] This one detail especially illustrates the correlation between changing personality and changes in the content of a religious system. This single reform expresses a change in the evaluation, status, and participation of the women in the synagogue cult.

In the controversy over the seating arrangement, the younger P[1] men among the executive committee (officers and directors) sided with the P[2] men, although the latter were the more active. During the first Yom Kippur after the dedication of the new synagogue the large middle section, reserved for family units, was almost empty except for P[2] families. These, of course, are far outnumbered in the group by P[1] families. The younger P[1] families, with only two exceptions, separated to sit in the outer male and female sections which were well filled. In other words, the younger P[1] parents, although in many instances sympathetic with the P[2] generation on the seating issue, actually behaved in conformity with the strict letter of the Law.

That the new synagogue is serving its functions and has brought in those who had been outside is indicated in the investigator's report: "Attendance at the new synagogue, on the high holidays, I was told, was 100 per cent, which I confirmed on Yom Kippur. There were approximately five hundred present at the *Kol Nidre* services on Yom Kippur eve, including many out-of-town relatives and friends. Whereas formerly local families went to their relatives in other cities for the high holidays, the new synagogue has reversed this movement. The average attendance at Sabbath services is about 125, which contrasts with the average of thirty in 1932."

ASPECTS OF RELIGIOUS WORSHIP IN THE CONTEMPORARY CONSERVATIVE SYNAGOGUE

IN the following pages we shall discuss some of the chief distinguishing features of religious worship in the contemporary Conservative synagogue. First to be considered is the *form* of worship. This includes external appearances, the language of prayer, synagogual arrangements, and the manner in which the Deity is addressed. There is next the *program* of worship: the public observance of the traditional holidays, festivals, and prayer services. Special interest centers about whether or not any new—and hence untraditional—occasions for divine convocation have been created. Lastly the *content* of worship, or the ideological framework of the prayers, services, and rituals, will be analyzed.

By separating form and content we mean only to suggest a distinction helpful in the setting up of an analytical framework. Actually there is an inseparable link between the two categories. Content defines form, while changes in form—made without apparent desire to change ideology—may deeply influence content. Form grades imperceptibly into content, content into form; to divide these two categories does not constitute a denial of the many interrelations and fusings which take place in actual fact. But the distinction is very helpful in making an introductory analysis. Full monographic treatment of the problem, however, would involve stressing interrelationships, fusings, and "unanticipated consequences."

§ *The Form of Worship*

The forms of worship characteristic of Orthodox Judaism differ widely from those common in Western countries, particularly in Protestant lands. In addition to this overall factor, it is notable that behavior during Orthodox worship is not in keeping with the particular cultural norms observed by the *American middle class.* Among Jewry, extreme informality in the religious setting and the continuance of "secular" behavior in "sacred" situations originally had no social class referent—such manners were exhibited by members of all classes in Eastern Europe. In the United States, however, with former lower- and lower-middle-class Jews adopting middle-class ways, and with the Jewish upper class no longer adhering to tradition, the old deportment comes to be thought of as *characteristic* of Orthodoxy as a system. Consequently, the individual is motivated to break with previous patterns not only because of possible theological objections, but by

---

Adapted from Ch. IV of *Conservative Judaism: An American Religious Movement* by permission of the publisher. (Copyright, 1955, by The Free Press.)

the very fact that his mobility has served to stigmatize much of his previous behavior—including that in the field of religion—as lower class and hence inappropriate to his new station.

Furthermore, since traditional Jewish worship is *actually* characterized by so many patterns which are, according to American norms, typed as being lower-class, the identification of Orthodoxy and social inferiority has been especially pronounced. While the ends of Jewish worship are approved by the general community inasmuch as they are considered to be identical with the goals of Christian devotion, some of the *means*—or devotional practices—used to attain them do violence to the conventional norms and aesthetic standards observed by middle-class persons. Were the traditional patterns of worship continued, middle-class Jews would be alone among middle-class people generally in practicing rites of a lower-class character. This disparity, then, introduces a strain in the institution and a readjustment becomes necessary. If the synagogue is to retain its middle class, standards during worship must at least approach those in general use. Essentially, new means must be devised or appropriated to enable old ends to be served. The following quotation illustrates the way in which Conservative Jews themselves have conceptualized this problem:

> When the Conservative Movement was organized, the Rabbis and the laymen, in order to build a Synagogue which would attract the young American Jew, were confronted with the problems of developing a service, which would be traditional and at the same time modern so that the American Jew would find himself at home.[1]

The form of worship may be studied under three headings: (1) changes in the status of *woman*, (2) introduction of *decorum* at services, and (3) reduction in *"commercialism"* during worship. Our analysis of these factors will highlight the view that the changes introduced by Conservatism constitutes a Western, bourgeois version of Jewish tradition necessitated by rapid upward social mobility and acculturation, and that furthermore the development of Conservatism has aided in the maintenance of some measure of equilibrium in the sub-community.

1. THE STATUS OF WOMAN. Perhaps the single most disruptive force, or "strain," to American-Jewish Orthodoxy has been the position of woman. Female subordination constitutes an important violation of Western norms. Furthermore, there is the consideration that the inferior position of woman is not only alarming when considered strictly normatively, but—viewed from the standpoint of institutional survivalism—it also presents a vital *organizational threat*. This is a consequence of the fact that males do not evince the same degree of religious interest as of old. Were they actively participating in worship and religious study, female subordination might constitute a serious annoyance, but it would hardly threaten institutional integrity. The gradual withdrawal from worship and religious study on the part of the male creates a void which must somehow be filled; women represent the logical group which can bridge the gap. To encourage their

participation, the norms of Judaism must be modified. Considered technically, the subordination of woman, inasmuch as it contributes to institutional instability, constitutes a "dysfunctional" element in the traditional system. Even though change will entail a serious violation of the religious code and the overcoming of much resistance, a *status quo* position would mean organizational suicide.[2]

It is highly significant to note that varying with class and other factors, religion in Western culture is predominantly an activity of *females*. For example, Robert and Helen Lynd found that women tend to take religion more seriously than men. Some 62 per cent of the membership of Middletown's largest church, they discovered, was female.[3] Leiffer has estimated that ". . . the average [Protestant] church has about 50 per cent more women than men in its membership."[4] Fichter suggests that the same situation is found among Catholics: women outnumber men by approximately seven to three in partaking of the spiritual activities of the parish.[5]

Unlike Christianity, Orthodox Judaism has not been able to make much use of the tendency in our culture for religion to maintain itself by appealing to a female public. While second settlement Orthodox synagogues may accept some financial assistance proffered by their ladies' auxiliaries, institutional rigidity prevents the utilization of any really large-scale reinforcement. It may well be that by the second settlement the Jewish woman is already more faithful in complying with the requirements of the sacred system than is her spouse.[6] One may observe in such areas that, unlike their husbands, some Orthodox women are reciting prayers or reading devotional literature faithfully each day (as females they are not under any religious obligation to do so). Indeed they receive no encouragement —formally or informally—for participating in such spiritual exercises. Their devotions are held in private and if not practiced on what could be described as a secretive basis, certainly the prayers are said in real seclusion. The same rituals are being performed concurrently at the synagogue by a diminishing group of males. It seems safe to say that the inability of Orthodoxy to use this "spiritual reserve" for the strengthening of its institutions, rather than permitting the effect of the activity of women to be dissipated because of highly informal structuring, has helped contribute to its own decline.

Against this background, the importance of the following observation is manifest: the overwhelming majority of Conservative synagogues seats men and women together. This is known as "mixed seating," or the family pew system. The adjustment of woman's position is an outstanding feature of the Conservative synagogue as well as the most commonly accepted yardstick for differentiating Conservatism from Orthodoxy.[7] This change is taken by the woman as symbolic of her new status, and was regarded by both sexes at the time of its adoption as a concession of crucial significance.

We are interested in some of the effects of this shift. Since the Friday evening service forms the backbone of the year-round worship program in Conservatism, the sex distribution at these services can be taken as a measuring rod.[8] According to the figures submitted by local synagogue officials, women already predominate among the worshipers. In 39 per cent of Conservative institutions women now form between 25 per cent and 49 per cent of the congregation on Friday night, while in 54 per cent of the congregations they constitute from 50 per cent to 74 per cent of those attending.[8a] Although it is admittedly difficult to measure whether or not the revision in woman's status has had real "functional" value—and if so to what degree—we suggest that it *is* helping in institutional maintenance. Women in the Conservative synagogue are taking up the slack produced by the male, whose decrease in attendance may well represent his acceptance of the general American pattern in the field of religious behavior.[9] The sex distribution during worship in Conservative synagogues may soon approach Western standards. The new norms, responsible as they are for the destruction of the unity of the Jewish sacred system, have provided a compensating factor. Jews are beginning to follow a pattern new to their group but implicit in the *American* system: much concern on the part of women for religion—an interest for which they are presumed to have a special affinity.

It is notable that as the Jewish woman reaches a new class level and becomes acculturated, she can turn to religion (or, more exactly, to attendance at public worship and participation in synagogue activities) as a leisure-time interest and as a symbol of newly won status. Under these conditions, the synagogue may serve as the focus for "deflected achievement" on the part of its female public. However, at the same time that this participation is taking place, the woman is neglecting the performance of many of the prescribed rituals (such as certain laws relating to the food taboos, or to Sabbath observance) which are incidental to her activities. Paradoxically, the strength of organized religion is augmented while personal behavior becomes increasingly secularized.

It should not be inferred that women in Conservatism are accorded perfect equality with their spouses. Although the sexes do sit side-by-side during worship and the women take part in all the responses indicated in the liturgy, they are still excluded from certain worship activities. To take the most significant instance, the ritual surrounding the handling and reading of the Torah scrolls is still generally reserved for males. This varies, however, according to the sanctity of the service. During the High Holidays the exclusion of females from the pulpit is almost complete. The procedure is modified at times during the less awesome Sabbath morning service. Women are frequently allowed considerable freedom at Friday evening worship, for the Torah scrolls are not particularly important in this service.

Thoughtful laymen have maintained that these variations indicate an inconsistency in the Conservative approach. For example, a leading Conservative figure in the Midwest has stated that:

A generation ago the young architect, the young engineer, the young doctor, the young lawyer, the young business man saw in Conservative Judaism a chance for genuine religious self-expression integrated with the best of thinking in the world at large. We saw the opportunity of giving equality to the women within the framework of our religious life. We gave them seats beside us, and since then, we have spent most of our time wondering about how we ever dared to be guilty of such a deviation. Our congregations still argue about the question of a mixed choir, not to speak of . . . calling a woman to the Torah. In this instance and in so many others, we feel that the past twenty-five years have not brought the fruition . . . to which we looked forward with such eager expectancy.[10]

But there has been no widespread agitation for perfect equality. Conservative women have generally been satisfied with their limited status—a great advance over the age-old segregation. Furthermore, the pattern of formal equality coupled with limited participation follows the model of many Christian denominations where the rites central to worship are also performed largely by males.

2. THE PROBLEM OF DECORUM. In Orthodoxy, quiet or intense recital of prayers and a "worshipful" attitude are not considered to be the only appropriate modes of religious behavior. In fact should a worshiper consistently adopt what would generally be considered a reverent demeanor, unless he had a well-established reputation for a very special kind of piety and occupied a seat along the Eastern wall of the synagogue (thus placing him close to the ark in which the Torah scrolls are kept), his deportment might well be the subject of intense criticism. Some resemblance to Jewish attitudes may perhaps be found among Catholics. In Italy, for example, great informality has prevailed at times among the congregation in spite of the liturgical service. In a far different setting, there are also some similarities in lower-class American Protestant sects and denominations, although Jewish worship lacks the high fervor and intensity characteristic of the services conducted by such groups. Essentially, however, the *form* of Orthodox worship does seem to be almost unique in its lack of solemnity.

If we study Jewish attitudes in the third settlement, we find that Orthodox worship is increasingly being stigmatized as unspiritual and lacking in proper decorum. This point of view is, of course, a function of the adoption of middle-class American norms of convention and aesthetics. Therefore in addition to modifying the position of women, the Conservative group has stressed a further reform: the presentation of a religious service which is "Jewish" but at the same time in conformity with the outward characteristics of worship—on the level of decorum—as practiced by other groups of a similar class level. The strong feeling about the decorum problem is conveyed by the following excerpt which purports to summarize public reaction to one of the first Conservative services held in the city of Milwaukee: "The synagogue was filled to capacity . . . all commended the dignity . . . that characterized the services and contrasted markedly with the disorder that they had come to associate with traditional forms of worship."[11]

How has decorum been introduced? In Orthodoxy the important services are led by the cantor. Such functionaries specialize in the elaborate rendition, frequently with the aid of a choir, of selected portions of the liturgy. The cantor has little interest in the behavior of the congregation other than during the time of his solos. Before beginning such prayers, he may pause and wait until order has been restored. If the form of the service is to be revised, it must be conducted by someone who will supply real leadership. The rabbi is the obvious choice to discharge this responsibility; it is his counterpart in the Protestant church who conducts the service. Thus the Conservative spiritual leader has come to be charged with planning the service so that it will proceed without interruption. He must see to it that there are no long pauses conducive to conversation, that the service is sufficiently varied so that boredom does not ensue with the attendant shift of interest away from the pulpit, and that breaches of decorum among congregants are quickly spotted and promptly dealt with.[12] In contrast to his Orthodox colleague, the Conservative rabbi actually *conducts* public worship.

To accomplish his task, the rabbi is assisted by a corps of ushers. They help seat the congregation (this is essential during the High Holidays when pews are reserved), and endeavor to keep the conversation of worshipers to a minimum. Also, the ushers must be on the watch to prevent individuals from moving about, for the Conservative worshiper is expected to remain in his seat at least during the important portions of the service. Visiting by infants and children, a feature of the Orthodox service which tends to create disturbance, is also restricted; children are expected to participate in the special services arranged for their benefit. Visiting in the main sanctuary on the High Holidays is usually confined to an especially arranged intermission.

It is not easy for Orthodox-bred individuals to accept these new forms of behavior all at once. While in recent years a certain degree of decorum could be assumed, during the 1920's when development of the Conservative pattern was in process, synagogue officials experienced real difficulty as they sought to enforce the new regulations. An official of a leading Cleveland synagogue, for example, stated at the time that:

> A great effort is being made to impress upon the congregation the importance of decorum. In many of the conservative Synagogues of America the services are [still] disturbed by constant whispering on the part of the audience. . . . [Our ushers] give to every worshiper upon entering the following card: "Worship without decorum is unworthy of an intelligent congregation. Please refrain from all conversation. . . ."[13]

That officials are still not satisfied may be surmised from a more recent source:

> Outweighing all these demands for appropriate appearance [of male wor-

shipers] are, however, the demands for appropriate conduct at the service. . . . demands should be pressed at all seasons of the year and should be hammered home in particular at High Holiday time.[14]

3. "COMMERCIALISM" IN THE SYNAGOGUE. The synagogue practices referred to under the heading of "commercialism" include: (a) "Shenodering," a general term referring to the pledging of money for the opportunity of participating in the Torah service. (b) The holding of auctions during holiday and festival services for the purpose of "selling" certain particularly honorific privileges; by stimulating competitive instincts, large amounts may be pledged. (c) The Yom Kippur appeal: fund raising which takes place during *Kol Nidre,* a particularly holy service. Since attendance is at a maximum and the worshiper is presumably in a receptive frame of mind, generous donations may be forthcoming. While these practices are related to decorum inasmuch as an additional diversion is created, they require separate treatment.

In the *shtetl* of Eastern Europe and in the areas of first and second settlement in the American city, there is little criticism of these practices. They are thought of as efficient devices for the raising of sums vitally needed to provide support for religious needs and communal charities. The distribuiton of the honors and the amounts of the donations (announced publicly) become the subject of much interested comment.[15]

It will be recalled that in Judaism there is no sharp division between sacred and secular, and consequently little development of separate norms for each area. This system conflicts with the Christian—and American— one which distinguishes between the sacred and the profane, defines which situations belong to each category, and provides for differential behavior. The "unspiritual" practices of the daily market place are excluded from the sanctuary on Sunday. Most Protestant denominations prefer to employ a relatively inconspicuous technique to raise some of the funds which they require. This is the passing (in silence) of a collection plate preceded by only a minimum, if any, amount of stimulation from the pulpit. While auctions, raffles, bingo games, and similar devices are still used to help finance churches, particularly Catholic ones, these activities are not carried on inside the sanctuary. If held on church property, generally they take place in the community hall or in some adjacent building.

It is not surprising then that as Jews internalize new norms, they tend to view their traditional methods of raising funds with increasing disapproval. Customary techniques are *now* felt to be singularly inappropriate to the religious setting. Thus as one Conservative publication states: ". . . there is no charitable expression in the English language that can connote the desecration of a Torah honor and the degradation of a House of Worship into a market place of vulgar vanities and rude commercialism."[16]

Since the clientele of the Conservative synagogue is on the whole prosperous, some of the old fund-raising devices can be dispensed with easily.

Membership dues come to provide an increasingly large proportion of congregational revenues.[17] Also, except for emergency needs, money for communal charities is no longer raised during services. Modification of the system is consequently taking place; features of the Protestant technique of the silent appeal are being adapted, although the ordinance which prohibits the carrying of money on the Sabbath and holidays complicates the process. However, individuals who receive honors are still generally expected to make a special contribution, but they are encouraged to do so in a "spiritual" manner:

> The principle of the "silent appeal" applies equally to the system of Torah donations. Many congregations have done away with the desecrating system of "airing" individual charitable impulses during the central part of the service— the reading of the Torah. They insist on anonymity in giving and thus cut the props from under all those displays of ill-starred fund raising campaigns that are dynamiting the very foundations of dignity in the synagogue. All announcements of pledges are eliminated. . . . Everyone however who is called to the Torah is handed an envelope which serves as a reminder and a convenient means of forwarding his donation. . . .[18]

Those congregations which have dispensed, in part or *in toto*, with the traditional method of raising funds are proud that their actions are now consistent with American norms. Thus: "We, in Congregation Rodfei Zedek, have set an example to Chicago Jewry, of the possibility of eliminating from our services direct appeals for funds, and embarrassing solicitations."[19] That the problem is still considered to be a vexing one can be gathered from the pointed remarks made by a lay synagogue official:

> Conservative Judaism maintains dignity in Judaism. . . . After all, why did we drift away from the so-called Orthodox point of view? Because we recognize that . . . [it] is obsolete in America. . . . We want to create a service that should be applicable to our children and to the future generations. . . .
> It is a very spiritual elevation when a man goes up to the Torah and he doesn't have to be bothered [with auctions and donations]. He should pay for it, and he should pay for it even more . . . [but a congregation] should not depend upon the individual whims of the person who comes up to the Torah. . . . a synagogue stands for dignity in Jewish life and let's uphold that dignity. . . . As far as "shenodering" is concerned, if it could be eliminated that stands for dignity. I was sorry to hear [at this convention] also that in some congregations they [still] have appeals on Kol Nidre night. Now, mind you, Kol Nidre night, the most holy night in the year, all of a sudden the rabbi gets up and makes an appeal . . . and immediately [the Jew] feels, where is he? Is he in a theatre? Or is he in a meeting place where the speaker is asking for an appeal for some organization?[20]

Ostensibly, most officials of Conservative congregations share this sentiment. When polled on the question: "Are you in favor of fund-raising during services?" only 29 per cent answered in the affirmative.[21] However, the system is too useful to be dispensed with in its entirety. Most congregations still employ *Kol Nidre* appeals. Apparently this occasion is a propitious one for fund-raising. Thus the choice between proper normative observance and ever-present institutional needs is frequently resolved in favor of the latter, and institutional maintenance acts as a vested interest blocking social change. It is regretted that the rabbi's sermon must in fact be an appeal for funds, but institutions whose overhead is large or who have pressing needs for expansion see no other way of meeting their requirements:

> Raising funds or standards on the High Holidays—that is the question. It is a dilemma that has plagued many congregational leaders who have awakened to the shame of commercialization of the holiest of divine services and who have to cope with the despairing problem of securing the ways and means for the upkeep of the congregation for the entire year. What a heart-breaking alternative![22]

Congregations experiment with techniques which allow for retention of the system, but at the same time reduce somewhat the degree of normative violation:

> . . . many synagogues, and especially large synagogue centers, [cannot] dispense with the Kol Nidre night appeals and . . . the sale of seats for the High Holidays in the immediate future. The problem confronting many synagogues is how to *spiritualize* and how to remove the obnoxious elements from the Kol Nidre appeal. . . . This is the Season of the year . . . when the Jew is imbued with the spirit of giving in order to maintain his house of worship. . . .[23]

It would appear that there are emotional factors present which block change in spite of the conscious will. The giving of charity, and particularly *its influence in assuring the individual's continued good fortune,* is a prominent motif in the cultural system of the East European Jew. Certain deep-seated attitudes, we know, tend to continue in spite of considerable acculturation. Thus it may be that the worshiper is still eager (although, wishing to conform with the norms, he professes quite the opposite) to make a public demonstration on the holiest day of the year of his eagerness to render a material gift to his Lord. Although "commercialism" may be distasteful, it may be even more of a personal threat were he to be deprived of the opportunity of making an offering. By restricting his donations throughout the year, the worshiper may *force* the scheduling of an appeal on *Kol Nidre* night.

§ *The Program of Worship*

1. TRADITIONAL SERVICES. In addition to form, the *program* of worship in the Conservative synagogue possesses some distinctive features in comparison with Orthodoxy. All Conservative synagogues conduct High Holiday services, and their halls are filled to capacity. While no special devices need to be employed in order to fill the seats, it is significant that not all of those who use synagogue facilities actually attend: it was found that only 74 per cent of the fathers of children registered in the religious school conducted by a Conservative synagogue in New York City partici-

pate in public worship during the High Holidays.[24] But it is generally believed that the High Holidays have retained their hold, and this is true in the sense that those who have some measure of religious interest do attend the services. The low ratio existing between the total number of seats in synagogues and temples and the total Jewish population results in the crowding of all available facilities.

With the exception of the High Holidays, however, the degree of interest in the traditional program of services is far from satisfactory. Conditions vary according to the size and location of the individual congregation, but on the whole the satisfaction felt about High Holiday attendance is missing when the other services are considered. Frequently, it is *not* that the year-round program of traditional services must be cancelled because of lack of attendance. Rather, it is that these services seem to appeal to a small group of comparatively uninfluential or peripheral individuals who represent only one age-grade in the congregation.

Conservative synagogues have not taken a complacent attitude toward this situation. In order to improve attendance, well-designed publicity is customarily sent out to members in advance of the services, and the worship program may be advertised in the public press.[25] Telephone squads are sometimes organized to call each home on the congregational roster and invite attendance. Also, the rabbi attempts to improve matters. He may see to it that duties usually handled by one person are divided among many, or that new activities are created in connection with the service— all on the theory that "use them or lose them." As an added feature, refreshments will be served. In many congregations guest rabbis and lecturers are invited to occupy the pulpit in the hope that a new face and a prominent reputation may attract additional worshipers.

Attendance at the traditional services is rarely increased by the employment of such promotional devices. The fact that at some of the services significant religious rites are performed helps to explain why the traditional worship program has been preserved. Such ceremonies, rather than the services themselves, apparently provide the motivation for the attendance of the majority. The *Bar Mitzvah* and Confirmation rituals serve to attract many relatives and family friends of the candidates; the *Yizkor* and the *Kaddish* prayers, said in memory of the dead, also draw worshipers.

To study these processes, we may start with the three daily services: the morning, afternoon, and evening prayers. According to information supplied by local officials in reply to the question "Do you have a daily service [in your congregation]?" only about half of the institutions hold these services (see Table 1).*

---

* The holding of a daily service is still typical of the very large congregation but some of the medium-sized institutions have already been forced to discontinue it. The

Table 1—Percentage of Congregations Conducting Daily Services*

	Morning Service	Evening Service**
	%	%
Yes	54	45
No	46	54
No Answer	0	1
Total	100	100
Number of congregations	(200)	

* Source: United Synagogue, *Survey*, I, p. 3.
**"Evening" includes also the afternoon service since the two are recited as a single unit, or with only a short intermission between them.

It is acknowledged that when attendance is well above the required minimum, many of the worshipers have come only for the purpose of reciting the *Kaddish* prayer.[26] The regular attendants are a group of elders, who were reared in the Orthodox atmosphere of the *shtetl,* and in the area of first settlement. Frequently these men were less pious before their retirement. Some of them—returning to the patterns of their youth—find the daily services to be an important means of reducing the "abyss of leisure" which they confront. Some might be worshiping in Orthodox synagogues but for the fact that they are living with, or near, their children who are active in the congregation.

Although most synagogues still conduct Sabbath services on Saturday morning, attendance is small: 57 per cent of the institutions report less than 50 regular worshipers, and 70 per cent less than 100.[27] However, the *Bar Mitzvah* ceremony works toward the perpetuation of this service. In very large congregations one or more candidates may be available on each Sabbath, and attendance may therefore reach impressive proportions. But like the daily service, the hard core of Saturday worshipers consists of "old-timers." Some congregations seek to improve conditions by stimulating the participation of children or young people. It is thought that they may also help to bring their parents back to the synagogue on Saturday morning. However, judging from the reaction to proposed reforms aimed at increasing the number of regular worshipers, most congregants remain apathetic.[28]

Attendance during festivals is also small. *Yizkor* on all of the festivals, and Confirmation on *Shavuoth,* the late spring holiday, do serve as reinforcement but ". . . in the majority of cases the general 'Holiday consciousness' is on the wane and is only feebly kept up by the memorial services provided by the Holiday calendar."[29] Furthermore:

distribution by congregational size of the 200 institutions replying to the *Survey* was as follows:

Congregations with a membership of 100 families or less:	18%
Congregations with a membership of 101-200 families:	25%
Congregations with a membership of 201-500 families:	37%
Congregations with a membership of more than 500 families:	20%

. . . organized worship is breaking down; daily services have practically disappeared in almost half of our congregations. . . . Saturday morning services have mostly become a perfunctory affair; Holiday Services on Passover, Sukkoth, and Shavuoth, in terms of attendance, are negligible.[30]

Officials feel that steps must be taken to arrest this decline:

The task then is clear: a new approach must be sought and new techniques must be developed . . . to give [*Shavuoth*] status in the appreciation of the rank and file, and to "sell" its values to our men, women, and children.[31]

To summarize, while the High Holidays have retained their appeal, the remainder of the traditional program of services does not fare well in the Conservative setting. This occurs despite the fact that the services may be publicized, that some have the advantage of being conducted in Westernized form, and that they are being reinforced by the celebration of various *rites de passage*. Judging from the age-levels of the worshipers, it appears that—barring the emergence of a religious revival of a certain type—decay will continue as surviving members of the old ghetto-bred generation diminish in number. This prediction would seem to hold true for the daily services in particular. Perhaps the women will come to play a more significant role at the festival and Sabbath services and thus help to keep them intact.

2. FRIDAY NIGHT SERVICES. While Conservative-minded individuals apparently are not very frequent participants in the traditional program of worship except at High Holiday time, they do retain the value of "Jewishness." From a sociological perspective, it can be said that they still require some form of collective behavior which will serve as a focus for common strivings and help periodically to renew group loyalties. This can be accomplished by participation in ceremonies symbolizing common sentiments. Such participation must be based on the regnant attitudes of the community. For example, the type of Sabbath observance prescribed in the sacred system is noticeably absent in the area of third settlement. What *has* remained among a certain group is a feeling of nostalgia for the Sabbath of old and a rather vague desire to indulge in some form of religious behavior which will be expressive of the Sabbath spirit.

Thus a new service has come to be introduced. Saturday morning worship is being supplemented—and in many congregations has already been supplanted—by a service held on *Friday night*. Friday evening worship permits the individual to engage in prohibited activities on Saturday and yet at the same time participate in some type of Sabbath observance. Friday night worshipers need not feel very guilty about absenting themselves from the traditional Sabbath service. Furthermore, the new Friday night service is free of the rigor and legalistic approach to observance characteristic of Orthodoxy. It represents an accommodation to the new norms assimilated by the Conservative group. . . .

The Friday night program in the Conservative synagogue is conducted in the form of a full worship service. It has largely replaced all other services in importance except those conducted on the High Holidays.[32] The trend toward Friday night is unmistakable, although it varies with the size of the congregation (see Table 2). In reply to the question, "When does the main Sabbath service take place in your synagogue?" the answers of officials of medium-sized congregations (201-500 families) were distributed as follows: 57 per cent replied "Friday evening," 14 per cent "Saturday morning," and 27 per cent considered both equally important. Smaller sized congregations voted overwhelmingly for Friday night in contrast to the larger-sized institutions where the trend is toward considering both services equally important.

Table 2—Main Sabbath Service by Size of Congregation*

Time of Main Service	100 Families or Less	CONGREGATIONS OF		Over 500
		101-200	201-500	
	%	%	%	%
Friday evening	84	69	57	36
Saturday morning	3	8	14	13
Both equally important	12	23	27	50
No answer	1	—	2	1
Total	100	100	100	100
Number of congregations	(200)			

* Source: United Synagogue, *Survey, I,* p. 8.

Part of the reason for the popularity of Friday night is traceable to the fact that the time at which it is held is a convenient one for many potential worshipers. But the special characteristics of the Friday evening service are also important factors. First, it is notable that inactivity on the part of the worshiper is a dominant characteristic of this service. The congregation in the traditional type of Jewish worship is a very *activist* body. Furthermore, a detailed knowledge of the liturgy, as well as the ability to read Hebrew fluently, is essential for participation. The Friday night Conservative service, however, demands much less from the worshiper. He is only required to join in some responsive readings and in various other types of prayers, and to sing familiar hymns. Merely a minimum familiarity with the Hebrew language and liturgy is needed. This service, then, represents an adjustment to the declining knowledge of the prayer book and the language in which it is written. As with most middle-class worship, the action on the pulpit is central. In conformity with overall trends in our culture, the individual is no longer an active participant, but is cast in the role of a spectator.[33]

The second central feature, one which fits in well with the general tenor of passivity, is that a sermon or address is almost invariably a part of these services. Furthermore it is a very *important* feature, for when asked about the "drawing-power" of the sermon, only 12 per cent of the laity stated that it plays no role in influencing their attendance.[33a] Since sermon topics are widely advertised and are designed with an eye to attracting worshipers, the subject of these discourses is of special interest. (See Table 3.)

Table 3—Sermon Topic Preferences*

Subject	Preferred by
	%
General problems of Jewry	76
Biblical interpretations	52
Religious observance	52
Ethical problems	44
Israel and Zionism	42
Political and social affairs	42
Psychological problems	29
Reviews of books and plays	20
Miscellaneous	3
No answer	2
Number of respondents (1145)	

* Source: United Synagogue, Survey, I, p. 24.

It is highly significant that the favorite choice of congregants is for "Jewish problems": sermons on the situation of Jewry considered largely from the viewpoint of their ethnic-group status. As for sermons strictly in the field of religion, discourses about the Jewish sacred system—with the stress on what laws and rites retain significance in the modern world—are popular. It is notable that the preference is for discussions of the problem of *religious observance* rather than theological doctrine. Developments in Israel and general social issues are also of some interest. But the fact of greatest significance is that "ethical problems" (the subject of many church discourses) is fourth on the list—congregants do not regard it as constituting *the* central focus for attention. Those who judge the Friday evening service by the standards of non-ethnic religious groups are disappointed that ". . . a three-quarter majority desires to make the pulpit a forum for airing the general problems of the Jewish people. . . ."[34] Actually, the preferences of the laity provide some confirmation of the hypothesis that the Conservative synagogue is in part a result of the desire of American Jews to continue with their ethnic group existence but to do so under the legitimation of religion. . . .

There is one other feature of Friday evening worship which is of considerable significance: after the service is concluded, a "social hour" is usually held.[35] Refreshments are served and socializing may continue for quite some time. Although attempts have been made to incorporate a formal program (such as a discussion on topics of current interest) into the social hour, in most institutions worshipers take a negative attitude toward such efforts. They feel that there has already been enough content of a serious nature by virtue of the rabbi's sermon.*

---

* Upon occasion, a discussion in the social hall may be substituted for the sermon.

Worship is thus not the only method of cementing group loyalties at the Friday evening service. The concluding portion of the proceedings is essentially organized along the lines of a voluntary association. The individual can meet his friends in pleasant surroundings, share with them in the partaking of food, and discuss family, clique, and group concerns. All of this takes place under the legitimation of religion. Synagogue leaders have recognized that both the worship and the *social* aspects contribute essential features to the Friday evening service:

The overwhelming majority of our congregations hold a late Friday night service. Moreover, it has developed, through the social hour usually following the service, into a most important instrument for the social intercourse of the congregational membership. By virtue of this dual function, it [the Friday night service] has become a yardstick for the effectiveness of a congregation and for its rabbinic or lay leadership.[36]

§ *The Content of Worship*

1. THE EMPHASIS ON FORM. As we have seen, Conservatism has made decided changes in the form and program of worship. Now we must turn to a consideration of the relationship between program, form, and *content.* Preparatory to this, however, some special analysis of the *actual* changes in form is necessary. Because some services have changed more than others, we require a number of further details before the content problem can be clarified in all its ramifications.

The maximum amount of change should take place at those services which are not heavily weighted with tradition. But this general principle needs supplementation. The fact is that at those services in the Conservative synagogue to which few *Conservative* Jews come, little if any change has taken place from the mode prevailing in the Orthodox synagogue. This is the situation in respect to daily worship, and even the Saturday morning service remains largely traditional in form.[37] Many feel that these services are merely vestigial survivals from Orthodoxy. In the larger congregations the daily services are generally the responsibility of the sexton rather than the rabbi. In fact, many Conservative rabbis do not attend regularly for they also share the viewpoint of their congregants that daily worship is appropriate chiefly for mourners and "old-timers"— that the demands of modern living make the schedule of three daily services obsolete. While in a number of places efforts have been made to increase attendance by making these services more Conservative, such reforms may prove to be dangerous. They can alienate the age-grade which now worships without attracting another group in its place. In summary, many congregations are able to carry on the full program of traditional religious services by the device of varying the form of their worship between Orthodoxy and Conservatism. Such flexibility has made Conservatism capable of satisfying disparate groups. Although some have objected by saying that "There is no logical explanation for having one Conservative Service one day and an Orthodox Service on the next,"[38] on the whole the arrangement has been well received.

The most highly adapted services, fully Conservative in form, are those held on Friday night and at High Holiday time.* Notwithstanding changes in form, the *content* of these services remains highly traditional. *Thus, even where the shift in form has been a radical one, there has frequently been no important change in content.* This requires explanation. First, however, we must provide some further documentation proving that a disparity between form and content actually exists. For example, in speaking about the changes introduced by his movement, the spiritual leader of a large Eastern congregation mentions only changes in the area of form. He suggests no comparable changes in content:

> Through a judicious choice of prayers; through responses both in Hebrew and in the vernacular; through congregational singing . . . through group participation at every level; through the introduction of readings, comments, explanations; through the shortened reading of the Torah [on the Sabbath], the trienniel cycle, giving greater opportunity to interpret and less opportunity for the wandering of interest . . . we have done much to make the Sabbath, Festival, and High Holiday services exhilarating.[39]

Unlike rabbis, Conservative laymen seldom attempt to analyze their movement in print. For an expression of their opinion on this problem, we must rely chiefly on unpublished materials. The personal document quoted below was written by a successful professional man who had the usual Orthodox upbringing. Upon moving from a second to third settlement area, he joined a Conservative congregation. In this extract, he communicates something of the effects which the radical shifts in form had upon him. Significantly, he too fails to note any changes in content:

> The biggest shock of all to me was the temple services on New Years and Yom Kippur. . . . I was born and bred in an Orthodox *shul* with the accompanying multitudinous prayers, jams of people and children all joined together in a cacophonous symphony of loud and sometimes raucous appeals to the Almighty. Here it was so different. A large group of Jews, men and women, sitting quietly together for hours at a stretch, subdued prayers, no rustling and bustling, no weeping and wailing, no crying children, just the music of the choir and cantor being the only loud sounds heard. Truly it was a revelation to me. I looked around the congregation and saw a large number of younger people sitting intently and reverently reading their *Machzors* [holiday prayer books]. They supplied you with a *talis* [prayer shawl] and *yarmelke* [skull cap] at the door. No carrying packages. The *Machzor* was clear, concise and arranged in order so as to be easily followed when the rabbi announced the page numbers. I soon immersed myself in the prayers and responsive readings. I listened to the sermons and understood what it was all about. . . . After the services I sat for a few minutes and pondered. What was the score? Which of the sects in Judaism is getting to the ear of Heaven first?
>
> It is so different for me. Like another world. Religiosity in the sense that I have been accustomed to is strangely absent. It will take me quite a time to accustom myself to things. . . . It's a bit confusing but very pleasant.

---

* The form of the Festival services appears to be intermediate between the Friday night and High Holiday services, and the daily and Sabbath morning services.

During the earlier days of the movement, when Conservative individuals were still quite sensitive to Orthodox opinion, congregational spokesmen also made explicit the fact that while they had changed the form and program of worship, they had retained much of the traditional content. One local spokesman stated that:

> The form of religious service in . . . [our] synagogue is conservative or modern orthodox, with sermons in English and responsive reading in English, hymns and prayers by cantor, choir and congregation both in Hebrew and English. *The traditional prayer book is used and the traditional ritual has been retained in all its essentials.* The family pew system has been adopted, and a social hour follows every Friday night service with a different member or organization in the center serving as hosts.[40]

2. FORCES BLOCKING ADAPTATIONS IN CONTENT. What factors are responsible for the gap existing between the modernized procedures and the traditional prayers? First there is the answer that although ritual is only a symbolic means of achieving a desired result, it tends to become an *end* in itself. The worshiper feels that only by using the *correct* (i.e., traditional) formula can he establish contact with the Deity and consequently have ". . . an effect on the concrete and spiritual world."[41] The Hebrew prayers—like all religious petitions—have achieved a certain sacredness; they have come to possess very strong emotional associations. Given additionally Judaism's legalistic framework, Eastern background, and age-old traditions, the reasons for some of the rigidity become clear. However, the pervasiveness of the lag between form and content in Conservatism is also related to (1) the characteristics of the period during which the movement emerged, (2) the role played by its rabbinical leadership, and (3) the kind of public which Conservatism has attracted. Starting with the first of these factors, for comparative purposes it is worthwhile to study the forces behind the pioneer revision of the Jewish liturgy—the one made by the Reform group in Germany. The aim of this movement was to harmonize the content of the prayer book with the *Zeitgeist*. But below the surface another motivation was present: the desire of Jews to qualify for political rights and increased economic opportunity. It was feared that themes found in the liturgy might be used as arguments to block emancipation and integration.[42]

In contrast with Reform, the growth of Conservatism took place *after* Jewish political emancipation had been granted. Thus there were no practical considerations dictating radical changes in content, such as the deletion of references to Zion out of fear of being charged with dual loyalties. The need to effect ideological readjustment could not come from the "outside"—a potent source for change among minority groups generally. The fact that Conservatism developed when Jewish emancipation was already a historical fact has had a profound effect in helping to insure the survival of traditional content.

If historical circumstance did not serve to generate pressures leading to change, it is conceivable that the impetus could have come from the rabbis. Constituting themselves into a bloc, perhaps *they* could have introduced revisions in content. While some students have overestimated the role of bureaucracies and pressure groups, such centers of influence and autonomy have at times been a strong factor in the decision-making process. In Conservatism, however, the influence of paid officials and of functionaries (the rabbis of local synagogues) on certain aspects of synagogue policy has been minimal. Good reasons exist which account for such ineffectualness. Historically, Conservatism has been a movement led by *laymen* rather than by rabbis. In many of the synagogues built in the areas of third settlement, major changes were instituted by the laity itself This was done either with the consent of the rabbis, or as frequently happened since many of these congregations were new institutions, functionaries were engaged *after* the innovations had been conceived of, if not implemented.[43] Only those rabbis were considered who were known as approving of the reforms. Conservatism was not the type of movement established by a cohesive leadership group revolting against the *status quo;* the spiritual leaders, like the laity, were merely "disaffected" from Orthodoxy. . . .

The Conservative spiritual leader grasped that the main desire of his membership was for a modification of Orthodox forms so that Judaism would be adapted to new surroundings. Accordingly, most functionaries have limited themselves to the instituting of decorous services. Their personal predilections, whatever they may be, have seldom been reflected in the *content* of congregational worship. Frequently, congregants are unaware of the ideas of their spiritual leaders outside the area of form. Thus a member of a Minneapolis Conservative congregation, interviewed in connection with a study of his local community, stated that the rabbi *had* assisted in modifying forms but he did not mention any leadership outside this area:

> I belong to the Conservative synagogue. Years ago all the men wore their own hats. There was no such thing as uniformity. I remember that I objected when the rabbi urged us to check our hats and wear skull caps. . . . Today I look back and wonder how I could possibly have objected.
> There used to be a lot of talking while the services were being conducted. Today it's really quiet and orderly. People used to get up and walk out at any time but the rabbi made them stop that, and it's really so much better now. We have ushers and they watch you pretty carefully so there is no disturbance of any kind.[44]

As regards the laity, they have generally been apathetic, or even opposed, to shifts in content. It is not difficult to trace the factors which help account for their attitude. Since Conservatism represents in part a response to embourgeoisement, it is the change to the *style of life* and worship characteristic of the new peer group which has been the chief concern. This holds true because ideologies and philosophical orientations change more slowly than less basic matters such as manners, dress, and aesthetic sensibilities. One Conservative rabbi who saw the emergence of the movement in a Midwestern community in the 1910's, himself noted somewhat caustically at the time that:

The Orthodox element consists largely of immigrants in the process of establishing themselves economically in the new land of their adoption. To the Conservative class belong those who have acquired either through systematic education or through social or business intercourse, sufficient culture to disgust them with the conduct of the immigrant classes. . . . Their breaking away from the older elements is *not* due so much to a desire to improve the content of Jewish life as it is to establish organizations that should be similar in form to those of their wealthier fellow Jews or their Gentile friends.[45]

Perhaps shifts in content will occur in the future, but the movement is still so young that the interests of its recently mobile adherents seem as yet chiefly limited to matters of form.

Implied above is the absence among the laity of many "intellectuals." Were such people attracted to the Conservative movement, it is possible that *they* would have opened the area of content to critical scrutiny. While it is true as a rule that intellectuals have generally taken little part in religious affairs, this has not always been the case. The early German Reform movement, for example, attracted a number of such individuals. For our purposes it is not necessary to set up criteria unambiguously differentiating "intellectuals" from "non-intellectuals," for the occupational distribution of the officers and board members of the congregations offers sufficient clues to the actual situation. In one study it was found that fully 55 per cent of the leaders are business owners, executives, or managers. (See Table 4.) Doctors, lawyers, dentists, accountants, and some engineers together with a few social workers account for almost all of the 30 per cent who are professionals. Academic people, writers, researchers, and other types of intellectuals have generally been poorly represented in the movement even though many such people now send their children to a

Table 4—Occupations of Congregational Officers and Board Members*

	Per Cent	
Owners or Top Executives of Big Business	4	
Owners or Top Executives of Medium Business	22	
Owners or Top Executives of Small Business	24	55
Other Business Officers or Managers	5	
Professionals	30	
White-collar Workers	4	
Blue-collar Workers	1	
Retired	1	
Other	3	
No Answer	6	
Total	100	
Number of Respondents (1787)		

* Source: United Synagogue, *National Survey on Synagogue Leadership,* p. 5.

synagogue because of their desire to provide them with a Jewish education. . . .

In summary, little demand for change in content has come from the middle-class Jew who fashioned the Conservative synagogue long after Jewish emancipation had been won. The movement has been led by successful business and professional men whose efforts have been devoted to "practical" matters; intellectual ferment has been missing from the Conservative synagogue. Furthermore, the decentralized character of Jewish life has served to limit the influence of the functionaries. Most rabbis have confined themselves to the application of changes in the form and program of worship calculated to harmonize synagogue modes with newly-achieved status. Conservative religious services are "Jewish" enough so that there is continuity with previous experience, but at the same time they take the new norms into account. The most popular adaptations have proven to be those which are in keeping with the spirit of the tradition, but whose *form* is different from the one followed in the immigrant synagogue. Conservatism mediates between the demands of the Jewish tradition, the feeling of both alienation and nostalgia toward first and second settlement areas, and the norms of middle-class worship. In effect it borrows something from each of these elements and synthesizes them into a new pattern.

JEROME E. CARLIN
AND SAUL H. MENDLOVITZ

THE AMERICAN RABBI: A RELIGIOUS SPECIALIST
RESPONDS TO LOSS OF AUTHORITY

IN any ongoing society there exists an area of sacred values and beliefs toward which a significant number of its members are oriented. Within the society there are certain individuals who are primarily concerned with the maintenance of, and adherence to, these sacred values and beliefs. These individuals we shall define as religious specialists. This paper is a report of the manner in which one contemporary religious specialist—the American rabbi—conceives of his role. More specifically, it will relate what a number of rabbis in a large American city told us about what they have done, are doing, and would like to do as religious specialists.

The role the American rabbi has fashioned for himself in the American Jewish community represents an attempt to cope with changes in the Jewish community which seriously undermined traditional authority structures and the legitimations and value systems upon which they relied. It is the central thesis of this paper that the American rabbi can best be understood as a religious specialist who is responding to this loss of authority.

The role of a religious specialist may be viewed in terms of the relationships existing between the following elements: (1) the system of ultimate values in the society of which the religious specialist is a member, (2) the basis, type and extent of authority given to, or created by, the religious specialist, (3) the functions or empirical activities performed in that role within the significant structures of the society.

A full discussion of this rather broad framework cannot be attempted here, but the following remarks will be helpful:

1. Two important dimensions of any ultimate value system are: (a) the degree to which the actor views his conduct as intimately related with the system of ultimate values, and (b) the degree to which the value system prescribes specific acts for the actor.

2. Authority, as it is most generally understood, has reference to the basic social fact that individuals are differentiated with respect to the possibility of their affecting each other's conduct. The religious specialist is said to have sacred authority because he legitimizes his authority in terms of an ultimate value system and because he is able to affect the behavior of others so that it will be in accordance with this system of ultimate values. There are three aspects of the authority of a religious specialist which should be kept in mind:

Published for the first time in this volume.

(a) The manner in which this authority is legitimated, e.g., by a claim of direct communion with the transcendental order, by ordination from a legitimate representative of the sacred, or by intimate knowledge of the rules governing sacred authority.

(b) The type or kind of authority that the religious specialist possesses: *Imperative authority* (characterized by the possibility of applying organized, relatively specific sanctions which include use of coercion), or *influential authority*, which by hortatory and exemplary conduct involves the imposition of unorganized, diffuse sanctions.

(c) The extent of the authority of the religious specialist—how many individuals act in accordance with the rules he espouses.

3. The functions of the religious specialist within the significant structures and their relationships to the other two elements will be made clear below. It should be noted, however, that these functions generally come to be legitimated in terms of the ultimate value system and, therefore, tend to become expressions of that system.

§ *Some Historical Considerations*[1]

The rabbi, as the distinctive and unchallenged religious specialist of the Jewish community, emerged from the Soferic-Pharasaic tradition by the end of the first century. While the rabbi, like priest and prophet before him, ultimately rested his authority on divine revelation, he is sharply distinguished from his predecessors by the manner in which he exercised and legitimated his authority. The authority of the priest was based on the claim that he was given, at the time of revelation, a divinely ordained hereditary office which empowered him to administer the sacrifices at the altar, to bless the congregation in the name of the ineffable God, and to bear the ark which contained the Law. In all three functions he was the intermediary between God and Israel, the administrator of the sacrificial cult. The prophet, although holding no office, claimed to have authority on the basis of the fact that he was directly inspired by God to speak, and that what he spoke was part of the divine revelation. He admonished and exhorted the people through preaching and teaching. The early rabbi, in contradistinction to priest and prophet, based his authority on an intimate knowledge of the written and oral law, both of which he claimed were divinely revealed. He was responsible for the elaboration of this body of sacred literature and was the creator and product of those institutions which bound the Jews together in the Diaspora—the school and the synagogue. As such he became the teacher, interpreter and judge of the Law.

These activities led to an important development of rabbinic occupational roles in which the teacher, the judge, the spiritual leader of the synagogue, and the official community leader became clearly delineated.

More significant, however, for our understanding of the peculiar nature and vitality of the authority of the rabbi, especially for the flowering of the medieval European rabbi, is the fact that this proliferation of rabbinic occupational roles was part of, and subordinate to, the development of a more encompassing and fundamental rabbinic role, that of "scholar-saint."*

What is involved in categorizing a religious specialist a scholar-saint? Viewed most generally, a scholar-saint is that type of religious specialist whose authority is based both on an intimate familiarity with the literature, values, and rules concerning the sacred area of a society, and on the fact that he lives his life in such a way so that he commands respect and, more importantly, inspires emulation from the other members of the community.

The attribute of saintliness, as it is used in this context, has reference to the quality of personal piety as part of everyday living in accordance with sacred rules. Asceticism, thought of as the release from everyday rules, necessary for the realization of some higher truth or identification, is not part of this notion of saintliness as it applies to the role of the scholar-saint. Although ascetism does appear and plays an important part in the history of the rabbinate (i.e., in the Hassidic movement and the institution of the Zaddik), it is essentially an aberration and has always been reabsorbed into the main tradition of the essential unity and identity of scholarship and personal piety.

Recruitment to the ranks of this type of religious specialist is not limited to individuals from a particular class in society; typically there is free entry. With respect to the rabbinate, any individual (historically, only male) able to master the vast learning and willing to live in accordance with the sacred rules is eligible to become a scholar-saint. There is also little formal hierarchical organization amongst scholar-saints, and the role itself remains functionally diffuse with little affinity for that degree of formality, specificity and organization necessary for the development into an occupational role.†

A full exposition of why the rabbi developed the role of scholar-saint shall have to wait for another occasion. A partial explanation, however, is

---

* The late Louis Ginzberg, one of the few scholars to give attention to the rabbinic role and to whom we are greatly indebted for the concept of scholar-saint, has stated in unequivocal and elegant language the fact that the rabbi was a scholar-saint: "We have now reached a point, which though it is usually ignored, is of fundamental importance in the history of the Jews of the antiquity and medieval times. It is the specifically Jewish view expressed in the old saying: 'Wisdom cannot become the portion of the evil hearted.' Character and learning according to this view are mutually dependent upon each other. Only he can be an original thinker of creative force whose character rises above the level of the common-place, for to use the words of a philosopher of modern times, 'Great thoughts spring from the heart.' This view grew to be so essential an element of the make-up in the Jew that for him the *saint and scholar became identical concepts*." (Ginzberg, Louis. *Students, Scholars and Saints*, [Philadelphia: The Jewish Publication Society of America, 1928], p. 83.) [Italics ours.]

† It may be that this lack of specificity of function and absence of bureaucratic involvement within the role increased the ability of the rabbinic scholar-saint (more so than other religious specialists) to adapt to differing historical circumstances.

to be found in the nature of the ethical value system of the medieval Jewish community. This system was based on a vast body of rules, precepts, and norms (created and continuously reinterpreted by unbroken generations of rabbis) which imposed the mantle of sacredness on practically all human activity. Elbogen has written, "Judaism made no distinct cleavage between the sacred and secular aspects of life. Problems of morality, family hygiene, diet, business relations, sexual life, education and dress, as well as the more distinctive religious elements of rituals were encompassed within Rabbinic authority."[2]

The obligation to know and teach the law and to live according to its precepts, although resting upon every Jew, became the special concern of the religious specialist, the rabbi. While this obligation called forth a remarkable degree of learning among all segments of the community (and the high proportion of Jews who studied and were versed in the tradition and rules is unique in the history of social achievement), it made of the rabbi a scholar.

The indispensable quality of piety or saintliness, basic to the rabbinic role, grew out of the same circumstances that gave rise to the necessity for scholarship. For as the tradition required living in accordance with the law as well as knowledge of it, so piety became a way of life for those religious specialists who sought to live in accordance with the mantle of sacredness with which all human activity had been covered.

It is important to note that the distinctive position and authority of the rabbi did not arise from the fact that he possessed skills that no one else possessed or performed functions that only he alone could perform, but from the fact that he excelled in those qualities and deeds which every member of the community aspired to realize. The rabbi became, in short, the embodiment of the cultural ideal.

It was the rabbi as scholar-saint who held the highest position of authority in the medieval Jewish community. This position was totally independent of whatever authority might accrue to him by virtue of any specific office he might hold in any particular rabbinic occupational post.[3] In fact, the appropriate, idealized performance of the scholar-saint role called for avoidance of official positions. Thus, Rabbi Elijah, the Vilna Gaon, the prototype of the scholar-saint, enjoyed the greatest prestige and position of any Eastern European rabbi although he never held office.[4]

This new sort of theocracy which dominated Jewish society, as Salo Baron has pointed out, was not based on any kind of officialdom or bureaucratic structure; it was a theocracy "not of professional or charismatic priesthood, but of rabbis recruited from all social classes, *whose claim to leadership consisted exclusively in learning and personal piety.*"[5]

At the same time that the scholar-saint role was reaching its most complete expressions, traditional institutions and traditional authority within the Jewish community were seriously threatened. Under the banner of the humanistic enlightenment which swept Western Europe in the eighteenth and nineteenth centuries, the individual Jew was given political and civil equality. The semi-autonomous status which the Jewish community had possessed for well over one thousand years, slowly but surely disintegrated. Jewish courts lost compulsory, and finally voluntary, jurisdiction over disputes between Jews; taxing power and other governmental functions were taken from the leaders of the Jewish community. Moreover, the capitalist revolution offered large numbers of individual Jews unprecedented economic possibilities; it also provided to sizeable portions of the Jewish community close contact with the values and norms of the bourgeois enlightenment.

The Emancipation, as the impact upon the Jewish community of the concatenation of the forces of humanistic enlightenment and capitalist revolution has come to be called,[6] posed a very serious problem to its religious specialist. Partly motivated by a desire to adjust Jewish tradition to the new science and humanism and partly spurred on by the wish to be accepted as social equals by other members of society, large numbers of members of the Jewish community began to question the structure of rabbinism and its most significant practitioner, the rabbinic scholar-saint. To this portion of the community traditional Jewish values, law, custom, ritual, and conduct became embarrassing, irritating, parochial, and irrational. The scholar-saint, who intimately knew and lived in accordance with this vast body of sacred rules, now became the object of much adverse criticism. As a result, the scholar-saint, the key figure in rabbinism, began to lose his prestige, his influence and his traditional functions in the Jewish community. It was thus that the rabbi came to face the problem of loss of authority.

Rabbinic roles in the United States have been created and defined under continuing conditions of emancipation. Thus the focus of our discussion concerning the contemporary rabbi will be the various ways in which he—as a religious specialist—is coping with the problem of the loss of authority. Viewing the rabbinic roles as a relationship between functions, authority, and a system of values, we shall present a detailed description of these elements as they have reference to the synagogue, the Jewish community, and to the non-Jewish community.

Our empirical investigation of the contemporary rabbi assumed that the "natural" classifications of Orthodox, Reform, and Conservative, as used in the American Jewish community, are basic data in connection with the rabbinate. Accordingly, we selected a stratified random sample of the rabbinate in a large American city. Our universe consisted of 162 ordained rabbis—30 Reform, 28 Conservative, and 102 Orthodox. Some twenty-five of the Orthodox were faculty members of a local seminary, and we treated them as a separate unit. In all, thirty-four rabbis were interviewed: eighteen Orthodox (two of whom were on the seminary staff), 8 Reform, and 8 Conservative. Interviews with the rabbis averaged from one and one-half to two and one-half hours, although there was a range from one-half hour to eight hours. A wire recorder was used for most interviews, and both authors were present and took an active part in the interview.[7]

Our study discloses that the rabbis within the three denominations are structurally organized and ideologically oriented so that for many purposes the denominational classification *is* useful in describing the American rabbinate. However, from the viewpoint of our central problem, namely, the way in which the American rabbinate has attempted to cope with the loss of authority, seven rabbinic roles emerge: (1) the Traditional rabbi, (2) the Free-Lance rabbi, (3) the Modern Orthodox rabbi, (4) the Intellectual Reform rabbi, (5) the Social Reformer rabbi, (6) the Traditionalistic Reform rabbi, and (7) the Conservative rabbi. Roles 1-3 are exercised by Orthodox rabbis, roles 4-6 by Reform rabbis. Role differentiation in the Conservative rabbinate was not extensive enough to warrant more than a single category.

The seven rabbinic roles will each be presented in turn, and we shall demonstrate that there is a pronounced development toward a common rabbinic role—one in which the professional aspires to scholar-saint status but incorporates functions and values new to the role as it was performed by the rabbi prior to Emancipation.

§ *The Traditional Rabbi*

We shall initiate our discussion with the Traditional rabbi, for it is from his role that the others emerge both historically and logically. In common with the other Orthodox rabbinic roles, the Traditional rabbi places a positive value in maintaining the totality of Jewish life as it was practiced prior to Emancipation. Unlike any of his colleagues, however, the Traditional rabbi is striving to maintain intact the scholar-saint rabbinic role as it was practiced in Eastern Europe.

The Traditional rabbi comes from some part of Eastern Europe where he was often rabbi for an entire Jewish community. Having left his native land when he was already middle-aged, he may be found today in what used to be the heart of the ghetto of our large American cities, an old man at the head of a dwindling congregation. Bearded, wearing the traditional long, black, gabardine robe of the Talmudic scholar, still most at home in the Yiddish tongue, he remains as much as possible in the role of the rabbi of the Old Country. Unable to cope with conditions of the New World, unwilling to swerve from his Orthodoxy, uncertain and dismayed as to how the traditional community is to be maintained, his view of the future of American Jewry and of the rabbinate is dim indeed. One such rabbi expressed the impossibility of his position as follows:

A young man came to me about twenty-six or twenty-seven years old, asking me to make an influence for him to get a *shul* [congregation]. I told him, "I give you advice, don't be a rabbi. Why? What you say if I give you my position. I go to my *shul* and give you the position of rabbi in my *shul*. I do you a big favor, yes? I tell you that I kill you. Why?" I tell him this way. "I am fifty-eight years old, the baby in my congregation is sixty-eight. How long can that exist? Ten years more, twelve years more—how long that can exist?" I said, "You are now twenty-six years—twelve years to have a *shul* and then you're thirty-eight, and by thirty-eight they'll throw you away."

The future looks even darker when this man recalls his prestige and authority in the Old Country:

A rabbi is good to be if you have the correct authority. The authority has been broken. A rabbi like in the old home, a rabbi for the town, we knew his word was law. We knew that the people must obey the rabbi, and if they have a *shaleh* [ritual question], to ask the rabbi; if they have a milk pot and it get mixed up then with the meat dishes, they needed the rabbi. Or it occurs an argument between some people, and the rabbi should decide; or in the smaller towns the rabbi helped build; he was in everything. He taught the people and learned with them in the morning, in the evening, and on *Shabbos* [the Sabbath]. The rabbi felt that he was needed and he was leader and he was satisfied with his position. They needed me and I they. But take a look at America—they are lost . . . their position, their correct position doesn't exist. It's that way throughout the country. Satisfaction is at a minimum.

The meager salary of the Traditional rabbi is indication enough that his feelings on this matter are founded on bitter experience. The Traditional rabbi receives a salary of $1,200 to $1,500 a year from the congregation.[8] This is augmented by monetary gifts and perquisites in connection with priestly functions, i.e., officiating at such ceremonies as Bar Mitzvahs, at marriages, and at burials. His income totals between $2,500 and $4,000.

Further illustration of the frustration and impotency of the Traditional rabbi is the extent to which he changes positions. It is not unusual for the Traditional rabbi to have held six positions by the time he is sixty years old. A few Traditional rabbis, despairing of ever finding a position which will suit them, attempt to form their own congregations and to operate the synagogue as a private business.

Quite frequently the Traditional rabbi finds himself at odds with his congregants, upon whom—it must be remembered—he is dependent for the renewal of his contract. His lay people may want to introduce changes which the Reform and Conservative groups have popularized. Family pews with men and women sitting together (a clear violation of Orthodox custom), and a late Friday night service (suspect because there is no precedent for it), are the major foci of dissension. One Traditional rabbi tells us how he felt about such a dispute:

I was against this [introduction of family pews and the late Friday night service]. After all I am an Orthodox rabbi. I said that things should be as they ought to be.

The lay people criticized him for being an "old-fashioned rabbi"; he felt he was just a "job-holder" without influence, without standing:

They gave me wages and that's all. They took in a lot of money but they would never give more to the Rabbi. Once in a while they threw me something. That's the way it is to be a rabbi in America.

Despite the fact that the functions of the traditional scholar-saint are no longer deemed valuable or desirable by the Jewish community and even though many of the functions of the scholar-saint have been taken over by state and secular agencies, the Traditional rabbi is unwilling, or perhaps unable, to change his functions. In response to the question of what he thought were the rabbi's most important functions, a Traditional rabbi gave us the following summary of his functions within the synagogue:

His most important job? First, he must observe prayer, and every morning and evening he must be in *shul*. Not only he must, but he is: "The beginning of wisdom is fear of the Lord." We must be clear. If the verse says that this is the most important job of the person, what's there to ask? If the ordinary Jew has this job, the rabbi certainly has this job: (pounding the table) "The beginning of wisdom is fear of the Lord."

First thing when he gets up in the morning he must go to *shul*. There a Jew asks him a question, 'Are the *teffilin* [phylacteries] any good?' There he is asked a question, "How should the services be conducted?" And there they ask the *rov* [rabbi] about a question in the house. There they find the *rov*. A Jew after *davening* [praying] comes in and asks a question about a chicken; maybe he has found a flaw in the bellybutton. Is the chicken *kosher* or is the chicken *tref* [non-kosher]? Before evening the *rov* must learn with the congregation. He sits and learns with them and observes that the services begin on time. *Mincha* [the afternoon service] you must not *daven* late, *Mariv* [the evening service] you must not *daven* early. They obey the *rov*. . . . Naturally, this is his job. And if two persons have an argument, it is the *rov's* job to make peace . . . they seek a judge, a law of Torah; if they don't go to the court they come to the *rov*. Of course in America they don't come so often, but when they don't come to the court they come to the rabbi. . . . The next thing he must *Mussir* them; that is, [he should instruct them that] they should behave correctly in the home, correctly in the family, behave correctly among people, and with God they certainly should behave correctly. That is the *rov's* job.

The Traditional rabbi realizes that the Talmudic scholar is no longer respected by the community. While preaching was not a function of the scholar-saint and was introduced into the rabbinate by the Reform rabbi, some Traditional rabbis have introduced the weekly sermon in order to compete with the newer rabbinic roles. He feels, however, that this is an undesirable function, smacking of entertainment and performing, and laments the fact that it has become an important criterion in the evaluation of the rabbi:

The main thing here the rabbi gives speeches, he is supposed to; sometimes the speeches please the people and sometimes they don't. They go out and say, "He's no speaker." I have seen myself people leaving from some of the biggest rabbis, great Talmudic scholars and they say: "No speaker. He's no speaker. He's no rabbi." So what's he worth? Nothing.

The Traditional rabbi does perform both priestly and pastoral functions, officiating at Bar Mitzvahs, marriages, and burials, and providing counselling when asked. As suggested above, these functions are important because they provide a goodly portion of the Traditional rabbi's income. However, the Jew who has no synagogue affiliation but desires an

Orthodox rabbi for certain ceremonial occasions does not tend to call upon the Traditional rabbi for these services.

The Traditional rabbi has some function in the modern Jewish community. For example, as a member of the Union of Orthodox Rabbis of the United States and Canada—the loosely organized body of European-trained Orthodox rabbis serving Yiddish-speaking congregations—he does what he can to supervise *Kashrut* [the dietary laws] in the community. However, in the non-Jewish community he has practically no functions at all. In fact, he tries to isolate himself from it:

> There's a certain expression, *Hamavdil*. It means separation between Israel and the other nations. We don't believe in good-will movements. They're just breaking the last fence we have between us and the *goyim* [non-Jews]. But we Orthodox rabbis, the further we can keep apart from the *goyim*, that's how we should separate ourselves.

With fewer and fewer people coming to his congregation for daily services, less and less demand for him to judge ritual problems or disputes between individuals, the Traditional rabbi claims little in the way of influencing his flock. There *are* Traditional rabbis who claim to have some influence in ritual matters in the synagogue. One rabbi stated that he at least had control of his pulpit:

> I've always allowed anybody to use the pulpit. There is only one time I haven't. On the second day of *Rosh Hashonah* [the New Year Holiday] they wanted a Reform rabbi to speak. I said he had nothing to do with the second day of *Rosh Hashonoh*. [The Reform group observe only the first day of *Rosh Hashonoh*.] If he wants to come like anyone else that's all right.

Another Traditional rabbi said that he had no control over the religious life of his members but that he thought that he might influence them to give charity:

> If I say anything about religion they won't listen, they won't obey. You know I have influence with lots and lots of people but only so far as it can go. I can give an influence if I tell them to give to charity, they will give; only if I tell them to hold the *Shabbos*, they won't hear me.

We asked the same rabbi about *Kashrut*:

> *Kashrut* they obey. At least they say so. If it's the truth or not, who knows? America's a free land. If they want to, they obey. Strength we don't have, strength that we should say, "You must. . . ."

All Traditional rabbis agree that in that which they conceive to be the most crucial area of Jewish life—observance of the Sabbath—they had very little influence:

> In my city in Europe if someone opened up [a store] on Friday night—that is, he was open ten minutes late—I went out and made him close up. Here all my *balabotim* [influential lay leaders], all my officers, have their stores open. I don't say anything to them because I know that they won't listen. I don't say nothing. I know the people don't listen to me. . . . I can't say what I should say.

Should I say, "Why do you keep your stores open on the *shabbos*? Close the stores!" they'll laugh me out of *shul*.

To add to his despair there is the fact that the Traditional rabbi feels what little influence he has left is being taken away from him by the Conservative movement:

> If they [the Conservative group] hadn't broken us we could hope the future would be better. They have laid waste the land. They stand on the side which breaks all holiness. They are to us worse than Reform. Why? Everybody knows what the Reform movement stands for. Conservative is half-Kosher, as they say, and thus is worse than the Reform. A Jew from us, a member of my *shul*, won't go to the Reform. They are tearing out the Jewishness, they are tearing out the Torah, and they are making out of it everything. . . . Do we go to them and take from them? We don't run to destroy their *Shulen*.

Thus we are forced to conclude that most Traditional rabbis are unable to exert much influence over the Jewish community. And yet, many Jews —although no longer Sabbath observers and even though they have abandoned most of the Orthodox ritual and belief—still refer to themselves as Orthodox Jews. If they are not religious, they at least want their rabbi to be so. The Traditional rabbi senses this: "You know the psychology of the people is that religion belongs to the rabbi." We asked this man: "You mean they are paying the rabbi to be *frum* [pious]?" "Yes, yes," he answered, nodding his head. "They let me be *frum*, and I let them be free." His only hope is the age-old hope of the Jew in time of suffering and distress—the faith in salvation through a redeemer. He concluded: "Let us hope there will come the time that Messiah will come."

§ *The Free-Lancer*

The Free-Lancer receives his name because he is the rabbi who, having *s'micha* [ordination], generally from an American *Yeshivah* [seminary], is rarely affiliated in a rabbinic capacity with any synagogue, school, or other arm of the Jewish community. He makes his living by selling certain rabbinic services to the large number of Jews who have no formal membership in a synagogue, or who are members of congregations or prayer-circles which have no rabbi. This activity has been labeled by the rabbinate as "free-lancing."

The Free-Lancer is generally a firm believer in the Orthodox tradition. He is, however, more acculturated than the Traditional rabbi, for he speaks English and wears modern clothing. He may or may not have a beard. But even more important than these outward dissimilarities, the Free-Lancer is not attempting to reproduce the old-world Jewish community in order that he may be its scholar-saint. In fact, he can best be distinguished from the Traditional rabbi in that he conceives of his role in the rabbinate as merely a business. His purpose is not community service, but the sale of *services;* his functions consist in performing religious rites for a fee. As one Free-Lancer put it:

Actually, I'm a specialist in weddings, funerals and burials, and dedicating monuments. I deal in intangible commodities. I feel that when I officiate at a wedding I am giving them something tangible. If I buy or sell goods, it's the same as dedicating a monument. I feel like I'm giving them something for their money.

Along with the ceremonies mentioned by the above respondent, the Free-Lancer may oftentimes be found at the cemetery anticipating an opportunity to be of service by chanting the prescribed ritual prayers on those occasions when it is customary for close relatives to pay their respects to the dead. He may even perform circumcisions. Sometimes, the Free-Lancer will take the pulpit of a small congregation to deliver a Bar Mitzvah address or even for a holiday period. The typical Free-Lancer, however, is careful to accept only those rabbinic positions which are temporary and do not involve communal responsibility.

Like the Traditional rabbi, he takes the scholar-saint as his model of what the rabbi should be; he rationalizes his refusal to accept more permanent responsibility in terms of the disregard and disrespect now manifested toward the rabbi. He is even more impressed with the futility and impotence of the American rabbinate than the Traditional rabbi:

> No matter how big a scholar you are, you have to cater to the whims of the *balabotim,* the big shots. The congregation has no consideration for their rabbi. They hired him and they do what they want with him.

Most Free-Lancers are quite obviously embarrassed and ashamed of their role. This is evident from the large number who refused to be interviewed, some of them with the statement: "You don't want me in your study." They realize that they are bringing disrepute to the rabbinate, and while they will not give up their free-lancing, they do not want their behavior to be reported. We asked one Free-Lancer whether opportunism was a problem in the rabbinate. He replied: "I'll refrain from answering that question because I feel that I am an opportunist." Pressed for an explanation of this remark, he said:

> I told you at the beginning of this interview that I'm not a rabbi, and I'm actually not the man to be interviewed. Certainly you should not judge the rabbinate by me. I'm the absolute exception from which no thesis should be constructed. The rabbis should not be judged by what I am. I'm not a practicing rabbi. I've made my living from free-lancing, from officiating at weddings, funerals and monuments. I'm not a rabbi.

The Free-Lancer phrases his willingness to remain in his role in terms of his inability to make a living in any other way. One of the more renowned Free-Lancers of the community told us that he had been in dozens of businesses, but that he could never make a go of it: "I'd save up a few dollars (from free-lancing) and then lose it in business and start over again to save, only to lose it again in business."

The Free-Lancer makes a good deal more money than the Traditional rabbi. One respondent told us that he had been offered $125 a week to raise funds for one of the Orthodox organizations, but he refused because ". . . they never paid enough, and anyway I didn't want to stay in public life." While this rabbi still maintains that he would like to give up free-lancing, he has by now given himself over exclusively to it. He declared in a satisfied manner that he had ". . . built up a large following."

Thus the Free-Lancer is essentially the rabbi who has made a "busi-ness" of religious ceremonies. He is the Traditional rabbi who holds no formal position, but engages in those aspects of rabbinics which a disinte-grating community still values.[9] Unwilling to suffer the hardship and dis-respect involved in attempting to regain the authority of the traditional scholar-saint rabbi, the Free-Lancer has turned his back on synagogue and communal responsibility. Whatever influence he might achieve through his officiating at weddings or funerals is exploited only for the particular event. Although he is aware that his activities may not be looked upon with favor by certain elements of the community, he is able to live with this criticism by defining his role as that of an expert technician providing services for a stipulated fee.

§ *The Modern Orthodox Rabbi*

Our discussion thus far has dealt with Orthodox rabbis who have been unable or are unwilling to cope with the problem of rabbinic authority posed by the Emancipation. Despite the fact that the community no longer values or requires the traditional rabbinic scholar-saint, the Tradi-tional rabbi refuses to compromise the role either by changing religious practices or by introducing new functions into the rabbinic role. The presence of the Free-Lancer only adds to the evidence of his failure. Yet an Orthodox community consisting of those who abide by traditional prac-tices and believe in traditional doctrines does exist in the United States. In the past three decades there has been developing a Modern Orthodox movement which appears to be taking over the task of rebuilding Ortho-doxy. Whatever its origins, this Modern Orthodox movement is now in the hands of the Modern Orthodox rabbi and it is to this rabbinic role that we turn our attention.

Perhaps the most appropriate way to begin our discussion is to indi-cate what the term "Modern Orthodox" does *not* mean. "Modern Ortho-dox" does not have reference to changes in ritual or belief. Although many Modern Orthodox rabbis have had a secular education, they are still staunch adherents to traditional Judaism. The Modern Orthodox rabbi be-lieves that the vast body of custom and law are sacred and should not be altered:

My faith is an intensely Orthodox faith and always has been and to the best of my knowledge it hasn't wavered. I am a believer in everything I understand that Orthodox Judaism expects us to believe.

While the term "modern" in this context does not indicate any ideological deviation, it does mean that the Modern Orthodox rabbi has been willing to assume many of the activities and functions introduced by the Reform and Conservative rabbi. Appearing on the American scene after the Reform and Conservative rabbi, he is aware that they have been able to attract a large number of persons with Orthodox backgrounds because of their "modern approach" and the new-found dignity in the Protestantization of rabbinic functions.* He realizes that the Traditional rabbi as well as the devout Orthodox layman are critical of this emulation and suspect him of introducing changes in tradition. To this the Modern Orthodox rabbi replies that the changes do not touch "traditional Judaism," and that he sees in them his only hope of attracting the Jewish masses back to traditional Judaism. In order to compete with the other religious specialists in the Jewish community, he has accepted the Protestantization of the rabbinic role by introducing preaching, pastoral, and where necessary priestly and community relations functions. From the viewpoint of understanding him as a religious specialist, this constitutes his modernity.

Superficially he has other modern attributes. There is little in the appearance of the Modern Orthodox rabbi to indicate his close kinship to the Traditional rabbi. He is bilingual, speaking English and Yiddish with equal fluency. He dresses in a manner befitting any professional man, and he is clean-shaven. His Hebrew education is extensive. Many have also received advanced secular training, and it is not uncommon to find a Modern Orthodox rabbi with a Master's degree in education as well as his *s'micha*. He is connected with the Seminary or some other educational body, or he has moved with the bulk of middle-class Jewry into the higher status areas of the city where he is active in building up synagogues and Jewish schools.

While the training which the Modern Orthodox rabbi received in his Yeshivah is more closely akin to that of the traditional scholar-saint than any of the other contemporary rabbis, he realizes very acutely that the Traditional rabbi's attempt to perform in this role has led to less and less rabbinic influence and authority. Aware of the myriad and powerful forces operating to militate against the kind of Jewish community he desires, he has given up scholarship for the all-important task of organizing educational institutions. Here is the statement of one of the top leaders in this movement, high up in Seminary life:

> One of our graduates who has failed to set up a good Hebrew school I would denounce all over the place. If he isn't studying, I might call him in and prod him into studying; but I would feel if he's got a good Hebrew school and a good set-up in the community, doing things for young people and creating a dignified Jewish service, even if he hasn't been studying much, I still say he's doing a good job.

The Modern Orthdox rabbi, in relegating scholarship to a secondary posi-

---

* See the material on the Reform rabbi for a full discussion of the Protestantization of rabbinic functions.

tion and stressing organizational and administrative tasks, has followed the lead of the Conservative rabbi:

> I spend a great deal of my time in administrative work because I am interested to see that certain projects get carried out. Whether it is in the construction of a fence around a children's play yard or a ritual matter, I like to feel that I have been a part of the activity and give the best advice I have to offer.

Administrative functions are increased by the number of activities the rabbi organizes or is able to attach to the synagogue. The synagogue often tends to take on the appearance of a community center, and as one Rabbi proudly boasted when he described his former congregation: "We had youth groups and a Sunday school; there were study groups for the Hadassah, B'nai B'rith and a lecture forum; volunteer war work, clothing for overseas—we handled them all." The importance of the administrative functions is to be found in the words of a young man who left the rabbinate precisely because he was unwilling to engage in all the activities that the successful Modern Orthodox rabbi feels is a necessary part of his functioning:

> As one of my members said, a small synagogue is like a general store. You have to be not only a preacher and teacher but must get new members and ads for the ad book and raise funds. Maybe you don't want me to talk about this now but I think the province of the rabbi is spiritual. I don't mix in the business end of the congregation and I don't want anyone mixing in the spiritual realm of the synagogue. The role of the rabbi is the spiritual end of the synagogue. I left when they asked me to get ads.

Every one of the Modern Orthodox rabbis interviewed looked upon education as his pet project. The respondent quoted below was planning for a large day school which will serve his entire area:

> I spend a great deal of my time in educational activities. I've built up a large day school here and I consider it one of my real accomplishments. Right now I'm working on the construction of a community day school with a neighboring synagogue.

The Modern Orthodox rabbi frequently behaves in the manner of the traditional scholar-saint. All Modern Orthodox rabbis attend morning and evening services, and all of them have instituted adult learning between the afternoon and evening services.

In our discussion of the Reform and Conservative rabbi we shall give a detailed description of the functions of many contemporary rabbis. Suffice it to say here that the Modern Orthodox rabbi has become an administrator of a synagogue, a director of youth activities, a pastor, a preacher, and a teacher. He marries, buries, and officiates at Bar Mitzvahs. In truth, he will perform any traditional or modern ministerial function which will bring people into his synagogue and schools.

Furthermore, it is true that the Modern Orthodox rabbi has introduced some changes in the services, again in order to compete with his Conservative and Reform colleagues. For example, the Modern Orthodox rabbi now has a late Friday night service and a weekly sermon in English. Unlike the Reform and many of the Conservative synagogues, this does not mean that the traditional service held before sundown is completely eliminated. It merely means he has added a "service" consisting of collective singing, a sermon, and perhaps a social hour with refreshments to the traditional service in the hope that he will be able to attract those Jews who have Orthodox leanings but would not attend traditional services because of their own lack of training as well as a lack of Protestant-like synagogue decorum.

With the increased number of functions as well as the utilization of new techniques, it is not surprising that the Modern Orthodox rabbi has achieved greater influence in the synagogue than the Traditional rabbi:

> I would say that the rabbi in the synagogue naturally carries a lot of weight. Obviously he is the center of authority unless he is an absolutely incompetent person.

However, this picture of increasing authority should not obscure the fact that the Modern Orthodox rabbi is not always the recipient of respect; he is not always able to accomplish his program. One rabbi, who has been in his present synagogue for thirteen years, put it bluntly: "I think only a fool can talk it into himself that he exerts an influence on the lives of his members." Another rabbi, who has left the synagogue field to work as an administrator in Orthodox education, was of the opinion that the influence of the rabbi embraced only ritual matters. "Besides ritual matters," he said, "that is, social matters, financial matters, even ideological matters, the rabbi has no authority."

His influence *is* being felt, however, in wider and wider areas. Many rabbis believe that they have even had an influence on the actual day-to-day lives of their members. One rabbi, for example, told us:

> I feel that I have helped to make people more charitable; that I've made a number of Jewish people more religious. I feel that I have helped to make a number of Jewish citizens more civic-conscious, without myself being always in the thick of civic activity. I feel that there are young men and young women in many parts of the country who understand their Judaism and Jewish life better because of my ministry and teaching. I know specifically of homes that are *kosher* that might not have been had I not been their rabbi, or somebody of my type. And I feel that there have been personal relationships established that account for more generous giving to charity, more intensive interest in Jewish life, and more devotion to many of our Jewish principles.

Within the Jewish community the Modern Orthodox rabbi devotes most of his time to the educational institutions. Either as professional educator or as active participant in drives to build more educational facilities such as Talmud Torahs, all-day schools, and Yeshivahs, he hopes that these instrumentalities will ultimately produce members for his movement. He may also be active in the Mizrachi, the Orthodox branch of the Zionist movement. While the Modern Orthodox rabbi is competing with the Reform and Conservative rabbi for congregants, like them he is aware that the powerful lay organizations within the Jewish community represent a competing influence:

> The Jewish Welfare Board . . . began (by) helping people in prison, which is the rabbi's job, and the armed forces, which is also the rabbi's job—as far as chaplains are concerned. Ostensibly . . . they engaged the chaplains and they recommended the chaplains, but really they began to make the chaplain a functionary of the Jewish Welfare Board. Now the Jewish Welfare Board has extended to the Center business. The Center also became a competitive force for the synagogue. The Center at first limited itself to recreational activities, then they took in adult education which is mostly rabbinical work . . . some of them have Hebrew schools. Some of them begin indirectly to decide religious matters. They don't say that openly but they do. And when one studies the survey that was made by . . . this fellow Janowsky you can see what's happened to the Jewish Welfare Board system in America.

With respect to the wider community there are some Modern Orthodox rabbis who believe — with the Traditional rabbis — that the Jewish community should not have any unnecessary contact with the non-Jewish world. There are those who see the necessity of participating in the wider community, but are too busily engaged within the Jewish community. In a small town, where there is no other rabbi, the Modern Orthodox type may serve as "ambassador to the Gentile world." This consists in delivering public addresses, participating in Armistice and Memorial Day ceremonies, and working for the Community Chest. One Modern Orthodox rabbi was a member of a team of clergy sent by the National Conference of Christians and Jews to preach good-will sermons in the South. A few have served as chaplains during the last war. On the whole, however, the Modern Orthodox rabbi has been much more concerned with his own particular synagogue and the associations in the Jewish community — all to the end of rebuilding a traditional community.

Despite many problems the Modern Orthodox rabbi looks toward the future with confidence. The following is typical:

> I am one of the optimists of Judaism . . . I think we are losing more and more of the masses from Judaism. That is, there are fewer and fewer people who keep *Shabbos* today than a generation ago, fewer people that go to a *mikvah* [ritual bath]; but we are gaining a more intensive and more intelligent group in smaller circles that will give us a more dynamic type of Judaism. We may be smaller in numbers, there may be more assimilation in the larger group, but there will be a more intensive Jewish life and a more intelligent Orthodox life in the smaller groups. And then, ultimately, I think from them will be a new growth.

In summary, then, the role of the Modern Orthodox rabbi centers about his desire to rebuild a traditional Jewish community. He conceives of the role of the rabbi in somewhat the same manner as the Traditional rabbi, but has introduced modifications in that role in order to regain the influence and authority it once possessed. Although he may consider the ultimate basis of his authority as resting in knowing and living the Law as the scholar-saint of old, his present emphasis on organization has led him to desert the traditional function of that role in favor of administrative tasks, preaching and pastoral work.

The Modern Orthodox rabbi has a greater influence in the synagogue than the Traditional rabbi and can be compared favorably with the Conservative and Reform rabbi in this regard. However, this does not say that his influence is very great. It is merely on the increase. He has little influence outside his own synagogue unless he heads a school or teaches in a Yeshivah. His influence in the wider community is probably negligible. His movement and his role are too young to make an accurate prediction of the ultimate form it will assume. It appears likely, however, that if any American rabbi is to reinstitute the scholar-saint rabbi of Eastern Europe, it will be the Modern Orthodox rabbi.

§ *The Reform Rabbinate*

During the early period of Western European Enlightenment and Emancipation, a new religious specialist — the Reform rabbi — appeared in the Jewish community. In direct contrast to the Traditional rabbi, the Reform rabbi explicitly rejected the rabbinic role of scholar-saint as it had been practiced in Eastern Europe. Arising in large part as a reaction to the problematic nature of rabbinic authority, the Reform rabbi participated in the formulation of a radically new value system and assumed a configuration of functions completely alien to the traditional scholar-saint role. We have chosen to call the changes in rabbinic functions introduced by the Reform rabbi the *Protestantization of rabbinic functions* because to a large degree it involved incorporating some of the major functions of the Protestant ministry. Preaching, and certain priestly functions such as conducting synagogue services, confirmations, marriages, burials, pastoral work, and certain types of community work are some of the functions new to the rabbinic role. In this section we shall discuss the Reform rabbinical role as it appears after more than a century of development in the United States.

Although the three contemporary types of Reform rabbis — the Intellectual Reform rabbi, the Social Reformer rabbi, and the Traditionalistic Reform rabbi — all differ in their claims for authority as religious specialists, they engage in similar functions within the synagogue. By and large, they have similar activities in the Jewish community and the non-Jewish community. We shall, therefore, first present a description of the functions held in common by the Reform rabbinate, following which the types will be distinguished.

The Reform rabbi presents a sharp contrast to most Orthodox rabbis in background, education and appearance. More likely than not, the Reform rabbi comes from a second or third generation middle- or upper-middle-class Jewish family. Apart from his seminary training, he usually has a limited

Jewish education. His secular education, however, has been extensive; it is not unlikely for him to hold a graduate degree in philosophy or one of the social sciences. His conversational language is exclusively English; whatever Yiddish he might know is not apparent. His dress and appearance is that of the successful professional or business man. He presently occupies a pulpit in a Reform Temple in a wealthy Jewish neighborhood, and he earns a salary of between $7,500 and $25,000 a year. In addition, the Reform rabbi generally receives in the form of perquisites and gifts from one-third to one-half again as much as his base salary. Gifts ranging from a box of cigars to a new automobile or a paid trip to Israel are not uncommon.

Although preaching had never been an important function of the traditional rabbinic scholar-saint, it is probably the most important single function of the Reform rabbi. "The importance of preaching," writes a Reform rabbi, "is felt just as strongly today as it was in the early days of the Reform movement — if not more so. . . . We must admit with Phillipson that 'the rabbi stands and falls in his pulpit work.' "[10] Since the sermon occupies a central position in the program of the Reform rabbi, it takes up a good part of his time and thought:

> The sovereign place given over to the sermon, from the early history of Reform until some twenty years ago still haunts us today. The sermon not only hovers over our day's work and sullenly regards every other duty as an intruder —but completely pre-empts our Thursdays and Fridays.[11]

Some Reform rabbis have come to regard the sermon as a "headache" because of the amount of time it consumes:

> Preaching, due to no fault of my own, has been for a long time the center of synagogue service. I found it that way when I entered it, you see. Now if you would ask if I prefer to eliminate it, certainly I would say that three-fourths of the headaches of the average rabbi would be removed if he wouldn't have to preach. If you would ask me whether I would rather not preach I would answer: "Certainly I would rather not because I have to perspire over sermons. I spend hours and hours first of all gathering material over a long period of time and then I have to write it out meticulously, which takes maybe six hours, and then to memorize it, which takes anywhere from three to five or six hours."

The content of the Reform rabbi's sermon covers a wide range of subjects: social and economic problems, racial and labor problems, the latest novel or play, psychiatry, philosophy, politics, and the care and feeding of children have all been discussed from the Reform pulpit. One rabbi informed us that he had spoken on Arthur Miller's *Death of a Salesman* on seven successive weeks.

Some Reform rabbis conceive the sermon as an instrument in shaping the moral lives of their congregants. These rabbis believe that only by means of inspirational themes can the sermon be effective in enhancing their influence as religious specialists. However, while our sample is admittedly small, it would be fair to say that the majority of the Reform rabbis we spoke with conceived of the pulpit as a lecture platform, and the sermon as a learned discourse only incidentally related to Jewish values. These "lecturers" believe that the rabbi can influence people through the sermon if the opinions expressed in it are "scholarly or scientifically arrived at through reading and study." One rabbi feels that his job is to analyze issues from the pulpit: ". . . to examine them thoughtfully and objectively and then take a stand, explain why he has taken that stand, give the reasons as forcefully and as logically as possible, and then leave it up to the congregation." While not all Reform rabbis would take as exaggerated a position as that expressed by the remark of the one respondent we present below, by and large they would agree with his central theme:

I believe in scholarship in the pulpit and I make that clear to my congregation. Anyone who wants sentiment or driveling hogwash will have to go someplace else. This may sound immodest but in a small town it would be a tragedy for my kind of approach to the rabbinate. I would have to worry about all the Mrs. Goldschmidts, not that this should not be done, but you would have to talk to these people on the fourth-grade level. . . . The point is when I give a talk, it is the university approach. My methodology and training permit me to do this.

Whether "lecturer" or inspirer, however, the Reform rabbi, like all rabbis, conceives of himself as a teacher. Many say that teaching is their primary function. "My first duty as far as the rabbinate is concerned," one Reform rabbi told us, "is that of teacher." Preaching, discussion groups, adult classes, Sunday school—all are part of these teaching functions. Although the Reform rabbi rarely teaches in the religious school, he takes it as his responsibility to see to it that the teachers are doing their job, and that the curriculum is what he wants it to be: "The rabbi certainly ought to show a major interest in his school even if he has professionals running it. I think the purpose of the school and the whole atmosphere of the school are his responsibility."[12]

Prior to Emancipation, the Jews had been a "nation of priests." That is, there was no theological obligation to obtain the services of a religious specialist for the vast bulk of religious ceremonies, and the high percentage of the population who were familiar with Jewish rituals prevented it from becoming a practical necessity. The Emancipation has made it obligatory for the rabbi to assume these functions, for his congregants no longer are able to carry on these activities. Thus, the Reform rabbi conducts the synagogue service. Aside from his sermon, he selects the prayers and leads responsive reading. Like other rabbis he also performs various priestly functions, among them those of confirming, marrying, and burying. The Reform rabbi is articulate on the technical problems raised by these *rites de passage*. He is very aware of the mundane arrangements which must "go right" in order to make his appearance there a success. In these activities he often seizes upon the opportunity to enhance the influence of the rabbinic role. In this connection one Reform rabbi frankly stated the following:

Well, the more young people I marry and they come into contact with me and the Temple, when they are ready to join a Temple, they will join my Temple more likely than someone else's. I'll be rather cold-blooded about it. I think you've got to think about building up good-will. I am thinking of the future.

These priestly functions of conducting religious and ceremonial rites blend into another function of the Reform rabbi. This is the pastoral function, an important area for the Reform rabbi. Pastoral visitation and counseling are both part of this function. Pastoral visitation includes visiting and comforting the sick and bereaved, paying visits on special occasions, such as birthdays, and finally, making "social calls."

The rabbi as pastor is with his people in their hour of sorrow — he must seek out the aged, the sick, and the bereaved:

> I feel that the biggest service the rabbi can render is his ability to go into the home of the sick man or the mourner's house and to bring help to people when they are in sorrow; when they feel that the world of tragedy has fallen about them.

He is also with them in their hour of joy — anniversaries, house-warmings, Bar Mitzvahs, confirmation receptions. As one respondent told us: "This gives the Rabbi a chance to identify himself with the family in their time of joy and honor. I also go to a home when they have some special birthday such as the seventieth. I visit couples when a baby is born." During grief situations the Reform rabbi feels that he may be able "to shape the repressed traditionalism of the adult generation" and that perhaps he will be able "to explain to the Vassar grandchildren the meaning of these traditions." During condolence calls he acts as spiritual adviser, personal confidant, and business consultant. Many rabbis have felt that their influence with congregants has been enhanced on such occasions. One rabbi, for example, although dubious of the effectiveness of preaching felt that: "When you have visited a sick room or you have taken somebody's hand, you feel as you go out that he is happier and feels better, especially when you learn later that you have meant a lot to him."

Almost every Reform rabbi we interviewed did some kind of counselling. In fact, most rabbis usually set aside a certain part of the day for this work. As pastoral counsellor the rabbi stands somewhere between the psychiatrist and personal confidant. He tries to handle less severe problems himself, sending the more serious cases to professional psychiatrists:

> The rabbi should be attuned to and keep up with psychological literature and be sufficiently trained in psychological and psychiatric problems to know when his influence as a minister ceases and the need for a trained clinical psychiatrist arises.

Some rabbis place great emphasis on the counselling functions, and one went so far as to define himself as a lay analyst:

> I am now one of the best-known lay practitioners in the field of personal problems. . . . I've reconciled more couples who were going into divorce and sent more people to psychiatrists than any other minister in town.

The Reform temple with a membership which may total as high as 1,500 families, an annual budget often reaching into the hundreds of thousands of dollars, with a large staff and numerous committees, is a big business. The Reform rabbi has recognized that a considerable portion of his time must be devoted to the task of running a large-scale enterprise:

A large portion of each week is spent in the administration of the Temple itself. By that I mean attending to such matters as the proper operation of finances, seeing that the membership is kept up . . . being in touch with the Men's Club, the Sisterhood, the various youth organizations, and so on, and seeing that they are all functioning well.

Many Reform Temples have hired executive secretaries in an effort to relieve the rabbi of routine administrative tasks. Although the rabbi is fearful of letting administrative functions take up too much of his time, he realizes the necessity of being in on the functioning of the organization, of making sure that his point of view is carried out in the running of the synagogue:

During my first year here I was not on the Board and I made it an issue on renewing my contract that I was to be at Board Meetings. . . . I felt that a congregation, after all, has a policy-making group and that's the Board. And I felt that certainly the Rabbi who devotes his full time to the work of the congregation ought to have a voice in the making of its policy.

Outside of the synagogue the Reform rabbi has functions in both the Jewish and non-Jewish community. Within the Jewish community he participates in a variety of fraternal, charitable, and Zionist organizations. In these organizations he may serve only to render the benediction at the annual dinner, or he may take an active role in the group. While most rabbis feel that their rabbinic status offers them entrée to these organizations, they realize that outside their own synagogue they are unable to sustain their influence.

In the non-Jewish community the Reform rabbi tends chiefly to act as an ambassador to the Gentile community. This is especially true of the Reform rabbi in the smaller communities:

We have a term called "Ambassador to the *Goyim*." I would say that it is one of the most important functions of the rabbi. Jews stick out more in a small town because everybody knows what everybody does. I would say that on the whole in the smaller and medium-sized congregations I would think that the rabbis spend more time on public relations than they do in the large community, and I would expect that their congregants expect them to do it.

Many Reform rabbis, in connection with their ambassadorial functions, become involved in interfaith work. They may be members of the National Conference of Christians and Jews or of a local council of churches and synagogues, and may also exchange pulpits with Protestant ministers. Undoubtedly the rabbi who devotes a large part of his time to working in non-Jewish organizations and activities gains added respect and influence among his own congregants. One rabbi pointed out this relationship very clearly:

> I had a fantastic reputation in the community. One year I was given the medal for the most Outstanding Citizen. My congregation was very genuinely appreciative of my work. They showed this by attending Friday night services and by personal loyalty. They were very loyal to me. They felt that I had added dignity to their relationship with the larger community.

It should be noted that it is the Reform rabbi who has almost a monopoly of these ambassadorial functions; both the Conservative, and especially the Orthodox, rabbi are usually willing to let the Reform rabbi handle these functions. As one Orthodox rabbi stated, "Good relations between the Jews and the Christians we've left to the Reform rabbis."

§ *The Intellectual Reform Rabbi*

The Reform rabbi has met the question of the loss of rabbinic authority by deviating most radically from the traditional scholar-saint role. For the totality of rabbinism, the Reform movement substituted a conception of Judaism as a set of universalized values, in many ways indistinguishable from the general values and beliefs of liberal thought in modern Western society. Gone was the vast body of specific rules and rituals to be found in rabbinism and to which the rabbinic scholar-saint had been able to point as divine. The Reform rabbi sought to base his authority within the philosophies of rationalism, idealism, humanism, and in line with the scientific method. In this way he began the process whereby he was to substitute his claim for authority in terms of knowing and living a sacred law by a claim for authority in terms of his intellectual ability. In effect he sidestepped the problem of rabbinic authority; the authority he claimed was that of an intellectual.

This intellectual orientation is the central theme of the belief of the Reform rabbi. Thus, for example, when we asked a Traditional rabbi what kind of a faith he had, he stared at us, as if to say, "What kind of a question is that to ask of an Orthodox rabbi?" When pressed for an answer he stated simply that he believed in the Torah. The very different kind of reply given by three Reform rabbis to our questions is reproduced below:

> Faith is a leap from the known to the unknown. You can't make that leap till you've mastered the known. . . . Truth is dynamic and evolving; the best a man can do is search for it. The quest for truth, you know Lessing talked about that.
>
> I happen to have a definite philosophical point of view about religion. You see I have what I call the combination of the Kantian and Bergsonian conception of that sort of thing.
>
> To keep up his faith I think the rabbi has to constantly study, read, be posted on current events, not only political and economic, but intellectual, literary, philosophic. The rabbi has to be a student *par excellence,* and if he is gifted at being a creative student and writer so much the better.

That the Reform rabbi sees himself in an intellectual role comes out in a variety of ways. The Reform rabbi is rarely satisfied with the title "Rabbi." Those who have received doctorates in philosophy, political science, psychology, or other fields, refer to themselves as "Dr. Cohen, Rabbi." Recall again the Intellectual Reform rabbi's approach to preaching. It is instruction—the imparting of information. He is interested in "scholarship in the pulpit," in giving the sermon "the university approach." His function in the pulpit is to examine issues ". . . thoughtfully and objectively and then take a stand, explain why he has taken that stand, give reasons as forcefully and as logically as possible and then leave it up to the congregation." He is, in short, a Ph.D. in the pulpit. His functions in the wider community as consultant, arbitrator, lecturer and book-reviewer, are further expressions of the intellectual theme.

But what kind of authority does the rabbi as intellectual possess? One rabbi summed this up for us in one short sentence: "He has the authority to talk on any subject he masters." Thus, on the basis of his familiarity with and mastery of various fields of thought, because he has studied the philosophers and schooled himself in psychology, economics, sociology, history and education, the Intellectual Reform rabbi feels that he has the right to be listened to and that his opinions should be weighed carefully:

> The days of the rabbi laying down *ex cathedra* a position and having it blindly followed by his parishioners is over. The most a rabbi can do, I believe, when a moral issue arises is to analyze it from the pulpit or the printed word, examine it thoughtfully and objectively and then take a stand; explain why he has taken that stand, whether he favors something or opposes something, give the reasons as forcefully and as logically as possible and then leave it up to the congregation.

Although the Intellectual Reform role is the most characteristic type within the Reform rabbinate, the Social Reformer type and the Traditionalistic Reform type are also present. Both may be considered to some extent as reactions against the Intellectual type which sought to submerge Jewish values into a general body of universal values; both hope to find some *raison d'être* for the rabbi, some legitimation for his functions and some basis for his authority in the traditions of Judaism.

§ *The Social Reformer Rabbi*

The Social Reformer is oriented toward the realization and fulfillment of liberal democratic values in contemporary society. Consequently he is vitally concerned with the issues of good government, international problems, the condition of schools in the community, race relations, labor relations, and crime and delinquency. He attempts to link traditional Jewish values with liberal democratic values by calling upon the prophetic tradition of Judaism—that part of the Jewish tradition which perhaps more than any other part champions the values of social justice—to legitimate his fight for the fulfillment of democratic ideals. His goal in the synagogue is to bring his congregants to an awareness of the necessity—a necessity which he emphasizes as grounded in their tradition—of working for liberal causes. He conceives of the entire program of the synagogue in terms of the implementation of this goal. He also realizes that a program of this nature may revitalize the interest of the congregation, particularly that of the younger members, in their tradition, thereby enhancing his influence as a representative of that tradition:

> By exercising the teaching skill and patience necessary to link contemporary issues to our ancient traditions, the rabbi will accomplish much more than he can by merely using the pulpit as soapbox and the synagogue as a recruiting agency for each new cause. He does something for the tradition, of course. He makes it relevant and thus congenial to the young man mentally alert. He gives the incomparable ethic of Judaism the only homage worthy of its glory, the homage of realization. But he does much more for the cause of liberalism as well, as he ties these movements into the enduring values of history and gives them a prestige and motivation they could never have gained from the current winds of doctrine.

The Social Reformer, though oriented toward the general community, does not neglect the synagogue, for the synagogue is his reference point and an organizational base for his efforts in the field of social action.

When we come to the question of the kind of authority that the Social Reformer possesses, we must remember that he sees himself as a leader in both the Jewish community and the general community. He integrates his position and activities by insisting that the maintenance and fulfillment of the values and beliefs of the Jewish community are dependent upon the realization of the generalized liberal democratic values as well as the goals of the wider community. His authority in one is therefore inextricably bound up with his authority in the other.

§ *The Traditionalistic Reform Rabbi*

The Traditionalistic Reform rabbi type includes those Reform rabbis who wish to go even further than the Social Reformers in their return to Jewish traditions. This movement, as one Traditionalistic Reform rabbi described it, is ". . . in the direction of a re-assertion of Jewish culture . . . and toward traditional values and forms which the older Reform has repudiated." The use of traditional rituals in the synagogue is particularly evident:

> There is now a purposive desire and policy on the part of Reform to recapture and restore more and more the color and life of historic Judaism. Early Reform scorned Purim as a nationalistic Jewish festival; today Purim is reintroduced with a shortened *megillah* [the *Book of Esther*], prepared in scroll form. Early Reform discountenanced the *shofar* [ram's horn], and endeavored to substitute for it a cornet or an organ call; today the *shofar* is reappearing, albeit with a mouthpiece.

These changes have affected role conceptions. Thus one traditionally oriented Reform rabbi, in answer to the question of what he conceived his functions should be, replied:

I think the rabbinate has neglected an important phase of its function which is primary, and that function, of course, is the religious function in integrating our people more intimately into their lives as Jews, as religious and observant Jews, and as Jews who belong to—and I am going to use Kaplan's definition for the moment—to a "religious civilization." . . . We now have the opportunity and the climate in which to build a Jewish communal life which had been sorely neglected so far. . . . I also feel that the rabbinate must give more attention to the entire problem of organizing the Jewish community into a more integrated structure than it is now—a community in which the synagogue will play a vital role.

These rabbis are not only devoted to rebuilding the Jewish community about the synagogue, but in their search for a legitimate basis of authority they envision themselves returning eventually to a scholar-saint role (this, of course, does not mean that they wish to return to Orthodoxy). In this connection Rabbi Morton M. Berman has said that:

There remains a field that is the special realm of the rabbi. It is Judaism. . . . here lies the unchallengeable authority of the rabbi that gives him warrant to teach, to judge and to speak in all phases of Jewish life. . . . As has always been the case in Jewish history, superior learning is still the principal basis for rabbinic authority. But our history has also shown that the extent of Jewish information is not the only condition of rabbinic authority. The other condition which cannot be dispensed with is personal piety. . . . The modern rabbi, if he chooses to be a rabbi, has to hearken to the voice of God in order that he may be heard by his fellow men. *He has to be a man of piety in addition to being a man of learning.*[13]

With this emphasis on the rebuilding of the Jewish community with the synagogue at its center, and with the conception of the rabbi as ultimately a scholar-saint, we begin to move out of the Reform and into the Conservative camp.

§ *The Conservative Rabbi**

The most recent of the three denominations of American Judaism—Conservative Judaism—has its roots in that portion of the ideology of Reform which saw Judaism as an historically evolving tradition. Despite this ideological inheritance, Conservatism arose in opposition to the radical Reform position, especially as this position was stated in the Pittsburgh Platform of 1885. While Conservatism has welcomed and sometimes fostered change in ritual, custom, and belief, it essentially placed a positive value on identification with the vast body of accumulated tradition. This midway position between the unswerving conformity of the Orthodox, and

---

* For more comprehensive view of the development of the Conservative rabbi see Marshall Sklare, *Conservative Judaism: An American Religious Movement* (Glencoe, Illinois: The Free Press, 1955), Ch. VI.

the radical departure from tradition by Reform, can be viewed as another major attempt to handle the breakdown of traditional authority due to the Enlightenment and Emancipation.

All the Conservative rabbis we spoke with were—like the majority of their congregants—children of Eastern European immigrants. All of them come from lower-middle-class Orthodox backgrounds, and have a firm foundation in the teachings of Orthodox Judaism. The Conservative rabbis we interviewed had all spent a number of years in an Orthodox Yeshivah. While half of our respondents received their ordination from the Jewish Theological Seminary of America—the official seminary of the Conservative group—the other half were recipients of ordination from Orthodox institutions. Sometime after receiving their training, the latter joined the Conservative ranks. In dress and appearance they look much like the Reform rabbi, but they are more likely to use a Yiddish expression or a "Jewish gesture." Many of them speak Yiddish fluently, though their conversational and pulpit language is English.

The Conservative rabbi, with his midway position between Orthodox and Reform, considers both secular studies and traditional rabbinic training as necessary prerequisites for the American rabbinate:

> Since the Jewish community is an integral part of the American community, it is only natural that the rabbi is a part of that community too. Thus the rabbi who knows only *Talmud* and *Mishnah* and not Dewey, Lincoln or Emerson, cannot expect to do well.

While no Conservative rabbi conceives of Orthodoxy as a threat to his movement, he does nevertheless still feel the necessity of answering the charges brought against him, namely, that he has deviated sharply from tradition. In part, he legitimizes the changes he has introduced in terms of non-traditional values; here the emphasis is upon a "dynamic Judaism, keeping pace with new events." Quite frequently, however, he resorts to legitimizing his activities not in terms of a more highly prized value system, but merely as that of a Traditional rabbi faced with the problem of a disintegrating and godless Jewish community. He feels he has made changes in order to rebuild a spiritual Jewish community. One Conservative rabbi who had held an Orthodox pulpit for three years and then joined the Conservative movement phrased it this way:

> I looked about me and almost never saw a young person. It was an abomination to me. Some of them were young but looked old. Those who had sons and daughters would invite me to their home for *Shabbos* so that we would break bread with them. The son and daughter never stayed with them. They went away. And I wondered: "Here I am a young fellow. What am I going to do here? What will I accomplish as a rabbi?" I was convinced some changes would have to be made.

Whatever qualms the Conservative rabbi might have in explaining his role to the Orthodox are absent in his reply to the Reform. Here the Conservative rabbi is clear that he is stemming an unhealthy departure from traditional Judaism. One Conservative rabbi told us how this notion was a significant factor in his decision to accept a rabbinic post:

Well, the opportunity they described was to influence the whole Midwest in the direction of a more positive Jewish life. The city had a reform tradition. There was no one in the town speaking English who stood before the community and dared mention the fact that he was a traditional Jew. The city had been dominated by Reform Judaism.

In this connection it is significant to note how another Conservative rabbi boasted about his ability to compete with Reform:

I took away all the children from the school of the Reform Temple. I built up a school, Sunday and Hebrew, so that they had no Sunday School. So that rabbi became incensed: What did the rabbi who is Conservative have to do with Sunday School? The Sunday School belongs to him, he thought. I arrested the flow [to Reform]. The young men who made good financially used to join the Reform Temple for social life. This was stopped. They became aristocrats here too.

In point of fact, however, the contemporary Conservative rabbi spends little effort or time in legitimizing his behavior. He is much too busy, for he is working to revitalize the Jewish community and to make the synagogue as its center. As we encountered him, the Conservative rabbi was primarily an organizer. "Build membership," "construct educational facilities and programs," "reorganize the dues structure," "plan a budget," "initiate a men's club and a sisterhood," "build up attendance at weekly Sabbath service," "make plans for a new building,"—these words come to the mouth of the Conservative rabbi when you ask him what he has been doing in his present position. One such man who has held three positions, each of which was a "promotion," was asked to describe his functions in each synagogue. Here is his reply:

Outside of preaching there was a great deal of administrative work, building up a congregation. I was responsible for the budget. I introduced the budget into that synagogue though I wasn't the first to think of it. When I came there were 110 families, now there are 375. [In the second synagogue . . . ?] Same duties as the last place except even more work was required there in the congregation building up membership. [In your present synagogue?] I'm responsible for new members, at least—well 95 per cent of them. Now the synagogue is in a solid financial position.

In his zeal as organizer and promoter, the Conservative rabbi has often engaged in activities which he feels tend to lower the dignity of his position as a religious specialist. He is uncomfortable in these activities, but he justifies them on grounds that this is the only method of obtaining the attention of a non-observing and rapidly assimilating community. He is the salesman of a not too highly valued commodity—a more or less traditional Judaism. Thus one man told us:

There has been an unfortunate change in the function and role of the rabbi. Whereas the whole momentum of Jewish life for the rabbi in Eastern Europe was positive, that is, it was something, today it is something else. He is warding off, working against assimilation. *In so doing he becomes a drummer, a fifer, a salesman, an advertising agent.* Let us remember, too, that drummers and fifers are not generals, they are drummers and fifers. He becomes a campaigner, an administrator of the community endeavors. *The rabbi becomes an extrovert and is a functionary at a ceremony. We see him at the opening of golf clubs, birthday parties, club meetings, weddings, and many such occasions.*

Another rabbi indicated the effect this kind of job has had on the rabbinic personality:

> Most of us have a little ham in us as well. There is Rabbi ———— who strokes back his wavy hair; I'm sure the hair is a nuisance but to him it's very effective in the pulpit. Rabbi ———— does the same thing with his locks. And then there are the affectations of speech we pick up. You see we are constantly alone and I suppose we get seduced by the public . . . the point is you have to put yourself across and in so doing you never know what you are guilty of.

Aside from the overriding consideration which the Conservative rabbi is now giving to his organizing activities, by and large his functions are similar to those of the Reform and the Modern Orthodox rabbi. The Conservative rabbi differs in these functions from the other rabbinic roles in terms of his conception of these functions and the content he places into them. Thus, like all contemporary rabbis who view the future with some optimism, the Conservative rabbi places teaching as a primary function. Here his "mixed" ideology is especially prominent:

> I think he should primarily be a teacher of Judaism as an interpreter of the tradition. I think he can really function and be of service there. I feel there is *nothing Jewish* and *nothing human* which should be foreign to him.

The Conservative rabbi sees scholarship not only as a necessary correlary function to teaching, but as part of the traditional rabbinic role which he values. He bemoans the fact that his organizational activities and some of the Protestantization functions do not now permit the exercise of Jewish scholarship:

> That's the tragedy now in the American rabbinate; that unless they have sterling characters and great determination, most of them cease to be rabbis. I mean they may be preachers or pulpit speakers or administrators but not rabbis in the sense of true scholars anymore. There are less and less scholars in the rabbinate every year.

While preaching began as a method of competing with the Reform rabbi, it has become as important a function for the Conservative rabbi as it is for the Reform rabbi. Although aware that it is not part of the traditional rabbinic role, few Conservative rabbis look forward to the time when preaching will no longer be a central function in the American rabbinate:

> I suppose the first requirement [of the rabbi] would be preaching; although it would not be fair to judge a rabbi by his ability or lack of ability in the pulpit, I think the congregation does. Secondly, I believe eventually a rabbi stands or

falls by his success or failure in the pulpit, not altogether, but to a large extent. Here he wields influence over a great many people at one time, and a half-hour sermon can make a great many people walk out inspired or have them walking out grumbling.

Interestingly enough, the rhetoric of the Conservative rabbi in connection with the sermon is markedly different from the Intellectual Reform rabbi. We do not intend to suggest that the Reform rabbi is less zealous in his attempt to present moral issues to his congregants, but, in our sample at least, the Intellectual Reform rabbi spoke of his preaching in terms of speaking before an "audience." The Conservative religious specialists consistently used "congregants" or "worshipers":

Preaching is a very important function. There are three things involved in preaching: teaching, changing wrong ideas, and motivating conduct. Either one or all of these is involved in preaching . . . if you have a consistent group of worshipers a point of view is gradually transmitted which molds people's lives.

The Conservative rabbi does as much pastoral work as his other activities will permit. For him, social visitation and counselling are all part of his grand plan to reactivate the synagogue as the central institution in the Jewish community. It is almost certain that as congregations achieve a stable membership (and in the years since this study was done many have actually accomplished this goal), the Conservative rabbi will assume more and more of these functions. However, as one man told us, as an organizer,

I didn't have time for it. There were years and years that I was hardly at the homes of my members. For years I went out to homes I hadn't been before to look for new members. Many a Jew used to tell me he wasn't home. One of them said, "Look at me, do I need a synagogue? I'm a Jew at heart!" I said that I'm not a heart specialist.

The Conservative rabbi has made the conducting of services one of his primary functions. He admits that the service has been traditionally run without the benefit of a rabbi, but points out that at present very few laymen are familiar enough with the services to handle them properly. He feels that the congregation has grown so accustomed to having the rabbi as its guide that it cannot do without him. He calls this "the Protestant element."

Changes have been made in the ritual of the synagogue which are considered heretical by the Orthodox. Such reforms as mixed pews, organ music, and shifts in the traditional prayers are looked upon by the Conservative rabbi as minor changes—he is willing to compromise on these matters because it satisfies his members. A Conservative rabbi recounted the following incident which illustrates his propensity to accept a compromise position between Orthodoxy and Reform:

There was the problem of the organ, of whether we should use the organ in the synagogue. They tried to introduce it in the synagogue long before I came. There was violent objection—someone actually took an axe to it. Most of the snags were ironed out in my day—*we worked out a compromise. I told them I didn't care one way or the other—there was no ideological problem involved for me.* Many of the laymen had set views, however, I finally told the people who did not come to the late Friday night services that they had not the right to tell us what to do unless they came. However, I promised them that the organ would not be played on Saturdays and on the holidays—that is when they came. After that there was no problem.

Not all changes in the services are legitimized in terms of appeal to membership. Although in the following illustration the changes might have been made to attract a large group who had hitherto not had an active share in the services, the rationale for change is made on the basis of values which may not be in direct conflict with Judaism but certainly have never been a prominent part of it:

> We have done some outstanding radical experiments. We have been leaders in the emancipation movement of Jewish women. We have brought women to the Torah [traditionally only an activity a man might perform], to read the blessings, and have introduced the Bas Mitzvah. [The Bas Mitzvah is an attempt to give women the same introduction into adulthood as the Bar Mitzvah.]

Perhaps one of the most significant departures from the role of the Traditional rabbi is to be found in the Conservative rabbi's activities with regard to daily prayer service. Unlike the Modern Orthodox rabbi, he does not attend nor feel it incumbent upon him to come to the daily morning or evening services. The Traditional rabbi and the Modern Orthodox rabbi maintained that it was the obligation of all Jews to attend services, and that certainly the rabbi must do at least what is expected of all Jews. Further, these rabbis envisioned the daily attendance at synagogue as an opportunity to become better acquainted with their congregants and hoped their presence would suggest that the congregants should come to them in the event of any personal difficulty. Contrast that attitude with the Conservative rabbi whose failure to attend daily services brought him into open conflict with his members:

> They [the members] denounced me to the Seminary on grounds that I came to *minyon* [public prayer with ten or more males present] only on Mondays and Thursdays. [A portion of the Torah is read during the Monday and Thursday services.] I refused to come to *minyon* daily. That was an issue, *minyon*. It's a sacrifice. Who feels like *davening* at seven o'clock in the morning? So I went Mondays and Thursdays; but sometimes I didn't go Monday and Thursday either. They said: "A rabbi who doesn't go, why should we worship?" It doesn't mean that the president or vice-president went. "But why should we worship if the rabbi doesn't?" You can understand that in a way. They feel the rabbi doesn't believe in daily prayer, public daily prayer. They can assume he *davens* at home; sometimes they suspect that too. Who knows what the fellow does in the morning? He doesn't come to *minyon*. So I would say that the rabbi sits late at meetings; how can you expect the rabbi to start the day at that ungodly hour, you see.

Although the Conservative rabbi does undertake activities within the Jewish community, he is ever mindful that for him the crucial institution is the synagogue. In his program to center the community about synagogue life, the Conservative rabbi takes an active part in organizing schools and recruiting persons to enter these schools. This will range from conducting adult education classes to encouraging young persons to enter the Jewish Theological Seminary of America. At the same time the rabbi may hold important policy-making and executive positions with Zionist groups, the United Jewish Appeal, the local Jewish federation, B'nai B'rith, or other philanthropic, political, and social organizations. Here he makes full use of his religious specialist role to direct Jewish life back to the synagogue. Furthermore, recognizing the full force of these and wider community organizations as possible competitors in his effort to achieve synagogue affiliation, he responds by incorporating many of their activities and attractions into his own synagogue program.

Within the wider community the Conservative rabbi participates in civic functions. Thus he turns up as a chaplain to an American Legion post, or as a representative on the mayor's commission for good housing. A few Conservative rabbis have been very active in "good government" movements, and by and large they take the "liberal" position in political affairs. However, unless the Conservative rabbi is in a small town, where he feels keenly the obligation to be an ambassador to the Gentile community, he is content to leave this task to the Reform rabbi or to the lay leaders of the Jewish community.

It has been our contention thus far that the Conservative rabbi constitutes a clearly delineated role with no subtypes within the denomination. He has been characterized as a religious specialist who faced the problem of the breakdown of traditional authority with a middle-of-the-road program; he fits between the Intellectual Reform rabbi and Traditional rabbi in the sense that he possesses values, functions, and aspirations from each role. However, inasmuch as there is evidence of widespread ideological divergence among the Conservative rabbinate, there is some justification for the argument that the Conservative rabbinate should be categorized either as Modern Orthodox or one of the Reform types. Thus at the conventions of the Rabbinical Assembly of America during the past ten years there have been serious clashes on what changes are permissible in Jewish law and ritual. Despite these divergencies, there is a central core of Conservative rabbis who have a similar response to the question of Jewish faith and who are in general agreement as to what should constitute Jewish practice. The emphasis is upon some reconciliation of scientific knowledge with belief in a significant number of traditional Jewish values:

I would say that the majority of them [conservative rabbis] are people who are possessed of a positive faith: they believe in a Supreme Being guiding the destinies of men, that the universe has a realistically spiritual pattern as the scientific and material pattern with which we have learned from the world of science. Our men will perhaps have a lesser degree of the supernatural that borders already on superstition. There's a good deal of the rational, the Maimonidean attitude, you know, a large degree of reason combined with your faith. I would say that's the most typical of our Conservative rabbis. That's how I feel myself.

There is, furthermore, complete agreement on the exemplar function which the Conservative rabbi must serve within the Jewish community. There is, for example, a world-famous Conservative rabbi, acclaimed by the general public as a tremendously impressive preacher, an extremely gifted organizer, a leader in the introduction of changes in ritual and values, who spoke wistfully and somewhat longingly about a rabbi who had been able to perform the scholar-saint role. After giving a full account of the many activities he had organized, the associations he had headed, and his fame as a public figure, he said:

> Now let me give you a different picture. Go to _____ City. There you find a man, Rabbi _____ by name. I saw and visited him. *He is no preacher, he is no community organizer, he is a scholar—still a little ghettoish-like looking. Yet you will find there is reverence for him.* You will find it. . . . With the average rabbi that is the most intensive and rewarding part of the job.

Other successful organizers in the Conservative rabbinate have voiced their desire to play an exemplary role. The following are typical:

> The rabbi should set an example of decent, honorable living. He should be the prototype of the good Jew.

> Well, the first function of the rabbi is to be a teacher, not only by conveying knowledge but primarily by example.

> A rabbi ought to be a man of great saintliness who by his very presence inspires cheerfulness and comforts people.

Finally, in support of our thesis that there is but one overall Conservative rabbinic role, we should like to mention only briefly the important function that the three organizations of Conservative Judaism, its seminary (Jewish Theological Seminary of America), its synagogue organization (United Synagogue of America), and its professional rabbinic organization (Rabbinical Assembly of America) are performing in this connection. From our observation of the Jewish community, we feel that these organizations are introducing a centralized administration in Conservative Judaism. While still young and beset with many problems, these organizations are presently laying the groundwork for control and discipline of individual members, for synagogue affiliation, and for rabbinic practices. This does not mean that there will be no controversy within Conservative ranks; in fact, it seems likely that ideological controversy is to be the next big development of the Conservative movement. However, we feel that this controversy will take place *within* the movement and that by and large it will have the effect of strengthening synagogue practice, Jewish observance, and the position of the Conservative rabbi.

Although the Conservative rabbi aspires to the scholar-saint role, the character and content of this role will differ from the traditional rabbinic scholar-saint. It will differ both in terms of the ideological base, which will include innovations in custom and law, and in its incorporation of the functions made part of the rabbinic role by the Reform rabbi. It is certainly clear that at the present moment the Conservative rabbi is not a scholar-saint. For the time being, at least, the Conservative rabbi makes his claim for authority as the religious specialist who has been busily rebuilding a Jewish community whose members had rapidly been drifting away from Jewish identification:

I would definitely say that the rabbinate has stemmed the tide of indifference to a measure where I personally feel a certain degree of satisfaction.

What is the extent of the authority of the Conservative rabbi? On this point it would be well to listen to the Conservative rabbi himself. One rabbi had this to say:

Very few matters will be decided on the basis of the rabbi's decision. There are some problems of an intermarital situation where the rabbi's opinion holds a great deal of weight. However, in general the rabbi has little influence. If the rabbi would speak out at immorality in business, none of his parishioners would listen to him. It's very difficult to be effective. Jewish life is not integrated and there are no real sanctions that can be brought against an individual. No one is accountable to the rabbi or for that matter to the Jewish community at large. It's certainly different than the little *shtetl* in Poland. I'm not advocating a return to those days, mind you. However, the little *shtetl* had much to recommend itself. Here there was an integrated community with sanctions and discipline. There was a wholeness which found all his actions judged with corresponding reaction by the entire community. That's so much different from today. Take a member of _____ Temple. He won't be asked how he handles his business or how much charity he gives a year. He's a member who pays his dues and that's sufficient for the congregation. . . .

The area of rabbinic authority has become limited to ritual questions and since there are very little ritual questions, there is actually very little area in which he operates with authority.

On the other hand, we received this reply.

I think the rabbi is more in leadership in the community than he ever was before. (Q.: Even back in Europe?) I think the rabbi's leadership is accepted much more than years ago. Even back in Europe. I think so. Never before has the rabbi been in the leadership in national Jewish organizations as much as he is now. Of course, I find precedent for it in Eastern Europe and Western Europe. But I think that the rabbi as leader is outstanding today in the modern Jewish community.

If we look at the Jewish community today, it would be hard to deny much of what the first rabbi has to say about the question of authority. In the city where our study was made Conservative Judaism can claim the membership of only about 10 per cent of the total Jewish community (this constitutes about 25 per cent of the synagogue-affiliated community). Furthermore, when pressed to describe the kind of people over whom he has had influence, or the kind of influence that he has had, the Conservative rabbi must admit that his area of influence has not been very large. Jewish scholarship, philanthropy, influence on some families to keep a "Jewish Friday night," assistance in a grief situation, and ritual questions, are the types of examples which the rabbi can give of his influence. He feels, however, that these are not the true measurements of his influence, for he knows one or two cases where he has exercised a dominant force upon some individual's life:

> There was a lawyer who had achieved success in the practice of law. He was known to be a bachelor and then I began to hear from some friends that he was very attached to a Gentile woman. They had been going out together for several years. One day another friend in the community told me, "Rabbi, I think you will be interested to hear this. You know so-and-so has broken that relation and in so doing he said, 'I have to decide between that young woman and the rabbi and I decided in favor of the rabbi.' "

While each Conservative rabbi has one such example which emphasizes his increasing influence, he is much more prone to talk about the total number of members he has brought into the congregation, the synagogue structure which has been built, and the organization he heads. Certainly the Conservative rabbi cannot be said to have made more than a good beginning in organizing the Jewish community about the synagogue.

With a historical perspective in mind, however, statements to the effect that the Conservative rabbi is an influence do not appear to be as fanciful as the statistics and evasive answers to the question of influence would indicate. We may recall that during the 1920's the prestige of the synagogue and the authority of the Traditional rabbi were minimal within the Jewish community. Secular associations were the main sources of influence and promised to supplant the synagogue in the event that the community continued to exist at all. It was at this time that the Conservative rabbi appeared on the scene. Announcing himself as a Traditional rabbi with the modifications already noted, he came forth to reorganize the community about the synagogue. The optimist in the Conservative rabbinate is expressing the feelings of an organizer who begins to see some of the fruits of his efforts. He looks back to twenty-five years ago and sees the tremendous growth of his movement in the interim. He thumbs through his appointment book and finds that his services are wanted not only by his own congregants—counselling, a meeting to see about increasing the budget for recreational activities, a session with the building committee who want his advice on some matter concerning the addition of the new wing—but also by the local Zionist group to take an active part in their program, and possibly by the local Jewish federation to help determine policy in charity allocation. Thus the Conservative rabbi feels that he has accomplished something substantial, and with the enthusiasm born of this accomplishment he may signify this satisfaction with an hyperbolic statement about his influence. It is certain at least, that he *has* had an active part in "stemming the tide of indifference."

Although financial remuneration is not by itself an index of influence, it should be noted that the Conservative rabbi is well paid. Of the nine Conservative rabbis interviewed, only two received below $7,500. If we include perquisites, the average Conservative rabbi earns between $10,000 and $12,000. This figure does not include special gifts which many rabbis receive. One gift, the subject of much comment among the rabbis, was a home constructed at a cost of about $75,000 and given to a local rabbi outright. This is unusual, but the trip to Israel or the new car are quite routine. Perhaps more significant than salary or gifts is the fact that the Conservative rabbi is in great demand. There are an insufficient number of Conservative rabbis to fill the posts open to them.

We can, perhaps, best summarize the role of the Conservative rabbi, in terms of its present function and its future aspirations for authority as a religious specialist, by quoting one of the men we interviewed. Following a four-hour session, we asked our respondent—whom we conceive to be the prototype of the Conservative rabbi—if he had any general comments to make on our study. This was his reply:

The rabbi in the United States has aspects of the old *Rov* and the Protestant pastor. A congregation expects pastoral attention; it also expects scholarship and attention to learning. The Eastern European Jews still look at me as an old-country Jew. When I come into Talmud class they still stand; I still serve them as a *Rov* would in Europe, the attitude of respect is the same. The other groups, well their attitude is more friendly and informal. The respect I get from them is for my opinion as a personal counsellor.

There's an intangible in the rabbinate but something very important. When a rabbi is a normal healthy Jew leading an adjusted life, he serves a tremendous purpose by merely existing. When people can admire you for just this, if they say "If I can only be like the rabbi, I'd be O.K.!" then the rabbi is doing a real job. By having a nice happy family and being respected, he gives status by just existing. This is very important in a mixed community. He becomes the symbol of the potentialities of American Jewish living, a symbol worthy of emulation.

§ *Conclusion*

The contemporary rabbi falls within the shadow of Emancipation and faces in varying degrees the problem of loss of authority. We have been particularly concerned with the question of what alternative roles the rabbi has developed in adjusting to his problem. Our empirical study has disclosed seven major contemporary rabbinic roles. Initially, we may note two extreme polar types representing two radically different types of adjustment—the Traditional rabbi and the Intellectual Reform rabbi.

The Traditional rabbi is characterized by his attempt to approximate as closely as possible the scholar-saint role of the Eastern European rabbi. He has been unwilling to swerve from his Orthodox belief or practice, to add new functions to his role or to change the basis of his authority. As a result he has little or no influence. He is extremely pessimistic about the future; his only hope is in the coming of Messiah. The Free-Lancer demonstrates the inability of the Traditional rabbi to cope with the problem of authority. Feeling that the task is hopeless, the Free-Lancer earns his livelihood from rabbinic functions but refuses to accept any responsible rabbinic role.

The Intellectual Reform rabbi has dealt with the problem of rabbinic authority by deviating most sharply from the traditional rabbinic scholar-saint role. He has, in fact, rejected that role and the value system on which it was based. For the totality of rabbinism he has substituted the generalized values of modern Western society, with all the latter's complexity, instability, and change. Having denied the authority of classical Judaism he seeks to base his authority within the philosophies of rationalism, idealism, humanism, and in the scientific method. In effect, he has sidestepped the problem of traditional rabbinic authority; he claims instead the authority of an intellectual. As an intellectual he is confronted by a highly generalized and ambiguous value system which severely limits the extent of his authority in that it does not readily permit the prescription of specific acts which had been so characteristic of rabbinism. In line with his intellectual role his most characteristic function is the imparting of general knowledge and the clarification of issues from the pulpit and lecture platform. His major functions as a religious specialist are those of the liberal Protestant minister whom he has emulated—preaching, priestly duties, pastoral work, and community service.

There have been four other rabbinic roles, the Modern Orthodox, the Conservative, the Social Reformer, and the Traditionalistic Reform, which have developed in the process of dealing with the problem of authority. These roles represent the rejection of both polar types of adjustment—the Traditional on the grounds that it fails to cope with the situation and the Intellectual Reform on the grounds that it is too radical a departure from the past. It is significant that important features of the role of the Modern Orthodox, Conservative, and Traditionalistic Reform rabbi indicate the emergence of a common rabbinic role. The earliest, most characteristic, and the most significant of the three has been the Conservative rabbi.

We have characterized the Conservative rabbi as standing somewhere between the two polar types. Like the Traditional rabbi he is desirous of playing a scholar-saint role. Unlike him, however, he is willing to make changes in both the traditional value system and functions in order to rebuild the Jewish community in which such a role would be possible. Although he still performs some of the functions of the Traditional Orthodox rabbi, in the main he has taken over the complex of functions engaged in by the Intellectual Reform rabbi. We noted the predominance of the organizing aspect of his role in all these activities. The character of the new value system is indicated by the fact that although he is unwilling to introduce changes in the ultimate values of traditional Judaism, he favors and permits changes in ritual and custom in his

. . . quest for an adaptation of Jewish traditional beliefs and practices to the tone, temper, and exigencies of contemporary living, the striving after a balance between historic Judaism and the modern world.[14]

Although he is still far from the scholar-saint role, as an organizer he has not only been able "to stem the tide of indifference" resulting from the Emancipation, but has had remarkable success in gaining adherents to his movement.

The other two rabbinic roles—the Modern Orthodox and Traditionalistic Reform—have to some extent accepted the model established by the Conservative rabbi. In his efforts to rebuild the synagogue as the center of the Jewish community the Modern Orthodox rabbi has also become an organizer and an administrator; he is willing to sacrifice scholarship to the building up of a religious school. Like the Conservative rabbi, he has been willing to make changes in traditional rabbinic functions. He has accepted the Protestant ministers' functions of preaching, priestly duties, pastoral visitation and counselling. Nevertheless, he is still at the synagogue for daily services and is generally on hand to perform the traditional functions of the Traditional rabbi. Although he recognizes modern science and philosophy, he hopes to keep intact the totality of beliefs and practice of classical rabbinism and eventually, therefore, to perform as a traditional rabbinic scholar-saint.

The Traditionalistic Reform rabbi, moving from the other polar type, the Intellectual Reform rabbi, has assumed a role very similar to that of the Conservative rabbi. This has meant that he has focused his energies on organizing the Jewish community about the synagogue, that he has introduced traditional ritual and values into his program and that he too aspires to play the role of the scholar-saint.

The Social Reformer, like the Traditionalistic Reform rabbi, has moved closer to traditional Judaism. He has as a primary concern, however, not alone the rebuilding of the Jewish community but also the realization of liberal-democratic values and goals which have been legitimized in terms of prophetic Judaism. He does not envision himself as scholar-saint but as an active organizer and leader of social action groups.

There are, then, three elements which appear to contain the most characteristic features of the Modern Orthodox, Conservative, and Traditionalistic Reform roles and which attest to the proposition that a common rabbinic role is emerging, namely: (1) all three types of rabbis have been characterized as organizers in so far as they are presently engaged in organizing and rebuilding the Jewish community about the synagogue; (2) all to a large extent perform a similar complex of functions, including preaching (in English), teaching, pastoral visitation and counselling, priestly functions, administrative functions, and engaging in numerous activities in the Jewish and non-Jewish community; (3) all aspire to a scholar-saint role.

Thus it appears that the scholar-saint role which from the time of the early rabbi was the most characteristic rabbinic role in the Jewish community, but which was submerged under the impact of Emancipation, is once again destined to re-emerge as the most characteristic rabbinic role. The new scholar-saint will, undoubtedly, differ from the traditional type. It seems likely that some of the functions which the contemporary rabbi has assumed—preaching, priestly functions, pastoral work, and some communal activity—will find a place in the new role. In so far as changes are introduced in the traditional value system they will have repercussions in the content of the scholar-saint role since that role bases its authority in knowing and living the Law. Furthermore, the fact that changes have been introduced into the value system will very likely raise the question of how and on what basis the value system will be eventually defined. This may involve an element of inherent instability in the authority of the new scholar-saint role. Whatever may be the uncertainty and indefiniteness of the new rabbinic scholar-saint role, authority will be based on knowing and living the Law, and to the extent that a community will be built up around the Law the rabbi will be its religious specialist.

IRA O. GLICK

THE HEBREW CHRISTIANS:
A MARGINAL RELIGIOUS GROUP

A LITTLE-KNOWN, yet unique, institution is the Hebrew Christian Church. It is composed of some seventy adult members (together with their children) who, though born of Jewish parentage, have been converted to Christianity. While the banding together of a group of religious converts is sufficient in itself to attract a good deal of attention, it is not for this reason that the Church and its members are of interest. Rather, it is the fact that these converts consider themselves to be Christians at the same time that they maintain that they are Jews. Thus they say: "We are Jews because we trace our lineage to Abraham the first Jew, and we are Christians because we have accepted Christ as our Savior." Reflecting this conception, the Hebrew Christian Church contains a mixture of Jewish and Christian elements and, as is indicated by its name, does seek to identify its members as being simultaneously Jewish and Christian. As such, it is a group which highlights many aspects of the social, cultural and religious position of the American Jew. The Hebrew Christian Church represents an extreme institutional attempt to solve the dilemmas inherent in this position.

§ *The Church and Its Members*

Although the Hebrew Christian Church was formally organized in 1934, its origins date back to the early years of the twentieth century, when a young Jewish immigrant from Roumania came to this country. His name was Herman Kaufman. He was the son of orthodox Jewish parents, and he settled in one of the smaller East Coast cities which had an established Jewish community. Now in his mid-sixties, Kaufman says that he had very little contact with Christians and absolutely none with organized Christianity until the time he unwittingly stopped to look at some Yiddish books displayed in a store window near his home. The store was actually a Christian mission especially designed to attract the attention of the Jewish immigrant; Kaufman found this out somewhat later after he was approached by the woman missionary. When she discovered that he was a recent immigrant and knew very little English she immediately offered to teach him the language. For the lessons, his instructress used the New Testament as a language test. Kaufman, who still speaks with a

---

Published for the first time in this volume.

The article is based on a larger study done in 1950-51 by the writer while he was a graduate student in the Department of Sociology, University of Chicago.

pronounced Yiddish accent, says: "I will be forever grateful to her for using the New Testament, for it is the best writing in the English language." It seems evident that Kaufman is grateful to her for another, more basic reason: using the subject matter of the book the missionary introduced him to the teachings of Christ. Several years after leaving his orthodox home, Kaufman was baptized a Christian, an event which largely shaped the course of his future life.

The years following his conversion were quite important for Kaufman. He was successful in persuading his Jewish immigrant wife (whom he still likes to refer to as a *kashera maidel*) to accept Christ as the Jewish Messiah, making her the first of some five hundred Jewish converts for whom he claims responsibility. When a Christian benefactor became interested in him, he was able to leave his job in a tailor shop for a better position and, in the process, to acquire several years of formal schooling. Then, "The Lord directed me to the seminary where I became an ordained minister." Shortly following his ordination in the early 1920's, Reverend Kaufman was called upon by a large Christian missionary organization to be director of the newly established Emanuel Center.

Emanuel Center is a Christian mission to the Jews utilizing a community-center approach in order to achieve its objective of bringing Jews to Christ. When first organized it was located in an immigrant Jewish neighborhood; due to a shift in the city's Jewish population the Center was forced to change its location. Some nine years ago it moved into a modern brick building situated on the edge of a densely populated, lower-middle-class Jewish neighborhood. It is clear that the choice of Kaufman as director of the Center was a wise one. His European Jewish background makes him much like the Jews who live in the area adjacent to Emanuel. He has a knowledge of Yiddish, and can read and to some small extent understand Hebrew. He is familiar with the traditions, customs, and laws of Judaism. Furthermore, in his role as a missionary to the Jews, he understands the difficulties encountered by the Jew who embraces Christ as the Messiah. For over thirty years Kaufman has continuously held the position of director, and from all indications has been successful in his work. Emanuel Center has become known as one of the outstanding models of the community-center approach in the field of Jewish evangelization. By carrying out a full program of activities closely supervised by trained missionary workers, a comparatively large number of Jews have been introduced to Christianity. Since many of these activities are especially designed for teen-agers, the Center has had most influence with Jewish youth of the neighborhood, some of whom subsequently acknowledged Christ as the Messiah. Today, these converts form the core membership of the Hebrew Christian Church.

Children from the neighborhood assemble at Emanuel during the after-school hours. Activities are accompanied by a conscious, though slow and subtle, process of indoctrination:

One of my friends joined the Scouts at Emanuel and one by one all of our friends joined. We were about twelve or thirteen years old at the time. Some of them dropped out later because they weren't interested in the religious aspect of it. I was. We had Bible stories, hymn singing, and things like that, and I liked it very much. I was at an impressionable age and I thought that the woman who led our Scout troop was wonderful. I grew very attached to her; she made a terrific impression on me. I wanted to know what made her so lovable, so I asked her. She told me that it was because she had something in her. I told her I wanted to have it too and that I wanted to know just what it was that she had within her. She told me that what she had was the way she believed, that Christ was the Jewish Messiah. I didn't understand it, but I said to her, "if you believe it, I'll believe it too."

Other members state that the initial attraction to Emanuel was the gym, the basketball games, the summer camp maintained by the Center, or the interest that Kaufman or his wife displayed in them. But whatever the original reason or the particular setting or activity in which the participant found himself, the techniques and devices brought to bear upon him by the workers seem to have been quite similar. If the individual did not enter as a member of a group he soon found himself in the midst of one. There the ostensible activity came to have religious overtones as the worker developed a close relationship with each individual. At some point the young person realized that the religious aspect of the program was of greater importance than the more obvious content. "When I came here I didn't know what it was," one member recalls, "and when I did learn I was disgusted. How could a Jew believe in Christ?" With feelings such as these the participant frequently left the Center; occasionally he remained, maintaining that it could not affect him:

We Jewish boys, we were between twelve and fourteen, all knew that it was a mission. Our parents warned us about going there; you know Jewish parents and what they think about missions. We said we would repulse it.

There can be little doubt that someone or something "repulsed" the influence of Emanuel in the great majority of cases. The statistics are not available, but of all those who at some time made use of the facilities offered at Emanuel, only a very small minority ultimately accepted Christianity. Furthermore, of those who confessed their belief in Christ, only a minute percentage remained to later undergo baptism. With this small group the problem for Kaufman and the Center staff was how to insure their continued adherence to the newly accepted faith. The solution was found in segregating believers from nonbelievers as much as possible. Rather than have the converts participate in the general activities of the Center, special groups were created where they had the fellowship of other young confessors. One such group, called the Queen Esther Club, contained all of the girls who had "found the Messiah." Here, and at the private summer camp, the program became overtly Christian with prayer meetings and Bible study—the young believers were not distracted by those who had not accepted the gospel.

This separation of believers from nonbelievers was not too difficult to accomplish, for once Christianity was accepted as the true religion, segregation was not only necessitated by reasons of internal strategy but was also imposed from without by the manner in which nonbelievers acted toward the new Christians. Church members found that a declaration of faith was rapidly followed by isolation from all social contact with Jews. It was most poignantly experienced with the individual's own family. As one member stated, "How does a Jew tell his parents that he has become a Christian?" He went on to say:

I didn't tell my father that I was a Christian until after I was in high school [four-five years later]. I remember quite vividly: it was two o'clock in the morning and I was in the dining room studying for exams. It was a very vivid experience. He came into the room and said, "I heard something terrible about you. I heard that you are a Christian." I still didn't have the courage to tell him that I was. I don't know what I said, but he said, "If you ever do such a thing, don't tell me about it; keep it to yourself until I am dead." I was very disturbed about it all but didn't say anything. Then a little later, we were alone in the house one afternoon, and I told him that I was a Christian. I had to tell him. He didn't say one word and stormed out of the house and didn't come back for supper. Oh, yes, before leaving he said that he was going "to those people," referring to Emanuel. I said, "Do you think that you can take out what's in my heart?" And since then he has always shied away from all religious discussions.

The scene depicted here is quite typical of what took place when the acceptance of Christ was announced—or, as more frequently occurred, was "found out." Parents reacted violently, and as most were Yiddish-speaking Jewish immigrants, this is not at all surprising. Typically, they belonged to a wide variety of Jewish fraternal organizations, though only a few seem to have attended a synagogue or to have observed Jewish rituals. In spite of their religious derelictions, they were distinctively Jewish in terms of their cultural attitudes and sentiments. More significantly, they expected their children to remain loyal Jews in much the same manner as they considered themselves to be, and for the most part these expectations were fulfilled. The brothers, sisters, and cousins of these converts became more Americanized and less traditionally Jewish than their parents, but they retained this identity.

The converts indicate that in the long run their relations with parents and family often improved as parents came more and more to accept the idea of the child's act. The initial estrangement between the convert and his family may thus be mitigated. It is, however, relations with friends and with the wider Jewish community that were but rarely re-established. Once it was known that the person had become a Christian, he was informally but effectively isolated from his old friends; his social contacts were thus confined to the small group of fellow-believers at the Center. As most of these conversions took place during adolescence, ostracism was first encountered at a time when the patterns of future social relations of a broader nature are so often determined. The Jewish youth of the community knew those who participated in the activities at Emanuel, and being aware of the aims of the institution, they soon differentiated between those who merely made use of its facilities and those who became involved in the religious aspects of the program. Being considered part of the latter group made for non-acceptance:

I had very few friends outside of Emanuel. In fact, I never had any other friends. The kids in school knew that I was a Christian and they shied away from people who were like that. They think they are queer, or odd, or peculiar.

Feelings such as these are quite common among the Church members. They speak of constant hostility from outsiders which for the most part was expressed in derisive and taunting remarks, but occasionally broke into physical violence.

The separation of the Emanuel converts from other Jews thus occurred at an early stage in their careers as Christians. It was determined by the adverse pressures from without as well as the desire of the Emanuel staff members to keep closer supervision of the newly-won adherents. As long as the converts were in their teens, this informal fellowship, with its peculiarly Jewish-Christian mixture, appears to have been effective. But after adolescence many began to gradually drift away from the group. When this happened they usually stopped leading an active Christian life. Only a few of the converts seem to have joined a Gentile church after they left the Emanuel group, and only a limited number of these seem to have been able to adapt to the fellowship which they found there. Most of them could not adjust to these new "Gentile" surroundings and consequently neglected their church membership and often lost their faith in Christ. The exact number of converts who thus slipped away after abbreviated careers as Christians is difficult to ascertain, but a survey made prior to the formation of the Hebrew Christian Church states that ". . . an alarming percentage had drifted after conversion . . ." and that only ". . . a small percentage were active Christians." What happened to those who lost their faith is also not known; it is probable that many reverted to the Jewish group, if not to Judaism itself. The members prefer not to speak of these people and in many ways look upon them in the same manner that converts are traditionally viewed by Jews. The act of leaving the ranks of the loyal followers always brings on the epithet of "traitor."

It was early in 1934 that the converts decided to accept Reverend Kaufman's suggestion to unite and to form a Hebrew Christian church. Whereas its original purpose was "to conserve the fruitage of the Jewish mission" (namely, Emanuel Center), it was not long before this conception changed. A short time later it was thought of as being the rightful place for all Jewish converts to Christianity, irrespective of the place or means of conversion. The Church thereupon invited other individuals born of Jewish parentage who recognized Christ as the Jewish Messiah to join its ranks, and today one finds among the membership those who were brought to Christ by agencies other than Emanuel. These people are in fact very different from the Emanuel converts. Their cultural and social backgrounds are heterogeneous; their careers as Christians, prior to their entry into the Church, were not of one pattern. Conversion came at different periods in each of their lives, and the reasons they give for the acceptance of Christ usually are associated with personal crises. Life as a Christian, rather than consisting of similar experiences, is unique for each of these people. Generally speaking, they are much less familiar with Jewish life, Judaism, or Jewish ceremonies and customs, than are the Center converts. The following story is typical:

There was really nothing Jewish in my upbringing. My father would always bring home a Christmas tree for the holiday and when the minister in the church near our home would give a sermon on Jews my father would attend services. . . . The few times that I saw my father go to the synagogue was on those days that you say the prayer for the dead, whatever it's called. And then he would stand there just like a dummy. As far as Judaism went my folks were no more Jewish than a dog on the street. The Jewish world meant nothing to me; my religion was nil.

The non-Center people speak of other conversions in their families as a rather frequent occurrence; they also mention a high incidence of name-changing and intermarriage. Typically, they lived in predominantly Gentile communities, whereas the Emanuel converts almost always resided in Jewish or semi-Jewish neighborhoods (this same pattern for both groups continued even after conversion). It is clear that Gentiles do not seem so strange to them, and all have had some experience in a Gentile Christian church. Thus relations with non-Jews are carried on with greater facility than is the case with members of the Emanuel group.

§ *A Status Dilemma*

The members of the Hebrew Christian Church maintain that their conversion is but a matter of knowing that Christ is the Messiah—the Jewish Messiah—and that by their acceptance of him they have thereby fulfilled the Jewish religion. Their membership in a Hebrew Christian Church, they claim, is not strange, for if they were to become a part of the Gentile Christian church they would not be fulfilling their role as Jewish converts. They add that unfortunately the Christian church has forgotten its true origins, and that consequently neither the Jewish convert nor Judaism in any of its pre-Christian forms are given their rightfully deserved place in the Christian scheme.

If Hebrew Christianity is not a strange phenomenon for the Hebrew Christian, it cannot be said that the same holds true for Jews or for Gentile Christians. Hebrew Christianity appears to almost all people exclusive of Hebrew Christians to be a contradiction in terms. In our society it is assumed that one is either a Christian or a Jew; to maintain that one is both is to present the outsider with a most difficult problem. Yet what the Hebrew Christian does is precisely to say that he is both Jewish and

Christian. He not only gives himself a name which undeniably identifies him in this manner, but at the same time he is consciously separated from all outsiders and surrounds himself with a series of rituals and ceremonies that unmistakably point to his attempt to be both Jewish and Christian.

Why, once conversion from Judaism to Christianity has taken place, do these people insist on being identified as both Jews and Christians? To answer this question, one must separate the members of the Church in terms of the agency which recruited them. It appears that for the Emanuel convert a complete break from the original Jewish group is too severe a step; instead, a more limited move from Judaism is chosen. This is not, in reality, too difficult to understand: with strong Jewish sentiments in both family and community and with little direct contact with the Gentile Christian world, a more gradual transition to the new faith and the social world it implies is much easier to make. Furthermore, the mission which served to introduce these people to Christianity was peculiarly "Jewish" in that its program—under the supervision of a Jewish convert who made use of his "Jewishness" to approach people—was directed to attract Jews to what was claimed to be only a higher form of Judaism. Membership in the Hebrew Christian Church permits these people to say that they are still Jews ("look at the name given to our Church") in spite of their acceptance of Christ.

To understand the membership of the non-Emanuel converts in the Hebrew Christian Church one must be familiar with the position of the Jewish convert in the Gentile Christian Church. These people give evidence that this position is most difficult to assume, for it appears that in most cases the convert's success depends on withholding the fact that he is of Jewish parentage. Once it becomes known that he is a *Jewish* convert, he is to the Gentile members primarily a Jew and is treated accordingly. As one member who had experienced Christianity in a Gentile church stated:

> The Gentiles think that the Hebrew Christian Church is a wonderful thing; they respect you very much for joining it [rather than a Gentile church]. They'd rather have you in a Hebrew Christian Church. . . . Sure, there's anti-Semitism among the ordinary Gentile Christians; if you're a Jew, you're a Jew, even though you have been converted. But these Gentiles are not real Christians.

Be they "real Christians" or not, the difficulty for the Jewish convert is apparent. Faced with such a problem, the convert may choose from several alternatives, each of which offers a limited solution to his dilemma. He may return to the Jewish group; he may find a place in Gentile surroundings by stressing his status as "convert" and presenting his testimony to his new Christian brethren in an effort to spur them on in their Jewish evangelization efforts; or he may seek out fellow-converts who share the same dilemma. Regarding the first alternative little can be said. It is certain that relapses to the Jewish group do take place, but it is not known under what conditions or to what extent these occur.

Several of the Church members exemplify the second alternative. As Jewish converts they went before Gentile Christian audiences, giving their testimony. They soon realized, however, that the vast majority of Gentile Christians are not interested in bringing Jews to Christianity and are not willing to be constantly confronted with the fervent messages and testimonies of zealous converts who want to see their former coreligionists brought to the new faith. This type of external conscience can be quite irritating, and in any event this "profession," already overcrowded, can absorb only a limited number of people. Furthermore, a career of bringing the message of Jewish evangelization to Gentile Christians precludes all possibilities of leading a "normal" life; the abuses from Christians and especially from Jews that one must take are far too great, while the benefits are extremely limited.

The third alternative is to seek out fellow-converts who share the dilemma and to organize or to become a part of a group of Jewish converts who for some reason are not in the main body of Gentile Christianity. The Hebrew Christian Church is such a group, and a portion of the members are people who have consciously chosen this alternative. This is not to say that they *prefer* being separated from Gentile Christians, for in many instances they do not. Rather, they have been forced to make a decision and have selected this alternative:

I once had the feeling that there is no difference between Jews [i.e., Hebrew Christians] and Christians [Gentile Christians], but later my opinion changed very much. Before, I had the feeling that there is no difference, that all are one in Christ. But after being persecuted as a Jew even though I had been a Christian for some time, well, you don't want to be different. And even though the Hebrew Christian Church emphasizes that we are all one in Christ, that really isn't so. We want to be in the Gentile Christian church, but we can't; even Reverend Kaufman knows that.

It is extremely doubtful whether any of the members would disagree with this statement, although they seldom speak out so openly about their present surroundings. More often they are heard to praise the Church as a "great thing," as a "testimony to both Jews and Gentiles." To show their loyalty to the group they at times point out that although originally converted to a particular denomination, they now realize that (at least for the Jewish convert) denominations are meaningless and that to be together with fellow-converts of Jewish origin is of more importance than being in any particular denomination:

I'm a Baptist, but I want to be with my people. Denominations aren't too important anyway. I joined this Church because all of the members are Jews. With Jewish people, it's not a matter of denominations, or at least that's the way I think about it. It's being converted to Christ, not to any particular denomination.

What becomes important, therefore, is the warm fellowship of other converts from Judaism obtainable in a Hebrew Christian Church.

The dual identification of the Church members as Jews and Christians focuses on the marginal character of Hebrew Christianity. It is a group situated between the Jewish and Gentile Christian groups in our society, and the Hebrew Christian simultaneously participates in some aspects of each of these cultures yet is not completely identified with either. All members are aware of this to some degree; the more perceptive are able to verbalize it:

We don't really give to Jewish charities. If all of the Hebrew Christians gave to Jews who would give to the work for Hebrew Christians? In Germany, before the last war, the Jews helped the Jews, the Gentiles helped the Christians, and the Hebrew Christians were not given any help. We Hebrew Christians had to help them out. I don't know why Jews or Christians didn't help the Hebrew Christians. *I guess we Hebrew Christians are in-between.* Nothing was done for the Hebrew Christians in Germany until the International Hebrew Christian Alliance came to help them. [Italics added.]

Marginality is not pleasant for the individual so placed. It easily leads to confusion and severely restricts the person's social relations with large numbers of people. Thus it is only in his own group, within the limiting confines of the Church and its membership, that the Hebrew Christian can arrive at a solution to his dilemma. The solution is to be found in the ideology of the group—an ideology which seeks to define in an ideal manner the status of the Hebrew Christian.

§ *The Ideology*

The belief system of the Hebrew Christian Church, as might well be expected, is primarily concerned with Judaism, Christianity, the relations between the two, and the role of the Jewish convert to Christianity. The key terms in this scheme are "Jewish" and "Judaism," "Gentile" and "Christian," "Hebrew" and "Gentile," and "Hebrew Christianity" and "Gentile Christianity." With the exception of the latter two, these concepts refer to social groups in our society and their respective belief systems which for most purposes of ordinary social intercourse have been adequately defined. The newcomer or visitor in the Church, whether he is Jewish or Gentile, will in a short time realize that for the Hebrew Christian this is not quite true, that he is in protest against these accepted and established meanings and usages. It will be noted that the Hebrew Christian has modified and redefined the existing terminology, has added new designations, and has emerged with a novel and interesting classification. While not completely articulated and in part only implicit, there is sufficient evidence from the expressions of the members that this constitutes his ideology.

To begin with, there are two levels to this scheme. The first refers to a biological, "racial" complex that one is born with and into, and that one cannot change; it is an inherited characteristic that transcends social and/or psychological usages and desires. On this level there are two "types," Jewish and Gentile, neither of which has been created or de-fined by man. Indeed, they have been created, preserved, and protected from any infringement by God himself. Thus, it is not by chance that one is born a Jew, for God has ordained it so; individuals so blessed, regardless of their wishes or the wishes of those about them, must remain classified as such because the will of God has so decreed. When asked about his being Jewish, the Hebrew Christian will invariably respond in terms of this scheme. "Do I consider myself to be a Jew yet? Of course! You're born a Jew, it's in the blood, I believe"; or, "It's a matter of race. If you're born of circumcision, of the seed of Abraham, you can't change that. Even in a Gentile Christian Church we're still Jewish; it's race." The second type on this "biological" level, the Gentile, refers to all persons who are not Jewish; that is, all persons not of Jewish parentage. Just as being born a Jew is God-ordained, so too is being born a Gentile; no matter what a person might do he cannot change this identification.

The second level has to do with belief systems, namely, paganism, Judaism, and Christianity—and is distinct from the first level in that it is not inherited biologically. Paganism and Judaism were the religions of Gentiles and Jews respectively before the coming of Christ and were trans-mitted by members of these groups to their offspring from generation to generation. Paganism was superseded by Judaism, Judaism by Christianity —all at the will of God. The Hebrew Christian is not overly concerned with paganism; instead, he concentrates on Judaism and Christianity.

Taking these key terms, the Hebrew Christian then proceeds to rank them. It is maintained that the criterion for such an ordering is the super-natural: what is preferred by God as it is known to man by revelation. Again, the structure is of divine rather than of human origin, and the Hebrew Christian claims that he is merely revealing it to all men who are either not aware of it or who do not follow it. On the first level, the "racial," the lowest position is that of Gentile; the Jew is in the dominant position, for God sought to reveal himself to the Jew and he is therefore of the "chosen people." On the second level, paganism occupies the lowest position; Judaism is a superior belief system for it has been brought to man by God. But Judaism is inferior to Christianity, for with the coming of Christ and the presentation of his doctrine Christianity became the pre-ferred belief and hence occupies the dominant position in God's rank order of theological systems.

Combinations of racial and religious traits determine an individual's position in this divine arrangement. The Gentile-pagan is the lowest; above him is the Jew who follows the tenets of Judaism. Until the time of Christ's appearance this was the total uncomplicated design; however, with the coming of the Messiah, the Gentile who accepted Christianity assumed the dominant position. The Gentile Christian rather than the Jew is therefore the favored of God, and it is partly for this reason, so the explanation goes, that God has continued to punish the Jews. Finally, the completion of this hierarchy finds the Hebrew Christian at the very top, for he is now racially *and* religiously superior in that he combines the highest traits of each level.

A related element in the Hebrew Christian ideology is its persistent attempt to show that the Jew who accepts Christianity is not in reality a convert. The explanation for this is arrived at by examining the "true" nature of Christianity. For the Hebrew Christian the New Testament is a Jewish doctrine—God gave it to the Jews first, by means of a Jew, and only afterwards to the non-Jews. Christianity, therefore, is simply Judaism in a more refined, ethically superior form. The minister, in his weekly sermons, constantly repeats this theme:

. . . the average Jew and the average Christian look upon Judaism and Christianity as two different religions belonging to two different peoples. Judaism, they say, is the religion of the Jew, and Christianity is the religion of the Gentiles. This unfortunate misunderstanding of the basic and historical meaning of the two words, "Judaism" and "Christianity," stands in the way of a real reconciliation between Jews and Christians. Christianity is not the religion of the Gentiles as some people think. Christianity is the Jewish religion as it was completed by the life and work of *Yeshua Hamuschiach,* or Jesus Christ, who came into the world in fulfillment of Messianic prophecy. It is of the utmost importance for us Jews to ascertain the truth as to what Christianity really is and to stop talking about it as "the Gentile religion."

The way this mistake can be discovered is, first of all, by examining the historical origin of Christianity. It is definite without the possibility of contradiction that Christianity began as a Jewish Messianic movement in Palestine. The founder and leader of the movement was *Yeshua Hamuschiach,* whose name was changed to Jesus Christ as the story of his life and work was translated into the Greek language. It is also well authenticated that his first followers were all Jews. . . .

Reverend Kaufman develops this theme by pointing out how the apostles decided that the new Judaism would not be for the Jew "'born of circumcision" only, but for the Gentile as well. This was agreed upon after it was seen how eagerly they received the gospel of Christ. However, Reverend Kaufman emphasizes, it was not a Gentile religion that was being promulgated by the apostles; it was a Jewish religion. The Gentiles who declared their faith in Christ accepted a superior form of the Jewish religion and became known as Christians. They did not become Hebrew Christians, for this term was reserved for Jews who acknowledged Christ as the Jewish Messiah, in the same manner that it is today used to designate Jews who believe in the Jewish Savior. Just as the first Hebrew Christians were followers of the "Jewish religion," so too are the present Hebrew Christians. Therefore, the Jew who becomes a Christian does not become a convert; on the contrary, it is the Gentiles who are the converts when they become Christians. Thus, members of the Church may say that:

The Gentiles didn't have anything at first; it was the Jews who did. . . . A Gentile becomes a Jew when he becomes a Christian. Christianity is a Jewish religion. The Gentile is a convert to Judaism; the Jew is not the convert. Truthfully, I feel that I accepted the Christian world, for if Christianity is a Jewish religion then the Gentiles were accepted by me.

While pointing out that the Hebrew Christian is the preferred of God because of his racial and spiritual superiority, and that being a Hebrew Christian does not imply conversion because Christianity is a Jewish religion, the members of the Church are also stating that they are better Jews than their "racial" brethren who adhere to the older form of Judaism. In accordance with this conception they say that Jewish ritual objects rightfully belong in their Church. Moreover, these same symbols would be in all Christian churches, Gentile as well as Jewish, if Gentile Christians were cognizant of the elementary fact that Christianity is a Jewish religion. The members, explaining the presence of this symbolism, point out that:

> The religion we have is true Judaism. The Star of David belongs on the curtain in our Church; it should be in every church. Judaism is the oldest religion and our feeling is that the Gentile comes to the Jew, as with the Bible. We want to keep that Jewish atmosphere in the Church; we want it in the rituals. When we build our own Church it will have right across of it, inscribed, "The Hebrew Christian Church" and a Star of David.

In addition to the Star of David, the Hebrew Christian Church makes use of other Jewish symbolism. On the front wall of the Church there hangs a large blue curtain on which is woven a candelabrum, superimposed upon a six-pointed star, the *Mogen David*, all enclosed by a white circle. From the seven points of the candelabrum red flames emerge to form the Hebrew letters *Yud, Shin, Vav,* and *Ayin*—thus spelling the word *Yeshua*, the Hebrew name of Jesus. Above the circle are inscribed the Hebrew words, *Anochi O'er Ha-olam,* and below, the English translation, "I am the Light of the World." A table before the slightly elevated platform at the head of the room displays an engraved *Mogen David,* brass candelabra, an open Bible in Yiddish, and two offering plates.

The Hebrew language is utilized in the church decor and ritual. It appears on the insignia of the Church and it is used in the course of the liturgy. Reverend Kaufman blesses his congregants with the traditional priestly invocation of *Yevorechacho Adonai Veyishmoracho,* even to the point of extending his arms and spreading apart his third and fourth fingers. No translation of the blessing is given. Hebrew is likewise employed in the sermons; seldom a week passes that the minister does not incorporate some Hebrew word or phrase in the course of his address. What makes this all the more striking is that the congregants do not understand the language; in fact, only a very few can read the Hebrew script by rote with even a minimum of proficiency. It must be concluded that Hebrew is merely symbolic of their origins and of their belief that Hebrew Christianity is the "true Judaism" and the "true Christianity." It is symbolic, just as is the *matzah* which they substitute for the usual Christian wafers during their communion service, or just as is their token support of Zionism and the State of Israel and their occasional contribution to Jewish charities. But the presence of these symbols should not result in the mistaken belief that the Hebrew Christian Church is "Jewish" in the manner the members maintain. For in its fundamental religious orientation it is Christian, and aside from the character of the membership and the presence of Jewish symbolism, the church does not differ from the ordinary Gentile Protestant church.

§ *Social Realities*

The ideology of the Hebrew Christian Church is best understood not in theological terms or symbols, but rather in the social realities which it reflects. Hebrew Christianity is a protest movement. It is in protest against the position which the Jewish convert to Christianity must occupy in our society. As such, it calls upon history and theology to justify the Hebrew Christians' attempt to transform the existing social world into one which he desires to bring about—a world in which the Jewish convert will have a recognized status. At present the convert faces a most difficult dilemma: if he has ties to his former Jewish environment from which he cannot completely dissociate himself, he finds it almost impossible to adjust successfully to his new Christian life. If, on the other hand, he is able to make the necessary break with his past, but in the course of his career as a Christian he is found to be of Jewish parentage, he is most often compelled to abort his "'Gentile" mode of living. Hebrew Christianity seeks to resolve this dilemma by providing the convert with a new *social* category where he can feel the comforting security of fellow-converts. From here he can explain to the world how Hebrew Christians look upon themselves: namely, "We are Jews because we trace our lineage back to Abraham, the first Jew, and we are Christians because we have accepted Christ as our Saviour." With the aid of his ideology he can tell the essentially hostile world of Jews and Gentiles which encompasses him that Hebrew Christianity is of divine origin, decreed by the God of Jews and Gentiles alike, and that he should be treated accordingly.

But neither Jew nor Gentile (except for those few engaged in Jewish evangelization) is willing to accept the legitimacy of the scheme or the new social creation of Hebrew Christianity. For them it is a gross contradiction, as a person is considered to be *either* a Jew *or* a Christian. This denial is expressed not so much on the theological level as it is on the social—the manner in which they act toward Hebrew Christians. The Jew, if he knows a person to be a Hebrew Christian, will treat him as if he were only a Christian, or, still worse, as a convert, a *meshumad*. The "Hebrew" part of Hebrew Christianity is not recognized. Among Gentile Christians the reverse is true; the Hebrew Christian is treated as if he were solely Jewish. Members admit, albeit reluctantly, that "for the Gentile, if you're a Jew [i.e., a Hebrew Christian] you're still a Jew. If you're a Jew they'll persecute you in the Gentile church." Possessing traits of two social groups, yet being treated by members of each group in terms of characteristics associated with the other, is most distressing. As one member put it, "It's rough being a Hebrew Christian; you have to fight the whole world."

It is for this reason that the Hebrew Christian tends to articulate his view of what the world should be like only within the confines of his own group and to a few trusted, benevolent outsiders. When with strangers he will seldom attempt to "pass" as a Hebrew Christian; instead, he will most often try to "'pass" as either a Jew or a Gentile, the choice depending on which identification he believes to be most advantageous at the moment. One member tells of a vacation he and his family spent in a rural area:

> We stopped in a small town general store and soon discovered that the owner was Jewish. When he found out that we were Jewish he was so glad to see us that he made us remain with him for the entire day at his home. . . . No, of course I didn't tell him that we were Hebrew Christians. I don't go around like that; it's obnoxious. You can't be obnoxious. If it would come up I'd tell the person, but I don't go around broadcasting it.

Another member, when asked whether he had told his parents of his conversion, replied that he did not reveal it for some time, and when he did do so he told his father but not his stepmother:

> You know your own parents and the Jewish people; you don't rush in and tell them that you're a Christian. I had to use tact. My stepmother still doesn't know that I'm a Christian. I didn't tell her and neither did my father; it would have ruined the marriage.

It is only in the restricted surroundings of the Church that the member can afford to reveal what he considers to be his true and complete self — his Hebrew Christian self. It is here that he can act toward his fellow-converts in terms of the group ideology and make plans for the perpetuation of his Church and his way of life. For, like the members of most other groups, the Hebrew Christian is not only interested in making a place for himself in society, but also desires to provide for future generations of Hebrew Christians.

Preservation and perpetuation of the group implies recruitment and growth, a task which can be accomplished in several ways. One is to attempt to influence all Jewish converts who are at present affiliated with Gentile Christian churches to reveal their true antecedents and thereupon to join the Hebrew Christian Church. This appeal is made primarily on the basis of pointing to the large amount of discrimination against Jewish converts which exists in Gentile surroundings. If the "facts" of discrimination are not known to such converts, the Hebrew Christian wishes to force it upon their attention. Numerous articles in the *Hebrew Christian Alliance Quarterly*[*] plead with converts to come forward and to reveal themselves in order to strengthen the cause of Hebrew Christianity. Instances of Gentile Christian discrimination against what are termed "Hebrew Christians," but actually referring to *all* Jewish converts, are cited. It is emphasized that the remedy is for Hebrew Christians to unite in a common fellowship.

In many respects this is known to be a futile cry, for if a convert succeeds

---

[*] The *Quarterly* is the publication of the national organization of Hebrew Christians, "Hebrew Christian Alliance."

in "passing" in a Gentile church the chances of his "return" to Hebrew Christianity are remote. A more realistic way of recruitment would seem to be in bringing the message of Christianity to Jews in the hope that they will be persuaded to accept the doctrine as the present members have. Conversion in this case is not to Christianity, but to Hebrew Christianity. The minister in his weekly sermons stresses the Christian duty of the members to bring the message of Christ to all Jews with whom they come in contact. But by and large his pleas are ignored. The Hebrew Christian would rather "pass" as a Jew when he is with Jewish people who do not know him, an attitude which precludes the possibility of speaking about Hebrew Christianity, and he finds it much too difficult to even bring up the subject of his own conversion when with his family, let alone attempt to win them to his faith. Furthermore, as a socially and economically mobile person — in much the same way as are his former co-religionists — he is cognizant of the inappropriateness of this type of behavior. With the exception of a few newer and younger converts, the average Church member strongly disapproves of such older methods of evangelization as house-to-house visitation, store-front and street meetings, and the distribution of tracts and pamphlets. The community-center approach as practiced by Emanuel is much more in accord with his tastes and aspirations. Even in this area he largely delegates the job of proselytization to fundamentalist Gentile Christians who are either paid or voluntary missionaries. It is these people, under the supervision of Reverend Kaufman, who conduct the Emanuel program and who are responsible for winning new converts to Hebrew Christianity. And, as we have seen, this number tends to be negligible.

There remains one further way of perpetuating (although not expanding) the Church, and that is for present members to raise their children as Hebrew Christians. To aid the parents a special educational program is conducted by the Church; every Sunday morning, following services, regular classes are held. During the week the children, if they live in the neighborhood, can spend much of their free time at the Center participating in organized activities. In addition, the parents informally instruct them in the teachings of the Church.

However, raising children to be Hebrew Christians is a difficult process. Hebrew Christians do not live in an isolated community and they have hardly enough offspring to confine their children to Hebrew Christian friends exclusively. These young people must, of necessity, associate with Jews and Gentile Christians of their own age. In these relationships they confront many problems that are similar to those faced by their parents, all of which have to do with belonging to an unrecognized social group. The similarity, however, is only on the surface, for the manner in which the children come to view these problems is quite different. These children were born and raised as Hebrew Christians and have never experienced life as Jews. They know nothing of a conversion experience and lack the conviction of the person who gives up his religion for another. They are aware of the fact that they are Christians, with some modifications in church symbolism, but they have never had the opportunity to be in a Gentile Christian church. They are clearly different from their Jewish and Gentile classmates and are treated accordingly, but having been born Hebrew Christians, they do not readily understand why they must be in this unpleasant position.

It is still too early to discuss with complete reliability the question of what happens to second generation Hebrew Christians. Yet from the few currently available cases there is a strong indication that these people are more remote from the Jewish and closer to the Christian group than are their convert parents. This is not surprising, inasmuch as they have never been Jews and have never had any intimate relationships with either Jews or Judaism. The Church, being essentially Christian, brings them closer to Gentile society. Many of their parents recognize this problem and its rather inevitable consequences. As a solution they say that they would like to re-create a "Jewish atmosphere" for their children — one similar to that which existed in their own parents' homes. But they do not quite know how this is to be done:

I feel that I'd like my children to have a Jewish background so that they can be a testimony to their people. You know that's the main reason for our Church—so that Jews will not say that we became Gentiles. I want my children to have the same background as I had; they should have the Jewish influence, the type combined with the Christian. . . . The best thing—what I want them to get—is a Hebrew Christian background like mine. That's why I want to move to the neighborhood where the Center is located, so that they can get that kind of background. I know a couple, the mother is Gentile and the father is Jewish, and the children don't feel Jewish at all. The girl says, "How can I feel that I'm a Hebrew Christian? I don't feel Jewish." Maybe it's the cultural background that I want my children to get; also, some of the religion. I'd like them to retain something so that they'll know that they're Jewish.

In spite of the fact that this mother sincerely desires her children to be Jewish — and therefore Hebrew Christian — in all probability she will fail. And, consequently, her children, as well as all others born and raised as Hebrew Christians, will be more Christian than Hebrew, more Gentile than Jewish. Already this is revealed in the marriage patterns of the few Hebrew-Christian-born members who have selected mates: whereas their parents almost always married a Jew who subsequently was converted or was already a Hebrew Christian, the children tend to marry Gentile Christians. When this occurs, affiliation is seldom continued with the Hebrew Christian Church. One mother, an non-Emanuel convert, commenting on her son's forthcoming marriage to a Gentile, stated:

He's marrying a Gentile girl, as you know, a Catholic, and Catholicism is pounded into them. Of course, I would prefer for him to marry a Hebrew Christian girl. My reasons are entirely Scriptural: God wants us to avoid trouble; he wants us to marry the same. I feel that I have a perfect right to be against this marriage, to pray to God that he should not allow it. If he doesn't stop it, then he has a reason for it, he has some purpose in letting it go through. But I know that I would like my son to remain with his own people—for him and for his own people. In unity there is strength.

This same trend is reflected even by the son of the minister. For his wife he selected a Gentile girl. And although now he is affiliated with the Church, following his ordination as a minister he spent several years in an all-Gentile church and community. It is true that he is still a Hebrew Christian, but for him this term means something different than it does for his parents. As with others of his generation, he is more Gentile and Christian than he is Jewish.

The tendency for the second generation to become almost exclusively Christian leads one to believe that in many respects the Hebrew Christian Church can be looked at as an intermediate step in the conversion of Jews to Christianity. While ordinarily thought of as occurring in the lifetime of one individual, and furthermore as taking place in a flashing moment of revelation and inspiration, it appears that here conversion takes two or possibly more generations. It is not the religious aspects of apostasy that requires so much time; it is rather the social features, which are much more involved and much more difficult to accomplish successfully. For conversion implies not only an acceptance of an abstract God, an impersonal church, and theological beliefs that are foreign to one's own heritage; more crucial is the fact that it necessitates an adjustment to a whole new series of personal relations, self-conceptions, and behavior patterns. In this life at least, these things are of far greater importance than religious concepts. Viewed in this manner, the Church and its ideology perform a substantial service for its adherents. However, as a movement, it cannot continue for long in the way in which it is now conceived. At present it is merely a wayside stopping place for one or two generations who enter, tarry a while, and then leave. Under such circumstances it must recruit new members, people who, if they and their descendants will not permanently affiliate themselves, will at least perpetually fill the ranks. This the Hebrew Christian Church does not seem to be able to do. We are therefore led to believe that the interesting phenomenon of Hebrew Christianity will at some future time cease to exist.

5

Psychological Aspects:
Group Belongingness
and Jewish Identification

INTRODUCTION

THE growing interest in the psychological sciences has been reflected in the Jewish field by the increase of research on problems of group belongingness and Jewish identification. This increase of research seems large only because there was so little material previously; it is still apparent that knowledge in other areas has accumulated at a faster rate than has been true for the study of group belongingness and Jewish identification.

Two predominant strands characterize these research efforts. The first grows out of the framework developed by Kurt Lewin. Lewin was a unique figure—a man responsible for pioneer developments in the general field who at the same time possessed a high degree of interest in Jewish problems. He was strongly concerned with therapy—in applying the psychological sciences to the problems of the Jew. The second strand developed outside of the Lewinian framework, and in fact the innovators had relatively little interest in Jewish life and problems. We refer to the researchers responsible for the volume, *The Authoritarian Personality*. Stemming from this work, there has been an attempt to relate authoritarianism to the problem of Jewish identification. While the concept of authoritarianism was originally developed to explain attitudes of majority-group members, it was not difficult to visualize the possibility that it might be helpful in understanding a minority group as well.

The first article included in the present section actually lies outside of these two lines of development. It represents research sponsored by an "action agency," and designed to assess a particular situation. Such data can, however, be reanalyzed so as to uncover relationships which are of more than transitory significance. Thus, the article by Marshall Sklare and Benjamin B. Ringer, "A Study of Jewish Attitudes toward the State of Israel," presents both a summary of certain aspects of Jewish opinion of a decade ago, as well as some of the variables which help explain these opinions. In addition to the psychological orientations presented, the article serves the important function of elucidating the opinion of Jews about the State of Israel, and to a lesser extent about the question of Zionism. This area is an important aspect of American Jewish life which is only touched on in other articles; the research reported by Sklare and Ringer constitutes one of the few empirical studies on the subject.

Marian Radke Yarrow's article, "Personality Development and Minority Group Membership," is more typical of relevant investigations in the field of social psychology. Her contribution includes both a careful review of pertinent theory as well as a report on a significant research effort. In framing her problem, Yarrow utilizes the approach of Kurt Lewin. Her article has special value in this regard, for Lewin's prestige served to interest people in his approach even though his writings on this particular subject were not based on the type of research which he conducted in other fields. In keeping with Lewin's scheme, Yarrow's stress is on the deprivational rather than the rewarding aspects of minority-group membership, on exclusionary patterns rather than on the degree of acceptance which flows from such membership, on the pressures which act on the minority-group child to throw him into conflict—rather than into adjustment—with his environment, on loyalties which are mutually exclusive rather than mutually supplementary. These tendencies are all apparent in the framing of the various "forced-choice" situations included in Yarrow's questionnaire.

The value of the approach cannot be doubted, but the necessity of supplementing it with a different framework may also be apparent. In any case, the present article not only constitutes an excellent example of one approach to the problem, but it has the added value of presenting the results of a questionnaire administered to three highly different groups. These results suggest some of the varied psychological consequences of different minority-group "atmospheres."

The articles by Joseph Adelson and Irwin D. Rinder represent attempts to measure Jewish identification, and to correlate such identification with other factors. In this connection, both authors employ the "authoritarian personality" scales. Also, Rinder and Adelson utilize the approach apparent in the Yarrow article. Thus, in lieu of a true sample of young people, they obtained respondents drawn from the varied socio-economic, generational, religious, and ideological groups in the Jewish community. As will be noticed, the results of Adelson and Rinder are not in perfect agreement with each other.

MARSHALL SKLARE
AND BENJAMIN B. RINGER

A STUDY OF JEWISH ATTITUDES
TOWARD THE STATE OF ISRAEL

IN the Spring of 1948, immediately after the new State of Israel was established in Palestine and soon after it had been recognized by the United States, the American Jewish Committee conducted a number of studies designed to assess the reactions of American Christians and Jews to these important events.[1] Among Christians, the investigation focused upon how much was known about these happenings, upon attitudes toward selected aspects of the Palestine situation, and upon the relationship of such attitudes to feelings toward Jews in general. Among Jews, the investigation also focused on the extent of knowledge about the Palestine situation and on reactions to the establishment of the State of Israel. In addition, an effort was made to determine whether the establishment of a Jewish State provoked conflicts in political loyalties.

The present article is concerned with only one phase of the larger study. It is confined to an analysis of the reactions of a sample of the Jewish population of Baltimore who were interviewed in May, 1948. We shall also compare the attitudes of our Jewish respondents with those of white Gentiles residing in the same community.

§ I. Methodology

The particular survey with which we shall be concerned was the second of two conducted in Baltimore by the American Jewish Committee (AJC) in cooperation with the National Opinion Research Center.

The first survey took place in November, 1947, and was designed to investigate attitudes toward minority groups. Interviews were conducted with a probability sample of 1,200 residents of Baltimore, 18 years of age and older. About 800 members of the sample were white Christians. Some 77 were Jews—a number corresponding proportionately to the distribution of Jews in the total population.

After the establishment of the State of Israel, AJC decided to return to Baltimore for a second survey in May of 1948. Among other things, it wished to discover how the establishment of Israel had affected attitudes toward Jews. AJC was, therefore, interested in reinterviewing the same

Published for the first time in this volume.

This paper constitutes a reanalysis of data gathered for "The Palestine Study," a research project of the Division of Scientific Research of the American Jewish Committee. Thanks are due to AJC for permission to publish this material.

group of white Christians who had served as respondents for the survey conducted the previous November. Due to a variety of reasons such as refusal to be interviewed again, change of address, and inability of the interviewer to find the respondent at home even after three visits, only 556 of the original 800 were in fact reinterviewed.

Another of the research objectives of the 1948 survey was to examine in detail the response of Jews to the establishment of Israel. In particular, knowledge was desired about the extent to which Jews with varied backgrounds differed in their attitudes toward Israel. It was therefore decided that not only should the original Jewish respondents be reinterviewed, but also a group of new respondents be added. (In keeping with their representation in the population, only 7 per cent of the November sample were Jews, a group which was too small for the elaborate analysis that was planned.) The May sample of Jews was thus greatly enlarged[2] and consisted of a total of 230 respondents, only 50 of whom had been interviewed in the first survey.[3] Because of the enlarged sample, data on changes in Jewish attitudes are available for only a minority of the Jewish respondents. Consequently, this paper will touch only incidentally upon the problem of attitude change; we shall instead concentrate on the uniformities and differences found within the May sample.

§ II. Information and Interest

The 1948 survey was conducted during the period in which the recently established State of Israel was being attacked by the surrounding Arab nations. Most Jews in our sample responded to the strife with considerable interest. When asked, "What do you consider the most important trouble spots in the world today?" the one most frequently mentioned was Palestine. Virtually all—94 per cent—made it one of their choices. This was more than twice as many as selected the next most frequent choice, Russia, a nation which was mentioned by only 41 per cent. Among Christians the reverse was true. Russia was mentioned more frequently than was Palestine. Seventy-one per cent chose Russia, and only 43 per cent voted for Palestine. Thus, among Jews Palestine occupied the center of the world stage while among Christians it was Russia.

Not only were most of the Jewish respondents aware of the fighting in Palestine, but in addition they did not keep this awareness to themselves. They made the conflict a topic of conversation; they discussed it with other persons. This is evident in their response to the following question: "Do you ever talk with other people about the Palestine situation?"[4] Eighty-four per cent replied that they did. More than one-third (37 per cent) said they brought it up frequently in conversation, and almost half (47 per cent) said they talked about it occasionally.[5]

In view of this widespread concern and discussion, it was not surprising to find that most Jews displayed more than a casual acquaintance with what was taking place in Palestine. They understood, for example, who the various participants in the conflict were and what role England played in the situation. To study the level of their general knowledge about the Palestine situation, we constructed an index from the following four items:

1. Knowledge of fighting taking place in Palestine.[6]
2. Which people are fighting each other in Palestine? (correct answer: *Jews and Arabs.*)
3. Has any of the above countries—that is, United States, England, or Russia —been active in governing Palestine for the past 30 years or so? (correct answer: *England.*)
4. Do you happen to know what is the name of the new Jewish State? (correct answer: *Israel.*)

More than three-quarters of the Jewish sample answered all four items correctly; every Jewish respondent was able to answer at least two. Most Jews thus possessed a real knowledge of some of the major features of the Palestine situation. Indeed, they had a much better understanding of the events than did most Christians. Among the non-Jewish sample only one-third answered all four items correctly. Another third answered three correctly. The remaining one-third responded correctly to only two, one or none of the questions.[7]

The familiarity of most Jews with certain major features of the Palestine situation did not mean that they were experts on its varied details. Few were as well informed on specifics as they were on items of more general information. Only 54 per cent could identify correctly the Jewish organizations or individuals who were in favor of setting up a Jewish State; even fewer (35 per cent) knew which organizations or individuals were *opposed* to setting up a Jewish State. Only 43 per cent could correctly identify the *Irgun.*[8]

These differences in level of information did not occur at random. They varied with such factors as level of education, age, sex, income and place of birth. Those who had completed high school or who had gone to college scored higher on the index of general knowledge and were better informed on the questions about detailed knowledge than were those with fewer years of formal education. Men were better informed than women; the native born knew more than the foreign born; and those under thirty-five were more knowledgeable than were those over thirty-five. In addition, people with higher incomes ($70 per week or more) were better informed than were those with lower incomes (less than $70 per week).[9] It is important to note, however, that even among the relatively less-informed groups, a significant number had kept up with the events and politics relating to the new Jewish State. Thus, among Jewish respondents who had *not* completed high school, more than two-thirds (69 per cent) were high on the general knowledge index. This is in decided contrast to the Christians, among whom only 51 per cent of those who *had* completed high school or more scored high on the same index.

§ III. Support

The Jews in our sample hardly approached the Palestine situation as might a detached observer who seeks information for "scientific purposes." In other words, their concern and interest were not devoid of emotional content. Thus, they made no pretense at neutrality, and their partisanship for Israel was clearly expressed. For example, virtually all respondents endorsed the establishment of the State of Israel. Approximately nine out of ten replied "Approve" to the following question: "The Jews have set up a new Jewish State in part of Palestine. Do you approve or disapprove of this action by the Jews?" A similar number thought the United States had been right in recognizing the new State ("The United States has just recognized the new Jewish State in Palestine. Do you think that this was the right thing to do, or the wrong thing to do?").

In the eyes of most, past support of Israel was not enough; they felt that the crisis situation which beset the new country necessitated a continuing effort. Furthermore, they were desirous of support by the United States Government. They both wanted and expected the Government to approve of Israel and to help it in its fight with the Arabs. For example, in answer to the question, "Do you think the United States Government should help the Jews in Palestine, should help the Arabs, or should help both or neither?," 62 per cent favored helping the Jews, no one favored helping the Arabs, 16 per cent favored the Government not helping either group, and 14 favored helping both.

In seeking the assistance of the United States Government, our Jewish respondents were not looking for a way to relieve themselves of responsibility. On the contrary, they were convinced that providing Israel with the needed assistance was first and foremost an obligation of the Jewish community.[10] The obligation they saw as theirs, and its fulfillment they viewed as imperative—all this irrespective of the general tide of opinion and of the specific attitude of the United States Government. Asked the question, "Even if the United States does not help the Jews in Palestine, do you think that the Jewish people in the United States should or should not help them?," 95 per cent signified that they should. Asked further, "In your opinion, would the Jews in the United States be right or wrong to try to help the Jewish State even if the United States were against helping it?," over seven out of ten felt that they would be right.[11]

How did Baltimore Jewry propose to help Israel? By what manner and means? The answer is primarily through *economic* means and only secondarily through *military* means. Virtually all would have Jews send money (91 per cent) as well as food and clothing (93 per cent). Somewhat fewer would approve of American Jewry sending munitions (80 per cent). And fewest—but still the majority—would favor sending fighting men (51 per cent).

Similar kinds of assistance would be welcomed from the United States Government, although fewer respondents expected from it the specific forms of aid they expected from Jews. Greatest support was for the sending of money (62 per cent) and for the sending of food and clothing (59 per cent). About half (51 per cent) would have the United States Government ship arms and ammunition, but only a minority (23 per cent) would have the Government take military action by sending soldiers. Most Jews, in other words, while wanting economic and other forms of assistance, did not expect or want the United States to go to war for the sake of Israel.

§ IV. Personal Involvement and Commitment to Jewish Life

Although the attitudes of most respondents reflected a *common* direction, consensus with regard to the *strength* or *intensity* of pro-Israel sentiment was absent. Thus, Baltimore Jewry did not share a uniform sense of urgency or a common desire to participate personally in the conflict. In fact, only a minority were completely preoccupied with the situation and totally committed to the cause. We have already noted that only somewhat over a third (37 per cent) said they made the Palestine situation a frequent topic of conversation. It was also found that only a minority were so concerned with the situation that they could see themselves as personally joining the struggle. We have reference in this connection to the 38 per cent who answered "Yes" to the pointed but "iffy" question, "If you could, would you yourself like to be fighting in Palestine?"

What accounted for these variations in involvement?[12] Why were some people much more concerned than others? One of the primary factors was found to be the strength of the individual's ties with Judaism and/or Jewishness. Included in the questionnaire were a number of queries thought to be indicative of such ties, and from these items an index of Jewish identification was constructed. The items were as follows:

1. Do you attend services at a Temple or a Synagogue? How often?
2. Are you a regular member of either a Temple or a Synagogue?
3. Are you a member of any Jewish organization?
4. Is Yiddish spoken in your home a good deal, fairly often, or hardly ever?

People who attended services regularly or fairly often, who were synagogue members, who were affiliated with a Jewish organization and who spoke Yiddish at home a good deal or fairly often, or who could qualify on any three of these four criteria, were considered as having a strong or *high* Jewish identification. The rest were considered to have a relatively *low* Jewish identification.[13]

Comparing individuals manifesting high Jewish identification with those manifesting low identification, we found that the former went further in their support of Israel than the latter. They were more personally involved in the conflict and were more willing to have the United States Government send arms and men to Israel. This tendency is apparent in Table 1.

Table 1—Commitment to Jewish Life Intensifies Involvement with Israel and Support of Military Assistance

| | LEVEL OF COMMITMENT TO JEWISH LIFE | |
	High	Low
% who share a high level of personal involvement with Palestine situation.[14]	50%	33%
% who agree that:		
U. S. Government should send *arms and ammunition* to help the Jews in Palestine	61%	46%
U. S. Government should send *soldiers* to help the Jews in Palestine	34%	16%
	(77)	(153)

It is interesting to note, however, that commitment to Judaism and Jewish life, while making for greater personal involvement, did not increase the likelihood of a pro-Israel orientation. It affected the *intensity* but not the *direction* of a Jew's response to Israel. Virtually all, irrespective of level of commitment, showed some favorable sentiments toward Israel: it was right for the United States to have recognized the new Jewish State in Palestine, and Jews should help Israel even if the Government was neutral or negative (see Table 2).

Table 2—Commitment to Jewish Life Has No Effect on Sharing a Pro-Israel Orientation

| | LEVEL OF COMMITMENT TO JEWISH LIFE | |
	High	Low
% who agree that:		
It was right for the United States to recognize the new Jewish State in Palestine	90%	90%
	(77)	(153)
Even if the United States does not help the Jews in Palestine, the Jewish people should *help* them.	96%	96%
	(76)	(151)

Thus, it is apparent that merely being Jewish was enough to evoke pro-Israel sympathies; however, it is equally apparent that something more was generally needed to transform these sympathies into active involvement with and support for Israel. A firm attachment to Jewish life and the sharing of strong sentiments and feelings about Jewishness played an important part in producing this involvement and support.

The importance of "sentimental ties" is further underscored when we look at the part played by "intellectual ties." Merely having an intellectual-ized concern with Israel did not in itself have any effect on involvement. This conclusion is apparent when the relationship between level of in-formation and involvement is examined. We see no connection between the two. Knowing more about Israel did not make for more involvement (see Table 3).[15]

Table 3—Knowledge Has No Effect on Level of Involvement

	LEVEL OF KNOWLEDGE ABOUT PALESTINE SITUATION	
	High	Low
% who share a high level of personal involvement with Palestine situation	39% (178)	38% (52)

However, if the informed person was in addition deeply committed to Jewish life, then his being knowledgeable about Israel did make a differ-ence. It increased the likelihood of his being intensely involved with the country. It was, therefore, only in the absence of commitment to Jewish life that knowledge failed to exert any influence on level of involvement. Apparently among the less committed, knowledge about Israel was merely part of a more general interest in world affairs. It was not, as in the case of the highly committed, an expression of a special concern with Israel (see Table 4).

Table 4—Knowledge of Palestine Situation Intensifies Involvement Only among those Highly Committed to Jewish Life

	LEVEL OF COMMITMENT TO JEWISH LIFE	
	High	Low
% who are highly involved in Palestine situation among those having:		
High level of knowledge about situation	52% (54)	33% (124)
Low level of knowledge about situation	43% (23)	35% (29)

Thus, commitment to Jewish life played an important part in the rela-tionship between knowledge and involvement. It functioned as a condi-tion which had to be present if knowledge was to intensify involvement with Israel. In the most simple terms, the Jew first had to have his "heart" in Jewish life if his "intellect" was to draw him closer to Israel.

§ V. The Problem of "Dual Loyalty"

In view of the sympathies which our respondents manifested for the State of Israel, one might wonder whether such attitudes posed any special problems in regard to their relationship to the United States. The question of "dual loyalty" has on occasion been raised. Queries such as, "How does the Jew reconcile his interest in Israel with his loyalties as an American citizen?," and "To what extent does he perceive any conflict between the two?" have been asked.

The data suggest that our respondents felt little, if any, incompatibility between their ties to the two countries. It was evident from our interviews that even those individuals strongly involved with Israel saw no conflict between their support of that nation and their allegiance to the United States. To them the issue of a Jewish State was distinct from the issue of the national identification of the American Jew. As one woman much concerned with the Palestine situation said:

> As far as I'm concerned, America is my home, but Jews should have a place they can call their home. I have no desire to leave America . . . but Jews should have a little place to call their own.

And, when a Jewish homeland was considered by Jewish respondents to be a necessity in order ". . . to give displaced persons a chance to live and rehabilitate themselves . . . ," respondents felt even less strain upon their identity as Americans. The replies would indicate that a Jew may give wholehearted support to the establishment of a Jewish State, and to helping insure its viability, while he reaffirms his allegiance to America.

Even our respondents' replies to the question which asked whether it would be right for Jews in the United States to try to help the Jewish State even if the United States were against helping the country revealed a reluctance to admit any incompatability between support of Israel and allegiance to the United States. Although the question would seem to raise that possibility and to require a choice between loyalties to the two countries, most of our respondents did not interpret the query in that light. Even though they answered that Jews would be right to help, they were not affirming greater loyalty to Israel than to the United States but were expressing their unwillingness to accept the premise that continued support of Israel might conflict with their allegiance to the United States. To them the statement that the United States would be against helping the new State did not imply that any basic issues of loyalty would be at stake or that any legal sanctions might be applied against Jewish help to Israel. It seemed simply a matter of course that Jews should help other Jews. Such action could not be harmful to the United States even if American policy was one of neutrality:

> We must help our own. Every family or group knows this. We are not hurting our Government by treachery, but we definitely are helping those who are oppressed and needy.

In other words, help for other Jews would do no harm to America. Jews are in need, and there is no conflict between loyalty to the United States and assistance to one's brethren.

However, a small group of respondents did consider that a conflict in loyalties might be involved if the United States opposed help to Israel. Why their perception of the situation differed from that of the others cannot be explained. Unfortunately, our data do not provide us with the kind of detailed information about the selective perceptions of our respondents which such an explanation would require. We do know, however, that in virtually all of the cases where a conflict was perceived, loyalty to the United States was reaffirmed. Though sympathetic to Israel, such respondents felt that under these conditions continued support might be construed as an act of disobedience to the Unted States Government and should as a consequence be stopped:

It would be wrong if the assistance placed this country in jeopardy. Our first loyalty is to the United States.

It's wrong if it's an act against the Government. I wouldn't want them to.

Naturally, if the Government would not want them to, it would be bad. I hope they will do their best for the Jewish people.

A similar reaffirmation of ties to America was observed in still another connection. Virtually all persons in our sample, despite their desire to help Israel, felt that their roots were in the United States and their primary loyalties to America. Few would sacrifice their ties to America for those to Israel. Indeed, even if given the opportunity, few would consider leaving the country. When asked "Would you yourself like to go to Palestine to live if you could, or would you rather stay in this country?," only 5 per cent said they would prefer living in Palestine.

Thus, for most Jews Israel and the United States stood for two different kinds of commitments and ties, neither of which clashed with the other and both of which were essential to their total image of themselves as American Jews. However, should they be faced with a situation where they would have to choose between the two countries—a situation which they were anxious to avoid—loyalty to the United States would prevail.

§   *VI. Nonsupport and Fear of*
      Heightened Anti-Semitism

As we have already seen, most of our respondents expressed support for the new State of Israel. Examination of the interviews of the small group of deviants who felt differently revealed a number of grounds on which they based their opposition. We have already commented on one of the more frequent: fear that support of Israel might bring the Jew into conflict with the United States Government. Closely allied with this as a major reason for nonsupport was the fear of a possible hostile reaction on the part of American Christians—not necessarily the Government itself —to Jewish assistance of Israel.[16] This is seen in responses to the question, "Do you think that the Palestine situation may cause more anti-Semitism in the United States, or will it make for less anti-Semitism, or won't it affect anti-Semitism in this country?"

While the nonsupporters of Israel were no more convinced than were its supporters that the conflict would affect domestic anti-Semitism—only about half in each group foreseeing any domestic repercussions (see Table 5)—among those who *did* predict an effect non-supporters were much more pessimistic about the direction which such an effect would take. They firmly believed that the conflict would intensify anti-Jewish sentiments.[17] The supporters of Israel held the opposite view. They were con-

Table 5—Expectation that Arab-Israel Conflict Will Affect Domestic Anti-Semitism
Is Not Significantly Correlated with Attitude toward Aid for Israel

	The United States Government		Even if the United States Does Not Help the Jews in Palestine, Jewish People in the United States	
	Should Help Jews	Should Not Help Jews or Don't Know[18]	Should Help Them	Should Not Help Them or Don't Know
% who feel that Arab-Israel conflict will have an effect on domestic anti-Semitism	51%	53%	52%	40%
	(175)	(53)	(219)	(10)

fident that the Palestine situation would serve to lessen anti-Semitism (see Table 6).

Not all proponents of aid who expected repercussions, however, shared these convictions. Some expressed fears similar to those voiced by the opponents of aid. They too were worried that the conflict might increase anti-Semitism. The presence of these anxieties was closely related to the *degree* and *kind* of support proffered by those who were pro-Israel (see Table 7).

Respondents who approved limited assistance to Israel were more pessimistic about the probable impact of the conflict on the domestic situation than were those who approved more extensive aid. Specifically, those who would have American Jews offer money, food and clothing but not fighting men were more fearful of anti-Jewish repercussions than were those who would even support the sending of fighting men.

Those respondents who did not favor giving aid or who favored limited

Table 6—Among Those Who Predict an Effect, Non-Supporters Foresee an Increase
in Anti-Semitism while Supporters Foresee a Decrease

	The United States Government		Even if the United States Does Not Help the Jews in Palestine, Jewish People in the United States	
Direction of predicted effect of Arab-Israel conflict:	Should Help Jews	Should Not Help Jews or Don't Know[18]	Should Help Them	Should Not Help Them or Don't Know
Increase in domestic anti-Semitism	38%	68%	44%	100%
Decrease in domestic anti-Semitism	62	32	56	0
	100%	100%	100%	100%
	(89)	(28)	(114)	(4)

Table 7—Among Those Who Predict an Effect, Presumed Direction of Effect Is Related to Kind of Support for Israel

	Even if the United States Does Not Help Jews in Palestine, Jews in America Should Help Them by Sending Food, Clothing and Money	
Direction of predicted effect of Arab-Israel conflict:	And Also by Going There To Fight	But Not by Going There To Fight
Increase in domestic anti-Semitism	35%	57%
Decrease in domestic anti-Semitism	65	43
	100%	100%
	(68)	(44)

help tended to worry that non-Jews would blame the Arab-Israel conflict for disturbing the peace of the world, and as one respondent stated:

> If there is trouble in this world, they will blame it on the Palestine situation.

They feared that the impatience or even anger of the non-Jew would be directed not only at Israel but also at Jews in other parts of the world, including the United States. Anti-Semitic sentiments could, accordingly, be expected to rise.

To offset or to minimize these repercussions from the conflict, these respondents would have American Jews assert their independence and separateness from the Jews of Israel. Some would do this by having American Jews refrain completely from helping Israel. Others were less extreme. They wanted American Jews to do something for Israel but would avoid having those things done or given which to their way of thinking might jeopardize their security and blur their identity as Americans in the eyes of the non-Jew. They would, therefore, confine aid to the philanthropic level—food, clothing and money.

On the other hand, those who favored all kinds of aid for Israel were inclined to see the matter from an entirely different frame of reference. To them the crucial thing was that a small nation was meeting the challenge posed by powerful aggressors and that a struggle for independence and survival was being waged by Jews for their own nation. They felt that the couraegous behavior of Israeli Jews was bound to evoke the admiration of non-Jews. As one respondent commented:

> The Palestine situation will cause more respect when they [the Christians] see Jews fight for a country.

As a result, they were convinced that Israel's struggle with the Arabs, far from stimulating anti-Semitism in America, would reduce it by enhancing the stature of the Jew. And, since the battle Israel was waging would benefit Jews in America and elsewhere in the world, it was entitled to full-fledged and unreserved support, including the sending of volunteers.

While it would appear from the above that the kind of aid a respondent endorsed was more a result than a determinant of his conception of the probable impact of the conflict on the domestic situation, it is equally apparent that the conception was itself largely a product of the respondent's basic attitude toward Israel. He projected into the future that which corresponded to his present feelings and concerns. If he was deeply attached and involved with Israel, then he was disinclined to see anything bad resulting from its struggle with the Arabs (see Table 8). He stressed the

Table 8—Among Those Who Predict an Effect, Level of Involvement with Israel Affects Direction of Predicted Effect

Direction of predicted effect of Arab-Israel conflict:	LEVEL OF INVOLVEMENT WITH ISRAEL	
	High	Low
Increase in domestic Anti-Semitism	28%	58%
Decrease in domestic anti-Semitism	72	42
	100%	100%
	(49)	(69)

identity of interests of world Jewry and Israel and pointed to the various benefits that would accrue to all Jews from the conflict. He felt, therefore, that Jews were obligated to provide all-out support for Israel. On the other hand, if the respondent was relatively uninvolved with Israel, he was inclined to distinguish between the interests of Israel and those of other Jews and to entertain the notion that the conflict might have harmful consequences for the Jew in America. He would, therefore, minimize these effects by having American Jews provide Israel with nothing more than philanthropic assistance.

§ VII. The Effect of Israel on Jewish Identification

Having examined reactions to assisting the newly founded State of Israel, we may next inquire into the impact of the fighting upon the feelings of Jews with respect to the problem of Jewish identification. Our respondents were asked, "Since the fighting in Palestine has been going on, do you feel any closer to the Jewish people as a whole, or don't you feel any closer?" Half of them reported that they now felt closer; half reported that they did not. Those who maintained that they did not could be classified into two distinct groups. About half, or 24 per cent of the total sample, claimed that they had always felt close to other Jews, and presumably could not be moved to feel any closer. The remainder indicated that they had not in the past, and did not now, feel any strong bond with other Jews.

Respondents who said that they now felt closer were asked to explain why. Frequently they indicated that they commiserated with the Jews fighting for a homeland:

> There are so many homeless Jews with no future.

> They've been persecuted. They should have a homeland.

> They're in distress and still having bloodshed after all these years.

Other answers seemed to express something in addition to sympathy, perhaps pride:

It's wonderful that the people are fighting for a country.

They're fighting for something they believe in and a worthy cause.

A number of comments could not be easily classified in terms of sympathy or pride. An example is the statement, "They're fighting for their very existence." Because many comments were of this unrevealing nature, it was not possible to ascertain the relative prevalence of specific sentiments behind a statement of greater closeness to the Jewish people. Actually, the wording of the comments suggests that "feeling closer" did not always represent intimate identification with the Jews who were fighting or who wanted a homeland. *"They've* been persecuted" or *"They're* fighting" indicates that considerable distance was still felt between the Jew safe in America and the Jew persecuted in Europe or fighting in Palestine.

There is evidence, however, that a certain proportion of those claiming that the Palestine fighting had drawn them closer to other Jews did experience greatly intensified feelings of identification. For, although these individuals were less likely to manifest strong Jewish identification than those claiming they had always felt close to the Jewish people (32 per cent with strong Jewish identification as compared with 46 per cent),[19] they were as highly involved in the Palestine fighting. Thus, of those who now felt closer to the Jewish people, 43 per cent claimed that they would be willing to go to Palestine to fight. A similar proportion, 40 per cent of those who said they had always felt close, were willing to make the same commitment.

Besides examining the effect of the Palestine conflict upon group identification, the study also inquired into its effect upon specific behavioral commitments to Jewish life. Respondents were asked whether they had joined any Jewish organizations during the preceding year. Out of the 230 persons interviewed, 28 people or 12 per cent said they had. Of the 28, a total of 15 had joined Zionist or pro-Zionist organizations. A total of three had joined an anti-Zionist organization, and the remaining ten joined groups which could be best classified as "non-Zionist." It is noteworthy that people who said they felt closer to Jewry as a result of the Palestine fighting were more likely to have joined Jewish organizations than were those who claimed that their feelings in this connection had not changed.

§ *VIII. Summary*

Pro-Israel sentiments were almost universally found among our respondents. The intensity of their sentiments, though, varied with the extent of their commitment to Jewish life. Those with the strongest attachment to Jewish life and Judaism were most likely to have a deep personal stake in Israel and to be vitally concerned with its fate. In addition, commitment to Jewish life played a crucial role in the relationship between level of information about Israel and involvement with the country. It had to be present if increased knowledge was to draw a person closer to Israel.

Being pro-Israel posed no threat, insofar as most of our respondents were concerned, to loyalty to the United States. The two countries stood for two different kinds of commitments and ties, neither of which clashed with the other and both of which were essential to our respondents' total image of themselves as American Jews. However, if a choice between the two countries had to be made, then loyalty to the United States would prevail.

A major worry expressed by the small minority who did not favor aid to Israel, and also by those only mildly pro-Israel, was that domestic anti-Semitism might be aggravated by the Arab-Israel conflict. This anxiety muted their enthusiasm for Israel and bolstered their resistance to helping the new country. The more ardent pro-Israel respondent felt differently. He expected the conflict to reduce anti-Semitism in America, and he would have American Jews provide all-out support for Israel.

Finally, the fighting in Israel seemed to have intensified the feelings of identification of a number of Jews. It made them feel closer to the Jewish people as a whole.

MARIAN RADKE YARROW

PERSONALITY DEVELOPMENT
AND MINORITY GROUP MEMBERSHIP

THERE is a long history of interest and concern regarding the influences of social minority status upon the individual. Few characteristics of the individual's social environment are more enduring and have effects (potentially) upon more aspects of his adjustment and achievement than his membership in a minority group (racial, national, religious) which occupies a position of recognized social underprivilege.

Despite this fact, the developmental problems of the child as a member of a minority group have received little systematic integration with, and investigation as, problems of socialization and personality development. Both the fields of minority group research and of socialization, it would seem, would be measurably enriched by such a liaison. Instead, "ethnic relations" have become somewhat of a separate "applied" field of social psychology, with attention being centered much more on the beliefs, affects, and intentions of the dominant groups toward the minority rather than upon the consequences of these reactions for the minority member. Data on the "majority" group are very useful and necessary for understanding the minority group, for they provide a picture of the reality of attitudes and of behavior potentials which comprise the psychological surroundings of the minority. They are not, however, sufficient for understanding the problem of minority status and minority-majority relations.

The present paper is directed to the problems which minority group children face in the process of growing up, problems in the formation of their personalities and in the learning of the social roles and values in terms of which they function in society. Several sources of theory and data provide us with frameworks for investigating the social and psychological situation of the minority child. One of these calls attention to the personality variable in intergroup relations. In particular, the work of Adorno, Frenkel-Brunswik, Levinson and Sanford on the Authoritarian Personality (1) demonstrates forcefully the relationship between personality and prejudice, and the link between ethnic attitudes and child-rearing backgrounds. While pertaining mainly to the "majority" group, this study has implications with respect to minority groups. One can assume that the individual's adjustment to the disadvantages of belonging to a deprived social group are also conditioned by factors of his personality structure and childhood experience. From this point of view, the conditions, structure,

---

Published for the first time in this volume.

and well-being of the minority group as a whole will in part depend on the individual personality structure of the minority member.

Another framework which is relevant for investigating developmental problems in minority status is found in the orientation of some cultural anthropologists. Their basic theoretical position is stated by Gillin (10): ". . . the individual learns to be the kind of person he becomes, and . . . most of what he learns is cultural material conveyed to him by the members of his group and their artifacts. The cultures . . . vary . . . , but each has the effect of producing a certain similarity in personality among the individuals who practice the culture. These similarities . . . owe their existence to the similarities in training and conditioning to which children of a given group are exposed. . . . If we know the child-rearing patterns of a society or social category, we are in a fair position to describe reliably the type of person we may expect to find in that society or category."

A number of studies undertaken from this point of view have concerned themselves with social class differences in child-rearing practices within the white and Negro races in American society (6, 7). They have been concerned principally with variations in the feeding and cleanliness training, the handling of dependency drives and the socializing of aggressive drives in different subcultures and with the associated personality outcomes. To the extent that a given social minority represents consistency of child-rearing, we would expect certain similarities in personality of minority children. However the child-rearing variables just mentioned are not likely to be the socialization variables in which there are the greatest differences between children of minority and majority groups, or which are the most uniquely crucial in the development of children of minority groups.

In a curious way, the personality-and-culture school, although working within a framework of culture and social group, has focused upon interpersonal situations in early childhood — how the culture is mediated to the child by the parent or parent surrogate. This emphasis on the parent-child relation, in one sense, tends to overlook the larger social context in which the social subgroups exists. It is necessary to go beyond this framework and to conceptualize the socialization influences peculiar to minority status in terms of social roles and group variables.

The special relation of individual and culture in the minority group was described and conceptualized, now many years ago, by Kurt Lewin (14). In his analysis of the social situation confronting the minority he has described the balance of forces toward and away from belonging to the group. Loyalties, ties and securities draw the individual toward his group. At the same time, factors disagreeable or disadvantageous in belonging to the group, and greater attractions outside, result in forces away from the group. In the minority, a negative balance of forces may develop as a consequence of the negative attitudes, the restrictions, and the social punishments imposed by the dominant majority. The minority member is likely to develop a "negative chauvinism" with respect to the group, to want to get away from the group and the things it represents in his mind, and to accept the attitudes and values of the "majority" group. This tendency is aggravated by the fact that he cannot move freely into the majority group; he is forced by the majority to stay within his own group. As Lewin generalizes further, the person for whom the balance of forces is negative will move, psychologically, as far away from his group as possible, but in so doing he will remain constantly on the barrier between the groups and constantly in a state of frustration and conflict. Conflict creates tensions, restless behavior and overemphasis in one direction or another. Aggressive feelings are engendered. They are likely to be directed not only toward the group of higher status but toward the person's own minority group and toward himself. Deep-seated conflicts of loyalties and goals are likely to arise. They are not likely to be fully understood by the individual himself.

The individual's state will in some measure be affected by the nature of the boundaries between his group and the dominant groups — whether they are perceived as impassable (as in the Ghetto) or relatively passable (with various kinds of connectedness and overlapping of groups). Particularly if the latter is true, if he can and does belong to and participate in other groups, some uncertainty of belonging and acceptance in the non-minority groups is likely to exist, as well as some marginality with respect to values, loyalties and expectations.

Lewin sums up the psychological importance of the individual's group membership as "the ground on which he stands, which gives or denies him social status, gives or denies him security and help. The firmness of the physical ground on which we tread is not always thought of. Dynamically, however, the firmness and clearness of his ground determines what the individual wishes to do, what he can do, and how he will do it." (14, p. 174).

Lewin's conceptualizations provide only the broad dimensions of the minority problem, but it gives a fruitful source of unexplored hypotheses and a framework for looking at empirical data on minority group reactions. The preceding formulations are sufficiently distinct but overlapping to serve as guides for investigating our problem.

Let us preview the discussion of the paper. This article has two objectives. The first is to consider a number of general problems of socialization, and to ask wherein membership in a minority group complicates the process. By examining what is known about social developmental processes and relating this information to the special circumstances of the minority child and his family, it is hoped that we can give new perspective to the specific developmental problem under consideration. The second objective is to examine the available empirical data on minority children and to interpret them within theoretical frameworks discussed above. It is assumed that the problems we are considering are not unique to any single social minority, and that by looking at the data of several groups we can more clearly understand the underlying processes in the minority child's development.

§ *Development of a Self-Concept*

Of primary significance in the child's personality development is his developing conception of himself. There is a common core of experiences for every child which contributes to the development of the self-pattern— the child's relationships with his parents, the try-outs by the child with his peers (in playing, in matching skills, in declaring likes and dislikes, in doing and being like others, in asserting uniqueness), and the child's experiences of authority and affection with adults.

When the child is told he is good or bad, when he is frustrated and prevented from reaching certain goals, when he is rejected or loved — each of these events and conditions becomes part of the experience out of which develop his feelings about himself. Often these rewards or punishments can be understood by the child as related to certain antecedents in his own behavior or to conditions which he can alter or maintain. Not infrequently, however, there are less clear and less alterable relationships. Such situations (e.g., not knowing why punishment is given, or why acceptance is withheld or inconsistent) present grave obstacles to arriving at a stable self-picture.

For each child there will be difficulties in the development of the self-concept, but for the minority child one can anticipate special obstacles. The minority child is likely to face many situations of the kind described above in which the relationships between his behavior and characteristics and the ensuing rewards and punishments are uncertain. For the minority child there is the central threat to the self-picture which comes with his developing awareness of his group's role in society, with the correlatives of negative attitudes, affects and pressures. This awareness may be learned directly through his contacts with society, or mediated through the parent. This raises the question of how the relationships with the parent of love, affection, authority, and control can intensify or modify the threats of minority group status upon the child's self-evaluations.

Research provides some data concerning how early and in what form minority membership becomes part of the young child's identity. Studies of children of nursery-school age and first and second grades indicate that group identifications are present at these ages. This is true for racial as well as religious and national differences. The studies of Goodman (11), Clark (4), and Radke, Trager and Davis (20) (using dolls or picture materials) find that Negro and white children notice racial differences in physical attributes, that many use racial terms, that they express a sense of differences in the social roles of Negroes and whites and express affective and value-laden materials congruent with adult prejudices. Negro children show more concern and awareness regarding their own racial membership than do white children. Even at the three-year-old level, conflicting preferences and rejections of their own race appear in some children.

Awareness of self as Jewish appears also in young children. Hartley, Rosenbaum and Schwartz (12) interviewed three and a half- to ten and a half-year-old children in New York City. The children were asked, "What are you?," and also, "What does Jewish mean?" Ethnic responses were frequent from the four a half year level and older, between two-thirds and three-fourths of the children giving such responses. The younger children described "Jewish" in concrete terms, while the older children tended more often to use abstractions. The authors comment that this is in line with the kinds of perceptual and intellectual capacities of children of these ages.

Radke, Trager and Davis (20) were able to compare responses of group-awareness of Protestant, Catholic and Jewish children (five-to-eight-year-old). The children were shown pictures of a church with children in front of the church, and a similar picture of a synagogue. The children were asked to describe the picture and, later, to tell something about the children in the picture after they had been identified as to religion. The children's familiarity with their religious groups was rated as showing extensive and elaborated information, having definite, specific but more limited ideas, or showing vague, uncertain or no ideas at all about the group symbol or label. Seventy-one per cent of the Jewish children were rated as having specific or extensive information about being Jewish, whereas the comparable percentages for Protestant and Catholic children when asked about their own groups were 25 per cent and 51 per cent, respectively. (The label "Protestant" was most unfamiliar, and the specific denominational labels were not used.) By way of illustration, several responses of Jewish children are quoted:

I'm Jewish and people that talk Jewish are. I don't know how. Only my mother and father . . . They don't go to church. They go to synagogue. That's what I go to. If anyone dies they read the Bible for a year. Stay home eight days. Sit *shiva* over them. . . . (7 years old)

Jews go to *schul* . . . I know Sandra and Jean are Jewish. They go to *schul* . . . I play with Italian people. My mother likes them better. Mark is Jewish and he always hits me. (8 years old)

The responses of Jewish children are further distinguished by intensified group consciousness and personal involvement; 47 per cent gave strongly positively toned responses, and 9 per cent equally strong rejecting responses. Dora (a second-grader) shows this reaction. She becomes tense and excited in responding to the pictures and questions:

I'm Jewish. I know all about it. Some stay home on holidays. You have to fast if your sins get bad. (Asked if she knows any Jewish children) No. They're all Italian except me (an accurate appraisal of the classroom) . . . Jews are the best people, mother said. You know I'm a Jew. . . . I'm not allowed to go (to church). Only synagogue. (Churches) ain't no good. Synagogue is better. Catholics don't like Jews. Make fun of Jews. I don't care if they don't like me. They better not make fun of me! . . . Jews are good and nice . . . (whispers) My teacher's a Jew (accurate).

From the preceding and other similar studies it can be concluded that compared with majority group children of the same ages, minority children (racial or religious) show earlier and greater differentiation of their own group as well as more personal involvement in the group identification. Along with identifications of their own group go frequent differentiations of other groups, and these often in negative terms. The phenomenon of "self-hatred" appears occasionally in the responses of young children, more often for Negro than for Jewish children. The ability of the child to differentiate groups does not mean inevitable differentiation in superior-inferior terms.

From research in child development it is well known that the child has developed a strong sense of self and of others by the time he reaches the preschool and early school years. The ethnic aspect of the self must, therefore, be part of a complex self-other picture. We know, too, from the work of Piaget (16) and others, that the child's abilities to use abstractions and to make classifications of events develop slowly, and are not well developed in the preschool and early school years. An understanding of being a member of a minority group involves, in part, these intellectual capacities. Various questions might then be raised about the clarity of the early ethnic concepts and the kinds of learning represented in the children's responses regarding group belonging.

Various forms of perception and levels of complexity are discernible in their reactions. Thus, "Jewish" sometimes appears in the child's thinking as a label associated with a specific act or object ("Jewish is candles" or "You pray when somebody dies."). It is for other children a characteristic of some people ("They know how to talk Jewish. I don't know how."). For other children it is an abstraction which classifies people ("I am Jewish." "There are only two Jews on my street, Herbie and Mark."). Analyses that have been made of young children's prejudices toward other groups show much the same kinds of thinking (Allport, 2). It has been pointed out, too, that children often learn group words that are used as epithets ("dirty Jew," "nigger," "wop"), and that the power of the word seems to be understood although the group referent may be unclear to them. References of this kind to one's own group do not appear in the interviews with young children of minority groups. Indeed, one would not expect them. However, observational data on the same children interviewed above showed the power of these epithets in interactions among children. Play and unorganized activities in school settings were observed (21). In these settings the group label occurred, on occasion, in angry interactions, such as "But you're a Jew," which was used as reason to reject. Regardless of the understanding of the child using the label, the significance for the minority child at whom it is directed should not be minimized. This kind of rejection is perhaps one of the most direct and thoroughgoing threats to the young child's self-picture.

Hartley *et al.* (12), in the study cited earlier have demonstrated other sources of confusion in the child's attempts to comprehend ethnic membership, namely in the intellectual difficulty in dealing with part-whole problems. These investigators asked a series of questions to determine how the child conceived of himself as Jewish and as American. A sample series follows: Are you American? Are you Jewish? Can you be both? When are you American? When are you Jewish?, etc. In the children's responses four kinds of perceptions of the two group belongings emerged. (1) The child sees himself as being only of the group in which he is momentarily observed; he cannot be both. (2) The child sees himself in one continuing membership, with the other momentary. (3) He sees himself always as being both. (4) He sees himself as belonging permanently to one, but with the potentiality for the other. It is not possible from the reported data to determine how closely age-linked these differences are. They illustrate, however, the complexities of various identities and roles which the child must learn, and learn to differentiate appropriately in different settings.

§ *Contexts for Learning Group Identity*

We should not consider the question of the early awareness of minority belonging only as a kind of problem of concept formation. The contexts in which this early learning occurs and the affective correlates and consequences of these contexts are of concern.

Extrapolating from knowledge of child development, it can be assumed that the affective beginnings of ethnic group identity, just as in other aspects of the child's early experiences, are extremely important in subsequent development. Particularly important is whether foundations are laid which foster feelings of insecurity that the child is unable to cope with, or which provide security and strengths for dealing with later difficulties.

There are two somewhat separate questions regarding the relationships of parent and child in a minority group which have a bearing upon the child's adjustment to the minority role. One concerns the kind or method of direct teaching about group-belonging or group culture *per se*. The other question concerns the feelings and behavior which characterize the relationship of parent and child. These dimensions of parental behavior which form the core of current theories of personality development and childhood experience are familiar: variables of warmth or possessiveness, acceptance or rejection, severity or laxity in training and discipline, differences in philosophy from authoritarian to democratic, and so on. Both of these questions are highly relevant to an understanding of the socialization process for minority children.

The first question is dealt with directly in a study by Radke-Yarrow, Trager and Miller (19) who attempted to learn from parents the kinds of training they provide for their children relating to racial and religious groups in our society. Parents (N = 101) of first- and second-grade children were interviewed about the kinds of restrictions and freedoms granted their children in social relationships with other groups, the kinds of explanations and admonitions given concerning group differences, the explanations or experiences intended to give understanding of own group membership, and the methods of handling problems of intergroup hostilities. These were parents of children whose conceptions of their own group (Jewish and Negro) have been reported above (20). The sample was urban, predominantly middle and lower-middle class. Only the responses of the Jewish ($N = 7$) and Negro ($N = 29$) parents will be examined here. In general, their responses are marked by distress and confusion. All but one of the Jewish parents and half of the Negro parents believed that their six-year-olds were conscious of racial and religious groupings, and provided observations to support their beliefs. The parents who denied an awareness by the child invariably contradicted themselves later in telling about their child's questions. A Jewish mother is quoted, after first saying that her daughter is too young to know: " 'Why am I Jewish?' she keeps saying. 'Why can't I have a Christmas like the Irish?' " Many parents recalled questions which their children had asked: "Why do I have to be a Jew?" "What color am I?" "Why aren't Catholics as good as us?" Very similar questions, it should be noted, were also asked by children of the majority groups.

The parents' attempts to deal with children's questions and with incidents in which hostility is directed toward the Jewish child or Negro child are woefully inadequate. One mother summed it up by saying, "We try to explain. They can't understand. It's a mess." Often the minority parent attempted to talk about the child's own group and other groups by "telling him there is no difference," or by saying, "we're all Americans"; or with vague acknowledgments of differences, such as, "God made different kinds," or "God created all equally only their faces were different in color." Others gave the child an explanation of his group in terms of group relations, "I would tell him colored are Jim-crowed." And only one mother in the total sample interviewed spoke of the whole way of living as being important in how the child learns to look upon differences among people. There is striking absence of any recognition of the need to handle the feelings and insecurities which may be expected as the child meets with difficulties.

These data only begin to identify some of the conditions of learning which minority group parents provide. We need to know more about the modes and frequencies of various direct and conscious methods of indoctrination used by parents which give the minority child a sense of self and an understanding of social relationships. We need to know, too, the kinds of results—in the mental health of the child—from the various kinds of training received.

Discussing the problems faced by parents in bringing up a child of any socially underprivileged group, Lewin (14) outlines a course of action which he deductively supports by an analysis of anticipated resultant tensions which would follow from alternative actions by the parents. He proposes that delaying recognition and minimizing the social problem aspect of group membership leads to greater difficulties for the child later on. An early, clear and positive feeling of belonging to the group is an essential foundation. This foundation would function to reduce the ambiguity and tension inherent in minority status. It would counteract the pulls away from the group and it would help to depersonalize the antigroup sentiments and actions encountered in society. This position derives from Lewin's more general position regarding the necessary clarity or firmness of "social ground" for the individual's security and direction. Systematic data have not been obtained to test this proposition. To do so would require careful spelling out in specific operations how the "early," "clear" and "positive" group-belonging can best be accomplished. This brings us to the second question raised, namely, the family context in which group identity is learned and the influence of parent-child relationships upon adjustment to minority membership.

Allport (2) speaks of children "adopting" and children "developing" group attitudes as a result of various parent behaviors. We have been concerned above with ideas and attitudes which may be *adopted* as a result of direct teaching; we now look to the styles of life and interdependencies of parents and child which may increase or decrease the probability that certain kinds of attitudes rather than other kinds will develop. Specifically, the question that concerns us here is how the parent-child relationship affects the child's view of himself and the world, and consequently his view of himself as a member of a minority group.

One important aspect of the parent-child relationship which has been examined in terms of resultant attitudes in the child, is the dimension of authoritarianism. This relationship has been described by Allport and also by Frenkel-Brunswik (9) as one in which the child cannot help but acquire suspicions, anxieties, and hatreds. The dynamics of this development may be described briefly as follows. With the authoritarian parent the child learns that human relationships are dominated by power and authority. Thus, he can readily acquire a view of the world in which status and power predominate. The discipline which this child receives is such that he submits rather than accepts or understands. It is not possible for him to express his impulses, with the result that he comes to mistrust them. As a frightened and frustrated child, he may "gain safety and security in oversimplified black-white schematizations and categorizations on the basis of crude, external characteristics" (Frenkel-Brunswik, 9). On the other hand, the child brought up in an atmosphere in which the parent is warm and democratic is more likely to be oriented toward his social world in terms of love, and is less likely to require rigid categorizations of others. This analysis has been made with respect to the prejudices and personalities of majority group children. It is transposable to the analysis of the minority child's orientations toward his own group-belonging and toward his social world of other, including dominant, social groups. Thus, theoretically, the frightened, frustrated minority child of authoritarianism, like the ethnocentric majority child, can also be expected to look upon status and power and "clean" categorizations as very important in his social world and to attempt to work out adaptations to his minority status in ways similar to the ethnocentric child described by Frenkel-Brunswik. Similar glorifications and vilifications of ingroups and outgroups may be anticipated. However, aggressions and glorifications may be directed variously. A chauvinistic orientation toward one's own group with aggressive rejections of other and dominant groups is one possibility. An alternative adjustment with the opposite kind of polarization is suggested by Lewin's (14) analysis of negative forces away from minority belonging: rejection of one's own group and intensified efforts to conform to dominant group standards and attitudes (the self-hatred syndrome).

It seems likely that the kinds of needs fostered in the parent-child relationship and the kinds of direct teaching by the parent can be expected to reinforce one another. Thus, it is hypothesized that in the harshly autocratic home, more than in the warm accepting equalitarian home, the minority parents' direct teachings concerning minority membership will be predominantly oriented around status, ingroup-outgroup hostilities, and dimensions of inferiority and superiority. While empirical data are wanting to test out these relationships in minority group socialization, theoretical analyses help to clarify the manner in which parental authority and affection relations may influence the child's learning of social status and social roles, and to point the way to needed research in these problems.

This brings us back to a question of parental influences, seen as a question of personality and culture. What are the various child-rearing patterns of the social minority groups? And how may they constitute different kinds of influences for children of different minority groups? Distinct patterns differentiating racial, national or religious minorities seem unlikely, since social class differences cut across ethnic lines, and class differences in child-rearing practices have been clearly demonstrated by Davis and Havighurst (7). It has been observed that with both Negro and Jewish groups (depending upon social class level), parental overprotectiveness toward the child is often characteristic. Stressed as well is the parent's strict discipline and insistence upon "good" behavior (not showing aggression, not being noisy, etc.). Coupled with the latter may be the parents' overconcern for achievement on the part of the child. The prevalence of these tendencies is not known. Yet one might reflect upon the parent-provided learning settings for the minority child and consider how, in various combinations, they provide different possibilities for personality and social development. Dai (5) explores precisely this problem in his analysis of the problems of Negro childhood. He presents a number of case histories showing how in dramatic proportions the "self-systems" of these youths and their reactions to all authority have developed out of their particular relationships with parental authority. He then goes on to show how their socialization has been affected by certain family and social conditions prevalent within the American Negro group which tend to increase the frequencies of certain kinds of parent-child relationships for the Negro child. Among the factors cited are the greater proportion of lower economic class families, the higher frequency of broken homes, and the prevalent pattern of maternal dominance in the family.

§ *Learning Social Roles*

While the child is acquiring an identity with respect to his minority group, he is concurrently learning many other social roles. In following his developing sense of group-belonging beyond the early stages of differentiation, we will want to keep in mind some of the other currents in the child's social development. The increasing importance of peer groups and the competition between peer and parent values must be reckoned with in understanding the child's social behavior. Role prescriptions linked with age and sex and social class levels are some of the potent determiners of his behavior and values. Within this context we will attempt to follow some of the developmental changes in the meaning of minority group-belonging.

To obtain empirical data on the changing psychological situation of the minority child at different ages and in different social environmental settings, Radke *et al.* (18) studied Jewish children ranging in age from seven to seventeen years. The research aimed at obtaining the child's conception of himself as it is linked with group membership, the kinds of social learning with respect to his minority role, the nature of his minority-derived conflicts and the kinds of defenses developed to meet these conflicts.

The children were seen together in small informal discussion groups. There were twenty-four groups of six children: a group of boys and a group of girls at each of four age levels, and from each of three different environmental settings. The age groupings were seven and eight, ten and eleven, thirteen and fourteen, and sixteen and seventeen years. The environmental settings for purposes of brevity will be referred to as "Orthodox," "Center" and "Community." They are differentiated in the table found on the top of page 462.

The discussions, appropriate to each age level, were about children's social participations and their general social likes and dislikes. In this context the investigator guided the discussion to issues of Jewish and non-Jewish interactions. This was stimulated by recounting a publicized local incident in which a gang of boys had attacked two friends (a Jewish boy and a non-Jewish boy) as they were returning to their homes one night. The incident was familiar and understandable at all ages, and it put non-Jews in roles of companion and of aggressor.

The group session was planned as follows. The incident was intended to stimulate discussion of intergroup relations. The discussion was per-

	Group A "Orthodox"	Group B "Center"	Group C "Community"
Social Class	Lower-middle & middle	Lower-middle & middle	Upper-middle
Ethnic composition of neighborhood	Predominantly Jewish	Predominantly Jewish	About 60% Jewish
Parentage	Mainly foreign-born	About half foreign-born	Mainly American-born
Religious and cultural observance	Strict Orthodox	Little strict observance, Conservative or Reformed denomination	Little cultural and religious observance
Formal Jewish education	Young children in parochial school. Teenagers in youth groups emphasizing orthodoxy	Little formal Jewish education	Very little formal Jewish education

mitted to develop spontaneously until "exhausted." The leader then probed for either the positive or the negative aspects of group relations, whichever had been given less attention by the children. The interviewer raised questions concerning what being Jewish meant to the children, somewhat as follows: "We've been talking about various things that happen to people who are Jewish and things that they do. What would you say being Jewish means to you?" The children were asked, too, how their parents felt about the things being discussed. The discussions were recorded by two observers.

At the end of the session the children were asked to fill out a questionnaire in which each child could, in a sense, crystallize the opinions that he and his peers had been expressing. The questionnaire described nine hypothetical situations, each of which required a choice of ingroup and outgroup alternatives and an explanation of the choices made. The questions were constructed around the following areas of decision: (a) creating, or not creating, islands for ingroup associations and culture (such as joining a club or neighborhood center in which membership is or is not limited along group lines, or choosing club activities along group lines); (b) choosing a general life setting (a neighborhood to live in); (c) incorporating group identity into "public," "American" settings (discussing Jewish culture in a school or wearing a Jewish insignia); and (d) expressing relative values (choosing to whom to give charity). The questionnaire items are as follows:

1. Suppose that there is going to be a new club that you can join. What kind of name would you like it to have—a name that is Jewish, or a name that is not Jewish?

   Jewish   Not Jewish
   Why?

2. If you could choose a badge or pin to wear to stand for the club, which

would you like—a pin or badge that stands for something Jewish or for something that is not Jewish?

Jewish   Not Jewish
Why?

3. Suppose this new club is going to act out a story. What kind of story would you like to act out—a story about Jews or a story that is not about Jews?

About Jews   Not about Jews
Why?

4. If your club decided to learn some new songs which would you choose —a Jewish song or a song in another language?

Jewish   Not Jewish
Why?

5. Suppose the new club can choose anything it wants to learn about. Would you choose something about Jewish life or about something that is not Jewish?

Jewish   Not Jewish
Why?

6. If you have to give a speech in front of your whole class in school, what would you like to talk about—a Jewish subject or not a Jewish subject?

Jewish   Not Jewish
Why?

7. If you had $5.00 to give away to help poor people who needed money to buy food and clothes, would you give it to help Jews, or to help all poor people?

Jews   All poor people
Why?

8. Suppose you moved to a different town named Rockville, which would you like to join—the Rockville Jewish Youth Center or the Rockville Youth Center?

Rockville Jewish Youth Center   Rockville Youth Center
Why?

9. If you moved to a different street would you like only Jews to live on the street, or both Jews and non-Jews?

Jews   Jews and non-Jews
Why?

The children were instructed to check one of the alternatives. In some instances children checked both groups, explaining their reasons for this choice.*

The children responded in the group interviews with considerable involvement. For many, it was probably the first time that they had examined and discussed at length their minority group membership. Once inhibitions were overcome, there were often intense expressions of feelings. As one child expressed it, "I like to get out everything that's in me." The

---

* The same questionnare was used with another group of children from the same social background as Group B [17]. A study by Chein and Hurwitz [3] also uses an adaptation of the questionnaire.

particular involvements vary, as we shall see, with the age and social background of the group. We will describe the children's responses to the interview and questionnaire; then we will re-cover the data analytically.

The incident which the leader used in initiating discussion is seized upon and elaborated, everyone attempting to talk at once. They recount many other incidents: gang fights, discriminations in camp, not being chosen as a partner or elected to a school office, and so on. Only the seven- and eight-year-olds with Orthodox backgrounds and attending parochial schools are silent and unresponsive. It is possible that they have been sheltered sufficiently to have avoided face-to-face intergroup hostility. For virtually all of the other children, particularly for the older age groups, the non-Jewish world is seen as essentially hostile territory, hedged with barriers and uncertainties. Their generalizations about this world are severe, such as:

All Christians have a little anti-Semitism in them. It doesn't come out unless they are disturbed.

Most Christians hate Jews.

The high class think it but don't express it. The low class is more expressive because it is under more pressure.

In dealing with the outgroup hostilities there are some common agreements among these children as to the outer facade that one assumes. It consists of responding to the hostility from the outgroup by doing nothing, "smoothing things over," not ruffling the surface. It is also the accepted procedure to maintain the situation so that nothing unpleasant will occur, so that the delicate balance is not disturbed:

At high school a non-Jew called a Jew a "kike." The Jew walked away but the next day acted as though nothing had happened.

In the other instance, the leader asked the thirteen- and fourteen-year-old girls in Group C if they shared information about religion with non-Jewish children. Silence followed this question, then: "Children don't discuss that. It's barred from conversation. Both avoid it."

Another form of adaptation to the perceived hostile environment is offered, namely, limiting contacts outside one's own group: "If you want to be on the safe side, you should stay with your own color and nationality." This kind of separation is proposed primarily by the teen-agers. They express the feeling that casual associations are all right, but that there are limits beyond which one must not go. "We campaigned for a non-Jewish girl for school office, but she was amazed when I said 'Hello' to her on the street." Children from Group A, the "Orthodox" group, also set limits, but give additional motives. They see contact outside their own group as a danger to their standards; they may be "tempted to break away."

This is the setting for living as minority members, as these children see it. What, then, is the meaning for them of the minority group itself? Predominantly, the children reflect their own group against a background of the dominant environment; that is, rarely is it described in and of itself without referring to the majority group. A thirteen-year-old boy in the group of Orthodox background does so, however. Responding to the question, "What does it mean to you to be Jewish?," he describes being Jewish as constituting a way of life and a set of ideals. His response is followed by an enthusiastic group reaction, "You hit it on the nose." The youngest children in this group describe Jewish belonging somewhat similarly, as observing certain laws and customs, but they show little affect toward the group. In the other groups the mode of responses is quite different. Some representative comments about the meaning of own group speak for themselves in this respect:

We're proud of it. We wouldn't admit we aren't.

In a group we're proud to be Jewish, when we are alone we are ashamed. I have walked in places where I have hoped to have nobody know.

These are defensive and anxious replies. Seldom are they challenged by children with more "positive" substance.

In everyday social interactions, children, especially young children, often explore differences among each other in "better than," "not as good as" terms. The many stories on the theme of "my father can do better than your father" are testimony to this tendency. It is exactly this mine-against-theirs kind of comparison that dominates the children's discussions of cultural and religious aspects of ingroup and "others." They are often unable to compare without strong value judgments. Both ingroup and outgroup customs are at times valued, and again derogated. The older children do not respond differently from the younger children in this respect. One might be tempted to think of this kind of response in terms of intellectual and affective regression. Their perceptions become dedifferentiated into the dimensions of good and bad.

Behind the severely judgmental tone which dominates the discussions can be seen conflicts and struggles which these children are having with multiple values and role prescriptions. Some of these conflicts and struggles are peculiar to minority status, but all share common elements of the ordinary struggles of growing up: the need to conform to the values of peers, the need to break away from parental dependence but with guilt in so doing, the confusions arising from the inconsistencies between society's ideals and society's practices. We can better study the nature of these conflicts if we turn now to the questionnaire data obtained individually from each of the children in the groups. The age of the child and the social environment in which he lives are considered in relation to his responses to group-belonging.

The questionnaire provides, first, a measure of how frequently, and in which circumstances, the child chooses his own group, the non-Jewish groups, or both groups for his associations, interests, or identifications (see Table 1). Ingroup choices, it is found, are high among the youngest children but show a general and considerable decrease with age. With one exception this is consistent in each of the specific situations described by the questions. Thus, choosing to have a neighborhood center to which only members of one's own group belong falls from *89* per cent for seven- and eight-year-olds to *44* per cent for sixteen- and seventeen-year-olds. Choosing to live on a street with only one's own group members falls from *49* per cent to *25* per cent for the same ages. Identifying with one's own group in a public-school setting by discussing a Jewish topic drops from *65* per cent to *25* per cent. In giving support to charity the trend is reversed: *22* per cent of the seven- and eight-year-olds give support only to the ingroup, in contrast to *60* per cent of the sixteen- and seventeen-year-olds.

Table 1—Jewish Children's Choices of Their Own Group

Choice Situation	Ages:	7-8 (N = 37)	PER CENT OF CHILDREN CHOOSING OWN GROUP 10-11 (N = 42)	13-14 (N = 36)	16-17 (N = 32)
a. Club Name		70	52	22	25
b. Club Pin		78	62	36	41
c. Club Dramatics		70	60	53	44
d. Club Music		74	38	31	34
e. Club Study		81	60	44	38
f. School Speech		65	31	17	25
g. Recipients of Charity		22	19	64	60
h. Neighborhood Center		89	55	61	44
i. Street To Live on		49	24	37	25

In the matter of overall choices of ingroup and outgroup, there are interesting response differences between the children coming from the three different environmental settings. Ingroup choices are highest in the Orthodox group (71 per cent of all the choices), and lowest in the Community group (21 per cent). The ages at which the steepest drops in ingroup choices occur differ by social subgroup. The drop is most marked at thirteen and fourteen years for the children from the Orthodox and Center environments. In the Community group, the change comes earlier, the sharpest drop occurring at the ten- and eleven-year levels. Age changes in general are smallest in the children from the Orthodox environments, who maintain relatively high ingroup choices at all ages. (Comparisons of the responses of the children from the three community settings are given in Table 2. Age groups are combined because of the small number at each age.)

One other gross comparison among the subgroups can be made before attempting to interpret these findings. A number of the children present an "absolutist" frame of reference in making their choices, giving the same choice on each of the questionnaire items. Whether it is a street to move to, a club to join, an emblem to choose, etc., the choice is always Jewish

Table 2—Choices of Own Group by Jewish Children from Different Social Environments

		PER CENT OF CHILDREN CHOOSING OWN GROUP					
		"Orthodox"		"Center"		"Community"	
Choice Situation	Ages: 7-11 (N-24)	13-17 (N-24)	7-11 (N-28)	13-17 (N-20)	7-11 (N-27)	13-17 (N-24)
a. Club Name	96	67	79	0	11	0
b. Club Pin	96	71	93	20	26	21
c. Club Dramatics	92	75	86	35	18	33
d. Club Music	83	71	61	10	22	13
e. Club Study	92	63	93	50	26	13
f. School Speech	79	38	46	10	19	13
g. Recipient of Charity	17	63	32	45	11	75
h. Neighborhood Center	92	71	82	65	41	25
i. Street To Live on	54	42	50	50	4	4

or never Jewish. The children at these extremes were compared by age and social enivronmental setting. It is chiefly the youngest children in the Orthodox and Center groups who make exclusively ingroup choices (two-thirds of the children). A few of the ten- and eleven-year-olds from the Orthodox and Center environments, and none of the Community children, respond in this way. On the other side of the coin is the response pattern in which the ingroup is *not* chosen. This reaction occurs primarily among Community children from the three oldest age groups, with a third to a half of these children showing this pattern.

To interpret the trends and differences observed, we will need to look at the satisfactions and pressures relating to minority group-belonging which are expressed by the children. These data are the reasons given by the children for their choices on the questionnaire items. A code was developed from the responses, with the following categories: (a) expression of fear, sensitivity and insecurity ["The ignorance of others (Jews) would lead me to be ashamed."] (b) loyalty and acceptance relating to own group ["Because I am eager to learn more and more about Jewish life and customs."] (c) rejections of own group ["Because I'm sick of hearing Jewish stories."] (d) rejection and hostility toward outgroup ["Because we don't like some Catholic groups."] (e) desire for wider association and understanding between groups ["Because it is good to know things about the life of other religions in order to understand them and get along better with them."]. The age changes in these responses are summarized in Table 3, which presents the per cent of children for whom the given category appears once or more in the total of a child's responses to the "why" questions.

The youngest children support their predominantly ingroup choices of alternatives with such statements as, "I like Jewish because I am Jewish," or express, with some belligerency, the idea that because it is mine it is better.

Children at this age in the "Community" group who tend to choose outside the Jewish category give such reasons as, "I like all people," or, "All people should play together." With similar directness and certainty the seven- or eight-year-olds from each of the environmental settings support their choice of providing help for all needy people by involving the principle of fairness: "I would give to all because it's not fair to give to one."

Children of this age show little variation in their reasoning from one questionnaire situation to the next. They seem to find a "rule" which applies pretty much without regard for any special requirements or conditions in the situation. Since the seven- and eight-year-olds very frequently mention their parents in the group interviews, it might be reasoned that the rules of values expressed on the questionnaire are adoptions from parents' teachings. We may interpret what they are saying as, in essence, "this is what we are in our family," "this is what my mother says is right."

Table 3—Reactions to Minority Group Membership by Younger and Older Children

	CHILDREN	
Expressions of:	7-11 Years	13-17 Years
	%	%
Fears, sensitivity, insecurity, regarding group-belonging	57	85
Acceptance and loyalty relating to ingroup	94	94
Rejections and derogations of ingroup	28	72
Aggression and rejection of majority group	41	28
Desire for more association and involvement in larger culture	81	91

But we know this is not the whole story. Children of seven and eight are influenced also by factors outside parental values and controls. They are aware of differences in their social world and are keenly alert to factors which entitle them to, or deprive them of, status and acceptance among their peers. Do, then, the responses described on the questionnaire reflect in these seven- and eight-year-olds their firm security in their group identity? Undoubtedly they do for some, but this is not always the case. These children expressed many apprehensions in their group interviews, where they talked about "name-calling" by the outgroup and disclosed images of how badly teachers and other adults of the outgroup can behave toward Jewish children. Their reactions to the questionnaire would seem, in part, to represent their imbeddedness in their family. It also represents in part their mode of defense: the outgroup may treat us badly but ours is really best.

By the age of ten or eleven, we have seen, many of the children's preferences have shifted away from the ingroup. At this period of childhood, when the youngster is thoroughly submerged in the peer culture and when conformity is the basic rule, his feelings of "difference" in minority belonging might be expected. In the ten- and eleven-year-olds' explanations the conflicts between conformity needs and parental and group loyalties are manifested in many ways. Expressed pleasures in observing Jewish customs are interspersed with expressed sensitivities as to what others will think if such differences are observed. Conflict is evident, too, in choices of an ingroup island of association or interest not for its intrinsic values, but in order to avoid the unsure and to permit one to be off one's guard ("Anything you say wouldn't be held against you." "You won't be in fights and it would be peaceful around.").

The minority child of this age is beset with other conflicting wishes and pressures. He expresses intense desires to learn more about, and to be a part of, the broader culture of his peers, though at the same time he is fearful that he will be hurt in these attempts. This striving for multiple identity is clear in the boy who says, "I would like everyone to know I don't belong to *only* Jewish things."

By adolescence the familiar conflicts of adult minority status are fully manifested. There are intensifications of the same conflicts expressed by the younger children as well as the addition of new ones. The most marked developmental change is in the tremendously increased differentiation or complexity with which the adolescent considers his minority role. His decisions on each of the questionnaire items tend to be more unique—a weighing of the special aspects and conflicts that each situation entails. He considers where and how prejudices of the outgroup are likely to be expressed, and how these possibilities can be minimized or avoided. He weighs which of several overlapping roles or memberships should take precedence in a given situation (Shall we vote Jack into the club because he is the school football star, or shall we rule him out because he isn't Jewish? If we're good Americans shouldn't we want everybody on our street or in our club?). He sometimes ponders his self-concept. Having criticized the ingroup in the stereotypes of the anti-Semite, he reflects "Where does that leave me?" At times he recognizes the expediencies of dissociating himself from minority membership in order to reach certain personal and social goals. He is more likely than younger children to conceptualize his personal dilemma in terms of "race prejudice," thus giving him a chance to depersonalize the experiences in which he is or fears to be rejected. This is not sufficient, however, to take care of the unclearness, threat, and ambivalence which are founded in the minority position. These varied responses fit into the framework of adolescence with its widening social contacts, interests, and skills, the keen importance of status among one's peers, and the growth toward independent adulthood.

Seventy-two per cent of the adolescents express aggression or rejection concerning their own group; 28 per cent express hostility toward the majority group. (The comparable percentages for children seven to eleven years old are 28 per cent and 41 per cent.) The tendency to reject one's own group and the weaker tendency to reject the majority group are probably symptomatic of the strength of peer-group conformity and acceptance needs, reinforced by adolescent rebellion against parental norms. In several of the groups the adolescents mimic their elders in a highly aggressive manner and with great amusement. They also raise doubts about the validity of their religious teaching, with consequent distress and anxiety.

The greatest amount of insecurity as minority members is expressed, too, by the adolescents. Eighty-five per cent, as compared to 57 per cent of the younger children, verbalize sensitivities and tensions in decisions concerning their associations and identifications. Undoubtedly the marginal social status of adolescence helps to account for this intensity of feelings with regard to minority status at this age. Already in a marginal role (neither child nor adult), the minority role brings with it an additional marginality.

With the present data, only a beginning is possible in understanding the conditions leading to various attitudes and adaptations to minority group-belonging. Social pressures concomitant with age changes have an effect. In addition, we can compare the reactions of children from the three different social backgrounds. The attitudes that we have compared along the age scale are presented in Table 4 in terms of the social environmental backgrounds of the children.

Table 4—Reactions to Minority Group Membership in Children
from Different Environmental Settings

Expressions of:	"Orthodox" Group %	"Center" Group %	"Community" Group %
Fears, sensitivity, insecurity, regarding group-belonging	65	84	69
Acceptance and loyalty relating to ingroup	100	95	88
Rejections and derogations if ingroup	23	57	71
Aggression and rejection of majority group	54	32	18
Desire for more association and involvement in the larger culture	71	86	100

From the standpoint of their "objective" environmental setting, the "Center" children, perhaps, more than the other groups are children of two cultures. They are surrounded by a Jewish culture, and, in their neighborhoods, Yiddish is as much a language of the street and store as English. However, at school and outside their neighborhoods they become more thoroughly aware of the larger culture. The older they grow the more obvious the differences are, and the more they rebel against the parent or grandparent culture. Insecurity is expressed most frequently by children in this setting; the older children of this group are the most negative and aggressive in the study. They are the ones who are most concerned with contrasts between ingroup and outgroup. By virtue of parochial school attendance and closer adherence to Jewish customs, the "Orthodox" children have had less contact with the majority group. The environment of the "Community" children, on the other hand, is one in which the norms of the majority group have been adopted and Jewish culture has less salience.

Desire for more involvement in the larger culture as well as expressed ties to one's own group are high in each setting, although the greatest outward movement and least ingroup orientation is found in the Community children. The reverse—highest ingroup orientation and least outward movement—is found in the Orthodox children. The groups differ also in the direction of their expressed hostilities. The Orthodox children spend most of their hostility upon the outgroup; the Community children direct theirs toward the ingroup.

In summary, the characteristics observed in the children of this study, at each of the ages and in each of the settings, are congruent with Lewin's conceptualization of the social-psychological situation of minority membership. The opposing forces (and often negative balance of forces) with respect to their own group are manifested in these children's insecurities and in their vacillations between wanting and rejecting, loving and hating, seeking and avoiding both ingroup and outgroup. A predominant lack of clarity as to the characteristics of their surroundings, their image of themselves and their expectations document Lewin's description of the unfirm "ground," so critical in preventing a satisfying and integrated adjustment.

These data provide the beginnings of a developmental study of the effects of minority group-belonging. There is much more to be learned about developmental aspects through more sensitive measurements of the individual child and through comparative materials from children of other minority groups in American society.

§ *Summary Interpretations*

We have undertaken to analyze some of the problems of minority group-belonging within the context of general socialization problems. We have viewed this process as one involving the development of the self-concept and the learning of social roles. This framework is intermediate between a study of the psychodynamics of the personality development of a minority member and a cultural analysis of minority group problems. The interlocking contributions of each of these approaches is necessary to a thorough understanding of the psychological impact of minority group status. There are in the literature a number of highly informative studies of the personality development of minority members, especially of the American Negro (13), but we are lacking sufficient comparative data on other minority groups to formulate in detail the psychology of minority group-belonging. Most especially we have few data obtained directly from childhood in the course of the child's development.

In the preceding analysis of the socialization of children of minority groups we have seen that the developmental problems of minority status are of the same *kind* and of the same *timing* as in normal processes of socialization. However, problems of self-other attitudes are accentuated, and learning and adapting to multiple social roles and reconciling parent and peer cultures are complicated by minority membership. Viewing these complications within the perspective of socialization, it is possible to formulate more meaningful questions which will guide further research in this area, and which can form the basis for planning child-rearing practices that will be most helpful to minority children. As problems of social-ization, we may ask such questions as: "How much less often (as compared to the majority child) do the minority child's motivations coincide with social rules?" or, "How much greater are the incompatabilities of social prescriptions for children of the minority than of the majority group?"

While emphasizing the essential similarities of problems in socialization of all children, it is important, too, to identify conceptually the particular added difficulties for minority children. Generally, in the learning which is required of children in order to assume and conform to many different social roles (such as those of age, sex, and class), positive motivations are involved. The child is rewarded, intrinsically or extrinsically, for the be-haviors which he adopts. However, many of the roles required of the minority child—as, for example, learning the patterns of restrictions, defer-ences, and cautions appropriate to minority position—bring no comparable rewards or satisfactions.

Many of the experiences out of which the child learns minority status and role are the result of circumstances in which the relation between antecedents and consequences are unclear. This is especially true for the young child. He has offered friendship to his peers and he is rejected. He has "done nothing," yet the attack turns on him. In the older child it is similar. Everything is going along fine, but one day he is called a dirty name or left out of the group. These kinds of experiences make cognitive learning difficult, if not impossible. Furthermore, the model which the minority parent is able to provide in this sphere of social living may itself reflect anxieties and conflicts, thus depriving the child of a much-needed base of security.

Research in other aspects of child development has indicated that given socialization pressures may bring about very different effects in the child, depending on the age at which these pressures occur. There are certain stages or periods at which the organism is especially vulnerable to certain influences. If this be the case, it should be taken very seriously into con-sideration in the study and rearing of the minority child. Thus, very different consequences—immediate and lasting—might follow depending, for example, on the age or stage of development at which social under-privilege or group discrimination becomes a reality to the child, or the age at which various needed supports are given or lacking.

The socialization problems of minority children are not merely of relevance to a numerical few in our population. Lois Murphy (15) has estimated that a third of the children in our culture are growing up as members of social minorities. Although these groups vary in the degree and dimensions in which minority status is imposed, it is assumed that many of the psychological effects are the same. Attention in the sciences of human development has been given to many other "special" children (the gifted, the retarded, the handicapped, the delinquent) and to many special conditions of childhood (the broken home, the institutionalized child, the overprotective mother). With equal seriousness and sophistication, the tools of research are needed in understanding the psychological impact of minority status upon the child.

References

1. Adorno, T. W., Frenkel-Brunswik, E., Levinson, D. J., and Sanford, R. N., *The Authoritarian Personality*, N. Y., Harper, 1950.
2. Allport, Gordon, *The Nature of Prejudice*, Cambridge, Addison-Wesley, 1954.
3. Chein, I. and Hurwitz, J. *The Reactions of Jewish Boys to Various Aspects of Being Jewish* (Mimeographed), N. Y., Jewish Welfare Board, 1950.
4. Clark, K. and Clark, M., The Development of Consciousness of Self and Emergence of Racial Identification in Negro Preschool Children, *Journal of Social Psychology*, 1939, *10*, 591-99.
5. Dai, Bingham, Some Problems of Personality Development Among Negro Children, pp. 545-66, in *Personality in Nature, Society, and Culture*. Edited by Kluckhohn, Murray, and Schneider, N. Y., Knopf, 1954.
6. Davis, A., American Status Systems and Socialization of the Child, pp. 567-76, in *Personality in Nature, Society, and Culture.*
7. Davis, A., and Havighurst, R. J., Social Class and Color Differences in Child Rearing, pp. 308-320, in *Personality in Nature, Society, and Culture.*
8. Dollard, J., *Caste and Class in a Southern Town*, New Haven, Yale University Press, 1937.
9. Frenkel-Brunswik, E., A Study of Prejudice in Children, *Human Relations*, 1948, *1*, 295-306.
10. Gillin, J., Personality Formation from the Comparative Cultural Point of View, pp. 164-75, in *Personality in Nature, Society, and Culture.*
11. Goodman, Mary E., *Race Awareness in Young Children*, Cambridge, Addison-Wesley, 1952.
12. Hartley, E. L., Rosenbaum, M, and Schwartz, S., Children's Perceptions of Ethnic Group Membership, *Journal of Psychology*, 1948, *26*, 387-98.
13. Kardiner, A. and Ovesey, L., *The Mark of Oppression*, N. Y., Norton, 1951.
14. Lewin, Kurt, *Resolving Social Conflicts* (ed. G. Lewin) N. Y., Harper, 1948.
15. Murphy, Lois B., Social Factors in Child Development, pp. 129-39, in *Readings in Social Psychology*, N. Y., Holt, 1947.
16. Piaget, J., *The Moral Judgment of the Child*, N. Y., Harcourt, Brace, 1932.

17. Radke-Yarrow, M., Developmental Changes in the Meaning of Minority Group Membership, *Journal of Educational Psychology*, 1953, *44*, 82-101.
18. Radke, M., Davis, H., Hurwitz, J., Pollack, P., *Group Belonging Among Various Subgroups of Jewish Children*. Unpublished manuscript, 1950. Used by permission of Commission on Community Interrelations of the American Jewish Congress.
19. Radke-Yarrow, M., Trager, H., and Miller, J., The Role of Parents in the Development of Children's Ethnic Attitudes, *Child Development*, 1952, *23*, 13-52.
20. Radke, M. Trager, H., and Davis, H., Social Perceptions and Attitudes of Children, *Genetic Psychology Monographs*, 1949, *40*, 327-447.
21. Trager, H., and Radke-Yarrow, M., *They Learn What They Live*, N. Y., Harper, 1952.

JOSEPH ADELSON

A STUDY OF
MINORITY GROUP AUTHORITARIANISM

RECENT studies in the psychology of prejudice have suggested the existence of close and meaningful relationships between attitudes towards the ethnic minorities and certain psychological dynamics. Perhaps the most important concept underlying this work has been "authoritarianism" (1); in its recent uses the term has had at least two senses: referring to a characteristic ideological orientation, and designating a complex of personality attributes which appear to be related to commitment to such an ideology. The impetus of the California study has given rise to a rapid proliferation of related researches, particularly in such areas as child development (4) and cognition, perception, and memory (3, 7, 8). Some criticism has been made of the implicit sociological and political assumptions involved in the major study (6, 9), and it is certain that many of the original findings will undergo modification. Nevertheless, the study's crucial importance is likely to go unchallenged; it has given empirical buttressing to the idea that ideological dispositions are closely related to general personality functioning.

The various studies of prejudice have, quite naturally, drawn their samples from the majority population—native-born white Christians. Yet if the notion of an "authoritarian personality" is to possess the generality its formulators propose, it would be necessary to demonstrate that these ideology-personality connections exist among other groups, including the ethnic minorities. Given minority group members disposed to the authoritarian orientation, what attitudes may we expect them to maintain concerning, for example, the significant aspects of minority group membership? Since the authoritarian ethnic is himself an object of prejudice we cannot expect that his political and social views will duplicate exactly those of the authoritarian majority; on the other hand, we may anticipate that the authoritarian *mode* of defining political and social issues will be discernible. If we assume that the authoritarian minority group member is given to cynicism, the derogation of others, projectivity, a preoccupation with strength and weakness, a concern with status, we must still discover

This is an expanded version of a paper which originally appeared in the *Journal of Abnormal and Social Psychology*, Vol. 48, No. 4, 1953, pp. 477-485. (Copyright 1953 by the American Psychological Association, Inc.) It is used here by permission of the A.P.A.

The paper is based on a doctoral dissertation submitted in September, 1950, to the Department of Psychology at the University of California. The author is indebted to Drs. R. Nevitt Sanford, Robert E. Harris, and Reinhard Bendix, under whose supervision the research was done, and to Dr. Else Frenkel-Brunswik and Miss Betty Aron for their many helpful suggestions.

[475]

what ideological forms, if any, these tendencies take. Which groups are seen as strong, which as weak? Which are seen as possessing high or low status? Upon which groups are ego alien attributes projected? How are ingroup and outgroup defined?

The present paper reports the results of a study of ideology and identification processes among members of the Jewish minority. It became clear early in the research that authoritarianism was a critical dimension underlying attitudes toward Jewishness, and that the above questions required asking and answering before even a partial understanding of the general problem was to be obtained.

§ *The Exploratory Study*

EXPLORATORY INTERVIEW.

It would have been possible, of course, to proceed directly to the formulation of hypotheses concerning the authoritarian definitions of Jewishness and to construct attitude scales to test these. It was deemed safer, however, to begin with the intensive interviewing of a small number of subjects (Ss). Seventeen Jewish college men, chosen from two fraternities, comprised the initial sample.

The interview schedules were designed to cover two general areas: the "clinical" section, organized along psychoanalytic conceptions, sought to obtain a brief compass of S's life history, stressing those early involvements thought to be influential in establishing consistent and idiosyncratic modes of self-other integration; the "ideological" portion had as its aim the delineation of beliefs and attitudes regarding Jewishness.

Examination of the interview protocols suggested a constellation of attitudes which appeared to characterize those Ss who, on the basis of clinical material and F-scale scores, were designated as authoritarian. A number of hypotheses concerning the nature of Jewish authoritarianism were formulated; what were thought to represent the essential statements of this ideology were put into attitude-item form. The construction and utilization of this scale will be discussed at length below. We shall begin by presenting the interview data in so far as they suggested the major variables in Jewish authoritarian belief.

INTERVIEW FINDINGS. *The Authoritarian Image of the Jew.* Intolerance of ambiguity, the propensity for sharp and dichotomous distinctions so fundamental to authoritarian thought, is represented in the image of the Jew. Like many of his Gentile counterparts, the authoritarian Jew speaks of two kinds of Jews: an ingroup, to which desirable characteristics are attributed, and a derogated outgroup. The terms of the dichotomy frequently vary from person to person; each interviewee employing it tends to emphasize particular traits as characterizing ingroup and outgroup. For some, the outgroup figure is a social climber, intent upon "crashing into upper circles";[1] others stress his being "cheap," or a "spendthrift," or "coarse," or "loud." Indeed some authoritarian Ss make a variety of accusations. Witness one evaluation of the several Jewish fraternities:

Our house gets the cream of the crop. You know, clean-cut, decent, refined. You've heard of (a prominent jurist). You've heard of him. His son is a member. The (A fraternity) are next. A nice bunch of kids. It's not a wealthy house but they keep their noses clean. They know how to behave. The (B's) are the worst. You know—cheap, wholesale, grubbing Jews. Their parents made money in the war. Garment business Jews. Loud, throw their money around. They give all the Jewish houses a bad name. I don't know about the (C's) and (D's). From what I hear, they really aren't fraternities in the real sense of the word. They're Hillel Jews. You know, just—Jews.

Underlying such statements we usually find some conception of status stratification. The "other" Jew may be seen as lower-class, unassimilated, poor, of the ghetto, the pariah; or he may be viewed as *nouveau riche,* vulgar, garish, loud, Eliot's Bleistein, the parvenu. Whether pariah or parvenu—the phrasing is Arendt's (2)—he is subsumed under a single rubric, namely, that he violates middle-class standards and expectations.[2]

The dichotomization process would appear to have certain functions for the authoritarian Jew. For one thing, the outgroup figure permits the mechanisms of projection and displacement to come into play. Furthermore, dichotomization provides a defense against hostile majority evaluation. The authoritarian sees himself as uninvolved in any "responsibility" for anti-Semitism. Prejudice against the group is viewed as "rational" (see below); its cause is the deviant behavior of the "bad kind of Jew." Still further, the definition of the self as a "good" Jew permits a kind of identification with the aggressor, a sense of affiliation with the Gentile, who is frequently perceived as a powerful and potentially threatening figure. The interviews suggest that many of the authoritarian's interactions with Gentiles are predicated upon this self-definition, so that there is occasional participation in Gentile anti-Semitism. Telling how he handled the prejudices of his Army compeers, one subject relates: "Sometimes you play along with them. If they were telling Jewish jokes I added some of my own."

Perhaps it is unnecessary to note that the authoritarian image of the outgroup incorporates the essential elements of the anti-Semitic stereotype; even the contradictions are retained, as in the attribution of both seclusive and intrusive motives. One important component of Gentile anti-Semitism is omitted; the Jew is never seen as a sinister or dangerous force. The theme of Jewish power, when it does appear, is greeted not with hostility, but with pride and admiration.

The Authoritarian Imagery of the Gentile. The figure of the Gentile is also a dichotomous one. There is a "bad" Gentile, bearing lower-class characteristics: the mass-man, ignorant, inarticulate, violent, envious. There is counterposed an image of the "good" Gentile, a middle-class figure, genteel and refined, with whom the authoritarian feels joined in the solidarity of decorum. This latter image, it should be said, is a variable one; in some interviews the good Gentile seems fraternal, a chum, a pal; the implication is of a cameraderie of disdain for both bad Jew and bad Gentile. In other interviews the seeming reference is to an older, more paternal figure, whom one approaches deferentially, whose opinion is sought; there are suggestions here that the figure is a power and a threat, and that the meet response is propitiation. In either case, the good Gentile is seen as competent to differentiate the two kinds of Jews, as responding to the one amicably and to the other with distaste. The lower-class Gentile, blind and raging, is held incapable of this distinction.

Anti-Semitism. Having accepted the anti-Semitic evaluation of the Jew, in so far as it designates the outgroup, the authoritarian accepts perforce the anti-Semitic solution of the Jewish problem. Anti-Semitism is seen as a "rational" or "natural" response to the behavior of the "bad" Jews. These individuals must, for example, renounce clannishness and learn to mingle with others; they must cease attempting to intrude themselves into Gentile circles. They must, above all, give up their deviant behavior. The immoral, the nonconformist, the radical, the intellectual, the crooked, the overreligious, the atheistic, these Jewish types and others, it is felt, provoke the Gentile and endanger the position of those Jews who conform. In general, the authoritarian Ss are fearful of conspicuous behavior on the part of Jewish individuals, except in so far as it is "conspicuously good." The authoritarian would flatten Jewish diversity to a somewhat featureless Babbittry. And so it is that many of these Ss would have the Jews combat anti-Semitism neither by organizational activity, nor propaganda, nor political enterprise, but, in the words of one interviewee, "by behaving themselves . . . being outstandingly good." (It may here be suggested that alien impulses are represented by "the Jews," and that the Gentile world is parental; the formula by which so many of our Ss have had to live—repression, conformity—is turned to ideological use.)

The dichotomous conception of Jew and Gentile underlies and gives meaning to authoritarian opinion as to the cause and cure of anti-Semitism. It is felt that deviant Jewish behavior may incite the unthinking Gentile to a violence in which ingroup Jews would become involved. Furthermore, it is problematic to what extent the good Gentile may be trusted. Though presumably aware that there are two kinds of Jews, the indecorous behavior of the one may cause him to lose patience with the entire group; or perhaps through some myopia he will, like his imperceptive co-religionist, fail to distinguish between the two kinds of Jew. At any rate, the authoritarian Jew is in fear, and he wishes to placate.

The desire to please and appease the powerful Gentile is reflected in the belief that organizational response to anti-Semitism, when it is necessary, should be of a quiet, secret, conspiratorial nature. Organizations such as the Anti-Defamation League should avoid stirring up public attention. Antiprejudice propaganda, as in the motion picture *Gentleman's Agreement,* is seen as potentially dangerous by "bringing things out into the light." The threatening environment, the "world as jungle" theme, typical of authoritarian thought, and presumably stemming, at least in part, from the projection of hostile impulses, is here given a peculiarly minority group slant.

STRENGTH AND WEAKNESS. A preoccupation with this theme, a characteristic one for authoritarian males, is represented in the protocols as a general tendency finding expression in diverse ideological areas. For example, the establishment of the state of Israel is considered important not because of humanitarian or political considerations but for the show of strength involved. Some Ss dwell upon the "weakness" of this or that kind of Jew, concentrating particularly upon those who deny being Jewish. Still others suggest that the only effective way of meeting personal anti-Semitism is through physical violence, though it must be said that other authoritarians specifically eschew such a tactic, apparently because it connotes a lower-class behavioral mode. (It may be conjectured that the strength-weakness polarity will be in even greater evidence among lower-class authoritarian Jews.)

The Nonauthoritarian. If we have so far ignored the ideology of the nonauthoritarian it is because their interviews are characterized by a failure to express the dimensions we have designated as authoritarian, rather than by any separate consistency. That is to say, these protocols are extremely diverse, although there are many instances of clear relationship between ideology and personality dynamics. If it is difficult to posit particular syndromes of nonauthoritarian ideology, it may be because the sample is too small to permit such a demonstration, rather than because the syndromes do not exist.

Certain tentative generalizations may be made, however. The nonauthoritarians seem possessed of a consciously "liberal" political orientation, under which they subsume the problem of Jewishness; the latter is seen in this larger context, an emphasis being put upon an economic interpretation of anti-minority prejudice. There is the attempt, too, to link Jewishness to the general minority problem; hence, the Negro's situation is frequently seen as having, in an impersonal sense, more fundamental importance.

It should be emphasized that the nonauthoritarian are not freer from conflicts and confusions about being Jewish; indeed, they frequently seem more disturbed than do the authoritarian, in part because of a lesser rigidity of defense and in part because their political beliefs are often at variance with underlying feelings concerning Jewishness. It is doubtful whether many individuals, Jewish or Gentile, can completely avoid incorporating our society's stereotype of the Jew. The point is that the authoritarian Jew accepts the stereotype and recasts it to meet the circumstance of his Jewishness; the nonauthoritarian Jew rejects its validity, fights its existence within himself, and is sometimes ridden by guilt when he is unable to do so completely.

It appeared from the interview protocols, then, that authoritarian Jewish ideology could be summarized in a number of statements: the Jews are divided into ingroup and outgroup, the latter being seen (in a middle-class sample) as violators of middle-class standards, as being seclusive, intrusive, offensive, nonconforming; the Gentiles are similarly dichoto-mized, the central notion being that anti-Semitism is a lower-class Gentile trait, to which the middle-class Gentile is not given; anti-Semitism is viewed as caused by the "bad" (nonconforming, offensive, etc.) behavior of the outgroup Jews; anti-Semitism may best be fought by a modification of the behavior of these Jews; propagandistic or organizational activity against anti-Semitism should be discreet in approach, so as to avoid an-tagonizing the powerful majority; political and economic solutions of anti-Semitism are rejected; there is a preoccupation with the themes of strength and weakness, expressed in a rejection of "weak" and an idealization of forceful Jewish characteristics and behavior.

§ Test of Hypothesis with Questionnaire

This configuration of attitudes and beliefs was hypothesized as constituting Jewish authoritarianism. Several alternatives were available for the testing of the hypothesis; the most convenient appeared to be the questionnaire method. It was proposed to construct a series of items which would represent the major aspects of the variable in question, and to administer these to appropriate groups in the university community. The success of the total scale would be judged by its reliability, internal consistency, and validity. The scale's validity was to be established by its correlation with the University of California F scale, which measures general authoritarianism (1).

THE QUESTIONNAIRE

The Likert method of scale construction was employed. Its advantages and disadvantages relative to others have elsewhere been discussed at length (1, 5). The Ss were offered six categories of response ranging from complete agree-ment to complete disagreement. No neutral category was given. The responses were transformed into a seven-point scoring system, with the middle score of four used for omissions.

So far as this was possible for the items for the scale (hereafter called "JA" for Jewish Authoritarianism) were taken directly from the interview protocols of authoritarian Ss; in most cases some slight revision was necessary. In some in-stances, however, item writing presented formidable difficulties. For example, those statements which expressed essentially anti-Semitic opinions had to be phrased so as to avoid violating the affirmant's sense of group belongingness. These items, furthermore, could not seem overinclusive in reference; they had to permit the authoritarian respondent to condemn some Jews (or even "the" Jews) without appearing to condemn himself or his ingroup.

A further difficulty stemmed from the fact that certain elements of the ideology are authoritarian only in that they are elicited spontaneously, or that they occur in a particular context. A case in point is the "strength-Israel" coupling. The authoritarian, in discussing the Palestinian conflict, failed to con-sider other than its aggressive implications, yet it was felt that they would be offended by an item suggesting that this is their only concern. It was necessary, then, to formulate the statement so as to permit the respondent to express pride in Israeli strength without having it appear that he is unmindful of other considerations.

The 22 items of the JA scale follow:

1. People who deny being Jewish do so out of a weakness in character.

4. Most Jews who meet a great deal of anti-Semitism bring it about by their own obnoxious behavior.

7. I was proud of the establishment of the State of Israel, mainly because it showed that Jews could be as strong and as forceful as anyone.

9. Jews can combat anti-Semitism by showing Gentiles they can behave like any other people.

12. Jewish organizations such as the Anti-Defamation League should do their work quietly and without stirring up public attention.

15. A Jew with good breeding and manners will always be accepted by Gentiles.

18. Motion pictures like "Gentleman's Agreement" do more harm than good in that they give people anti-Semitic ideas they did not have before.

20. Considering the coarse behavior of certain Jews, if I were a Gentile I would probably be anti-Semitic.

23. Anti-Semitism is fostered by powerful groups to divert attention from social and economic injustice.

26. Because I am a Jew I feel I have to be a bit more careful about what I do and say.

29. The best solution to the Jewish problem is in changing the economic basis of our society.

31. Anti-Semitism would decrease if more Jews would make an effort to adopt American ways.

34. A lot of anti-Semitism is caused by the number of Jewish radicals.

37. I have often been embarrassed by the anti-social conduct of certain Jews in public life.

40. Well-educated Gentiles are rarely anti-Semitic.

43. Too many Jews try to intrude themselves into circles where they're not wanted.

45. A good way to fight anti-Semitism is to expose publicly instances of prejudice.

47. Anti-Semitism could be eliminated if we could somehow get rid of the immoral and crooked Jews.

48. I am most proud of the Jews for their strength in enduring persecution.

51. The Jewish group in this country would get along better if many Jews were not so clannish.

53. I feel personally ashamed when I see Jews making themselves conspicuous in public places.

55. There are many Jews to whom anti-Semitic statements do apply.

THE QUESTIONNAIRE SAMPLE

The questionnaire study was conducted, by and large, among members of the university undergraduate community. The use of such a sample of course limits the scope of generalization, but there are advantages in subject accesssibility and homogeneity. Moreover, the hypotheses to be tested were formulated from interviews with a college group, and it was felt that their initial testing should be carried out among such a group.

The sample is further limited in representational breadth, for on the whole Ss are members of exclusively Jewish groups—fraternities and sororities, the Hillel Foundation, a Zionist club. This circumstance is somewhat less disabling than it may at first appear to be, for the study's purpose was not to survey Jewish collegiate opinion, but to test certain suppositions concerning the relations of attitudes to other variables. Still, it cannot be gainsaid that the sample does not tap those individuals—perhaps a majority of the college population—who are uninvolved in Jewish organizational activity.

Several alternatives were considered for remedying this deficiency; one of these was to mail questionnaires to those listing themselves as Jewish in the college directory, but it was felt that there would be but a poor rate of return, and from a select group. Another possibility was to distribute the questionnaires in college classes, but this, it was felt, might be embarrassing to some. Two procedures were finally adopted; first, two Jewish students living in cooperative boarding houses were contacted and agreed to distribute the tests among the Jewish residents. The returns, however, were poor; about 40 per cent of the men's and 55 per cent of the women's group were willing to respond. (The men's questionnaires were not returned in time for inclusion in the present body of data.) Furthermore, it was the impression of both distributors that the group which did respond contained a disproportionate number of individuals with active Jewish interests and affiliations.

The second alternative chosen was to distribute the questionnaire to friends, and to have them solicit their friends. This group, which we have called "unaffiliated" (none of its members were connected with Jewish groups), differs from the others in that it contains some graduate students (by and large, in the psychological professions) and some nonstudents who are vocationally affiliated with the university (a stenographer, two psychiatrists, a psychiatric social worker). Despite its seeming diversity, this subsample is, with respect to certain variables, extremely homogeneous.

In Table 1 are given the frequencies and percentages of response to personal information items for each of the subgroups. The total number of subjects is 241, of which 149, or roughly 60 per cent, are members of fraternities or sororities. This high percentage was unintended, and stems from the fact that the non-fraternal groups did not provide as many Ss as was expected.

Three fraternities were tested; the number of individuals from this source was 99. Of those available for testing, only one refused to participate; hence there is almost a complete representation of the potential population. Referring to the table, it may be noted that the modal fraternity member is Reform Jewish, attends services only on holidays, prefers the Democratic Party, and is of native-born parentage. The sorority sample totals 50, and all of those available participated. With respect to the tabled categories, this group is essentially similar to the fraternity sample.

The Hillel questionnaires were obtained during a dance, which had been preceded by religious services. We would estimate that between 60 and 70 per cent of those in attendance were tested, but we have no way of knowing whether these Ss are a fair sample of Hillel membership, or to what extent or in which direction they are different from those who attended but did not fill out the questionnaire. The modal number of this subgroup is denominationally Conservative, politically Democratic, of foreign-born parentage, and often a participant at religious observances.

The Zionist group is in most respects similar to the Hillel sample; indeed, there were at least 10 members who had previously taken the questionnaire at the Hillel dance, and we have learned that most of the 19 who did not attend this affair ordinarily participate in Hillel activities. The girls' co-operative group, though theoretically unaffiliated, seems actually very similar to the previous two. The unaffiliated group is, modally, without denomination, religiously unobservant, extremely liberal politically, and of foreign-born parentage.

THE QUESTIONNAIRE FINDINGS. The odd-even coefficient of reliability for the JA scale (when corrected by the Spearman-Brown formula) is 0.79. This value may be considered adequate for an initial attempt, and in view of the multidimensional nature of the attitude in question. In revising the scale, the attempt would be made to omit or rewrite those items which,

Table 1—Frequencies and Percentages of Response to Various Categories among the Sample Subgroups

(Total N = 241)

Category	Fraternity N	%	Sorority N	%	Total F-S N	%	Hillel N	%	Zionist N	%	Co-op. N	%	Unaffiliated N	%	Total Non F-S N	%
Sex																
Men	99	100			99	66	28	62	10	53	11	100	9	53	47	51
Women			50	100	50	30	17	38	9	47			8	47	45	49
Denomination																
Reform	49	49	30	60	79	53	11	24	4	21	3	27	0	0	18	20
Conservative	29	29	14	28	43	29	18	40	7	37	5	45	3	18	33	36
Orthodox	4	4	3	6	7	5	6	13	2	10	1	9	0	0	9	10
None	17	17	3	6	20	13	10	22	6	32	2	18	14	82	32	35
Religious Attendance																
Regularly	2	2	2	4	4	3	4	9	1	5	0	0	0	0	5	5
Often	10	10	7	14	17	11	20	44	6	32	4	36	0	0	30	33
Only on holidays	68	69	35	70	103	69	15	32	7	37	5	45	5	29	32	35
Never	19	19	6	12	25	17	6	13	5	26	2	18	12	71	25	27
Political																
Republican	15	15	7	14	22	15	1	2	0	0	0	0	0	0	1	1
Democrat	51	52	29	58	80	54	23	51	8	42	8	72	9	53	48	52
Progressive	5	5	2	4	7	5	9	20	4	21	3	28	7	47	21	23
None	28	28	12	24	40	27	12	27	7	37	0	0	1	6	20	22
Parental Nativity																
Both U. S.	48	48	22	44	70	47	9	20	6	32	4	36	3	18	22	24
Both Foreign	29	29	17	34	46	31	32	71	13	68	5	45	12	71	62	67
Mixed	22	22	11	22	33	22	4	9	0	0	2	18	1	12	8	9

because they fail to correlate with the total scale, serve to lower its reliability.

The "Discriminatory Power" (D.P.) technique of item analysis, introduced by Likert, was employed to assay the degree of relationship between item score and total scale score. The use of this method permits a great saving in computational time, as compared with item score-scale score intercorrelation, while providing a close approximation of this correlation. In using the technique, a comparison is made between each of the item means of the extreme high and low quartile groups. The greater the difference in mean score, the more does that item correlate with the total scale. For items scored by a seven-point system, the difference between the extreme quartile means should amount to at least two points in order to indicate acceptable significance. This is so when the item mean for the total distribution is between three and five; items whose total mean is above or below these values require lower discriminatory powers, for it is plain that a D.P. of two suggests a much sharper differentiation when the total item mean is six than when it is four.

Table 2 provides the relevant item analysis data for the scale. The column headed DP$_{JA}$ lists the differences in scores between the extreme quartiles on JA, while the DP$_F$ column does the same for the extreme scorers on F. If the JA scale is indeed highly correlated with the F scale, an effective item should discriminate the extreme quartiles on both. Considering first the DP$_{JA}$ values, we note that the mean D.P. is 2.33, indicating that, taken together, the items are fairly efficient in discriminatory power.

Table 2—Jewish Authoritarianism Scale: Its Means and Discriminatory Powers for Total Group

		MEAN				Mean for
No.	Item	H.Q.	L.Q.	DP$_{JA}$	DP$_F$	Total Group
1.	deny weakness	5.40	4.05	1.35	1.79	4.96
4.	obnoxious	4.95	1.48	3.47	2.01	3.20
7.	Israel forceful	4.58	3.18	1.40	1.48	4.23
9.	like other people	5.93	2.03	3.90	2.85	3.84
12.	work quietly	4.42	1.55	2.87	2.04	3.06
15.	good breeding	4.23	1.80	2.43	2.18	3.13
18.	"Gentlemen's Agreement"	2.18	1.47	0.71	0.32	1.94
20.	If I were a Gentile	3.57	1.42	2.15	1.18	2.36
23.	powerful groups	4.12	2.98	1.14	0.21	3.95
26.	more careful	4.68	2.73	1.95	0.54	3.63
29.	economic basis	5.78	4.23	1.55	0.84	5.60
31.	American ways	4.68	1.22	3.46	2.05	2.86
34.	Jewish radicals	4.68	1.72	2.96	2.49	3.19
37.	public life	5.50	2.77	2.73	1.79	4.05
40.	well-educated Gentiles	5.33	2.38	2.95	2.56	3.95
43.	intrude	4.55	2.07	2.48	2.31	3.33
45.	expose publicly	3.58	3.08	0.50	0.12	3.58
47.	immoral and crooked	3.47	1.10	2.37	1.90	1.96
48.	enduring persecution	4.92	3.57	1.35	1.64	4.50
51.	clannish	5.78	2.17	3.61	2.55	4.12
53.	conspicuousness	5.98	2.68	3.30	1.76	4.31
55.	statements do apply	5.93	3.23	2.70	1.32	4.49
	Mean	4.74	2.41	2.33	1.33	3.64

Of the 22 items, five have a D.P. above 3.0, nine have D.P.'s between 2.0 and 3.0, six are between 1.0 and 2.0, while the remaining two are below 1.0. The mean item mean is 3.64, which is near the neutral point of 4.0.

Examining the table more closely, we may observe that the five items whose D.P. is above 3.0 have in common the derogation of outgroup Jews; explicitly or otherwise these Jews are seen as provoking and meriting anti-Semitic response. It is apparent in retrospect that the scale is overly weighted with this type of item; twelve of the twenty-two propositions express overt hostility towards the Jews. To some extent this is justifiable, for such a condemnation is the core of Jewish authoritarian ideology. Nevertheless, certain dimensions of the attitude are underrepresented. The imagery of the Gentile, certainly an important constituent of authoritarian ideology, is directly expressed in but one item (well-educated Gentiles). This proposition has a high DP_{JA} (2.95), ranking sixth, and a DP_F of 2.56, which ranks second. These values suggest that the variable expressed by the item is significant enough to merit greater representation within the scale.

The seventh item in rank order of D.P. is Number 12, which asserts the need for discreet antidiscrimination activity. Contrasting with this effectiveness is Number 45, which appears to state a similar proposition in reverse fashion, but which is the poorest item in the scale, having a DP_{JA} of only 0.50. By hindsight again it is apparent that it permits ambiguous reading; some of the nonauthoritarian may feel that public exposure is an inadequate method of combatting anti-Semitism, when compared with other alternatives.

Three of the items (18, 31, 47) have total means below 3.0 and one (24) is above 5.0, although several others approach these points. Item 29 may be noted because the extreme affirmation it received (its mean is 5.60) was totally unexpected. It is probable, however, that the item is ambiguous, in that it is written so as to allow the respondent to interpret "economic basis of our society" idiosyncratically. Quite naturally, those items whose means are extreme have low D.P.'s. The rather aggressively stated Number 47 ("immoral and crooked"; the phrasing was borrowed from an omitted F scale item) deserves mention because its D.P. is 2.37, despite its exceptionally low mean of 1.96. The proposition was almost totally rejected by the low quartile; 57 of 60 scored the statement −3.

Turning now to the DP_F column, we observe that the values, quite understandably, are lower than for DP_{JA}. The mean DP_F is 1.33, suggesting what will later be verified, that the JA scale is highly correlated with F. Further, it is generally true that the rank order of DP_{JA} scores approximates closely that for DP_F. There are three striking exceptions wherein DP_F is greater than DP_{JA}. Examining these items (1, 7, 48), we observe that each is in some way expressing the "strength-weakness" theme. It is likely that we are here dealing with a dimension somewhat separate from the rest of the scale, whose major theme is middle-class conformity.

What of the inadequate items, those whose D.P. is below 2.00? We have already indicated that some of these suffer from a too general agreement or disagreement; several others apparently represent the separate dimension of "strength"; still others appear to be ambiguously or carelessly worded. It seems quite probable, however, that the "economics" hypothesis must be rejected. Both items emphasizing the relationship of anti-Semitism to economic stratification have low D.P.'s, although one of these, as we have seen, attracted general affirmation.

Table 3—Differences in JA Score Associated with Listed Categories

Category	N	M	SD	CR	P
Sex					
Men	146	81.8	19.1	1.33	>.05
Women	95	78.3	20.4		
Fraternal					
Frat. Men & Women	149	90.0	14.1	11.4	<.001
Non-Frat. Men & Women	95	64.9	18.0		
Parental Nativity					
Both U. S.	89	86.8	21.0	3.89	<.001
One or both Foreign	152	76.4	18.3		

We may turn, finally, to a consideration of the relationships of the JA scale to other variables. A critical, though initial, test of its validity is in the extent of its correlation with the University of California F scale; the Pearsonian coefficient is 0.67, with an S.E. of 0.06.

In Tables 3 and 4, we may note the differences in JA score associated with the categories derived from face sheet data:

1. Fraternity and sorority members score higher than those not so connected. Moreover, in a comparison of the fraternal, Hillel and Zionist, and unaffiliated groups, the first scores highest, the last lowest.

Table 4—Differences in JA Score Associated with Listed Categories

Category	N	M	F	P
Fraternity Men	99	90.4	48.5	<.001
Sorority Women	50	89.3		
Non-Frat. Men	47	63.9		
Non-Sor. Women	45	66.0		
Religious Denomination				
Reform	97	87.8	14.3	<.001
Conservative	76	80.4		
Orthodox	16	78.3		
None	52	67.2		
Political				
Republicans	23	95.4	17.8	<.001
Democrats	128	83.2		
Progressives	30	60.5		
None	60	78.8		
Religious Attendance				
Regularly or Often	56	78.6	14.9	<.001
Only on Holidays	135	85.7		
Never	50	68.4		
Fraternal	149	90.0	92.6	<.001
Hillel-Zionist	64	67.5		
Unaffiliated—Co-op	28	60.2		

2. The Reform Jewish score highest of the denominational groups, while the religiously unaffiliated score lowest.

3. Those who attend religious services only on holidays are the highest scoring group; those who never attend are the lowest.

4. The Republicans are the highest group in the political stratification, while the Progressives are lowest.

5. Those Ss both of whose parents are American born have higher scores than those with one or two foreign-born parents.

6. There is no sex difference.

These results appear to conform with the over-all impressions of the writer and other observers concerning the prevalence of the attitudes in question among the groups which were studied. It would seem that the central differentiating criterion is group membership. In Table 1 we noted certain characteristics which appear to be predominant in the fraternity groups: Reform Judaism, religious observance only on holidays, a comparatively high degree of political conservatism, second-generation American nativity; it is these categories which have the highest JA scores.

Before we proceed to the discussion of a related problem — that of the relationship between authoritarianism and ethnocentrism — it is to be noted that our results appear to lend support to the contention that authoritarianism is a variable which underlies a variety of attitudes and shows its effects among other groups than the ones studied in the original California investigation. The particular attitudes involved in Jewish authoritarian ideology are genotypically similar to non-Jewish authoritarian attitudes, in the sense that both can be understood with reference to such features of personality organization as authoritarian aggression and submission, the need for dichotomous and invidious distinctions, and so on. The interview data collected for this study — space does not permit its presentation here — indicate clearly that the early interpersonal situations of the authoritarian Ss were similar to those described in the Berkeley study.

Several caveats should be entered; these pertain to the generalizability of the obtained results. It is quite certain that the components of Jewish authoritarianism elicited by this study do not nearly exhaust the range of possibilities. They are a function both of the topics covered in the preliminary interview schedule and of the middle-class adolescent sample employed. What the JA scale emphasizes are the attitudes of a group which, because of its uncertain social position, stresses conformity to a particular array of middle-class norms. The item analysis indicates further that the theme of aggression is underplayed in the scale as now constituted, and that this theme may represent a separate dimension. Other investigators undoubtedly will demonstrate that other attitudes belong to this complex. The result of this investigation has not been so much to survey the range of factors involved in the ideology in question as to indicate its articulation with the extant body of theory concerning authoritarianism.

§ *Authoritarianism and Ethnocentrism*

How does Jewish authoritarianism relate to Jewish ethnocentrism? Examining the item content of the JA scale, we may be led to wonder whether we are dealing with a particular variant of Jewish "self-hatred." The rhetoric of many of these items, the rancor and disdain which they express, may make it appear that authoritarian Jews have a low degree of attachment to Jewishness or to the Jewish community, however defined. On the other hand we know that among majority-group individuals authoritarian and ethnocentric attitudes appear together, apparently because of intrapsyhic factors. How, then, do these two variables relate to each other in the case of a minority group?

If we return to the interview protocols for some illumination of the problem, we find no clear evidence of a relationship one way or the other. Some authoritarian subjects seem to show a minimal commitment to Jewishness, while some seemed highly involved; a similar diversity is found among the non-authoritarian.

In order to resolve the problem, it was necessary to develop a scale for the measurement of Jewish ethnocentrism. The following elements were thought to be involved: a desire to maintain the Jewish group as an intact entity; an opposition to behavior which would endanger the group's cohesion and separateness; a voluntary commitment to Jewish affiliation, and a sense of gain from such a commitment; chauvinism, or the tendency to believe in Jewish superiority, particularly as regards intellectual competence. The choice of these specific sentiments was empirical, in the sense that the interview material indicated their concurrence.

The fourteen items of the Jewish ethnocentrism (JE) scale follow:

3. I have often wished I were not Jewish.
6. I can hardly imagine myself marrying a Gentile.
11. Because the Jews have endured so much persecution, those who survive today are innately superior to other groups.
14. I prefer to have Jews as my friends.
17. I would have nothing to do with a person who denied being Jewish.
22. There is no justification for a Jew changing his name.
25. I think it is disgraceful when Jews adopt Christian customs, such as Christmas trees.
28. It is important to instill strong feelings of Jewishness in Jewish children.
33. Given a choice, I would rather join a Jewish organization than a mixed one.
36. I prefer to contribute to Jewish charities.
39. I feel quite proud whenever I hear or read of an accomplishment by a Jew.
42. On the whole, there are more advantages than drawbacks to being Jewish.
49. An unusually large number of Jews excel in the arts, sciences and professions.
56. On the whole, Jews are superior intellectually to other groups.

The data pertaining to the JE scale may be briefly summarized. The corrected split-half reliability coefficient is 0.82, a satisfactory figure. Use of the D.P. technique shows that the scale is internally consistent; the few items which have a low D.P. (11, 39, 49) all express chauvinistic sentiments, a strong indication that chauvinism has at the best a low correlation with the rest of the scale.

To test the validity of the scale, we must see whether it differentiates among subjects who differ in behavior and group membership related to Jewishness. Members of Jewish organizations, for example, should score higher than those who have no such affiliation. Table 5 presents a number of these differences:

Table 5—Differences in JE Score Associated with Listed Categories

Category	N	M	F	p
Denomination				
Reform	97	56.5	17.9	<.001
Conservative	76	59.6		
Orthodox	16	67.2		
None	52	46.5		
Religious Attendance				
Regularly or Often	56	61.6	70.2	<.001
Only on Holidays	135	59.6		
Never	50	40.4		
Parental Nativity				
Both U. S.	89	53.1	2.50*	<.02
One or both foreign	153	57.6		
Organizations				
Fraternal	149	55.7	40.3	<.001
Hillel-Zionist	64	61.1		
Unoffiliated—Co-op	28	47.7		
Sex				
Men	146	55.5	0.81*	>.05
Women	99	56.9		

* Critical Ratio

These results point to the scale's validity; those individuals score highest who show the greatest degree of in-group oriented behavior. It may well be, of course, that the scale is not measuring "ethnocentrism," but some other, more or less related variable: "group identification," for example, or "degree of assimilation." The argument for calling it a measure of ethnocentrism rests essentially on the item content.

We may now return to the problem of the relationship between authoritarianism and ethnocentrism. The Pearsonian correlation between the two scales is 0.16. Thus the relationship is negligible, for this sample at least; the two attitudes vary independently of each other.

What bearing do these results have on the general problem of minority group identification? The data are of course too limited to allow us even to attempt a definitive formulation. Their value is negative, cautionary; the results argue that the phenomenon of group affiliation is more complex and elusive than it is sometimes suspected to be.

In some of the early writing in this area we find the tacit assumption that group identification is a unidimensional variable. In the case of the minority group, identification is considered to vary along a continuum extending from group self-hatred at one extreme to the opposite pole of intense ingroup affiliation. Such a formulation is eminently rational; but it is contradicted by the low positive correlation between ethnocentrism and authoritarianism. The JA scale is in its item content very close to what is ordinarily termed "Jewish self-hatred"; yet, as we see, it is possible for persons scoring high on the scale to feel themselves committed to the Jewish group, as they define it.

Of course this result is anomalous only if we employ a definition of group identification which is rational and unidimensional. If we consult our common-sense understanding of the phenomenon, we recognize quickly enough the problems it provokes. It does not allow for ambivalence, which is especially prominent among minority group members; it assumes that all group members share more or less the same definition of the group; it assumes that each group member has a stable, consistent definition of the group. These assumptions may or may not be correct — very likely they are not. In any case, we cannot — at this moment of our knowledge — accept a definition of group identification which must assume them correct.

From the point of view of future research strategy, we may raise the question whether it is useful, at least at this time, to press for purely quantitative measures of group affiliation. To do so now may be premature. By concentrating on the problem of "how much" identification, we may lose sight of the more central task of exploring the individual's total relationship to the group. To put it another way: our major problem is to isolate the variables which will best define the connections between individual and group.

Using data from the present study, we can observe concretely some of the difficulties attending a quantitative approach to group affiliation. The ethnocentrism scale (JE), because of its ability to differentiate criterion groups, may be considered an adequate measure of "degree of group belongingness" or some equivalent of the same. Employing this scale alone we can identify a substantial, though heterogeneous group of individuals who score low (bottom quartile), and who may be presumed to have a minimal commitment to Jewishness. However, if we introduce the authoritarianism scale we find that the group of low scorers contains at least two distinctive subgroups, one high and one low (extreme quartiles) on JA.

Looking at the demographic data we find that the low JE-high JA group consists largely of individuals of upper-middle-class background, who belong to fraternities and sororities, and whose parents were born in this country; the low JE-low JA group is composed of individuals whose background is lower-middle class or working class, who are extremely liberal politically, who do not belong to organized groups, and whose parents are foreign born.

In both instances, then, there is a low degree of affiliation with Jewishness. But almost certainly the antecedent social processes are dissimilar. Quite as important is the fact that the "style" or "phenomenology" of identification is different in the two groups, so much so as to call into question whether we are dealing with the same phenomenon in both cases. In one instance, low affiliation is associated with a considerable contempt and hostility towards a good share of the Jewish group; in the other there is, at the least, a conscious sense of neutrality and dispassion towards the Jews. It is almost certain that "the Jew" is defined quite differently by the two groups. It is also probable that "low affiliation," in the two cases, has separate implications for actual behavior (such as in the readiness to marry out of the group). All in all, we see that the use of a single scale of "belongingness" tends to obscure essentially different ways of relating to the group.

A similar situation is found at the other extreme of the ethnocentrism scale, among the high scorers. Again we find two distinct subgroups, depending on the JA score. Those high on both scales are fraternity members, of upper-middle-class background; they are about evenly split in denomination, between Reform and Conservative; in about one-half of the cases both parents were born in this country, while for the other half one or both are foreign born. The low JA-high JE group is largely of lower-middle and working-class origin; its members belong to Hillel, and to Zionist organizations; the denominational membership is one-half Conservative, one-quarter Reform, and one-quarter None; parental nativity is almost entirely foreign. Once more we find that a particular scale position on "belongingness" is associated with strikingly diverse social origins and statuses. Again we can assume differing definitions of the Jewish group, as well as a probable difference in the phenomenology of identification. And again it is probable that these differences will result in separate behavioral dispositions in matters involving Jewishness.

All of this suggests that we may do well in future research to work towards multidimensional typologies of group identification. What we have done here is to sketch a loose and provisional model of Jewish group affiliation, a fourfold scheme based on two variables. Very likely these two scales (or variants of them) will be useful in developing a definitive formulation of the phenomenon; almost certainly other measures will need to be introduced. The use of typology allows us to approach the actual complexity of the processes of group identification.

§ *Summary*

A sample of seventeen Jewish college men was interviewed intensively for the purpose of formulating hypotheses as to the nature of Jewish authoritarian ideology. Statements thought to represent this ideology were included in a 22-item Likert-type scale which was administered to 242 Jewish college students.

The interviews suggested that among the constituents of Jewish authoritarianism were the following: the Jews are divided into ingroup and out-group, the latter being seen (in a middle-class sample) as violators of middle-class standards, as being seclusive, intrusive, offensive, nonconforming; the Gentiles are similarly dichotomized, the central belief being that anti-Semitism is a lower-class Gentile trait, to which the middle-class is not given; anti-Semitism is viewed as caused by the deviant behavior of the outgroup Jews; anti-Semitism, it is felt, may best be combatted by a change in the behavior of these Jews; it is believed that organizational activity against anti-Semitism should be discreet, so as to avoid antagonizing the powerful majority; political and economic solutions of anti-Semitism are rejected.

The scale of Jewish authoritarianism is internally consistent, possesses a corrected odd-even reliability of .79, and is valid to the extent that its correlation with the California F scale is .67; the scale differentiates certain sociological groups.

A fourteen-item scale to measure Jewish ethnocentrism was also developed. The correlation with the scale of Jewish authoritarianism is 0.16, indicating that the two measures vary independently of each other. This result suggests that Jewish group identification cannot be formulated as a unidimensional variable, one which extends from group "self-hatred" to intense ingroup affiliation. In view of the complexity of the phenomenon, it is argued, the problem must be approached through the use of a multidimensional typology. This approach is demonstrated by using the scales of authoritarianism and ethnocentrism in combination. A fourfold model is developed, one which points to qualitatively different types of relationship to the Jewish group.

References

1. Adorno, T. W., Frenkel-Brunswik, Else, Levinson, D. J., & Sanford, R. N. *The authoritarian personality.* New York: Harper, 1950.
2. Arendt, Hannah. *The origins of totalitarianism.* New York: Harcourt Brace, 1951.
3. Fisher, J. The memory process and certain psychological attitudes, with special reference to the law of prägnanz. *J. Pers.,* 1951, *4,* 406-420.
4. Frenkel-Brunswik, Else. A study of prejudice in children. *Hum. Relat.,* 1948, *55,* 157-166.
5. McNemar, Q. Opinion-attitude methodology. *Psychol. Bull.,* 1946, *43,* 289-374.
6. Riesman, D. Some observations on social science research. *Antioch Rev.,* 1951, *11,* 259-278.
7. Rokeach, M. Generalized mental rigidity as a factor in ethnocentrism. *J. abnorm. soc. Psychol.,* 1948, *43,* 259-278.
8. Rokeach, M. Prejudice, concreteness of thinking, and reification of thinking. *J. abnorm. soc. Psychol.,* 1951, *46,* 83-91.
9. Srole, L. Social dysfunction, personality, and social distance attitudes. Paper read at Amer. Sociol. Soc., 1951.

IRWIN D. RINDER

POLARITIES IN JEWISH IDENTIFICATION:
THE PERSONALITY OF
IDEOLOGICAL EXTREMITY

§ *Frame of Reference*

THE entrance of immigrant groups into the United States initiated changes on the part of the members of these groups which is best described as "Americanization." This change may be conceived as taking place on two different levels: (a) acculturation, or the relinquishment of the language, customs, food habits, and social expectations of the old culture and the adoption of substitute cultural items from the American milieu; and (b) identification, or the feeling of membership and subjective belongingness, from the old ethnic group toward the new American society.

Progressive change can and usually does proceed apace for both these processes; Park's (9) concept of the race relations cycle (where, following contact, continuing interaction goes through phases of competition, conflict, accommodation, and assimilation) is the systematic statement of this phenomenon. The general validity of the cycle concept in its American application has been affirmed by such studies as *The Polish Peasant in Europe and America* (17), *Old World Traits Transplanted* (10), *The Ghetto* (20), and more contemporaneously, *The Social Systems of American Ethnic Groups* (19). Although acculturation and identification usually proceed simultaneously, this is not a necessary relationship, for one may change without the other. The emphasis in earlier works was often on the modal adjustment of minority groups, i.e., the unilinear trend toward assimilation, though some note was taken of the possibilities of deviation from the trend. Thomas and Znaniecki studied intensively the individual who could not become reorganized after being moved from one culture to another but in whom uprootedness became a life-pattern. In considering the phenomenon of "the return to the ghetto," Wirth took note of a regressive current within the cycle for Jews who met resistance and rebuff in their assimilatory attempts. Sociologists have long known that certain "social types" were constructed by minorities to label their awareness of individual deviations from the cycle, i.e., those who were

Published for the first time in this volume.

This article is based upon a portion of the author's thesis, "Jewish Identification and the Race Relations Cycle" (unpublished Ph.D. dissertation, Department of Sociology, University of Chicago, 1953). The author is indebted to Prof. D. T. Campbell for his aid throughout this project.

[493]

moving too fast or too slow relative to their group. The *meshumad*, Bohemian, or striver might illustrate the former; the *caffone*, greenhorn, and Uncle Tom the latter.

§ The Problem

The members of successive generations of ethnic groups may be seen as ranging along a continuum of identification extending from an original ethnic, through an intermediate mixed ethnic-American, to an identification wholly or predominantly American (i.e., non-ethnic). Distribution along this continuum is not random but is primarily a function of length of exposure and experience with the competing models of ethnic and American roles and self-concepts. (See Figure 1.)

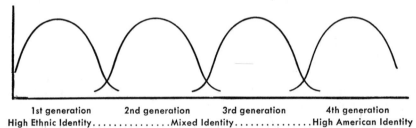

1st generation   2nd generation   3rd generation   4th generation
High Ethnic Identity.............Mixed Identity.............High American Identity

Figure 1—Idealized Representation of the Identificatory Trends over Successive Generations in the Race Relations Cycle

The differences in emphasis in the identification manifested by various generations may be studied for evidence of the cycle process, or the range of differences in identification to be found within any one generational group may be examined as expressions of individual differences in commitment to an ethnic ideology or identification. It is this latter interest which constitutes the focus of the present study. Specifically we are interested in the range of identifications found in a group controlled for third generation, Eastern-European Jewish origin. The range of hypothesized identifications may be conceptually divided into (1) an average group centering about the norm, (2) which extends on the one side into an over-identified Jewish group, (3) and which on the other grades into an under-identified Jewish group. These categories are analogous to Stonequist's marginality resolution typology of the intermediary role, the nationalist role, and the assimilationist role (16).

The major hypothesis of this study is that there is a rapprochement, a functional psychological equivalence between the polarities of over- and under-identification. Both represent the repression or denial of that which is felt as threatening to the self in contrast to the acceptance and creative synthesis of the total self found in the intermediary role (14). Regardless of the direction of deviance from the norm, whether toward over- or under-identification, we feel that the psychodynamic of personality or style of response is the same. The measure of personality employed to test this hypothesis is the F-scale, specifically designed to study the authoritarian personality (2). The authoritarian syndrome—summarized in the variable "intolerance of ambiguity"—includes such characteristics as intolerance of ambivalence, dichotomous thinking, repressed hostility, rigid all-or-nothing formulations, etc. This conceptual tool seemed congruent with the mechanism which seems involved in the reaction patterns of over- and under-identification, i.e., the inability to tolerate or retain an ambiguous Jewish-American identification which is manifest in the repression of one or the other facet of the problem complex.

§ *The Measurement of Jewish Identification*

The problem to be investigated necessitates having a tool which could reliably and validly measure Jewish identification. The instruments already in existence were reviewed and items adapted from them (3) (4) (5). None of these was suitable in its entirety for our purpose, and the instrument finally constructed contained some variations on conventional attitude methodology.

Since Jewish identification consists of a number of potentially independent axes or subtypes of identification, provision was made for tapping those most relevant, namely general,[1] religious, racial, national, and cultural feelings of Jewishness. Twenty-three items were distributed through these categories with each item presented as a problem in identification with four alternative responses, these representing choices or solutions characteristic of the following:

A. Strong, monistic Jewish identification
B. Moderate, pluralistic Jewish identification
C. Moderate, pluralistic non-Jewish identification
D. Strong, monistic non-Jewish identification

Examples of this item-alternative format are the following questions representative of each of the subscales. On the actual test the order of the alternatives was randomized and not keyed.

(General) To be told one is not a "typical" Jew . . .
(A) is plain out-and-out insulting.
(B) is insulting but also embarrassing if the speaker intended it as a friendly remark.
(C) shows that the speaker is a victim of stereotyped thinking.
(D) is something of a compliment in that it shows your acceptance.

(Religious) To be a Jew in the full sense of the word . . .
(A) requires the observance of the religious rituals, practices, etc.
(B) only requires one to participate in those religious activities which one finds satisfying and rewarding.
(C) doesn't require the performance of any special activity whatsoever, if one is so inclined.
(D) requires the elimination of halfway measures; one should either be completely Jewish or forget the whole thing.

(Racial) Jewish people unable to have children of their own should adopt . . .
(A) only children of known and proven Jewish ancestry.
(B) any child, providing they make some attempt to preferably get one of Jewish background or ancestry.
(C) any healthy child, whom they may raise as their conscience dictates.
(D) a child who doesn't look Jewish, if they have their choice between one that does and one that does not look Jewish.

(National) When I hear the national anthem and see the flag of Israel . . .
(A) they thrill me as does nothing else.
(B) they thrill me more than most similar ceremonies do.
(C) my response is about the same as it is to other similar ceremonies.
(D) whatever else I feel is accompanied by a measure of uneasiness.

(Cultural) The Jewish culture . . .
(A) is a priceless heritage which is unmatched by the culture of any other group.
(B) is a thing of great antiquity which has certain value and beauty for those who feel some attachment to it.
(C) is one among many of the world's cultures, which taken together, comprise proof of man's creativity.
(D) is a tribal product which is now a burden to many Jews.

Respondents were asked to endorse two of the four alternatives in their order of preference and several scores were derived from the various combinations of endorsements which resulted. Our present concern is the quantitative strength of Jewish identification score and this was obtained through the Likert-type weighting of the alternatives so that various combinations of A, B, C, and D responses received values ranging from 12 to 1 indicating progression from high to low (i.e., strong to weak) feelings of Jewishness.

Validation of the instrument was effected through the use of criterion groups. Five groups with whose Jewish identification the writer had *a priori* familiarity cooperated in taking the test battery. Mean scores were computed by groups for each of the subscales as well as for the total score. The differences between groups were not only in the direction anticipated but were highly significant statistically in terms of the analysis of variance.[2] The groups, all resident in Chicago, ranked as follows from high to low:

1. The *"Leadership"* class at the *College of Jewish Studies* is a group of young persons attending evening sessions of a course designed to train and equip them with group leadership skills. The course consists of the enlistment of social-scientific knowledge and techniques in the enhancement of the role of leader in the Jewish community. This is a group of *third* generation, *Eastern* European origin.

2. The *"History of Religion"* class at the *College of Jewish Studies*. These students wish to augment their knowledge of the historical development of Judaism. The group is slightly older than the "Leadership" group, which is in its late teens. This religion class is predominantly composed of persons of *second* generation, *Eastern* European origin.

3. *Office personnel* of the *Anti-Defamation League*, consisted of secretarial and administrative workers satisfying the criterion of *third* generation, although

two were of *Western* rather than *Eastern* Europe origin. Employment by the organization indicates no particular degree of Jewish identification beyond a certain minimum.

4. The *University of Chicago group* consisted of residents in the University's Prefabricated Housing Project who were contacted on the strength of the impressionistic selection of their names for "Jewishness" in addition to a number whose ethnic identity the author was familiar with. This was a group of graduate students and young professional academic people of varying identifications; mostly *third* generation, *Eastern* origin.

5. The *American Council for Judaism* was selected as the group likely to have the lowest overall identification score because of this organization's avowed credo that Judaism is a religion and is or should be nothing else, and that the goal for American Jews should be "integration." Respondents from this group were predominantly of *Western* European origin and either of *third* or *fourth* generation. Groups 3 and 5 had a higher average age than the preceding groups.

Table 1—Mean Weighted Identification Scores by Criterion Group

Group	N	General	Religious	Racial	National	Cultural	Total
"Leadership" class	9	7.7	7.0	7.6	8.5	10.2	8.1
"History of Religion" class	11	7.3	6.6	6.9	8.2	9.6	7.7
Anti-Defamation League	12	7.0	6.9	6.4	7.1	8.4	7.1
University of Chicago Prefabs	29	5.8	5.2	6.0	6.7	7.6	6.2
Amer. Council for Judaism	23	4.8	6.0	5.3	3.2	5.3	4.9
F (variance ratio)		18.0	1.7	6.5	40.0	24.6	26.0

This instrument, with a hypothetical score range of 0-12 (expressing the total score as an average item weight) actually obtained group scores ranging from 3.2 to 10.2 (see Table 1). Another general observation is that the instrument *does* rank groups in the identical order in which they were arranged on the basis of the researchers' general familiarity with the sociology of the Jewish community.

Another interesting point about Table 1 is that with the exception of the Religious subscale, all five groups consistently occupy the same rank order on the several subscales of identification. This is evidence of the high correlation between subscales which, in turn, indicates that Jewish identification is—to some extent at least—a generalized attitude or syndrome of attitudes.

A number of specific observations may be made relative to scores inspected through a horizontal rather than a vertical reading of the table. Although this horizontal reading (or subscale comparison) is not as statistically justifiable as the vertical (for it assumes a topic-to-topic equality in wording item-alternatives), it is of interest in the light of our knowledge regarding these criterion groups. It has been noted that the rabbinical students at Hebrew Union College obtained a higher score in religious identification than any other group. Furthermore, the American Council for Judaism which ranks lowest in every other area of identification, is exceeded in lowness of Religious identification only by the University of Chicago group (whom we know to be highly secular and humanistic rather than religious in emphasis). Again reading horizontally, we see that the American Council for Judaism obtained its lowest rating on National identification and its highest on Religious identification. To one familiar with the anti-Zionism of the Council (its major *raison d'être*) and its insistence that the only proper Judaic identification is the religious one, this contributes not only to our confidence in the validity of the research instrument, but also suggests that the subscale referents are validly labelled. Furthermore, the reliability of the test was determined through the test of item homogeneity, i.e., split-half comparability. The instrument yielded a satisfactory overall reliability of .87 although the separate subscales, being smaller, had individually lower reliabilities.

We conclude that there appears to be a generalized attitude syndrome of "Jewish identification" toward which each of the sub-scales contributes a component, while each shows an association with total score. However, the association between subscales, while significant, is not so compellingly high that we cannot also deduce that some independence obtains between the separate facets of identification. Thus, the criterion groups, whose identifications were more particularistic with regard to different subscales, showed some low and even negative subscale interrelationships rather than a generalized identification complex.

§ *Identification, Acculturation, and Ethnocentrism*

The results discussed from this point on refer to a group of eighty-eight persons selected out of a larger sample because all satisfied the requirement of third generation, Eastern European origin. This group contains some of the original respondents of the criterion groups plus others from two Jewish fraternities and two Jewish sororities at Northwestern University as well as the members of a Jewish service and philanthropic organization. Our test battery included a Social Distance Scale, adapted from Bogardus. It inquired into our subjects' willingness to engage in various activities with Gentiles ranging from living in the same neighborhood to intermarrying.[3] The patent interpretation is that there is a positive correlation between identification and social distance, i.e., the stronger the ethnic identity the greater is the in-group or ethnocentric sentiment. The subscale for Racial identification had the highest of any subscale correlation with Social Distance and also the highest on several social psychological measures of authoritarianism and rigidity. This indicates that the exclusive or parochial axis of racial identification has a particular attractiveness for the insecure.

Another instrument employed was the Inventory of Religio-Cultural Practices, a checklist of thirteen practices indicative of traditional Jewish ritual behavior. The list included the maintenance of a Kosher home, lighting Sabbath candles, synagogue attendance, marriage, burial, confirmation, etc.[4] In addition to asking respondents to indicate their own religio-cultural practices, the inventory also provided data on several generations since it inquired into the practices of grandparents and parents, one's own personal practices, and preferences for one's children. As anticipated by the cycle hypothesis, there was a continuous diminishment of practices over these generations showing the effect of acculturation and/or assimilation. An interesting and important finding was that although our respondents' practices score correlated with their identification score, the practices scores of their parents, and even more so those of their grandparents, showed no association with their own contemporary identification. We learn from this that the identificatory differences within our research population of third generation Jewish Americans may not be attributed to differences in their rather uniform family cultural backgrounds, and thus systematically explained away. Rather, differences in Jewish identification in the formally homogeneous ethnic group which is our research population are genuinely idiosyncratic and of social psychological significance. The various measures which have been referred to in this section are presented in Table 2.

Table 2—Correlation Analysis of the Inventory of Religio-Cultural Practices, Social Distance, and the Measures of Identification

			JEWISH IDENTIFICATION			
Measures	General	Religious	Racial	National	Cultural	Total
Social Distance	−.01	−.38	−.46	−.38	−.41	−.54
Cultural Practices						
Grandparents	.10	.23	−.06	.10	.16	.16
Parents	.29	.26	.01	.21	.25	.29
Self	.44	.53	.33	.38	.48	.59
Children	.47	.51	.30	.39	.48	.60

§ *Testing the Hypothesis*

Our major inquiry concerns Jewish-American identity conceived as an ideological situation which is essentially marginal since the possibility of conflict is present in its dualism. This conflict could be handled by our third generation respondents—or any generation of mixed ethnic-American identity—in one of two ways, i.e., they could either repress the problem through the exaggeration of one identification at the expense of the other, or they could realistically attempt to retain and develop some synthesis of the two. Our hypothesis is that despite their ideological divergence, persons who overreact to their Jewishness by either denying or asserting it resemble each other in the psychological quality of their response. By obtaining a sample group controlled for generation and place of origin and obtaining a range of identifications within this context, it becomes possible to note the modal identification which serves as the norm or benchmark of adjustment. It is only with reference to this range and this empirically obtained norm that it becomes possible to denote objectively (rather than polemically) over- and under-identification. The hypothesis anticipates that these extremes will score more closely on the F-scale than will either to the ideologically more intermediate but psychologically more different group.

Employing the scores obtained with the Jewish identification test and scores derived from a shortened version of the F-scale (using the twelve most discriminating items), we found that an insignificant measure of linear regression or simple correlation obtained. However, further computation revealed that a curvilinear association between the two did exist as anticipated (see Table 3). Both a significant departure from linearity

Table 3—Curvilinearity between Total Identification and F Score

Variable	Correl. Coeff. (r)	Correl. Ratio (n)	TOTAL IDENTIFICATION Means for Various Levels of Identification Low..High									
F scale	.07	.65	5.0	4.8	3.7	2.5	3.0	4.1	3.4	3.1	4.4	5.8

(7.10) and a high and significant correlation ratio or *eta* (6.36) were demonstrated with significance beyond the 1 per cent level. Here, then, is literal and graphic confirmation of the French proverb "les extrèmes se touchent."

Further confirmation of the hypothesis about the interrelatedness between ideological extremeness and personality constriction was sought through the use of an independent non-verbal measure of personality. Psychologists have been aware for some time of the unity and consistency of response that is personality and have been able to study it on many levels of behavior, e.g., physiological, perceptual, cognitive, and ideological. On the perceptual level, Thurstone's (18) factorial study resulted in the isolation of the specific tests which best measured various factors involved in perception. The test for speed of closure and that for flexibility of closure were then found capable of assessing personality and were utilized in the present study for that purpose (11). The two scores were combined in a formula which cancelled out their common ability component (intelligence) and maximized the elements of pressure for perceptual closure and flexibility. The resulting score is a measure of "tolerance of ambiguity"—the opposite of authoritarianism. This measure was significantly correlated with the F scores (—.33) and in the anticipated direction. Analysis of this perceptual score for U-shaped curvilinearity with Jewish identification revealed a pattern of good curvilinearity in mean score progression but fell a little short of significance at the 5 per cent level. Considering that these were such different and imperfect measures, this was regarded as encouraging and suggestive.

§ *Discussion and Summary*

A number of studies have discovered a positive relationship between personality constriction and extremes of Jewish identification. In several instances, under-identification to the point of self-hatred (Jewish anti-

Semitism) was found correlative with authoritarianism or clinical evidence of a similar nature (12, 15). In another study, Himmelhoch (7) found ethnocentrism or strong in-group identification and out-group hostility correlated with authoritarianism as measured by the F-scale plus clinical evidence. Adelson's (1) conclusions were somewhat at variance with these others and with the present study in that his not too highly identified fraternity subjects showed a rigid conformity with middle-class values combined with the highest authoritarian scores of any of his subjects, whereas his more highly identified Jewish subjects who were Zionists or members of Hillel scored lower on authoritarianism. However, Adelson's lowest group on authoritarianism were the unaffiliated, of assumed lowest identification. Perhaps some of the disparity between these and other findings could be reduced if generation, cultural background, etc., were held constant.

In addition to these empirical studies, others have sensed the relationship between ideology and personality. Hoffer (8) is explicit about the psychological kinship of those on the ideological fringes, be they right or left. Greenberg (6) makes the same point with particular reference to both Jewish self-hatred and Jewish chauvinism. This study has reported on an effort to control for cultural background while gathering an array of ethnic identifications; on the construction of an instrument for measuring this identification; on various correlates of identification; and on the verification of the hypothesis that subjects toward the ideological extremes of Jewish over-identification and under-identification will perform similarly and more highly on the F-scale than those of more intermediate commitment.

References

1. Adelson, J. "A Study of Minority Group Authoritarianism." *Journal of Abnormal and Social Psychology,* 1950, 48, pp. 477-85.
2. Adorno, T. W., and others. *The Authoritarian Personality.* New York: Harper and Bros., 1950.
3. Campisi, P. J. "A Scale for the Measurement of Acculturation." Unpublished Ph.D. dissertation, Department of Sociology, University of Chicago, 1947.
4. Chein, I., and Hurwitz, J. A *Study of Minority Group Membership: The Reaction of Jewish Boys to Various Aspects of Being Jewish.* New York: Jewish Center Division of the National Jewish Welfare Board, 1950.
5. Geismar, L. "The Construction and Use of a Scale to Measure Ethnic Identification." Unpublished Master's thesis, Department of Sociology. University of Minnesota, 1950.
6. Greenberg, C. "Self-Hatred and Jewish Chauvinism." *Commentary,* 1950, 10, 426-33.

7. Himmelhoch, J. "Tolerance and Personality Needs: A Study of Ethnic Attitudes among Minority Group Students." *American Sociological Review,* 1950, 15, 79-88.

8. Hoffer, E. *The True Believer.* New York: Harper and Bros., 1951.

9. Park, R. E. "The Race Relations Cycle in Hawaii." *Race and Culture,* Glencoe: The Free Press, 1950, pp. 194-95.

10. Park, R. E., and Miller, H. A. *Old World Traits Transplanted.* Chicago: Society for Social Research, University of Chicago, 1925.

11. Pemberton, C. "A Study of the Speed and Flexibility of Closure Factors." Unpublished Ph.D. dissertation, Department of Psychology, University of Chicago, 1951.

12. Radke-Yarrow, M., and Lande, B. "Personality Variables and Reactions to Minority Group Belonging." *The American Psychologist,* 1951, 6, p. 329 (abstract).

13. Rinder, I. D. "Jewish Identification and the Race Relations Cycle." Unpublished Ph.D. dissertation, Department of Sociology, University of Chicago, 1953.

14. Rinder, I. D., and Campbell, D. T. "Varieties of Inauthenticity." *Phylon,* 1952, 13, 270-85.

15. Sarnoff, I. "Identification with the Aggressor: Some Personality Correlates of Anti-Semitism among Jews." *Journal of Personality,* 1951, 2, 199-218.

16. Stonequist, E. V. *The Marginal Man.* New York: Chas. Scribner's Sons, 1937.

17. Thomas, W. I., and Znaniecki, F. *The Polish Peasant in Europe and America.* Chicago: University of Chicago Press, 1918.

18. Thurstone, L. L. *A Factorial Study of Perception.* Chicago: University of Chicago Press, 1944.

19. Warner, W. L., and Srole, L. *The Social Systems of American Ethnic Groups.* New Haven: Yale University Press, 1945.

20. Wirth, L. *The Ghetto.* Chicago: University of Chicago Press, 1928.

6

Some Cultural Aspects
and Value Orientations

INTRODUCTION

THE problem of value orientations, and by implication the question of what, if any, type of special culture is shared by American Jews, has thus far not been the subject of extended discussion. Some attention was given to this question in the section on demographic aspects, specifically in the discussion on social mobility, but it is only the present group of articles which focuses very directly on the area of cultural patterns and value orientations.

Our emphasis in the present section is on patterns and orientations which are special to the Jewish group, or which are more commonly encountered in the Jewish group than elsewhere. This emphasis is made with all due regard for: (1) the difficulty of equating patterns more commonly discovered among Jews with "Jewish" culture patterns, and (2) the additional difficulty that cultural differences discovered between Jews and non-Jews may be a function of "extraneous" factors such as class and status differences. Ethnic-religious differences are, to be sure, highly relevant in explaining differences in patterns of stratification—the point is that culture patterns and value orientations may actually result from differences in stratification. When matched groups are available, all of this becomes perfectly apparent. Unfortunately, such matched groups are *not* always available; it is frequently necessary to compare gross populations.

To clarify any possible misunderstanding, it should be noted that the procedure which we follow in this section has the limitation, by inference at least, of *underestimating* the points of similarity between Jews and their neighbors. Some of these similarities are apparent from material in previous sections. In any event, it is worth underlining the fact that similarities are equally as important as differences. For our purposes, however, exploring differences is the more useful procedure. As will be apparent, the material presented in this section constitutes only a beginning in the definitive assessment of what is an exceedingly complicated subject. Because the possibility of vague generalization is ever present in this area, we have sought to include a good deal of quantitative material, particularly in such areas as alcoholism, mental illness, and delinquency. And in order to place the section in proper perspective, we have deliberately chosen two contrasting articles in the field of voting behavior. They demonstrate how the same facts may be interpreted by stressing cultural aspects and value orientations, or by utilizing a highly dissimilar framework. While the major part of this section is devoted to such problems as delinquency, mental health, and alcoholism, as well as to voting behavior, it is understood that these areas may not necessarily represent *the* most strategic way to attack the subject matter of the section. All of the articles, however, do make a substantial contribution to an understanding of the subject.

David Mandelbaum's "Change and Continuity in Jewish Life" is based on a lecture, and thus his article is less formal in tone than most of the others. Not being confined to any one aspect of the problem, and not concerned particularly with the area of social problems, the Mandelbaum material serves to introduce the other articles. The author does not present any new research, but rather draws upon the published data in very skillful fashion; he succeeds in highlighting a number of basic themes which have been mentioned by one or another investigator. The attempt to relate organizational forms to value systems, and the East European cultural heritage to the present system of shared values, is particularly noteworthy.

At one place in his article Mandelbaum alludes to the need for further evidence about the nature of parent-child relations in the Jewish family. Ideally, a separate section should be included in this book devoted to such aspects of the American-Jewish family as: family structure, the definition of roles and functions of the various members of the family, child-rearing patterns, parent-child relationships, the impact of general norms upon the American-Jewish family, interrelations between family and community, the division of functions between family and community in shaping the "Jewishness" of the child, and the role of socio-economic and generational factors in Jewish family patterns. While there is a sizeable fiction literature on the American-Jewish family, unfortunately specialists in the field of the sociology of the family have devoted very little attention to the Jewish group. There are no large-scale studies which can be reported on, but nonetheless some significant material is available. As an example of such material we include an article by the psychotherapist Martha Wolfenstein, entitled "Two Types of Jewish Mothers." It is based on case histories of two families of different generation and of contrasting character. Some of Wolfenstein's interpretations can be formulated into propositions for testing in family-research projects, though other ideas—more strictly analytic in character—are not so easily translated into hypotheses for research. It should be emphasized in this connection that the generation whose dominant socialization took place in the *shtetl* of Eastern Europe is now quite advanced in age. Since the Jewish community is increasingly a second-third generation community, systematic study of the immigrant generation cannot long be deferred.

Two articles on delinquency are included: Sophia Robison's "A Study of Delinquency among Jewish Children in New York City," and Jackson Toby's "Hoodlum or Businessman: An American Dilemma." The Robison study is based on data gathered from the docket book of the Children's Court of New York City. The methodology illustrates the fact that while the Decennial Census and many other such sources are of limited usefulness for the study of Jewish problems, data from official agencies can sometimes be used for researches in the area of Jewish studies. Another feature of the article is the comparisons between the data gathered for 1930 and for 1952. Robison's figures suggest some significant contrasts between the contemporary pattern of delinquency and that of a previous generation. It appears that a substantial proportion of the earlier delinquents committed crimes of a less serious nature—crimes which are hardly reprehensible according to Jewish cultural norms. In fact, such offenses as peddling without a license might be thought of as preparing the individual, as it were, for future social mobility. All of this is in contrast to the contemporary picture. The economic prosperity of the present era makes peddling rather obsolete; a greater proportion of today's delinquent Jewish youngsters indulge in behavior which is uniformly regarded as anti-social. But overriding all of these considerations is the evidence which points to an exceedingly low rate of delinquency among Jewish youth.

What is the explanation for such a phenomenon? It is to this problem that Jackson Toby addresses himself. He contrasts Jews and Italians—the same groups utilized in the Strodtbeck article in Section 2. Toby's approach stresses the Jewish respect for education; he does not suggest some of the more varied perspectives developed by Strodtbeck. Perhaps one of his most valuable points is contained in a concluding footnote where he suggests how some foreign cultures may facilitate adjustment in the American educational and occupational systems. Actually, what many view as the highly successful adjustment of Jews to American society accounts for the frequent use of the Jewish group for comparative and cross-cultural studies.

The article by Jerome K. Myers and Bertram H. Roberts, "Some Relationships between Religion, Ethnic Origin and Mental Illness," continues the line of thinking pursued by Toby, for Myers and Roberts seek to discover those patterns of Jewish culture which explain some of the differences which they find in the rates of mental illness. Their data have one great advantage: investigators generally base themselves on admissions to mental hospitals; the Myers and Roberts data, however, include individuals who are suffering from psychoneurotic disorders and who are in private treatment with a psychiatrist. In discussing their figures they properly emphasize that the high "rate" of psychoneurosis among Jews may well be traceable to acceptance of psychoanalytic psychiatry; their suggestions as to why this particular therapeutic process is less objectionable to Jews than others are highly interesting. The problem of Jewish family structure is touched on by Myers and Roberts, but since the necessary material is not available, they can do little more than speculate as to the special characteristics of the American-Jewish family, and of its socialization practices.

While rates of delinquency and mental illness among Jews have received some attention, the field in which there has been perhaps the greatest interest is alcoholism. Charles R. Snyder, an investigator on the staff of the Yale Center of Alcohol Studies, is one of the individuals who has paid a good deal of attention to the Jewish group in connection with this problem. Snyder's work is distinguished by attention to theoretical questions as well as the use of quantitative materials. His work represents an excellent example of how a specialized topic may provide clues to larger problems in the study of acculturation. Since the stress in the excerpt which we reproduce is on interaction between Jew and non-Jew, significant material is included on how new culture patterns are learned, and on the situations which make people resistant or accepting of change. By implication, the Snyder material may suggest some of the unanticipated consequences of intergroup contact and secularization—consequences which may be apparent only in future decades.

The limitations of the Snyder material lie chiefly in the absence of a first-generation group of respondents who are strongly secular in orientation. Such a group would help clarify whether the cause of Jewish sobriety is adherence to religious norms or adherence to a Jewish value system which is supra-religious. Also, it would be helpful to have more sensitive indicators of Orthodoxy than the one employed in the study.

As research in the area of political behavior has come to involve the careful inspection of election returns, and in particular their analysis ward by ward, the question of the political predilections of ethnic groups has been the subject of increasing study. In recent years differences in political preferences as between Jew and non-Jew, and the explanation for such differences, has received some attention. One type of explanation for the differences is illustrated by an excerpt from a monograph by Lawrence H. Fuchs devoted to the political behavior of American Jewry. Fuchs' emphasis is on values shared by a minority group which predisposes them to view domestic and international issues in a special light. His position has been challenged as being founded more on speculation than on empirical research; it is indeed true that the linkages between the actual facts of Jewish voting behavior and his theoretical orientation seem plausible enough at times, but are not conclusively demonstrated. For example, his survey data (most of which are not reproduced here) offer no demonstration of a correlation between adherence to a Jewish value system and a belief in liberalism. Nevertheless, Fuchs' material serves a very worth-while purpose both in drawing attention to the significance of the area of voting behavior for the study of the value systems of the Jews, as well as in illustrating some of the current thinking *about* values. This thinking can be applied in any number of areas.

Werner Cohn presents a strongly contrasting view in his article "The Politics of American Jews." He does not project any *values* as explanations for Jewish liberalism—values which are presumed to be characteristic of Jewish culture and are assumed to be held by the bulk of American Jewry. His emphasis is on the non-Jew rather than the Jew, on anti-Semitism (actual or feared), on the historical position of the Jews in the modern era, and on barriers between Jews and Christians as members of groups separated both by social and supra-social barriers. His approach, too, requires further validation before it may be fully accepted. It may well be that both the Cohn thesis and the Fuchs thesis are of value in explaining voting behavior of the American Jew; there is need for an investigation which will test both factors simultaneously and seek to give each its proper weight.

CHANGE AND CONTINUITY
IN JEWISH LIFE

IN other times and places, the hostility of the surrounding society was certainly one factor in keeping Jews within their group. The dogma of the church or mosque might encourage would-be converts, but the attitudes of the people would fend them off. Moreover, a change by a Jew could not be a piecemeal one: either the threshold was crossed or it was not. Once across the boundary into the other culture and society, the Jewish transferer found himself in a strange and quite alien system and, perhaps more important, in a totally new group, cut off from the family and friends of his previous existence. To cross that boundary was a far more perilous adventure than was the socially approved emigration to a new land. Few men or women, then and now, could have strong enough motivation to shear off one's own history, to leap into a strange culture and to stand alone in a new society, naked of family and friends.

Yet too much can be made of such containing pressure. Jewish communities have existed over a long time in places where the outside pressure was not great and still they adhered to their Jewish ceremonies and the rest of Jewish culture, as did Jews elsewhere. The writer once studied a Jewish community in Cochin, in the far south of India, whose ancestors have lived in amiable and tight proximity with their neighbors in the region for over a thousand years. The greater number of them closely resemble their Hindu neighbors in physical type and in most outward characteristics. And Hinduism makes no objection to an eclectic participation in worship and ritual. These Cochin Jews very easily could have taken over one Hindu trait after another until their Judaism disappeared. And yet they did not. They remained and remain Jews.[1]

To take another example, at a vast geographic and cultural remove, the Jewish community in San Francisco has been established for more than a century. Here also, according to an interesting essay on this community, there has been relatively little compaction from the outside and increasingly little cultural divergence with others of similar socioeconomic status in the city. And here also the Jews remain Jews in identification,

In April, 1954, Prof. Mandelbaum delivered the annual Oscar Hillel Plotkin lecture at North Shore Congregation Israel, Glencoe, Illinois, entitled "Change and Continuity in Jewish Life." This lecture was expanded somewhat and then printed in booklet form by the Oscar Hillel Plotkin Library of the Congregation. The portion reproduced here represents the last half of Prof. Mandelbaum's lecture. It is used here by permission of the author and the publisher.

keep community functions (though altered from those of their European forebears) steadily alive.[2]

Hence outer containment is hardly a sufficient answer to the question why Jews want to remain Jews. . . . Among a variety of mankind, an inner group unity is built by ceremonies, among other factors. With Jews no less than others, such cohesion develops. Moreover, it appears to be a unity with some special characteristics. Before we consider these characteristics, it is well to note that the question just stated has too often been wrongly put to get an illuminating answer. Not why do Jews want to continue as Jews, but why should they cast off Jewish identity, is frequently the more strategic question.

Because it is in that form that the question commonly presents itself— if it does at all—to American Jews. Thus the article on the Jews of San Francisco tells of the problem faced by some parents who have not had any formal religious affiliation until their children want to attend the neighborhood Sunday school (of whatever denomination) along with the other children. "Parents are continually approaching their [sic] rabbi with this problem, and even when long travelling distances are involved, are anxious to have their children receive a Jewish Sunday school education."[3]

Parents in that situation quite anxiously want their children to preserve social identity as Jews—or at least to have an option in such identity. This is partly because cultural-religious diversity is not particularly penalized. What is disadvantageous is not to belong to any one of the established religious categories. The comment of a Jew in Yankee City on this matter may be quoted as representative of similar declarations which have been reported in field studies and in journalistic pieces. "The young men have found out that even to have the Christians like us, we should go to the synagogue. A Jew who is an honest Jew and takes an interest in his synagogue, that is, in his community, is really liked better by the Gentiles. A Christian who is a customer of mine told me that he would have more faith in one who was an observing Jew than in one who denied his religion."[4] While there are no statistical data on the prevalence of this view, various studies indicate that the environing society does encourage Jews to be Jews. As in Yankee City, so it is widely true in America, that all ethnic and religious groups are constrained to conform with the social system, and the system as it has now developed encompasses three recognized and established sets of churches, Protestant, Catholic, and Jewish. Jews in factories as well as in stores have told that they fare better with their non-Jewish neighbors and fellow-workers if they are forthrightly Jewish. Children too, are expected to fit into one of the three categories and they may feel themselves much disadvantaged if they have not attended any Sunday school.

There is also another force which attracts and impels these parents to maintain ties with the Jewish community, not only for the sake of their children but as much for themselves. It is the particularly high value which Jews tend to place on affiliation with, and approval of, the in-group. All societies must inculcate concern with in-group approval in order to maintain a going social organization. It is an idea worth testing against a wide array of evidence that Jews are particularly concerned with maintaining and participating in the web of social relations; that Jews, more than most other peoples, find personal satisfaction in keeping up the social structure and, conversely, that the prospect of deliberately cutting oneself off from one's Jewish affiliations awakens considerable guilt, even more so than would be true for Armenians, say, or Mormons. Further, it appears that this special weighting of the importance of the in-community has long been true and may be one of the significant underlying continuities in Jewish culture.

This is not to wave aside as unimportant the continuity of religious belief, theological tenet, ethical principle, or historic tradition. It is rather to bring to notice a pervasive theme which is less explicit though perhaps not less effective.

The theme can be detected throughout the chapters of a book on *shtetl* culture, *Life Is with People*, which gives the proper clue in its very title. To the East European Jew of earlier decades, life was nothing if it was not with people, with his people, with his community circle within the larger society. Over and over again, in various contexts, we find passages which express this concept. "For each individual, the ideal center of gravity is not in himself, but in the whole of which he is an essential part."[5] Each one is not only a part of the whole, but feels himself to be an essential part, so that if he severs himself from the social whole, he knows that both he and the group are the less for the severance. Not all men were of the same social worth, status differences were important and there was considerable drive and scramble for prestige positions. But almost all status could be achieved; very little was merely inherited or otherwise ascribed to the individual.

Moreover, there was a minimal equality for each person which both he and the society jealously preserved. No man should sink below that level of basic equality, should demean himself or be demeaned so as to be permanently and in all respects subordinate within the Jewish community. Therefore it was beyond the bounds of decency to inflict real shame on another person, to impair his fundamental equality with other Jews. "Shame is horrible to the *shtetl*."[6] The individual was imbued both with a strong sense of his individual worth as a member of the group and with a strong sense of responsibility to play his proper role in the group.

There were many voluntary associations in the *shtetl*, people banded together to carry out some specific purpose. It is noteworthy that the purpose was almost always one of maintaining the social equilibrium, of preserving the minimal status of each person within the Jewish community. There were associations to provide loans for the poor, to provide dowries for needy brides, to educate orphans, to give the dead a proper (and strictly egalitarian) burial, and many another of similar charitable aim. Mainly lacking were associations which would directly advantage the participants. There were few, if any, groupings for aesthetic, athletic, or economic purposes, or for the pleasures of the senses. Associations for learning did benefit the participants but the benefits derived from these were considered to be for the good of the community as well.

Charitable associations played so large a part in the community's life because the readiness to help one's fellows was built into the individual's motivational system and into the society's institutional and religious systems. "The patterns of giving and receiving represent a key mechanism in the *shtetl,* basic to individual relations and to community functions, and paramount in the ethical system to which all relations and all functions are referred. Giving is both a duty and a joy; it is a source of heavenly approval and also a source of earthly prestige."[7]

The fortunate one is the person who can give; giving maintains the social web of the community and insures that each member can hold his head high. The dynamics of benefice—as Dr. Natalie Joffe has called the process—are complementary rather than reciprocal. Parents are donors and should not receive from the children. The children can make return by passing benefits to their children. "Within the home, as in the larger community, giving must move in a descending spiral, never in a closed circle of bestowal and reciprocation." And the giving, Dr. Joffe notes, serves not only to enrich the donor and succor the recipient "but also to perpetuate the community and maintain the status quo."[8]

. . . The theme of individual worth, responsibility and fundamental equality spread wide through the culture. In religion there were no special priestly intermediaries between man and God. Each man, preferably indeed in the company of his fellows, addressed his Creator directly. The very covenant between man and God was thought of as something of a bilateral pact with a certain equality between the contracting powers in regard to mutual obligations and rights. Insofar as the covenant was considered an agreement between stronger and weaker, "The very inequality strengthens the right of the Chosen People to ask for help, since the strong has an obligation to the weak."[9]

The assumption of this basic equality pervaded all human relations. The equality was a potential in that high status was equally open to all who could validate such positions by their efforts: it was a constant reality in that no man (or woman in her, formally subordinate though actually powerful, sphere) should be demeaned, deprived of his rightful social role as a Jew among Jews. No human authority was taken as final, no leader was above criticism, every individual could rely on his own judgment in choosing among disputed ideas.[10] With this self-reliance went a widely shared sense of personal importance in carrying on the society and a strong desire to help perpetuate its traditions and organization. There were indeed other facets of *shtetl* life, frequently bitter internal divisions, and there were individuals who felt choked by the ritual and social restraints. Such discordant processes may have been fostered by the very lack of ensconced human authority and by the individual's sense of independence.

The scriptural tradition bore out this stress on equitable and equable social relations. Psalm XV, which was said to summarize all the 613 divine commandments, is concerned with proper relations among people, not with ritual, devotion, or the fate of the soul. The passage from the Mishnah in the introductory section of the morning prayers, a passage of particular importance, does enjoin study and certain ritual observances, but also stresses charity, social obligations, making peace between man and man.[11] These are but two examples among very many of the scriptural stress on the same societal theme.

Societies have been differentiated by one anthropologist into those which find the court of last appeal in matters religious in the social act and those which find it in the private emotional experience.[12] Jewish society has clearly weighted the social deed above the private emotional experience. Despite many individual and situational exceptions, this tendency seems valid over a broad concourse of Jewish history.

Yet there are other peoples who also highly value their social structure and jealously seek to maintain it. For example, recent studies of Japanese and of orthodox Hindus highlight their concern with the social framework. While they place as great an emphasis on society as did *shtetl* Jews, there are differences in the particular locus of high value. Japanese seem most concerned with the proper interlocking of component parts of society; orthodox Hindus seem engrossed in the preservation of one's status in the hierarchy; while *shtetl* Jews seem to have been absorbed with keeping the society going as a constituency of independent and fundamentally equal persons. The Japanese kind of emphasis seems to have been suited to effective organization for the accomplishment of specific tasks, the Hindu to cultural and societal stability, the Jewish to adaptability and social continuity.

In many ways the American environment was most congenial to this central value of *shtetl* culture. Here the larger society, as well as the Jewish enclave, was open to individual achievement—if not completely open, then much more so than were the European societies of the time. Here too authority was more tolerated than reverenced. Individual self-reliance and independent initiative were not culturally discouraged. There were other prevailing beliefs which were quite congruent with those held in the *shtetl*. Learning was widely encouraged and believed important for all. The good things of the world were considered both infinite and attainable, as they were in the view of the *shtetl*. Then there were favoring social and economic factors. Jews, unlike most immigrant groups, came from a town trade-craft economy rather than from a village-agrarian economy. They took readily to the trade opportunities in the expanding American towns. And the expanding American economy continued to enlarge their opportunities.

Small wonder that Jews quickly adapted to the main currents of American culture. The adaptation was rapid both for the earlier wave of German Jews, whose European milieu had not been quite as encapsulated as was the *shtetl,* and for the East European Jews who came from *shtetl* society. In the United States their concern with societal maintenance was not confined to the Jewish group, and more than a few Jews in practically every place where there was a Jewish settlement became notable for civic enterprise and concern with the city's welfare. For example, in the essay on San Francisco's Jewish community it is remarked that Jews were conspicuous for their sense of community from the beginning. The first two welfare organizations in the city were set up by Jews. As they prospered they made large contributions to the general community life.[13]

The contributions were more than just financial. San Francisco is not a typical American town, but the civic sense of some of its Jewish population and their influence in the fine arts, in education, perhaps in the decorative arts such as dress, has been duplicated in many another American city. The concentration of Jews in a few of the largest cities (not far from half in New York City alone) has restricted the range of influence, but American Jews have probably made some distinctive contributions to, just as they have participated in, middle-class American ways of life.

In common with other middle-class Americans, they have shared in the secularization of life of the last century and especially the last half century. Because some emigrants from the *shtetl* shifted directly from a theologically oriented culture into a thoroughly secular one, it has seemed that such secularization was particularly true of American Jews. But the process had been going on in the *shtetl* as well; it has in some degree been true of most American religious groups. If the doctrines of Israel's divine election and mission have been dimmed in America, it may be noted that some long-cherished doctrines of the Roman Catholic Church have also—and not entirely dissimilarly—become modified in America from their purport in nineteenth-century Sicily or Ireland.

Despite all the change in doctrine and synagogue, the theme of maintaining Jewish society and culture still is strong; at least it is strongly heard and forcibly urged. The survival of Jews as Jews is a note of transcendent importance to a good many articulate Jews. It seems, both from the current literature and anthropological field observations, that "survival" still can bring forth an overriding emotional response among Jews. . . .

The individual's responsibility to maintain the social tradition and the traditional society seems to be a live and continuing theme. It appears explicitly in programmatic, hortatory statements; to take one example among very many, there is a passage in Professor Eli Ginzberg's *Agenda for American Jews* which notes that "the behavior of the [American] Jewish group as a whole has attested to its ability and willingness to follow tradition which holds that every Jewish community is the brother and guardian of every other." At the present time, Ginzberg continues, it is particularly true that one remains a Jew by his own actions because "the community is without sanctions and the affirmation of one's Jewishness is solely a matter of personal responsibility."[14]

The theme is implicit in the anthropological field observations. Thus, for Minneapolis, Gordon reports, "Institutional life of the Jewish community is strong. The degree of Jewishness is often measured by the number of Jewish organizations to which one belongs. Status is acquired thereby."[15] And in Yankee City the anthropologists saw how deeply felt was the need for an adequate Jewish institutional setting when there was a unified group effort to acquire a new synagogue-community center building. . . .[16]

It may be presumed that the high pitch of enthusiasm simmered down to normality in subsequent years, but it also appears that normally the Jews, more than other ethnic or religious groups in Yankee City, are much concerned with the maintenance and continuity of the traditional culture and society. The Irish, the Greeks, the Armenians and the other ethnic groupings of Yankee City are also interested in preserving the old tradition and continuing the ethnic social relations; but among none of them does this concern appear as strong an urge as it does among Jews. This is the impression which one gets from the Yankee City data, an impression which should be tested and documented in various American localities by research specifically designed for the purpose. Such research will have to distinguish between what is generically American and what may be more specifically characteristic of American Jews. Because it is not only the Jews in Minneapolis who acquire status by joining numerous organizations nor are only the Jews in Yankee City concerned with the survival of their historic tradition. The data now available indicate, to the present writer, that Jews are more concerned with the maintenance of their group and act on that basis.

If that impression is demonstrated to be valid by further research, and if additional evidence shows this value to have been an important continuity in Jewish life, there will still be the question of how such continuity could possibly have been maintained despite the great changes in the explicit way of life. One clue may lie in the relations between parents and children, especially between mother and child. The quality of the mother-child relation as it is described for the *shtetl* seems to be relevant to the contemporary Jewish family in America. Despite the widely esteemed *obiter dicta* of Gesell and Spock, there is much that is crucial in parent-child situations which still eludes the child care concordance. These are relations which are pervasive in scope and deep in root; they may have continued similar in quality and in grand result as between the old *shtetl* and the modern suburb.

Something of the quality of this relationship is illustrated in an old Yiddish folk tale (the motif occurs in the folklore of other peoples as well) which I heard as told recently by a mother visiting her son and his family. It gives the moral in stark and unearthly terms, as folk tales do. The tale tells of a demanding wife who finally capped her iniquitous career by demanding the tongue torn out of her mother-in-law's head. The son, for reasons sufficient to the tale, finally did the terrible deed and as he was carrying it back to his wife, he stumbled and fell. Whereupon the tongue spoke and said, "O my dear son, have you hurt yourself?"

Studies of parent-child relations which would give useful comparative evidence on this score have not yet been made. But we do have other kinds of evidence, some of which have been mentioned above, that bespeak continuity.

Jews were not given to alcoholic excess in the *shtetl*, nor are they in America. Perhaps the reason in both periods is the same: to be drunk is to lose control of one's social self and such disruption of societal ties, even temporarily, is so repugnant as not even to be a temptation. In both periods, excess in any form is rare, except such excess, as in learning, which bolsters society. Asceticism of the senses made no sense in the *shtetl* —perhaps because no useful societal outcome results therefrom, however elevated the individual may thereby feel—and among the *shtetl's* descendants in America there seems to be no inclination toward curbing the biological needs, as the Kinsey statistics indicate.

Philanthropy was regarded as the very badge of Jewishness in the *shtetl*[17]; it rewarded the individual giver by channeling his energies toward maintaining the equilibrium of the society. Philanthropy still is prized among American Jews; the average contribution among American Jews is substantially above that estimated for the whole population,[18] and may also be more when calculated by various income levels.

Affiliation with the Jewish community is still not to be lightly discarded, and many American Jews who make only a token gesture of such affiliation by attending high holyday services, nonetheless religiously cling to this token. Thus in the early thirties the present writer studied the Jews of a town in Connecticut. It was then striking how few attended daily and Sabbath services in the synagogue and how many—almost all of the 629 men, women, and children—came to high holyday services. It was clear that that attendance was for a good many a symbolic gesture of reaffirmation with the Jewish group. Non-attendance implied that the absent one was cutting loose from the community, and very few wanted to do so.[19]

Very few want to do so in this decade. The available statistics on intermarriage are quite convincing on this score. True, there are indeed about 5 per cent who do intermarry, and some of these pass out of the Jewish community. Others, not intermarried, also leave the Jewish group. But in general the continuity of Jewish affiliation, whether reckoned as a religious or an ethnic association, is proportionately greater than that of most other American groups.

This continuity appears to some Jewish commentators . . . as the carrying on of the outer husk only, of a shell which is now being filled with a new content that is totally unworthy of the historic past. But the number and vigor of these commentators in themselves attest that the old tradition is not totally dead. The history, the ethic, the scripture are continuing and lively subjects of discussion and teaching. It may be that only a very small proportion of American Jews now participate in such activities as compared with the proportion in *shtetl* society, but the great majority do not try to discourage these activities and a good many contribute the money which helps keep them going. Dr. Siskin's article on acculturation ends with an eloquent paragraph of tribute to those American Jews who are devoted to the culture and society of Judaism, who are "a stubborn remnant that will stand, an island in an alien ocean."[20]

The island shows little sign of diminishing. There is yet to be felt the full effect of what an historian has called the principle of third-generation interest. He noted that among Americans of immigrant origin "what the son wishes to forget the grandson wishes to remember."[21] It is likely that not a few grandsons will take strong interest in the grand tradition which their grandfathers practiced.

Beyond these present generations, we can only speculate. We can be quite confident that the succeeding generations will be moved by the same human needs for a tradition, an inner society, and a religion, which dominated the generations of the past. Whether they will continue to cherish the Jewish tradition, there is no way of knowing with certainty. Anthropologists know that some ancient traditions, religions, social orders have ended, and living descendants of folk who carried on a venerable way of life may take on a very different culture. But Judaism seems to be one of the tougher traditions, and far from moribund, despite some current appearances.

The forces which formerly consolidated Jewish society may not reappear in strength, but new ones may develop. In recent decades, the nightmare of Hitlerism was one such factor and, on the positive side, the establishment of the State of Israel was another. It seems hardly likely that Israel will continue to play the same consolidating role for American Jews that it has in the recent past. The native-born Sabra whose generation will before long take over the leadership of the Israeli state, cannot but have a different outlook from that of his American Jewish contemporaries. The same societal theme of life may continue to animate both, but it will very probably be expressed in different ways.

In present-day America, there has been many an obvious change from the former Jewish way of life. But, as we have seen, great and perhaps comparable changes have come about before in Jewish history without spelling the end of Judaic culture or Jewish society. Hence the statement . . . that among the first native-born generation of Jews in Yankee City, "the Judaistic system is seen completely shattered" needs revision both as a particular description and as a basis for generalizing. Similarly the historian, Handlin, may overstate the case when he writes that it is hard now to see in the organized life of the Jewish community any concern with the values of its traditional culture.[22]

The organized community not only makes gestures (perhaps even effective advances) in the direction of carrying on the explicit values of traditional learning, but there also appears to be a continuity of implicit value. The American Jews, by and large, are content to remain Jews, satisfied that they are Jews. This is quite like the *shtetl* notion, though it may rise out of some different circumstances. One different circumstance is that anti-Semitism is not the factor it was. It is by no means totally absent from the American scene, but its virulence is far different from its strength in a Polish village of the last century.

The comparative data, as from India and from America, make doubtful Dr. Gordon's statement that if anti-Semitism ceases to be a problem and source of worry to the Jew, if he is wholly accepted in the larger society, "the forces that now draw him closer to his fellow Jew may disintegrate."[23]

The binding forces appear to be strongly generated from within the Jewish group. The continuity of Jewish society in America seems, from all evidence, well established. This social continuity may stem from continuity of concern with the maintenance of the social structure. If this be so, the long continuity of Jewish life is related to something more than just the adaptability which Dr. Zigmond's article proposes as the secret of survival.[24] Secrets of longevity, as usually offered, seldom turn out to be the sole causes. Most men who have survived to an exceedingly old age are not loath to impart the secret of their survival, whether it be drinking or nondrinking, smoking or nonsmoking, exercise or its abhorrence. Secrets of cultural and social survival may be similarly suspect, but an epigrammatic statement in the book on the *shtetl* may contain a good deal of sharp analysis in brief compass.

The authors tell of the continued acculturation of Jews and say, "Each impact that chips at the outer edge may serve simultaneously to strengthen the core."[25] That core, as we have noted, entails several integrating forces. There is the human force which brings men together to enact ceremonies and other group functions, and rewards them individually for doing so. There is the Jewish force which not only provides traditions, scriptures, and explicit ethics, but very importantly fosters the prime value on social maintenance and the individual's responsibility to carry on this value. In the American environment this core value seems still potent. Indeed it is nourished both by the favorable material and social circumstances and by the presently prevailing American sentiment that Jews stand steadfast as Jews.

The outer edges, at least, of Judaism have indeed been changed under the impact of American culture. Jewish society has taken on many new forms and appurtenances—donor luncheons, monster rallies, and the like. But there do seem to be certain cultural values which continue to be expressed through these new forms as they have been expressed, through older forms, by the many long generations of Jews.

MARTHA WOLFENSTEIN

TWO TYPES OF JEWISH MOTHERS

The cases reported here were observed in the Child Guidance Institute of the Jewish Board of Guardians in New York City. I saw both Mrs. L. and her daughter Karen in psychotherapy once a week for two and a half years. Mrs. S. was similarly in treatment with me for a period of two years. Her son Stan was treated by another therapist, whose detailed case notes were utilized for this study. I am greatly indebted to the Jewish Board of Guardians for their kind permission to use the material from these cases.

I SHOULD like to present here the picture of two mothers, one of Eastern European Jewish origin and the other of an American Jewish family. Markedly different mother-child relations appear in the two cases, which can be regarded as expressing different cultural patterns. These mothers were seen over a period of two or more years in a child-guidance clinic, where their children were also in treatment, and both were primarily concerned about quarrelsome relations with their children. It would have been ideal if these two cases could have been matched in respect to age of the mother, age and sex of the child, socioeconomic status of the family, and so on, so that the cultural background would have been the main variable. Unfortunately, the clinical material which comes one's way is not so neatly arranged for research purposes. However, in assessing the culturally characteristic aspects of the two cases, I have drawn on considerable antecedent research on Eastern European Jewish culture,[1] as well as on other observations of American and Jewish mothers,[2] research on old American non-Jewish families,[3] and an analysis of American child-training literature.[4]

Mrs. S is a stout, ruddy-faced woman of fifty-one who speaks with a marked Yiddish accent. She came to this country as a young woman. Born in Russia, she was the fourth of a family of eleven, three of whom died in childhood. She had little schooling, which she regrets; her intelligence appears to be superior. She retains close ties to her family of origin, sharing a house with her older sister, who is "like a mother" to her. Her husband, also of Eastern European origin, is a workingman, whom she describes as excessively good-natured—everyone takes advantage of him—and for whom she has considerable contempt. She has three sons to whom she is intensely devoted. It is on account of her youngest son, Stan, who is fourteen, that she has come to the child-guidance clinic. Stan has frequent violent quarrels with his mother, cursing and insulting her, after which he

Reprinted from *Childhood in Contemporary Cultures*, edited by Margaret Mead and Martha Wolfenstein, by permission of the author and the publisher. (Copyright, 1955, by the University of Chicago Press.)

cries and implores her forgiveness. Mrs. S. weeps when she talks about these scenes, exclaims how it hurts her, how it is killing her, speaks of her intense feelings as a mother and her life of sacrifice for her children.

Mrs. L is a slender, youthful-looking woman of thirty-four. She is second-generation American (her parents having been of Eastern European origin) and the eldest of a family of five, all of whom are living. She is a college graduate. Her family unit excludes her family of origin; she feels that involvement in the affairs of her mother, brothers, or sisters would conflict with giving proper attention to her husband and children. Her husband was born in Eastern Europe, came to this country as a boy, got his schooling here, and is also a college graduate. He is an office manager. They have two little girls. The elder, Karen, who is nine, is brought for treatment. The parents are concerned about her hostility toward her mother. Mrs. L speaks of Karen's "negativism," then reproaches herself for her "rejection" of Karen during her early years. When Mrs. L relates family upsets, she usually assumes a humorous tone as if she would like to turn it all into an amusing anecdote.

I should like to consider certain contrasting attitudes of these two mothers, first in respect to the image which the mother has of the child. Children pass through various stages of development, as, for instance, the helpless infant, the school child bent on acquisition of skills, the rebellious adolescent. Cultures differ in their emphasis on one or another phase of development, taking the characteristics of the child in a particular phase as constituting his essential nature. The way in which the mother conceives her own role varies accordingly. If the image of the helpless infant predominates, the mother must feed and care for him and guard him from harm; she cannot leave him to take care of himself. This conception of the mother-child relationship may persist through all phases of the child's development. If, on the other hand, the phase or aspect of the child's life which has to do with acquisition of skills is most strongly emphasized, the mother's role is more that of an educator, and the child is encouraged to be independent from an early age.

Mrs. S continues to think of her adolescent son as a helpless infant, who cannot be trusted to do anything for himself and who, if left to his own devices, will injure himself, probably irreparably. She is constantly worried about his health: he is in danger of catching cold from not buttoning up his jacket or not wearing his scarf or sleeping with the windows open. When she cautions him about these things, he flies into a rage, yelling that he is not a baby. (Her anxieties reinforce his own adolescent fears about himself, that he may have damaged himself by masturbation. This contributes to making the mother's expressions of worry about the son's health intolerable to him.) To this mother her big athletic boy is still as fragile as an infant, just as vulnerable to the hazards of the environment, and just as dependent on the mother's vigilant care in order to survive. Similarly, when it comes to buying clothes, which he would like to do by himself, she is sure that he will be cheated if she does not go with him. When he wants to get a summer job, she is convinced that he is too young, that the only possible job for him would be one which she would arrange for him to get in her sister's store. About his studies, she again expresses mainly fears that he is damaging himself, either endangering his future prospects by not studying or ruining his health by studying too late at night.

If we attempt to relate this maternal attitude to the Eastern European Jewish background, we can see factors there which made for the fixation of the mother-child relation on the earliest infantile phase. In the traditional Jewish community the mother was not the educator of her dearly beloved sons. At about the age of three the little boy was snatched from the arms of his weeping mother and sent to school. Learning was the province of the men exclusively.[5] The time when the mother could have her son to herself, to love and care for, was when he was a baby, before the world of men and of learning claimed him. For the older boy she had no comparably important role to play. Her image of the child remained complementary to her own role, which was not that of an educator but one of feeding the infant, anxiously protecting his fragile organism, aware of his helplessness, his inability to survive without her constant care.[6] One might say that just as a child tends to become fixated on a certain phase of development if it is extremely gratifying or to regress to it if a later phase is too frustrating, so similarly a mother may remain fixated to the maternal role corresponding to that phase of the child's development which was most gratifying for her and to regress to this in the face of frustration in later phases.[7]

The Jewish religion has as a major motive the consolidation of father-son relations through the submission of the son to paternal authority. There is one god, the father, not the son or the mother deified by Christianity. The custom of the Eastern European Jewish community of separating boys from their mothers at such an early age was in the interest of inducing submission to paternal elders. Before the development of the oedipal phase, with its rebellious impulses toward the father, the boy was already subjected to the tutelage of men, the rod of the teacher, and the word of God. The separation from the mother curtailed opportunities for expression of the oedipal attachment to her. As a result, the mother knew her little boy much better in the preoedipal phase, when he was passive to her ministrations, than in the oedipal phase, in which boys develop more active impulses toward their mothers; and the boy on his side had more opportunity for expressing the earlier than the later strivings toward the mother.

A reality factor in the European Jewish situation which contributed to the mother's anxiety about her child was the high infant mortality rate. In Mrs. S's case, three of her siblings had died in childhood. Such experiences reinforce anxiety about the fragility and vulnerability of the infant.[8]

While Mrs. S's sons were born in this country and brought up under different conditions of life from those of her original community, it would seem that Mrs. S perpetuates the model of her own mother, from whom she learned the maternal role. This role, as the mother of babies, did not include educational functions, and even less could Mrs. S assume those in a strange country where she knows little of what her children must learn.

From Mrs. L, on the other hand, we hear: "When will Karen grow up? Why is she still so babyish?" When she feels less dissatisfied with her daughter, she reports that Karen is beginning to assume some responsibilities. Mrs. L is greatly concerned about skill and accomplishments. She complains that Karen is clumsy, that she lacks manual dexterity, and also that she is not socially adept. When Karen is nine, her mother is already thinking about her independent adult life. If Karen's relations to her family are disturbed, then she may not have good relations to the opposite sex later on. That is why Mrs. L feels that Karen should have treatment. Later Mrs. L is thinking about sending Karen away to college, though she is only at this time in the sixth grade.

The American family has been characterized by Margaret Mead as a "launching platform," the place from which the children take off for their own independent existence. The mother is not supposed to hover protectively over her little one but to speed him off on his tricycle to join his age mates. Recent American child-training literature has stressed the motor and exploratory impulses of the infant, his tendency from a very early age to get going and master his environment.[9] Mothers who study Gesell check whether their children are demonstrating the appropriate skills from month to month. The aspect of the growing child as one who acquires skills is strongly emphasized. The mother's role is to facilitate the acquisition of skills, to preside over the child's learning. In America the role of teacher is to a high degree a woman's role, both at home and in school.[10]

Mrs. L exemplifies this maternal attitude. She is troubled because her child does not show so much skill or so much independent activity as the mother expects. We do not hear from Mrs. L the anxieties about the child wearing enough sweaters or possibly catching cold and so on which so constantly haunt Mrs. S.

Another major question in respect to which maternal attitudes vary is this: How vulnerable is the mother in relation to the child? How much can the child's behavior hurt or wound her? In the case of Mrs. S, the thought is repeatedly expressed that her children can kill her. Though she sees her son Stan as a helpless and fragile baby, who needs her constant care to stay alive, she also sees him as terribly strong and powerful, capable of killing her. When he quarrels with her, she tells him that he is "aggravating" her to death. The doctor has said that, because of her high blood pressure, aggravation could kill her. She frequently tells Stan about a woman who lived across the street whose son actually aggravated her to death. On one occasion when Stan was angry at her, she went out on the porch without a coat and thought she caught cold. In his rages, he tells her to drop dead. She answers him that she will; if he is like that, what does she have to live for? Following a quarrel she often feels sick. She retires to her room and lies down. When Stan comes in and tries to mollify her, she does not speak; she acts as if she were dead.

Death wishes toward the parents, who are at the same time deeply loved, are inevitable in human childhood. And with the child's illusions of omnipotence there is the fantasy that these wishes can kill. In the S family this is not just a guilt-ridden fantasy of the child, it is even more a firm belief of the mother. By his show of anger against her, her son is attacking her very life. The quarrel itself is an act of murder.

A number of factors contribute to this maternal reaction. Mrs. S deeply represses any negative feelings of her own toward her mother and toward her children. She would never have behaved toward her mother the way her son behaves toward her. Recalling her own childhood and how the children would never have dared to answer their mother back, Mrs. S remembered how her sister, after having been punished by their mother, muttered to herself: "It should happen to me"—meaning that what she wickedly wished to the mother should fall on her own head. Hostile feelings were turned back against the self. Perpetuating her strong positive ties to her mother, Mrs. S still lives with her older sister, who is like a mother to her. In relation to her children she also denies any negative feelings; she is never aware of anything but self-sacrificing love toward them.[11] The fate of these unacknowledged hostile feelings would seem to be that they are projected onto her children. The hostility which she dared not admit toward her mother assumes terrifying proportions in her son and is directed toward her. The unadmitted negative feelings which she has toward the son are similarly projected and contribute to her belief that he will fatally damage himself.

Mrs. S is vulnerable not only to the attacks of her son against her but to his tendency to damage himself, which is equally destructive to her.[12] If by not following her admonitions he catches a cold and makes himself sick, who will suffer? She will. The two of them are inextricably bound together in life and death. Mrs. S has also told her son that if she dies, he dies. Presumably he could not survive her, either because of his helplessness or because he would die of guilt and grief.

If we look for a model of the mother-child relationship as Mrs. S experiences it, a situation in which the child is at the same time most vulnerable and most capable of killing the mother, we may find this in childbirth. It is then that the child's life is most endangered, while the child in turn causes the mother intense suffering and endangers her life. For Mrs. S every emotionally fraught scene with her son would seem to be a repetition of childbirth. We may ask what circumstances make for such a strong fixation on this experience. For a mother who is impelled to relive it in this way, we may guess that it represents a very deep gratification. In the Eastern European Jewish community the importance attached to having children was tremendous. A wife who produced no children could be divorced.[13] Mrs. S expressed the traditional pride in maternity. She frequently clasps her hands to her large bosom and exclaims: "I am a mother." However, the high value attached to being a mother does not necessarily carry with it such an intense emotional fixation on the act of birth itself.

In trying to account for this, I would propose the following hypothesis. Traditional Jewish life involved strong defenses against sexual impulses. The preponderance of rituals and avoidances hedging every act strongly suggests a compulsive character structure, profoundly impressed with the dangers of sexuality. At the same time it was recognized that complete genital abstinence was not feasible. Sexual thoughts could obtrude themselves and disturb serious occupations, particularly the ideal pursuit of the man, that of constant study. Thus the sexual act was to be performed to free the man's mind from disturbing thoughts. It seems likely that sexual relations were thus carried out as quickly as possible, to get the thing done and out of the way, that sex was brief and isolated from the rest of life. It was shameful, for instance, for a man and wife to see each other naked.[14] There can have been little erotic elaboration under such circumstances, and one may suppose that the aim of satisfying the woman was absent.

For the sexually unsatisfied wife the great genital experience was childbirth. Then she received from her son the intense and prolonged genital stimulation which she did not get from her husband. But, since she also participated in the regression from full genitality, her image of sex was a sado-masochistic one. Thus her great sexual experience, that of childbearing, was fraught with the dangers of killing and being killed. (While these dangers are actually present in childbirth, they do not under other circumstances assume such emotional importance.) If we suppose that these hypothetically reconstructed relations are exemplified in the case of Mrs. S, we can understand why she is impelled to repeat painful scenes with her son, scenes which have the conscious significance that he may kill her and thus also bring about his own death and which unconsciously reproduce the experience of childbirth.

In contrast to this, Mrs. L does not attribute to her children the power to destroy her. They can be a terrible nuisance and annoyance, but they are not that dangerous. Quarrels are less climactic, more trivial and imminence of fatality does not haunt the daily routine. Mother and child are less isolated in intense struggle with each other; quarrels as recounted by Mrs. L appear to revolve around many external details and circumstances and to include other persons.[15] Thus Karen comes home from school and complains about her teacher; Mrs. L tries to justify the teacher, and Karen becomes enraged with the mother for taking the teacher's side. Karen and her sister get into a dispute about which one finished her milk first, and Karen shouts so loudly that her mother threatens her with the strap. On another occasion the little sister calls the mother an ass, and the mother spanks her. Karen yells that her mother is mean and cruel until the mother spanks her, too. There are daily quarrels about Karen's not getting dressed promptly enough in the morning, and so on. Mrs. L is exasperated with Karen, but she does not express the thought that Karen could aggravate her to death.

What are the emotional factors in this mother which make for this more moderate estimate of her child's power to damage her? Unlike Mrs. S, Mrs. L does not completely repress her own hostility toward either her mother or her children. She has many outspoken reproaches against her own mother. She does not maintain the same high level of filial piety which we noted in Mrs. S, who still lives on the closest terms with a good mother-figure, her older sister. Mrs. L frequently wards off with resentment what she takes to be unfair claims of her mother on her. She recalls how little her mother has helped her and holds many things against her mother from childhood days. Thus she justifies the negative feelings which she acknowledges toward her mother. Similarly in relation to her daughter, she admits that the child was, to begin with, a terrible burden which she resented. While she blames herself for having felt this way, she readily acknowledges how much of a burden Karen remains for her, and on one occasion confessed that she sometimes wishes that Karen were dead. Since these hostile feelings toward her own mother as well as toward her daughter are to some extent consciously acknowledged, they do not have to be projected onto the child. Thus the child is not invested with mother-killing or with self-destroying tendencies from the mother's own unconscious. As we noted before, Mrs. L is much less concerned than Mrs. S with her child's health and does not see Karen as wilfully exposing herself to colds or in other ways endangering her life.

Mother and child in the L family are not a symbiotic pair, with their fates inseparably intertwined, but two mutually independent persons. The mother is not fixated on the phase of the child's helpless infancy or the situation of childbirth but is urging her child toward increasing independence and looks forward eagerly to the greater independence she herself can enjoy, for instance, when she gets the children off to camp for the summer. Also, the mother's anger is less turned back against herself and less libidinized. When Mrs. L gets annoyed with Karen, she seethes inwardly until she cannot restrain herself from hitting the child; then she feels relieved. She experiences a catharsis. This seems to be in keeping with major American patterns about aggression. There is the feeling that aggression should be turned outward, that it is good to get things off your chest, and that an overt fight clears the air. The venting of anger seems to be experienced as a simple excretory act: something is got rid of, and one feels relieved. Anger here appears to be relatively uninvolved with sado-masochistic fantasies. Neither of the combatants is pictured as weak. The relation between parent and child is felt to be a symmetrical one. (When Karen's mother calls her a "nitwit," Karen calls her mother an "idiot." Karen also calls her mother a "brat.")

Karen, on her side, has the inevitable wishes, fantasies, and fears of her mother's death. But these are isolated from the day-to-day quarrels with the mother. They are expressed in reactions to movies and television shows which fascinate and sometimes frighten her, in which the wife dies and the husband marries his girl friend. Karen writes a play in which a grown-up married daughter becomes enraged with her mother for trying to make her get a divorce (Karen has frequently urged her father to divorce her mother), and the daughter murders the mother. However, her actual quarrels with her mother do not appear to be a manifest dramatization of such fantasies. It is not as in the case of Stan who shouts "Drop dead!" to his mother and so induces in the mother an access of illness, when she retires to her bed and acts as if dead. Karen's mother remains upright and active; she does not comply with the child's unconscious fantasies.

In so far as the thought of killing enters into the quarrels between Karen and her mother, it takes the form of the child's fantasy that the mother is killing her. When the mother hits her, Karen sometimes screams: "You're killing me!" and in the next breath, "You can't hurt me!" Thus the child's death wishes toward the mother are projected onto the mother. It is again the reverse of the S family, where the mother's hostile impulses (toward both her mother and her child) were projected onto the child, who was seen as killing her. (We may also suppose that Mrs. S really believes that her son is bringing her to an early grave, while Karen has less of a serious anticipation of her own death when she accuses her mother in this way.) The projection of the child's bad wishes onto the parents has been observed to be a typical motive of American film plots. There, in oedipal dramas, a mother-figure tries to seduce the hero, and a father-figure tries to kill him. To take one example out of many, in *Gilda*, the beautiful wife of the hero's boss sought to win the hero's love, and the boss made an attempt on the hero's life. The hypothetical connection which we have suggested between this type of film plot and American family life is the following: American children are expected to surpass their parents. As the children see themselves as potentially on a higher level than their parents, they are more easily able to ascribe to the parents the bad impulses which they repudiate in themselves.[16] Karen seems to exemplify this American pattern in her projection of her bad impulses onto her mother. In the S family, on the other hand, where the European image of parental sanctity persists, bad impulses are seen as concentrated in the child.

While parents are inevitably moral authorities for their children, there are many variations in the manner of expressing and acknowledging this authority. Parents may be regarded with awe as righteous judges, or their fallibility may be unmasked. They may demand ceremonial respect, or they may feel uneasy in the role of authority and play it down. For Stan, his mother retains the power to pardon or condemn. After he has quarreled with her, he pleads for her forgiveness. If there have been angry words over breakfast, he cannot leave for school until she gives him a forgiving kiss. This reconciliation and pardon seem to have the effect of undoing the crime implicit in the quarrel. He is not only freed from the burden of his wickedness, but he is reassured that his mother does not remain in deathlike withdrawal. When his mother condemns him, he is liable to feel that this is a just sentence. In yelling dirty words at her he feels that he is implicitly confessing his masturbation and his bad sexual thoughts. The mother responds by calling down the punishment of God on him, and the boy feels that this is what he deserves. Thus his mother remains an external conscience for him, confirming the state of his soul. Mrs. S has no doubts about her own righteousness. She never alternates condemnations of her son with self-accusations. She recalls the respect she had for her own parents and cannot understand the lack of equal respect in her son.

Mrs. L is much less sure of being in the right. She acknowledges that her tolerance or intolerance of Karen's annoying behavior varies with her mood, whether she feels sick or well, or whether she has had a quarrel with her own mother. Karen is outspoken in her conviction that her mother's punishments are not an expression of superior justice but of impulsive feelings. When Mrs. L hits the children, Karen shouts that her mother is a maniac, "She hits because she likes to hit!" Karen never asks for her mother's forgiveness following a quarrel but after a short time "forgets" it (according to the mother) and is affectionate and cheerful again. The mother here is neither a just punisher nor a source of absolution. Just as the quarrel does not assume the significance of a crime, so also it is not a moral drama involving repentance and pardon.

It has been observed that in American families and in American life generally, no one likes to assume a role of authority.[17] A superordinate position makes one feel uneasy. There is a tendency to make all relationships approximate to symmetry. President Eisenhower's favorite news photograph of himself shows him laughingly shaking hands with his small grandson, who bows as the grandfather bows to him.[18] In American families the parents listen to the children rather than requiring the children to listen to them in quiet deference.[19] Parents who do not like to arrogate to themselves a superior authority tend to minimize moral justifications in their handling of their children. This is again reflected in the images of parent-figures in American films. Manifest parents of the hero or heroine are likely to be mild, ineffectual background figures. Characters who stand for the parents in a more disguised way, such as the hero's boss and the boss's wife, are often dangerous, violent, and immoral. Thus the punishing aspect of the parents is separated off as an attack without moral justification.[20] It is in this spirit that Karen takes the occasional angry blows of her mother: "She hits because she likes to hit."

The strong emotions engendered in family conflicts may be a source of intense (though unadmitted) gratification, or they may be felt as a disruption of a desirable façade of calm and efficiency, as senseless and exaggerated reactions, deprecated in retrospect as much ado about nothing. As might be inferred from what we already know, our two mothers differ greatly in their reactions to emotional scenes. Mrs. S preserves and repeatedly relives the intense emotions evoked by familial happenings. As she relates a quarrel with her son, the scene is alive for her, no word or gesture is forgotten, and her tears flow afresh as she exclaims: "I can't stand it, it hurts me, it's killing me." On the manifest level she suffers, but less consciously she enjoys these scenes and is thus impelled to re-evoke them so that she can feel again the gratifying pain which they arouse.

The emotional atmosphere of Mrs. L's discourse is quite different. There are no tears. Mrs. L's characteristic expression is an amused smile, and the tone she assumes as she recounts family upsets is a humorous one. The emotional quality of quarreling scenes is not re-evoked but is transformed in the retelling. In retrospect the feelings of anger and distress (especially of the child—the mother tends to minimize her own) appear unreasonable, disproportionate, absurd. Mrs. L strives to turn upsetting scenes into comic anecdotes. There is less enjoyment here of the painful feelings which a quarrel produces; to derive pleasure from it in retrospect, Mrs. L must transform the emotional tone of the scene and reduce its intensity by treating it humorously. Probably also Mrs. L experiences less pain in the quarrel itself than Mrs. S does, since Mrs. L assumes more the role of an aggressor than of a victim. In so far as quarrels are disturbing for Mrs. L, she tends to blank them out in memory. In her reports there is a displacement of emphasis from the central emotional drama to trivial peripheral details. Thus, if she and Karen have quarreled because she wanted Karen to try on a skirt she was making for her and Karen did not want to interrupt her play, Mrs. L goes into great detail about the pattern and the material she used for the skirt but forgets what she and Karen said to each other in their anger. The angry episode is like an alien thing which has obtruded itself into the reasonable and unemotional tenor of life; Mrs. L rectifies and smoothes over this break by eliminating it in memory.

Suffering is the major theme of Mrs. S's life. When she is not preoccupied with Stan's attacks on her, she recalls the misfortunes of her second son, who, after having started on a brilliant career, got into trouble and ruined his chances. Again and again she remembers with tears his early successes and re-evokes the tragedy of his downfall. "It hurts me, I have such pity on him, I could die." At other times she speaks of her eldest son, who has never caused her any trouble and who is doing quite well. But his wife makes unreasonable demands on him and does not understand him, and he is very hard pressed financially, and again it hurts Mrs. S. When family parties are organized on various occasions, there are always some painful repercussions as someone was not invited who should have been, or someone did not come who should have come, and Mrs. S participates in the hurt feelings which are thus engendered. Every encounter, fraught as it is with intense emotion, assumes a dramatic quality in Mrs. S's telling of it.

There is little of this dramatic quality in Mrs. L's account of her life. As she details the external aspects of events, playing down their emotional undertones, nothing seems very important. One wonders what really matters here? If one looks for a pervasive theme, one finds it perhaps in the issue about order and disorder. Mrs. L feels that in her parents' house everything was in disorder. Her mother was a bad housekeeper. Innumerable relatives trouped in and out. The family was constantly moving. Nobody ever knew how much money they had. The father gambled. Escaping from this disorder, Mrs. L married an extremely meticulous, fussy, precise, methodical man. However, she is unable to meet successfully his requirements for perfect order; in her there persists an unresolved conflict on this issue. While she does not overtly rebel against her husband's standards, she derives great covert gratification from her daughter Karen's messiness. Over and over she relates Karen's feats of sloppiness. When Karen gets undressed, she leaves one shoe under the kitchen table, the other in the middle of the living-room floor, and so on. Karen eats mashed potatoes with her fingers. When she is supposed to take a bath, she sits in the tub reading a comic book and forgets to wash herself. These and other similar habits of Karen's exasperate her father. While Mrs. L repeatedly complained about them, she laughed so genuinely at the same time that when it was pointed out to her that she vicariously enjoyed Karen's sloppiness, she was able to acknowledge this to be true. Karen's inability to conform to time schedules (getting dressed in the morning, getting to bed at night) is a source of daily conflict, especially with the father.

The mother herself has residual difficulties about punctuality. But she finds relief from her inner conflicts about orderliness by externalizing them; Karen acts out disorderly impulses while the father embodies restraints against them. Mrs. L gives the impression of strong, persistent ambivalence toward early cleanliness training. On the one hand, she rebelled against it, this rebellion being justified by later disillusionment with her parents, who failed to live up to a high standard of orderliness.

On the other hand, she felt impelled to strive toward such a standard and sought reinforcement for this striving in her husband. In Karen, understandably enough, there are similar conflicts. At the same time that she is so messy at home, she always has the job of the housekeeper at school. She manifests some very finicky reactions, becoming disgusted to the point of nausea at excretory smells, even her own, and expressing similar disgust at the sight of her little sister picking her nose.

I would suggest the following hypothetical basis for the emotional orientation of these two families. In both cases there seems to be a considerable concentration on motives of the anal phase.[21] But in the S family the sector of these motives which is emphasized is the sado-masochistic one. There are strongly libidinized fantasies of killing and being killed, with the mother's predominant image of herself as suffering and dying because of what her children do to her. In the L family, another sector of anal motives is in the ascendant, namely, those having to do with dirt and messiness and the defensive struggle toward cleanliness, neatness, and order.[22] This conflict between messiness and order lends itself less to melodramatic expressions. It is likely to take the form rather of endless, nonclimactic nagging about petty details. Instead of the tragic maternal reproach, "You are killing me," it is, "Take your bath, Karen. It's already quarter to nine. . . . Karen, take your bath. It's five minutes to nine."

In traditional Jewish culture, strong defenses were erected against aggression. Innumerable rituals guarded against the break-through of aggressive impulses.[23] One may suppose that the impulses thus warded off had a strong sadistic quality. These impulses were to a large extent turned inward. The Jews underwent endless sufferings, which they accepted in a spirit of exalted masochism as inflicted by a God who loved them above all others. This submission to paternal authority was haunted by rebellious impulses which appeared as doubts about religious rules to which exceptions could always be found; and the doubts were in turn fought back by ever more refined formulations of the rules. The Jewish religion concentrated on regulating relations between men, between a sole father-god and his sons. There are covert indications of sadistic impulses of children toward mothers which also had to be held in check. Thus one motive behind the taboo against eating meat with milk may have been a defense against the impulse of the infant to bite and eat the milk-giving breast. Adam and Eve were expelled from Eden for having eaten the apple (a breast symbol). However, the major emphasis of religious ritual and observance was on male relationships. Women, excluded from study and argumentation about the law, may thus have expressed the same sado-masochistic motives, which men elaborated in highly ritualistic ways, in more free-flowing emotional relations with their children. Men accepted their sufferings from God, women from their children.

This sado-masochistic concentration appears to be absent in American culture. Opportunities for turning aggression outward have been manifold, nor does aggression seem fraught with terrible dangers. The possibility of injuring women has little plausibility where women appear as very strong.[24] On the other hand, cleanliness has been an outstanding American value. Current advertising for soaps and deodorants plays on the doubt about ever achieving perfect bodily cleanliness and the belief that one must be utterly clean in order to be loved. The emphasis on cleanliness training, which here seems so major, is one which involves, on the side of the mother, the image of the child as one who can learn and, on the side of the child, strong conflicts in relation to strict maternal demands.[25] These conflicts have in the past been notably resolved in reaction formations against the original messy impulses, giving rise to the clean, orderly, methodical, hard-working individual, who got things done when they had to be done. At present there is less maternal resoluteness in the demand for cleanliness, and the traditional reaction-formative type of character is no longer in the ascendant. However, I would suggest that there is a certain basic attitude toward excreta which remains the same. Excreta are impersonal things which one has to dispose of in appropriate ways. The relation between mother and child in which things play a major role provides a model for other relationships which are not sheerly between persons, but where persons are mutually involved in the management of things. I would speculate further that where a more sado-masochistic relation prevails, excreta are often equated with beloved persons who have been incorporated and who are being destructively got rid of.[26] This would fit the Eastern European Jewish pattern, in which there are few impersonalized quarrels about the orderly or disorderly management of things but where conflicts tend to have the significance of destroying the opponent.

I have tried to present here two contrasting pictures of some aspects of Eastern European Jewish and American Jewish mother-child relations. The question arises as to how the transition is achieved from the one to the other. Further investigation would be required to provide the answer to this. I have relatively little information about the mother of Mrs. L. From what I know, although she came to this country as a young girl, she seems to have perpetuated the Eastern European model of maternity less than Mrs. S. For instance, she was less anxious about her children and left them more to take care of themselves. As far as the S family is concerned, we can see a marked transition from the Eastern European Jewish pattern in the behavior of the son, in his overt expressions of aggression against the mother. Stan suffers severe conflicts about aggression. He strives to deny the mother's belief that his aggression can kill her. "Nobody ever died of aggravation," he argues. At the same time he tries to justify his aggressive feelings against his parents in terms of what he considers mistreatment in his childhood, and so on. He is striving for the American position that it is permissible to rebel against one's parents. But this remains difficult for him, since in the culture from which the parents come such rebellion is tantamount to murder.

In discussing the L family I have throughout referred to presumable general features of American culture. The question may be asked: What is Jewish in the L family? Here I must bring in the character of the father, whom I have dealt with very little. This father, of Eastern European Jewish origin, appears to exemplify a strong identification with his mother.[27] Thus, since he has been in bad health in recent years, he reproaches Karen for the aggravation she causes him by saying that it will shorten his life. However, he seems to have some conflicts about this, attempting at times to conceal from Karen that he feels exhausted after a prolonged dispute. Mrs. L is outspoken in her condemnation of her husband for attempting to impose such a burden of guilt on the child. Perhaps he realizes vicariously for her her residual masochistic tendencies, which she consciously repudiates. She denies any thoughts that annoyance with Karen can affect her health, and she does not recall any comparable reproaches from her own mother. We may note further that the strong-mother weak-father combination which we find in the L family corresponds to a frequent American family constellation.[28] However, the specific qualities of this father, who is physically weak while he remains intellectually superior, have a marked Jewish aspect.

To sum up, we have seen here, in a fragmentary way and with much admittedly speculative interpretation, two contrasting maternal patterns. The Eastern European Jewish mother sees her child at any age as terribly vulnerable, a baby incapable of taking care of himself, who would perish without her constant vigilance. At the same time the baby appears as terribly strong, capable of killing the mother. We saw in this a fixation of the mother on the earliest phase of the child's life, and particularly on the experience of giving birth, and also a tendency to project onto the child the mother's unacknowledged hostility toward him and toward her own mother. The mother is a righteous figure, capable of damning or giving absolution. She is a suffering person, being incessantly wounded and killed and deriving her major unacknowledged emotional gratification in this masochistic way. The American Jewish mother here described sees her child mainly as an independent being, who should stop as quickly as possible being babyish and proceed to acquire skills. A different aspect of the growing child is emphasized, that having to do with learning, and the child is not seen as fragile. The mother acknowledges hostility toward the child and toward her own mother and does not project them onto the child, who is accordingly not seen as self-damaging or as destroying the mother. In the conflicts between mother and child, the mother appears as less surely righteous, and the child can attribute gross unmoralized aggressive impulses to her. This is in keeping with American parents' avoidance of a dominant authoritative role, the tendency toward symmetry in parent-child relations, and the possibility for children to ascribe their own condemned motives to the parents. Instead of the sado-masochistic image of the quarrel as a murder, a central issue is the more impersonalized one about order and disorder. One of the foremost unsolved problems raised by this essay, as a subject for further research, is the question of how the transition from the Eastern European Jewish to the American Jewish family is achieved.

References

Abraham, Karl. 1942. *Selected Papers of Karl Abraham.* Translated by D. Bryant and A. Strachey. London: Hogarth Press and Institute of Psychoanalysis.

Bateson, Gregory. 1942. "Morale and National Character." In *Civilian Morale,* ed. Goodwin Watson, pp. 71-91. Boston: Houghton Mifflin Co.

Bibring, Grete. 1953. "On the 'Passing of the Oedipus Complex' in a Matriarchal Family Setting." In *Drives, Affects, Behavior,* ed. Rudolph Lowenstein, pp. 278-84. New York: International Universities Press.

Coleman, Rose W., Kris, Ernst, and Provence, Sally. 1953. "The Study of Variations of Early Parental Attitudes." In *The Psychoanalytic Study of the Child,* VIII, 20-47.

"Eisenhower's Favorite Picture of Himself," *New York Times Magazine.* January 10, 1954, cover photograph.

Freud, Sigmund. 1942a. "Character and Anal Eroticism." In *Collected Papers,* Vol. II. London: Hogarth Press and Institute of Psychoanalysis.

———. 1942b. "Obsessive Acts and Religious Practices," *ibid.*

Gorer, Geoffrey. 1948. *The American People: A Study in National Character.* New York: W. W. Norton & Co.

Infant Care. 1945 and 1951. Children's Bureau, Washington, D.C.

Jones, Ernest. 1948. "Anal-erotic Character Traits," *Papers on Psychoanalysis,* pp. 413-37. London: Baillière, Tindall & Cox.

Loewenstein, Rudolph. 1951. *Christians and Jews: A Psychoanalytic Study.* New York: International Universities Press.

Wolfenstein, Martha. 1953. "Trends in Infant Care," *American Journal of Orthopsychiatry,* XXIII, No. 1, 120-30.

Wolfenstein, Martha, and Leites, Nathan. 1950. *Movies: A Psychological Study.* Glencoe, Ill.: Free Press.

Zborowski, Mark, and Herzog, Elizabeth. 1952. *Life Is with People: The Jewish Little Town in Eastern Europe.* New York: International Universities Press.

SOPHIA M. ROBISON

A STUDY OF DELINQUENCY
AMONG JEWISH CHILDREN IN NEW YORK CITY

THIS paper reports on a study made of juvenile delinquency among Jewish children in New York City in 1952. Certain relevant statistics for non-Jews are also cited. In addition, comparisons with delinquency among Jewish children in New York City in 1930 are also presented.

The findings for 1952 are based on an analysis of the Juvenile Court docket book of four of the five boroughs which comprise New York City. Richmond, the borough for which no count was made, comprises an area in which few if any Jewish children are known to the local Juvenile Court. Furthermore, less than 1 per cent of New York Jewry reside in this borough.[1]

Data on Jewish children for this study could be gathered due to the fact that in the docket book of the Children's Court each child is identified as to his religious affiliation. Our researchers searched the dockets and noted down all cases where a child was identified as Jewish. For 100 of the cases, supplementary data were obtained (this material was gathered from records of social-service agencies). All data for 1930 are drawn from the author's study, *Can Delinquency Be Measured?*[2]

§ *The Number of Delinquents*

We discovered that in 1952 delinquency petitions were filed in the four boroughs of New York City for a total of 226 Jewish families. These were families residing in the borough in which their children were brought to Court; some thirteen Jewish children who were not referred to the Court in their borough of residence were not included in our count. It should also be noted that since the basis of the count in this study is the family, if more than one child in a given family was in difficulty, that family is counted only once (in only six families were two or more children involved). Furthermore, in thirteen instances the same child was known to the Court more than once in the course of the year; and since our statistics are by family, repeaters are of course counted only once.

In 1952, juvenile offenses in New York City totalled 5,762.[3] Thus Jewish children in the Court represent about 3 per cent of the total. What

Published for the first time in this volume.

This paper is based upon a report done under the auspices of the Jewish Board of Guardians of New York City. The author is grateful to the Board for permission to publish these data.

proportion of the child population of New York City, then, is Jewish? In the study conducted by the Health Insurance Plan of Greater New York in 1952, it was found that 27.2 per cent of the white population under fifteen years of age was Jewish.[4] We must conclude that the rate of juvenile delinquency among Jews is very low; if Jewish children were delinquent in correct proportion to population size there would have been almost ten times as many Jewish delinquents as in actual fact. Admittedly, among other subgroups in the New York City population, such as the white Protestants (or even better, the white middle-class Protestants), low rates may also be encountered. All such matters need further study, and whether the disproportion we have noted might be encountered in some other segments of the population of New York City must remain an open question. It is doubtful, however, whether any other religious group in New York City can rival the Jews as regards infrequency of delinquency.[5] It would appear that this holds true even if factors such as race and socio-economic status are controlled.

Jewish leaders are aware of the fact that delinquency is a problem of distinctly minor proportions in the Jewish community. Despite this, the fear has been expressed that Jewish youth of today are far less law-abiding than those of a generation or two ago. Data on this question, as well as about the geographical distribution of Jewish delinquency in New York City, are supplied in Table 1. As is apparent, there was a tremendous drop between 1930 and 1952 in the number of Jewish cases known to the Juvenile Court. If we assume that these two years can serve as trend indicators, then delinquency is not only a minor problem in the Jewish community, but it is one which is diminishing at a spectacular rate. In 1952 Jewish children in the Court represented less than 3 per cent of the total, though they comprised 25-30 per cent of the total juvenile population. This was not the situation two decades earlier: in 1930 Jewish children accounted for almost 20 per cent of all cases brought to the attention of the Court.[6]

Table 1—Jewish Children Referred to Court

| Borough of Residence | 1952 | | 1930 | | Change |
	Number	Per Cent	Number	Per Cent	1930-1952
Total	226	100.0	1392	100.0	−1166
Manhattan	23	10.0	208	15.0	−185
Bronx	66	30.0	291	21.0	−225
Brooklyn	106	46.0	856	61.0	−750
Queens	31	14.0	37	3.0	− 6

There are striking differences in comparative borough rates as between the two intervals. Thus, only 23 Manhattan families were known to the Court in 1952, in contrast to 208 in 1930. At the other extreme, in the Borough of Queens, only six less cases were referred to the Court in 1952 than were known in 1930. The significance of these two sets of figures a generation apart is obviously related to the size of the population-at-risk in 1930 and 1952. While Manhattan has been losing Jewish population, Queens has been gaining Jewish population at a very rapid rate.

§ *Offenses, Disposition, and Petitioners*

An understanding of the significance of the statistics previously quoted can be greatly enriched by analyzing *who* petitioned the court, *what* kind of charge the petitioner advanced, and *how* the case was disposed of. Perhaps the best starting point is the question of the type of offense which the youngster was charged with.

The distribution of offenses for the 226 Jewish cases is given in Table 2. The rank order of these cases is as follows: (1) wrongful appropriation of property, (2) ungovernable behavior, (3) injury to persons, (4) sex offense, (5) habitual truancy, and (6) acts of carelessness or mischief. There were no cases of runaways, and none of peddling or begging.[7] The main finding is the overwhelming preponderance of cases labelled "wrongful appropriation of property."

Table 2—Major Offense Categories, Jewish Delinquents, 1952 and All Delinquents Referred to the Children's Court, 1951

Offense	1951 (All)		1952 (Jews)	
	Number	Per Cent	Number	Per Cent
Total	5606	100.	226	100.
Wrongful Appropriation				
of property	3023	54.	97	43.
Burglary	1687	30.	47	20.
Robbery	344	6.	15	7.
Stealing	614	11.	10	5.
Auto Stealing	378	7.	25	11.
Injury to persons	329	6.	22	10.
Sex offense	530	9.	19	8.
Ungovernable behavior	528	9.	46	20.
Habitual truancy	442	8.	16	7.
Running away	254	5.	—	—
Acts of carelessness				
and mischief	473	8.	11	5.
Peddling	—	—	—	—
Other and not reported	27	—	15	7.

In comparison with the Court totals for 1951, Jewish children in 1952 ranked higher in the following categories: (1) auto theft (11 per cent in comparison with 7 per cent), (2) ungovernable behavior (20 per cent in comparison with 9 per cent), and (3) injury to persons (10 per cent in comparison with 6 per cent). On the other hand, burglary in the Jewish group accounted for 20 per cent of the offenses, in comparison with 30 per cent of the offenses committed by the total group.[8]

Even more significant, however, is the fact that a comparison between the 1930 Jewish figures and the 1952 Jewish statistics shows a dramatic shift in the category of offenses. In 1930, the leading offense which brought the 1,392 Jewish children to the Court was peddling or begging without a license. Thus, this category accounted for more than a third of the 1,085 Jewish children known to the Brooklyn Court in that year.[9] Thus, the inference appears to be warranted that even though the total number of cases in 1952 was very small in proportion to the estimated distribution of Jews in the population, the Jewish child who was brought to the Court in 1952 came because his behavior was more similar to that of the non-Jewish delinquent than was true two decades earlier. In essence, a greater proportion of Jewish children in trouble with the law in 1952 exhibited violent and aggressive behavior.

As regards the party who petitioned the Court, the police were the most frequent petitioners, initiating almost half of the petitions (see Table 3). Jewish youngsters were, however, less frequently the subject of a police petition than was the case with non-Jews; Court statistics reveal that in 1952 the police served as petitioner in 70 per cent of all adjudicated cases.[10] The police are more apt to be the petitioner in offenses against property; parents are more apt to be the petitioner in cases of ungovernable behavior.

Table 3—Petitioner of Jewish Delinquents Referred
to Children's Court in 1952

Petitioner	TOTAL	
	Number	Per Cent
Total	226	100.0
Parent	24	10.6
Police	104	46.0
Citizen	58	25.7
Other Relatives	6	2.7
All others	34	15.0

We may now turn to the highly important question of the disposition of the petition (see Table 4). In 1952 only a minority of the Jewish cases (35 per cent) were dismissed, either immediately on hearing or after investigation. The majority of children were either placed on probation or committed (actually the majority were placed on probation—only 56 of 146 non-dismissed cases were committed). All of this is in decided contrast to 1930. Then, two-thirds of the Jewish cases (67 per cent) were dismissed. Thus, if the percentage of probation and commitment may be considered an index to the seriousness of the behavior, matters have changed considerably. Again, the point is reinforced that although the relative number of delinquent Jewish children was markedly smaller in 1952 than in 1930, the type of behavior for which Jewish children were known to the Court in 1952 was much more serious from the standpoint of the community at large.[11]

Table 4—Disposition of Delinquency Petitions of Jews
in Children's Court, 1952 and 1930

Disposition	Total—1952		Total—1930	
	Number	Per Cent	Number	Per Cent
Total	226	100.0	1392	100.0
Dismissed	80	35.4	934	67.1
Probation and Commitment	146	64.6	458	32.9

§ Some Familial and Personal Characteristics of the Delinquent

A full social portrait of the Jewish youngsters referred to the Children's Court in 1952 cannot be attempted here. We shall, however, delineate a number of relevant characteristics. Thus, as regards the parents' nativity, in 21 per cent of the families both parents were foreign-born. However, these foreign-born persons probably resided in the United States for a considerable period of time. To cite only one fact in this connection, in the 100 cases where supplementary data were gathered there was practically no mention of inability to speak English.

Of the 100 cases, approximately 60 per cent of the children were living with both parents at the time they were brought to Court. Another 20 per cent were living with their mothers, and the remainder resided with step-parents or elsewhere. Two-children families represented the median as well as the mode, except in Brooklyn where the median was three. Only two children out of the total group of 100 were born out of wedlock. Comparable figures for the general Court population would, no doubt, show a much higher incidence of larger families, of broken homes, and of children born out of wedlock.

Reports on the 100 cases where supplementary data were gathered (and where the child was living with both of his parents or with his mother) reveals that in almost half of the homes the earnings of the bread-winner totalled $80 or more per week. The income of some of those earning less appeared adequate in view of the fact that the rent was low and the family small. The comparable figures for all cases in the Court are weighted in the other direction—a predominance of families on relief or in marginal economic circumstances.

Occupation of the breadwinner was given in the records of 59 of the 100 families. Among the Manhattan fathers, one was a manager in a department store. There was a small merchant, a taxi driver, an elevator operator, a house painter, and an auto mechanic in the group. The occupations of the Queens fathers, whose incomes were higher than those obtaining in the other boroughs, included such categories as businessman, manufacturer, and importer. In the total group there were none reported holding unskilled jobs of the type characteristically found in immigrant groups. In only rare instances were the mothers working.

Turning to characteristics of the individual children, we discover that for the total group of 226 only 11 per cent were under twelve years of age at the time of their Court appearance. Grade in school is noted in the docket, and inspection of the age-grade distribution of these 226 children reveals no marked discrepancies. However, because the New York City schools have a 100 per cent promotion policy, there is no assurance that educational achievement is commensurate with grade attained. Of the 100 children on whom more detailed data were gathered, reading difficulties were noted on the records of twelve of the cases. I.Q. ratings were available in 47 of the 100 case records studied. While complete reliance should not be placed on the ratings because of the wide variety of tests employed as well as occasional variations in test scores reported for individual children, it is likely that if mental retardation had been suspected this condition would have been checked by more careful testing. Only four Jewish children had I.Q.'s below 80, and only one was below 70. Some 60 per cent of these Jewish children had I.Q.'s over 90 (20 per cent of the total Jewish group had I.Q.'s over 110). In contrast, for all children brought to the Court in 1952 only 5 per cent had I.Q.'s over 110, and only 30 per cent had I.Q.'s above 90. We thus discover that the Jewish group is characterized by approximately twice the general proportion of normal and above-normal I.Q.'s. As distinguished from the total group, Jewish children do not appear to be characterized by such problems as reading disability or low I.Q.[12]

As for place of residence, in almost two-thirds of all the health areas in New York City there was not a single Jewish child referred to the Court. In 1930, however, only a little less than one-fourth of the health areas had no Jewish children in Court, and in slightly more than a third of the health areas there were five or more cases. By way of contrast, during 1952 only eleven health areas had five or more Jewish cases in Court. Obviously, health-area rates for Jewish delinquents have little meaning when in the course of a whole year only one health area (Brooklyn 58.10) had as many as eight Jewish children in the Court. In fact, even combinations of health-area totals by health-center districts in which there are concentrations of Jewish population (as for example such notably Jewish sections as Brownsville or Flatbush in Brooklyn, the lower East Side or the middle West Side in Manhattan, Crotona or the Concourse in the Bronx), show no appreciable clusters of Jewish delinquents. Although neighborhoods may, because of such physical aspects as the predominance of business, markets, railroad tracks or park areas, determine the form of delinquent behavior, the facts presented here contradict the hypotheses that neighborhood—as such—has much to do with the production of delinquents.

§ *An Overall View*

In comparison with the statistics for 1930, and the estimated population-at-risk, Jewish delinquency in New York City has not only markedly declined but its distribution within the boroughs has changed. Many health areas which in 1930 registered some delinquent cases had none in 1952. No health area in 1952 had more than eight cases and the majority had only one in the course of a year. In regard to family characteristics, the assembled data on Jewish cases contradict most of the generalizations about delinquents. The majority did not come from broken families, or from families on relief, or those in which the mothers were working. Parents were literate, the children were born in wedlock, and with the exception of a relatively few cases, families were small. These Jewish delinquents were not retarded; comparatively few had reading problems. On the basis of the fact that the total number of Jewish cases are so small, and are so different in respect to family and child characteristics from the total delinquent population, the inference appears warranted that the infrequent Jewish delinquent resembles the non-Jewish delinquent only in his type of behavior.

These findings would seem to point up the necessity for a more definitive analysis of the types of behavior and problems which bring children who are members of the Jewish subculture into the Juvenile Court. Also, the study suggests the possibility that an investigation of family and group solidarities, and of cultural characteristics, may be more rewarding than the current frontal attack on so ill-defined an entity as "delinquency."

HOODLUM OR BUSINESS MAN:
AN AMERICAN DILEMMA

DESPITE the high standard of living enjoyed by the United States, stealing is a major problem. In 1950 a million thefts were reported to the police in two thousand American cities (combined population: seventy million people).[1] Burglaries, robberies, car thefts, and other forms of larceny outnumbered homicides, rapes, and aggravated assaults sixteen to one.

§ *Social Disorganization:*
A Factor in Hoodlum-Type Stealing

Why should so much predatory crime occur in such a rich country? The age and socio-economic status of arrested offenders provide some clues. American thieves are usually young hoodlums from slum neighborhoods.[2] One explanation of their youth and neighborhood of residence is that people are more prone to act upon their antisocial impulses when external controls over them are weak. Thus, adolescents steal more than older or younger people because they are less likely to be under the influence of a family unit; they are becoming emancipated from the family into which they were born but have not yet married and become involved in a new family unit. Similarly, slum dwellers steal more than suburbanites because stealing is not universally frowned on in deteriorated neighborhoods as it is in wealthier communities. In short, predatory crime occurs when social vigilance is reduced.

Case histories of hoodlum-type thieves generally support the "social disorganization" explanation of stealing. Commonly, the street-corner rowdy grew up in a chaotic household.[3] His parents exercised ineffectual control over him. This did not necessarily come about because of indifference, but rather because they were overwhelmed by their own difficulties, such as: chronic warfare in the household; death, desertion, or serious illness of the breadwinner; mental deficiency or disease; alcoholism; gambling; promiscuity; or too many children for an unskilled father to support or a harried mother to supervise. Such problems not only reduce the effectiveness of parental control. By curtailing income and forcing the family to occupy the least desirable housing, they are also indirectly responsible for ineffective community control. A slum is a neighborhood where houses are old, overcrowded, and in need of major repairs. But it

---

Published for the first time in this volume.

is also a place where people with incapacitating problems are concentrated. Preoccupied with their difficulties, they are simultaneously ineffective parents and apathetic citizens. "Horse rooms" and "cat houses" are able to locate in slums for the same reason that youngsters are permitted to "hang out" on street corners: troubled people do not care. Thus, it is no accident when reformatory inmates come from backgrounds where neither family nor neighborhood influences posed a strong obstacle to taking other people's property.

§ *Differential Attraction to the Hoodlum Role*

The weakness of parental and community controls cannot, however, account for the fact that girls pass through adolescence and live in slums just as boys do, yet do not steal to the same extent. Nor does the weakness of external controls explain why only a minority of slum youths steal persistently enough to get caught. Others grow up under similar circumstances and seem reasonably law-abiding. More must be involved in the creation of a hoodlum than the lack of vigilance of family and neighbors. What goes on *inside* the young tough? Is he mentally sick? A small percentage of the thefts which come to the attention of juvenile and criminal courts can be accounted for in this way. The psychiatrist explains how a need for love may drive a boy to take women's lingerie from clothes lines. However, the hoodlum typically does not fit the psychiatrist's portrait of a neurotic; he steals because his friends steal.

Why should he choose such friends? Their thefts are petty and crudely executed. A professional con man or safecracker would be ashamed to commit crimes so lacking in craftsmanship. They burglarize a grocery store; they drive off a car and "strip" it of radio, heater, and tires; they break into a house while the owner is away and look for valuables; they beat up a drunk on a dark street and take his wallet. Sooner or later they will be imprisoned, for not only are they unskilled, but they are chronically "broke" and thus they cannot bribe law enforcement officers or hire topnotch lawyers. Nor do they have friends in high places who will intercede with police or prosecutor. Unlike racketeers who steal because enormous profits outweigh the risks of apprehension, hoodlum-type thieves can look forward to a trifling income and to long years in custody.

§ *Status Discontent*

What possible explanation can there be for such self-defeating behavior? When asked why he steals, the hoodlum says, in effect, "Bad companions," "For excitement," or, "I needed money." Yet other youths find nondelinquent friends, different kinds of excitement, and other ways to make money. Actually, stealing is only one phase of his rebellion against conventional values.[4] He and his friends curse, destroy property maliciously, philander, create public disturbances, band together in gangs to fight other gangs, and are insolent to teachers, policemen, and social workers. They seem bitter, resentful. What is their grievance? Apparently it is that their lives offer no hope for legitimate success.[5] As children, they went to the movies and learned that American men should own convertibles and handsome clothes. They also learned, as they got into the teens, that their own prospects for "getting ahead" were poor. Somehow they had lost the chance to enjoy a luxurious style of life. Defacing property is their way of striking back. "Borrowing" flashy cars is their way of tasting the good things America promised them.

True, in the United States even slum youths are well off by comparison with the poor of Europe or Asia. But this is small comfort; they compare their lot with that of the most successful and glamorous Americans, not with the downtrodden of other continents. Relative to American movie stars and captains of industry, they feel underprivileged, and it is how they *feel* that counts. Resentment against a social system has little to do with the objective deprivations it imposes. Resentment arises when deprivations are greater than people believe they *ought* to be.[6] In the United States, where the ideal is social ascent, poor climbers may be more bitter than poor eaters in other societies. And, paradoxically, the considerable amount of upward mobility in America increases rather than decreases the resentment of those trapped at the bottom; after all, it dramatizes their failure. Faced with the alternatives of blaming themselves or of feeling robbed of their birthright, they prefer to choose the latter.

§ *Educational Achievement and Social Mobility*

They have a case. Youths become trapped at the bottom of the socio-economic heap largely because they did poorly at school. In all fairness, however, it should be remembered that the basis for school adjustment is laid in the home and the community. If a child's parents and friends hold education in awe and encourage him to bend every effort to learn from his teacher, he will value gold stars and high grades and being "promoted." If the child is sent to school because the law requires it (and because his mother wants to get him out from underfoot), he may regard the classroom as a kind of prison. Thus, family background is important to the youngster's adjustment in the crucial first years of school.[7] Parents who see to it that their son keeps up with his work in primary school may make it possible for him to pursue a business or professional career later. Parents who permit their boys to flounder in the early grades unwittingly cut them off from the main path of social ascent.

Even an intellectually superior youngster can become a school "problem" if he is not properly motivated in the early grades. Forced to come at set times, to refrain from pinching his neighbors, to keep quiet so that the teacher can instruct the class as a group, he perceives school as a discipline imposed on him rather than an extension and development of his own interests. If no one at home or in the neighborhood makes school effort seem meaningful to him, he lacks the incentive to learn regardless of his intellectual potentialities. The vicious circle of neglect and failure cumulate. Within a few years, he is retarded in basic skills such as reading, which are necessary for successful performance in the higher grades. Whether he is promoted with his age mates, "left back," or shunted into "slow" programs, the more successful students and the teachers consider him "dumb." This makes school still more unpleasant, and his disinterest increases.

By adolescence, an unsuccessful student may well decide that he is fighting a losing battle. Is it surprising that he becomes a truant and a disciplinary problem in class? Having learned little in school except how to annoy the teacher, he has neither the prerequisites for further education nor the courage to attempt to make up his deficiencies. It is too late for him to use the educational route to a high standard of living. But what other routes are there? Professional sports? The entertainment world? Politics? The opportunities in those fields are limited. More frequently, youngsters think they can escape from a pattern of defeat by withdrawing from school and going "to work." They find, however, that educational failure is predictive of occupational failure. The youth who quits school upon reaching the age when state law no longer compels attendance is unrealistic if he expects a well-paid, interesting job. The early school-leaver gets unskilled work that offers little chance for advancement: stock clerk, delivery man, soda jerk, pin boy in a bowling alley. (His failure to complete high school, the competition of older and more experienced workers, and the stipulations of the child labor laws make employers reluctant to hire him—unless no one else is available.) He does not get along with supervisors any better than he did with teachers. He changes employment frequently. After several months of frustration, he may lose interest in steady work and instead take odd jobs when pressed for money.

§ *The Hoodlum: A Rebel against Permanent Low Status*

Psychically uncommitted to school or job, such a boy "hangs out" on the street corner with other unsuccessful youngsters. He needs their approval as a compensation for the rejection of school authorities and employers. The price for their approval runs high. He must show that he is not "chicken," i.e., cowardly. The way in which he can do this is by manifesting a reckless willingness to steal, to fight, to try anything once. He must repudiate the bourgeois virtues associated with school and job: diligence, neatness, truthfulness, thrift. He becomes known as a "loafer" and a "troublemaker" in the community. When family and neighbors add their condemnations to those of teachers and employers, all bridges to respectability are burned, and he becomes progressively more concerned with winning "rep" inside the gang. For him, stealing is not primarily a way to make money. It is a means of gaining approval within a clique of outcasts. The gang offers a heroic rather than an economic basis for self-respect. Of course, if a holdup or a burglary nets a substantial amount of money, the hoodlum has the best of both worlds. But for most hoodlums, the income from crime is pitifully small. Only occasionally does a gang member graduate into the ranks of organized crime, as Al Capone did, and thereby become a financial success. Capone was as exceptional among hoodlums as Rockefeller was among businessmen.

Further insight into the motivation of the hoodlum results from contrasting him with the law-abiding adolescent. Clinical study reveals that the impulses to steal and murder and rape are universal.[8] Apparently, the difference between the law-abiding adolescent and the hoodlum is not that one has impulses to violate the rules of society and the other does not. Both are tempted to break laws at some time or other. Laws prohibit what circumstance may make attractive: driving an automobile at eighty miles an hour, beating up an enemy, taking what one wants without paying for it. The hoodlum yields to these temptations; the boy living in a middle-class neighborhood does not. How can this difference be accounted for? Do shade trees, detached houses, and other advantages reduce envy, hatred, and maliciousness? Or is it rather that the middle-class youth has more to lose by giving rein to deviant impulses? Not only does he have a spacious home to live in, nutritious food to eat, and fashionable clothes to wear. More important, he has status. He comes from a "good" family. He lives in a "respectable" neighborhood. His teachers like him; he gets good marks and he moves easily from grade to grade. These social victories provide a reasonable basis for anticipating future achivements. He expects to complete college and take up a business or professional career. If he applied his energies to burglary instead of to homework, he would risk not only the ego-flattering rewards currently available but his future prospects as well.

In short, youngsters vary in the extent to which they feel a stake in American society. For those with social honor, disgrace is a powerful sanction. For a boy disapproved of already, there is less incentive to resist the temptation to do what he wants when he wants to do it. Usually, the higher the socio-economic status of the family, the more the youngster feels he has to lose by deviant behavior. For instance, middle-class children are more successful in school, on the average, than lower-class children. On the other hand, *some* lower-class youngsters fare better in school than *some* middle-class youngsters. To determine the stake which a youngster has in conformity it is necessary to know more than the level which his family occupies in the economic system. His own victories and defeats in interpersonal relations can be predicted only roughly from family income or father's occupation.

Some individuals have less stake in conformity than others in every community, but communities differ in the proportion of defeated people. A community with a high concentration of them has an even higher crime rate than would be expected from adding up the deviant predispositions of its individual members. Thus, the small incidence of stealing in suburbs is due not only to the scarcity of youngsters with little stake in conformity, but also to the fact that a potential rebel is surrounded in school and in the neighborhood by age mates who are motivated to compete within the framework of the established social system. They frown upon stealing because *they* do not need to rebel. On the other hand, in deteriorated neighborhoods, the concentration of defeated persons is greater. Therefore, a youngster needs a larger stake in conformity in the slum than in the suburb in order to resist temptation. In short, there is a social component to the stake in conformity; the youngster meets defeat in isolation but does not usually become delinquent unless he obtains the support of his peers. In neighborhoods where most boys feel capable of competing in the educational-occupational status system, those who do not may be unhappy—but are not usually delinquent.

Especially in slum communities, then, the less the boy's stake in conformity, the more likely he will join with other outcasts in antisocial behavior. On the other hand, if he can be given a vested interest in a law-abiding role, he could be detoured away from gang membership. This approach to delinquency prevention might well begin at school. Recall that the pattern of defeat found in the records of hoodlums starts in the classroom. Is it feasible to provide dull pupils as well as bright ones with victories? Can casualties be avoided in a mass production educational system where youngsters differ in abilities, backgrounds, interests? Although, in principle, more widespread distribution of recognition may prevent vicious circles from starting, it is not easy for the teacher to see to it that everyone gets his quota of recognition. In the first place, the teacher can hardly help favoring youngsters who show respect for her and are living examples of her skill at communicating knowledge. In the second, the status hierarchy of the classroom depends on the attitudes of the children as well as those of the teacher. Suppose, for instance, that a Negro child is regarded with contempt by his white classmates. Or suppose that a child from an economically marginal home is made to feel ashamed of his shabby clothes. The results of the educational process cannot be standardized by techniques analogous to those used by quality control experts in making uniform the end-products of the assembly line.

§ *A Natural Experiment in Crime Prevention*

Would an all-out attempt to improve school adjustment have an appreciable effect on American crime? No one knows for sure. In so far as such an attempt were directed by school authorities alone, it might be too little and too late. Parents may be better able to motivate a child to put forth effort in school than the most skillful teacher or counselor. But an interesting historical comparison shows what an orientation favorable to school achievements can do, at least potentially, by way of crime prevention. Jews and Italians came to the United States in large numbers at about the same time—the turn of the century—and both settled in urban areas.[9] There was, however, a very different attitude toward intellectual accomplishment in the two cultures. Jews from Eastern Europe regarded religious study as the most important activity for an adult male. The rabbi enjoyed great prestige because he was a scholar, a teacher, a logician. He advised the community on the application of the Written and Oral Law. Life in America gave a secular emphasis to the Jewish reverence for learning. Material success is a more important motive than salvation for American youngsters, Jewish as well as Christian, and secular education is better training for business and professional careers than Talmudic exegesis. Nevertheless, intellectual achievement continued to be valued by Jews—and to have measurable effects. Second-generation Jewish students did homework diligently, got high grades, went to college in disproportionate numbers, and scored high on intelligence tests.[10] Two thousand years of preparation lay behind them.

Immigrants from Southern Italy, on the other hand, tended to regard formal education either as a frill or as a source of dangerous ideas from which the minds of the young should be protected.[11] They remembered Sicily, where a child who attended school regularly was a rarity. There, youngsters were needed not only to help on the farm. Equally important was the fact that hard-working peasants could not understand why their children should learn classical Italian (which they would not speak at home) or geography (when they would not travel in their lifetime more than a few miles from their birthplace). Sicilian parents suspected that education was an attempt on the part of Roman officials to subvert the authority of the family. In the United States, many South Italian immigrants maintained the same attitudes. They resented compulsory school attendance laws and prodded their children to go to work and become economic assets as soon as possible. They encouraged neglect of schoolwork and even truancy. They did not realize that education has more importance in an urban-industrial society than in a semi-feudal one. With supportive motivation from home lacking, the second-generation Italian boys did not make the effort of Jewish contemporaries. Their teachers tried to stuff the curriculum into their heads in vain. Their lack of interest was reflected not only in low marks, retardation, truancy, and early school leaving; it even resulted in poor scores on intelligence tests.[12] They accepted their parents' conception of the school as worthless and thereby lost their best opportunity for social ascent.

Some of these youngsters did not reconcile themselves to remaining on the bottom of the heap; they rebelled. Second-generation Italian boys became delinquent in disproportionately large numbers. In New York City, 39 per cent of the white delinquents of foreign-born parents in 1930 were of Italian origin, although less than 22 per cent of the white families with foreign-born heads were of that ethnic group.[13] In Chicago, second-generation Italian boys in the years 1927-33 had an appearance rate in the Cook County Juvenile Court *twice* as high as white boys generally.[14] Among older and more serious offenders, too, a disproportionate representation of Italian-Americans occurred. In 1933, second-generation Italian men were committed to state prisons and reformatories proportionately more frequently than the average second-generation American.[15]

Second-generation Jewish youths had less reason to become hoodlums. Whether they lived in slums or not, they usually perceived a constructive alternative to continued lower-class status. Their parents kept legitimate channels of social ascent open for them by inculcating the traditional attitude of respect for education and by transmitting the business know-how gleaned from hundreds of years of urban life in Europe. Why should they have rebelled against success in the marketplace as a criterion of status? Their chances in the marketplace were excellent. As a matter of history, although Jewish immigrants took menial jobs and lived in over-crowded ghettos during the first two decades of the twentieth century, their *children* became overwhelmingly middle class. The shift from unskilled and skilled trades worked at by one generation, to clerical, managerial, and professional occupations in the next, probably was not duplicated by any other immigrant group.[16] Jewish parents did not consider themselves engaged in crime prevention, but consequences do not have to be foreseen to be real.

Did second-generation Jewish youths avoid delinquency, as these considerations suggest? Data on the offense rates of Jews are difficult to come by.[17] Official agencies in the United States rarely identify offenders by religious affiliation and do not consider Jews to be a nationality.[18] Some statistics on Jewish offenders exist, however, and, fortunately, they refer to periods shortly after large-scale Jewish migration to the United States —so that they are, in effect, second-generation rates. In New York City, for example, Jewish youngsters constituted in 1930 about a quarter of the white delinquents—although the Jewish population at large was estimated to be about a third of the total white population of the city.[19] To be sure, only nine-tenths of the Jewish delinquents in 1930 were the offspring of foreign-born parents, but it is unlikely that a recalculation of the Jewish delinquency rate for youngsters whose parents were born abroad would have made an appreciable difference.[20] Out of 394,080 prisoners sent to the prisons and reformatories of the 48 states from 1920 to 1929, 6846 (1.74 per cent) were Jews.[21] (The Jewish population of the country was estimated then to be 3.43 per cent of the total.) Crude though these data are, they show that the probability of becoming a hoodlum was not the same for second-generation Jews and second-generation Italians.

§ *Summary*

When forced by an injudicious choice of parents to live in poverty, some unknown proportion of American boys will resent it. They will want to acquire the clothes, automobiles, and home furnishings displayed in the movies. If a business or professional career is feasible, resentment makes them ambitious; perhaps they add a new chapter to the rags to riches saga. If they cannot perceive themselves utilizing legitimate channels of advancement, this same resentment may drive them to lash out against society; they become a menace to life and property. The cultural tradition from which youngsters come is relevant to this alternative because success in school is a prerequisite to business or professional careers, yet success in school does not depend on ability alone. It depends also on the attitudes toward formal education that children assimilate in the home and the neighborhood. For an underprivileged boy who has introjected the glittering goals of the American Dream, his ethnic background may be the crucial factor in the channeling of discontent with low status.[22] Whether he becomes a hoodlum or a lawyer may hinge on the accident of Italian or Jewish origin. Ironically, while Jewish "ambition" has been the subject of much discussion, friendly and unfriendly, the low Jewish crime rate has not been recognized as the outcome of the same cultural resources which makes "ambition" possible. Eyebrows have also been raised over the large number of Italian offenders, whereas the difficulties of Italian youth in American schools—and the resulting obstacles to social ascent— reveal Italian "criminality" to be the other horn of a characteristically American dilemma.

Perhaps American society can learn from its Jewish subculture that placing a high valuation upon intellectual achievement is an indirect approach to crime prevention. If it proves feasible to keep open the educational path to middle-class status for more youngsters, adolescent hoodlumism can be expected to decrease. Such a program is no panacea. In the first place, dull children cannot excel in school work no matter what the social pressure. Their problems will increase, as a matter of fact, the greater the emphasis on academic accomplishment. In the second, children growing up in disorganized families, living in slum neighborhoods, or exposed to race prejudice will continue to be problems to themselves and others. What *can* be said in favor of education for social ascent is that it attempts to cope with an ailment specifically related to delinquent rebellion, namely, status frustration. It seems paradoxical that in the United States, some youths become hoodlums instead of businessmen, not because they lack the ability to succeed legitimately or disdain money, but because they find out too late the relationship between school adjustment and middle-class status.

JEROME K. MYERS AND
BERTRAM H. ROBERTS

SOME RELATIONSHIPS BETWEEN RELIGION, ETHNIC ORIGIN AND MENTAL ILLNESS

A RECENT trend in research into the etiology of mental illness is the investigation of social and cultural factors, with religion and ethnic origin receiving particular attention. Interest in this area covers a wide range, extending from the influence of religious and ethnic group cultures upon personal adjustment to the subtleties of the social component in interpersonal relations and the individual's subjective reaction to his ethnic or religious status. These problems are of special interest in an heterogeneous society like America, where ethnic and religious differences are important determinants of behavior.

Previous research indicates that mental illness is distributed unevenly among religious and ethnic groups. Most of these studies dealt with first admissions to mental hospitals (2, 8, 11), and a few were based upon Selective Service examinations (5). In the present study[1] we surveyed an entire urban population to determine the distribution of psychiatric illness among religious and ethnic groups.[2] Since previous studies were completed ten to thirty years ago, our findings can be expected to reflect some of the trends brought about by advancement in psychiatric treatment and other changing social conditions.

§ Design of the Survey

A survey was made of all patients residing in the metropolitan area of New Haven, Connecticut, who were under the treatment of a psychiatrist on December 1, 1950. A schedule was filled out for each patient from his record in a mental hospital or outpatient clinic, or through an interview with his psychiatrist. In order to cover the entire population under psychiatric treatment on this particular date we contacted all the practitioners, clinics, and hospitals in the state and nearby regions, as well as national hospitals treating New Haven patients. A total of 1,963 cases were found with 1,393 located in public hospitals, 37 in private hospitals, 159 in clinics, and 374 being treated by private practitioners.

A direct inquiry was made about the patient's place of birth and religion, and the ethnic origin of his parents. The psychiatric diagnosis proposed by the practitioner or the record was validated by our research psychiatrists and converted into the Veterans Administration diagnostic scheme.[3] Since consensus was difficult in certain of the subcategories, the

Published for the first time in this volume.

differences were resolved by combining these subcategories under a more general heading. For this reason the psychoneurotic disorders include the psychosomatic and character disorders. Alcohol and drug addictions were also grouped together, as were the affective disorders and the illnesses of senescence. The small number of organic mental illnesses necessitated their inclusion under one heading. The final form of the diagnostic scheme which has been carried through the entire study is presented in Table 1.

§ *The Community*

Metropolitan New Haven is a polyglot manufacturing community of approximately 250,000 population. The Italians and Irish are the largest ethnic groups, comprising about one-third and one quarter of the population, respectively. Two other groups, the British-Americans and Jews, make up about one-quarter of the population between them. There are also smaller numbers of Germans, Negroes, Poles, and Scandinavians. Approximately three-fifths of the community is Roman Catholic, one-third Protestant, and one-tenth Jewish.

Since large-scale European immigration ceased only thirty years ago, and internal migration into the community by Negroes from the rural South and Puerto Ricans is still underway, the ethnic groups are by no means equally acculturated and assimilated. The British-Americans, or Old Yankees, who founded New Haven over three hundred years ago, set the pattern and objectives for the acculturation of all other groups. Although the "old" immigrants, such as the Germans and Scandinavians, are highly acculturated and assimilated, the "new" immigrants who began arriving in the 1880's and the Negroes remain differentiated in many ways. Of the more recent groups, the Jews have been most successful in their acculturation, especially in the economic and educational systems. However, they have not been assimilated into the community's social structure and have developed a parallel religious and social life separate from the Gentiles. There are also vertical divisions within the Gentile social structure according to race, religion, and ethnic origin.[4] For example, there are eight different Junior Leagues in the community for appropriately affiliated upper-class young women. The highest-ranking organization is the New Haven Junior League, which draws its membership from "Old Yankee" Protestant families whose daughters have been educated in private schools. The Catholic Charity League is next in rank and age, drawing its membership from Irish-American families. In addition to this organization there are Italian and Polish Junior Leagues within the Catholic group. Within the Protestant division of the community there is a Swedish and a Danish Junior League. Upper-class Jewish and Negro families, as well, have their own Junior Leagues (9). Thus, race, religion and ethnicity are powerful differentiating factors in the New Haven social structure.

§ Findings

RELIGION AND MENTAL ILLNESS. The distribution of psychiatric illness among the three major religious groupings is shown in Table 1. Compari-

Table 1—Distribution of Psychiatric and General Population According to Diagnosis and Religious Affiliation

	Catholic		Protestant		Jewish	
	No.	%	No.	%	No.	%
General population	6,736	57.5	3,869	33.0	1,108	9.5
Total psychiatric population	1,059	57.0	576	31.0	223	12.0
Psychoneurotic disorders	189	46.2	122	29.8	98	24.0
Alcohol and drug addiction	61	68.5	28	31.5	0	0.0
Schizophrenia	506	60.8	245	29.4	81	9.7
Affective disorders	86	55.1	53	34.0	17	10.9
Psychosis with mental deficiency	56	61.5	23	25.3	12	13.2
Disorders of senescence	100	55.9	67	37.4	12	6.8
Epilepsy	25	71.5	9	25.7	1	2.9
Other organic	36	53.8	29	43.4	2	2.8

son of the psychiatric population with a control group consisting of a 5 per cent systematic sample of the general population reveals a significant statistical difference in the distribution of total mental illness, the psychoneurotic disorders, and alcohol and drug addiction.[5] In addition, significance is approached in the distribution of the organic illnesses. As can be seen in Table 1, Jews have a much higher rate of neurosis than Catholics or Protestants, while Catholics have the highest rates for alcohol and drug addiction. Organic illnesses, on the other hand, tend to be more frequent among Protestants. No differences were found, however, in the distribution of schizophrenia, the affective disorders, psychosis with mental deficiency, and illness of senescence. Since our previous research has demonstrated that social class is also a determining factor in the distribution of mental illness, we checked all our significant findings to see if this factor was operating to produce the religious differences.[6] The results indicated that social class differences in the distribution of the three religious groups were generally not responsible for the uneven rates.[7] The only instance where the religious differences disappeared when we controlled for class was among Class V psychoneurotics. This did not, however, account for the fact that neurotic disorders among Jews were two and one-half times above expectation, since only 12 per cent of all neurotics were found in the lowest class. Among the 88 per cent of neurotics found in the other four classes, the Jewish rate was consistently higher, as seen in Table 2. In contrast to the high rate of neurosis, it is remarkable that there were no Jews found among the alcohol and drug addicts.

We compared our findings with those of Malzberg and Dayton, who used first hospital admissions (2, 8). As would be expected, our rates are higher for psychoneurotic disorders, since we included ambulatory patients. In all other categories our findings are substantially the same as

Table 2—Percentage Distribution of Psychoneurotics and General Population by Religion and Social Class*

RELIGION	SOCIAL CLASS							
	I-II		III		IV		V	
	General Population	Psycho-Neurotics	General Population	Psycho-Neurotics	General Population	Psycho-Neurotics	General Population	Psycho-Neurotics
Jewish	21	29	13	38	7	18	4	2
Catholic	28	17	47	31	63	64	73	74
Protestant	51	54	40	31	30	18	23	23
Total	100	100	100	100	100	100	100	99

* The number of neurotic cases by class is as follows: I-II-93, III-104, IV-157, V-47. Eight cases could not be class typed because of insufficient data. Classes I and II are combined because of the small number of cases in Class I.

those of other investigators. In contrast to what is stated in two textbooks of psychiatry (3, 14), we did not find a higher rate of affective disorders among Jews. A similar observation was made by Malzberg (7) in 1930.

ETHNIC ORIGIN AND MENTAL ILLNESS. The patient's ethnic origin was determined by the nationality of his father.[8] However, the answers to the schedule questions regarding the parent's ethnic origin cannot be taken as entirely valid, since they represent subjective impressions to some extent. In addition, no distinctions are made according to the number of generations the person's family has been in America. Therefore, we limited our analysis to four relatively distinct groups—the Irish, Italian, Negro, and Jewish.[9] As there are no general population figures dealing with ethnic origin, we compared the distribution of diagnoses between ethnic groups within the psychiatric population. (See Table 3.)

Significant differences were found in the distribution of mental illness among these four groups. As already indicated, Jews were high for psychoneurotic disorder and low for alcohol and drug addiction. The Italians were low for alcohol and drug addiction while the Irish were high. It is now clear that the high rate of alcoholism among Catholics mentioned previously is to be attributed to the Irish group, since Italians and Irish make up the great majority of Catholics in New Haven. It was interesting to find that Negroes were extremely low in their proportion of affective disorders (15). Finally, six of the eight Negroes with organic disease had

Table 3—Distribution of Psychiatric Population According to Selected Ethnic Groups and Diagnosis

	Irish		Italian		Jewish		Negro	
	No.	%	No.	%	No.	%	No.	%
Psychoneurotic disorders	50	15.5	93	23.4	98	43.9	10	11.1
Alcohol and drug addictions	35	10.9	3	0.8	0	0.0	8	8.9
Schizophrenia	153	47.5	192	48.4	81	36.3	50	55.6
Affective disorders	23	7.1	35	8.8	17	7.6	1	1.1
Psychosis with mental deficiency	12	3.7	21	5.3	12	5.4	3	3.3
Disorders of senescence	42	13.0	36	9.1	12	5.4	9	10.0
Epilepsy	0	0.0	3	0.8	1	0.4	1	1.1
Other organic	7	2.2	14	3.5	2	0.9	8	8.9
Total	322	99.9	397	100.1	223	99.9	90	100.0

general paresis; however, this represents a dramatic decline in total numbers in comparison with earlier studies (2, 8). All other findings are substantially the same as presented in these studies.

IMMIGRATION AND MENTAL ILLNESS. Since immigration into the United States has been very low during the last three decades, the average age of the foreign-born population is considerably higher than the native-born. We therefore controlled for age, since it is sometimes related to the form of psychiatric illness, by limiting our analysis to persons over twenty years of age according to specific age groupings.[10] Although we do not have specific immigration data for Jews, the findings presented in Table 4 concerning the differences between native- and foreign-born will apply to the Jewish population, which is mainly first and second generation in this age group.

There is a significant difference in the distribution of mental illness among the native- and foreign-born, with a higher proportion of foreign-born in the total psychiatric population and in the diagnostic categories of affective disorder, illnesses of senescence, and the organic illnesses. However, the higher rate of disorders of senescence among the foreign-born is due to their higher average age. A significantly higher occurrence

Table 4—Distribution of Psychiatric and General Population, 21 Years of Age and Over, by Nativity and Psychiatric Diagnosis

	Native-Born No.	Native-Born %	Foreign-Born No.	Foreign-Born %
General population	135,568	79.5	34,900	20.5
Total psychiatric population	1,363	77.0	408	23.0
Psychoneurotic disorders	313	93.2	23	6.8
Alcohol and drug addictions	70	85.4	12	14.6
Schizophrenia	643	76.9	193	23.1
Affective disorders	102	65.4	54	34.6
Psychosis with mental deficiency	67	84.8	12	15.2
Disorders of senescence	91	50.3	90	49.7
Epilepsy	32	91.4	3	8.6
Other organic	45	68.2	21	31.8

of psychoneurosis is found among the native-born. In the remaining diagnostic categories there are no significant differences between the native- and foreign-born. The similarity between these findings and those reported by Dayton (2) is remarkable if neurosis is excluded from the comparison.

§ *General Discussion*

It is important to note that this survey is not a true prevalency study of psychiatric illness: it is limited to those people with mental illness who are under the treatment of a psychiatrist. It would be inaccurate to infer that the distribution found here is a direct reflection of what might be found if the community were surveyed on a random, door-to-door basis. It is therefore necessary to consider the factors which might differentiate this psychiatric population from such a prevalency sample. For example, there may be significant differences among the religious and ethnic groups in their awareness of psychiatric symptoms. Similarly, there may be variation in their acceptance of psychiatry as the optimal treatment for mental symptoms. Such considerations must be held in mind in evaluating the significance of our findings.

It was interesting to find that the social variables under consideration had no effect on the distribution of schizophrenia or psychosis with mental deficiency. On the positive side, our investigation revealed an increased frequency of psychoneurotic disorders. Part of this can be immediately credited to the inclusion of ambulatory patients in our study. However the acceptance of psychiatry and psychotherapeutic treatment is undoubtedly a growing trend in the United States. As a new development requiring some informed intellectual comprehension, it would be expected that the better educated would have first exposure to the trend. This would explain the higher rate of psychoneurotic disorder among the native-born, who have reached a higher educational level than the foreign-born.

It is our opinion that the acceptance of psychoanalytic psychiatry is an important factor accounting for the extraordinarily high rate of psychoneurosis among Jews. The explanation for this must be considered in terms of the ethnic structure and tradition of the Jewish group in addition to its religious organization. There appears to be little conflict between the acceptance of Jewish religious doctrine and psychoanalytic theory. The accent here must be placed upon the common level of acceptance, for it is true that Jewish theological beliefs are in conflict with the atheistic orientation of Freud's writings. Within the last decade, however, there has been diminishing emphasis on this aspect of psychoanalytic theory by its proponents. In fact, efforts have been made to reconcile the differences between psychoanalysis and religion, as best indicated by Joshua Liebman's *Peace of Mind*. From the Jewish patient's standpoint, there is seldom any direct conflict between his religious values and the therapeutic process. In contrast, there is more opposition to psychoanalysis among Catholics. Although the higher levels of the Church have accepted the major components of psychoanalysis, omitting the atheistic orientation, there continues to be opposition among the local clergy as well as certain lay groups. This negative view of analytically oriented psychiatry is especially prevalent among the Irish Catholics. As evidence, not a single patient of Irish birth was receiving psychotherapy for a neurosis.

In modern times the widespread acceptance of scientific medical treatment has become an important component of the Jewish way of life. In the case of physical illness, Jews usually try to obtain the best available care, regardless of cost or sacrifice for the family. Consequently, in the face of a mental or emotional difficulty, these families are likely to seek the most competent and advanced psychiatric treatment, which is considered by many to be psychoanalysis and its derivatives. Jews, of course, have played a very important role in the development of psychoanalysis. They have made many of the major contributions to its theory and presently represent a large proportion of the analytically oriented psychiatrists. It is probable, therefore, that Jewish patients look favorably upon going to a psychiatrist with the same background as themselves.

Jewish cultural values seem to support many components of the psychotherapeutic process. Many people are coming to regard psychotherapy as encompassing a warm and accepting understanding of the patient's difficulties. This humanitarianism, which is not necessarily part of psychoanalytic theory, is similar to the atmosphere fostered in Jewish family life in the face of personal difficulty. This non-judgmental acceptance of the patient in a sympathetic fashion is also an orientation strongly featured in the training of psychotherapists. Further, as the patient proceeds into treatment, it is desirable that he should express his anxiety rather than suppress it or take precipitous aggressive action. Such behavior in treatment is similar to the traditional Jewish manner of expression.

It has been suggested that the process of psychotherapy, which is mainly a verbal exploration of the individual's emotional difficulties, is facilitated by the historical intellectualism of the Jewish people. Our research indicates that this was not necessarily the patient's orientation, as the majority did not know what the actual therapy process would be when they first approached treatment. However, this technique of adjustment might well have been an element which attracted Jewish physicians to the field of psychiatry. In summary, we must state that although these explanations for the high rates of psychoneurosis among Jews in terms of the acceptance of modern psychiatry seem plausible, we cannot be certain that the actual occurrence of the illness is not substantially higher in this group.

The general decrease we found in organic mental disease, especially among Negroes, is due to the decline of general paresis as a result of improved chemotherapy and an enlightened acceptance of modern medicine. The high rate of alcoholism among the Irish population and its absence among Jews has repeatedly been found (1). If this finding is compared with the inverse rates of psychoneurosis it appears that there is some kind of cultural determination in the formation of symptoms. A recent study of Jewish servicemen by Nodine and Roberts sheds some light on this problem (10). They found that Jewish servicemen will drink great amounts of alcoholic beverages on single occasions to conform with the social activities around them. In contrast to the Irish servicemen, however, they do not use alcohol as a crutch or support for certain personal and social frustrations. In reaction to oppressive authority or in the face of an aggressive challenge expressed directly in anger or indirectly in competition, the Irishman will take a drink whereas the Jew seeks complete sobriety. From a psychopathological standpoint the Irishman's use of alcohol to handle aggression has great potential danger in contributing to the development of alcoholism.

A further finding which needs explanation is the distribution of affective disorder. This illness was found to be more frequent among the foreign-born and apparently of diminishing occurrence in the Jewish group. The trend in affective illness, which is one of the major forms of psychosis, is not easily explained in terms of current knowledge of etiological factors which includes genetic as well as interpersonal processes.

Generally the explanation for social-psychological phenomena is sought in terms of the ego's reaction to external reality and the manner in which social factors color childhood experiences. The former implies the ego's capacity to control the social manifestations of internal impulses in deference to external pressures. Since behavior is modified in this way, it can be expected that neurotic symptoms which are often interpersonal communications will be influenced by social pressures. This process was inferred in the discussion of the occurrence of alcoholism among the Irish and its absence among Jews. Our finding represents an example of cultural conditions expressing a suppressive and displacing effect upon the symptomatic manifestations of psychic disorder.

The explanation of the diminishing occurrence of affective disorder among Jews and the native-born might be in terms of the development and socialization of the child. According to psychoanalytic theory, the affective illness is based upon a fixation in the first four years of life. Hence, if social forces have some effect upon the formation of this illness, it must be that they are brought to bear upon the dynamics of the family. More concretely, this would mean the role and responsibility assumed by various members of the family and the quality of the parent-child relationship. This is conceivable, since the American family structure differs considerably from the European, particularly in the middle class where it is less patriarchal due to the rising status of women. Early childhood experience in America also differs in many other ways from the European pattern. It has been suggested elsewhere that the great stress placed upon child-feeding has been an important factor in the causation of affective illness among Jews. The acculturation of the Jewish family in America, where problems of actual subsistence are less important, has tended to play down this practice. We can only speculate that such changes as these operating within the family dynamics have brought about the diminution of affective illness among Jews and native-born Americans.

In conclusion, religious and ethnic factors seem to relate to mental illness in three important ways. First, before assimilation and acculturation are achieved, child-rearing practices differ among religious and ethnic groups leading to variations of the basic personality (6). Similarly, previous forms of behavioral expression influence the manner in which a cultural group communicates a state of mental distress. Finally, the acceptance of the medical delineation of mental illness with its therapeutic procedure represents a modern value which is more rapidly accepted by certain religious and ethnic groups than others.

References

1. Bacon, S. D., *et al.*, *Studies of Drinking in Jewish Culture*. New Haven: Laboratory of Applied Physiology, Yale University, 1951.
2. Dayton, A. N., *New Facts on Mental Disorders*. Springfield: Charles C. Thomas, 1940.
3. Henderson, D. K., and Gillespie, R. D., *A Textbook of Psychiatry*, 7th ed. London: Oxford University Press, 1950.
4. Hollingshead, A. B., "Trends in Social Stratification: A Case Study," *Am. Soc. Rev.*, 17: 679, Dec. 1952.
5. Hyde, R. M., and Chisholm, R. M., "Studies in Medical Sociology, III: The Relation of Mental Disorder to Race and Nationality," *New England J. of Med.*, 23: 612, 1944.
6. Kardiner, A., *The Individual and His Society*. New York: Columbia University Press, 1939.
7. Malzberg, B., "The Prevalence of Mental Disease Among Jews," *Ment. Hyg.*, 14: 926, 1930.
8. Malzberg, B., *Social and Biological Aspects of Mental Disease*. Utica: State Hospital Press, 1940.
9. Minnis, M. S., "Cleavage in Women's Organizations: A Reflection of the Social Structure of a City," *Am. Soc. Rev.*, 18: 47, Feb. 1953.
10. Nodine, R. and Roberts, B. H., "Social Factors in the Psychodynamics of Alcohol Behavior." Unpublished manuscript.
11. Pollock, H. M. *et al.*, *Heredity and Environmental Factors in the Causation of Manic-depressive Psychosis and Dementia Praecox*. Utica: State Hospital Press, 1939.
12. Redlich, F. C., *et al.*, "Social Structure and Psychiatric Disorder," *Am. J. Psychiat.*, 109: 729, Apr. 1953.
13. Roberts, B. H., and Myers, J. K., "Religion, National Origin, Immigration and Mental Illness," *Am. J. Psychiat.*, 110: 759, Apr. 1954.
14. Rosanoff, A. J., *Manual of Psychiatry and Mental Hygiene*. 7th ed. New York: John Wiley and Sons, Inc., 1944.
15. Tooth, G., *Studies in Mental Illness in the Gold Coast, Colonial Research Publications* (No. 6). London: His Majesty's Stationery Office, 1950.

CULTURE AND JEWISH SOBRIETY:
THE INGROUP-OUTGROUP FACTOR

JEWISH experience with beverage al-
cohol poses some crucial questions for all who are concerned with the
problems of alcohol which beset modern society. The drinking of alcoholic
beverages is widespread among Jews and has been so since ancient times.
Percentage-wise, there are probably more users of alcoholic beverages in
the Jewish group than in any other major religio-ethnic group in America.
Yet as has been shown repeatedly both in this country and abroad, rates
of alcoholism and other drinking pathologies for Jews are very low.

Two further considerations must be added to this paradox in order to
clarify its significance and to suggest the kind of research which might
prove fruitful. First, there is no lack among Jews of acute psychic tensions
of the sort which are popularly supposed to cause drinking pathologies.
In comparison to certain groups exhibiting an excess of alcohol problems,
Jews have a proportionate share of neuroses and psychoses. In addition,
perhaps it may be said that they have an undue share of anxieties which
have their origin in broad social and historical circumstances. Hence, psychological explanations of drinking pathologies which are exclusively
phrased in terms of disproportionate needs to relieve psychic distress seem
patently contradicted by the facts of Jewish experience. Secondly, the
heterogeneity of Jews in terms of physical or racial characteristics casts
doubt upon any kind of bio-racial explanation. This doubt is considerably
strengthened by the failure of science to uncover any specific hereditary
mechanisms sufficient to account for drinking pathologies. These considerations thus highlight the possibility that at least part of the explanation
for Jewish sobriety may be found in the cultural tradition of the Jewish
people. While there is no logical need to deny a conditional role to bio-
psychic factors in the genesis of drinking pathologies, the facts augur well
for the sociological approach in attempting to understand the Jewish experience and, by implication, alcohol problems in general.

The present study is part of a larger research plan designed to extend
our knowledge of American Jewish drinking patterns and to test differ-

This paper appeared in slightly different form in the *Quarterly Journal of Studies
on Alcohol,* Vol. 16, No. 4 (December, 1955), pp. 700-42, and is used here with their
permission as well as with the permission of the author. The paper is part of a series
published in this journal by the author under the general title "Culture and Sobriety.
A Study of Drinking Patterns and Sociocultural Factors Related to Sobriety among
Jews." This series constitutes Part IV "Studies of Drinking in Jewish Culture," appearing in the *Quarterly Journal of Studies on Alcohol.*

ent explanations of the rarity of drinking pathologies in this group. To place this chapter in perspective, brief comment on the most promising line of explanation in the light of our overall findings* seems warranted.

Of the various theories advanced, the one projected by Bales (1, 2) appears to have the greatest explanatory value. On the most general level, his theory holds that group rates of extreme drinking pathologies are resultants of the interaction of three major sets of contributing factors. The first of these may be called *dynamic factors,* referring to the group incidence of acute psychic tensions or needs for adjustment sufficient to provide the driving force in drinking pathologies. The second consists of *alternative factors,* that is, culturally defined possibilities of adopting behavior patterns other than excessive drinking which are nonetheless functional equivalents in channeling and relieving acute psychic tensions. The third set may be designated as *orienting factors,* or the kinds of normative attitudes toward drinking itself which are carried in the cultures of different groups. Obviously these factors are exceedingly difficult to weigh in a given empirical situation. Nevertheless, in his specific discussion of the Jewish group, Bales emphasized the orienting factor of the particular normative attitudes toward drinking which are embedded in the rituals of Orthodox Judaism as being sufficient to account for the *difference* between Jewish rates of drinking pathologies and the rates for certain other groups with quite different normative attitudes.

Those who are familiar with traditional Judaism will at once recognize how extensively and firmly drinking is woven into the traditional rituals of the annual cycle of holy days and festivals, the *rites de passage,* and the observances of the Sabbath. They will also be cognizant of the extension of religious symbolism to drinking situations apart from formal acts of sanctification. Indeed, normative Judaism generally locates the act of drinking squarely in the network of sacred ideas, sentiments, and activities. In the context of this tradition, drinking is defined as symbolic, expressive, and communicative rather than as convivial or hedonistic in character. It will perhaps not strain the imagination overly much to suppose, with Bales, that early training and continued participation in religious drinking rituals help structure in the character stable attitudes toward drinking; that such attitudes are incorporated in the personality together with the most powerful religious ideas and sentiments of the group and are renewed and vitalized in the ceremonies and rituals which best express and reinforce these ideas and sentiments later in life. In any event, it was Bales' view that this body of tradition develops drinking attitudes of a quality and intensity sufficient to counter the development of hedonistic or addictive drinking.

---

* The reader is referred to the other articles in the present series (see *Quarterly Journal of Studies on Alcohol,* Vol. 16, Nos. 1-3, and Vol. 17, No. 1) for a detailed specification of these findings and of the evidence bearing upon them. These materials will shortly be published in monograph form and may also be found in (31).

This line of reasoning clearly links the distinctive sobriety of the Jews with the Orthodox religious tradition and its corpus of ritual and ceremony. Our own research, utilizing present-day diversity in Jewish religious affiliation and practice, checked this point of view systematically. Our findings to date are supportive: intoxication and signs of more extreme drinking pathologies are conspicuous by their absence among the more Orthodox, despite their extensive use of wines, spirits, and beers. However, as religious affiliation shifts from Orthodox to Conservative to Reform and to Secular, signs of drinking pathologies show marked and systematic increase. Moreover, these changes cannot be attributed to the direct influence of social class or generational factors. This is important because a host of studies, including our own, have shown differentiation among Jews in this country in their religious affiliation and practice along class and generation lines. Statistical analysis indicates, however, that continued sobriety is to be found wherever the Orthodox tradition is vital—albeit in attenuated form —regardless of social class or generation status. The earmarks of drinking pathologies become significantly evident where this tradition has been discarded, particularly if this is true in the earliest stages of socialization. All of this is not to say that Jews—other than the Orthodox—are debauching themselves with drink. Rather, there appears to be a trend toward convergence with wider societal drinking averages, normal or pathological— a trend, which corresponds with a decline in the vitality and impact of the Orthodox Jewish religious tradition. It is data of this kind which lend plausibility to Bales' point of view.

There are, however, other possible explanations of our findings. Also, there are aspects of Jewish tradition other than ritual drinking which comprise relevant parts of the total cultural orientation toward beverage alcohol. In the material which follows, we will seek to evaluate theories which in various ways have sought the explanation of Jewish sobriety in the relations of Jews to the larger society. This will involve us in an analysis of those particular aspects of Jewish culture which, while bearing on drinking behavior, are intimately connected with the ingroup-outgroup situation, that is, with the status of Jewry as a minority group.

§   *Some Theoretical Considerations*

The theories of Kant (17), Fishberg (9),[1] and others emphasize the ingroup-outgroup situation as decisive for Jewish sobriety.[2] Kant wrote:

> Women, ministers, and Jews do not get drunk, as a rule, at least they carefully avoid all appearance of it, because their civic position is weak and they need to be reserved. Their outward worth is based merely on the belief of others of their chastity, piousness and separatistic lore. All separatists, that is, those who subject themselves not only to the general laws of the country but also to a special sectarian law, are exposed through their eccentricity and alleged chosenness to the attention and criticism of the community, and thus cannot

relax their self-control, for intoxication, which deprives one of cautiousness, would be a scandal for them.

Whatever the inadequacies of this point of view, the minority status of the Jew cannot be dismissed as of no consequence for Jewish sobriety. Nearly all students of Jewish drinking behavior have attributed significance to this situation in one way or another. Even Bales (2) suggests that the fear of retaliation from dominant groups may provide reinforcement to a norm of sobriety which he thinks derives ultimately from religious beliefs and practices. A survey of the literature on the influence of the ingroup-outgroup situation on Jewish drinking behavior, however, makes it especially clear that speculation has far outrun the accumulation of supporting evidence. By and large there has been cavalier indifference to the need for basing theories on firm factual foundations. Only Glad (11) attempted direct verification of Kant's type of theory which explains Jewish sobriety as a minority sect reaction to fear of censure from powerful majorities. Glad interprets his own evidence as nonsupportive of the theory, but for reasons discussed elsewhere (31) Glad's findings are inconclusive.

There is some further indirect evidence bearing on this problem. Bales (2) made a painstaking analysis of what he calls the empirical adequacy of Kant's argument and, like Glad, concluded that the facts do not support the theory. However, the facts upon which Bales based his rejection cf Kant's theory are not facts concerning ingroup-outgroup influences on Jewish drinking behavior. The facts which in Bales' opinion challenge the empirical adequacy of Kant's explanation are drawn from histories of alcoholics. Bales reasons that, in the last analysis, Kant's theory attributes sobriety and the absence of alcoholism among Jews to the operation of the cognitive faculties—that is, the Jews, although they drink frequently, avoid excess and addiction by rationally assessing the consequences. This presumed rational assessment is made in the context of the actual or potential censure to which members of the disadvantaged Jewish minority are exposed. But experience with alcoholics does not support an assumption that knowledge of the dangers and undesirable consequences of excessive drinking enables the exercise of good judgment or "will power" sufficient to prevent alcoholism. Accordingly, Bales concluded that Kant's explanation and the analogous explanations of others are empirically inadequate.

Bales' criticism of the "rationalist fallacy" in these arguments is astute and suggestive. It highlights the naïveté of trying to explain the consistent sobriety of the Jews without some disciplined understanding of the nature of alcoholism. The critique also points to a body of facts which must be accounted for, at least by implication, in any adequate explanation of Jewish sobriety. Bales' reasoning, however, tends to obscure the need for a thorough analysis of the influence of the ingroup-outgroup situation on Jewish drinking behavior. This results from the implicit assumption that the nature of that influence is of the sort which Bales imputes to Kant's brief description and that the Jewish response is actually a purely rational one. This assumption, however, has no systematic evidence to support it. In Bales' argument this assumption is connected by a chain of inferences to facts on the etiology of alcoholism, and Kant's type of theory is accordingly found wanting. But Bales' readmission of Kant's explanation as a secondary factor in Jewish sobriety testifies to his own reluctance to dismiss ingroup-outgroup relations as of no importance for the sober response of Jews to beverage alcohol.[3] We must therefore question whether the assumption of a rational response to imminent censure or danger exhausts the significance of the ingroup-outgroup situation for Jewish sobriety. It seems that the resolution of the problems engendered by Bales' criticism of Kant's theory lies in further factual investigation of the influences on Jewish drinking of the Jewish ingroup, the Gentile outgroup and the relations between Jews and Gentiles.

Yet another facet of the ingroup-outgroup situation remains to be considered. The outgroup has been held by some observers to exercise a demoralizing influence on Jews in their use of alcoholic beverages. Fishberg (9) and Myerson (24), for instance, assert that the assimilating Jew who has increasing contacts with Gentiles is more prone to drunkenness and alcoholism than his compatriot of the ghetto.[4] The implications are clear: relations with the outgroup, which have been seen by Kant, Fishberg and others as a major cause of Jewish sobriety, are seen also in an entirely different light as the source of increasing intoxication and alcoholism among Jews. The evidence supporting this latter view is sketchy. It consists largely of clinical impressions and a few statistics which suggest greater inebriety among relatively assimilated Jews. But little or nothing has been revealed of the conditions under which changes are induced in Jewish drinking behavior and attitude, or the actual role of ingroup-outgroup relations in the process.

It is apparent that several questions of fact must be answered before a general evaluation of the impact of the ingroup-outgroup situation on Jewish drinking behavior can be made. For example, can immediate social pressures from the outgroup be inferred from a difference in Jewish drinking behavior in ingroup and outgroup contexts? Are these pressures handled differently by various categories of Jews and, if so, why? Do Jews perceive social pressures regarding drinking in terms of ingroup and outgroup? Are these perceptions related to stereotypes of Jews and Gentiles which are part of the Jewish cultural tradition? If so, what is the nature of these stereotypes and what functions do they serve? Does the vitality of these stereotypes depend upon strong group identification and participation in other aspects of Jewish culture? Can the findings on these various points be woven together with evidence which indicates such a decided difference in the relative sobriety of Orthodox and non-Orthodox Jews? How then, is the significance of the ingroup-outgroup situation for Jewish drinking behavior to be assessed? These are the kind of questions which we will attempt to answer, if only in a preliminary way.

§ *Intoxication in Ingroup and Outgroup Contexts*

The question has been raised whether or not there is a difference in response to alcohol when Jews drink with members of the ingroup or in outgroup contexts. A behavioral difference in this respect should be indicative of the nature of ingroup and outgroup influences on Jewish sobriety. Suggestive evidence is to be found in the reports of our sample of New Haven Jewish men[5] on the social contexts in which episodes of intoxication occurred. Of course, pinning down all these contexts is an impossible task when respondents have been intoxicated frequently. Descriptions were actually obtained for only 40 per cent of the instances of intoxication reported by men in this sample. Of these instances, however, 60 per cent took place either in military service or in college, with military service predominating. It is not certain that the social composition of the drinking group was preponderantly Gentile in all instances of intoxication in the service or in college. But the answers of several men questioned on this point indicate that the companions were frequently non-Jewish. Moreover, of the seventeen in this group who had been intoxicated more than five times in their lives, twelve experienced some or all of the episodes of intoxication in the service or in college.[6] When it is borne in mind that drinking actually occurs more often in ingroup than outgroup contexts, the fact that a substantial proportion of intoxications occurs in outgroup contexts assumes considerable significance. Without obscuring occasional instances of intoxication in Jewish settings, as at a Bar Mitzvah or wedding, the evidence points to the influence of the larger Gentile society in modifying Jewish patterns of moderate drinking and sobriety.

Because many of the Jewish students in the College Drinking Survey (34) sample attended colleges where a plurality or substantial minority of the student body are Jews, military service probably represents a more extreme outgroup situation than does college for these students. Consequently, a comparison of the patterns of drinking and sobriety in veterans and nonveterans among the Jewish students should be indicative of ingroup-outgroup influence. A reflection of these influences is to be found in the fact that of those Jewish veterans who reported on the regularity or irregularity of their drinking patterns in military service, 65 per cent had had an irregular pattern as against 35 per cent with a regular pattern. Of course regularity or irregularity may mean many things, and there is no assurance from these data that Jewish students were more prone to intoxication while in the service. Subsequent questions on differences between current civilian drinking and practices while in the service revealed that 49 per cent of the veterans now drink less, 37 per cent about the same, and only 14 per cent more than while in the service. Still there is possible ambiguity in statements concerning "drinking more" or "drinking less," which may refer to frequency of drinking rather than to quantities consumed. But from what is known of Jewish interpretations of "drinking more" or "drinking less" there is little doubt that quantity was foremost in the minds of these students. Hence, a substantial proportion of Jewish veterans who reported drinking more in the service were almost certainly expressing an increase in the quantities of alcoholic beverages consumed in particular drinking situations and not just an increase in frequency of drinking.

The soundness of this interpretation is indicated by the fact that Jewish student veterans reported substantially higher frequencies of intoxication than nonveterans. On the one hand, only about a fourth of the nonveterans reported having been drunk twice or more, or tight more than five times. On the other hand, about half the veterans had exceeded these limits. Uncritical reliance on gross differences in intoxication between veterans and nonveterans, however, may be misleading. Veterans in college tend to be older than nonveterans and consequently have had more time to accumulate experiences of intoxication.[7] Age differences must therefore be taken into account before differences in intoxication among the Jewish students can be attributed to the service situation. To determine the effects of age differences, veterans and nonveterans were divided into two age classes (according to whether or not they were above or below the mean age for the sample of Jewish students) and were further classified by extent of intoxication. The resulting distribution is shown in Table 1 and it is clear that veterans in both age classes exceed nonveterans while differences by age are inconsequential.[8]

Table 1—Frequency of Mild Intoxication (Tight More than Five Times) in
Veterans and Nonveterans among Jewish Students,
by Age Classes (in Per Cent)

Age	Veterans	Number Reporting	Nonveterans	Number Reporting
21 or less	49	(29)	25	(336)
Over 21	54	(101)	24	(45)

The difference in extent of intoxication between the veterans and nonveterans is particularly noteworthy because it does not apply to college students as a whole. On the basis of their general study of drinking among college students, Straus and Bacon (34) concluded that there are no significant differences in intoxication between veterans and nonveterans when age differences are taken into account. This is not the case with Jewish students. Apparently military service is related to greater experience of intoxication while age difference is insignificant within the narrow age range of these students.

§ Social Pressures

More direct evidence of the differential influences of social environments on Jewish patterns of drinking and intoxication is contained in sections of the New Haven interviews. The seventy-three Jewish men in the

New Haven sample were asked whether they had been criticized for their drinking practices, either for "not drinking enough" or for "drinking too much." In reply, forty-one said they had felt criticism for not drinking enough, while only sixteen reported criticism for drinking too much. Forty-seven respondents identified the sources of these pressures. Analysis of the results (Table 2) indicates that Jewish men perceive the Jewish group as exerting pressures in the direction of moderate drinking and sobriety, while the non-Jewish milieu is perceived as the primary source of pressures to drink to excess.

Table 2—Sources of Social Pressures on New Haven Jewish Men To Drink More or Less

Pressure	Jewish	Mixed	Non-Jewish
To drink more	2	11	18
To drink less	15	1	0

Chi-square $= 35$, $P < .01$

The content and sources of the pressures summarized in Table 2 deserve further attention. With the exception of one case which is equivocal, all Jewish men who had been criticized for drinking too much reported the source of criticism as specifically Jewish and familial. "The folks used to think I drank a little too much," or "My wife doesn't like me to drink at all," were typical comments. By contrast, criticism for not drinking enough was confined almost exclusively to the categories of friends, acquaintances and business associates. Also, several men who reported criticism from mixed sources for not drinking enough added qualifications such as "mostly non-Jewish." Of the two men who reported exclusively Jewish criticism for not drinking enough, one said he was teased on Passover for just touching the wine to his lips, whereas the traditional rule calls for drinking the better part of four cups. The other indicated a jocular form of criticism from relatives—"We need lots of schnapps 'cause old X is here," hardly to be interpreted as an expectation that the respondent should actually drink larger amounts. Reactions to this kind of ingroup criticism are essentially humorous. But outgroup criticism of not drinking enough may evoke responses of moral indignation, resentment and resistance. Typical are reactions such as these: "They call me a sissy, but I don't care." "They try to get me to take more, but I never do." "It's just none of their business!"

These data are sufficiently unambiguous to permit some important inferences. In the first place, twice as much felt pressure to drink more was reported than to drink less. This suggests the covert nature of the social pressure on adults within the Jewish group and the implicit acceptance of the sobriety norm. But should overt social pressure be brought to bear on the individual by other Jews, it will more than likely be in the direction of moderate drinking and sobriety. This does not mean that Jewish men never find themselves in the position of refusing a drink offered by a Jewish host. However, such a situation would not ordinarily generate sufficient tension to leave an emotional residue which would be expressed as a feeling of social criticism. In the second place, a substantial number of Jewish men feel that the social milieu does bring pressure on them to drink more than they ordinarily drink. But these pressures are perceived as emanating primarily from the outgroup. In sharp contrast, the outgroup is seldom or never perceived as exerting explicit pressure toward moderate drinking and sobriety.

§ *Variations in Response to Outgroup Pressures*

In the light of the facts on the social sources of pressures to drink less moderately, the more frequent intoxication among Jews in military service and college can perhaps be understood as a response to outgroup pressures. Our New Haven data, however, indicates a decided absence of intoxication in the course of daily contacts with non-Jews within the community. This raises the question as to why Jewish men often yield to outgroup pressures in the service and in college, but only rarely in the course of ordinary events. Certainly intracommunity contacts between Jewish men and Gentiles are frequent and there is evidence in our interviews that drinking is sometimes involved in these situations. The interview materials also confirm that in these latter situations social pressures are often brought to bear on Jewish men to drink beyond the limits to which they are accustomed. Our view is that the solution of this problem hinges on the different types of socially structured situations and relations which arise between Jews and non-Jews within the community, in military service and in college.

1. SOBRIETY IN INTRACOMMUNITY RELATIONSHIPS. While supporting data cannot be presented in quantitative form, there is reason to believe that role and situation are more often instrumentally defined by Jewish men during intracommunity contacts with non-Jews than during military service or in college. There is also reason to believe that an instrumental definition of the situation helps to constrain the drinker from intoxication. If these assumptions are valid, constraints should be at a maximum where social pressures to drink more are experienced by Jews in the course of daily intracommunity relations with Gentiles.

The idea that an instrumental orientation exerts constraints in the drinking situation stems in part from Glad's (11) suggestions based on his comparative study of Jewish, Irish Catholic and Protestant attitudes toward drinking. Glad proposed that Jews tend to be oriented toward long-range goals in contrast to the Irish who are more concerned with proximate goals. Among Jews, recognition, achievement and understanding take precedence over proximate goals like warmth, friendliness, and concern for how people feel, which Glad believes are more valued by the Irish.

Glad therefore suggested that in most situations Jews drink as an incidental means to the achievement of the long-range goals, and that heightened concern with those goals necessitates constraint in the drinking situation. But lacking more refined measures of value emphases in these two cultures, such generalizations seem hazardous. Also, in Glad's construction there is some implication of indifference on the part of Jews to proximate goals such as warmth, friendliness and concern for the feelings of others, for which there is no factual basis. There would seem, however, to be factual justification for asserting a cleavage in Jewish life whereby the satisfaction of proximate goals is confined to relations with Jews, while the satisfaction of goals giving rise to an instrumental orientation is more characteristic of relations with Gentiles. Certainly in the eastern Europe of a few generations ago the expressive and affective life of Jews was of necessity, as well as voluntarily, restricted to family, ghetto and ethnic community. Relationships with Gentiles were largely defined by the Jews' precarious "middleman" role between nobility and peasant masses.[9] Concern with economic survival daily forced Jews out of the emotionally satisfying and protective ghetto, but in the capacity of "economic man." There was little approach to the cultivation of primary-group ties on the part of either Jews or Gentiles. Moreover, ethnic cleavage tends to persist in the modern American community, although in attenuated form.[10] In daily community life the affective and expressive relations of Jews are still to a large extent confined within the boundaries of family and ethnic group. Our New Haven data suggest that, by contrast, relations with non-Jews tend to be instrumentally defined; in intracommunity contacts with non-Jews, New Haven Jewish men are typically in business roles (sales and service and professional roles) characterized by functional specificity and affective neutrality. The situational goals are the contract, the sale, making a good impression, and the larger goals of money, recognition and status which these imply. In these situations, cognitive interests are given primacy. It is imperative "to be on one's toes" and "keep one's wits about one" in order to manipulate objects and persons in the situation to the desired end. Consequently, an element of renunciation and discipline is introduced; the individual feels pressure not to "give in" to modes of gratification like intoxication which disrupt cognitive processes and interfere with the achievement of larger objectives.[11]

Evidence of an instrumental structuring of relations with non-Jews and the constraints which this definition exerts on drinking was spontaneously given in the course of interviews with New Haven Jewish men. The following interview excerpts illustrate these points quite explicitly:

[Mr. X, a salesman, 50 years old:] I sell. I'm out on the road. I could get a drink in every home I go in. They're [non-Jews] always offering but I usually give them an excuse. I tell them I'm on doctor's orders not to drink. In that way I don't insult anyone. [At a later point in the interview:] I don't get to know my customers that well. You can't get too familiar with them or they start to take advantage of you. They want to treat you like one of the family but you have to draw the line.

[Mr. Y, 47 years old, an executive in the transportation field in a capacity which brings him into personal contact with a wide range of the firm's customers, largely non-Jewish:] When I do drink nowadays it's a question of entertaining business-wise, and "occasions." . . . When I'm entertaining [in business connections] I feel you've got to keep a certain amount of decorum. You're talking to people. After all, you're doing it for a purpose!

[Mr. Z, 60 years old, owner of a small building firm, states that he does a good deal of his drinking in "business" and with "business associates" who are predominantly non-Jewish. Under these circumstances, he says:] I'll do what the rest are doing. If they're having high-balls, I'll sit in and hold on to that glass for sociability. . . . A man shouldn't drink, but there are times a man has to drink. But the less you drink, the better. People shouldn't take more than two drinks on any occasion. Two drinks should be the limit. . . . I entertain a lot but that's not any personal expense. We buy liquor at Christmas and other times but that's business, not personal. With business associates, I'll go wherever they take me. I try to make them feel as pleasant as possible.

It would be erroneous to suppose that the instrumental orientation expressed in these excerpts is something distinctively Jewish. Obviously this attitude is required by many roles in society, occupied by Jews and non-Jews alike. It would be equally erroneous to imply that all intracommunity relations between Jews and Gentiles are instrumentally defined by Jews. In the modern American community, social contacts frequently arise between Jews and Gentiles which fall within the range of primary-group relations. However, in choosing intimate non-Jewish friends, Jews may avoid those who drink excessively and who might put pressure on them to do likewise. The following excerpt illustrates this process of selection where friendship alternatives are open:

My closest friends are Jewish [but] . . . my friendships have spread out in recent years to include many non-Jews. [He lives in a very mixed neighborhood. But he adds:] None of my friends are excessive drinkers!

What is important, however, is that an instrumental orientation may exert a constraining influence on intoxication among Jews at precisely the point where they are likely to be urged and pressed to drink in a hedonistic fashion, namely, in contact with Gentiles. It is also important that, while anxiety about the loss of cognitive orientation is evidently a deterrent to intoxication in these situations, the cognitive emphasis is in the nature of a means to other ends rather than an end in itself. There is no obvious relation between this emphasis and the general valuation of mental faculties deriving from the Jewish tradition of learning and study.

In considering Jewish resistance to pressures to drink excessively in the course of intracommunity contacts with non-Jews, the proximity of the Jewish family and Jewish community should not be forgotten. These, presumably, act as negative sanctions on intoxication. Stable relations with family and ethnic community may also strengthen the Jewish man's personal sense of Jewishness with which, as we shall try to show later, the concept of sobriety is intertwined. Indeed, as long as family and community sanctions are imminent and the sense of ethnic identification strong, outgroup pressures to drink more may intensify adherence to the sobriety norm. A stubborn feeling that "they [Gentiles] cannot break me" seems to be reflected in the remarks of several respondents, and an instrumentally structured role relationship would simply reinforce this resistance. Changes from norms of moderate drinking and sobriety should occur where emotional investment is shifted to the non-Jewish outgroup, where ingroup sanctions are no longer imminent and where an instrumental orientation no longer constrains. In circumstances of this kind, resistance to outgroup pressures may be expected to weaken. Anticipated is a tendency toward conformity with patterns of drinking or intoxication characteristic of the particular group or stratum with which the individual identifies.

2. INTOXICATION IN MILITARY SERVICE. These conditions for change are closely approximated in military service and to a lesser extent in college, and the facts suggest that Jews actually are more prone to intoxication in these contexts. However, data on the contexts of intoxication need to be supplemented by qualitative impressions before the impact on Jewish drinking behavior of situations like military service can be fully appreciated. In the service Jews are severed from the intimate milieus of family and community which support patterns of moderate drinking and sobriety. They are impelled by circumstances to make primary-group identification with non-Jews whose drinking patterns are at variance with their own. Conformity to norms of relatively heavy drinking is evidently often a condition of acceptance into these intimate, tightly knit primary groups which studies of army life (30) suggest are essential for the maintenance of individual morale. As one New Haven man expressed it:

> I started in the Army like a lot of others. No one in my old gang drank. I started drinking more in the Army with the attitude of trying to be one of the boys. [Actually this man drank frequently before entering the service. His reference is to hedonistic drinking.]

Moreover, military service not only disrupts normal social relations and routines but apparently often undermines instrumental, goal-directed activities. This tendency is reflected time and again in the assertion by Jewish men that they drank more in the service because there was nothing else to do. The following comment is not at all atypical:

> I drank more in the Army. There wasn't much else to do. When you were in town you went to bars with the Company. You'd sit and drink and listen to records. I usually get sick before I lose control but this completely excludes the Army. I guess I've passed out a few times, at that, in the Army.

Military service, too, is a context alien to the eastern European Jewish tradition and especially the Orthodox religious tradition.[12] A perusal of the reports of the New Haven Jewish men on their military experience often gives the impression that they were "fish out of water." General discomfiture, together with the disintegration of goal-directed activities and experience of social pressure, is clearly expressed in this case:

> I did a fair amount of drinking in the Army. Everytime we'd get a week-end pass we'd drink. Why? Didn't have a hell of a lot else to do. My buddies in the Army would criticize me [for not drinking enough]. You'd want to stay sober enough to get back to the truck, and they wouldn't care. They weren't Jewish— damned uncomfortable I was in the Army!

Sometimes military service appears to be an acutely anxiety-producing situation for Jewish men. Cut off from emotionally supportive relations with family and ethnic community and from the community of values which give daily routines and instrumental activities their meaning, some Jewish men become extremely anxious and confused. In isolated instances, alcohol was sought as a means of escape from an alien and distressing situation, as the following excerpt testifies:

> Two or three times in the Army I just went out, left camp, had a few drinks— from that point I don't remember until I got up the next morning. In the Army I was depressed and homesick. I went out and got drunk. They called it psychoneurosis. Then, I snapped out [after a medical discharge]. Didn't drink any more after that. [He means that he did not drink hedonistically subsequent to his military experience; he currently drinks alcohol about 125 times a year.]

However, acute loss of orientation and accompanying anxiety may be the exception rather than the rule. Perhaps more typically Jewish men drink heavily in military service to gain acceptance into Gentile primary groups toward which it is meaningless to assume an instrumental attitude and from which basic emotional supports are sought because there is no alternative. . . .

3. RESPONSE OF DIFFERENT RELIGIOUS CATEGORIES. Is there a marked difference among Jews of different religious affiliation in response to the situational pressures to drink immoderately which arise in military service? Different responses to the same situational pressures might indicate varying intensities of inner sentiments supporting Jewish norms of moderate drinking and sobriety. Similarities, while not vitiating the role of inner attitudes, would certainly point to the importance of the social environment in sustaining or modifying these norms. Unfortunately our

Table 3—Frequency of Intoxication (Drunk Twice or More) in Veterans and Nonveterans among Jewish Students, by Nominal Religious Affiliation (in Per Cent)

	Veterans	Number Reporting	Nonveterans	Number Reporting
Orthodox and Conservative	33	(15)	12	(125)
Reform and Secular	62	(21)	35	(89)

New Haven data are insufficient to permit refined conclusions on these points and the small number of Orthodox veterans in the student sample seriously limits the possibilities of generalization. Clues are nonetheless forthcoming from the data in Table 3 on the extent of intoxication of veterans and nonveterans among the Conservative and Orthodox combined in a single category, and the Reform and Secular, likewise combined. Although significant differences appear between these religious categories irrespective of veteran status, there is also significantly more intoxication among veterans when religion is held constant.[13] While insufficient to nullify differences between more and less Orthodox Jews, the service situation evidently exerts a powerful influence towards heavier drinking which is responded to by all the religious categories.

The burden of the evidence appears to be that the internalization of norms and ideas antithetical to hedonistic drinking is often insufficient to sustain patterns of moderate drinking and sobriety in the face of strong situational counterpressures, such as those which arise in military service. Evidently, conscience alone cannot guarantee conformity to behavioral patterns which are at variance with primary-group norms. The moral consensus of the primary group appears to be a potent factor determining the character of the individual's drinking behavior. The obverse implication of an increase in intoxication in the service is, of course, the overwhelming importance to Jewish sobriety of regular participation in a Jewish milieu which supports norms of moderate drinking and sobriety. Where the sober dictates of individual conscience and primary-group consensus are in harmony, as in the Orthodox religious community, the likelihood of continued sobriety would appear to be greatest despite extensive drinking.

4. INSULATION OF ORTHODOX JEWS FROM OUTGROUP PRESSURES. The data in this section also point to an important latent function of the broader religious complex in sustaining Jewish norms of moderate drinking and sobriety. Orthodox norms circumscribe the social life of observant Jews so as to minimize the emergence of close, primary-group relations with Gentiles. This is readily apparent in the prohibition on intermarriage, in dietary restrictions, and the like. But no less important is the totality of norms which channel the Jew's emotional and expressive life within the confines of the Jewish community.[14] By curtailing the development of primary-group ties with non-Jews, Orthodox Judaism insulates its adherents from outgroup pressures to drink immoderately. Orthodoxy does not do away entirely with social contacts between Jews and Gentiles. Thus mere social contact with Gentiles is hardly a cause of intoxication among Jews. But Orthodox Judaism tends to narrow the bases of Jews' contacts with outsiders largely to the economic area where instrumental attitudes predominate. The effects of this circumscription are twofold. On the one hand, the potential influence of primary-group relations with non-Jews in modifying drinking behavior is mitigated. On the other hand, the structure of the permitted role relationship may itself induce additional constraints in the drinking situation.

The observant Jew is thus doubly protected from outside pressures to drink hedonistically, while within the confines of the Orthodox community consensus supports sobriety and the act of drinking is ritually controlled. With the continuation of ethnic cleavage but a decline in religious motives for drinking, the instrumental drinking described by Glad (11) is perhaps becoming more important to Jews. Accordingly, continued separatism and the value complex from which instrumental attitudes derive may represent a second line of defense against intoxication. But where the insulating function of Judaism disintegrates and instrumental orientation is disrupted, moderate drinking and sobriety apparently often give way to convivial and hedonistic drinking.

§ *Ethnocentrism and Jewish Sobriety*

All of this leads us to juxtapose two sets of facts. First, as shown elsewhere (31), strong moral condemnation of intoxication is prevalent among the more Orthodox Jews; second, as we have seen, Jews associate social pressures toward moderate drinking with the ingroup and toward "more" drinking with the outgroup. Actually, these ideas and sentiments are indicative of underlying cultural stereotypes of sober Jew and drunken Gentile and of the incorporation of sobriety in the ethnocentrism of the Jewish group. The exact character and prevalence of the stereotype, as well as the forces maintaining or modifying it all constitute subjects which are of some consequence in the study of Jewish sobriety.

1. STEREOTYPES OF SOBER JEW AND DRUNKEN GENTILE. The elucidation of Jewish stereotypes can be started by considering the responses of Jewish men to questions pertaining to beliefs about Jewish and Gentile drinking practices. In the New Haven interviews, the Jewish respondents were directly asked whether they thought Jews drink more, less or about the same as Gentiles. On the basis of responses to these questions, it may be concluded that the prevailing belief is that Jews drink less than non-Jews. Of the sample of 73 men, 54 asserted this to be the case. Not a single man asserted that Jews drink more than non-Jews and only 7 felt that Jews and non-Jews drink about the same, while the remaining 12 refused to offer a definite opinion on this point. In questioning respondents, no attempt was made to specify whether "more" or "less" referred to the incidence of drinking, frequency of drinking or amounts consumed. Where respondents made assertions about the simple incidence and frequency of drinking among Jews and Gentiles, these were usually consistent with their beliefs about drinking to excess. In other words, it was implied that the incidence and frequency of drinking among non-Jews is greater than among Jews, which is by no means necessarily the case.

It must be observed at once that questions about drinking among Jews and non-Jews induced considerable conflict in respect to particularistic and universalistic values. A few excerpts from the interview records will illustrate the nature of the competing values:

Definitely [Jews drink less], but I can't think in those terms.

I don't see any reason why they [the Jews] should be any different from anyone else.

I think everybody should drink less than they do.

I didn't study it. I'm not looking into it. There are all kinds of fish in the sea.

Give me half a minute to think. I'm an authority? Jews are a minority. There are fewer Jews. I think they're about the same. I think the Irish drink more than Italians. Poles drink. Jews are human. Jewish peddlers used to drink when they were cold. Jews shouldn't be an exception. They're no chosen people.

That may be just prejudice. I don't like to make general statements.

I'd hate to say. Most of my friends, Jews and non-Jews, drink about like I do. Hard to tell, it's up to the individual.

There's an old saying among Jews of my class—my father has an old theory that Jews drink less than Christians. It's hard to say. It might be so. I don't mean this with a racial bias, it just might be that Jews drink less.

That's something I wouldn't say, I couldn't say, but I think they do [drink] less. There are very few drunkards among the Jewish race.

I don't think it has anything to do with nationality. I don't want to bring it in. If Christians were raised in a non-drinking environment they wouldn't either.

Well, I don't think necessarily less—they—I think you can base it on occupation, on per cent. There's more Gentiles patronizing taverns, grilles, etc., than Jews.

These examples are sufficient to show that, while the prevailing Jewish belief is that excessive drinking is a Gentile characteristic, there are strong competing values which make it difficult for many Jews to admit discussion of the matter in these terms. The conflict between universalism and particularism is nothing new in Jewish culture. It has been the fundamental paradox of normative Judaism since ancient times.[15] In all probability the protracted minority status of the Jews has sensitized them to this value conflict and current democratic ideologies have reinforced the universalistic side of the coin. Time and again the themes that "we're all human," and "it's up to the individual," and "these things are not racial or nationality matters" are to be found alongside statements of a highly particularistic and ethnocentric nature in the interviews.

In the historical experience of the Jews in Europe, there was probably considerable objective basis for Jewish beliefs about excessive drinking among Gentiles. At least historians of Jewish life in eastern Europe, such as Dubnow (7), relate that the Gentile peasantry became intoxicated with tiresome regularity. In America, where there are many millions of abstainers, the objectivity of these Jewish beliefs is open to some question, although abstinence sentiment is most apparent in rural areas while American Jews are predominantly urban.[16] What is sociologically significant, however, is not the objective truth or falsehood of these beliefs but whether or not they are believed. As Thomas and Thomas (36) observed, "If men define situations as real, they are real in their consequences." Of further significance is the question as to whether or not Jewish beliefs about drink-

ing among Jews and Gentiles are linked with basic moral ideas and sentiments. The problem is whether or not these beliefs reflect concepts of
ethnic virtue whose emotional importance is magnified by reference to
opposite characteristics in outsiders.

In an effort to probe deeper into this problem, the New Haven Jewish
men were asked whether they had the idea in childhood that sobriety was
a Jewish virtue, drunkenness a Gentile vice.[17] In response to this question,
twenty-seven of the seventy-three men answered yes, thirty-eight answered
no, and eight said they did not remember or could not answer. Taken at
face value, these findings seem partially to contradict the results and inferences from the more matter-of-fact question as to whether Jews drink
more or less than non-Jews. But in the face of further evidence the
apparent contradiction fades away. Later in the interview, Jewish men
were asked whether or not they were familiar in childhood with stories,
songs, poems or sayings which suggested sobriety as a Jewish virtue,
drunkenness as a Gentile vice. As an example, the little ditty "Shikker
iz a Goy" (Drunken is a Gentile) was frequently cited. Despite the logical
inconsistency, responses to this question reversed the trend of answers to
the previous question on sobriety as a Jewish virtue, drunkenness as a
Gentile vice. A majority of forty-eight men answered that they were familiar as children with such folk beliefs, only seventeen replied that they
were not, while eight said either that they did not remember or could not
answer.

The increase in affirmative answers to the second of these two questions
is associated with the relinquishment by some Jewish men of universalistic
attitudes in the interview situation. This turnabout accompanied the respondent's recognition that the interviewer knew the prevailing folk beliefs and that it was therefore no longer necessary to conceal ethnocentric
ideas behind a universalistic front.* This process of relaxation in the interview situation may be illustrated by some examples. One elderly man who
said that Jews and Gentiles drink "about the same" asserted later that
drunkenness is "more a Gentile characteristic," although he felt obliged
to qualify this by the phrase, "in a way." When the interviewer subsequently inquired whether he knew "Shikker iz a Goy," he was surprised
and delighted, and insisted on singing the entire song, as well as some
other ditties of similar import, for the interviewer's benefit. In another
case the respondent tenaciously denied awareness of any differences between Jews and Gentiles. At the mention of the song "Shikker iz a Goy,"
however, he exclaimed, "Say, you must have really studied this!" and went
on to say that he had long been familiar with these notions. Nevertheless,

---

* Interviewers were both Jewish and non-Jewish; the majority of the interviews
were conducted by non-Jews. Whatever the interviewer's identity, this was only revealed
if the interviewee specifically asked about it. Because the leading non-Jewish interviewer
had a name which could be taken as "Jewish," many respondents tended to assume that
he was a Jew.

some Jewish men were either reluctant or refused to give up their universalistic attitude. Moreover, the insistent qualification that "they [the folk beliefs] didn't leave any impression on me" was often heard. In one interview, a relative of the respondent happened to be present when the interviewer mentioned "Shikker iz a Goy." The respondent, who had answered in the negative to the preceding question on the imputation of drunkenness to Gentiles, just shook his head: "Never heard of it!" At this his relative remarked, in amused astonishment, "Aw, come on—everybody knows that! Why, mother used to sing me to sleep with it when I was a baby!" The respondent smiled a bit sheepishly but continued shaking his head, indicating with a wave of his hand that he was ready for the next question.

The qualitative import of Jewish stereotypes could easily be lost among statistics and anecdotes. Thus it may be well to give the content of the little song, "Shikker iz a Goy," which has been translated from the Yiddish as follows:

> The Gentile goes into the saloon, the saloon,
> And drinks there a small glass of wine;
> he tosses it off—his glass of wine.
> Oh—the Gentile is a Drunkard—a drunkard he is,
> Drink he must,
> Because he is a Gentile!
>
> The Gentile comes into our alley, our little street,
> And breaks the windows of us poor Jews;
>   our windowpanes are broken out,
> For—the Gentile is a Drunkard—a drunkard he is,
> Drink he must,
> Because he is a Gentile!
>
> The Jew hurries into the place of prayer;
> An evening prayer, a short benediction he says,
>   and a prayer for his dead.
> For—the Jew is a sober man—sober is he,
> Pray he must,
> Because he is a Jew.[18]

It would be an exaggeration to impute great historical or educational significance to this song itself. It evidently originated in the Russian ghettos and is unquestionably not known to many Jews. However, the linkage of sobriety with Jewish identity, drunkenness with Gentile identity is so explicit that it seems doubtful that such a ditty could gain much currency unless it were congruent with generally held Jewish concepts and values. Moreover, the ideas expressed in "Shikker iz a Goy" are quite consistent with Clark's (5) recent satirical "Portrait of the Mythical Gentile," an attempt to depict the essence of current Jewish stereotypes of Gentiles. As his opening remark, under the heading "Gentile Appetites," Clark characterizes prevailing Jewish beliefs as follows:

All Gentiles are drunkards. They have not only debauched themselves, but have made drunkards of many Jews. The Gentile drinks enormously, but without savor, being insensitive to vintage and admixture.

The substance of these findings is that sobriety has been incorporated into the ethnocentrism of the Jewish group. In his classic discussion Sumner (35) pointed out that the principal function of ethnocentrism is the clarification and intensification of a group's norms and sentiments through the magnification of their opposites as characteristic of disliked or hated outsiders. Following Sumner's reasoning, stereotypes among Jews of sobriety and drunkenness in terms of Jew and Gentile clarify sobriety as "our way" and intensify the emotional sentiments supporting it with broader feelings for things Jewish as opposed to things which are not.

Sumner, however, referred in his discussion of ethnocentrism to a relatively undifferentiated "primitive society" and probably presupposed a solidarity which cannot be taken for granted in the heterogeneous nominal Jewish group of today. The influence of Jewish stereotypes as a deterrent to intoxication may well depend upon the vitality of a larger network of ethnocentric ideas and sentiments which are not equally distributed among nominal Jews. In the minds of many Jews beliefs that Gentiles drink more than Jews may be propositions which have little or no relevance apart from their objective status as true or false.[19] Before such beliefs can regulate drinking behavior through the dictates of conscience and social sanction they must be imbued with emotional value and moral significance. Whether or not reinforcement for a norm of sobriety stems from Jewish stereotypes would seem to depend on the kinds of ideas and sentiments which are more generally mobilized by the symbols of ingroup and outgroup—Jew and Gentile. To touch on the implications of this problem requires more extended discussion of the probable role of ceremonial Judaism in giving definition and emotional support to Jewish group symbols, ethnocentric norms and ideas.

2. SIGNIFICANCE OF THE ORTHODOX DEFINITION OF THE JEWISH SITUATION. The ceremonial observances of Orthodox Judaism are interlaced with a system of basic religious ideas which, while universal in much of their ethical import, are nevertheless ethnocentric in character. It is the basic ethnocentric ideas of traditional Judaism which in large measure define the situation of the religious Jew in society at large. These premises define the Orthodox Jew's position vis-à-vis the criticism and hostility of the wider society, which have been referred to extensively in the literature on Jewish drinking behavior, as well as toward its attractions. Our supposition is that stereotypes of sober Jew and drunken Gentile take on emotional connotations which reinforce a pattern of sobriety through association with these broader ethnocentric ideas and supporting sentiments.

While Orthodox Judaism has no monopoly on ethnocentrism, the ethnocentric concepts of traditional Judaism are not to be understood solely as a defensive reaction to discrimination and rejection by society. Ortho-

dox Judaism has made capital of the ingroup-outgroup situation. The
Orthodox view presupposes a special and sacred covenant of the Jews
with God. Much of the message of the Scriptures is devoted to the ideas
that the Jews are chosen, separate and sacred, with a special mission and
purpose in this world. Orthodox injunctions set apart and insulate Jews
from profane contact with outsiders. Tradition exhorts the pious Jew to
exemplify the superiority of Judaism and belief in the one true God by
strict conformity to the Law (the Torah). Orthodox Jews know that there
will be censure and retaliation from outsiders and catastrophe in this life.
This is interpreted, in accordance with Biblical concepts, as the instrument
of God's judgment for failure to live up to the dictates of the religion.[20]
The traditional Jewish point of view, together with its general social implications, is well expressed by Moore (23) as follows:

> God "hallows his Name" (makes it holy), therefore, by doing things that
> lead or constrain men to acknowledge Him as God. And as it is God's supreme
> end that all mankind shall ultimately own and serve him as the true God, so it is
> the chief end of Israel, to whom he has in a unique manner revealed himself,
> to hallow His name by living so that men shall see that the God of Israel is
> the true God. This is the meaning of the kiddush-ha-shem, the hallowing of the
> Name. . . . The opposite of the hallowing of the Name is the profanation of
> the Name (hillul-ha-shem). It includes every act or word of a Jew which
> disgraces his religion and so reflects dishonor upon God. The world judges
> religions by the lives of those who profess them—the tree by its fruits. It was
> thus that the Jews judged other religions; the vices of the heathen prove the
> nullity of the religions which tolerated such behavior, and even encouraged it
> by the examples of their gods. A favorite topic of Jewish apologetics was the
> superiority of Jewish morals, not merely in precept but in practice, and they
> argued from it the superiority of their religion, thus inviting a retaliation which
> the heathen world let them experience in full measure. Individuals, sects, re-
> ligions, which profess to be better than others must always expect to have their
> conduct observed with peculiar scrutiny and censured with peculiar severity.

The sociological significance of this passage is that in the total context
of ingroup-outgroup relations the pious Jew feels a generalized pressure
or motivation to live in accordance with the dictates of his religion—a pressure which arises in part from his own ethnocentric assumptions.

In some respects, Moore's conclusions as to the principal motive to
moral conduct in Judaism parallel Kant's explanation of Jewish motives
for sobriety. As between these eminent thinkers, however, there is a difference in emphasis which is pertinent here. Kant mentions the ideas of
"chosenness" but he stresses the "outward worth" of the Jew, based on the
belief of others in his "separatistic lore." He seems to imply that it is
simply a concern for status or worth in the eyes of outsiders which motivates Jews to reserve. Then Kant's argument takes an ambiguous turn. He
writes of the Jews' fear of "intoxication which deprives one of caution" in
apposition with outgroup censure and criticism. Kant's remarks thus become open to two kinds of dubious interpretation.

The first doubtful line of reasoning is that the individual Jew or the

Jewish group has experienced, and consequently eschews (or, on the basis of experience realistically anticipates and therefore eschews) direct criticism, censure or retaliation from Gentiles while in a state of intoxication or for achieving such a state.[21] The evidence that has been presented here on the character and sources of direct ingroup and outgroup pressures in respect to drinking, as well as on Jewish responses to and perception of these pressures, makes it difficult to sustain such an interpretation.

The second and subtler line of reasoning appears in the writings of Haggard and Jellinek (13) as follows:

> The most reasonable of these explanations [of Jewish sobriety] seems to be the one given by Kant, who thought that the Jews, forming isolated groups within other nations and being exposed to constant censure, must avoid, in the interests of racial welfare, anything that would make them conspicuous. Their temperate use of alcohol is an unconscious defense against the censure of their race.

How the avoidance of conspicuousness in the eyes of others could be a criterion for the selection and perpetuation of Jewish norms, including the temperate use of alcohol, is difficult to see. The bulk of Orthodox Jewish observances are conspicuous to many Gentiles. Indeed, to staunch anti-Semites the totality of Judaism is conspicuous, and it is to be doubted that the devout Jew who observes his Sabbath is blissfully unaware of the situation. As for the standard of "interests of racial welfare" to which Haggard and Jellinek allude, if this refers to individual or group wisdom of an essentially prudential character or to a standard *ex post facto* imposed upon the group by an observer, it is of doubtful value in explaining Jewish sobriety. But if it means that ideas of welfare are associated with temperance in drinking among Jews, we can only agree, with the proviso that they are probably associated also with the "intemperate" use of alcohol by certain other groups. The attachment of the idea of group welfare to particular ways is, of course, exactly what Sumner (35) considered to be the common or defining characteristic of the mores. However, what is or is not imbued with the idea of welfare by Orthodox Jews is not determined by the avoidance of conspicuousness.[22] Jews might indeed have appeared less conspicuous to many Gentiles had they been more prone to drunkenness, their very sobriety being a point of differentiation, at least in their own eyes.[23] Nor does the fact that hedonistic drinking and intoxication are officially censured in Christianity, as well as in Judaism, mean that a striving to live up to Christian norms is the motive for Jewish sobriety. Adherence to traditional Judaism is certainly intimately bound up with ideas of group welfare, and in the Orthodox view welfare in turn is indicated by the status of relations with outsiders. But what is welfare to Orthodox Jews—that is, what ways of behavior are imbued with the element of welfare—is primarily determined by the Law and the criterion of conformity to the Law, whose norms are defined as fixed and immutable, revealed by God and embodied in tradition.[24] Acts which are believed to threaten welfare are above all acts which deviate from and negate the ingroup religious code, the more so if they do so conspicuously in the eyes of both Jews and Gentiles. The importance of this emphasis, as opposed to a general Jewish need to avoid conspicuousness in the interests of racial welfare, is that it leads to different predictions as to the behavior of religious and irreligious Jews in the face of outgroup censure and criticism.

These considerations lead, then, to a third interpretation latent in Kant's argument, which becomes clear in conjunction with the passage from Moore, cited above. Moore in no way detracts from the importance of outsiders as a source and reference for the Jew's moral judgments of behavior and as a stimulus to conformity with ingroup norms. But where Kant fails to be explicit, Moore emphasizes the basic idea of moral superiority in Judaism which gives the pious Jew a sense of inner worth or dignity in being Jewish. The principles of the hallowing and profaning of the Name derive their power to motivate moral conduct among Jews in a hostile environment from the initial premise of moral superiority. Theoretically, the enhanced motivation to conformity with Jewish norms is a resultant of the interaction of the fundamental ethnocentric idea together with the censure and hostility of outsiders. In this view, the Jew who is deeply committed to the premise of Jewish moral superiority simply intensifies conformity to his own distinctive cultural norms in the face of outgroup pressure and criticism. He intensifies also his scrutiny of the moral conduct of fellow-Jews in the light of Jewish norms. In association with these ethnocentric ideas and relations of hostility with outsiders, cultural definitions of sobriety as a Jewish virtue, drunkenness as a Gentile vice, should enhance motivation to conform to Jewish norms of moderate drinking and sobriety.[25]

3. CEREMONIAL PARTICIPATION AND THE MOBILIZATION OF SENTIMENTS IN SUPPORT OF GROUP SYMBOLS AND ETHNOCENTRIC IDEAS. The character of Jewish response to outgroup censure would seem, however, to be determined by the intensity of sentiments supporting basic ethnocentric ideas. Lacking belief and emotional conviction as to their own moral worth in being Jewish, many Jews may tend more toward conformity with wider societal norms when faced with outgroup criticism and censure. Evidently this is what Sartre (29) means when he says: "What stamps the inauthentic Jew is precisely this perpetual oscillation between pride and a sense of inferiority, between the voluntary and passionate negation of the traits of his race and the mystic and carnal participation in the Jewish reality." But given the sense of inner worth and value in Jewishness, Jews may simply emphasize those aspects of behavior, including sobriety, which are culturally defined as distinctively Jewish. A basic problem is thus how the symbols of Jewishness come to command the moral sentiments so as to sustain the sense of inner worth and motivate conformity to Jewish ideals.

It is our own hypothesis that, more than any other feature of Jewish life, participation in the ceremonials and rituals of Orthodox Judaism fosters the sense of inner worth together with ethnocentric ideas and moral sentiments. Theoretically, ceremonial and ritual are especially effective because of the particularly strong internalization of group symbols, norms and ideas which takes place through this kind of activity. As Durkheim (8) observed, the social functions of ceremonial and ritual have to do primarily with the maintenance of group solidarity and the integration of group symbols, norms and ideas with supporting emotions or sentiments.[26] According to Durkheim, ceremonial and ritual are everywhere accompanied by sacred as opposed to utilitarian attitudes, and characteristic sentiments of reverence and respect. Durkheim ultimately identified these sentiments with veneration for the authority of society itself rather than with the intrinsic properties of the sacred symbols, objects or states of nature they are assumed to represent, as had earlier writers. He perceived, however, that the connection of norms and ideas with supporting sentiments of solidarity and moral authority is achieved through the use of collective symbols (and particularly the major symbols of the authority of the group itself) in the context of ceremonial activity. In Orthodox Jewish ceremonial and ritual the sacred symbols of God are endlessly reiterated and so also are the various symbols of the Jewish group itself. Through ceremonial participation Jews reenact their solidarity with the group and renew their contact with the overwhelming symbols of its moral authority. The familistic character of many ceremonies also dramatizes and reinforces the system of authority in the family, integrating "concrete" or "real" authority with the "abstract" symbolism of the moral community. There is no need here for a detailed exposition of this symbolism. What is pertinent is simply that the symbols of the moral community are prominent and that the internalization of these symbols (that is, their connection with the sentiments of solidarity and moral authority) is enhanced through ceremonial and ritual activity. From this point of view Jewish ceremonial and ritual patterns are conceived of as more than forms for the expression of religious ideas and sentiments. They are also a mechanism which transmits and sustains basic Jewish cultural values. Presumably ceremonial observance strengthens the value of Jewishness, as well as the moral sentiments which group symbols command. We believe, too, that ceremonial participation, or socialization within this tradition, facilitates the internalization of the Orthodox definition of the Jewish situation in relation to the larger society. Theoretically, then, stereotypes of sober Jew and drunken Gentile should elicit the most powerful moral sentiments supporting a norm of sobriety among more observant Jews, while participation in ceremonial and ritual should enhance motivation to conform to this norm in the context of tense ingroup-outgroup relations.

4. EFFECTS OF CEREMONIAL PARTICIPATION ON THE INTENSITY OF SENTIMENTS SUPPORTING ETHNOCENTRIC MARRIAGE NORMS. There are no data

by which to test directly the extent to which stereotypes of sober Jew and drunken Gentile activate sentiments which support norms of moderate drinking and sobriety among Jews. Nor can the precise relationships between ceremonial observance and the mobilization of these sentiments be determined. Actually, all the evidence on reduced condemnation of drunkenness and increased intoxication with declining Orthodoxy is consistent with the point of view set forth above. The problem is that declining Orthodoxy also correlates with changes in other aspects of Jewish culture —such as ceremonial drinking—aspects which may independently contribute emotional support to norms of moderate drinking and sobriety. Hence, it is exceedingly difficult to isolate the specific contribution of ethnocentric ideas and sentiments.

A partial resolution of this dilemma lies in the demonstration that sentiments supporting ethnocentric ideas are strongest among the more ceremonially Orthodox in respect to behaviors unrelated to drinking and intoxication. In this connection, data on marriage preferences from our New Haven study are highly suggestive. The intensity of sentiments opposing marriage between Jews and Gentiles is probably an especially good index of commitment to broader ethnocentric ideas because intermarriage so obviously threatens the integrity of the Jewish moral community.[27] Ordinarily, students of acculturation and assimilation pay particular attention to ethnic behaviors and attitudes regarding intermarriage on the assumption that these data reflect the continued solidarity or dissolution of the group. Available statistics (3) indicate a high rate of inmarriage among Jews, although the rate of intermarriage has fluctuated widely in different times and places, reaching a recent peak in pre-Nazi Germany, where Orthodox Judaism was in relative decline. Statistics gathered in New Haven (19) suggest that intermarriages are less than 10 per cent of all Jewish marriages. The data from the New Haven interviews show also that Jewish men, irrespective of ceremonial observance, share the belief that Jews should marry Jews rather than Gentiles. Our immediate concern, however, is not with intermarriage rates as such. It is rather with the strength or intensity of sentiments supporting the belief that inmarriage is desirable, as these may relate to ceremonial observance. Our hypothesis is simply that the intensity of sentiments supporting this ethnocentric belief among Jews diminishes with declining ceremonial observance.

In the New Haven interviews a series of questions put before the Jewish men were designed to elicit the relative intensity of sentiments supporting the inmarriage norm. The respondents were first asked to assume that they had a son of marriageable age who had met a congenial girl with whom he had common interests. They were then presented with five hypothetical situations and requested to indicate the degree of their preference for a girl of either Jewish or Protestant origin (although not necessarily religiously observant in either case). In each situation a value conflict was introduced by associating the Jewish girl with an undesirable personal or social characteristic while the Protestant girl was described as socially and personally desirable. Preferences in each situation were recorded on a four-point check list of intensity, as follows:

1. I would much prefer her to be Jewish even if she . . . (the particular undesirable characteristic).
2. I probably would prefer her to be Jewish even if she . . . (the particular undesirable characteristic).
3. I probably would prefer she not . . . (have the undesirable characteristic) than that she be Jewish.
4. I would much prefer she not . . . (have the undesirable characteristic) than that she be Jewish.

Responses to each question were scored 1, 2, 3 or 4 (a score of 1 being the strongest preference for Jewishness) and the scores on the five questions were summed into an index of intensity of sentiments.[28] The minimum score of five, therefore, indicates the strongest preference for Jewishness. A maximum score of 20 would indicate strongest preference for a Protestant girl in the face of the undesirable characteristics associated with the Jewish girl. The mean and median scores of the 58 men who gave adequate informaiton on all five questions were 8.2 and 8.0, respectively. Theoretically, a neutral score would be 12.5. Thus the central tendency of the sample is in favor of marriage with the Jewish girl despite her undesirable characteristics.

The hypothesis that ethnocentric sentiments are strongest among the ceremonially more observant was tested by constructing two categories of strong and weak sentiments and comparing the distribution of the Jewish men in these categories according to degree of ceremonial Orthodoxy.[29] Men with index scores of 8 or less (i.e., below the mean) are considered to have "strong sentiments" favoring inmarriage, while those with scores above 8 are considered to have "weak sentiments" in support of this norm. It is clear from Table 4 that the intensity of sentiments supporting an ethnocentric marriage norm progressively weakens with declining ceremonial observance. . . .[30]

Table 4—Intensity of Sentiments Supporting Ethnocentric Marriage Norms among New Haven Jewish Men, by Degree of Ceremonial Orthodoxy

	Strong Sentiments	Weak Sentiments
Most Orthodox	9	3
Intermediate	18	11
Least Orthodox	3	12

There is not a one to one correspondence between relatively high frequencies of intoxication and high scores on the index (indicating weak ethnocentric sentiment). Some Jewish men with high scores have seldom or never been intoxicated. However, of the men reporting on marriage preferences who had been intoxicated more than five times in their lives, seven had scores of 10 or more on the index while only four had scores below 10. These findings suggest that a weakening of ethnocentric sentiments, although not in itself productive of intoxication, may be among the necessary conditions for increasing intoxication among Jews.

More generally, the findings suggest that the relative value of Jewishness is enhanced by ceremonial observance and that the sentiments supporting ethnocentric ideas are stronger among ceremonially Orthodox Jews. It is plausible to infer from these facts that the imagery of sobriety as a Jewish virtue, drunkenness as a Gentile vice, elicits strong moral sentiments in support of norms of moderate drinking and sobriety through association with a broader network of ethnocentric ideas and sentiments which are deeply internalized in the personalities of the more Orthodox Jews. As ceremonial observance wanes, however, stereotypes of sober Jew and drunken Gentile may lose their power to mobilize and reinforce emotions supporting these norms because the symbols of Jewishness lose the inner emotional significance achieved through ceremonial participation. Just as the sentiments supporting ethnocentric Jewish ideas about marriage lose their intensity, so, we suggest, do sentiments elicited by stereotypes of sober Jew and drunken Gentile, and for essentially the same reasons.

5. EVALUATION OF THE ROLE OF GROUP STEREOTYPES. With these concepts in mind, we may essay a more general evaluation of the role which stereotypes of sober Jew and drunken Gentile may play in Jewish sobriety in conjunction with the Orthodox definition of the situation and relations of hostility with outsiders.

To the religious Jew sobriety is a Jewish virtue. It is a measure of the Jew's worth, not directly in the eyes of Gentiles, who are reputedly prone to drunkenness, but in his own eyes and in the eyes of members of his group. Sobriety is a standard, among others, by which the degree of fulfillment of obligations to God and to the Jewish religious community may be determined. To the pious Jew intoxication is antithetical to the dictates of his religion. It is incompatible with the performance of daily rituals which demand consciousness, caution, self-control and discipline lest the Name be profaned. The religiously observant Jew has ritualized the use of beverage alcohol; he has brought drinking within the sphere of the most powerful social controls and moral sentiments. As Kant suggested, intoxication does deprive one of caution and it is linked in the mind of the devout Jew with loss of self-control and the commission of any number of acts which may be profane, unclean, aggressive, sexual, and otherwise improper in nature. For the religious Jew retaliation from the outgroup is inseparably connected, symbolically, with all relaxation of moral standards and religious discipline. Tensions between ingroup and outgroup therefore provide a tremendous rationale and motive for applying negative social sanctions to intoxication and for creating an atmosphere in which sobriety is expected of all.[31]

Beyond this, to the Jew who takes pride in his religion, intoxication and the drunkard are symbols of outgroup moral degeneracy and targets for scorn and derision. In the imagery of the group, to be a drunkard is to profane oneself, to become like the irresponsible Gentile. The hypothetical sanction is extirpation. Among the strictly observant, Jews who outmarry are considered dead. Funeral ceremonies are held and future contacts with the defectors are taboo. Similarly, in the symbolism of the group, intoxication and the drunkard are identified with ceasing to be a Jew. In this context the implications of a well-known Jewish folk saying become clear: "A Yid a Shikker, zoll geharget veren!" [A Jew who's a drunkard, may he get killed!] It is not just that the Jewish drunkard may expect to be or will be killed by a hostile outgroup; he deserves death!

The imagery of sobriety as a Jewish virtue, in sharp contrast to the sinful drunkenness of Gentiles, has further implications once the Orthodox Jewish definition of outgroup retaliation as punishment for the relaxation of religious discipline is taken into account. Through this system of ideas hedonistic drinking and intoxication become connected with all the realistic and imaginary anxieties and fears of extreme punishment from Gentiles which are so manifestly present in the Jewish group. Acute intoxication may thus symbolize more dramatically than other modes of deviant behavior a state of helplessness and vulnerability which cannot be offset through the exercise of that self-control and moral discipline which Judaism enjoins. The obverse of this situation is the fear of releasing all the aggressive and retaliatory impulses which are relentlessly checked by the Orthodox religion and the exigencies of a powerless minority status. Consequently, the counteranxieties elicited by the very idea of intoxication may be extraordinarily powerful.

It may be suggested, however, that with declining ceremonial and ritual observance the sentiments associated with beliefs about sober Jews and drunken Gentiles tend to wane. Powerful group symbols lose emotional support. The "outer" moral authority of Jewishness and its correlate of inner worth lose significance, while anxieties about retaliation and the expression of aggression are lessened along with the relaxation of Jewish moral standards and religious discipline. To individual Jews the cognitive and emotional meaning of these ideas derives from a broader context of identification with Judaism. It is worth reemphasizing that this identification is most clearly expressed, sustained and transmitted through Orthodox religious ritual and ceremonial.

6. PERSISTENCE OF GROUP STEREOTYPES BEYOND RELIGIOUS BOUNDARIES. There is, of course, an ethnic cleavage which persists beyond the boundaries of religion. In the process of socialization many Jewish children internalize and carry on traditional Jewish attitudes which parents still share despite the abandonment of ceremonial observances. Moreover, anti-Semites incessantly manage to discover or conjure up characteristics which set apart even secular Jews from their fellow-citizens. Among Jews them-

selves there is recognition of a common descent and of an ethnic heritage, although many Jews are evidently in doubt as to the nature of this heritage.[32] Of late, considerable fanfare has been sounded over Jewish nationalism with the ascendance of the State of Israel to legitimate political status among the nations. For the more secular in the American Jewish community, philanthropic and political activities, in contrast to specifically religious activities, enhance the sense of Jewish group membership. In this connection it is pertinent to note that acknowledgment of stereotypes of Jewish and Gentile drinking appears to be related to continued sobriety despite the abandonment of most ritual observances.[33] But suggestive as these facts may be of the influence of ethnic stereotypes on Jewish sobriety beyond the traditional community of religious participation, they should not obscure the likelihood that these stereotypes are most pervasive and powerful within the religious community. It is in terms of cultural continuity with the Orthodox religious tradition that these beliefs and their normative influence can be best understood.

§ *General Effects of the Ingroup-Outgroup Situation*

The tentative general conclusions to be drawn from the present research with respect to the influence of the ingroup-outgroup situation on Jewish drinking behavior and sobriety are these: It is not direct censure for intoxication from outsiders, or the realistic possibility of censure or retailiation while in a state of intoxication, which is most significant for Jewish sobriety. In the American cultural setting, direct social pressures from outsiders concerning drinking apparently work in the opposite direction. They tend to induce convivial and hedonistic drinking among Jews, rather than moderate drinking and sobriety. Jews actually conform to these outgroup pressures precisely where relations of solidarity with the Jewish community are situationally disrupted or permanently attenuated. By contrast, it is the Jewish group which exerts direct social pressures inducing moderate drinking and sobriety. The effectiveness of these ingroup pressures apparently varies directly with the solidarity of Jews with the Orthodox religious community.

But none of these effects can be divorced from the more general context of tensions which exist between Jews and Gentiles in society as a whole. Intergroup tension may intensify Jewish ethnocentrism and heighten conformity to traditional norms among more religious Jews. When refracted through Orthodox ideology, the threat of conflict and anxieties about retaliation probably stimulate ingroup moral discipline. Acute intergroup tension may also reduce Jewish participation in Gentile society and motivate a return to the ingroup and a renaissance of traditionalism among the less religious, more assimilated Jews. As one New Haven Jewish respondent put it:

When times are good the Jew forgets his religion, but then the Goy gets his fur up and it's back to the old ways.

Consequently, sobriety having the status of a Jewish virtue, adherence to this norm may be affected by the vicissitudes of tension and antagonism between the Jewish ingroup and the Gentile outgroup in society at large. It is our belief that in these terms Kant's explanation of Jewish sobriety makes sense. To be stressed, however, is the fact that the basic ideas and ceremonials of traditional Judaism have a certain autonomy or vitality which is not immediately contingent on ingroup-outgroup tension and it is with these ideas and practices that Jewish sobriety is most intimately associated. Before the response of Jews to the ingroup-outgroup situation can be understood in respect to the drinking of alcoholic beverages and other behaviors, the incidence and impact among Jews of these cultural patterns must be taken into account.

These tentative conclusions are compatible with broader sociological conceptions of the nature and consequences of relations between status groups in society at large. In their recent general discussion of this subject, Stone and Form (33) call attention to the fact that a group's self-respect is not always commensurate with the social honor which it is accorded by society. They reiterate Max Weber's observation that the sense of dignity experienced by a group may bear no correspondence to its objective position in the actual status hierarchy. As Weber says: "Even pariah peoples who are most despised are usually apt to continue cultivating in some manner that which is equally peculiar to ethnic and status communities: the belief in their own social honor."[34] Following Weber's thought, Stone and Form go on to observe:

> The sense of dignity that transcends the negatively privileged position of a status group is anchored in the future, often contingent upon the fulfillment of a mission. . . . When the characteristic sense of dignity or personal worth of members of status groups and aggregates is examined with reference to their objective status, and gross intransigencies are disclosed, the conditions for what Hughes has termed "status protest" have been established. Where there are great disparities between dignity and objective status, a group may reject existing status arangements and establish itself as a status group outside the ongoing status structure of the community.[35]

The historical condition of the Jews in Western civilization might be characterized as one of chronic status protest in this sense. However, the disparity between inner worth or dignity and objective status (which is the condition for status protest) is not solely a consequence of the hostility and contempt of society. It is also a function of the ethnocentric ideas of the Jews themselves. These ideas are most clearly embodied and transmitted in the Orthodox religious tradition and internalized most effectively through Orthodox Jewish ceremonial and ritual observance. It is also possible that through the elaboration of ceremonial and ritual Jews have given expression to the need to reject existing status arrangements and to establish themselves in large measure outside the ongoing status structure of the wider society. Adherence to Jewish norms of moderate drinking and sobriety is, as we have shown (31), intricately bound up with Orthodox ceremonial and ritual observances. Deviation from these norms may thus be broadly conceived as a complex function of the vitality of ceremonial Judaism considered together with the objective position and subjective evaluation accorded to Jews by society.

§ *Clarification of the Roles of Ritual Drinking and Other Factors*

Our analysis would be seriously misleading if the imagery of sobriety as a Jewish virtue, together with broader ethnocentric ideas and sentiments and the pressures arising from ingroup-outgroup relations, were conceived of as causing the sobriety and virtual absence of drinking pathologies among Jews in some ultimate or final sense. No such thought is intended. Under certain conditions these factors are assumed to provide strong motivation and reinforcement to a norm of sobriety and, accordingly, constitute part of a complex of sociocultural variables which must be considered. But other features of Jewish culture may certainly contribute to the effective social regulation of the use of beverage alcohol. In this connection we share Bales' belief that the extensive ritualization of drinking in Jewish religious ceremonial is of the utmost importance.[36] Especially to be noted is the fact that traditional Jewish religious symbolism quite explicitly links the major ethnocentric idea with the ritual drinking situation. Thus the Sabbath Kiddush concludes with these words (27): "For Thou hast chosen us and sanctified us above all nations, and in love and favor hast given us the holy Sabbath as our inheritance. Blessed art Thou, O Lord, who hallowest the Sabbath." Yet in focusing attention on ritual drinking there is a tendency to lose sight of other factors. It might easily be concluded from Bales' discussion that ritual drinking by itself creates all the powerful ideas and sentiments in traditional Jewish culture which are opposed to intoxication and hedonistic drinking. And at times Bales himself seems to advocate this narrow conception. However, he does mention secondary factors in Jewish sobriety and refers to the "underlying ideas and sentiments" associated with the ritual use of wine as providing the "primary emotional impetus" to the hatred of intoxication and barriers to the formation of addictive motives among Jews.

Actually, there is a twofold significance to ritual drinking in Bales' argument which is not always clear. On the one hand, ritual drinking may be conceived as giving form and expression to religious ideas and sentiments integral with a larger pattern of ceremonial and ritual observance. Because of his involvement in a wider pattern of ceremonial and ritual observances, the pious Jew approaches alcoholic beverages with a generalized ritual attitude. On the other hand, insofar as ritual drinking is experienced early and practiced continuously in life, this specific mode of drinking has the effect of reinforcing in the personality the ideational and emotional connections between the acts of drinking and the most powerful sentiments and symbols of social control in the Jewish group. In short, the traditional prescriptions to drink ceremonially reinforce the connections between the ideas and sentiments associated with the generalized ritual attitude and the act of drinking itself. A stable attitude toward the drinking of alcoholic beverages is consequently molded which does not leave the outcome of drinking to chance, individual experiment, fear or ignorance.

But there is still the knotty problem of the generalization of a controlled attitude toward drinking. This problem is most broadly illustrated by the fact that human behavior is so flexible that patterns of ceremonial drinking can alternate with patterns of convivial and hedonistic drinking within the same cultural framework.[37] Why, then, has there been no such alternation or dualism in Orthodox Jewish life?

Part of the solution to this problem probably lies in the fundamental idea of Orthodox Judaism as a "total way of life" through which all man's activities are to be sanctified. Orthodox Judaism presses for integration, for the permeation of all facets of life with sacred symbolism. The possibility of this kind of integration appears to be bound up with a pattern of close communal living. The hostility and discrimination of outsiders has contributed to this integration by forcing Jews to live under the compact social conditions congenial to it. The tendency toward permeation of all activities with religious values is clearly evident in the Orthodox requirement that the Jew must pronounce a benediction before drinking any beverage in any circumstance. This custom obviously facilitates the extension to the drinking situation of ideas and sentiments of reverence and respect and the larger moral meanings associated with being a religious Jew, even though the situation is not otherwise of an essentially religious character. But reinforcing the tendency toward a controlled use of alcoholic beverages, which is immanent in the extension of a ritual attitude, are the ethnocentric ideas and sentiments and pressures arising from the ingroup-outgroup situation. Through the network of ethnocentric symbolism and sentiments the idea of sobriety becomes integrated with the feeling of moral superiority in being Jewish. Orthodox Jews have claimed legitimacy for their religion and defended Judaism through the cultivation of and adherence to what they conceived to be a morally superior discipline. In this perspective, stereotypes of sober Jew and drunken Gentile define intoxication among Jews as a threat to the basic claims and defenses of Judaism and as a threat to the particular personalities whose self-esteem and integration derive from the religion. It seems likely that, in association with collective stereotypes, the inner meaning of intoxication for the Jew himself is the degradation of Jewishness. For the Jew to become intoxicated symbolizes the futility of the Jewish moral struggle in a society which holds Jewishness in disesteem. Perhaps, then, these additional factors help to explain the apparent sobriety of ghetto Jews who used alcoholic beverages in convivial situations, as wedding celebrations, in which drinking might have taken a hedonistic turn. Very likely some Jews were not so pious in these circumstances as always to bless the beverages prior to drinking. But to become intoxicated under these conditions would have been "un-Jewish."[38] Evidently, the inner and outer social pressures "not to let down" on this *point d'honneur* were and still are very strong for Jews who are solidary with the Jewish community.

The complex reinforcing factors conducive to Jewish sobriety may persist, of course, even where the ceremonial use of alcohol is in decline. Obviously, ritual drinking directly depends upon the vitality of the larger religious and ceremonial pattern. Beyond this, ceremonial and ritual evidently are also a powerful mechanism for giving Jewishness and ethnocentric ideas strong inner emotional meaning, while Orthodox beliefs provide a definition of the situation which motivates sobriety in the context of tense ingroup-outgroup relations. Consequently, we suspect that these additional factors lose their power to motivate sobriety among less Orthodox Jews whose identification with traditional Judaism is weak or who situationally identify with Gentiles on a primary-group basis, as in military service or in college. It may be suggested, however, that these additional factors helped to preclude the extensive development of patterns of convivial or hedonistic drinking in alternation with the ceremonial and religious use of beverage alcohol in the closely knit Jewish community.

It is important to note that, theoretically, the effectiveness of norms, ideas and sentiments in regulating intoxication depends upon their internalization in the personality. They must be anticipated in the drinking situation itself. Social sanctions from members of the group after the individual has reached a state of intoxication or developed a pattern of inebriety are not of primary significance. To be effective, the regulatory norms, ideas and sentiments must be elicited immediately in the drinking situation and be supported by the consensus or social expectancies of the surrounding milieu. In fact, Bales stresses the specific act of ritual drinking precisely because he believes that the internalization of a controlled attitude toward drinking is facilitated by the overt and repeated practice of drinking in a religious context, and in our opinion this is correct. However, the internalization of the reinforcing ideas and sentiments to which we have alluded need not necessarily depend upon the experience of intoxication or even the experience of drinking. The broader process of socialization is sufficient to structure these elements in the personality. Through the internalization of ideas and sentiments associated with Jewishness and the Jewish situation, and ideas of sobriety as a Jewish virtue, drunkenness as a Gentile vice, Jews bring to the drinking situation powerful moral sentiments and anxieties counter to intoxication. That these factors do not derive from the specific experience of drinking does not preclude their being a part of the normative orientation toward the act of drinking itself. We might say, then, that through the ceremonial use of beverage alcohol religious Jews learn how to drink in a controlled manner; but through constant reference to the hedonism of outsiders, in association with a broader pattern of religious and ethnocentric ideas and sentiments, Jews also learn how not to drink.

References

1. Bales, R. F. Cultural differences in rates of alcoholism. Quart. J. Stud. Alc. 6: 480-499, 1946.
2. Bales, R. F. The "Fixation Factor" in Alcohol Addiction: An Hypothesis Derived from a Comparative study of Irish and Jewish Social Norms. Doctoral dissertation: Harvard University, 1944.
3. Barron, M. L. The incidence of Jewish intermarriage in Europe and America. Amer. sociol. Rev. 11: 6-13, 1946.
4. Bernheimer, C. S., ed. The Russian Jew in the United States: Studies of Social Conditions in New York, Philadelphia, and Chicago, with a Description of Rural Settlements. Philadelphia: Winston, 1905.
5. Clark, W. Portrait of the mythical gentile: One stereotype breeds another. Commentary 7: 546-549, 1949.
6. Dollard J. Caste and Class in a Southern Town. New Haven: Yale University Press, 1937.
7. Dubnow, S. M. History of the Jews in Russia and Poland from the Earliest Times to the Present Day. Transl. by I. Friedlander. Philadelphia: Jewish Publication Society of America, 1916-20.
8. Durkheim, E. The Elementary Forms of the Religious Life: A Study in Religious Sociology. Trans. by J. W. Swain. London: Allen & Unwin, 1915.
9. Fishberg, M. The Jews: A Study of Race and Environment. New York: Scott Publishing Co., 1911.
10. Gerth, H. H. and Mills, C. W. From Max Weber: Essays in Sociology. New York: Oxford University Press, 1946.
11. Glad, D. D. Attitudes and experiences of American-Jewish and American-Irish male youth as related to differences in adult rates of inebriety. Quart. J. Stud. Alc. 8: 406-472, 1947.
12. Glazer, N. Why Jews stay sober: Social scientists examine Jewish abstemiousness. Commentary 13: 181-186, 1952.
13. Haggard, H. W. and Jellinek, E. M. Alcohol Explored. New York: Doubleday, 1942.
14. Hughes, E. C. Social change and status protest. An essay on the marginal man. Phylon 10: 58-65, 1949.
15. Infield, H. G. The concept of Jewish culture and the State of Israel. Amer. sociol. Rev. 16: 506-513, 1951.
16. Jellinek, E. M. A document of the Reformation period on inebriety:

Sebastian Franck's "On the Horrible Vice of Drunkenness," etc. (Classics of the Alcohol Literature.) Quart. J. Stud. Alc. 2: 391-395, 1941.

17. Jellinek, E. M. Immanuel Kant on Drinking. Quart. J. Stud. Alc. 1: 777-778, 1941.

18. Jellinek, E. M. Recent Trends in Alcoholism and in Alcohol Consumption. New Haven: Hillhouse Press, 1947. Also in Quart. J. Stud. Alc. 8: 1-42, 1947.

19. Kennedy, R. J. R. Single or triple melting pot? Intermarriage trends in New Haven, 1870-1940. Amer. J. Sociol. 49: 331-339, 1944.

20. McKinlay, A. P. Ancient experience with intoxicating drinks: non-classical peoples. Quart. J. Stud. Alc. 9: 388-414, 1948.

21. McKinlay, A. P. Ancient experience with intoxicating drinks: non-Attic Greek states. Quart. J. Stud. Alc. 10: 289-315, 1949.

22. McKinlay, A. P. Attic temperance. Quart. J. Stud. Alc. 12: 61-102, 1951.

23. Moore, G. F. Judaism in the First Three Centuries of the Christian Era: The Age of the Tannaim. 3 Vols. Cambridge, Mass.: Harvard University Press, 1927-30.

24. Myerson, A. Alcohol: a study of social ambivalence. Quart. J. Stud. Alc. 1: 13-20, 1940.

25. Parsons, T. The Social System. Glencoe: Free Press, 1951.

26. Parsons, T. Essays on Sociological Theory, Pure and Applied. Glencoe: Free Press, 1949.

27. Philips, A. Th., transl. Daily Prayers. New York: Hebrew Publishing Co., n.d.

28. Riesman, D. A philosophy for 'minority' living. Commentary 6: 413-422, 1948.

29. Sartre, J. P. Portrait of the inauthentic Jew. Commentary 5: 389-397, 1948.

30. Shils, E. A. The study of the primary group. In: Lerner, D., and Lasswell, H. D., eds. The Policy Sciences: Recent Developments in Scope and Method. Stanford: Stanford University Press, 1951.

31. Snyder, C. R. Culture and Sobriety. A Study of Drinking Patterns and Sociocultural Factors Related to Sobriety Among Jews. Doctoral dissertation: Yale University, 1954.

32. Snyder, C. R. and Landman, R. H. Studies of drinking in Jewish culture. II. Prospectus for sociological research on Jewish drinking patterns. Quart. J. Stud. Alc. 12: 451-474, 1951.

33. Stone, G. P. and Form, W. H. Instabilities in status. The problem of hierarchy in the community study of status arrangements. Amer. sociol. Rev. 18: 151-163, 1953.

34. Straus, R. and Bacon, S. D. Drinking in College. New Haven: Yale University Press, 1953.

35. Sumner, W. G. Folkways: A Study of the Sociological Importance of Usages, Manners, Customs, Mores and Morals. 2d Ed. Boston: Ginn, 1940.

36. Thomas, W. I. and Thomas, D. S. The Child in America: Behavior Problems and Programs. New York: Knopf, 1928.

37. Thorner, I. Ascetic Protestantism and alcoholism. Psychiatry 16: 167-176, 1953.
38. Warner, W. L. and Srole, L. The Social Systems of American Ethnic Groups. (Yankee City Series, Vol. III.) New Haven: Yale University Press, 1945.
39. Zborowski, M. and Herzog, E. Life Is With People: The Jewish Little-Town of Eastern Europe. New York: International Universities Press, 1952.

LAWRENCE H. FUCHS

SOURCES OF JEWISH INTERNATIONALISM
AND LIBERALISM

ON November 3, 1942, the voters of four Boston wards went to the polls to vote on, among other things, the somewhat academic question of the formation of a democratic world government. It was hardly a surprise that the voters of Boston's second most Jewish ward were more enthusiastic about the idea of world government than voters elsewhere.[1] The reputation of the Jew for internationalism and cosmopolitanism, a reputation for which he has suffered much at the hands of both Hitler and the Communists, is well deserved. "Every influence and contact and experience has made him a universalist and an internationalist . . . he has participated out of proportion to his numbers in movements for international justice, understanding, and humanitarianism, and has been receptive to social philosophies with a world view such as socialism, communism, and a world state."[2] The wellsprings of Jewish internationalism are not hard to find.

§ Why Internationalism?

The Jews, having been dispersed over the face of the globe for 2,000 years, have rarely been welcome or at home anywhere. First as traders, then as moneylenders, then as shopkeepers they were tolerated in the professions that were either too risky for Christians or prohibited to them. In these capacities Jews kept traveling and were in almost constant contact with one another. Consequently, the language, culture, folklore, and religion which the Jews developed are in many important respects transnational.

The modern state system has brought only occasional relief from persecution to the Jews. Since the seventeenth century, all European states have at some time or other sponsored anti-Semitic legislation as a matter of state policy. In the last eighty years anti-Semitism has increased rather than diminished—pogroms in East Europe, the Dreyfus affair, and more recently the monstrous persecutions of Hitler and Stalin. There have been periods of surcease from national, state-sponsored anti-Semitism. For the past 100 years no state-originated liabilities have been placed on Jews in English-speaking countries. Even the dictators Cromwell, Napoleon, and Peron in their own times eased the burdens placed on Hebrews in an effort to make them enthusiastic nationalists. But while Jews have become "good" Americans, Argentines, Frenchmen, and Germans, they are still not secure in the

Reprinted from *The Political Behavior of American Jews*, pp. 171-203, by permission of the author and the publisher. (Copyright, 1956, by The Free Press.)

world of nationalism. They know that even liberal national states like the United States and France cannot prevent unofficial persecution. More importantly, they know from experience in Germany and Russia in recent decades that liberal national states cannot prevent the destruction of Jews as a people within illiberal states.

Consequently, American Jews are anxious that the United States, a country whose beneficence towards Jews in international affairs has been well demonstrated, play a strong role in international politics. At the same time they are anxious for the development and strengthening of the United Nations, and so they have taken an unusual interest in the U.N. genocide convention, the international bill of rights, and the strengthening of world organization generally.

§ *Why Liberalism?*

The international history of the Jewish people, their cosmopolitan character, and their insecurity in a world of nation states may explain the extraordinary Jewish interest in the Marshall Plan, the U.N., and Point 4; but although the Jews are internationalists in matters of foreign policy, they need not be liberals at home. In 1940, the Poles were as strongly interventionist as the Jews. In 1944, Americans of Yankee stock tended to be strong supporters of the United Nations and the Anglo-American alliance. But Poles and Yankees divided on class lines on most New Deal issues, while the Jews did not. Why were the Jews liberals at home even after they had climbed to the top of the class ladder?

§ *Social Class and the Jews:*
A "Vilified and Persecuted Minority"

Such a question actually begs a prior issue. Were the Jews really perched on top of the class ladder, as alleged by national survey and area studies? . . . When W. Lloyd Warner and Leo Srole studied ethnic groups in "Yankee City," they rated ethnic groups in a class system based upon criteria concerning occupation, residence, and social class. They found that Jews had a much higher occupational prestige score than the natives (Yankees). But Jews as a group were not as high in social class as natives, and Jews did not live in as desirable neighborhoods as natives or Irishmen.[3] Even more importantly, Warner and Srole introduced the concept of subordination. The degree of subordination of an ethnic group was based upon the following five factors: (1) freedom of residential choice; (2) freedom to marry out of one's own group; (3) extent of occupational restriction; (4) access to associations, clubs, etc.; and (5) vertical mobility. While the Jews were rated very high in the class system of Yankee City because that system gave great weight to such objective factors as amount of income and occupational prestige, the Jews rated very low in the system of subordination simply because of discriminations practiced against them. A hierarchy of six categories was established by the authors within the racial type "light caucasoid," and English-speaking Jews fell into the fifth category while European Jews fell into the sixth and last category.[4]

Such results confirm the findings of social distance tests. The results of these latter tests have not varied much since 1926 when Emory S. Bogardus introduced them. Then, Prof. Borgardus asked 1,725 Americans in a stratified sample to state their attitudes toward forty ethnic groups. German Jews ranked twenty-sixth from the top, Russian Jews twenty-eighth. Twenty years later the social distance scale was given to 1,950 persons in six different regions. This time Jews ranked twenty-third in a list of thirty-six ethnic groups. In another study of 1,672 white university students, Jews were rated fifth out of the nine ethnic groups being evaluated: native-born white, foreign-born white, Chinese, Indian, Jew, Filipino, Japanese, Negro, and Mexican in that order.[5] No matter how high Jews are placed on the socioeconomic status or class scales which are based on occupation and income, they are unwanted by vast numbers of Christians. Although 16.3 per cent of the nation's medical doctors and 10.9 per cent of the nation's lawyers may be Jews,[6] many Jews still cannot easily live where they want to, go to the schools of their choice, marry whom they please, or be respected for what they are.

It really matters little whether Jews are rated in a class system based on social distance tests and subordination or on occupational prestige in order to see that Jews as a group are made deeply insecure by the constant pressures of hostile Christian majorities. As Jean-Paul Sartre has put it, "An Israelite is never sure of his position or his possessions. He cannot even say that tomorrow he will still be in the country he inhabits today, for his situation, his power, and even his right to live may be placed in jeopardy from one moment to the next."[7] His feelings of insecurity are extensive.[8] Even in free and pluralistic America the Jews are engaged in a continuing quest for security. There are very few who do not sense that the security of the Jewish group depends in great measure upon the largess of liberal government.

Since the Jews feel and know insecurity even when they are well-to-do and powerful, they are able to empathize with others who are discriminated against and insecure. It is no coincidence that the three books written since 1948 on the problem of legislation affecting Negro rights have been written by Jews.[9] Jews and Jewish organizations have always taken an extraordinary interest in Negro rights. One of the reasons German Jewish immigrants were drawn to the newly formed Republican Party nearly one hundred years ago was that Party's stand on the slavery issue. Jews who had worn badges of slavery or inferiority for centuries were prone to sympathize with American Negroes in their plight.

Knowledge of extreme persecution has made Jews acutely sensitive to the persecution of others. Moreover, Jews sense that inroads on the freedom and well-being of others may soon be followed by onslaughts on themselves. That is one reason why they have been in the forefront of civil liberties movements, and why their reaction to McCarthyism has been distinctly negative. It is difficult to imagine a large body of Catholic and Protestant clergymen representing *well-to-do* congregations *unanimously* passing a resolution denouncing Senator McCarthy and urging that his committee chairmanships be taken from him. Yet, this is just what the Central Conference of American Rabbis, representing 600 Reform Rabbis in every section of the country, did in June 1954. The Rabbis also denounced the use of the term "fifth amendment communists" and protested the use of loyalty oaths. One Rabbi, probably repeating the thoughts of many Jews, compared McCarthy to Hitler.

Discrimination against Negroes and attacks on the civil liberties of others are felt by the Jews to be incipient attacks on them. Throughout history, political and social reaction in other matters has been associated with persecution of the Jews, as Louis I. Newman has shown. And general authoritarianism has invariably brought anti-Semitism in its train.[10] In short, part of the explanation of Jewish liberalism must lie in the fact that anti-Semites are illiberal in political and social matters, as the authors of *The Authoritarian Personality* have shown.[11] If extreme anti-Semites tend to think strongly that Negroes ought to be segregated, that the government has no responsibility for the welfare of the people, and that free speech ought to be curtailed, Jews are not likely to agree with those views.

But this cause and effect relationship can also be turned on its head. Reactionaries may be anti-Semites because they think Jews are liberals. If that were true it would imply that Jews were liberals in matters of politics for other reasons besides their own group insecurity. It might signify that Jewish interest in the growth of the liberal state would exist even if the Jews were not "the most vilified and persecuted minority in history."[12] It may be that authoritarian Christians are anti-Semites because, as Maurice Samuel has insisted, they find the liberal and egalitarian implications of Jewish values intolerable.[13]

§ *Values and Votes*

Do Jewish group values tend to make the Jews liberals in the context of American politics? Some suggestive answers to this query come from a recent study on the cultural consciousness of Jewish youth. Its author, Werner J. Cahnman, asked questions of groups of Jewish and non-Jewish teenagers in an effort to discover the components of cultural consciousness in Jewish youth. Although he found that discrimination against Jews was a factor in the development of cultural consciousness, it was not the primary factor. Instead Cahnman concluded that "The primary twin elements of such consciousness are emotional nationalism (Zionism) . . . and humanitarian socialism."[14] Continuing, he wrote, "The sensitivity to discrimination among Jewish youth is increased because of the image of a just society which is at the back of their minds."[15] The Jewish teenagers were not only more concerned than their non-Jewish playmates about such things as race prejudice and the need for co-operation among minorities, but also about the infringement of civil liberties, the spread of militarism, and such problems as the unequal distribution of wealth and the need for minimum wage legislation. While such items as these last two, under the heading of "social abuse and social reform," were mentioned in 11.2 per cent of the Jewish replies, they were completely absent from the answers of the non-Jewish control group. One of the implications of the study is that Jewish "humanitarian socialism" is prior to discrimination against the Jews. The source of these attitudes lie not merely in a reaction to persecution, but in Jewish group values themselves.

Values are the criteria by which goals are chosen. If the Jewish youth Cahnman questioned actually had an image of a just society in the back of their minds (and the non-Jewish teenagers did not) even before they were treated unjustly, then the source of the Jewish attitude probably lies in Jewish values.

What are the distinctive values of America's Jewish subculture? To judge from a vast impressionistic literature and a growing systematic study of Jewish culture, those things most valued by Jews as Jews are: (1) Learning (*Torah*); (2) Charity (*Zedakeh*); and, for want of a better phrase or word, (3) Life's pleasures (non-asceticism). In probably no other American subculture is so high a value placed upon learning and intellectuality, or upon the helping of the poor by the rich and the weak by the strong, or upon living a good life upon earth in full use of one's body. These three values, taken together or regarded separately, have helped to guide Jewish political behavior in recent decades along what in the discourse of our times would be called "liberal lines."

Learning (*Torah*). The importance given to learning and knowledge finds expression among contemporary Jewry in many ways. The learner, or student, or rabbi has always been given the highest status in Jewish community life. In a recent study of Polish Jewry it was found that the learner or student was still accorded the highest status in the community.[16] In this country, settlement workers in immigrant quarters have always noticed the exceptional value which Jewish parents put on schooling for their children.[17] Talcott Parsons believes that intellectuality is the Jew's most distinguishing trait, and that "the strong propensity of the Jews to enter the professions can certainly, at least in part, be looked upon as a result of their traditional high regard for learning."[18] Albert Einstein similarly was convinced that any special notice which Jews may have won in intellectual endeavors is due "to the fact that the esteem in which intellectual accomplishment is held among the Jews creates an atmosphere particularly favorable to the development of any talents that may exist."[19]

The high value which Jews place on learning is also manifest in figures for Jewish attendance at colleges and universities and in the grades of Jewish students. In this country and in Europe the Jewish passion for learning results in unusually high attendance at the universities and similar centers of higher education. A recent study on college admissions in the United States shows that Jewish high school seniors are more anxious to continue their studies than their Christian classmates.[20] A veritable legion of studies show that Jewish boys and girls make better grades and achieve higher intelligence scores than non-Jewish students.[21] Such differences cannot easily be ascribed to differences in hereditary endowment, but can be explained by the strong value which is placed on learning and knowledge in Jewish culture.

Although Thorstein Veblen thought that the unusual "Intellectual Pre-eminence of Jews" would disappear after the establishment of a Jewish state, there is evidence of the continued emphasis which Jews put on learning for learning's sake. Even in Israel itself, many of the leaders of the government have been noted for their scholarship and intellectual achievement.[22]

Charity (*Zedakeh*). The second in the important trilogy of Jewish values is *Zedakeh,* the Hebrew word for charity. . . . Of the three values, this one has the most relevance to the politics of our time. Its most precise meaning is not charity in the English sense of that word. Most students of Jewish culture would agree that its real meaning is not charity but justice; "social justice" would be more accurate.

The heritage of *Zedakeh,* even though American Jews may not be familiar with the word itself, is deeply rooted in Jewish community life. Louis Wirth wrote, "The relation between the giver and the receiver of charity was a peculiar one in ghetto society. Charity was more or less synonymous with justice, and to give to the poor, the orphans, and the helpless was a religious duty."[23]

To give is still a *mitzvah* (blessing) in Jewish community life, and *Zedakeh* is still highly prized. In a recent and well-received study of Jewish life in the towns of Eastern Europe it was concluded that *Zedakeh* was valued second only to learning. As the authors wrote, "Praying three times a day does not make you a Jew. You have to be a Jew for the world. That means you have to do something for other people as well."[24] In still another study of the value system of East European Jews, Natalie Joffe observes differences in the traditional Western attitudes toward reciprocity and the Jewish attitudes:

> For a society within the framework of the Western cultural tradition, East European Jewish culture exhibits a minimum of reciprocal behavior. Wealth, learning, and other tangible possessions are fluid and are channeled so that in the main they flow from the "strong," or "rich," or "learned," or "older," to those who are "weaker," "poorer," "ignorant," or "younger." Therefore all giving is downward. . . .
>
> It is mandatory for the good things of life to be shared or to be passed downward during one's lifetime. . . . It is one of the greatest blessings in the

world to put what you have at the service of others, be it wealth, learning, or children.[25]

Although *Zedakeh* enjoins the individual Jew to help the weak and the poor, Jewish charity has been more than just alms-giving by individual benefactors. It has been considered part of the governance of the community itself. In some countries in the Middle Ages Jews "were obliged by law to provide for their poor, or were made jointly responsible for taxes or fines imposed on members of the community. . . . Thus, in the course of centuries, the support of the poor by the rich became a custom, a duty of the rich, and a right of the poor."[26] This tradition of corporate charity has been carried over into the philanthropic enterprises of English and American Jewry.[27]

In explaining the continuing solidarity of the Jewish people, Albert Einstein placed the Jewish respect for *Zedakeh* above everything else. Although he stated the proposition too strongly, there is a partial truth in his claim that "The bond that has united Jews for thousands of years and unites them today is above all, the democratic ideal of social justice, coupled with the ideal of mutual aid and tolerance among all men."[28]

Life's pleasures (non-asceticism). A third Jewish value which is frequently stressed in the literature on Jewish culture is probably best understood when put negatively. It is non-asceticism. As Rabbi Morris N. Kertzer writes, "Judaism does not accept the doctrine of original sin. . . . Nor do we consider our bodies and our appetites as sinful."[29] Jews place a high value on *a pleasurable life in this world.* Since Jews do not consider their bodily appetites as sinful, their behavior in matters of sex, drink, and food is affected accordingly.

In the Jewish villages of Eastern Europe "sexual enjoyment is considered healthy and good. . . . He [God] made man with sex organs and appetites, the exercise of them must be good."[30] Werner Sombart once compounded evidence on low rates of illegitimate Jewish births with quotations from the *Talmud* and *Bible* to argue that Jews were essentially ascetic in temper,[31] but he was very much mistaken. Jewish proscriptions are generally against the excessive use of bodily appetites, not against their use at all. And while it is true that Jews tend to have relatively few illegitimate children, the explanation lies partly in the widespread acceptance by Jews of birth control measures and their emphasis on sex within the marital relationship. For example, Kinsey found that American Jews have more marital intercourse than non-Jews at all age levels except the youngest.[32] Even more significantly, Kinsey and his associates reported that Jews talk more freely about sex than Christians.[33]

Though the Jew is temperate in matters of drink, as recent scholarship shows, the Jewish teetotaler is hard to find. The Jewish attitude toward the use of alcohol appears somewhat ambivalent. There is nothing the Jew despises in Christians so much as drunkenness, unless it is ignorance of stinginess. While the Jews loathe drunkenness, they do like to drink, especially sacramental wine. In fact, the Jews are enjoined to drink at various festivals and ceremonies. The Jewish attitude is not ascetic. It is well summed up in a colloquy which two young Jewish boys had in one of Angoff's novels as they watched Woodrow Wilson in a triumphal parade.

Moshe and Kislov felt elated about Wilson. They were as excited as little boys.
"I sometimes wonder," said Kislov, "what a man like Wilson does when he wants to rest, relax."
"Who knows? He doesn't drink, of that I'm sure," said Moshe.
"You don't mean never. A little *Kiddish* [drink of sacramental wine] he no doubt has sometime," said Kislov.[34]

The Jewish attitude toward food is less restricted. Most Jews are sensuous about food. There are few vegetarians among them. In short, the Jewish spirit and temper are non-ascetic because of the value which most Jews have always placed on the enjoyment of life's pleasures.

§ *Jewish Values in America*

The question which comes to mind is: Are these values of learning, *Zedakeh,* and life's pleasures Jewish values only? Is not America a well-educated, charitable, and pleasure-seeking society? While it is true that these things are valued in American society, they are not the dominant values of our Protestant-American culture as they are in Jewish culture. According to Robin Williams there are four tests which may be given to determine the importance of values in a culture. Williams asks: What will people pay for? What do they pay attention to? What do they reward and punish? What explicit statement of value do they make?[35] By all four tests it is quite clear that learning, *Zedakeh,* and the enjoyment of life on this earth are more valued by most Jews than by most non-Jews. These values are more extensive, have lasted longer, are sought and maintained with more intensity, and bring more prestige to those who carry them in Jewish culture than in non-Jewish culture.

So important are the love of learning and *Zedakeh* to Jewish tradition that the Jewish prayer book asserts that these two plus the worship of God constitute the three principal tenets of Judaism. It is true that there has been a passion for education in America which is unmatched in any other country in the world, but as Harold Laski has written, "It has been . . . an intensely pragmatic matter. . . ."[36] Whether or not it is true, as Laski asserts, that the American frontier tradition is responsible for the American stress on practical knowledge (life is the best education) there does exist in America a current of anti-intellectualism which runs alongside of the American public school tradition and which has found frequent expression in American politics in recent decades. While Americans generally disparage the "impractical" intellectual and academician,

Jews tend to accord him the highest respect. It is fairly common for poor Jewish families to give a portion of their meagre savings to help support some bookish Rabbi who does nothing but study the *Talmud* in some dilapidated tenement. Such a man would probably be called a "waster" by most Christian Americans. It is the practical man who achieves status in America, the man who can build a better mousetrap or at least meet a payroll. That is why, for example, America's greatest scientific achievements are in the technological realm and not the area of pure science. It is why politicians can provoke a wry smile from most American audiences by a reference to "fuzzy-minded intellectuals." In America the passion for education has been hitched to America's drive to make things and do things. In the Jewish subculture the passion for learning stands on its own.

It is also true that charity and humanitarianism are respected in the United States. Americans readily pour millions of dollars into the heart fund, the polio fund, the tuberculosis association and similar charities every year. But the Christian view of love (*Zedakeh*) as applied to politics has been considerably mitigated by the political implications of the Calvinistic notion that people get what they deserve, and that prosperity is a mark of moral virtue. The political influence of *Zedakeh* has also been curtailed by the impact of Social Darwinism on Protestant America. The idea that weakness or poverty is a mark of everlasting biological unfitness is contrary to the very essence of *Zedakeh*. Yet, William Graham Sumner urged such an idea on Protestant America with considerable success. The notion that poverty, for example, is an index of biological and moral degeneration lent itself admirably to the defenders of the status quo for a half century after Appomattox. This is not to say that American society is not a charitable society. But charity is not generally accorded as a matter of right. The recipients of charity ought to "deserve" it, not merely need it.

As for non-asceticism, American society is no doubt getting more sensual. . . . Just how sensual American culture has become may be seen from the billions of dollars Americans spend on entertainment, cosmetics, food, labor-saving devices, and liquor each year. Still Christian America, particularly Protestant America, must contend with its bleak Puritan heritage. There is not the same free acceptance of physical pleasures that one finds in the Jewish culture. In fact, the case can be made that Jews have been disproportionately influential in the de-Puritanizing of America because of the special place of Jews in Hollywood, the legitimate theater, advertising, publishing, and the ladies' garment trades.[37] One student of culture conflict actually believes that the non-asceticism of the Jews and the asceticism of Gentiles has been the crucial difference and primary cause of tension between Hebrews and Christians in the United States. He concludes, "The areas of western European culture that have been colored by Protestant Christianity are essentially ascetic in temper;

Jewish culture, on the other hand, is sensuous—good food, fine clothing, a fine home."[38]

§ *The Political Implications of Jewish Group Values*

"Values are modes of organizing conduct—meaningful, affectively invested pattern principles that guide human action."[39] In what ways do Jewish values guide Jewish behavior in American politics? Considered separately, it is possible to see how each dominant value has had influence in shaping the Jewish position on issues and candidates in recent decades.

Zedakeh has more to do with politics directly than the Jewish love of learning and of life's pleasures. For *Zedakeh* deals with the distribution of power, which, after all, is what politics is about. In explaining the reverence of Jews for Franklin Roosevelt, Rabbi Ferdinand Isserman explicitly maintained that the Jewish *Zedakeh* was responsible. Of F.D.R., Isserman said:

> . . . he was partisan to protect, to uphold the rights of the weak. He did not plead for sympathy for the weak, he spoke of their rights. Judaism knew no charitable concept which meant that generosity and goodness of soul induces men to help the weak. It knew tsekodah, righteousness, not charity. Righteousness means the rights of men. It was said that Roosevelt was partial to the Negroes. So he was. They were the weak. . . . It was said that he sided with oppressed people. So he did. . . . Roosevelt shared the prophets' faith in the rights of the weak. . . .[40]

Zedakeh, as well as Jewish insecurity, would help promote Jewish sympathy for the Negro and help induce a favorable attitude toward progressive taxation, Roosevelt's war on the economic royalists, social security, and most of the programs which constituted the New Deal. It would also explain the favorable attitudes of Jewish businessmen and professional men toward an extension of power to labor, as long as they thought of laborers as being relatively weak or underprivileged. It would also explain the results of the liberalism or altruism test which we gave to the voters of Boston's "Jewish" Ward 14 in 1953, the much greater willingness of the Jewish voters to be taxed to aid the less fortunate in Kentucky or even in Africa and Asia.[41] *Zedakeh* would also explain why 62.7 per cent of the voters of Jewish middle-class Ward 14, and only 34 per cent of the voters of Yankee upper-middle class Ward 5, and 51.4 per cent of the electors in Irish middle-class Ward 15 in the city of Boston voted to give pensions to deserving citizens over sixty-five in 1942. It would explain why 76 per cent of the votes cast in Ward 14 in 1950 on the issue of raising the minimum wage were favorable as compared to only 47 per cent of those cast in Ward 5 and 74.5 per cent of the vote in Ward 15. It might even explain why 86 per cent of the voters in Ward 14 were in favor of absentee voting for disabled persons while only 76.6 per cent and 82.7 per cent of the electors in Ward 5 and 15, respectively, agreed when the question was put to a referendum in Boston in 1944. The enthusiastic Jewish

response to the New and Fair Deals cannot be put down to Jewish insecurity alone, economic, psychological or otherwise. *Zedakeh* played its
role in shaping Jewish political behavior in recent decades because of the
structuring of political issues. It is difficult to see the relevance of *Zedakeh*
to the silver-gold issue or the tariff issue, even though germaneness might
exist. But how quickly *Zedakeh* comes into play on such questions as unemployment compensation, shorter work, higher wages, relief, WPA, and
so on.

The Jewish reverence for learning has also played a role in making
the Jews political liberals in recent decades. It has influenced the Jewish
response to individual candidates as well as to specific issues. In another
of Angoff's novels, the ancient Jewish Alte Bobbe "was very pleased that
Woodrow Wilson was elected President. She said, 'He has so much grace
and learning. Ah, it's a wonderful country where a professor, a learned
man like that, can become the head man.' "[42] . . . The very learned and
intellectual manner of Adlai Stevenson, reputed to have lost him votes
among non-Jews, won approval among Hebrews. Twenty-two and one-half
per cent of the reasons given by Jewish Stevenson voters in Ward 14 for
preferring the Governor concerned his personality and his intelligence
compared to only 13.8 per cent of the reasons given by Gentile Stevenson
voters. One Jewish housewife remarked "Stevenson spoke so beautifully.
He was so educated. But then Eisenhower was a college man too."

It was the Jewish love of learning and intellectuality which, at least in
part, assured their positive response to the Roosevelt "brain trust." The
idea of professors in government did not seem incongruous to them as it
did to many Gentiles. For centuries they had been taught that the most
learned men ought to run the affairs of the community. They were not repulsed by the notion of planning in government as were many of their
fellow Americans. Charity, welfare requires planning. That is a Jewish
tradition. If the state is to take an active role in assuring the welfare of its
citizens, it ought to put the best brains to work planning how this will be
done.

On still another important group of issues the Jewish value of intellectuality helped promote the "liberal" position among Jews. On civil liberties
issues the Jews became fierce defenders of intellectual independence. While
almost 12 per cent of the Jewish voters in the Ward 14 sample were in
strong agreement that even Nazis and Communists ought to have free
speech, not a single Gentile respondent was in strong agreement with that
position. To be sure, the insecurity of the Jews prompts their anxiety about
civil liberties, but the value which Jews place on knowledge plays a role
as well.

The non-asceticism of the Jews has also influenced the general Jewish
position on the political issues of our time. On certain questions such as
the liquor question or the birth control issue, it is easy to see how the
non-asceticism or this-worldliness of the Jews directly influenced their posi-

tion. The value which Jews place on life's pleasures was responsible for relatively high anti-prohibition votes which the voters of Ward 14 recorded in twelve referendum votes on that issue since 1928. In all but two of those referendum contests the vote against prohibition was always higher in Jewish Ward 14 than in any other middle-class ward in the city, including the Irish wards. When the voters of Boston were asked through a referendum question if they favored the giving of birth control information by doctors to patients in need of it, the favorable vote in the Jewish wards was proportionately six times as high as it was in most Catholic areas, and higher than in Yankee Ward 5.

But how has the non-asceticism of the Jews helped to make them political liberals as that term has been used in recent decades? The answer is that by its emphasis on this-worldliness and the enjoyment of life here and now, Jews have been made more receptive to plans for a better life, for reconstructing society, for remaking man's environment, for socialism, for millennialism. Taken together with the other Jewish values of learning and *Zedakeh,* the non-asceticism of the Jews has, along with their insecurity, helped to produce a distinctive Jewish political style, a style which has characterized the liberal position in our time.

§ *The Jewish Political Style*

As Rabbi Philip Bernstein puts it in his popular book, *What the Jews Believe,* "The Jewish outlook is by its very nature optimistic, progressive, forward-looking. . . . It prods Jews constantly to strive for a better world, to be in the thick and at the front of movements for social reform. Even the very Jewish radical who may ignore his Jewishness is the product of its messianic fervor."[43] This outlook, a product of Jewish insecurity and the Jewish value system, constitutes a political style, an approach to the issues of social organization. Implicit in this style is the view that man and his environment are malleable, that he is much more the creator of history than its creature. Implicit, too, is the notion that man's environment and his polity are made for him. Implicit is a dynamic view of law, that it is changing and made for man. It is more than accident that three of the five great legal names which Americans associate with sociological jurisprudence are Jewish names: Brandeis, Cardozo, and Frankfurter. (The others are Stone and Holmes.) And especially implicit in such a style is the belief that what happens in this life on this earth is very important, what happens here and now matters very much.

§ *Christian Emphases*

Contrast this view with that which the Christian theologians Bernard I. Bell and Reinhold Niebuhr assert is the orthodox Christian position. Bell raises the question, "But is man capable of getting better and better by his own natural development or is he doomed to failure unless God intervenes? It makes a great deal of difference which of these alternatives is correct, a difference not only in theoretical doctrine but also in one's attitude toward living, one's source of hope and happiness, in social action, too."[44] Christianity has been split in its answer to this question. Judaism has not. Orthodox Christianity stresses the concept of redemption only through God's intervention. In recent years the Neo-Calvinists have lamented the failure of Christians to hold fast to this fundamental theological tenet. They have insisted that any departure from the Christian emphasis on complete dependence on God for the betterment of his condition has led to what Bell calls "the exaggerated optimism about man which . . . is the chief cause of our decay."[45] The failure of too many Christians to adopt what Niebuhr calls "Christian realism" in understanding man's sinfulness, his egocentricity, and utter helplessness without God has in his judgment led Americans too often into the fallacies of communism and utopian ideas for world government.[46]

But the fact is that American Jews, not Christians, have served these causes far out of proportion to their numbers. The Neo-Calvinists have exaggerated the political effects of liberal and heretical Christianity. After all, the vast majority of Christians still believe that man is stained with original sin and cannot be redeemed without God's grace. When the American sociologist, Lester Ward, stressed that man's power over nature was unlimited he was rejected, while the ideas of William Graham Sumner dominated the thinking of the Supreme Court for more than forty years. Dependence on God for the improvement of man's condition has been coupled in the orthodox view with the idea that faith and repentance—not works—brings redemption. Of course, many Christians have stressed works too, and it is impossible to speak of a single Christian position on any of these issues—so various and individualistic is Christian theology. The Catholics have had a long tradition of working among the poor, and in recent decades there have been many labor priests and waterfront priests, backed by Papal encyclicals, active in movements for social and economic reform. In the United States they have been joined by the followers of the Social Gospel movement led by Washington Gladden and Walter Rauschenbush. From the Social Gospel and similar movements came a Protestant emphasis on secularizing religion, on work in settlement houses, recreation centers, adult education, and political reform. Quaker concern has always manifested itself in humanitarian works. In the late nineteenth and early twentieth century, "liberalism" stressing the goodness of man, works, and social action was an important theological current running through all of the major Protestant denominations. It would certainly be a mistake to underestimate the role of liberal and secular Christianity in American life.

But it would also be a mistake to exaggerate it. While a number of Catholic leaders have been in the forefront of social action on behalf of the oppressed, Catholic law teaches resignation and moderation to the poor. Catholic Church leaders in the United States have been militantly anti-Socialist. More important than the Catholic political mood are the Protestant influences on American politics. The only major Protestant movement which has been optimistic about man and stressed his powers to improve life through social and political action has been the Social Gospel.

From the Anabaptists to the Fundamentalists, the political implications of the important Protestant theological movements, with the exception of the liberal "heresy" of the nineteenth century, have been conservative. Calvinism, Lutherism, Puritanism, Evangelicalism, Fundamentalism, and contemporary neo-Calvinism—all have tended to oppose the notion of social betterment through the state. Indeed, the Anabaptists reluctantly admitted that the state was necessary at all, and refused to assume any responsibility for it. Lutherans and Calvinists stressed the sinfulness of man. Crucial to the early Anglican position was the concept of justification through faith. Puritanism, which influenced all of the major Protestant denominations to some extent, emphasized asceticism. Fundamentalism has usually meant extreme social conservatism and suspicion of scientific and secular influences. The Evangelical movement in the first half of the nineteenth century insisted on the sinfulness of man, salvation through faith, and the need for conversion.

It is true that many of the leading evangelists were busily engaged in the front lines of various reform movements during this period, but these movements were usually aimed at the suppression of personal vice and immorality. They had nothing to do with the role of the state in society. Almost every single one of the leading evangelists opposed Andrew Jackson while supporting Sabbatarianism, temperance, and anti-slavery. In their theological writings Lyman Beecher, Charles Finney, Calvin Colton, Albert Barnes, and other evangelists showed considerable innovation, but they were politically conservative to a man. They worried over the souls of the poor but opposed poor relief, limitations on child labor, and extensions of the suffrage.[47] In fact, the great *theological radicals* (in their day) who have had the largest influence on American Protestantism—Calvin, Luther, and Wesley—were, unlike the Hebrew prophets of ancient times, *politically conservative.*

Surely, the Quakers and the Unitarians have been influential in American life; but who would argue that Quakerism has played a larger role in shaping American politics than Puritanism, or that a handful of Unitarians have had the impact of a movement such as Fundamentalism, which dominates whole sections of the country! Quaker concern may make Herbert Hoover a great private humanitarian, but other influences determine his politics.

Still, it will be said that Christian liberalism must have had considerable impact if only to judge by the violent reactions of the Fundamentalists and Neo-Calvinists. It did have a large impact, but its influence was mainly theological and not political. The debate between liberals and fundamentalists was primarily over such matters as biblical criticism and the deity of Christ. Liberal theology reached its zenith during the early decades of the twenties, the very years when conservatism dominated American politics. Liberal theology at least implied that a truly Christian society could be achieved here on earth, but not necessarily through social action. For example, one way of exercising Christian responsibility was through individual "stewardship." This did not mean taking literally Jesus' extreme denunciation of wealth, but it did mean that the wealthy Christian should part with some of his money through philanthropy. But charity, like exploitation, was not the concern of the state, and the Christian theory of stewardship bears no resemblance to *Zedakeh.*

While liberal theology did not necessarily mean liberal politics, it sometimes did. Individual Quakers such as John Howard who struggled for prison reform and William Wilberforce who fought slavery were indeed motivated by religious force. Horace Buschnell and Washington Gladden stressed the social implications of Christianity. The Social Gospel was "a new application of the Christian ethic to the demands of a new historical situation"—the industrial age.[48] In fact, many theologians stressed the teachings on social justice of the Hebrew prophets Amos and Micah. But unlike Amos and Micah, the Christian liberals did not demand a recasting of society. Most of them only hoped to make life more bearable on earth, and for a great many the emphasis was still on the world to come. Even Wilberforce preached to the impoverished to accept their lot in life, and Rauschenbusch never supposed that the kingdom of God could be produced by man's efforts. The Social Gospel was a popular movement in the United States for fifty years from 1870 through 1920, but it appears to have affected American politics only slightly throughout its growth. It reached its height in 1908 when it was symbolized by the organization of the Federal Council of the Churches of Christ in America. Ironically, that was the year William Howard Taft, a Unitarian and the candidate of the conservatives, defeated fundamentalist theologian and "liberal" politician William Jennings Bryan for the Presidency.

The optimism of the liberal theology of the late nineteenth century has fallen into disrepute in the aftermath of the great depression, genocide, two degrading world wars, and the terrors of world communism. The Neo-Calvinist writings of Reinhold Niebuhr, J. V. Langmean Casserly, and others have re-emphasized the traditional Christian view of sinful man and its insistence that faith is the key to salvation. There can be little doubt that the Christian emphasis on faith and repentance as contrasted with the Jewish stress on works has influenced American political behavior. As one Jewish writer recently pointed out, faith is essentially personal and works are inherently social.[49] Contrast the recent urging of the executive director of the Rabbinical Assembly of America to rabbis to raise questions and criticize social institutions with the oft-held Lutheran position that Christ's kingdom is not of this world, "and that therefore it is the preacher's duty to preach repentance and faith and not to concern himself with worldly affairs."[50] Because faith is personal and works are usually social, the Christian efforts at social and economic reform, great as they have been, have been dwarfed by the energies which Christians have spent on the saving of souls. Enormous Christian effort goes into missionary work and pastoral counseling, while the Jews hardly pay any attention to these affairs at all. Catholics place strong emphasis on the confessional. And the Church is prepared to make its peace with any social order, authoritarian as well as democratic, so as to concentrate on its main job of personal salvation.

Because of the orthodox stress on the sinfulness of man and the necessity of faith for redemption, many Christians view as the greatest of all impieties any effort by man to bring about what God has promised. Thus, Arnold Toynbee has criticized the restoration of the state of Israel as a prideful usurpation of Divine Will. For the same reason the English historian, like many Neo-Calvinists, has termed the communist movement a "Christian heresy" because it strives to produce the kingdom of God on earth without God, thus denying the capacity of the Almighty to do the task alone. But if the communist movement is in a sense a Christian heresy, it is also Jewish orthodoxy—not the totalitarian or revolutionary aspects of world communism, but the quest for social justice through social action.

Although there are many exceptions, Jews have tended to emphasize the interrelatedness of religion with social organization, while numberless Christians have believed that their temporal interests could be divorced from their religious convictions. By comparison with the Jews the Christians have been otherworldly. Contrast, for example, the notion held by many Christians that celibacy (as sharp a break from this world as one can make) is the highest form of life with the view which Rabbi Bernstein says Jews hold—that "The reward of the good life is the good life."[51] Undoubtedly, there are hundreds of thousands of Christians who agree with Bernstein and his coreligionists, but there are also hundreds of thousands who do not. In a recent book on Christianity and social problems, H. Ralph Higgens describes three typical Christian approaches to social questions, not one of which is held by any sizable number of Jews.[52] The first he calls the "hands off view." Injustice and suffering are to be endured since they are unavoidable "and are to be used by the Christian as spiritual musclebuilders." The second is the "first aid kit approach" used to salve the wounds of an unjust social order. The third holds that nothing much can be done until all men have been converted. Each of these views, as Higgens points out, is melancholy and based on a concept of selfish man. The fact that these are not the only Christian views is borne out by Higgens' own plea for Christian action on social problems, stressing the relevance of Christian morality to social life in the tradition of liberal theology.

The main point is that while there are many Christian approaches to social and political questions, the Jewish position has been relatively unified. While orthodox Christianity stresses man' sinfulness, repentance, and otherworldiness, the Jews appear to have emphasized man's potentialities, works, and life here and now. Orthodox Christian theology has tended to color American politics with a conservative cast from which Jews have been largely exempt. On the other hand, Jewish cultural and theological values have promoted a liberal and radical political style.

It cannot be urged too often that there are many exceptions to the general tendencies described above. Thousands of Methodists, Episcopalians, Presbyterians, Baptists, and Catholics to say nothing of Unitarians and Quakers are, in Bernstein's words, "optimistic" in politics, "strive for a better world," and are "in the thick . . . of movements for social reform." But tendencies there are, and among Jews aggressive and optimistic reformism in politics is found much more often than among their Christian countrymen.

None of this is to say that Christian theology is responsible for making America conservative. In fact, just the opposite is true. The United States is a liberal-democratic state, and the Judeo-Christian emphasis on love, justice, and human dignity is in no small measure responsible for democracy itself. But there is a conservative position within the framework of American politics which can be categorized by such notions as the importance of order, the sanctity of private property, the futility of social change, and the Herbert Hoover type of rugged individualism. These elements of conservatism in American politics may be mainly secular in origin, but they meet with little resistance from the major strains of Christian theology and with a great deal of opposition from Jewish cultural and theological values.

§ *Jewish Solidarity in Politics*

Accepting the view that Jewish insecurity and the Jewish value system primarily account for the political liberalism of American Jews in recent times, the query remains, "Why do Jews take their values and norms from the ethnoreligious group they belong to in making political judgments? Why don't they relate their political behavior to the norms of other reference groups they belong to, their class groups or occupational groups?"

Like all of us, Jews relate to many reference groups.[53] Jewish doctors may adopt either Jewish norms or those of the AMA in judging proposals for socialized medicine; Jewish lawyers may adopt Jewish norms in judging the use of the Fifth Amendment by crypto-communists or they may use those of the American Bar Association; Jewish taxpayers may employ Jewish values as points of reference for judging tax legislation or they may follow the views of a taxpayer's association. The available evidence shows that an unusual number of Jews do derive their political attitudes and opinions from being Jewish. It is that which makes them political liberals and internationalists. Why is it that membership in the Jewish group, apparently without regard to the depth of one's involvement in that group, is so vital in determining the vote behavior of Jews?

There are basically two answers to this, and one of them has already been provided. The Jewish religion and culture are centered on the here and now as the Christian religions and cultures are not. And there is evidence that younger Jews believe that the Jewish religion should become less and less concerned with theology and ritual and more and more concerned with secular social and economic problems.[54] But the fact that Judaism is this-worldly does not mean that Jews will apply Jewish norms to worldly affairs in competition with other norms.

The main answer lies in the unusual cohesiveness and solidarity of the Jewish group. Through centuries of dispersion, persecution, and even genocide the Jews have persisted as a people. The Jews have survived because of the extraordinary will to survive. They have resisted conversion, eschewed intermarriage, and scorned suicide. In the ghettos they developed a strong feeling of common responsibility. Perhaps more than anything else it was the ghetto experience which produced cohesiveness among the Jews. As Louis Wirth explained in his monumental study on Jewish ghetto life:

What makes the Jewish community—composed as it in our metropolitan centers of so many heterogeneous elements—a community is its ability to act corporately. It has a common set of attitudes and values based upon common traditions, similar experiences, and common problems. In spite of its geographical separateness it is welded into a community because of conflict and pressure from without and collective action within. The Jewish community is a cultural community. It is as near an approach to communal life as the modern city has to offer.[55]

Wirth wrote in 1928, when the American ghettos were beginning to disintegrate and the flow of orthodox Jews into the ghettos had just about stopped. But the spectre of anti-Semitism came to replace these unifying factors and to prevent the divisive effects of assimilation. Anti-Semitism made considerable headway in the 1920's and 1930's. Exclusion from good housing and better residential areas was extended. The quota system at schools, in professions, and in clubs barred Jews from access to influence and prestige. Then the depression and the rise of Hitler exacerbated tensions between Jew and Gentile. Over 100 anti-Semitic organizations sprouted during the 1930's, and Gerald L. K. Smith, Father Coughlin, and Gerald Winrod applauded Hitler's attempts to destroy European Jewry. The solidarity of the Jews was reinforced by these events, and the tight cohesiveness of American Jewry was assured for at least a few decades. Jewish doctors, lawyers, laborers, peddlers—all were made conscious of their Jewishness whether they wanted it or not. Their insecurity as Jews served to emphasize Jewish values as points of reference for political action. After the war the growth of Zionism in the United States reinforced cohesiveness still further. The total membership in Jewish voluntary organizations grew from 807,000 in 1935 to 1,085,000 in 1941 and 1,436,000 in 1945, a much higher rate of increase than for all voluntary associations in the United States. . . .[56] Meanwhile, Jewish charities received a sudden burst of support which went far beyond the average national increase despite the fact that the ghettos in the big cities continued to disband and circulation figures for the Yiddish press went steadily down.

The events of our time have not only promoted Jewish unity, but they have made the Jews the most politicized group in the United States. During most of the nineteenth century American Jews were relatively indifferent to politics. Apathy resulted partly from a lack of issues which interested Jews, partly because Jews were so busy doing other things, and partly because of the reluctance of Sephardic and German Jews to enter politics as such. While Rabbinical sermons in the twentieth century are highly secular, mid-nineteenth century Rabbis generally objected to what they called "politics in the pulpit."[57] The Jewish pulpit was usually silent on such topics as free trade, labor unions, and governmental relief. Today, leading Rabbis speak out boldly on almost every major political question. The anti-Semitism and Zionism of recent decades have promoted group consciousness, which, in turn, has made Jewish values influential in shaping the political behavior of American Jews.

There are other contributing sources of Jewish liberalism, but they are probably not of major significance. Lewis Browne has forcefully stated the proposition that Jews are liberals and radicals in politics because they are an urban people.[58] American Jews are concentrated in the urban centers, but many of them were village and peasant folk in East Europe before they came to America. And the fact remains, within the cities other groups are sharply divided in politics on economic class lines whereas the Jews are not.

§ A Personal Conclusion

Some readers may object that I have asserted the liberalism of the Jews and discussed the sources of Jewish liberalism in too sweeping a manner. Need it be said that there are thousands, perhaps hundreds of thousands of American Jews who are not liberal? Of course there are Jewish reactionaries, but these are the exceptions. Still, it ought to be remembered that this book is about Jews in a specific place and a specific time, and that even in a few short years these generalizations may fall. . . . It may be that Jewish liberalism and internationalism are on the wane, and that the Jewish political style is less often found than it was fifteen years ago. The latter seems especially true. But in recent years, as during the first twenty years of the Republic, American Jewry has taken the liberal position in politics, and generalizations about the causes of Jewish liberalism ought not to be abandoned merely because they are large. Since they seem to be true, I would happily acquiesce in Albert Einstein's judgment that "Abandonment of generalization [in the field of politics] . . . means to relinquish understanding altogether."[59]

THE POLITICS OF AMERICAN JEWS

IN OCTOBER, 1954, the Gallup organization reported an interesting difference between Jews and non-Jews: while 49 per cent of all the Americans polled had expressed a preference for the Republicans over the Democrats, only 20 per cent of the Jews polled had done so. This result was particularly striking, as those socio-economic groups in which Jews are highly represented—the professional, business, and white-collar groups—contained, in general, the most Republicans. That Jews, according to these and other figures, are largely Democratic is symptomatic of the fact that their political behavior is not consistent with what are presumed to be the interests of the occupational groups to which many of them belong.

No other group has been so overwhelmingly attached to New Deal politics—or so overwhelmingly opposed to anti-New Deal politicians. In a study by Gallup done in June, 1954, 31 per cent of a national sample of Americans was "intensely disapproving" of Senator McCarthy; 38 per cent of all Democrats felt that way; but among American Jews, fully 65 per cent opposed McCarthy "intensely."

Jews are used to thinking of themselves as liberals, and they know that among their Jewish friends and acquaintances it is simply taken for granted that one is "liberal" and "progressive" rather than "conservative" or "reactionary." It seems interesting, nevertheless, to see just how and why such attitudes have come to prevail. Since we know from historical and scientific data—as well as from personal experience—that Jews in other countries tend by the consistency of their "liberalism" to mark themselves off from non-Jews in much the same manner in which American Jews do, our search for an explanation should lead us, first, to the Old World.

Before the French Revolution there was no problem of political attitudes among Jews: they lived in autonomous communities where they were governed mainly by their own elders. Thus, legally and socially, they constituted a separate people living within, but not "being of," the other peoples of Europe. European countries were still Christian then in a formal sense, and there was no such thing as citizenship for non-Christians.

Within the French Revolution, however, European politics divided

---

Published for the first time in this volume.

The article is based on the author's Ph.D. dissertation: "Sources of American Jewish Liberalism—A Study of the Political Alignments of American Jews" (New School for Social Research, 1956).

into a "left" and a "right" along an axis that involved a new, secular concept of citizenship. The left began to propound the view that nationhood rather than religious affiliation should determine citizenship; whether an individual was Catholic or Protestant should have no bearing on his rights and obligations as a Frenchman, Englishman, German, or any other kind of national, toward the nation-state. This view was extended to include Jews, who in the course of the 19th century became legal citizens of their respective countries all over Western and Central Europe (only Czarist Russia remaining stubbornly "Christian" in its concept of citizenship).

There remained, however, a rightist opposition in all the European countries—conservative parties that clung to the view that the state must be Christian. Not one of these—from the bitterly anti-Semitic Monarchists in Russia through the staunchly Catholic *"Noires"* in France to the amiable Tories in England—could reconcile itself to Jewish political equality. Consequently, while emancipation (the name given to the process by which civil equality was conferred upon Jews) did away with geographical "pales of settlement"—at least for Jews outside Russia—it created a new kind of "pale" in the political area: since adherence to the Christian religion was made a prerequisite for joining the parties of the right, Jews had no alternative but to side with those of the left.

This new political "pale" was only one of a number of signs that the purposes of the emancipation had not been entirely fulfilled. For no matter what laws or even explicit ideologies decreed, Jews were never able to become part of a European nation in a full sense. Emancipation may have given new forms to Christian-Jewish relations, but it could not overcome the social distance between the Jews and the plebian masses of Europe. That persisted as before.

As the psychoanalyst Rudolph Loewenstein has pointed out (in his book *Christians and Jews*), though official Christian doctrine need not of necessity be either friendly or hostile toward the Jews, the effect of Christian teachings has invariably been to stimulate anti-Semitism among the mass of non-theological plebeians. When people are taught from earliest childhood that there is an intimate and ambivalent relation between God and the Jews—God's son being a Jew, the Savior having been denied (or worse!) by the Jews—strong and ambivalent feelings toward the latter are bound to arise. And where conditions of life have made intelligent reflection difficult and scarce, and there is but little to modify aggressive impulses—which is the condition of life for the vast majority of humanity—Christian ambivalence toward Jews usually extends to violent hatred.

To distinguish this plebeian type of anti-Jewishness from those ways in which official Church doctrine can itself be called anti-Semitic, I call it *secondary* Christian anti-Semitism, since plebeian anti-Semitism is derived from, but does not directly express, Christian religious teachings. It is interesting to note that throughout the Middle Ages, during which the Catholic Church was doctrinally anti-Semitic (i.e., when it practiced what

I would call a *primary* Christian anti-Semitism), the Popes again and again sought to protect Jews from the physical threat of plebeian or *secondary* anti-Semitism. While primary anti-Semitism is doctrinal and theoretical, the secondary variety is physical, "racial," and frequently violent. It was this secondary type of anti-Semitism, as we shall see, that complicated the relations of Jews to most of modern politics.

In parties of the moderate and constitutional left, Jews were often able to play prominent roles as intellectuals, journalists, and parliamentarians; one recalls names like Lasker and Rathenau in Germany and Crémieux and Blum in France. Undoubtedly, moderate democratic movements have claimed the allegiance of the overwhelming majority of Europe's Jews. When a strictly Orthodox rabbi, Dob Berush B. Isaac Meisels, was elected, with Catholic help, to represent Cracow in the provisional Austrian Reichsrat of 1848, he took his seat to the left of the aisle. Observing the surprise of the presiding officer at seeing an Orthodox rabbi among the liberals of the left, Meisels remarked, *"Juden haben keine Recht"* (Jews have no right); this describes—*mutatis mutandis*—the situation to this day.

It was the most normal thing for a Jew to support one of the moderate left parties. These movements not only defended the civil rights of Jews against attack by conservatives; they defended law and order against attack by plebeian movements. (Law and order—even if of an anti-Semitic kind—were usually preferred by Jews to the capriciousness of revolutionary situations which, by rousing the lower classes to direct action, would often end up in pogroms.)

But moderate liberalism was far from being able to solve either the general problems of European Jews or the personal ones of Jewish liberals. The very qualities of liberalism which made Jews acceptable to it (and vice versa), namely the emphasis on rational, intellectual, legal, and parliamentary processes, generally limited its influence to the more superficial conscious layers of the mind. The moderate left in Europe lacked both the religious-traditional roots of the conservatives and the quasi-religious appeal of what we know as totalitarian movements. One can never be exclusively and entirely a liberal in the sense in which one can be exclusively and entirely a conservative or a Communist; liberalism, being a "merely" rational point of view, embraces no more than those issues which are easily susceptible to the ministrations of reason; other, "deeper" questions, values, feelings, and instincts remain untouched by it. That is why the political movements of their choice could not help Jewish liberals to raze the spiritual barriers between themselves and Christians. Within the moderate left, Jew still tended to remain Jew, and Christian Christian.

In those cases, moreover, in which Jews became prominent as liberal politicians they made exceptionally vulnerable targets for anti-Semitic attack. The imposition of a rational way of life, always distasteful to the plebeian, was particularly resented when the advocates of this way of life could easily be viewed as strangers to the traditional, religiously derived values of the country. The terrible campaign of hate conducted against Walter Rathenau in the early days of the Weimar Republic, culminating in his assassination, is only the most striking example of the vulnerability of Jewish liberal leaders.

The situation was very different—though no less complex or ambivalent —among the more radical left movements. Since these constituted themselves in effect as post-Christian faiths, previous religious affiliations were presumably irrelevant within their ranks. And in fact radical movements— from the Jacobin Cult of Reason through Marxism and Anarchism to the Bolshevism of our own day—have often been able to offer Jewish participants a measure of communion with non-Jews that was altogether impossible among the moderate left groups.

The radical parties were the organizations of what Toynbee has called the "internal proletariat," i.e., of those who continued to live within Western society though in increasing measure spiritually alienated from it. The social dilemma of the post-emancipation period made Jews particularly prone to join such movements: for, whereas the autonomous Jewish community organizations and the kind of Jewish life they guaranteed had been largely destroyed, the countries where this happened, though ruled by secular states, still remained Christian in their essential patterns of social cohesion. Jews found themselves with all the legal trimmings of equal citizenship—the passport, the right to vote and to hold property, etc.—but still socially isolated and suspect.

This was truer, of course, in some countries than in others. In Russia there had not even been legal emancipation, and a Jewish intellectual, his talents spurned by Russian society, found it easy to make common cause with those who were burning to destroy, once and for all, the whole system of Czarism. The prominence of Jews in the leadership of the 1917 Bolshevik revolution constituted an ultimate reflection of the social position of Russian Jews throughout the 19th century. Trotsky, commander of the Red Army; Zinoviev, first president of the Communist International; and Kamenev, first president of the Soviet Republic—these names indicate what happens when society rigorously denies able and educated men scope for the exercise of their talents.

Germany presents a much milder case. Jews had become legally emancipated there, though they were not fully accepted either by the ruling aristocracy or the commons. German Jews became prominent not only in radical politics, but also in the liberal parties and in liberal journalism. But as we see from the biographies of Eduard Lasker and Walter Rathenau, the pariah status of the German Jews exerted a constant pressure upon them toward radicalism; German society would not—either in the 19th or the 20th century—tolerate a Jew as a normally functioning politician.

The political problems of French Jews, despite all appearances to the contrary, had many similarities with those of the Jews in Germany. After the revolution, France did not formally exclude Jews from government service (as Germany did, to some extent, until the Weimar Republic), but there remained a social exclusion which restricted the career of any would-be Jewish politician to the parties of the left. And even being on the left could not mean the same thing for a Jew that it meant for a non-Jew. In Catholic France, a Jew was *forced* into a radical secularism which few other republicans would match. "Men of Catholic background," writes D. W. Brogan in *France Under the Republic,* "even if otherwise completely alienated from the Church, still tended to think that a religious education was a good thing for their wives and daughters. . . ." Little wonder, then, that the extreme and "proletarian" left (in the Toynbean sense) always contained a large proportion of French Jews.

Radical leftism thus had many attractions for Jews and exercised a large influence on them in practically every European country. Yet at the same time the movements of the radical left constituted a dire threat to Jews. Radical movements appealed directly to the passions of the plebeian masses, and there is a long history of pogroms which shows that any such appeal, no matter what its source, tends to arouse the primitive, "secondary," plebeian type of anti-Semitism in addition to other passions. While revolutionary Jews of 18th-century Paris helped to bring about the fall of the Bastille, revolutionary peasants plundered Jewish houses in the countryside; while Jews were engaged in the grim business of throwing bombs at Czars under the auspices of Russian terrorist organizations, some of their political friends went so far as to address appeals to the peasantry to "arise, laborers, avenge yourselves on the landlords, plunder the Jews, slay the officials"; while a Jew was commander-in-chief of the Red Army in 1918, the Bolshevik-led peasants staged a pogrom in the Ukraine.

Toward the beginning of the 20th century, however, anti-Semitism became rarer in the radical leftist movements than it had been before. One of the reasons for this was that Marxism, with its emphasis on consciousness and control, generally gained ascendancy over Anarchism and Syndicalism with their emphasis on the deed; history has shown that the greater the role of rational purpose and control in a radical movement, the less it accommodates plebeian anti-Semitism. The other reason for the decline of leftist anti-Semitism—and the subsequent history of Bolshevism proves that it was only a decline and no final disappearance—was the rise of a new kind of plebeian movement on the right that made anti-Semitism its specialty. The new anti-Semitic mass parties served to drain the radical parties of their more violent anti-Semitic elements, and forced socialist radicals, in the ensuing sharp conflicts with their plebeian competitors on the right, to clarify their principled opposition to anti-Semitism.

By now we have learned from the history of Bolshevism that its apocalyptic kind of socialism can tolerate plebeian anti-Semitism more readily than can the parliamentary socialism of the Second International. But even Bolshevism—mainly because of its historical ties to Marxism—cannot afford to sponsor the kind of ruthless and unabashed anti-Semitism that was the official program of such parties of the plebeian right as Hitler's in Germany, the Iron Guard in Rumania, and the Arrow Cross in Hungary. Because such parties were among the bitterest opponents of Bolshevism in pre-war days, the latter was able to assume the role of a protector in the eyes of many Jews. The popular image of politics as ranging from an extreme left to an extreme right that were in unbridgeable opposition to each other—this popular fallacy (for it is most certainly a fallacy) is to a very large extent based on the different attitude towards Jews of the two kinds of totalitarian movements.

Let me now summarize the factors that have influenced the character of Jewish participation in European political life. There was, first of all, the general left-right division, with Jews restricted to the left. Probably a majority of the Jews who were at all politically active adhered to the moderate democratic movements. These movements, insofar as they upheld the principles of the Enlightenment, represented the sheerly political interests of Jews, but they could not in any way reduce the persisting underlying social estrangement of Jew from Gentile.

The radical movements offered, apparently, a rapprochement; traditional religious barriers were presumably irrelevant within the post-Christian faiths. It developed very early, however, that any movement seeking to appeal to the plebeian masses would, willy-nilly, arouse the primitive, secondary-Christian, or "racial" type of anti-Semitism. The relations between Jews and the radical left therefore remained inherently ambivalent.

The European Jews were thus caught between the lukewarmness of the moderate parties and the fire of the radical ones. The former were relatively free from anti-Semitism, but could do very little in a positive way to assure the Jew of an integrated, organic place in society. The radicals promised to wipe the board clean of everything including Christianity, which seemed to promise an end to Jewish social isolation, with all becoming brothers of all, but often these movements succeeded most in wiping the board clean of Jews.

When Jews first began to come to the United States in important numbers, after the Civil War, they found an environment in which the traditional Jewish-Christian tensions had been uniquely relaxed. The great diversity of denominations and sects within American Christianity had precluded the establishment (even in a nonlegal or informal sense) of any one church or religious body. Consequently, not only did the differences between Christians and Jews appear—at first sight—as not much more fundamental than the differences among Christians themselves, but the very concept of a Christian state was lacking to the American political tradition.

There always were conservative parties in this country, but their programs never excluded the participation of Jews, and there was no national, pre-Revolutionary tradition of social exclusion. American politics never contained the elements of a primary anti-Semitism, and consequently individual Jews were free to—and to some extent actually did—participate in any American political organization to which their ordinary social and economic interests inclined them. As we shall see presently, however, a number of historical factors—specifically, the persistence of secondary anti-Semitism as well as the identification of American Jews with world Jewry—combined to make Jewishness relevant in the matter of political choice even in this country.

During the Civil War, Jews apparently were found among the partisans of the South as often as among those of the North, and among Democrats as often as among Republicans. In those years American Jews were still few and far between; until about 1870, they probably never numbered more than one-third of one per cent of the population. To a very large extent they were thought of—and thought of themselves—as individually functioning participants in American politics; no one was much concerned over any possible relevance of their Jewishness to their balloting.

But in retrospect we can detect such a relevance. We know, for instance, that Jews in general recoiled very early from any participation in the radical Abolitionist movement, whose fanaticism appealed directly to plebeian malcontents and enlisted veterans of previous radical movements: radical Protestant revivalists, Know-Nothings, anti-Catholics. Jews, significantly, stayed away from the Garrison movement; whether or not they remembered the European lesson, they seemed to apply it: once popular passions—of whatever sort—were aroused and allowed to run unbridled they invariably turned anti-Semitic in any environment where children were taught that the Jews had betrayed Jesus.

It was within the general atmosphere of radical Abolitionism, too, that the most conspicuous expression of official anti-Semitism in American history took place. In the midst of the Civil War, General Grant, irked by the activities of Jewish traders around army camps, issued an order banning all Jews—residents as well as transient traders—from behind Union lines in his department. President Lincoln had to intervene personally to revoke the order; and when the Democrats sought to have Grant censured by Congress, Abolitionist Republicans, not wishing to let it appear that the Democrats could be right about anything, killed the motion.

After the Civil War, the Jewish population of the United States began to swell rapidly, the relatively small flow from Germany becoming augmented by a strong stream from Eastern Europe. These immigrants from Russia and Austria were strongly influenced by their radical intellectuals,

and for many years they formed the backbone of the Anarchist and So-
cialist movements in this country. By 1886 the Jewish community in New
York had become conspicuous for its support of the third-party (United
Labor) mayoralty candidacy of Henry George, the theoretician of the
Single Tax. From then until the second decade of the 20th century, Jewish
districts in New York and elsewhere were famous for their radical voting
habits. The Lower East Side repeatedly picked as its congressman Meyer
London, the only New York Socialist ever to be elected to Congress. And
many Socialists went to the State Assembly in Albany from Jewish districts.
In the 1917 mayoralty campaign in New York City, the Socialist and anti-
war candidacy of Morris Hillquit was supported by the most authoritative
voices of the Jewish Lower East Side: the United Hebrew Trades, the
International Ladies' Garment Workers' Union, and most importantly, the
very popular Yiddish *Daily Forward.* This was the period in which extreme
radicals—like the Anarchists Alexander Berkman and Emma Goldman—
were giants in the Jewish community, and when almost all the Jewish
giants—among them Abraham Cahan, Morris Hillquit, and the young
Morris R. Cohen—were radicals. Even Samuel Gompers, when speaking
before Jewish audiences, felt it necessary to use radical phrases.

What created this situation? First of all, there was the reason mentioned earlier: a radical faith could promise a more meaningful, that is to
say a spiritual, emancipation for Jews. But to this we must also add the
special meaning which a transit from Czarist Russia to the United States
had for a Jew.

As we have noted, there had never been a real attempt at Jewish emancipation under the Czars, and the Jewish intelligentsia in the Russian
empire grew up in an atmosphere of extreme hostility toward the state;
this was further nourished by contact with the Russian intelligentsia, who
likewise were alienated for the most part from Czarist society. One result
of this radical feeling of estrangement from the state and the majority of
society was the abundance of extreme and utopian ideas that were developed and debated in illegal organizations.

Such ideas do not change overnight. When the Jewish intellectual came
to the United States, he was suddenly given an opportunity to theorize
openly and to his heart's content. He took full advantage of it: for many
years, the Lower East Side was one big radical debating society.

There always remained, of course, a good number of Jews who dis-
sented from the general radicalism. The Orthodox Yiddish press (whose
circulation was small in comparison with the *Daily Forward*) was generally Republican in its political preferences. Unlike Rabbi Meisels of
Cracow, who had felt there could not properly be such a thing as a "right"
among Jews, the Orthodox Yiddish journalists of this first generation felt
that, in a country like the United States, their conservatism in Jewish
matters could best be complemented by conservatism in politics too. As
we shall see, two more decades of American experience changed this view;

like the rest of the American Jewish community, the Orthodox Yiddish newspapers in the 30's swung over to Roosevelt. And anyhow this Jewish conservatism could never quite be like the conservatism of Gentiles. Even when there did not seem to be any compelling domestic reasons for Jews to line up with the left, there always were disturbing events abroad. No Jew, for instance, no matter how conservative, could have a kind word for the Czar; and the pre-Bolshevik February revolution of 1917 was hailed by every section of the American Yiddish press, including the Orthodox.

As far as Jews of German origin were concerned, the evidence indicates that until the First World War the majority were affiliated with the party of Lincoln. Whether they voted Democratic or Republican, German Jews in America never became identified with either the lusty and uninhibited radicalism or the equally uninhibited Orthodoxy of the East European Jews. Until roughly the time of the New Deal, the Germans formed American Jewry's genteel 20 per cent.

The 30's mark a new chapter for the American Jewish community. The sons and daughters of the East European immigrants started to found their own businesses, go to college, and enter the professions, thus limiting the Jewish working class more and more to the older generations. And as the social distinctions between German and East European Jew began to fade, while Jewish radicals became moderate and liberal—a tendency in which they were joined by softened conservatives—the social fusion of "uptown" with "downtown" became complemented by a political one. The result was a phenomenon which I would like to call "American Jewish Liberalism," and which soon identified itself with the New Deal.

To most American Jews, Roosevelt represented the great antagonist of Hitler. By the time of the 1936 Presidential elections, almost all sectors of Jewish public opinion had come out for him. Not only did the previously Republican Orthodox Yiddish press switch to Roosevelt, but Jewish Socialists, led by the *Daily Forward,* for the first time abandoned the Socialist ticket in order to support him. It was predominantly Jewish Socialist and trade union leaders who formed the American Labor Party, to enable the old-time radicals to vote for Roosevelt on a "non-capitalist" ticket and thus with a better conscience. Judge Jonah J. Goldstein is reported to have summarized matters as follows: "The Jews had three *velten* [worlds]—*die velt, yene velt,* and Roosevelt."

Yet the reasons for such overwhelming Jewish support of FDR in the early and middle 30's are not at all as obvious as one might imagine. As late as January 1937, Roosevelt asked Congress for an arms embargo against Republican Spain. When Italy attacked Ethiopia, he had imposed an arms embargo that worked to the latter's disadvantage, while refusing at the same time to limit American arms shipments to Japan, who was then engaged in her early campaign against China. It was not until October of 1937, in fact—almost a full year after the 1936 elections—that Roosevelt, in his famous "Quarantine the Aggressors" speech, gave any indication that he would use the power and influence of the United States to oppose the Axis powers.

Before 1937, then, it could not have been his *overt* anti-Hitlerism that so endeared Roosevelt to American Jews. In actual fact, it was something much more interesting for our present inquiry: it was an *imputed* anti-Hitlerism that was based on the characteristically Jewish (that is to say, European) concept of a political left.

When Roosevelt spoke of himself as being "a little to the left of center," he must have confirmed the impression which the bulk of his Jewish supporters already had of him. The New Deal made its mark in this country with the kind of "welfare" program which Jewish Socialist leaders had been advocating for some time: legal encouragement of trade unions, unemployment insurance, social security—the kind of program, in short, which was often associated with Socialist parties. The political spectrum in Europe at that time, as manifest to the naked eye, ranged from the left, whose extreme consisted of the Communists, to a diametrically opposed right, whose extreme was thought of as "fascist." While this spectrum concept could never give a very profound explanation of political realities, it was a powerful force in shaping political attitudes in Europe, and though most Americans tended to pay little attention to it, it has been a potent factor in determining the political allegiance of American Jews to this day.

One of the most fateful consequences of the fixation on the left-right spectrum was to place the Communist movement within the pale of respectability. Browder's slogan that "Communism is 20th-Century Americanism" did not sound so incredible to people who regarded the New Deal as a force of that same left which included—at its extreme, it is true—the Communists. The New Deal administration tended to confirm this impression by recognizing Soviet Russia in 1933, and more importantly, by bringing people who were very close to the Communist Party into government posts.

The general atmosphere of the "anti-fascism" of the 30's, in which the line between the Communists and the others "on the left" was vague and shifting, had a much greater effect upon Jews than upon non-Jews. There is little doubt that Hitlerism caused many Jews to fall back, in some disorder, upon a line of defense which appeared to be a natural one to those who judged according to the outward categories of European politics. *The New York Times* recently quoted a statement that well expresses the feelings of a great many Jews at that time:

> Questioned by newspaper men, Professor ———— said he never was a member of the Community party, but admitted he might have unwittingly attended Communist-front meetings during the Nineteen Thirties. He said that, as a Jew, he felt very strongly against Nazism and the persecution of Jews in Germany and that he had done his best to fight Hitlerism. During the Nineteen Thirties, he added, he might have become associated with Communist-front organizations that were also combatting Nazism.

The Stalin-Hitler pact made a great many Jews recoil from the Communist movement in disgust and dismay, but Hitler's attack on Russia a year and a half later served rather quickly to heal these scars on the "left." With the Russian army locked in combat with the Nazis, the prestige of the USSR and the Communists reached an all-time high. Jewish Socialists who protested against the execution by the Russians of Alter and Erlich —the two most beloved Socialist leaders of the Polish Jews—were thought of as rather tactless. With the possibility of millions of Jews being saved thanks to the "heroism of the Red Army," it seemed like an act of ingratitude to make a fuss about two individuals.

We are now in a position to understand the four major themes in postwar political feeling among American Jews: the support of the liberal wing of the Democratic party; the strong attachment to Israel; the persisting bitterness toward Germany; and an attitude toward Communism that, while as a rule hostile, had something ambivalent in it.

These various aspects of postwar American Jewish Liberalism tended to reinforce one another. Pro-Israeli sentiment, for instance, went well with support of liberal Democrats: Eisenhower's administration had shown far less friendliness to Israel than did Truman's. An overwhelming antipathy to Senator McCarthy was another understandable expression of Jewish liberalism: first and foremost there was the Wisconsin Senator's role as the great anti-Rooseveltian of current American politics; then there was his identification with what is thought of as the "right wing"; finally, there was the fact that in his highly publicized "investigations" many individual Jews figured as targets.

With regard to the ambivalent attitudes of American Jews toward Communism and Russia, we have the information provided by a number of rather carefully constructed opinion polls. Ten years ago, the figures show, 63 per cent of non-Jewish Americans felt "warm" or "friendly" toward Russia, while 84 per cent of Jews felt so; and while 15 per cent of non-Jews expressed a "frigid" feeling, only three per cent of Jews indicated this extreme degree of hostility. In December of 1950, 13 per cent of the "white Christian" population favored equal rights for Communists, while 38 per cent of the Jewish population did (among Negroes, the figure was 20 per cent). More recent studies, however—especially those done immediately after the disclosures of Russian anti-Semitism—have reduced these differences, and it is this writer's guess that at the present moment American Jews are as hostile toward the Russians as non-Jews are, maybe even more hostile now that Communist Russia has emerged as an implacable enemy of Israel. But certain underlying differences undoubtedly remain.

There is still among American Jews a different kind of feeling toward Communists and those accused of Communism from that of most American non-Jews. Most older American Jews knew the radical environment of the early days of the East European Jewish immigration; those who are younger went through the Popular Front days of the 30's and the Second

World War. While not necessarily friends, the Communists were generally regarded as comrades-in-arms within the left. The quarrels with them—and nobody has quarreled as bitterly with the Communists as Jewish Socialists have—always had aspects of a family quarrel. (That does not mean, of course, that these quarrels were not as literally murderous as family quarrels can be.)

Moreover, many American Jews know what Communists look like and how they think; they have eaten with Communists at the same table, have argued with them deep into countless nights. For these American Jews, Communists are human beings. Compare this picture with that of the picture of Communists entertained by the bulk of Americans. Not only is Communism alien to them, but Marxism itself is largely outside their cultural traditions. American workers, unlike their European counterparts, never had to worry about choosing between Communists and Socialists in the unions. And the question whether Marx, if alive, would be a Socialist or a Communist is not a very important one in the everyday life of most Americans. But for Europeans it is, and the American Jewish community has been—certainly it was in the 30's—closer to Europe in this respect. When the American public rejects Communism, it does so largely because it sees in it an alien philosophy; when American Jews reject Communism, they frequently do so because they see it as a noble ideal of brotherhood gone sour. Both processes might end up in a "frigid" response to a public opinion poll, but the respective meanings of that response are profoundly different.

But I do not think that the Jewish relation to Communism remains much of a problem right now; in the first place, Communists no longer stand forth on either the national or international scene as confirmed opponents of anti-Semites; in the case of the Arab-Israeli conflict, in fact, Communists, both inside and outside the Soviet orbit, have tended to side officially with the Arabs. And the line taken by Moscow and China in the Suez crisis has probably done even more to turn Jews all over the world into bitter opponents of Communism. Furthermore, Communists are no longer in positions where they can influence a "liberal" movement; the lines between pro- and anti-Communist liberals are being drawn more and more sharply. It has become practically impossible to be an "innocent" fellow-traveler—or, to put it more exactly, to claim innocent motives for fellow-traveling.

Meanwhile, Jews in the United States have become more politically integrated with their surroundings than anywhere else; this relatively favorable development is due, in my opinion, to the religious heterogeneity of the country and to the absence of the tradition of a Christian state. Consequently, America has known few examples of that desperate, radical, "proletarianized" kind of Jewish intellectual once so common in the Marxist movement of Europe. And yet we do have the phenomenon of American Jewish Liberalism; we do have a set of American Jewish political mores that distinguish Jew from Gentile in very many cases.* (Not all Jews, of course, think the same way on political matters, but those who dissent from the majority's political mores are invariably aware of the fact of their dissent; their very disagreements must, insofar as such persons are Jews, be formulated with reference to the views of the majority.)

I regard this American Jewish Liberalism as the expression of what American Jews feel is their insecure place in the worldwide Gentile environment. The evidence indicates that there is a relation between Jewish insecurity and the relative importance of Jewish Liberalism; the strength of this complex of political ideas—or rather, reactions—was at an all-time high during the Hitler period. Its future, as I see it, depends more on factors in the Gentile world than on those operating among Jews alone.

It would be an error, in my opinion, to compare the assimilative possibilities of American Jews with those of any other American minority. No other American minority produced a man who came to be regarded as God by the whole Christian world while being regarded as no more than a human being by that minority itself. This historical fact or peculiarity is not something the Jews are likely to be separated from as a result of any of the social processes now observable.

Jews and Christians are separated by an ancient social barrier that is religious in nature. I use the word "religious" here in a sense broader than any institutional or theological category: I mean a separation which remains rooted in minds on both sides at as deep a level as religious feeling per se. This separation does not make it impossible for Jews and Christians to live together peacefully; nor does it preclude cooperation in all kinds of activities. But voting differently, feeling differently about politics, seeing the meaning and significance of politics differently—these, I suggest, are inescapable concomitants of the age-old and persisting social barrier between Jew and Christian.† And since the Messianic dawn in which there will be neither Christian nor Jew is not yet in sight, it is probably best to learn to live with this fact rather than disregard it or pretend it is not there.

---

* I have before me the report of a study conducted in 1956 in Chicago by Mr. Maurice Guysenir, from which the table below is taken. His figures are more recent than any I have cited so far.

	Per cent of Jews naming a Democratic candidate as their Presidential choice	Per cent of non-Jews naming a Democratic candidate as their Presidential choice
High SES (Socio-economic status)	66.0	15.9
Middle SES	74.1	17.9
Low SES	95.0	21.9
Average	72.0	18.5

Mr. Guysenir's study makes it clear that Jews continue to differ strikingly from non-Jews in their political preferences.

† This does not mean that we may not expect—indeed, we have already seen—an increase in the number of American Jews voting Republican. Such an increase would perhaps indicate a growing conservative tendency among Jews. But it is also possible for it to indicate a growing liberalizing tendency among Republicans.

NOTES

JEWISH IMMIGRATION AND ACCOMMODATION TO AMERICA

Bernard D. Weinryb

1. The figures are apparently of the sort that the late Louis Wirth once termed "guesstimates." The estimates for the Jewish population at the middle of the century run between 50,000 in 1848 to 150,000 in 1855. For 1877 the figure of 229,000 Jews is mentioned, while M. A. Kursheedt, Secretary of the Russian Immigrant Relief Fund in New York, maintained in October 1881 "there are not over four hundred thousand Jews in this country" (Z. Szajkowski *Publication of the American Jewish Historical Society* [hereafter *PAJHS*] XL, p. 266). It would appear that the Jewish population trebled during some thirty years; this would probably entail an immigration of some 100,000 during the time. This supposition is strengthened by Kursheedt's assertion that "the natural influx of Jewish emigrants is probably from three thousand to five thousand annually"; by K. Fornberg's computation that in the years 1869-1881 some 34,000 Jews came to the United States from Russia (*Yearbook of American Branch of Yivo*, II, pp. 9, 11); and by the exaggeration of the American correspondent of *Hamagid* who wrote (July 6, 1870) that every day thousands of Jews are arriving.

2. Cf. Oscar Handlin, "Our Unknown American Jewish Ancestors," *Commentary*, February 1948, pp. 106-107; *Report on a Conference on the Jewish Experience in America*, May 22-23, 1948 (mimeographed); and B. D. Weinryb, "American Jewish Historiography: Facts and Problems," *Hebrew Union College Annual*, XXIII (1950-51), pp. 222 ff.

3. Similar tendencies are to be found in Palestine-Israel. The fifth *Aliyah* [wave of immigration] of the 1930's is characterized as a German one, though in terms of numbers the German-Jewish immigrants constituted only a minority. Similarly with the third (1919-1923) and fourth (1924-1930) immigration waves, which are usually classified as "Russian" and "Polish" respectively.

4. John W. McConnell, *The Evolution of Social Classes*, Washington, D. C., 1942, pp. 26-29.

5. A good example is the relation to the "Galician" Jews among the Russian-Polish Jewish immigrants at the first quarter of our century.

6. Jacob R. Marcus, *Early American Jewry*, II, Philadelphia, 1953, p. 72.

7. Ernest Stock, "Washington Heights 'Fourth Reich,'" *Commentary*, June 1951, p. 581.

8. *Ibid.*

9. Maurice R. Davie, *Refugee in America*, New York, 1947.

10. Oscar Handlin, *The Uprooted*, Boston, 1951, p. 5.

11. Cf. also S. N. Eisenstadt, "Analysis of Patterns of Immigration and Absorption of Immigrants," *Population Studies*, VII (1953), pp. 167-180.

12. Georges Mauco, "The Assimilation of Foreigners in France," *Cultural Assimilation of Immigrants* (Supplement to *Population Studies*, March 1950), p. 15.

13. Eisenstadt, *op. cit.*, p. 176.

14. See Rudolf Glanz, *Jews in Relation to the Cultural Milieu of the Germans in America up to the Eighteen Eighties*, New York, 1947, p. 20.

15. Cecil Roth, *A History of the Marranos*, Philadelphia, 1932, p. 169.

16. *Ibid.*, p. 176.

17. *Ibid.*, p. 247.

18. Cf. Marcus L. Hansen, *The Atlantic Migration 1607-1860*, Cambridge, Mass., 1940, pp. 71 ff.

19. R. Mahler, *Divrey Yemey Yisrael, Ba-doroth Achronim*, I, Merhavya, 1952, pp. 83-85.

20. Cf. Roth, *op. cit.*, pp. 146 ff., and *passim*.

21. Since the early Kehilloth in the United States did not have legal powers, American Jewish historians generally follow the cliché of regarding them as voluntary organizations. However, from the point of view of a strongly motivated and religiously minded group, *herem* and exclusion was

quite enough power, for it made it impossible for Jews to continue to exist as Jews. It should be recalled that the community controlled the holding of religious services; the burial place; social services; distribution of Kosher foods, matzoth. ethrogim, probably also all ritual objects, since for such a small group it would have been unprofitable to handle them on a commercial basis. Marcus (*op. cit.*, p. 434) follows the general trend among historians but adds a qualification: ". . . affiliation was to a large degree compulsory in American Jewish Community."

22. Mahler's attempt to make Seixas almost a modern Zionist is the result of a misunderstanding of the character of the traditional Jewish sermon, beset as it was with the motif of "return" (see R. Mahler, "Yahaduth America Ve-Raayon Shivath Zion Bitkufath Ha-mehapecha Ha-amerikanith," *Zion*, XI, pp. 107-134). On the other hand, unlike the reformers of the second half of the nineteenth century, neither Seixas nor his congregation saw in the return-belief any offense to their patriotism.

23. Cf. B. D. Weinryb, "Noah's Ararat Jewish State in its Historical Setting," *PAJHS*, XLIII (1954), pp. 170-191.

24. Cf. B. D. Weinryb, "Gormin Kalkaliyim ve-Sozialiyim Ba-haskalah Hayehudith Bagermania," *Knesseth*, Tel Aviv, 1938, pp. 416 ff.

25. This was mostly limited to the large cities; the majority of the Jews in these regions lived in villages.

26. If, for instance, in Bavaria, an anti-Semite—the judge Johann Friedrich Siegmund v. Holzsehuher—learned this language and published in it, with German characters, a number of booklets and books for the purpose of anti-Jewish propaganda (writing under the assumed Jewish name of "Itzig Feitel Stern") this may prove that this Judeo-German was still in wide use in the 1830's and 1840's.

27. *Israelitische Annalen*, 1839, 1840.

28. Adolf Kober, "Jewish Emigration from Württemberg to the United States of America, 1848-1855," *PAJHS*, XLI, pp. 253-268.

29. In Wuerttemberg, of 206 individuals whose age is mentioned (1848-1855), 61% were below 20 years of age and 12% were of the age-group 20-30.

30. Aaron Wolfsohn (1756-1835), the co-editor of *Hameassef*, in ridiculing Polish-Jewish piety, tells of a Polish *lamden* (learned Jew) who did not believe in the existence of America and regarded stories about it as comparable to heretical tales ("Sicha be-Eretz Hachayim," *Hameassef*, VII, p. 123). If this story has any actual meaning it would seem that the Polish Jews who actually went to America were not overly learned or pious.

31. A German or Polish Jew may have been himself unlearned, but he was "assured" of survival and the "normal existence" of things by the fact that others were steeped in Torah.

32. Mose Weinberger, *Hayehudim Va-Hayahaduth B'New York*, New York, 1887, p. 28.

33. *Allgemeine Zeitung des Judentums*, XI (1847), p. 23. See also Kober, *op. cit.*

34. Quoted in J. R. Marcus, *Early American Jewry*, II, Philadelphia, 1953, pp. 153-154.

35. *Ibid.*, p. 176.

36. The more frequent use of Hebrew (and Yiddish) phrases and expressions in minute books and other community documents, which is observable at the end of the eighteenth century, may have come from this penetration of Ashkenazim into Sephardic communities, and their rise to leadership status.

37. It should be remembered that the "forty-eighters," and those who left Germany for political rather than economic reasons, constituted an exceedingly small group.

38. For particulars see B. D. Weinryb, "German Jewish Immigrants to America," in *Jews from Germany in the United States*, New York, 1955, pp. 103-126.

39. Abram V. Goodman, "A Jewish Peddler's Diary," *American Jewish Archives*, III, 3, (June 1951), pp. 96-104.

40. Rabbi David Einhorn claimed that the whole Reform movement in America would stand still or fall depending on whether or not German was used in religious services.

41. It should not be overlooked that the same synagogue was also designed to avoid alienating the Americanized elements of the second generation.

42. B'nai B'rith, for example, refused to allow a number of Jews from Poland and Russia to establish a lodge, declaring them unfit to belong to the organization, since they were anxious for orthodoxy and "too uncivilized" (*Hamagid*, March 2, 1881).

43. An attempt to reconstruct the culture of the *shtetl* as an integral unity (see Mark Zborowski and Elizabeth Herzog, *Life Is With People*, New York, 1952) can at best be regarded as a gross oversimplification.

Of similar quality are the tendencies of the last decade or so (stemming from a psychological reaction to the destruction of European Jewry during World War II) to idealize the past. All such attempts are dictated by nostalgia and romanticism; they constitute gross exaggerations if not falsifications.

44. The more liberal press which sometimes defended Jewish immigration (see, for example, the *New York Herald,* Sept. 15, 1891; Dec. 10, 1891) was not often expressing *vox populi.*

45. Cf. Oscar Handlin, "How U. S. Anti-Semitism Really Began," *Commentary,* June 1951, pp. 541-548.

46. See Irving A. Mandel, "The Attitude of the American Jewish Community toward East European Immigration," *American Jewish Archives,* III, pp. 11-36; Z. Szajkowski "The Attitude of American Jews to East European Jewish Immigration," *PAJHS* XL, (1951), pp. 221-280; B. D. Weinryb, "East European Immigration to the United States." *The Jewish Quarterly Review,* XLV, pp. 497-528.

47. Quoted in Zosa Szajkowski, "The Attitude of American Jews to East European Jewish Immigration 1881-1893,"

PAJHS, XL (1951), pp. 225 ff.

48. *Ibid.,* p. 227.

49. *Ibid.*

50. *Jewish Exponent,* Philadelphia, Aug. 5, 1887, p. 8. Cf. *ibid.,* Sept. 9, 1887, p. 7.

51. From New York: 1887: 1,082 (3.5% of those arriving at the port of New York); 1888: 1,396 (5.2%); 1889: 1,118 (4.9%); 1890: 1,204 (4.5%).

52. Harold Silver, "The Russian Jew Looks at Charity, 1890-1900," *Jewish Social Service Quarterly,* IV (1927), pp. 129-144.

53. B. Hoffman, *Fifzik Yohr Cloakmacher Union,* New York, 1936, p. 22.

54. M. Z. Raisin, *Dapim mi-Pankaso shel Rabi,* New York, 1941, p. 171.

55. Non-Jewish immigrants had done the same thing when they encountered difficulties (cf. M. L. Hansen, *The Immigrant in American History,* p. 47).

56. Raisin, *op. cit.,* p. 167.

57. S. Niger, "Meyer altheynmish vi Amerikanish," *Die Zukunft,* April 1940.

58. *Morgen Journal,* Sept. 9, 1914. For particulars, see Joseph Rappaport, *Jewish Immigrants and World War I* (Unpublished Ph.D. dissertation, Columbia University, 1951).

AMERICA IS DIFFERENT

Ben Halpern

1. Cited in C. Bezalel Sherman's article, "Nationalism, Secularism and Religion in the Jewish Labor Movement," *Judaism,* Fall 1954 (Tercentenary Issue), p. 355. The statement occurs in a manifesto issued by "Abraham Cahan, Organizer," on behalf of the Hebrew Federation of Labor of the United States and Canada, which was published in *Die Arbeiter Zeitung* (New York), December 5, 1890, two months after the Federation's founding convention. The full text is reproduced in E. Tcherikower's *Geshikhte fun der Yidisher arbeter-bavegung in die Fareynikte Shtatn* (New York, 1945), Vol. II, pp. 499-502.

2. When American anti-Semites avail themselves of election periods in order to conduct their propaganda, they do, of course, formulate "programs." The provisions relating to Jews in these documents are usually more vituperative than programmatic in character, and they combine obvious, though rather feeble, imitation of European models with some specific American features, reflecting animosity against

American Jewish organizations. I owe the following typical examples to the courtesy of my friend Jack Baker of the Anti-Defamation League: In William Dudley Pelley's (The Silver Shirt) weekly, on September 5, 1934, appeared "The New Emancipation Proclamation—The Silver Shirt Program." It proposed "racial quotas on the political and economic structure" in order to prevent Jewish office-holding "in excess of the ratio of (Jews) . . . in the body politic." All Jews, and all foreign-born persons not "completely naturalized," were to be registered, under severe penalties for evasion. All Jews were to be compelled to "forswear forever . . . Jewish allegiance," and any Jew apprehended in giving support to Jewish nationalism was to be criminally prosecuted for sedition. (Quoted in Gustavus Myers, *History of Bigotry in the United States* [New York, 1943], pp. 405-6.)

The 1948 election platform of Gerald L. K. Smith's Christian Nationalist Party called for "the immediate deportation of all supporters of the political Zionist movement" and the outlawry of "this international machine and all its activity." Such "Jewish Gestapo organizations" as "the so-called Anti-Defamation League, the American Jewish Congress, the so-called Non-Sectarian Anti-Nazi League, the self-styled Friends of Democracy" were to be dissolved. Immigration of "Asiatics, including Jews, and members of the colored races" was to be stopped. The partition of Palestine was opposed. The party program published by Smith in 1952, however, had no such specific references to Jews.

The nine point "Program of the National Renaissance Party" (published in the National Renaissance *Bulletin*, October, 1953, pp. 3 and 4) proposed, under point 1, to "repudiate the operetta-State of Israel;" in point 2, "to enforce a strict policy of racial segregation in America"; and in point 3 "to bring about a gradual deportation of unassimilable elements . . ." *viz.*, the "Puerto Ricans, Negroes, Jews and Asiatics"; in point 4, to bar Jews "from all political and professional posts" and to forbid marriage between Jews and "members of the dominant White Race;" and in point 6, to base American foreign policy upon a "German-American alliance in Europe; a Moslem-American alliance in the Middle East; and a Japanese-American alliance in Asia" (Reproduced in the U.S. House of Representatives, Commitee on Un-American Activities, *Preliminary Report on Neo-Fascist and Hate Groups*, Washington, Dec. 17, 1954, pp. 21-2).

See also Richard Hofstadter's comment on the tendency of the political attitudes of the "new American right" to express themselves "more in vindictiveness, in sour memories, in the search for scapegoats, than in realistic proposals for action" ("The Pseudo-Conservative Revolt" in *The New American Right*, ed. Daniel Bell, ed. [New York, 1955], p. 44, and note similar observations in other sources referred to by Hofstadter (*Ibid.*, p. 54, note 7.)

3. See Graetz's narrative of the "Synhedrion" in Paris and the events leading up to it, *History of the Jews* (Jewish Publication Society translation, Philadelphia, 1895), Vol. V, pp. 474-509.

4. The quip of the famous Orientalist Chwolsohn—that he was converted out of conviction, the conviction that it was better to be a professor in Petersburg than a *melamed* in Shnipishok—is only one of a long line of cynical anecdotes (going back

at least as far as Heine), which illustrate the psychology of many such conversions.

5. David Shub (in *The Jewish Daily Forward*, New York, May 15, 1955) says that this sentiment was attributed by Zionists to the Jewish Socialist leader Vladimir Medem (1879-1923), and was always denied by Medem and his associates. Whatever the origin of the quotation, which I have not been able to check further, it became a popular byword succinctly expressing an attitude of which Russian and Polish Jews had had several striking evidences among revolutionaries.

A pamphlet inciting to pogroms was issued by the revolutionary *Narodnaya Volya* group, and though it was withdrawn subsequently, there was a continuing discussion of the advisability of using anti-Semitism to foster a revolutionary atmosphere. The shock effect of this event on the Russian Jewish *intelligentsia* is described in Abraham Liessin's "Episodes," in the Yiddish Scientific Institute's *Historishe Shriften*, Vol. III (Vilna-Paris, 1939), pp. 196-200. It was from this same time that we date the reaction of a significant group of Russian Jewish intellectuals against the ideal of Emancipation and the rise of the counter-ideal of Auto-Emancipation.   ,

6. See, however, Judd L. Teller's article, "America's Two Zionist Traditions," in *Commentary*, October, 1955, pp. 343-52. This article emphasizes the existence of a pre-Herzlian Zionist "tradition" in America, represented by Mordecai Emanuel Noah and Emma Lazarus. It also highlights the difference in attitude between some native-born (or American-educated) early Zionists, like Louis D. Brandeis and Julian W. Mack, and the Eastern European outlook of immigrant Zionism. In common with many writers during the recent Tercentenary celebrations of American Jewry, Teller strains the data perceptibly in an effort to make episodes add up to a native American Jewish tradition; but the differences he emphasizes between the Zionism of the immigrant ghetto and the Zionism of "Uptown" Jews is a significant one, in view of the similarity of the latter to the neo-Zionist mood of today. Illustrations of early "native American" Zionist views will be found in a source book on Zionist thought, *The Zionist Debate*, edited by Arthur Hertzberg, which is being prepared for publication.

SOME ASPECTS OF JEWISH DEMOGRAPHY

Ben B. Seligman

with the assistance of Aaron Antonovsky

1. This rough total is based on estimates of Jewish population in 1,237 communities, obtained through the aforementioned poll, files of the United Jewish Appeal, surveys conducted by the Jewish Welfare Board and the files of the Council of Jewish Federations and Welfare Funds.

2. Sophia M. Robison, ed., *Jewish Population Studies* (New York: Conference on Jewish Relations, 1943). Dr. Robison's survey included studies on the Jewish communities of Trenton and Passaic, Buffalo, Norwich and New London, Pittsburgh, Detroit, Chicago, Minneapolis and San Francisco.

3. In only some of the community studies reviewed here were single-year age groupings included in the statistical report (Indianapolis, Passaic, Port Chester, New Orleans). Lacking such primary information, it was difficult to compare the various studies because of the varying age-class intervals established by each investigator. Special local problems apparently motivated the particular choice of an age-class interval. Thus, one investigator might be interested only in those persons under 25 years for purposes of studying youth activities, or another in those persons between ages six and fourteen in order to help analyze a problem relating to Jewish education. Yet it was necessary to compare the communities on some uniform basis, if even tentative generalizations concerning their Jewish populations were to be offered. This was achieved by constructing cumulative percentage graphs for each community on a scale sufficiently large to permit an interpolated reading back to a uniform age grouping established for all the studies.

4. In Newark an interesting shift is discernible. The highly productive age groups, 25 to 35, apparently prefer to reside in the city rather than in the suburbs, whereas the 35 to 45 age groups exhibit a contrary preference.

5. See L. Rosenberg, "Age Distribution of the Jewish Population in Ontario," *Information and Comment* (Canadian Jewish Congress), No. 8, March, 1939, especially Table 2. The largest age groups in 1941 were 20 to 34 years.

6. Benjamin B. Goldman and Alvin Chenkin, *The Jewish Population of New Orleans:* 1953, New York: CJFWF, 1954.

7. The statistical device employed for analyzing this aspect of population structure is the sex ratio, expressed as the number of males per 100 females.

8. Table 4 indicates that, in some communities at least, the proportion of divorces in the Jewish population is much smaller than in the general population.

9. Cf. Ruby J. R. Kennedy, "Single or Triple Melting Pot? Intermarriage in New Haven, 1870-1950," *American Journal of Sociology*, LVIII (July, 1952), pp. 56-59.

10. In using census data, one is confronted with the dilemma of using "families," which excludes people living alone, or "households," which may include non-related individuals as long as they dwell in one housing unit. Since the Jewish community data includes one-person families, "households" is a more comparable term.

11. *Statistical Abstract of the United States, 1951,* Tables 31, 33, pp. 24-25.

12. The Newark data are presented in detail in Table 9-A, *American Jewish Year Book*, Vol. LI, 1950, p. 19. The mean number of children per family in the city was 2.19; in the suburbs, 1.90.

13. It has been suggested that this type of enumeration secures a more accurate picture of the average size of the Jewish family. However, to obtain an entirely valid analysis, it would be necessary to distinguish between "completed" and "incompleted" families; otherwise younger families which might still have children in the future would be subsumed into the total picture. Further, this approach excludes the "single person" families, which is a sociological fact of some significance. It does help, however, in giving some idea of fertility in the Jewish population.

It ought further be noted that differences in the definitions of "household" and "family" as utilized in the various decennial censuses and in Jewish population studies may exaggerate the divergence between the average family size of Jewish and non-Jewish families. For example, grandparents may remain in the same domicile with children and grandchildren in rural and suburban areas to a greater degree than in urban areas, thus markedly increasing the average "household" size. With the Jewish population predominantly urban, and taking into account the urban predilection for small apartments, we may have here a factor explaining in part the ostensibly smaller Jewish family. This, of course, requires further investigation.

14. Cf., Ben B. Seligman, "How Many Jews in 1970?," *National Jewish Monthly,* April, 1955.

15. Nathan Goldberg, "Jewish Population in America," *Jewish Review* (Jan.-Dec. 1948); *idem, Population Trends Among American Jews* (American Jewish Congress Public Affairs Pamphlet II, No. 5, April 1948); *idem,* "The Jewish Population in the United States," *The Jewish People: Past and Present,* Vol. II (New York 1948).

16. *Information and Comment,* No. 7, June 1948, published by Canadian Jewish Congress.

17. Mortimer Spiegelman, "The Longevity of Jews in Canada, 1940-1942," in *Population Studies,* December, 1948, p. 292 ff. Goldberg, in *The Jewish People, op. cit.,* comments briefly on Jewish longevity, but his data go back to 1910 and 1931.

18. The writer suggests that specific death rates for Jewish populations might be arrived at through a population survey by asking respondents for information on recent deaths in the family. This implies, of course, a well-designed questionnaire as well as skillful interviewing. This was attempted in a recent health survey of New York City conducted by the Health Insurance Plan of Greater New York.

19. *17th Census, U.S. Summary* (vol. II, part 1) Table 50, p. 99.

20. *Ibid.,* Table 53, p. 101.

21. Cf., *Statistical Abstract, 1948,* Table 208, p. 193. The only studies which pro-

vided such detailed information were those for Newark, Portland and Charleston.

22. The statistical data on this may be found in the original reports. They are not reproduced here because of their cumbersome character.

23. The remainder were unoccupied. *Statistical Abstracts, 1951,* p. 721.

24. It is because of this that the columns in Table 15 are not strictly comparable.

25. The 26-30 groups show a different trend. A larger proportion of all whites were enrolled in school than of Jews (8.6 and 1.2 per cent, respectively). This is attributable to the fact that the 1950 Census changed its reporting in that year and included in the data for each community all students attending school there. This included all those attending New Orleans schools under the G.I. Bill in 1950. The study of the Jewish population, however, did not include Jewish students from out of town staying temporarily in New Orleans for studies.

26. Nathan Goldberg has made considerable use of these tabulations in his studies of the relation between family size, nativity of parents, and mother tongue. Cf. *op. cit.* in Note 15.

27. An example of outright identification of persons of Russian origin as Jewish may be found in *Social Areas of Los Angeles,* by E. Shevky and M. Williams, published by the University of California Press.

28. Yiddish-speaking groups appear to perpetuate their native tongues to a lesser degree in the second and succeeding generations than in other groups; *Cf.* T. L. Smith, *Population Analysis,* (McGraw-Hill, 1948), p. 86.

THE JEWISH POPULATION OF NEW YORK CITY: 1952

Ben B. Seligman

1. See my other article in this volume. Interested readers will wish to compare a number of the tables contained in the previous article with those presented in this one.

2. Thanks are due to the Health Insurance Plan of Greater New York for permission to duplicate the IBM cards of the Jewish respondents. The interest of Dr. Paul M. Densen of the HIP organization is

also gratefully acknowledged.

3. Cf. "The Religio-Cultural Background of New York City's Population," by N. R. Deardorff. *Milbank Memorial Fund Quarterly,* Vol. XXXIII, No. 2 (April 1955), pp. 152-160.

4. Cf. *American Jewish Year Book,* Vol. 56, 1955, p. 121.

5. Henry Cohen, *Jewish Population Trends in New York City,* Federation of

Jewish Philanthropies of New York, 1956. This publication was issued in mimeographed form and is fourteen pages in length. Subsequent citation of the report by Cohen refers to this publication.

6. In the absence of birth and death rate data it is difficult to visualize how this might be computed.

7. Cf. "Social Characteristics of American Jews, 1654-1954" in *American Jewish Year Book*, Vol. 56, 1955, p. 25.

8. Deardorff, *op. cit.*, p. 159.

9. Derived from Deardorff, *op. cit.*, p. 158.

10. *American Jewish Year Book*, Vol. 56, 1955, p. 120.

SOME CHARACTERISTICS OF DETROIT AREA JEWISH AND

NON-JEWISH ADULTS

David Goldberg and Harry Sharp

1. Owing, in part, to the clustered residential pattern among Jews, it is virtually impossible to estimate with certainty the number of Jews in the Detroit area from the results of an area-probability sample survey such as is used in this research. A difference of one per cent (well within sampling error) in the sample proportion of Jews would change the estimate by about 25,000 persons. A recent paper by Albert Mayer and S. Joseph Fauman ("Estimates of the Jewish Population by the Death Rate Method," appearing in the *Jewish Social Studies*) estimates the Jewish population of greater Detroit as 75,000 persons.

2. The Detroit Area Study's sample is based on a three-stage probability model. The selection stages are census tracts, blocks and dwelling units. Tracts and blocks are selected with probabilities proportional to size. Census information is obtained from every adult in the selected dwelling. Substitution of sample addresses is not permitted. The sample universe, i.e., the tracted area of greater Detroit, includes 89 per cent of the population of the Detroit Standard Metropolitan Area as defined by the United States Census.

3. An area-probability sample has greater variability than a simple random sample when the particular characteristic or population group in question is concentrated in a few geographic areas. In computing sampling errors for this paper, allowance was made for the clustering effect of the characteristics described. Although the variances were often considerably larger than might be expected in a simple random sample, all differences in proportions between Jews and non-Jews which are men-

tioned in the text are large enough to be statistically significant at the 5 per cent level unless otherwise noted.

4. See Philip Jaffe, "Differential Mortality in Detroit, 1940-1950" (Unpublished M. A. Thesis, Wayne University, 1953).

5. Clyde V. Kiser and P. K. Whelpton, "Differential Fertility Among 41,498 Native White Couples in Indianapolis," *Milbank Memorial Fund Quarterly*, XXI (July, 1943), pp. 221-280.

6. For example, see Carl M. Rosenquist and S. Thomas Friedman, "Jewish Population Trends in the United States," *Social Research*, XVIII (June, 1951), pp. 203-218.

7. For a summary of relevant studies and an original contribution to the literature, see S. Joseph Fauman, "Occupational Selection Among Detroit Jews," *Jewish Social Studies*, XIV (June, 1952), pp. 17-50.

8. Liston Pope, "Religion and Class Structure," *Annals of the American Academy of Political and Social Science*, CCLVI (March, 1948), pp. 84-91.

9. Fauman (*op. cit.*) also notes the existence of a much higher educational level for young Jews than for non-Jews of comparable ages.

10. Although there is a difference of about 20 per cent in the proportion of home owners among Jews as contrasted to Catholics and white Protestants, the difference is not statistically significant because of the extreme clustering of this characteristic.

11. As used here, the term "formal organization" is synonymous with "voluntary group." The church or synagogue, a special type of formal group, is not included in this definition.

OCCUPATIONAL SELECTION AMONG DETROIT JEWS

S. Joseph Fauman

1. *American Jewish Year Book,* Vols. XLIX-LI (Philadelphia 1948-50); Robison, Sophia M., and Starr, Joshua, eds., *Jewish Population Studies* (New York, 1943); Fauman, S. Joseph, "The Factors in Occupational Selection Among Detroit Jews," pp. 17-18 (Unpublished Ph.D. dissertation, University of Michigan, 1948).

2. U. S. Census, 1940, *An Alphabetical Index of Occupations and Industries,* prepared by Alba M. Edwards under the general supervision of Leon E. Truesdell (Washington, 1940).

3. See Baron, Salo W., *A Social and Religious History of the Jews* (New York, 1937) and other studies of Jewish history from a sociological point of view. See also Meyer, Henry J., "The Structure of the Jewish Community in the City of Detroit" (Unpublished Ph.D. dissertation, University of Michigan, 1939) for a discussion of the effect of Jewish occupational patterns upon Jewish behavior in the City of Detroit.

4. The concepts of value system and of value orientation that are used in this study are derived from Robert C. Angell's *The Integration of American Society* (New York, 1941). The following quotation gives the essence of the concept: "The basis of understanding that makes society possible is a common world of experience. The persons concerned have similar ideas with respect to the nature and function of objects and similar expectations with reference to the behavior of persons because they have been affected by a common milieu." (p. 8). The Angell study as a whole is an example of value-system analysis.

5. U. S. Census Monograph No. VII, *Immigrants and Their Children,* prepared by Niles Carpenter (Washington, 1927).

6. See Warner, W. Lloyd, and Srole, Leo, *The Social Systems of American Ethnic Groups,* (New Haven, 1945) for a discussion of these points.

7. Baron, Salo W., *The Jewish Community,* (Philadelphia, 1942); Aronson, David, *The Jewish Way of Life* (New York, 1946) p. 116; and Fishberg, Maurice, *The Jews* (New York, 1911).

8. *Michigan Census of Population and Unemployment,* (Lansing, Michigan: State Emergency Welfare Relief Commission, 1936-37) Ten Bulletins, Works Progress Administration. Also see Fauman, *op. cit.,* pp. 23-31, for a complete description of

the sample, the manner in which it was drawn, and the way in which Jews were identified. The original study discusses in detail the effect of age, residence, and other factors upon the sample.

9. Fauman, *op. cit.,* Ch. II; Michigan Census, *op. cit.*

10. Meyer, *op. cit.*

11. See Deming, W. Edwards, *The Statistical Adjustment of Data* (New York, 1943), Chs. I and VII, for a discussion of the assumptions and procedures involved in the adjustment of data. The particular problem of adjusting cells to known marginal totals is treated in Ch. VII. The method used here is similar to the discussion given by Deming.

12. See Davidson, Percy Erwin, and Anderson, H. Dewey, *Occupational Mobility in an American Community* (Stanford, 1937).

13. See Clark, Carrol D., and Gist, Noel P., "Intelligence as a Factor in Occupational Choice," *American Sociological Review,* Vol. III (October, 1938). Another article in which Gist collaborated stresses the same factor from a somewhat different point of view. See Gist, Pihlblad, and Gregory, "Scholastic Achievement and Occupation," *American Sociological Review,* Vol. VII (1942) pp. 752-63.

14. Meyer, *op. cit.*

15. Davidson and Anderson, *op. cit.,* p. 164 *passim.* Also Bell, Howard M., *Youth Tell Their Story* (Washington, 1938); McGill, Nettie P., and Matthews, Ellen N., *The Youth of New York City* (New York, 1940); Rogoff, Natalie, *Recent Trends in Occupational Mobility* (Glencoe, 1953). According to Rogoff's analytic technique the procedure best suited for the analysis of mobility generationally is to compare two generations of fathers and sons, and to analyze also the effect of race, age of son, and nativity of father while holding constant occupational structure in the two periods. But no ethnic or religious differentiation of fathers and sons in the white groups is made—apparently from lack of data. Rogoff concludes that (p. 106) "The likelihood of occupational movement did not depend greatly on the occupational origins of the sons, but the *destinations* they achieved did depend on their origins. . . . But the positions into which they moved varied with their occupational ori-

gins. This was especially true in 1940, indicating that the processes by which men selected and were selected for occupations were more closely related to social origins in 1940 than they had been in 1910." Actually the differential rate of mobility and immobility of sons of Jewish and non-Jewish parents in Detroit shown in Table IV demonstrates that the variation in subgroups within a population may be far greater and perhaps more significant than the similarities in the total group experience in two points in time. The Rogoff approach, valuable though it is, does not answer the question of how, in a given time and place, occupational selection and mobility of youth operate within and between groupings in the community. Our data seem to demonstrate that occupational destinations are much more than a result of occupational origins. Further, our data show education as the most important single factor influencing occupational destinations while, at the same time, quantity of education is not related to occupational origins.

16. Davidson and Anderson, *op. cit.*

17. Fauman, *op. cit.*

18. Fauman, *op. cit.*, pp. 54-57.

19. MacIver, R. M., ed., *Civilization and Group Relationships* (New York, 1945), Ch. VI, has a good discussion of the interrelationships between group advantage and education in the United States. See also Rogoff, Natalie, *op. cit.*, for a contrary view of the influences upon occupation of sons.

20. See the previous section for a discussion of the role of father's occupation in the occupational adjustments of Jewish sons. What is said there about Jewish skilled sons may also apply to clerical sons as well.

21. Fauman, *op. cit.*, pp. 67-68.

22. Fauman, *op. cit.*, p. 69.

23. Parkes, James, *The Emergence of the Jewish Problem, 1878-1939* (New York, 1946).

24. See Fauman, S. Joseph, "The Jews in the Waste Industries in Detroit," in *Jewish Social Studies*, Vol. III (1941) pp. 41-56, for an example of the way in which these habits affected one of the present-day occupations of Jews in America.

THE AMERICAN JEW

AND THE ATTAINMENT OF MIDDLE-CLASS RANK:

SOME TRENDS AND EXPLANATIONS

Nathan Glazer

1. See articles by Ben B. Seligman, *American Jewish Year Book*, 51, 1950, p. 28; 52, 1951, p. 12; 54, 1953, p. 14. [Hereafter *AJYB*.]

2. A. J. Jaffe and C. D. Stewart, *Manpower Resources and Utilization*, New York, 1951, p. 190.

3. The author, together with Herbert Hyman and S. M. Lipset, has analyzed two public opinion polls conducted in New York and its vicinity in 1948 and 1951 by the National Opinion Research Center. The statement in the text is based on these studies. A full report of what these studies reveal about New York Jews is in the files of the *AJYB*. A much larger sample study of the population of New York City was conducted subsequently, and data from this research are reported on in the present volume in the contribution of Ben B. Seligman. The new material supports the statement in the text.

4. These studies are from Sophia M. Robison, ed., *Jewish Population Studies*,

New York, 1953; Seligman in *AJYB* (op. cit.), 51, 1950, p. 28. The information on New Orleans is from Julian K. Feibelman, *A Social and Economic Study of the New Orleans Jewish Community*, Philadelphia, 1941.

5. Jaffe and Stewart, *op. cit.*

6. Charles Reznikoff and Uriah Z. Engelman, *The Jews of Charleston*, Philadelphia, 1950, pp. 263-64.

7. See footnote 3. Once again, this point is confirmed by the data in Seligman's paper.

8. These figures are from the study referred to in footnote 3. The study analyzed in Seligman's paper shows 9% of Jewish families with incomes over $8,000. This is unquestionably more reliable than the figures in the text, which was based on much smaller samples.

9. Ernest Havemann and Patricia Salter West, *They Went to College*, New York, 1952, p. 187.

10. We have no figures on occupations

of fathers of all Jewish college graduates. However, a study of female college graduates shows a smaller proportion of professionals among the fathers of Jewish students than among the fathers of non-Jewish students, and it is reasonable to assume the same would be true for the fathers of male college students. Robert Shosteck, *Five Thousand Women College Graduates Report*, B'nai B'rith Vocational Service Bureau, 1953, pp. 8-9.

11. Louis M. Terman and Melita T. Oden, *The Gifted Child Grows Up*, 1947, p. 298.

12. Havemann and West, *op. cit.*, pp. 187-89.

13. L. Wallerstein, "The Jewish Doctor," *Commentary*, 19, 1955, pp. 244-50.

14. Mirra Komarovsky, "The Voluntary Associations of Urban Dwellers," *American Sociological Review*, 11, 1946, pp. 686-98.

15. Herbert Goldhamer, *Some Factors Affecting Participation in Voluntary Organizations*, Ph.D. thesis, Sociology Department, University of Chicago, 1942, p. 54.

16. Gerhart H. Saenger, "Social Status and Political Behavior," *American Journal of Sociology*, 51, 1945, pp. 103-13.

17. J. B. Maller, "A Study of the Jewish Neighborhoods of New York," *Jewish Social Service Quarterly*, 10, 1934, pp. 271-76.

18. Nettie Pauline McGill, "Some Characteristics of Jewish Youth in New York City," *Jewish Social Service Quarterly*, 14, 1937, p. 267.

19. Louis Bultena, "Church Membership and Church Attendance in Madison, Wisconsin," *American Sociological Review*, 14, 1949, p. 385.

20. Jaffe and Stewart, *op. cit.*

FAMILY INTERACTION, VALUES, AND ACHIEVEMENT

Fred L. Strodtbeck

1. This report is based upon the "Cultural Factors in Talent Development" project conducted under the direction of the author largely at Yale University. The contributions of Bernard C. Rosen, Florence Sultan, and Leslie L. Clark are gratefully acknowledged as staff members during the development of the questionnaires and procedure, and the collection and analysis of data. George Psathas, Robert A. Ellis, and William Vosburg conducted a number of the interivews in connection with courses they were taking under the writer's direction. Margaret J. Robertson did the bulk of the computing, Marian R. Winterbottom performed the *n* Achievement scoring, and Hava Bonné Gewirtz assisted the writer at the University of Chicago in preparing this manuscript. The writer wishes to express his debt to Orvill G. Brim, Jr., who, during the year immediately preceding the data collection, performed a notable job of evaluating prior work in the field.

2. From an address to the Society for Social Research, June, 1956.

3. See Charles R. Snyder's exhaustive analysis of factors which account for the low inebriety rates among Jews (14). Since this literature is not comparative between Italians and Jews, it is outside our present interest.

4. This summary is from B. Tregoe's "An Analysis of Ethnic and Social Class Differences," an unpublished manuscript based upon research materials collected by the staff of the Laboratory of Human Development, Harvard University.

5. We wish to acknowledge a special debt to Florence Kluckhohn for guidance in a continuing concern for comparing cultural values, a concern which is more fully expressed in F. Kluckhohn, F. L. Strodtbeck, and J. Roberts, *Value Orientations in Five Cultures*, a volume which will be published shortly by Row, Peterson & Co.

6. The assistance of Florence Kluckhohn, Talcott Parsons, and Samuel A. Stouffer, joint directors of this seminar, is gratefully appreciated.

JEWISH SOCIAL WORK IN THE UNITED STATES: 1920-1955

Herman D. Stein

1. See Eisenstein, Ira, "Patterns of Living of the Jewish People on the American Scene," *Jewish Social Service Quarterly* [hereafter *JSSQ*], Vol. XXX, Fall 1953.

2. See Taussig, F., Kepecs, J., Dubin, M., Hyman, H. J. and Lurie, H., "The Effect of the Economic Depression on the Standards of Jewish Social Work Agencies"

JSSQ, Vol. VIII, Sept. 1931, pp. 18-33.

3. Grossman, Marc J., "Jewish Social Work in the Economic Depression," *JSSQ*, Vol. VIII, Dec. 1931, p. 87.

4. See Kohs, Samuel C. "Whither the Jewish Family Agency?" *JSSQ*, Vol. XXIV, Sept. 1947. This author has been consistent in his point of view. He raised similar questions in 1933. Note his "Current Fallacies Regarding Jewish Social Work," *JSSQ*, Vol. IX, June 1933.

5. A similar point is made by Marcel Kovarsky, who quotes a comment apropos of the Springfield survey: "A sectarian service, by its very existence, is an instrument of Jewish survival regardless of its specific content." See Kovarsky, Marcel, "Current Purposes and Goals of Jewish Family Agencies," *JSSQ*, Vol. XXX, Spring 1954.

6. Morris, Robert, "An Approach to a Rationale for Jewish Social Service," *JSSQ*, Vol. XXX, Fall 1953, p. 60.

7. See Wagner, Margaret W., "The Aged," New York, *Social Work Year Book*, 1951, p. 45. Note also Tibbitts, Clark, "The Aging," *Social Work Year Book*, 1954, p. 38.

8. See Fox, Flora, "Home Care Programs for the Aged," *JSSQ*, Vol. XXIX, March 1953, in which she describes some of the pioneer work of the Central Bureau for the Jewish Aged in New York City.

9. Solender, Sanford, "Implications of Current National Trends for Jewish Health and Welfare Services," *JSSQ*, Vol. XXX, Fall 1953, p. 28.

10. Seventy-one per cent of all residents in homes reporting to the CJFWF in 1954 were seventy-five years of age or over. *Yearbook of Jewish Social Service*. New York, CJFWF, 1955, p. 26.

11. *Ibid.*, pp. 28-29.

12. Richman, Leon H. "Trends in Child Care," *JSSQ*, Vol. XXIX, Dec. 1952.

13. Janowsky, Oscar I., *The JWB Survey*. New York, Dial Press, 1948.

14. *Ibid.*, pp. 246-47.

15. *Ibid.*, pp. 276-77.

16. Solender, Sanford, "Services to the Community and Its Youth," *American Jewish Year Book*, Vol. 54, New York, 1953, pp. 142-45.

17. By 1951, community centers were operating 201 day camps serving over 40,000 children. See *ibid.*, p. 144.

18. *Yearbook of Jewish Social Service*, 1955, p. 31.

19. See Zelditch, Morris, "Jewish Health Migration," *JSSQ*, Vol. XXIV, Sept. 1947.

20. The JDC is known familiarly as "der joint" among Yiddish-speaking communities, and was thus called in DP camps. In French-speaking communities, it is referred to as "le joint."

21. From 1945 to 1954 the JDC assisted in the resettlement of over 600,000 persons, representing more than 60 per cent of all of Jewish immigration during the postwar period.

22. Ginzberg, Eli, *Report to American Jews*. New York, Harper & Bros., 1942, pp. 22-29.

23. See Goldsmith, Samuel A., "Local Organization for Refugee Service," *JSSQ*, Vol. XVII, Sept. 1940, pp. 119-31.

24. USNA issued a number of manuals for community groups dealing with the educational, occupational, and social-cultural integration of the refugee. See, for example, *Organizing a Community Americanization Program*, 3rd ed., New York, USNA, March 1953.

25. *The USNA Story*, 1933-1953. New York, USNA, March 1954.

26. Gurin, Arnold, "Jewish Communal Services," *American Jewish Year Book*, Vol. 56, 1955, p. 263.

27. *Ibid.*, p. 255.

28. By 1931, it was possible for one social work executive to write: "The average lay board member is notoriously incompetent. In some quarters membership is merely a matter of family inheritance. It is up to the professional to build up his board." Grossman, Marc, *op. cit.*, p. 86.

29. Miller, Norman, "The Jewish Leadership in Lakeport," in *Studies in Leadership*, ed. by Alvin W. Gouldner, New York, Harper & Bros., 1950, p. 215.

30. See Amidon, Beulah, "What Can I Do?," *The Survey*, March 1949, p. 137.

31. Waldman, Morris D., "Training for Jewish Communal Welfare," address delivered at National Conference of Jewish Social Welfare, May 24, 1940 (published in *Harry L. Gluckman Memorial Lectures*, New York, 1941).

32. Bernstein, Philip, "Training for Jewish Communal Service," *JSSQ*, Vol. XXIV, Sept. 1947.

33. For a specific set of predictions, see Hexter, Maurice J., "The Next Twenty-Five Years in Jewish Communal Service," *JSSQ*, Vol. XXXII, Fall 1955.

THE ORIGIN AND GROWTH OF A JEWISH COMMUNITY IN THE SUBURBS:

A STUDY OF THE JEWS OF PARK FOREST

Herbert J. Gans

1. This article is based on a study done in 1949-50 with the help of a grant from the College of Jewish Studies, Chicago. In preparation for the present article, a brief restudy of Park Forest was done in May, 1955; this material is presented as a postscript. For the present version, some further analyses of the original data were also made. In addition, comparative material from other studies, published since the original research was completed, was gathered; this material has been placed in the footnotes.

2. In what follows, the terms "Jewish community" and "subcommunity" will be used interchangeably. For an excellent discussion of the concept of subculture, to which all of this is related, see Milton M. Gordon, "Social Structure and Goals in Group Relations," in Morroe Berger, Theodore Abel and Charles Page (eds.), *Freedom and Control in Modern Society*, New York, 1954, pp. 141-157.

3. The garden city movement—founded by Ebenezer Howard in England at the turn of the century—advocated the building of small communities with their own industries, to combine what were considered to be the social and psychological advantages of small town living with the requirements of an urban economy (see Howard's book, *Garden Cities of Tomorrow*, London, 1902). Leaders of this movement were instrumental in the construction of two garden cities in England. They have influenced, either directly or indirectly, the new towns built near London after World War II, the U. S. Government's Greenbelt towns built during the 1930's, and private developments such as Radburn (New Jersey), Park Forest, the Levittowns and several industry-built communities. Some of these are analyzed in Clarence Stein, *Towards New Towns for America*, Chicago, 1951.

4. The plans for Park Forest (which were revised during construction) are described in "American Community Builders," *The Architectural Forum*, August 1948, pp. 70-74, and by H. Henderson and S. Shaw, "City to Order," *Collier's*, February 14, 1948. Many other articles on the community have appeared in various architectural journals and general magazines

since that time. The best report on life in Park Forest is an insightful journalistic-sociological study by William H. Whyte, Jr., "The Transients," *Fortune*, May-August, 1953. See also, Herbert J. Gans, "Planning and Political Participation," *Journal of the American Institute of Planners*, Winter 1953, pp. 1-9, and "Political Participation and Apathy," unpublished M.A. thesis, Division of the Social Sciences, University of Chicago, June 1950.

For studies of English communities similar to Park Forest, see Ruth Durant, *Watling*, London, 1939; Harold Orlans, *Utopia Limited*, New Haven, 1953; and Leo Kuper et al., *Living in Towns*, London, 1953. For studies of American communities, see Robert K. Merton, "Social Psychology of Housing," in Wayne Dennis (ed.), *Current Trends in Social Psychology*, Pittsburgh, 1948, pp. 163-217, and his forthcoming *Patterns of Social Life: Explorations in the Sociology and Social Psychology of Housing*, with P. S. West, and M. Jahoda; William Form, "Status Stratification in Low and Middle Income Housing Areas," in "Social Policy and Social Research in Housing," *Journal of Social Issues*, Issues 1 and 2, 1951, pp. 109-131, and "Status Stratification in a Planned Community," *American Sociological Review*, October 1945, pp. 605-613. Two as yet unpublished studies of the Levittowns are Marie Jahoda et al., *Community Influences on Psychological Health* (tentative title), and John Liell, "Levittown: A Study in Community Development and Planning," Ph.D. dissertation, Department of Sociology, Yale University, 1952.

5. This description of the residents of Park Forest is based on participant observation as well as some fifty interviews with residents chosen at random (though not from a statistically designed random sample), for a study of political participation.

6. The total number of known "mixed marriages" was estimated at twenty-four, or 17 per cent of the Jewish population. Despite the efficiency of the community grapevine, this estimate is probably conservative. Of the twenty-four couples, about a third participated in the Jewish community.

7. This group of one hundred also included twenty who said they were not interested in the Jewish community. However, they had Jewish friends and were at least part of the communication network of the Jewish group.

The data presented here are based on about six months of observation in the village, including attendance at many meetings, on conversations with Jewish residents, and on full interviews with one person in each of forty-four Jewish families and partial ones with ten more. Although some tabulations based on the results of the questionnaire are presented in this paper, a large body of data remains to be analyzed.

8. The sample on which the data presented in this section is based was stratified between a group of leaders and actives selected from all factions of the community for the analysis of community processes, and a group of residents most of whom were known not to be leaders, chosen at random from the mailing list. In the original sample, actives were overrepresented; but with a knowledge of the proportion of actives and inactives in the total community (based on the judgments of a number of informants), this sample was brought closer to representativeness, *post facto*, by the random elimination of some interviews with actives.

9. Of the eight who would not divulge income information, the writer's estimates placed one below the median and five above it. The incomes of the remaining two could not be estimated.

10. The generational analysis using formal genealogical categories is complicated by the fact that Jewish immigration from Eastern Europe lasted over two generations. Furthermore, the immigrants were themselves of two generations, being either children or adults. Also, since Eastern European Jewry was then already acculturating in the wake of urban-industrial change and Western cultural influences, immigrants may have been of two or more *cultural generations* (i.e., "generations" defined in terms of deviation from the traditional culture). Consequently, an analytically meaningful concept of generation would have to include several factors, and a generational description of a second generation Jew would not be complete without an analysis of his parents' age at arrival and their cultural orientation at the time of his upbringing. Such an analysis of the Park Forest material remains to be done.

11. See W. Lloyd Warner and Leo Srole, *The Social Systems of American Ethnic Groups*, New Haven, 1945, Ch. 3. An analysis of income and occupational status of F-1 and F-2 generations indicated no differences between them, but F-2 people had slightly more education.

12. An impressionistic comparison of income and status (defined in terms of several consumption and leisure activity patterns) was made, based on the writer's judgment of the respondent and his household. The figure of $7500 was arbitrarily set as a minimal "upper-middle-class income." The following tabulation, which must be considered preliminary, indicated that inactives at the upper-middle-class income level would not necessarily follow the life-styles of that status:

| *Families with "Upper-Middle Incomes"* | *Consumption-Social Status* | | | |
	Upper Middle	*Middle Middle*	*Lower Middle*	*Total*
Actives	3	1	0	4
Inactives	3	6	0	9
All	6	7	0	13

Here, as elsewhere in the article, the definitions of lower- and upper-middle class are adapted from the images developed by W. Lloyd Warner and his associates in the Yankee City studies. Middle-middle describes a group of urban and now suburban white-collar workers with at least some college education whose consumption behavior is marked by the same dependence on the mass media as the lower-middle class, but on a more autonomous basis, and at a higher "brow level." However, they do not achieve, nor indeed seek, the consumption styles and especially the community activity patterns of the upper-middle class. They are the primary audience for much of the mass media fare and advertising beamed at the "young moderns." Probably the majority of Park Foresters may be thus classified.

13. Some of the Jewish families showed a decided preference for end units, which were slightly more expensive. The extent to which this choice was due to desire for isolation rather than the need for an extra bedroom for older children or the ability to pay higher rents, was not studied. The homeowners who came later live on a more traditional but curved street plan. For a highly generalized description of the court life see William H. Whyte, Jr., "How

the New Suburbia Socializes," *Fortune*, August, 1953, pp. 120-122, 186-190. For a rigorous study of certain limited aspects of the social life of a housing project, see Leon Festinger, Stanley Schachter, and Kurt Back, *Social Pressures in Informal Groups*, New York, 1950.

14. A systematic stratification analysis would probably show that those with upper-middle-class aspirations tended to find friends outside the court; this in part also explains the behavior of the Jewish residents.

15. No one has ever studied why one community or subdivision gains Jewish residents while another area is avoided. Dr. Julian L. Greifer reported that in the Philadelphia area:

> Some of the new private housing developments have become almost exclusively populated by Jews, as friend followed friend, and relative moved near relative. . . . I know of several pioneering Jewish families that settled in new suburban communities but after a few years moved back, at great personal loss, to localities more heavily populated by Jews. Apparently the failure of additional Jewish families to settle in the new communities isolated the pioneers from Jewish contacts and communal institutions.

"Relationships in a Large City," *Jewish Social Studies*, July, 1955, pp. 269-70. One factor in this decision is probably the ethnic identity of the developer. If he is Jewish he is likely to advertise in Anglo-Jewish papers, as well as invite friends to move into his project.

16. In 1953 the president of A.C.B. became the international president of B'nai B'rith.

17. In most cases, however, the recognition as well as many other parts of the community formation process were handled by the women, for they were in the community all day long while the men commuted to Chicago. This sexual division of the social labors held also in the non-Jewish community.

18. The kind of friendship relationship discussed here is not the intimate lifetime friendship as it is classically defined, but rather a companionship in transitory surroundings (like a college dormitory or army camp) which is intimate while the surroundings are shared but may end when they are not. On the other hand, it may lead to permanent relationships, especially

if the parties involved are travelling toward the same social goals. It would be interesting to discover whether contemporary social trends encourage such companionship rather than the permanent type of friendship.

19. Some comment should be made about the cohesive and social pressure functions of the mailing list. This list was carefully compiled soon after the formation of the lodge, and kept up to date so as to include everyone known or suspected to be Jewish. The existence of the community was stressed by frequent mailings which went even to people who rejected all contact with the Jewish group. Later, Sunday school announcements were sent to everyone, as its caretaker reported:

> Just to show people what was being done in the Jewish community and to keep their interest up. No names should be taken off the list just because people hadn't shown interest.

20. Warner and Srole, *op. cit.*, Ch. 7, especially pp. 210 ff.

21. Religious-cultural activities, as distinguished from social ones, are those involving both sacred and secular patterns of Judaism, either in traditional or contemporary forms. Social activities refer to sociability situations where the important factor is the participation with other Jews rather than the cultural theme of the activity (which is likely to be drawn from American leisure culture).

22. Class-structured differences over the definition of community organization and overorganization were also a factor here.

23. Although the terms were inaccurate in relation to accepted usage, it is true nevertheless that from the parents' perspective adult orientation would mean involvement in religious affairs, while child orientation would not, and would therefore have "secular" implications for them.

24. Our emphasis.

25. This attitude indicates the extent to which Jews still consider themselves to be members of a religious group (though they do not observe the religion), and do not perceive the fact that they belong to an ethnic group, even though this latter is their major Jewish characteristic.

26. A small group of highly educated Jewish Park Foresters took the fact that children recognized no ethnic differences as a departure for an attempt to organize a Sunday school which would teach comparative religion, and de-emphasize the

ethnic and denominational differences between Jew and non-Jew. The project failed to materialize for lack of support.

27. While this problem is hardly a new one, the presence of so many small children, and of picture windows in Park Forest, exposed what in the cities is hidden by the visual anonymity of apartment life and the existence of Jewish neighborhoods. For some historical background, see Melvin Landsberg, "That Christmas Problem," *Commentary,* December, 1954, pp. 558-61.

28. The areas of second settlement which Marshall Sklare describes as the source of Conservatism. See his *Conservative Judaism: An American Religious Movement,* Glencoe, 1955, pp. 66-72.

29. The level of observance in Park Forest may be illustrated by the fact that most of his Jewish neighbors considered him to be very Orthodox.

30. In this connection, it would be interesting to discover the extent to which parental (i.e., immigrant) attitudes on socio-economic mobility, child-training, and other areas of activity also influenced these respondents.

31. Historical studies of American Jewish communities indicate that the first institution set up was generally the burial society. In Park Forest, devoid as it was of old people, and with a death rate close to zero, the first need for a religious functionary seems nevertheless also to have been stimulated by functions connected with burial and memorial rites.

32. It should be noted that this paragraph was written in 1955 with the hindsight of events since 1949.

33. For a useful definition of clique, see W. Lloyd Warner and Paul Lunt, *The Social Life of a Modern Community,* New Haven, 1941, pp. 110-111.

34. Ethnic distinctions were almost nonexistent in the all-male activities. Bowling teams, baseball leagues, and poker clubs were organized on a court basis. In this connection one of the women observed:

The boys are real friendly, I imagine they don't think about it [ethnic distinctions] but the women have different feelings. Women have little to do; they talk about it in the afternoons.

The extent to which class factors rather than ethnic factors determined participation in these activities was not studied.

35. For a discussion of Jewish-non-Jewish relationships, and of anti-Semitism in Park Forest, see the writer's "Park Forest: Birth of a Jewish Community," *Commentary,* April, 1951, pp. 337-38.

36. Some of the respondents had rejected Judaism as a culture and religion, had not joined any of the formal organizations of the Park Forest Jewish community, but yet remained in the informal community. However, since the cliques were not formed on ideological bases, those alienated from Jewishness and from participation in the formal community were not excluded.

37. Compare the letter, "Jews and the Community," by Deborah Dorfman, *Commentary,* January, 1955, p. 85.

38. No systematic comparative study was made of this phenomenon; the generalization is based on participant observation of Jewish and non-Jewish leisure activities of various "brow" levels, and the examination of close to 200 living-room bookshelves in the community. Note also the comments by Nathan Glazer, "Social Characteristics of American Jews 1654-1954," in the *American Jewish Year Book,* Vol. 56, New York, 1955, p. 33.

39. See Russell Lynes' classic essay, "Highbrow, Middlebrow, Lowbrow," in *The Tastemakers,* New York, 1954, Ch. 13.

40. Compare this with Berelson's description of the typical library user:

From related investigations, the most probable interpretation of the differences in interest and activity involves a general characteristic which might be called cultural alertness. Studies . . . have repeatedly identified a certain group of people who engage in all sorts of cultural activities, in the broad sense, more than does the rest of the community. They read more, and listen more and talk more; they have opinions and feel more strongly about them, they join more organizations and are more active in them, and they know more about what is going on and . . . they are generally more sensitive and responsive to the culture in which they live.

"The Public Library, Book Reading and Political Behavior," *Library Quarterly,* October, 1945, pp. 297-8, quoted in his *The Library's Public,* New York, 1949, p. 49.

41. These Jews shared many of the characteristics which Robert K. Merton has attributed to the cosmopolitan influentials. While Merton made no distinctions between Jews and non-Jews, the Jew's historic role on the fringe of the social struc-

ture has perhaps directed him into cosmopolitan (if not influential) roles. Some of the conflicts within the Park Forest Jewish community (and also in Park Forest generally) can be understood in terms of conflicts between locals and cosmopolitans. Park Forest differed from the community studied by Merton in that a large number of cosmopolitans who were among the first arrivals in Park Forest saw the then unformed community as a place in which they might attempt to implement some of their cosmopolitan ideals. They thus took on many of the characteristics of "locals." In time, these cosmopolitans relinquished their positions to more genuine locals, for their utopian aspirations were rejected by the more conservative residents. See Robert K. Merton, "Patterns of Influence, A Study of Interpersonal Influence and of Communication Behavior in a Local Community," in *Communications Research 1948-1949*, ed. by Paul F. Lazarsfeld and Frank N. Stanton, New York, 1949, pp. 180-219.

42. Milton Gordon has described these as "passive ethnic intellectuals." See his "Social Class and American Intellectuals," *Bulletin of the American Association of University Professors*, Winter 1954-1955, p. 527.

43. The role of the non-Jewish intellectual in the Jewish group is discussed in Chandler Brossard's "Plaint of a Gentile Intellectual," *Commentary*, August, 1950, pp. 154-156.

44. Robert Park originally applied the concept to the Jews in his essay "Human Migration and the Marginal Man," *American Journal of Sociology*, May, 1928, pp. 881-893. This is reprinted in his *Race and Culture*, Glencoe, 1950, pp. 345-356. See also Everett Hughes, "Social Change and Status Protest; An Essay on the Marginal Man," *Phylon*, First Quarter 1949, pp. 58-65; Everett Stonequist, "The Marginal Character of the Jews," in Isacque Graeber and Steuart H. Britt, *Jews in a Gentile World*, New York, 1942, pp. 296-310; and Thorstein Veblen's perceptive essay, "The Intellectual Pre-Eminence of Jews in Modern Europe," in *Political Science Quarterly*, March, 1919, pp. 33-42. David Riesman has elaborated on the theme in "Some Observations Concerning Marginality," reprinted in his *Individualism Reconsidered*, Glencoe, 1954, pp. 153-65.

45. See, for example, the analysis of reading and class in the Yankee City class structure in Warner and Lunt, *op. cit.*,

Ch. 19, and similar analyses in *Middletown, Middletown in Transition, Elmtown's Youth,* and other community studies.

46. For a conceptual discussion, see Milton Gordon in Berger, Abel and Page, *op. cit.,* p. 151.

47. The Park Forest experience suggests that the rabbi is called in once the process of community formation, or a first stage in it, has been completed. For an excellent analysis of the extent to which the contemporary rabbi fills some of the roles of the professional, see Marshall Sklare, *op. cit.,* Ch. 6.

48. This may help to explain the fact that intermarriages usually involve Jewish men more often than they do Jewish women.

49. This description is a preliminary one which is not based on systematic study; it has been included here primarily for summary purposes.

50. While Park Forest would normally have been considered only a stopping point for many of the upper-middle-class people before they purchased their own home in a more statusful suburb, the interviewing indicated that more of the leaders and active members considered the village as a permanent residence than the inactive ones. Later, many of these people had become homeowners in the village. The development of an area of custom-built houses clustered around the residence of the A.C.B. president on the highest elevation in the village may have helped to keep these people in Park Forest by providing an area of fourth and fifth settlement for them. About half of the thirty-five units in this section were occupied by Jews.

51. Whether the politically active Jews were socially more mobile than similarly active non-Jews of the same socio-economic level is not known.

52. In most urban communities, Jews have been relatively inactive in politics, and competed for elective offices in numbers less than their proportion in the population. This has been explained by the low status of the urban politician. In the suburbs, however, where political activity is largely voluntary and statusful, Jewish participation has been high. Compare William Form, "Status Stratification in a Planned Community," in *American Sociological Review*, October, 1945, p. 612, where he points out that in Greenbelt, Maryland, Jews were over-represented among the officers of the town, and were even accused of "monopolizing offices."

See also Samuel Koenig, "The Socio-Economic Structure of an American Jewish Community," in Graeber and Britt, *op. cit.*, p. 242.

53. This section is based primarily on data gathered during the author's revisit to Park Forest. Interviews were held with a dozen informants, most of them in leadership positions, and some tabulations were made of congregational membership characteristics. While the informants were selected from among all the points of view in the community, their reports on the activities of the leadership must be considered more reliable than their comments on the attitudes and behavior of the inactive, and especially the unaffiliated members of the Jewish community. The material included about these people is presented as hypotheses which could be tested only by further community-wide interviewing. However, the presentation is restricted to those hypotheses which the writer feels would be upheld by more rigorous research.

54. This was largely due to the fact that two-thirds of the homes for sale were priced between $11,000 and $14,000, that is, for the lower-income buyers of the suburban housing market. The actual difference between the 1950 and 1955 residents was probably smaller than the one described by the residents, since a myth had developed in the village which pictured the pre-1950 community as inhabited largely by intellectuals and professionals.

55. For the most part, Jewish families have moved into higher-priced homes, and the availability of these has kept many renters in the village. The influx of new Jewish residents has been timed partly by the construction schedule. For example, when a new section of $19,000 units was opened in 1954 following a period of concentration on lower-priced homes, so many Jewish tenants and newcomers who had been waiting for houses flocked to buy, that the first "Jewish neighborhood" was developing in the village, and was being referred to as "Little Jerusalem" in the Jewish community. In this connection, an American Jewish Committee study recently reported that 40 per cent of the Jewish parents of "Riverton," an Eastern city, wanted to live in predominantly Jewish neighborhoods. See Marshall Sklare and Marc Vosk, *The Riverton Study: How Jews Look at Themselves and Their Neighbors*, New York, 1957, p. 37.

56. Several of these have been described

by *Commentary* writers. See Harry Gersh, "The New Suburbanities of the '50's," *Commentary*, March, 1954, pp. 209-221; Evelyn Rossman (pseud.), "The Community and I," *Commentary*, November, 1954, pp. 393-405; and Morris Freedman, "New Jewish Community in Formation," *Commentary*, January, 1955, pp. 36-47.

57. This figure was equal to that estimated some years ago as the proportion of all American Jewish families holding synagogue memberships. See Herbert Parzen, "Religion," *American Jewish Year Book*, Vol. 52, New York, 1951, pp. 86-87. However, the Park Forest figure is lower than that reported for some other suburban communities. Gersh (*op. cit.*, p. 218) quotes a percentage of "fifty plus" for a Westchester county suburb, and an unpublished estimate for Glenville, New York, is as high as 70-80 per cent (see L. H. Grunebaum, *Perplexities of Suburban Jewish Education*, mimeo., Scarsdale, N. Y., 1954, p. 9). Socio-economic, age, and generational differences may account for the variations.

58. As in 1950, this form of parental loyalty remained strong. The rabbi encouraged the practice by noting the Yahrzeit dates of every member, and calling them to his attention.

59. These attendance figures resemble national estimates. Compare also with the report on Glenville, New York:

Beth-El has a membership of about 1100 families. . . . Friday evening service is attended by about 100 worshippers, or less than five per cent. . . . There is a hard core of people who come . . . fairly regularly. . . . Yet to say that as many as 400 different adults attend services sometime during the year might be an optimistic overestimate. . . . On the two High Holy Days . . . over 2,000 people then crowd into the Legion Hall. (Grunebaum, *op. cit.*, p. 4.)

Rossman reports virtually the same pattern:

There may be 30 or 40 people on an ordinary Friday, 75 to 100 if there is a guest to speak at the social hour and a telephone committee has called everyone in the community. The older Orthodox people come out of loyalty. . . . New people just moved to town come hoping to find friends and clients . . . the officers . . . say they feel obliged to show their faces . . . a small group of couples try to come to services regularly. . . . Yet there are few Jews . . . who do not come to the temple at least once a year. (*Op. cit.,* pp. 402-3.)

60. From a fund-raising criterion, the annual bazaar was the most successful event. This was in part because many of the Jews were store owners or distributors and thus could donate merchandise for the bazaar. Many of the items were sold at bargain prices.

61. Much the same lag in male organization was reported in the New England suburb. See Rossman, *op. cit.,* p. 398, as well as Morton Sterne, "Country Club Judaism," in *Congress Weekly,* May 4, 1953, p. 6.

62. Although this high enrollment may be similar to that found in other suburbs, it was probably much higher than the ratio characteristic in cities. According to Harry Lurie: ". . . . there are no country-wide statistical data on the proportion of Jewish children attending Jewish schools. . . .Local studies indicate that enrollment may vary in different cities from 25-65%." "Jewish Communal Life in the United States," in *The Jewish People: Past and Present,* Vol. IV, New York, 1954, p. 206.

63. Park Forest Board of Jewish Education, *Your Community School for Jewish Education,* mimeo., Park Forest, 1955, pp. 1-3.

64. *Ibid.*

65. *Ibid.*

66. While both schools claim the desirability of the children's affiliation with the synagogue, they have distinctly different techniques for achieving this aim. The community school wants to make temple experience meaningful to the child and provide incentives for participation that relate to his own aspirations. The temple school approach is based on a more traditional one used with adults—emphasizing the necessity of attendance. The conflict between child orientation and adult orientation is evident even in questions of educational methods.

67. As in 1950, the differences between child and adult orientation were described as secular and religious ones during the public debates.

68. See Sterne, *op. cit.*

69. See footnote 41.

70. These factors would help to explain why the temple was built at the earliest possible moment, even though some leaders warned of the danger of premature building, and predicted—not without justification—that the building would be too small for educational and even some social functions.

71. Their expectations were based on actual conditions. A recent survey of religious education in 195 communities showed that 94 per cent of the Sunday schools and 82 per cent of the weekday schools were conducted under congregational auspices. Uriah Engelman, "Jewish School Enrollment," *American Jewish Year Book,* Vol. 56, New York, 1955, p. 250.

72. The group which favored rabbinical authority was in the majority. Thus it was probably not coincidental that the first rabbi, who lacked the experience and personal characteristics to fill this role, resigned his post, and that the present incumbent is a forceful speaker with a formidable record of training and experience, who stated his willingness to assume an authoritative role.

73. See William H. Whyte, Jr., "The Consumer in the New Suburbia," in *Consumer Behavior,* edited by Lincoln Clark, New York, 1954, p. 7.

74. See Marcus L. Hansen, "The Third Generation," *Commentary,* November, 1952, pp. 492-500. Nathan Glazer discusses Hansen's findings in "Ethnic Groups in America: From National Culture to Ideology," in Berger, Abel and Page, *op. cit.,* pp. 158-173.

75. For some personal observations see the articles by Gersh and Rossman. The phenomenon of "sticking out" does not apply to all suburbs, for there are in Chicago, as well as in other urban areas, suburbs in which rapid and large scale settlement by Jewish families has led to suburban versions of the Jewish neighborhoods of the city. While there are no reliable data to verify this point, it seems that in such suburbs the rate of formal community organization is much lower. Rossman reports a decrease in participation in formal organizations as the Jewish population of her suburb increased in size.

76. Reports from other comunities support the child-orientation hypothesis. See, for example, Gersh, *op. cit.,* p. 220, and Freedman, *op. cit.,* p. 46. Also, the report on Glenville, N. Y. mentions "the large passive majority which does little more than send its children to Religious School" and presents a case study of parental lack of interest in the children's school, and the conflict in the home because of parental desire to avoid involvement. The author offers this as "a valid composite picture of the environment of at least half our students." Grunebaum, *op. cit.,* pp. 4, 10, 15.

Further illustration of its existence can be found in the protest literature. See, for example, Rabbi William B. Silverman, "Are We Becoming a Juvenile Jewry?" *American Judaism*, November, 1954, p. 5. A sermon by Rabbi Albert Goldstein on the subject is quoted in the Silverman article. According to a letter from Rabbi Goldstein, this sermon has been reprinted in scores of temple bulletins.

77. An additional seven families were "mixed marriages." While this group of residents is probably not a representative sample of the post-1949 newcomers, the intermarriage rate resembled that found in 1949 (see footnote 6).

78. Again, the fact that the present rabbi came to Park Forest from a Hillel directorship was not a manifest factor in his selection, but is perhaps a latent one in his adjustment there.

79. Rossman and Freedman both report on the great proportion of social and leisure activities as compared to religious ones in the suburban congregation. The former quotes an informant as saying: "The older people worry about religion. The younger ones want good times" (Rossman, *op. cit.*, p. 397). The change in function has served as an institutional reinforcement.

80. See here the comments by Gersh, *op. cit.*, pp. 217 ff.

81. A temple officer estimated on one Friday night that of the sixty people present, only nine were there strictly to attend a religious service.

82. Despite the feeling of some leaders that the congregational membership would have voted down the proposal to set up a temple school, the institutional need of the congregation was such that given the six-year history of intensive effort at its organization, the power structure of the Jewish community, the increasing numbers of children, and the relative indifference of the community to organizational matters, the temple leadership would eventually have been able to set it up.

83. The Board of the temple consisted wholly of men, with the exception of one woman who sat primarily as her husband's representative since he was frequently out of town in his role as international president of B'nai B'rith. The Board of Jewish Education, on the other hand, had a number of women members.

84. The extensive involvement of women in the social and educational functions of the temple may be a factor in the recent revival of the question of the ordination of women by the Reform movement. See Rabbi Barnett Brickner, Presidential Address, Central Conference of American Rabbis, 1955, as reported in *National Jewish Post*, June 24, 1955.

85. The concept of a religious revival assumes an implicit comparison with a previous golden age of religiosity, for the existence of which there is little empirical evidence. While Eastern European Jews were undoubtedly more religious than their descendants, it was noted previously that they were already affected by acculturation pressures, and perhaps those so affected were more likely to be attracted by the promise of America.

86. In a forthcoming book, Nathan Glazer suggests, with some justifications, that sociologists attempt to explain the behavior of American Jews solely as an ethnic group, while ignoring their existence as a religious group. The present article follows the ethnic-group emphasis, primarily because it attempts to analyze the attitudes and behavior of the lay members of the community who are normally little concerned with ideology or theology, and whose behavior seems to be explicable without the use of religious concepts.

It is not possible here to do more than speculate about the religious beliefs of most Park Forest Jews, for this subject was not investigated specifically. There are few confirmed atheists or agnostics in the population, and not many more for whom the topic is one of major concern. If asked by an interviewer, most people would probably suggest their belief in a Deity, as well as indicate their relative indifference to the question. At the same time, however, they are likely to be conscious of the religious tenets of Juadism, and of their deviations from them. The resulting occasional pangs of conscience are not intense enough to inspire changes in behavior (although in crisis situations they may result in a turning to religious behavior-patterns experienced in childhood). Instead, such sentiments of guilt, or perhaps nostalgia, may cause people to feel that they ought to have a congregation and hire a rabbi, or at least it makes them responsive to the requests and urgings of those who are more personally concerned. They may even welcome a synagogue as a symbol of the religiosity they feel they owe their parents, their children, and themselves. Once assured of its existence, however, they feel no great need to share in its religious functions. Their behavior resembles that of an urban citizenry which votes the bonds for a museum proposed by *Kultur*-conscious representatives and takes pride in its presence, but rarely enters its portals. If there were any concerted objection or antagonism to the temple, this might indicate that the institution still had considerable emotional influence—albeit negative—on persons with

this attitude. However, the widespread indifference to the question of a temple in 1949, as shown in Table 8, suggests its lack of functional relevance to their adult roles. There was no indication in 1955 that the existing temple had persuaded them of its relevance or that some other institution, not now available, might achieve this.

THE JEWISH ORGANIZATIONAL ELITE OF ATLANTA, GEORGIA

Solomon Sutker

1. Atlanta is a Jewish community of intermediate size. The small Jewish community with a population of a few hundred to approximately five thousand rarely contains all the types of Jewish organizations to be found in the larger communities, whereas the intermediate communities with Jewish populations up to 25,000 do tend to have most of the specialized associations that can be located in the largest areas. The Jewish community of Atlanta, which is of the intermediate type, was selected for study as it was one of the few localities in the southeastern region that is large enough to contain the variety of organizations common to American Jewish life today, yet small enough to be studied by one person. It was not chosen as a representative Jewish community of intermediate size since insufficient information was available to the writer at the start of his research work to make any determination of such representativeness. The material that was gathered and compared with data from various secondary sources later indicated that the Atlanta Jewish community in many ways illustrates many of the changes occurring in Jewish community life in the larger cities of the nation, although it also exhibits certain idiosyncratic traits. These include the effects of the regional character of the city, the entirely middle class occupational pattern of the Jewish population, and the great emphasis that is placed on three Jew-

ish social clubs as the centers of social life of the community.

2. This typology is an adaptation of one devised by Karl Mannheim in *Man and Society in an Age of Reconstruction* (New York: Harcourt, Brace and Company, 1940), pp. 82-83.

3. It is part of the trend in our secularized, specialized and urbanized society to become increasingly dependent upon managerial technicians to operate important aspects of our economic life, our social service agencies, the educational system and government bureaus on various level from local to international.

4. The educational level of the young Jewish adult in Atlanta is quite high. Thus of 259 Jewish males, age twenty through thirty-nine, 59.1 per cent had attended college.

5. Although Atlanta and other large southern cities have the forms of Jewish community life that are to be found in the largest cities of the nation, they may have a less intensified socialization of the young into the traditions of Judaism. The fact that the heaviest Jewish population concentration is in the North may be one element affecting this socialization process, since the chances for interaction between Jews are greater in the areas with the densest population concentration.

6. H. H. Gerth and C. W. Mills, eds. and trs., *From Max Weber* (New York: Oxford University Press, 1946), pp. 190-244.

THE ROLE OF SOCIAL CLUBS IN THE ATLANTA JEWISH COMMUNITY

Solomon Sutker

1. See Carey McWilliams, *A Mask for Privilege, Anti-Semitism in America* (Boston: Little, Brown and Company, 1948), for a discussion of the position of the Jew in the social life of many American communities.

2. A new community center is now being completed. It replaces the old Jewish Educational Alliance which dates back to 1911.

3. Some years ago, the top stratum of the S. Club had operated a golf club. It had very few members and proved to be

too expensive a facility for this group. Some of the wealthier Eastern European Jews were admitted in order that the club might continue operations, but the organization was ultimately unsuccessful. Part of the reason for the demise of the golf club was that some of the original members objected to the admittance of the new group.

4. It is likely that the ratio of Zionists has increased in both organizations since 1945-1946. It was after this time that the American Council for Judaism was started as an organized effort to fight the Zionist movement. The supporters of the Council were usually members of the S. Social Club, but at the same time other German-Jewish members of this social club have joined the Zionist organization. Thus the situation appears to be that while attitudes toward Zionism became more polarized in the S. Social Club, the M. Social Club has been characterized by a relative unanimity of pro-Zionist support.

THE DEVELOPMENT OF A JEWISH UPPER CLASS
IN PHILADELPHIA: 1782-1940

E. Digby Baltzell

1. The larger study will be published shortly by The Free Press. In preparing the material on the Jewish community, I received both encouragement and guidance from my friend Edwin Wolf, II, of the Ridgeway Library; I am much in his debt. The responsibility for any errors in fact or interpretation rests, of course, entirely with me.

2. E. Digby Baltzell, "Who's Who in America and The Social Register: Elite and Upper Class Indexes in Metropolitan America," in Class, Status and Power, edited by Reinhard Bendix and Seymour Martin Lipset (Glencoe: The Free Press, 1953), p. 173. See this article for a more complete development of our theoretical structure.

3. Who's Who in America (Chicago: The A. N. Marquis Company, 1940), Vol. 21. Social Register, Philadelphia (New York: The Social Register Association, 1940).

4. No index used in the social sciences, of course, is completely accurate. All the men named here were listed in Who's Who except Morris Wolf. As he was the senior partner in the top Jewish law firm in the city—a firm which includes Sterns and Solis-Cohens as well as Wolfs—this is certainly a weakness in our index. As the Wolfs are such an important upper-class Jewish family, I have included Morris Wolf within the elite as if he were listed in Who's Who. Let us never be bound and blinded by our too often mechanistic methods in the social sciences!

5. See Jacob Rader Marcus, Early American Jewry (Philadelphia: The Jewish Publication Society of America, 1951), Vols. I and II.

6. Henry Samuel Morias, The Jews of Philadelphia (Philadelphia: The Levytype Company, 1894), p. 11.

7. See list of original subscribers to the Dancing Assemblies in: Joseph P. Sims, editor, The Philadelphia Assemblies 1748-1948 (Philadelphia: Privately Printed, 1947), p. 10; and J. Thomas Scharf and Thomas Westcott, History of Philadelphia, 1609-1884 (Philadelphia: L. H. Everts & Co., 1884), Vol. II, p. 864.

According to Morias, op. cit., p. 34, David Franks was a member of Mikveh Israel but was "lax in his adherence to Judaism, and married outside the pale of his religion."

8. Dixon Wecter, The Saga of American Society (New York: Charles Scribner's Sons, 1937), p. 153.

9. See Henry Samuel Morias, op. cit., pp. 15-16.

10. For a more detailed discussion of the building of Mikveh Israel on Cherry Alley, see Jacob Rader Marcus, op. cit., Vol. II, pp. 125-131.

11. Henry Samuel Morias, op. cit., pp. 70-71.

12. The Philadelphia Club 1834-1934 (Philadelphia: Privately Printed, 1934).

13. Ibid.

14. Dixon Wecter, op. cit., pp. 153-154.

15. Ibid.

16. Francis J. Brown and Joseph S. Roucek, One America, The History, Contributions, and Present Problems of our Racial and National Minorities (New York: Prentice-Hall, Inc., 1953), p. 663. Between 1841 and 1850, 434,626 Germans came to America; between 1851 and 1860 this figure had increased to 951,667.

17. See Carl Wittke, *Refugees of Revolution, The German Forty-Eighters in America* (Philadelphia: University of Pennsylvania Press, 1952), pp. 78-91.

18. Rufus Learsi, *The Jews in America* (New York: The World Publishing Company, 1954), p. 64.

19. Henry Samuel Morias, *op. cit.*, pp. 294-295.

20. *Ibid.*, p. 64.

21. *Ibid.*, p. 193.

22. *Ibid.*, p. 194.

23. *Ibid.*, pp. 135-138.

24. *Ibid.*, pp. 112-120.

25. "The Rich Men of Philadelphia," *Income Tax of the Residents of Philadelphia and Bucks County for the Year Ending April 30, 1865* (Philadelphia, 1865), pp. 5-9.

26. *McElroy's Philadelphia City Directory for 1859* (Philadelphia: Edward C. and John Biddle, 1859).

27. Rufus Learsi, *op. cit.*, p. 124.

28. *Ibid.*, p. 114.

29. *Ibid.*, pp. 131-135.

30. *Gopsill's Philadelphia City Directory, 1882* (Philadelphia: James Gopsill, 1882).

31. *Ibid., 1900.*

32. *Boyd's Blue Book* (Philadelphia: C. E. Howe Co., 1890).

33. This information as to Charles T. Yerkes' Philadelphia address at this time was obtained from the curator of the Dreiser Collection at the University of Pennsylvania Library.

34. *Boyd's Blue Book*, 1890.

35. Henry Samuel Morias, *op. cit.*, pp. 109-110.

36. See *Boyd's Blue Book* editions during 1880's and in 1890. Prominent families often named their summer residences along with their city addresses.

37. Dixon Wecter, *op. cit.*, p. 438n. Most writers on the subject believed that 1877 marked the beginning of the modern American practice of exclusion of Jews from summer resorts, hotels, and clubs. In that year Joseph Seligman was openly excluded from the Grand Union Hotel in Saratoga. When Seligman, a distinguished financier, friend of both presidents Lincoln and Grant (who offered him the post of Secretary of the Treasury), and one of the major financiers of the North in the Civil War, was told by the Grand Union manager that "no Israelite shall be permitted in the future to stop in the hotel," the "news" made headlines all over the country. See Rufus Learsi, *op. cit.*, pp. 172-173.

38. Between 1882 and 1914, some two million East European Jews came to America. Almost twenty-million other immigrants arrived in America during this period.

39. See H. L. Mencken, *The American Language, Supplement I*, (New York: Alfred A. Knopf, 1945), pp. 601-614.

40. According to H. L. Mencken, the most commonly accepted etymology for *kike* was thus stated in *American Speech* in 1926 by J. H. A. Lacher:

> In Russia there began some forty years ago a fierce persecution of the Jews. . . . Many found their way to the United States. . . . Here they offered keen competition to their brethren of German origin, who soon insisted that the business ethics and standards of living and culture of these Russians were far lower than theirs. Since the names of so many of these Eastern Jews ended in *-ki* or *-ky*, German-American Jewish travelling men designated them contemptuously as *kikis*, a term which, naturally, was soon contracted to *kikes.*

For the above and other claims and counterclaims as to origins, see *ibid.*, pp. 614-617.

41. Henry Samuel Morias, *op. cit.*, p. 193.

42. See obituary notices of Ellis A. Gimbel, *Philadelphia Evening Bulletin*, March 17, 1950.

43. See Oscar Handlin, *Adventure in Freedom, Three Hundred Years of Jewish Life in America* (New York: McGraw-Hill Book Co., Inc., 1954), pp. 143-174.

44. *Fortune*, Vol. XIII, No. 6 (June, 1936), p. 186.

45. *Ibid.*, p. 186.

46. The history of the Federation was obtained in an interview with Mr. Roman Slobodin, director.

47. *Report of the Federation of Jewish Charities of Philadelphia and its Affiliated Organizations, For the Year Ending April 30, 1920*, Vol. XIX. Upper-class families still held the dominant positions in the Federation: Louis Wolf was President, Jacob Gimbel, Honorary President, Samuel S. Fels, Honorary First Vice-President, and the Directors included Fleishers, Gimbels, Lits, Snellenburgs, Wolfs, and Cyrus Adler.

48. *Report of the Federation*, April 30, 1923.

49. *Ibid.*, A List of the Annual Subscribers to the Federation as of July 15, 1925.

50. *Polk's Philadelphia Blue Book, Elite*

Directory and Club List (Philadelphia: R. L. Polk & Co., 1924), p. 624.

51. Information on the founding of the Locust Club was obtained from the club's president in 1955, Raymond A. Speiser.

52. See The Philadelphia Evening *Bulletin,* March 21, 1956.

THE ATTITUDE OF THE SMALL-TOWN JEW
TOWARD HIS COMMUNITY

Joseph Greenblum and Marshall Sklare

1. See, among others, Lee J. Levinger, "The Disappearing Small-Town Jew," *Commentary,* August, 1952, 157-163; and Benjamin Kaplan, *The Eternal Stranger— A Study of Jewish Life in the Small Community,* New York, Bookman Associates, 1957.

2. For details about the sample and the characteristics of the respondents, see Robert Shosteck, *Small Town Jewry Tell Their Story,* Washington, B'nai B'rith Vocational Service Bureau, 1953.

3. Our analysis is confined to the American data. The fact that the Bureau considered all cities of less than 100,000 population as "small towns" is understandable. Inasmuch as American Jewry is concentrated in a handful of metropolitan cities, middle-size communities come to be thought of as "small-towns.'

4. These two items are combined in a single index and utilized in the analysis in a later section of the paper. There is one additional item: "Chances of having a satisfactory social life." It is, however, of limited utility since it is impossible to ascertain whether the social life being referred to is with fellow Jews, with mixed groups, or with Christians. This item is also commented upon in a further section of the paper.

5. We found this item to be highly related to the ratings in Table 1: more specifically, it was strongly associated with an index of Community Facilities Ratings (constructed from the first three items in Table 1), with a Jewish Facilities Ratings Index (constructed from the next two items), and with each of the last four items in Table 1, as well as with an index built from the last two items. Robert C. Angell ("The Moral Integration of American Cities," *American Journal of Sociology,* July 1951, Part 2) employed a similar item as one of a series on "general satisfaction with the community" ("Respondent would rather live here than anywhere else"), but instead of relating this to determinants, he viewed it as one of several broad aspects of community life (grouped under the concept "moral integration"), in order to characterize the community as a unit.

6. The item read: "Chances for having a satisfactory social life here are. . . ." Alternative responses were "good," "fair," "poor." "Good" responses were classified as satisfied, "fair" and "poor" as dissatisfied. This division allowed sufficient number of cases for purposes of comparisons. Although the item does not ask for a rating of the respondent's own social life, it was expected that one's personal experience would be strongly reflected in the evaluation of the community.

7. This point was made to us by Benjamin B. Ringer in a private communication. He also suggested an alternative hypothesis to explain some of the differences that persist in Table 5. Thus, within the smaller city, despite the fact that the level of social satisfaction is the same, the socially dissatisfied Jew in the smallest minority community is less disaffected with his general community than the socially dissatisfied Jew in the larger minority community because of greater compensations from the economic situation: the former may be more economically rooted and/or more satisfied with his economic condition.

8. A glance at Table 6 will reveal that such a possibility is indeed remote. Relatively more respondents in nearby communities live in larger Jewish communities than those who are more isolated.

9. At one extreme of the index are those respondents whose communities possess *all* three of the following: full-time rabbi, weekly services, and a Hebrew school. At the other extreme are those with: no rabbi, no services or services on High Holidays only, and no formal Jewish schooling. All other combinations fall into the intermediate category.

10. Each of the three items entering into the index was associated with overall attitude to community.

11. For a discussion of the concepts of

"reference group" and "relative depriva-
tion," see Robert K. Merton and Alice S.
Kitt, "Contributions to the Theory of Ref-
erence Group Behavior," in Robert K.
Merton and Paul F. Lazarsfeld (eds.),
*Studies in the Scope and Method of The
American Soldier,* Glencoe, The Free
Press, 1950, pp. 40-105.

12. The data would suggest that the
introduction of such facilities in the communities with no facilities that are nearer
to a large Jewish center would cause a
drop in disaffection. Substantiating this
statement, however, would involve a "be-
fore-after" test.

13. There are two methodological problems. First, since there is no apparent
time-order relation between them, one
wonders which of the two variables, devaluation or disaffection, is the dependent
variable. Peter Blau (*Public Opinion
Quarterly,* Vol. 19, No. 1 [Spring, 1955],
pp. 100-105) has suggested a technique
of resolving this problem. He introduces
a third variable which is clearly antecedent and related to each of the two problematic variables. This antecedent variable
is then controlled in testing for the spuri-
ousness of the relationship between the
two variables in question. Each of the
problematic variables is then controlled
in turn, while retesting the relation between the antecedent variable and the
other problematic variable. Disappearance
or diminution of the original relationship
establishes the dependent variable. Applying this technique to our problem, and
utilizing the index of Jewish community
organization as the common antecedent
variable, we find disaffection to be the
dependent variable. This is in accordance
with our hypothesis.

If devaluation is indeed an intervening
variable, the differences in Table 8 should
shrink or disappear when the index of
Jewish Facilities Evaluation is held constant. But when this is done, the cases
become too few in those cells which are
crucial for an adequate comparison and
test (i.e., in the categories, "less" minority organization which are also either
"high" or "intermediate" on the Evaluation index). Among the devaluators, i.e.,
those "low" on the index, the pattern of
differences in Table 8 still obtains. It is
therefore problematic whether devaluation
is a condition of the pattern, thus necessi-
tating respecification of the original relationships, or whether the Evaluation index,
as a whole, has little effect. It is possible
that devaluation, as a small segment of
the intervening process which also includes the reference group processes
alluded to above, will have little effect on
the differences in Table 8 even when sufficient cases are accumulated. Only a more
adequate test of the hypothesis, including
more direct indicators of reference community processes, will be able to resolve
this problem.

JEWISH PARTICIPATION IN THE LIFE OF MIDDLE-SIZED
AMERICAN COMMUNITIES

John P. Dean

1. Our material is based on data from
the Cornell Intergroup Relations Studies.
Our sources include the following: (a) Reports of participant observers living in the
Elmira community during the Cornell Intergroup Relations Studies conducted in
that city from 1948 to 1951. We are indebted to the following participant observers: Phyllis Geiss, Melvin Kohn, Rhee
Lyon, Alex Rosen, and Bernard Rosen. (b)
Replies to a questionnaire administered
to a cross-section (150) of the Jewish community in Elmira. Subsequently, a group
of seventy Jewish men over thirty years old
were interviewed on their community participation. (c) Field trips to eighteen other
communities where we interviewed leaders
in the Jewish community. These communities were all middle-sized American cities
with populations between 25,000 and 150,-
000. (d) Information gathered from Jewish community leaders in a sample of 239
communities stratified by region and size
of city throughout the nation. For details
as to size of these communities and the proportion of Jews to non-Jews, see Table 1.

The content of this paper should not be
construed as applying to larger centers of
Jewish population concentration in the
major metropolitan areas of the country.

A STUDY OF ORTHODOXY IN MILWAUKEE:

SOCIAL CHARACTERISTICS, BELIEFS, AND OBSERVANCES

Howard W. Polsky

1. Howard Polsky, *The Great Defense: A Study of Jewish Orthodoxy in Milwaukee* (unpublished Ph. D. dissertation, Department of Sociology, University of Wisconsin, 1956). For details about general methodology see Chapter 1, particularly the reference to Howard Becker, *Through Values To Social Interpretation* (Duke University Press, Durham, North Carolina, 1950). For details about the particular type of scalogram which we utilized see Chapter 10, particularly the citation of the work of Robert McGinnis.

Thanks are due to the Wisconsin Society of Jewish Learning for covering some of the costs of the study.

2. *The Milwaukee-Wisconsin Market,* prepared by *The Milwaukee Journal,* 1954.

Averages are for rented homes only.

3. The question, "What is the main reason for your belonging to the Orthodox synagogue?" was included in the questionnaire. The following are the categories into which most responses were coded: way brought up, family sentiment, belief in Orthodoxy, convenience of geographical location of synagogue, liking of atmosphere of synagogue, liking for rabbi, and desire to maintain synagogue. The results are not presented here because of the author's belief that a more probing type of question would have to be designed to obtain reliable answers. Also, this type of question does not seem well adapted to use in a telephone interview.

MINORITY GROUP IN TRANSITION: A STUDY OF ADOLESCENT

RELIGIOUS CONVICTION AND CONDUCT

Bernard C. Rosen

1. Research in this field has not kept pace with the apparent growth of interest in religion in postwar American society. Out of a total of 779 studies reported in the American Sociological Society's 1949 Census of Research, 2 per cent were in the Sociology of Religion; in 1952 the percentage was still 2 per cent. As an area of research the Sociology of Religion ranked 14.5 in 1949 in a total rank of 20 fields; by 1952 it had dropped to 17.5.

2. See, for example, M. Nathan, *The Attitude of the Jewish Student in the Colleges and Universities Toward His Religion,* Bloch, N. Y., 1932; N. Goldberg, "Religious and Social Attitudes of Jewish Youth in the U.S.A.," *Jewish Review,* 1943, 1, pp. 135-168; M. Greenberg, "The Jewish Student at Yale: His Attitude toward Judaism," *YIVO Annual of Jewish Social Science.* Vol. 1, pp. 217-40.

3. The U. S. Census does not ask the respondent's religion. The data on Jews for the most part have been collected by private agencies and are at best intelligent approximations. See S. M. Robison, *Jewish Population Studies,* New York, Conference on Jewish Relations, 1943, and W. L. Sperry, *Religion in America,* New York,

Macmillan, 1946, especially pp. 108-109. Since random sampling procedures were not employed in this study, care should be taken in generalizing from these data.

4. For a description of the *shtetl,* or Jewish "little town" of Eastern Europe as it existed up to World War I, and to some extent World War II, see Mark Zborowski and Elizabeth Herzog, *Life is With People,* New York, International Universities Press, 1952. For the role of rituals in everyday life see Chapter 2, Part I, and Chapter 3, Part II.

5. The Haskalah Movement was of course the great exception. See Jacob Raisin, *The Haskalah Movement in Russia,* Phila., Jewish Publication Society, 1913. But, in general, Western learning was so little esteemed that Peretz, the great twentieth century Yiddish writer, as a schoolboy could read Dickens only on the sly (see Maurice Samuel, *The Prince of the Ghetto,* Knopf, New York, 1948). Note Zborowski and Herzog, *op. cit.,* for a discussion of the curriculum of the Hebrew school (the *cheder*), pp. 88-123.

6. See Robin M. Williams Jr., *American Society,* New York, Knopf, 1951, pp. 426-28.

7. Hollingshead noted the same pattern among the non-Jewish youth of Elmtown. See his *Elmtown's Youth,* New York, Wiley, 1949, p. 247.

8. The writer is indebted to Dr. Peter Rossi of the University of Chicago for his assistance in constructing the scales. For purposes of scaling, responses were arbitrarily dichotomized so that responses termed traditionalist include those which are thoroughly traditionalist as well as those which only roughly approximate this.

9. Milton Steinberg, *Basic Judaism,* New York, Harcourt, Brace and Co., 1947, pp. 91-96.

10. Gunnar Myrdal, *An American Dilemma,* New York, Harper, 1944, pp. 3-4. See also, R. Williams, *op. cit.,* pp. 409-16.

11. Geoffrey Gorer, *The American People,* New York, Norton, 1948, pp. 202-08.

12. Gardner Murphy, *Personality,* New York, Harper, 1947.

ASSIMILATION OR SURVIVAL:

A CRISIS IN THE JEWISH COMMUNITY OF YANKEE CITY

by W. Lloyd Warner and Leo Srole

1. The classificatory scheme of ethnic generations used by the authors is as follows: P^1, the immigrant generation which entered the United States at an age over eighteen; P^2, the immigrant generation which entered the United States at an age of eighteen or under; F^1, the native-born offspring of P^1 and P^2; F^2, the native-born offspring of F^1. [Editor's note.]

2. A lower-class district. [Editor's note].

3. The synagogue was divided into three sections. The section on one side of the sanctuary was reserved exclusively for males, and the one on the opposite side exclusively for females. A center section between these two outer sections was reserved for family groups (i.e., males and females were permitted to sit together). [Editor's note.]

ASPECTS OF RELIGIOUS WORSHIP IN THE

CONTEMPORARY CONSERVATIVE SYNAGOGUE

Marshall Sklare

1. A comment by Joseph Weinstein in U. Syn. [United Synagogue of America]. *Proceedings of the 1950 Biennial Convention* (New York: U. Syn., n.d.), p. 86. Weinstein adds: "Here is where special problems presented themselves and the Ritual Committee came into being." (*Ibid.*) We will cover the major innovations introduced by these Committees; they have also instituted a great number of minor changes designed to bring the service into adjustment with the new aesthetic norms.

2. According to the rationale developed for the sacred system, division of labor in the religious area was calculated to strengthen the system itself. The woman, by virtue of her household responsibilities,

presumably lacked the required leisure for prayer and study—her participation in such activities would have been a threat to family life. Thus the assumption by the males of these duties *promotes* religious values. Such a point of view, while typical of the East and expressing its mores, entails severe dysfunctional consequences in the West.

3. Robert S. and Helen M. Lynd, *Middletown* (New York: Harcourt, Brace & Co., 1929), p. 355. Since synagogue membership is recorded by families rather than by individuals, no valid comparison with Christian denominations based on the sex ratio of the membership can be made.

4. Murray Leiffer, *The Effective City*

Church (New York: Abingdon-Cokesbury Press, 1949), p. 186. Cf. Gerhard E. Lenski, "Social Correlates of Religious Interest," *American Sociological Review*, XVIII (1953), 533-44.

5. Joseph H. Fichter, *Southern Parish*, Vol. I, *Dynamics of a City Church* (Chicago: University of Chicago Press, 1951), p. 254. The only spiritual activity in which men were represented in equal or better proportion was in attendance at retreats, an enterprise in which women find it difficult to participate because of their family responsibilities.

6. This is obviously related, among other things, to the fact that since these women confine themselves largely to domestic duties, they hardly have the opportunity for culture contact open to males by virtue of the masculine occupational role. Another factor is that the proper observance of the sacred system presupposes a certain degree of leisure, or at least the possibility of self-regulation of working hours. It would be safe to assume that, in contrast to Eastern Europe, here it is the females rather than the males who have the most leisure, and also the greatest opportunity for self-scheduling.

7. For a report on one of the few Conservative congregations which have not permitted mixed seating, see the *National Jewish Post*, VII, 8 (April 18, 1952), 1. In recent years mixed seating has become an issue in some Orthodox, or so-called "traditional," congregations.

8. Data about this, and some subsequent points in this chapter, are taken from U. Syn., *National Survey* (New York: U. Syn., 1950).

8a. *Survey*, I, p. 9.

9. Thus, services like the one held on Saturday morning where the attendance ratio is still highly in favor of the males (see *ibid.*, p. 36), or in which females do not participate (as in the daily service), represent the weakest links in the worship program. Of course many other factors, in addition to the present one, are involved in the decline of these services.

10. Julian Freeman, "Address," delivered before Conference of National Association of Jewish Men's Clubs, New York City, April, 1949. Note the experiment in advancing the position of woman which took place in one congregation: See *U. Syn. Review*, V, 5 (January, 1950), 4. Cf. Women's League of the U. Syn., *Proceedings—1950* (New York: Women's League of the U. Syn., n.d.), p. 135.

11. *U. Syn. Recorder*, IV, 1 (January, 1924), 14.

12. It is also necessary that the worshiper does not attempt to address the Deity in the traditional style, for this would constitute a breach in decorum. The Conservative Jew prays while the Orthodox worshiper "davens" (*daven* in Yiddish means "pray," but it connotes worship of a particular character). The difference in mood conveyed by the two terms illustrates the transition from the individualistic, informally-conducted, worshiper-centered Orthodox service, to the disciplined, mannered, and pulpit-centered rites of the Conservative synagogue.

13. *U. Syn. Recorder*, V, 3 (July, 1925), 20.

14. U. Syn., *High Holiday Planning for Your Congregation* (New York: U. Syn., n.d.), p. 20. This publication presents much material on the decorum problem in Conservatism. It is in effect a catalogue of the methods which have been used in the modification of Orthodox worship patterns. It includes an interesting "test" entitled: "How Good Are You on Your Synagogue Etiquette?"

15. Cf. Mark Zborowski and Elizabeth Herzog, *Life Is With People* (New York: International Universities Press, 1952), pp. 54-56, 206-07.

16. U. Syn.., *Sabbath Observance Kit—Number 2* (New York: U. Syn., 1951-52). The quotation is from pamphlet 4 in the *Kit*, entitled, "Yours Is the Honor: A Guidance Manual for Torah Honors," p. 6.

17. Also, there is less psychological motivation for the procedure inasmuch as the honorific worth of participation in the Torah honors has been devalued. Some of the services at which they are distributed, such as on the Sabbath and festivals, are now attended by only a relatively small group of worshipers..

18. U. Syn., *High Holiday Planning for Your Congregation, op. cit.*, p. 39.

19. *Ibid.*, p. 37.

20. A comment by Joseph Eister in U. Syn., *Proceedings of the 1948 Biennial Convention* (Typescript), pp. 194-97.

21. U. Syn., *National Survey on Synagogue Leadership*, (New York: U. Syn., 1953), p. 51.

22. U. Syn., *High Holiday Planning for Congregation, op. cit.*, p. 36.

23. A comment by Joseph Goldberg, Executive Director of the Brooklyn Jewish Center, U. Syn., *Proceedings of the 1948 Biennial Convention, op. cit.*, p. 160. (Em-

phasis supplied.)

24. Jacob S. Golub and Noah Nardi, "A Study in Jewish Observance," *The Reconstructionist*, XI, 9 (June 15, 1945), p. 11. This congregation does not stress the type of membership plan which automatically entitles one to High Holiday seats.

25. *Survey*, I, pp. 45-52, gives some information about promotional techniques. Much of the literature issued by the United Synagogue deals with such matters. Promotional techniques are used most frequently in connection with the Friday evening services rather than with the traditional services.

26. *Ibid.*, p. 3, and U. Syn., *Proceedings of the 1950 Biennial Convention, op. cit.*, p. 87. For techniques sometimes employed to gather the quorum required for public worship, see *Survey*, I, pp. 3-5. That a number of congregations have cancelled their daily services during the last decade seems clear from the figures printed in R.A., *Proceedings*, VIII (1944), 151. The Sunday morning breakfast and *Tefillin* clubs conducted by a number of synagogues are interesting examples of attempts to reinforce the daily services. See *Survey*, I, pp. 4-5.

27. *Survey*, I, p. 35. There are a few congregations in the East (the section of the country where tradition is strongest) which make the Saturday morning service the main weekly service. A few do not even conduct a late Friday night service. Congregations of this type help account for the 7 per cent whose Saturday worshipers number 300 or more. But note Arzt's statement: "With the virtual disappearance of the pious grandfather of yesteryear, the Sabbath morning service is on the verge of being abolished. Only the artificial stimulus of a socially popular *Bar Mitzvah* ceremony enables it to show sporadic signs of life." (Max Arzt, *Increasing Effectiveness of Our Synagogues* [New York: U. Syn., n.d.], p. 3.) Some congregations are already incorporating aspects of the *Bar Mitzvah* ceremony into the Friday night service, although the main ritual is still generally scheduled for Saturday morning. The boy may be assigned some part in the Friday night service, and his participation helps to increase attendance. At the same time the significance of the occasions for the candidate is multiplied since he appears at one of the more popular and well-attended services.

28. *Survey*, I, pp. 40-41.

29. *Ibid.*, p. 53. While *Yizkor* is also recited on Yom Kippur, it is not needed as a High Holiday attendance-builder. The same principle applies to the Friday night service: while the *Kaddish* prayer is read, it also does not represent a vitally-needed reinforcement.

30. U. Syn., *Proceedings of the 1950 Biennial Convention, op. cit.*, p. 58. Other services, such as *Selihoth*—prayers said before the High Holidays and serving as a prelude to them—are on the decline in Conservative congregations.

31. U. Syn., *Shavuoth Planning for Your Congregation* (New York: U. Syn., n.d.), p. 1.

32. See *Survey*, I, p. 10. According to the slogan which many congregations seek to popularize: "Friday night is synagogue night." Ninety-five per cent of all Conservative congregations schedule a Friday evening service. (*Ibid.*, p. 8.) Note that many Orthodox synagogues now conduct Friday evening services. In some cases this is currently their main weekly service. It should be noted that by the time Conservative congregations were founded, a considerable number of Reform temples had already switched their main Sabbath service to Friday night. This shift in Reform from Sunday morning to Friday evening constitutes a significant trend in Jewish religious life which cannot, however, be detailed here.

33. The most thought-provoking volume published in recent years which deals with such trends is David Riesman, *The Lonely Crowd* (New Haven: Yale University Press, 1950). We speak here of the general tenor of the Conservative service; it is true that laymen are still encouraged to perform the various duties involved in the holding of public worship.

33a. *Survey*, I, p. 23.

34. *Ibid.*, p. 26.

35. See *ibid.*, pp. 46-47. This is sometimes referred to by the Hebrew expression *Oneg Shabbat*.

36. *Ibid.*, p. 8.

37. See *ibid.*, pp. 35-44 and R.A., *Proceedings*, VIII (1944), 153-55. See also Elias Charry, "Baruch Adonoi Yom Yom," *Conservative Judaism*, VIII, 1 (November, 1951), 14-19. Rabbi Charry points out that ". . . the daily service is the last stronghold of the 'orthodox' in the Conservative congregations. . . . the 'old-timers' have here retained control." (*Ibid.*, 16.)

38. Anonymous comment quoted in *Survey*, I, p. 42. At times the division

between the Orthodox periphery and the Conservative core group is explicitly recognized. During the High Holidays in some congregations the "old-timers" do not participate in the service held in the main sanctuary, but rather are allowed to hold their own Orthodox service in another part of the building.

39. Charry, *op. cit.*, 15.

40. *U. Syn. Recorder,* VIII, 1 (February, 1928), 25. (Emphasis supplied.)

41. W. J. Goode, *Religion Among the Primitives* (Glencoe: The Free Press, 1951), p. 49.

42. This point was made by Ismar Elbogen. It is cited by Robert Gordis in his significant article, "A Jewish Prayer Book for the Modern Age," *Conservative Judaism,* II, 1 (October, 1945), 1-20. Rabbi Gordis concludes that ". . . practical considerations rather than philosophical ideals were at the roots of the objection to the

traditional liturgy." (*Ibid., 5.*)

43. Cf. Eugene Kohn, " 'Conservative Judaism'—A Review," *Conservative Judaism,* II, 4 (June, 1946), 12.

44. Albert I. Gordon, *Jews in Transition* (Minneapolis: University of Minnesota Press, 1949), p. 166. While most Orthodox worshipers pray in their street-hats, many Conservative congregations insist that the male worshiper check or store his street-hat and wear the more inconspicuous and "tasteful" skull cap. This is just one of the many minor readjustments to the new aesthetic norms which is part of the Conservative pattern. While each one is minor, in sum they make the "atmosphere" of the Conservative service very different from that of Orthodoxy.

45. Samuel Cohen, "Jewry in the West," *Jewish Theological Seminary of America Students Annual,* Vol. I (New York: J.T.S., 1914), pp. 76-77. (Emphasis supplied.)

THE AMERICAN RABBI: A RELIGIOUS SPECIALIST RESPONDS

TO LOSS OF AUTHORITY

Jerome E. Carlin and Saul H. Mendlovitz

1. For a more complete documentation of the historical context, see *The Rabbi: A Sociological Study of A Religious Specialist,* by Carlin, Jerome E. and Mendlovitz, Saul H. (Unpublished Master's thesis, University of Chicago, 1951).

2. Ismar Elbogen, "Judaism," *Encyclopedia of the Social Sciences,* ed. E. R. Seligman, VIII (1935), 431.

3. It was not uncommon for the rabbi who held an occupational post to find himself subject to other more powerful individuals and groups within the community.

4. See, Cohen, Israel, *Vilna,* Philadelphia: The Jewish Publication Society of America, 1943.

5. Baron, Salo W. *A Social and Religious History of the Jews.* 3 vols. New York: Columbia University Press, 1937, Vol. 2, p. 288. (Italics ours.)

6. See, for example, Baron, Salo, "Jewish Emancipation," *Encyclopedia of the Social Sciences,* Vol. VIII.

7. It might be noted that the technique of two interviewers proved to be very useful. To begin with, having had different experiences in the Jewish community, we were differentially sensitive to portions of our schedule; this made for more complete and comprehensive coverage of the sched-

ule. More important, perhaps, was the conscious exploitation of interviewer roles. Interviewer A was given the task of asking general questions and in the main to keep the interview guided in accordance with the schedule; interviewer B was given the job of intense probing. Interviewer A thus assumed a passive or permissive role while Interviewer B would ask the pointed and "embarrassing" question, assuming the role of an antagonist vis-à-vis the informant. The antagonist role offered the opportunity to raise issues which one interviewer might not have been able to do without endangering the interview situation. However, the presence of another interviewer who acted as a mediator between the rabbi and antagonist, or when it was warranted actively disagreed with his fellow interviewer, minimized this danger.

8. It is likely that Traditional rabbis in medium and small cities receive higher salaries but fewer perquisites.

9. It should be noted that many Traditional rabbis were or are engaged in freelancing. Their presence in a synagogue post should not be construed to mean that they are any more motivated by spiritual values or community service than the Free-Lancer. They may have merely been unsuccessful in

other occupations and preferred the security of a salary no matter how small, to the hardship of adjusting to the modern world or catering to a clientele in the highly competitive business of free-lancing.

10. Hertz, Richard C., "The Rabbi Yesterday and Today." Printed under the auspices of the North Shore Congregation Israel, Glencoe, Illinois, 1943, p. 7.

11. Weinstein, Jacob, "The Rabbi as Preacher," Lecture delivered at Hebrew Union College, Cincinnati, 1950, p. 2.

12. The Modern Orthodox rabbi and Conservative rabbi might very well delegate the actual teaching of the children to professionals if they were able to raise the budget for such a staff; certainly where these rabbis had a large budget they tended to do less and less actual classroom teaching.

13. Berman, Morton M., *The Role of the Rabbi*, New York: Jewish Institute of Religion, 1941, pp. 14, 15, 17.

14. Milton Steinberg, "Current Philosophies of Jewish Life in America," *The American Jew*, ed. by Oscar I. Janowsky (New York: Harper & Bros., 1942), p. 216.

A STUDY OF JEWISH ATTITUDES TOWARD THE STATE OF ISRAEL

Marshall Sklare and Benjamin B. Ringer

1. Samuel S. Flowerman was the Director of AJC's Division of Scientific Research at the time. Other members of the staff connected with "The Palestine Study" included Eunice Cooper, Helen Dinerman, Patricia Kendall, Thelma Herman MacCormack, Dean Manheimer, Marion Strauss, and Ruth Landes.

2. For each of the original 77, interviewers were instructed to query two additional people of the same age group. Where a block contained only Jewish families, additional respondents were obtained from the adjacent block. When both Jewish and non-Jewish families occupied a block, interviewers asked the original respondents where other Jewish families lived on that block and selected the additional respondents from among these. When an original Jewish respondent was not available, another person of the same sex and age was substituted. The use of this type of quota method to expand a sample involves a number of methodological problems, but it was felt that the procedure did insure a representation of Baltimore Jewry adequate for our purposes.

3. Because of reasons similar to those noted for the non-Jews, 27 of the original respondents could not be reinterviewed.

4. Since the study was conducted so soon after the State of Israel was established, the term "Palestine" was still very much in use and was therefore employed in the interview. In our analysis of the data, however, we will frequently use "Israel."

5. It is interesting to note that our respondents, though they made the Palestine situation an important topic in their conversations with other people, did not depend primarily on these conversations for getting news about the conflict. They turned to the formal media of communications, principally the press. This is evident in their response to the following question: "Do you get most of your news about Palestine from the newspaper, radio, magazines or where?" Their most frequent choice was the newspaper—66% selecting this medium. Their second and third choices were radio (41%) and magazines (9%), respectively. "Talking to people" was the fourth choice—only 6% mentioned it. (The various percentages exceed 100 since some mentioned that they utilized more than one news source.)

6. Respondents were considered to have knowledge that fighting was taking place in Palestine if they replied "Palestine" to either of the following two questions: "15. What do you consider the most important trouble spots in the world today?" or "16. (If Palestine not mentioned above [in answer to Question 15]): Are there any places where fighting is going on?" or if they answered "Yes" to the following question: "17. (If Palestine not mentioned in answer to Question 15 or Question 16): How about Palestine—is there fighting going on there?"

7. The Jewish and Christian respondents were each divided into two groups: (1) those possessing *high* knowledge (correct on all four items), (2) those possessing *low* knowledge (correct on three or less).

8. *Irgun Zvai Leumi* ("National Military Organization"), widely regarded as a terrorist group.

9. The close relationship between education and the two factors of income and age

raised the possibility that the latter's correlation with level of information might be spurious, that it might be solely a function of education—age and income having no independent effect on level of information. Unfortunately, there were not enough cases to permit our testing this by controlling for level of education.

10. This concurred with the trend of Christian opinion. Gentiles too were more willing to recommend aid by Jews than by the United States Government.

11. We have no way of knowing whether the Jewish population of Baltimore was more pro-Israel than was that of other cities; however, it is apparent that a pro-Zionist orientation was fairly widespread among Baltimore Jewry. For example, more than half of the sample, 57 per cent, stated that they had favored a Jewish State even before the advent of Hitler. Half of our respondents belonged to Jewish organizations classified as Zionist or pro-Zionist.

12. The "involvement" with which we are concerned refers to favorableness toward and closeness of ties with Israel. It is not to be confused with saliency of interest in matters bearing on Israel. Possession of a highly salient interest in Israel does not necessarily require a very favorable attitude toward the country. For example, members of the American Council for Judaism, though pre-occupied with Israel, are among its severest critics. Obviously, such persons would not score high on our involvement index (see footnote 14), although they might score high on an interest or even on our general knowledge index.

13. Strength of identification was highly correlated with nativity, education and age. Foreign-born Jews were much more likely to manifest strong Jewish identification (57%) than were native-born (21%); the less educated were more likely to fall into this group (46%) than the better educated (21%); and people over thirty-five (52%) rather than people under thirty-five (12%).

14. The Index of Personal Involvement was composed of the two previously-mentioned items: "If you could, would you like to be in the Palestine fighting, too?", "Do you ever talk with other people about the Palestine situation?" along with a third: "Since the Palestine fighting has been going on, do you feel any closer to the Jewish people as a whole, or don't you feel any closer?" Those who had at least two of the following responses: "Yes" for the first question, "A great deal" for the second, and "Yes, closer" for the third

were defined as having a *high* personal involvement in the Palestine situation.

15. It is interesting to note that among non-Jews there was a positive correlation between knowledge about the Palestine situation and support of Israel.

16. There were several other reasons offered by respondents for opposing aid to Israel. One, voiced by only a few, was expressed in terms of "Realpolitik." Israel was too small to expect to survive in a world of larger and more stable nations:

> I don't think a Jewish State has any right to be. It's based on incorrect reasoning on the part of Jews that they can maintain a small nation on the same footing as the nations are today.

In addition, there were a few who disapproved of the new State because they felt that Jews were properly a religious and not a national group:

> Jews are a people of a certain religion and not nationality. The Jews in Europe who are enslaved should be allowed into many countries.

While thus "rationally" opposed, these people tended, nevertheless, to want to help the Jews in Palestine. Furthermore, they could understand and sympathize with the desire of American Jews to help the Jewish State in spite of their opposition to its establishment:

> From a . . . brotherly-love standpoint, they [the Jews] would be right to help the Jewish State.

Their position was analogous to that taken by those Christian liberals who objected to a Jewish State for political or intellectual reasons but who nevertheless sympathized with Jewish aspirations for statehood.

17. Among non-Jews, factors such as a low level of prejudice, high educational level, and high level of information went hand-in-hand with interest in the Palestine situation and support for Israel. On the other hand, a high degree of prejudice and low educational level went hand-in-hand with lack of interest in Palestine and opposition to Israel.

No evidence was found to support the hypothesis that the Palestine situation was causing an increase in anti-Semitism. In fact, there is some evidence—requiring further validation—that the reverse may have been true. There is also no evidence to support the hypothesis that the Palestine situation resulted in any basic feeling among Christians that Jews were lacking in loyalty to the United States. Here, too, the reverse seems to hold. Most Christians expressed confidence in the national loyalty of American Jews. Among the least prejudiced, it appeared that esteem for Jews increased with improved Jewish fortunes in the war between Israel and Arab nations.

18. This is taken from our questionnaire item: "Do you think the United States Government should help the Jews in Palestine, should they help the Arabs, or should they help neither?" We have also reclassified the original responses to fit our revised version. Included in our category, "Should help Jews," are those who responded in the following manner to the original question: "Help Jews" or "Help both Jews and Arabs." Since no one chose "Help Arabs," our category, "Should not help Jews or don't know," includes only those who in response to the original question said, "Help neither" or "Don't know."

19. Those who claimed that they did not feel close to the Jewish people were least strongly identified as Jews. Only 21% manifested strong Jewish identification.

A STUDY OF MINORITY GROUP AUTHORITARIANISM

Joseph Adelson

1. In the section discussing the interview results all words and phrases enclosed within quotation marks designate direct quotes from the protocols.

2. An important qualification must here be made. Both groups of Ss—interview and questionnaire—consist of college students who must be presumed to share middle-class values, as that term is commonly used. The findings reported here should be interpreted with this in mind. While it is possible that the Jewish authoritarianism variables will hold for most middle-class Jewish groups, it is much less likely that they will be applicable to lower-class Jews. This is especially cogent in light of Srole's findings (9), which seem to question whether authoritarianism, as described by the Berkeley group, is applicable to lower-class individuals.

POLARITIES IN JEWISH IDENTIFICATON: THE PERSONALITY OF IDEOLOGICAL EXTREMITY

Irwin D. Rinder

1. General Identification is conceived of as a residual category for such less specifically motivated identification as might result from devotion or sense of loyalty to parents, reaction to anti-Semitism, etc.

2. The one subscale which did not discriminate between our criterion groups was that for Religious identification. A group from Hebrew Union College, the Reform rabbinical seminary, did score significantly higher on this sub-scale. This suggests that the scale itself is meaningful but that our criterion groups, different as they were in other respects, may actually have been similar in their religiousness.

3. The Social Distance Scores ranked the criterion groups in the same order in which they had been ranked intuitively and again by the identification test, thus contributing to the further validation of the test.

4. Scores on this instrument once again ranked the criterion groups as anticipated, indicating that this inventory itself could serve as a rough behavioral measure of identification.

CHANGE AND CONTINUITY IN JEWISH LIFE

David G. Mandelbaum

1. David G. Mandelbaum, "The Jewish Way of Life in Cochin," *Jewish Social Studies*, I (1939), 423-460.

2. Earl Raab, "There's No City Like San Francisco," *Commentary*, X (1950), 369-378.

3. *Ibid.*, p. 376.

4. W. Lloyd Warner and Leo Srole, *The*

Social Systems of American Ethnic Groups (New Haven: Yale University Press, 1945), p. 216.

5. Mark Zborowski and Elizabeth Herzog, *Life is with People* (New York: International Universities Press, 1952), p. 124.

6. *Ibid.*, p. 149.

7. *Ibid.*, p. 194.

8. Natalie F. Joffe, "The Dynamics of Benefice among East European Jews," *Social Forces*, XXVII (1949), 238, 242.

9. Zborowski and Herzog, *op. cit.*, p. 212.

10. *Ibid.*, pp. 78, 120, 217, 420.

11. Milton R. Konvitz, "A Letter to David Daiches," *Commentary*, XI (1951), 431-432; Moshe Decter, "The 'Old Country' Way of Life," *Commentary*, XIII (1952), 603-604.

12. David G. Mandelbaum, ed., *Selected Writings of Edward Sapir* (Berkeley: University of California Press, 1949), p. 350.

13. Raab, *op. cit.*, p. 371.

14. Eli Ginzberg, *Agenda for American Jews* (New York: King's Crown Press, 1950), p. 27.

15. Albert I. Gordon, *Jews in Transition* (Minneapolis: University of Minnesota Press, 1949), p. 303.

16. Warner and Srole, *op. cit.*, pp. 207-208.

17. Joffe, *op. cit.*, p. 239.

18. C. S. Bernheimer, "What is a Jewish Community?" *Jewish Social Service Quarterly*, XXVIII (1951), p. 226.

19. David G. Mandelbaum, "A Study of the Jews of Urbana," *Jewish Social Service Quarterly* (1935), p. 231.

20. Edgar E. Siskin, "The Impact of American Culture on the Jew," *Central Conference of American Rabbis Yearbook*, LXII (1952), p. 378.

21. M. L. Hansen, "The Third Generation in America," *Commentary*, XIV (1952), p. 495.

22. Oscar Handlin and others, "Seven Professors Look at the Jewish Student," *Commentary*, XII (1951), p. 532.

23. Gordon, *op. cit.*, p. 305.

24. Maurice L. Zigmond, "Judaism in Its Cultural Setting — An Anthropological View," *Yearbook, The Central Conference of American Rabbis*, LXII (1952), p. 359.

25. Zborowski and Herzog, *op. cit.*, p. 165.

TWO TYPES OF JEWISH MOTHERS

Martha Wolfenstein

1. Zborowski and Herzog, 1952; also unpublished material in the files of Columbia University Research in Contemporary Cultures.

2. I refer to observations made during several years as a school psychologist in private schools in New York City, where the large majority of the families were American Jewish; also to other cases at the Jewish Board of Guardians.

3. Unpublished material in the files of Columbia University Research in Contemporary Cultures.

4. See "Fun Morality" in the volume in which this article originally appeared (p. 168); also Wolfenstein, 1953.

5. Zborowski and Herzog, 1952.

6. An alternative has been observed to the tendency of this type of mother to see the child as always the same, namely, for the mother to hark back to the time of his early childhood as a golden age from which he has subsequently declined. It would seem that these two attitudes can also coexist: the child appearing invariant as far as health is concerned (always fragile and needing vigilant care) but changing in respect to goodness, becoming less loving toward the mother, less exclusively preoccupied with pleasing her.

7. Cf. Coleman, Kris, and Provence, 1953.

8. Infant mortality, however, is not decisive for the view that children are very fragile. Many deep-lying fantasies contribute to the image of the child as weak or strong (cf. "Image of the Child in Contemporary Films" in the volume in which this article originally appeared, p. 277).

9. *Infant Care*, 1945 and 1951.

10. Gorer, 1948.

11. Information about Eastern European Jewish mothers indicates much verbal expression of ambivalence toward their children. "In the mother's moods, opposites are almost simultaneous. If the child pesters her . . . her sharp 'devil take you!' or 'go into the ground!' will merge swiftly into a blessing, 'you shall grow strong and healthy for me!'" (Zborowski and Herzog, 1952, p. 334). Presumably in such swift undoing of the expression of a hostile wish, the mother

did not allow herself to become aware of its significance. When the child turns such expressions of hostility back toward the mother (this being apparently an American development), her overwhelming sense of the seriousness of these words derives some of its force from her own acknowledged hostility toward the child (as well as toward her own mother) which she projects. When the child says, "Drop dead!" the mother's reaction that this can kill her may not be a direct attribution of magical force to the words but rather the feeling that if the child is hostile toward her, this so wounds her to the heart that she can die. In the case of Mrs. S. it seems that she does on her side curse her son when provoked, but she does not acknowledge any feeling but that of wounded love toward him; her curses do not carry the force that his do.

12. This fantasy, that the mother will suffer and die if the son's self-damaging tendencies are carried through, may express an expiation: as if the mother unconsciously acknowledges her projected hostile tendencies and feels she must pay for them.

13. Zborowski and Herzog, 1952.

14. *Ibid.*

15. In contrast to this, typical quarrels in the S family are more narrowly focused in her mother-son relation. At a word from the mother—"Button your jacket" or "You should get some sleep now"—Stan flies into a rage—"Don't treat me like a baby "—and the fight is on. Where, as in the L family, a larger sector of the external world is likely to be included in the terms of the quarrel, a greater sense of reality guards against the

intrusion of melodramatic fantasies.

16. Wolfenstein and Leites, 1950.

17. Gorer, 1948.

18. *New York Times Magazine,* 1954.

19. Bateson, 1942.

20. Wolfenstein and Leites, 1950.

21. Freud, 1942*a*; Abraham, 1942; Jones, 1948.

22. In a similar way Rudolph Loewenstein (1951) contrasts German and Jewish characters, finding in the Germans a preponderance of defenses against dirtiness, in the Jews the concentration of defenses against aggression.

23. Freud, 1942*b*.

24. Similarly, one may contrast the attitudes toward women in British and American films. The British preoccupation with the danger of unleashing sadistic impulses toward women and the need to guard against such impulses find no counterpart in American films, where women are more than able to take care of themselves (cf. Wolfenstein and Leites, 1950).

25. Wolfenstein, 1953.

26. Cf. the little boy cited by Karl Abraham (1942, p. 427) who, when angry with his nurse, threatened to "ka-ka" her over the river. "According to the child's view the way to get rid of a person one no longer liked was by means of defecation."

27. As indicative of Mr. L's maternal identification, he says that he feels tied to Karen by an umbilical cord (when she is very demanding of his attention and he feels he cannot get away from her) and that he feels as if she had drained all the milk out of him (when he is exhausted by her demands).

28. Bibring, 1953.

A STUDY OF DELINQUENCY

AMONG JEWISH CHILDREN IN NEW YORK CITY

Sophia M. Robison

1. See Alvin Chenkin, "Jewish Population in the United States, 1955," in *American Jewish Year Book,* Vol. 57 (1956), p. 121.

2. New York, Columbia University Press, 1936.

3. Information from paper based on the Harrower-Peck Intake Project presented at the American Orthopsychiatric Association Annual Meeting, March 13, 1954.

4. Neva R. Deardorff, "The Religio-Cultural Background of New York City's Population," *Milbank Memorial Fund Quar-*

terly, Vol. XXXIII, No. 2 (April 1955), p. 160.

5. The Chinese are the only exception to this statement.

6. Unfortunately, there are no demographic data for 1930 comparable to those which became available as a result of the study sponsored by the Health Insurance Plan of Greater New York (this is the study which is analyzed in the article by Deardorff, previously cited). It is estimated, however, that in 1930 Jews constituted about one-third of the population of New

York City (see the methodological note in Robison, *op. cit.*).

7. Though the data are not included in Table 2, we find that there are variations in the proportions of these offenses as between the different boroughs.

8. Since the distribution of offenses for the total group was not available for 1952, we must cite the figures for the previous year.

9. Because of th? way in which the 1930 tabulations were published, it is impossible to allocate the incidence of the other types of offenses in the Jewish group (see Robison, *op. cit.*, for further details). However, the Jewish group in 1930 was unique as regards the high proportion

charged with peddling or begging.

10. This figure was furnished by the Court Statistician to the State Department of Correction, Division of Probation, State of New York.

11. The Court's action in 1952 varied both according to the sex of the offender and the borough in which his case was heard. The borough of Brooklyn, for example, was credited with the highest percentage of dismissed cases. In the dismissed group, all but six were boys. This reflects, no doubt, the greater readiness of the community to apprehend boys in contrast to girls (the ratio of boys to girls in the 1952 Jewish group was approximately six to one).

12. See Harrower-Peck, *op. cit.*, p. 16.

HOODLUM OR BUSINESS MAN: AN AMERICAN DILEMMA

Jackson Toby

1. U. S. Bureau of the Census, *Statistical Abstract of the United States: 1952*, Washington, 1952, p. 136.

2. Clifford R. Shaw and Henry D. McKay, *Juvenile Delinquency and Urban Areas*, Chicago: University of Chicago Press, 1942.

3. Harry M. Shulman, "The Family and Juvenile Deliquency," *Annals of the American Academy of Political and Social Science*, January, 1949, pp. 21-31.

4. Albert K. Cohen, *Delinquent Boys: The Culture of the Gang*, Glencoe, Illinois: The Free Press, 1955.

5. Robert K. Merton, "Social Structure and Anomie," *Social Theory and Social Structure*, Glencoe, Illinois: The Free Press, 1949.

6. The concept of relative deprivation was developed by Samuel A. Stouffer to account for seemingly paradoxical patterns of dissatisfaction among soldiers in World War II. Samuel A. Stouffer, *et al.*, *The American Soldier*, Vol. I, Princeton: Princeton University Press, 1949, pp. 124-130, 172-173, 178-182, 208-211, 250-254, 279-280, 525-527, 542-543, 562-564.

7. Bureau of the Census, *Sixteenth Census of the United States (1940) Monograph on Population Education: Educational Attainment of Children by Rental Value of Home*, Washington: Government Printing Office, 1945. See also Jackson Toby, "Educational Maladjustment as a Predisposing Factor in Criminal Careers: A Comparative Study of Ethnic Groups," unpublished

Ph.D. Dissertation, Harvard University, 1950, Chapter 4, "Group Factors in School Integration or Mal-Integration," pp. 93-122.

8. Franz Alexander, "Development of the Ego-Psychology," in *Psychoanalysis Today* (ed. by Sandor Lorand), New York: International Universities Press, 1944, pp. 143-150. Also, see Paul Schilder, "Problems of Crime," in *ibid.*, pp. 342-353.

9. United States Bureau of the Census, *Immigrants and Their Children, 1920*, Washington: Government Printing Office, 1927, p. 62. An official comparison of the rural-urban distribution of Jews and Italians is not possible with United States data. In Canada, however, 96.45% of the Jewish population was urban in 1931 as compared with 81.55% of the Italian population. Dominion of Canada, Bureau of Statistics, *Rural and Urban Composition of the Canadian Population*, Ottawa: 1938, p. 81.

10. For documentation, see Jackson Toby, *op. cit.*, Chapter 7, "The Orientation to the School Contributed by the Jewish Cultural Tradition," pp. 178-207.

11. Leonard Covello, "The Social Background of the Italo-American School Child: A Study of the Southern Italian Family Mores and Their Effect on the School Situation in Italy and America," unpublished Ph.D. Dissertation, New York University School of Education, 1944.

12. Nathaniel D. M. Hirsch, "A Study of Natio-Racial Mental Differences," *Genetic Psychology Monographs*, Vol. 1

(1926), pp. 239-406; Covello, *op. cit.*; Sophia M. Robison, *Can Delinquency Be Measured?*, New York: Columbia University Press, 1936, "Truants," pp. 127-155.

13. Robison, *op. cit.*, p. 182.

14. Shaw and McKay, *op. cit.*, p. 154.

15. Donald R. Taft, "Nationality and Crime," *American Sociological Review*, Vol. 1 (1936), pp. 724-736.

16. Nathan Goldberg, *Occupational Patterns of American Jews*, New York: The Jewish Teachers' Seminary and People's University, 1947.

17. Not only is it difficult to identify Jewish offenders, but in the United States it is no small problem to count the Jewish population at large. The Bureau of the Census does not collect information on the religious affiliation of individuals. As a result, the number of Jews in the United States is something of a mystery. Estimates are available, especially in large cities where the bulk of American Jewry lives, but no one knows how accurate these are. Even in New York, Boston, and Chicago, detailed data on age composition and nativity do not exist. Since an accurate count of the base population is necessary in order to compute a crime rate, Jewish crime statistics in the United States must be considered approximations even in those instances where the Jewish offenders have been validly identified.

18. In so far as Jews *are* identified in population survey, e.g., the Canadian Census, it is because they call themselves Jewish or are considered Jewish by others. Thus, their solidarity with other "Jews" is measured rather than their commitment to Jewish values. From the point of view of preventing crime, however, whether the individual has introjected the intellectual achievement values of the Jewish cultural tradition is more relevant to his developing a stake in conformity than the fact that he calls himself "Jewish." In the United States and Canada, where ethnic groups are in process of assimilation, the values of the ethnic tradition may be sloughed off by an individual before he disaffiliates in solidarity terms. This is particularly true of Jews because prejudice may enforce a solidarity upon them that is unjustified by common adherence to the ethnic tradition. In short, there is reason to believe that a statistical effort to document the crime-preventing effect of the Jewish cultural tradition cannot fully succeed; statistics about Jewish offenders and about the Jewish population at large employ an operational definition of "Jewishness" geared to solidarities rather than cultural commitment.

The author's survey of the case histories of a sample of Jewish juvenile delinquents tended to confirm this line of reasoning. These youngsters were, in their attitudes toward school and their occupational aspirations, much like juvenile delinquents from other backgrounds. That is to say, they did not have the orientations which one would expect of youngsters immersed in the Jewish cultural tradition.

19. Robison, *op. cit.*, p. 72; pp. 222-226.

20. Julius B. Maller, "The Maladjusted Jewish Child," *Jewish Social Service Quarterly*, Vol. 9 (1933), pp. 285-295.

21. H. S. Linfield, "Jewish Inmates of the State Prisons of the United States," *American Jewish Year Book*, Vol. 33, Philadelphia: Jewish Publication Society of America, 1931.

22. This analysis goes counter to the culture-conflict explanation of the high crime rates of second-generation Americans. According to the culture-conflict theory, the second-generation individual is neither fully integrated in the ethnic sub-culture nor in the American social system. Hence he may not be responsive to the norms of either. A high crime rate results from this failure of social control and the concomitant production of disorganized personalities. In the opinion of the writer, this theory is too promiscuous in its assumption that culture *difference* leads to culture *conflict*. Some foreign cultures may blend with the American socio-cultural mileu. For second-generation children from such backgrounds, the differences between their ethnic tradition and dominant American values may be a challenge leading to creativity and a new synthesis. Thus, for Jews, their cultural background facilitates adjustment in the educational and occupational systems. Other ethnic traditions may be relatively immiscible vis-à-vis the American socio-cultural milieu. Children of Sicilian-born parents who cling to traditional orientations may do so at the expense of their adjustment within the American social system. To put the same point in another way, the controversy between assimilationists and cultural pluralists may be partially resolved by making reference to specific ethnic traditions. Some may be so radically different in value from those of the United States that choices must be made. Others may be sufficiently compatible that value co-existence is not only possible but salutary.

SOME RELATIONSHIPS BETWEEN RELIGION, ETHNIC ORIGIN
AND MENTAL ILLNESS

Jerome K. Myers and Bertram H. Roberts

1. Conducted by the Yale University Departments of Sociology and Psychiatry, the project was aided by USPHS Mental Health Act Grant MH 263, "Relationship of Psychiatric Disorder to Social Structure." Also participating in the research were A. B. Hollingshead and F. C. Redlich, principal investigators, H. A. Robinson, and L. Z. Freedman.

2. See Roberts and Myers (13) for further details of the study.

3. Adapted from the Veterans Administration Nomenclature: TB 10A-78.

4. See Hollingshead (4) for a detailed discussion of the divisions in the community's social structure.

5. The Chi Square test was used in all calculations to determine whether significant difference existed between frequency distributions. Significance was defined at the .05 level, although in most cases it was less than .01.

6. See Redlich *et al.* (12) for details of these findings. In brief, an inverse relation was found between the distribution of the psychoses and neuroses by social class; the higher the social class, the greater the extent of neurosis and the less the amount of psychosis. For example, in the highest classes (I and II) 65 per cent of the psychiatric patients were neurotics and 35 per cent were psychotics; in the lowest class (V) the corresponding percentages were 8 and 92.

The community was divided into five social classes, utilizing Hollingshead's *Index of Social Position* which is based upon the three factors of education, occupation, and ecological area of residence. A brief description of these classes is as follows: Class I—families of wealth, high educational status, and considerable prestige in the community. Class II—families in which the adults are, for the most part, college graduates and are professionals and executives. Class III—small business owners, salesmen, white-collar workers, and some skilled workers; they have generally attained a high-school education and some have had a few years of junior college or business school. Class IV—semi-skilled workers and factory hands, the majority of whom have not completed high school. Class V—unskilled factory hands and laborers, with a grammar-school education or less, who live in the tenement and cold-water flat areas of the city.

7. We controlled for the influence of social class in the following manner: for every diagnostic category we made a Chi Square test of the religious distribution of the psychiatric and the general population within each social class.

8. The mother's ethnic origin was the same as the father's in 90 per cent of the cases.

9. Negroes are included, although strictly speaking they represent a racial group.

10. Data on nativity and age distribution for the general population were obtained from 1950 U. S. Census reports. Three age groups were used for purposes of analysis: 21-30, 40-59, 60 and over. Because of space considerations, we have presented data for the entire adult population in Table 4, instead of all the specific age groupings, since the pattern was usually the same in all groups. However, if the age difference between the foreign-born and native-born populations distorts these general findings, we so indicate in the text.

CULTURE AND JEWISH SOBRIETY: THE INGROUP-OUTGROUP FACTOR

Charles R. Snyder

1. Fishberg's views as relevant here are best expressed in Bernheimer (4).

2. The Jewish group is designated as an "ingroup" so as to suggest consciousness of group identity vis-à-vis the larger Gentile society (the outgroup), and in recognition of a cultural tradition which embodies in many ways an ethnocentric view. However, these terms are intended only as ideal types. By no means do all nominal Jews experience an equivalent sense of "ingroupness," and distinctions in this respect have an important bearing on Jewish drinking behavior. For elaboration of these concepts, see Sumner (35).

3. See also Bales (1).

4. The demoralizing influence of outsiders and the identification of hedonistic drinking with assimilation (more accurately, with idolatry) is not a new idea or simply an observation of modern theorists but one that has long standing in Jewish culture, as the following tradition indicates: " 'And they called the people unto the sacrifices of their gods: and the people did eat and bowed down to their gods [Numbers 25:2].' They [the Midianites] followed his [Balaam's] advice. . . . They put up shops for them and placed therein prostitutes and in their hands were all manner of attractive things. . . . And a young woman issued forth bedecked and perfumed and lured him and said, Why do we love you and you hate us? . . . Thereupon she gave him the wine to drink, and Satan burned in him. . . . When he asked her for sexual intercourse she said, I will not submit until you slaughter this to Peor and bow down to him. And he replied, I will not bow down to an idol. She said to him, You are only uncovering yourself. And he was mad with passion for her and did so." This tradition, with variations and amplifications, occurs in numerous ancient Talmudic and Midrashic sources, cited in Snyder (31).

5. The basic materials for this study were obtained from two sources. First, from interviews with a random sample of seventy-three New Haven Jewish men. Second, from questionnaires administered to a larger sample of male Jewish college students as part of the College Drinking Survey (34). Details of sampling procedures and conventions used in the analysis and presentation of data may be found in (31). Attention must be called, however, to the fact that Jewish students in the Survey were not drawn from any single locale or college setting. The sample of Jewish students represents an aggregate of Jewish youth scattered in 18 different colleges in various parts of the United States. Moreover, some selection was introduced in the sampling procedures of the College Drinking Survey. Of outstanding importance to this study was the inclusion of Orthodox Jewish students in greater proportion than their probable proportion in the American Jewish population might warrant. Because of these sampling procedures and the intrinsic limits of the universe under study, findings from the Jewish student sample cannot be thought of as direct measures of the incidence of sociocultural traits in the American Jewish population. Nor are findings from this sample directly indicative of

characteristics of particular communities, as are the findings from our New Haven sample. Even generalizations about drinking and other characteristics of Jewish college students based on this sample must be asserted cautiously.

Despite these qualifications, the sample of Jewish students is of decided value in studying relations among sociocultural phenomena pertinent to this research. For example, if intoxication varies inversely with religious participation among Jews, this should be evident in data from both the New Haven and the student samples. Our basic interest is precisely in relations of this kind and their interpretation, rather than in traits of particular Jewish communities, college students, or the American Jewish population as such. Thus, it does not matter that there are disproportionate numbers of Orthodox or frequent religious participants among the Jewish students sampled.

6. In the case of a thirteenth man it could not be ascertained whether intoxication occurred during this period. Actually, our data on experience in military service are not as satisfactory as they might have been because specific and detailed questions on service experiences were not included in the interview schedule. After the first interview, however, the interviewer made it a point to probe possible connections between intoxication and service experience.

7. On this point, see Straus and Bacon (34).

8. Chi-square of the difference by veteran status is 18.54, *P* (at 2 degrees of freedom) is less than .001. To simplify presentation, only data on milder intoxication are shown in Table 1. Data on more severe intoxication, showing an analoguous difference by veteran status, are presented in Snyder (31).

9. In describing contacts between Jews and non-Jews in the eastern European *shtetl*, Zborowski and Herzog (39) have this to say: "The market represents the chief contact between the Jew and the non-Jew, who for the *shtetl* is primarily the peasant. Aside from the market and scattered business negotiations, they inhabit different worlds. . . . The seeds of all their relations are in this market place contact." On the middleman role of the Jews in eastern Europe, see Dubnow (7).

10. For a brief description and documentation of the persistence of ethnic cleavage between Jews and Gentiles in America, see Snyder and Landman (32).

11. For a general definition and discussion of an instrumental orientation and the constraints arising therefrom, see Parsons (25). In discussing various possible modes of orientation of an actor to a situation Parsons warns that the cognitive, cathectic and evaluative modes are present in every situation, but adds that there is a "relative primacy of the different modes." What is important for our purpose is that if the actor's orientation is instrumental, cognitive interests have primacy and expressive or gratificatory interests which might disrupt the cognitive process are subordinated.

12. There is a long history of Jewish protest against military service in eastern Europe, a protest which stemmed partly from pacific religious ideals and partly from reaction to the deliberate attempts of despotic governments, such as the regime of Nicholas I of Russia, to crush Judaism and assimilate the Jews through the imposition of long and harsh terms of military service. For evidence of this situation in 19th century Russia and Poland, see Dubnow (7). The traditional rejection of temporal power as a means of maintaining Jewish "moral hegemony" is discussed by Riesman (28).

13. Chi-square of the difference in drunkenness along religious lines, holding veteran status constant, is 19.28, P (at 2 degrees of freedom) is less than .001. Chi-square of the difference by veteran status is 10.18, P (at 2 degrees of freedom) is less than .01. Analogous data on milder intoxication have been omitted here but are presented in Snyder (31).

14. The insulating character of Orthodox Judaism has been discussed in the recent sociological literature by Warner and Srole (38).

15. Cf. Moore (23).

16. For evidence of the concentration of abstinence sentiment in rural areas see Jellinek (18).

17. It was hoped that referring the question to childhood would remove some of the guilt felt for entertaining such an idea and thus allow freer discussion. Moreover, we wished to know whether or not these were beliefs of long standing.

18. Translated by Bales (2). While Bales cited this song and the "stigmatization of the Goyim as drunkards," he did not develop the possible reinforcing effects which this stereotyping may have on Jewish sobriety. Rather, he turned to a consideration of the menace which the drunken peasants constituted to the Jewish town dwellers in Czarist Russia, and to the question of whether or not Jewish sobriety was a response to this situation.

19. In fact, the writer has observed situations where references to the characteristic sobriety of Jews apparently motivated nominal Jews to drink immoderately.

20. God's punishments for disobedience as well as the rewards for conformity to the Law are stated in no uncertain terms in Leviticus, and the role of outgroups in this process is very clear: "Ye shall be slain before your enemies: they that hate you shall reign over you" (26:17); "And I will bring a sword upon you, that shall avenge the quarrel of my covenant" (26:25); "And I will scatter you among the heathen, and will draw out a sword after you: and your land shall be desolate" (26:33); "And ye shall perish among the heathen, and the land of your enemies shall eat you up" (26:38).

21. This first line of reasoning is quite clearly exemplified by Fishberg in Bernheimer (4). At one point Glazer (12) also seems to favor this kind of argument, although he modifies it somewhat by saying: "It is not consciousness of the siege that prevents any individual Jew from taking one more drink—motivation is more complicated than that. But it is the consequences of the siege, passed down from generation to generation. . . ." The case of the American Negro is particularly instructive as a test of the theory that simple avoidance of retaliation or censure can motivate the sobriety of relatively defenseless minorities. Authorities agree that the Negro in America, occupying an inferior social position, has been the butt of criticism from whites and often the object of persecution. Individually and collectively Negroes are vulnerable to punitive caste controls and occasional outrages against person and property. Yet, as Dollard (6) points out in his discussion of the psychic compensations or "gains" which accrue to Negro lower-class caste status, the behavior of lower-class Negroes in "Southern Town" is quite permissive in respect to the expression of aggression and sexuality and, apparently, drunkenness. . . . On the whole, the evidence at least indicates that in urban areas, where Jews are also concentrated, intoxication is quite common among Negroes and that subordinate minority status is of itself insufficient to induce a pattern of sobriety. It is possible, however, that where the more ascetic forms of Protestantism have gained strong adherence among Negroes, and where there is striving among them to dif-

ferentiate from the lower classes and emulate white middle-class "respectability," pressures to sobriety will be intense and enhanced by consciousness of race difference

22. For situationally or permanently assimilating Jews, however, what is or is not conspicuous in terms of wider societal norms may be of the utmost importance to perceived welfare and in determining behavior.

23. The evidence cn Jewish stereotypes suggests that this is very much the case. The thesis can even be entertained that non-Jewish criticism, far from being actually or potentially directed at intoxication and ensuing behavior, was directed at the uncompromising sobriety of the Jews. A recent comment by Glazer (12) is suggestive: "Something happened and it's hard to say whether it was that the Jews began drinking less or the rest of the world began drinking more. . . . In any case, sobriety, was added to the catalogue of traits that annoyed the Gentiles." The tacit assumption of this statement is quite the opposite of Kant's. It implies that Jews might have been less the butt of criticism had they seen fit to "let their hair down" and get drunk now and then, although the "damned if you do, damned if you don't" principle might well have prevailed. That the Jews early distinguished themselves and were distinguished by their sobriety among surrounding peoples is suggested by a variety of facts. For instance, the Hellenic society and culture which enveloped Judaism for centuries after the Macedonian conquest hardly looked on intoxication with disfavor, as McKinlay (21,22) has demonstrated. Evidence on drunkenness among such peoples as the Persians, the Babylonians and certain Semitic peoples in the Mediterranean region has also been compiled by McKinlay (20). Of greater significance is historical evidence of excessive drinking in more recent times by European peoples among whom large numbers of Jews have lived in comparative sobriety. For example, according to Sebastian Franck (16), inebriety was common to both sexes and among all classes in 16th century Germany, the prevailing attitude being one of indifference. Franck even noted the contrasting sobriety of the Jews and attributed their wealth to their "abstinence." The drunkenness of the eastern European Gentile peasantry has already been noted. Apparently, drunkenness often accompanied the most violent expressions of anti-Semitism in those countries, and it is constantly noted in this connection and derided by Jewish historians such as Dubnow (7).

24. It is not intended to imply that Judaic norms have in no way been subject to modification, reinterpretation and alteration, and that realistic adjustment to changing life conditions has had no role in this process. Our point is simply that the Orthodox emphasize the immutability of the religious system and associate individual and group welfare therewith.

25. Probably it was in this sense that two of the New Haven Jewish men asserted in an "off the record" manner, at the conclusion of their interviews, that the need to "keep up a good front" and "save face" before Gentiles was a basic motive in Jewish sobriety. These men do not, of course, go on to point out that what constitutes "good front" or "face" is determined by the values of the ingroup.

26. A good summary of Durkheim's ideas, as they are pertinent here, is contained in Parsons (26).

27. Unless there is conversion to Judaism.

28. This index is not, properly speaking, a scale of intensity of sentiments. The supposition was that a simple summation of scores would sufficiently differentiate extremes of strong and weak sentiment. Confirmation of the present findings through the use of refined scale techniques is greatly to be desired. The writer is indebted to Dr. Jackson Toby, of Rutgers University, for the design of these questions.

29. As defined in terms of ritual drinking experience. "Most Orthodox" men were defined as those brought up in homes where the Kiddush was regularly observed and who were observing the Kiddush at the time of interviewing. "Intermediate" men were reared in homes where the Kiddush was regularly observed but who, in later life, had abandoned the practice. "Least Orthodox" men were defined as those who neither observed the Kiddush regularly nor were brought up in homes where the Kiddush was regularly observed.

30. P is less than .01.

31. There is some question as to whether or not beliefs about retaliation and catastrophe as instruments of God's judgment for Israel's failures actually gained a real foothold among the Jewish people until the powerlessness of the group was concretely experienced by several generations in the Diaspora. This is intimated in Moore (23).

Thorner (37) suggests, however, that even prior to the Diaspora "Their [the Jews'] strategic position in the Fertile Crescent invited attack from the great warring empires, another situation which intensified the group solidarity and alertness to Yahweh and his Commandments. . . . Thus both prior to and during the Diaspora a gradually internalized value-system with its demand for a rationally controlled impulse-life subordinate to what were considered higher ends came under constant threat of attack and was thereby consolidated." The further working out of this aspect of Orthodox ideology so as to motivate and rationalize the solidarity of the Jews as God's chosen people in the Diaspora is alluded to by Reisman (28): "Occasionally, the group's 'nerve of failure' was supported by the notion that its very powerlessness proved the Jews to be in fact the Chosen of God. In this way, defeat itself could strengthen the faith of the 'saving remnant' of Jews."

32. The confused state of conceptions of the Jewish cultural heritage is mirrored in Infield's (15) effort to define contemporary Jewish culture. Virtually the only substantive feature which Infield finds common to contemporary Jews is "the odium of defection," although he proposes some questions whose answers might yield more abstract common denominators.

33. Data are presented in Snyder (31).

34. Cited in Gerth and Mills (10).

35. The concept of "status protest" is developed by Hughes (14).

36. Our reference here and in the ensuing discussion is to Bales' ideas as set forth in his dissertation (2) and reiterated in summary form (1).

37. The Tarahumara of Central America aptly exemplify such an alternation: At certain culturally appropriate times and places alcoholic beverages are consecrated and used for religious purposes, while at other times the same beverages are used in semiorgiastic fashion apparently devoid of sacred significance. Norms, ideas and sentiments do not seem to carry over from the one context to the other (Dr. Jacob Freed, personal communication).

39. On this point, see Zborowski and Herzog (39).

SOURCES OF JEWISH INTERNATIONALISM AND LIBERALISM

Lawrence H. Fuchs

1. Because of a quirk in referendum procedure, only four wards voted on the measure to call an international convention to write a world constitution. The result: Ward 5 (Yankee and upper-middle class) 73% approved; Ward 12 (Jewish and middle class) 82.3%; Ward 15 (Irish and middle class) 71.2%; Ward 20 (Irish-Yankee and upper-middle class) 66.8%.

2. J. O. Hertzler, "The Sociology of Anti-Semitism Throughout History," in *Jews in a Gentile World*, edited by Isaque Graeber and S. H. Britt, (New York: Macmillan, 1942), p. 76.

3. W. Lloyd Warner and Leo Srole, *The Social Systems of American Ethnic Groups* (New Haven: Yale University Press, 1945), p. 96.

4. *Ibid.*, p. 290.

5. This material is reported on and discussed in *Ethnic Relations in the United States* by Edward C. McDonagh and Eugene S. Richards (New York: Appleton-Century-Crofts, Inc., 1953), pp. 152-153. Another discussion of social distance scales may be found in *Groups in Harmony and Tension*, by Muzafer Sherif and Caro-lyn W. Sherif (New York: Harper & Bros., 1953), pp. 78-79.

6. McDonagh and Richards, *op. cit.*, p. 171.

7. Jean-Paul Sartre, *Anti-Semite and Jew*, translated by George W. Becker (New York: Schocken Books, 1948), p. 132.

8. For studies which show psychological insecurity of Jews compared to non-Jews, see Abraham P. Sperling, "A Comparison between Jews and non-Jews," *Journal of Applied Psychology*, Vol. XXVI (1942) pp. 828-40; May Sukov and E. G. Williamson, "Personality Traits and Attitudes of Jewish and non-Jewish Students," *Journal of Applied Psychology*, Vol. XXII (1938), 487-92; also Seward Keith and Meyer Freedman, "Jewish Temperament," *Journal of Applied Psychology*, Vol. XIX (1935), pp. 70-84.

9. These three books are: Louis C. Kesselman, *The Social Politics of FEPC—A Study in Reform Pressure Movements* (Chapel Hill: The University of North Carolina Press, 1948); Morroe Berger, *Equality by Statute* (New York: Columbia University Press, 1952); Louis Ruchames,

Race, Job and Politics (New York: Columbia University Press, 1953).

10. Louis Israel Newman, *Jewish Influence on Christian Reform Movements* (New York: Columbia University Press, 1925), p. 20.

11. T. W. Adorno, Else Frenkel-Brunswick, Daniel J. Levinson, and R. Nevitt Sanford, *The Authoritarian Personality* (New York: Harper & Brothers), Chapter 5.

12. This is Justice Frankfurter's phrase from the opening of his dissenting opinion in the famous flag salute case, *West Virginia V. Barnette,* 319 US 624, pp. 646-647.

13. Maurice Samuel, *The Gentleman and the Jew* (New York: Alfred Knopf, 1950).

14. Werner J. Cahnman, "The Cultural Consciousness of Jewish Youth," *Jewish Social Studies,* Vol. XIV (July, 1952), pp. 198-199.

15. *Ibid.,* p. 200.

16. Mark Zborowski and Elizabeth Herzog, *Life is with People* (New York: International Universities Press, 1953), Part III, Chapter I.

17. Frederick A. Bushee, *Ethnic Factors in the Population of Boston* (New York: Macmillan Co., 1903), p. 21; Robert A. Woods, ed., *Americans in Process* (Boston: Houghton Mifflin & Co., 1903), pp. 144, 353; Robert A. Woods, ed., *The City Wilderness: A Settlement Study by Residents and Associates of the South End House* (Boston: Houghton Mifflin & Co., 1899), pp. 37, 232.

18. Talcott Parsons, "The Sociology of Anti-Semitism," in *Jews in a Gentile World,* ed. by Graeber and Britt, *op. cit.,* p. 106.

19. Albert Einstein, *Out of My Later Years* (New York: Philosophical Library, 1950), p. 250.

20. Morton Clurman, "How Discriminatory Are College Admissions?," *Commentary,* Vol. 15 (June, 1953).

21. See the following: N. Nardi, "Studies in Intelligence of Jewish Children," *Jewish Education,* Vol. XX (1948), pp. 41-50. The I. Q. of Jewish children in New York was found to be much above the average of a non-Jewish control group regardless of home environment factors.

E. Clark, "Motivation of Jewish Students," *Journal of Social Psychology,* Vol. XXIX (1949), pp. 113-117. In a study of 6,774 freshmen at Northwestern University it was found that Jewish students, especially the boys, received higher grades than non-Jews even when aptitudes as measured by aptitude tests were held equal.

L. M. Terman, *Genetic Studies of Genius* (Palo Alto: Stanford University Press, 1925), p. 648. At the time of his study Terman found twice the percentage of bright Jewish boys and girls as were found among Gentiles.

22. The first prime minister, Ben Gurion, was a student of Greek philosophy. His successor, Moshe Sharett, is an accomplished linguistic scholar. The first President, Chaim Weizmann, was a chemist of renown. Isaac Ben Zvi, now Israeli President, has been a scholar all his adult life. The Knesset is as packed with historians and economists as our Congress is studded with lawyers.

23. Louis Wirth, *The Ghetto* (Chicago: University of Chicago Press, 1928), p. 81.

24. Zborowski and Herzog, *op. cit.,* p. 230.

25. Natalie F. Joffe, "Non-Reciprocity Among East European Jews," in *The Study of Culture at a Distance,* edited by Margaret Mead and Rhoda Métraux (Chicago: The University of Chicago Press, 1953), pp. 386-387.

26. Arthur Ruppin, *The Jews in the Modern World* (London: Macmillan & Co., Ltd., 1934), p. 352.

27. See Israel S. Chipkin, "Judaism and Social Welfare," in *The Jews, Their History, Culture and Religion,* edited by Louis Finkelstein (New York: Harper & Brothers, 1949), Vol. 1, Chapter 16, p. 713; Boris Bogen, *Jewish Philanthropy* (New York: 1917); Ephriam Frisch, *An Historical Survey of Jewish Philanthropy* (New York: The Macmillan Company, 1924); Cecil Roth, *The Jewish Contribution to Civilization* (Cincinnati: The Union of American Hebrew Congregations, 1940), Chapter 12, "The Greatest of These is Charity."

28. Einstein, *op. cit.,* p. 249.

29. Morris N. Kertzer, "What is a Jew?", *Look,* June 17, 1952.

30. Zborowski and Herzog, *op. cit.,* p. 135.

31. Werner Sombart, *The Jews and Modern Capitalism,* translated by M. Epstein (London: T. Fisher Unwin, 1913), pp. 235-236.

32. Alfred Kinsey, *Sexual Behavior in the Human Male* (Philadelphia: W. B. Saunders, 1949), p. 492.

33. *Ibid.,* p. 496.

34. Charles Angoff, *In The Morning Light* (Boston: The Beechurst Press, 1952).

35. Robin Williams, *American Society* (New York: Alfred Knopf, 1952), Chapter

11, "Culture Orientation in American Society." In the use of the term "value" the writer relies heavily upon the discussion found in this chapter by Williams.

36. Harold Laski, *American Democracy* (New York: Viking Press, 1948), pp. 322 ff.

37. For example, three of the eight principal movie companies are controlled by Jews. In three others Jews play a major role in management and ownership. Jews publish the magazine *Esquire*, which was the first important magazine of its type. The crimes at which Jews excel (the only crimes) according to crime statistics, are in the area of gambling and bookmaking. Jewish control of the ladies' garment industry and influence in advertising have no doubt helped to usher in the brassiere ads which may be found *ad infinitum* in our most respectable newspapers and magazines.

38. Graeber and Britt, *op. cit.*, p. 235.

39. Williams, *op. cit.*, p. 373.

40. Max Kleinman, *Synagogue Tributes* (New York: Bloch Publishing Co., 1946), pp. 72-73.

41. 56.9% of the Jews and 39.8% of the Christians agreed that they ought to help pay for the roads and education of people in Kentucky. 44.5% of the Jews and 28.9% of the Christians agreed that they ought to be taxed to help raise standards of living in Asia and Africa.

42. Charles Angoff, *Journey to the Dawn* (New York: The Beechurst Press, 1951), p. 419.

43. Philip S. Bernstein, *What the Jews Believe* (New York: Farrar, Straus and Young, 1950), p. 73.

44. Bernard I. Bell, *Crowd Culture* (New York: Harper & Brothers, 1952), p. 111.

45. *Ibid.*

46. Reinhold Niebuhr, *Christian Realism and Political Problems* (New York: Charles Scribner's Sons, 1953). See Chapters I and II and p. 183.

47. For a complete discussion of the evangelical movement in the North see Charles C. Cole, Jr., *The Social Ideas of the Northern Evangelists, 1826-1860* (New York: Columbia University Press, 1954).

48. John Dillenberger and Claude

Welch, *Protestant Christianity* (New York: Charles Scribner's Sons, 1954), p. 245.

49. Joseph R. Narot, "Judaism, Christianity, and Salvation," *The Reconstructionist*, Vol. XX (April 23, 1954), p. 16.

50. William Warren Sweet, *Religion in the Development of American Culture, 1765-1840* (New York: Charles Scribner's Sons, 1952), p. 38.

51. Bernstein, *op. cit.*, pp. 4, 65. Writes Bernstein (p. 4): "Most Jews have assented to the judgment of an olden Rabbinic teacher who [said] . . . 'One hour of repentance and good deeds in this world is better than the whole life of the world to come.'"

52. H. Ralph Higgens, *Christianity and America's Social Problems* (New York: Comet Press, 1952), p. 8.

53. I have accepted the definition of the Sherifs that reference groups are "simply those groups to which the individual relates himself as a part or to which he aspires to relate himself psychologically." (*op. cit.*, p. 161). For a discussion of reference group material see Theodore Newcomb, Eugene L. Hartley, and others in *Readings in Social Psychology* (revised edition; New York: Henry Holt & Co., 1952), Part IV, B.

54. Meyer Greenberg, "The Jewish Student at Yale," in *Race Prejudice and Discrimination,* ed. by Arnold M. Rose (New York: Alfred Knopf, 1951), p. 317. Nathan Goldberg, "Religious and Social Attitudes of Jewish Youth in the U.S.A.," *Jewish Review,* Vol. 1 (December 1943), pp. 139-141.

55. Louis Wirth, *op. cit.*, p. 279.

56. Leo Bogart, *The Response of Jews in America to the European Jewish Catastrophe,* 1941-1945, Unpublished M.A. Thesis, University of Chicago, 1948, p. 46.

57. Robert I. Kahn, *Liberalism as Reflected in Jewish Preaching in the English Language in the Mid-Nineteenth Century,* Ph.D. Thesis, Hebrew Union College, 1949, p. 71.

58. Lewis Browne, *How Odd of God* (New York: The Macmillan Co., 1934), Chapter VI, especially pp. 216-222.

59. Einstein, *op. cit.*, p. 252.

DATE DUE

NOV 19 '69			
MAY 11 '70			
MAY 6 74			
MAY 6 '77			
DE 2 '81			
AP 6 88			
NO 11 '92			
DE 13 95			
GAYLORD			PRINTED IN U.S.A.